Conflict After the Cold War

Edited by one of the most renowned scholars in the field, Richard Betts' *Conflict After the Cold War* assembles classic and contemporary readings on enduring problems of international security. Offering broad historical and philosophical breadth, the carefully chosen and excerpted selections in this popular reader help students engage in key debates over the future of war and the new forms that violent conflict will take. *Conflict After the Cold War* encourages closer scrutiny of the political, economic, social, and military factors that drive war and peace.

NEW TO THE FIFTH EDITION

- Original introductions to each of 10 major parts as well as to the book as a whole have been updated by the author.
- An entirely new section (Part IX) on "Threat Assessment and Misjudgment" explores fundamental problems in diagnosing danger, understanding strategic choices, and measuring costs against benefits in wars over limited stakes.
- 12 new readings have been added or revised.

Richard K. Betts is the Arnold Saltzman Professor of War and Peace Studies in the Department of Political Science, the director of the Institute of War and Peace Studies, and the director of the International Security Policy Program in the School of International and Public Affairs at Columbia University.

Praise for the Fifth Edition

For students of international relations and security, and those who teach them, the fifth edition of Betts' *Conflict After the Cold War* is the indispensable volume. It is a superb collection of foundational and contemporary readings on the causes of war and peace, curated to stimulate serious thinking about today's conflicts as well as tomorrow's. Pulling it all together are Betts' ten commentaries, each one an illuminating gem of thematic overview, scholarly synthesis, and critical insight.

Timothy Crawford, *Boston College*

The new edition of Richard Betts' book brings together an impressive collection of classic readings with contemporary work on modern and currently emerging challenges. It works perfectly in exposing students to both theoretical concepts and practical policy problems. With well-edited selections, students can understand the key ideas of competing viewpoints without exhaustive reading.

John W. Dietrich, *Bryant University*

In this new edition, Richard K. Betts, one of our shrewdest and wisest observers of international affairs, has assembled a varied and illuminating set of readings to help students and other readers better understand the major issues of war and peace in the second decade of the contentious and confusing twenty-first century.

Michael Mandelbaum, *The Johns Hopkins School of*
Advanced International Studies; Author of Mission Failure:
America and the World in the Post–Cold War Era

A generation after the Cold War, Richard Betts' *Conflict After the Cold War* remains the gold standard of international security readers. Grounded in classical theory and immersed in contemporary issues, Betts' blend of world leaders, philosophers, and scholars offers a three-dimensional foundation for classroom discussion that is both informative and provocative.

Richard W. Maass, *University of Evansville*

Conflict After the Cold War is a carefully selected, tightly inter-related, and crisply summarized collection of theoretical and substantive articles that introduce the reader to the key conceptual approaches to the study of international conflict. It illustrates how those different theoretical approaches offer contrasting explanations for key historical episodes and suggest different policy responses to future problems. No stone is left unturned: Causes of conflict at the international, domestic, and human levels are all addressed. Betts' introductions to key sections of the book are clear and comprehensive, serve to highlight the theoretical debate, and connect each section to the overall theme of the book. Reflecting a lifetime of careful scholarship and teaching, this book is a gift to undergraduate and graduate students, and to the faculty tasked with teaching them the fundamental of international politics.

Barry R. Posen, *Massachusetts Institute of Technology*

Conflict After the Cold War is an indispensable resource for any course on international security. The blend of contemporary and classic writings, presented by a leading thinker, helps students understand the causes of war and peace and the elements of sound security policy. All aspiring strategists should read, and re-read, this volume.

Michael Beckley, *Tufts University*

There is no better source of essential readings on the topic of war and security. *Conflict After the Cold War* introduces students to many seminal works that form the foundations of contemporary thinking in international relations. I highly recommend this book to those wishing to gain a deeper understanding of realist and liberal thought on anarchy, power, and domestic and international institutions. Excellent readings throughout the book help explain a diverse set of issues related to international conflict, such as economic interdependence, terrorism, and climate change.

David Lektzian, *Texas Tech University*

Richard Betts has assembled an essential collection of essays for any student of security studies. Expertly organized and introduced, the new edition of *Conflict After the Cold War* provides historical and contemporary perspectives on a wide range of security challenges.

Brian Urlacher, *University of North Dakota*

This collection of readings is both timeless and timely, offering an urivaled introduction to the core questions and concepts of international relations. By assembling and judiciously excerpting classic texts into one handy volume, Richard Betts has done a real service to the field.

Rosemary Kelanic, *Williams College*

Conflict After the Cold War

Arguments on Causes of War and Peace

Fifth Edition

RICHARD K. **BETTS**

Columbia University

Routledge
Taylor & Francis Group

NEW YORK AND LONDON

Published 2017
by Routledge
711 Third Avenue, New York, NY 10017

and by Routledge
2 Park Square, Milton Park, Abingdon, Oxon, OX14 4RN

Routledge is an imprint of the Taylor & Francis Group, an informa business

© 2017 Taylor & Francis

The right of Richard K. Betts to be identified as author of this work
has been asserted by him in accordance with sections 77 and 78 of the
Copyright, Designs and Patents Act 1988.

Second edition published by Longman, 2002
Third edition published by Pearson Education, Inc., 2008
Fourth edition published by Pearson Education, Inc. 2012, and Routledge, 2016

Library of Congress Cataloging-in-Publication Data
A catalog record for this book has been requested

ISBN: 978-1-138-29068-6 (hbk)
ISBN: 978-1-138-29069-3 (pbk)
ISBN: 978-1-315-23137-2 (ebk)

Typeset in Sabon
by Apex CoVantage, LLC

Printed and bound in the United States of America by
Edwards Brothers Malloy on sustainably sourced paper

CONTENTS

PREFACE

A generation has now passed since the Cold War. Expectations of dramatic change in world politics have come full circle. The apparent outbreak of peace after the Berlin Wall opened inspired great hopes but proved brief. Since the turn of the century political violence has undermined stability and progress within many countries. Even the potential for war between major powers, a threat that seemed to have vanished for most of the post–Cold War period, has emerged again. The shock of September 11th; wars in Iraq, Chechnya, Afghanistan, Libya, Sudan, Congo, Syria, and many other places; the murderous assaults of Islamic State and Al Qaeda; reassertion of Russian power in Georgia, Crimea, and Ukraine; and Chinese muscle flexing in the western Pacific make the world seem as dangerous as ever to the generation born since the Cold War. Yet all this global violence so far remains at levels far lower than what occurred in the first half of the twentieth century or was feared in the second half. By the standards of the previous generation we have only moved from Cold War to Hot Peace. As deadly and messy as the world looks, things could get much worse.

On the other hand, many have faith that current conflicts are temporary aberrations, restricted to backward regions beyond the West, and that they will succumb to a historical tide of peace as the benefits of global economic integration and political liberation unfold. Optimists see the surge of reactionary Islamist terrorism as a delaying action against ultimately irresistible modernization, and far less dangerous in its material effects than in its psychological impact. They see war between Russia or China and the West as utterly improbable because the world has learned from the folly of the twentieth century, and they believe international institutions and material interest will keep rising tension manageable.

Which way will these shaky global conditions move? Forward to broader and deeper peace, as seemed possible right after the Cold War? Backward to cataclysmic conflict among major powers? Or will the world stumble along indefinitely with an array of small but brutal wars within divided countries and episodic terrorism against more stable societies of the West?

The danger of war may not be the single most important issue facing mankind. The potential for catastrophic climate change, pandemic disease, or global economic collapse competes for concern. But the potential for major war is clearly among the top few concerns of international politics. If weapons of mass destruction continue to spread, the question will become even more pressing. So how do we find the answer? For either forecasting or shaping the future any answer depends on assumptions about what conditions, events, or initiatives tend to cause war or peace.

For many, the assumptions about what causes conflict or cooperation are intuitively obvious. Indeed, most pundits and statesmen promote policies they think will work on the basis of unexamined assumptions about causes and effects. If the assumptions are wrong, the policies will fail, or even make things worse. This volume is designed to shake students out of unthinking confidence in facile assumptions. It aims to expose them to the timeless questions and recurrent debates about what causes war or peace, to show them that most current ideas are actually variations on old themes, and to impress upon them that classic disagreements by thoughtful theorists about what either logic or history should tell us still have much relevance. As much as possible, readings were selected that argue with each other, to make students realize that what seems self-evident or obvious to many people can be challenged in serious ways. Pedagogically, the purpose is to make students step back from certainty, to question what seems to be common sense, and to think about what more they need to know to have informed opinions on the subject.

To do this, Part I presents contrasting basic arguments about what the driving forces in world politics are, and how they affect the odds of conflict or cooperation, as well as a frankly fearful view of the dark side of technological progress. Parts II and III outline the main competing traditions in theory of international politics: realism and liberalism. Part IV adds perspectives on psychological and cultural causes, more subjective sources of decisions about war that may sometimes override the materialist and conscious motives that dominate realist and liberal explanations.

Getting into more detail, Part V presents contrasting arguments variously grounded in the basic realist and liberal traditions about why the logic of free economics and international interdependence naturally encourages peace (Angell, Schumpeter, Rosecrance, Ikenberry), or how economic interests can leave ample motives for conquest (Machiavelli, Blainey, Lenin, Milward, Waltz). Part VI suggests how political development and ideological change create frictions that foster violence. Ideas about national identity and self-determination can put groups at each others' throats (Gellner, Mansfield and Snyder), raising questions about which is the lesser evil: deliberate separation of antagonistic ethnic groups, or forced national integration. Kaufmann and Kumar argue on opposite sides of the latter question.

The next two sections are about the workings of war itself, and how they channel other causes and constraints. In Part VII, Jervis and Levy present different assessments about how judgments of the difference in effectiveness of offensive or defensive modes of combat affect decisions about war. Waltz offers an unconventional view about how the most destructive weapons may make the world safer rather than more dangerous. Byman and Cronin debate the balance of costs and benefits in the application of a new conventional technology (aerial drones) to strategy for counterterrorism.

Part VIII on unconventional war covers the topics that have dominated the recent national security agenda in the world's most powerful states, especially the United States: terrorism, guerrilla warfare, and counterinsurgency. Is terrorism simply a nihilistic and nonsensical atrocity, or is it a strategically rational instrument, however awful? Martha Crenshaw and Osama bin Ladin offer sobering cases for the latter view. Lawrence of Arabia, Mao, Huntington, and Galula then analyze the classic interaction of objectives, strategy, and tactics in revolutionary or guerrilla warfare. Cohen, Crane, Horvath, and Nagl distill the official American military rationale for counterinsurgency, while Gentile argues that the mission is a fool's errand.

The new Part IX links the lessons of the past to the present most explicitly. Perhaps the uncertainty shaping the risk of war that is both most intense and most enduring is the question of how to assess the potential threat posed by an adversary. Too much suspicion may make conflict a self-fulfilling prophecy, while too much empathy may leave one prey to an aggressor who is more predatory than assumed. The agonizing differences and choices involved in threat assessments and the strategies that flow from them are illustrated by contrasting attempts to make sense of the challenges posed by great powers—Germany in the twentieth century and Russia today—and revolutionary movements in Vietnam and Afghanistan.

The concluding section, Part X, flags issues that have emerged only in very recent times—new potential sources of political violence due to environmental degradation and competition for natural resources, and the complexity of threats to almost all of modern society's basic activities due to dependence on cybersecurity. Then it concludes with essays that link speculation about the future to the overarching visions and theories featured at the beginning of the book.

NEW TO THIS EDITION

Twelve new items provide consideration of issues posed by potentially revolutionary developments in technology and cultural cleavage, the rise of Chinese power, liberal arguments for the pacifying effects of international institutions and economic interdependence, effects of new military technologies such as drone aircraft, the burgeoning priority of cybersecurity, and the dilemmas involved in anticipating threats:

- Fred C. Iklé, "The Dark Side of Progress," in Part I.
- G. John Ikenberry, "China's Choice," in Part V.
- Debate between Daniel Byman ("Drones: Technology Serves Strategy") and Audrey Kurth Cronin ("Drones: Tactics Undermine Strategy") in Part VII.
- Martin C. Libicki, "Why Cyberdeterrence Is Different," in Part X.

An entire new section, Part IX: Threat Assessment and Misjudgment: Recurrent Dilemmas, explores fundamental problems in diagnosing danger, understanding strategic choices, and measuring costs against benefits in wars over limited stakes. How do statesmen know whether the adversary is a predatory aggressor who must be deterred or defeated by mobilizing military power against it, or has defensive motives behind its worrisome actions, in which case forceful opposition might trigger the war it is meant to prevent? Why do statesmen make bad judgments about how to fight revolutionary opponents in unconventional wars? Paired items illustrate how these uncertainties produced varying types of mistakes in the past hundred years and could again:

- Documents on contrasts between British officials' thinking about German policy before World Wars I and II, and how they erred in opposite directions: memoranda by Eyre Crowe and Thomas Sanderson in 1907, and communications from Ambassador Neville Henderson during the 1938 Munich crisis.
- Contrasting Russian and anti-Russian assessments of Moscow's motives in annexing Crimea and intervening in Ukraine: Vladimir Putin's speech of March 18, 2014, interpreting Russian action in Crimea and Ukraine as legitimate and defensive, and Eliot Cohen's dramatically opposite assessment.
- A classic post-mortem by James C. Thomson, Jr. on the American disaster in Vietnam, and a pre-mortem by Stephen Biddle on potentially similar mistakes in Afghanistan.

ACKNOWLEDGMENTS

This volume owes much to three sets of people:

- The Columbia University students and teaching assistants in my course "War, Peace, and Strategy," for whom the book was originally designed;
- The staff of the Arnold A. Saltzman Institute of War and Peace Studies, especially Ingrid Gerstmann, who have eased my task as director; and
- My family: Adela M. Bolet, my wife, and my now-grown children, Elena Christine, Michael Francis, and Diego Fitzpatrick Betts, who kept me happy enough to get the work done.

I am also grateful to the staff at Routledge who made the transition of publishers remarkably painless.

Visions of Conflict and Peace

The end of the Cold War shocked observers everywhere. Some reacted with confidence that the future would be prosperous, progressive, and peaceful. Others feared that historic patterns of disorder and conflict would return. The essays in this section outline several contrasting visions—two optimistic, three pessimistic—that were influential soon after the Cold War. These visions each turned on differing assumptions about what fundamental drivers of human behavior would trump others, and they reflect many of the ideas and suppositions underlying the specific discussions in the rest of this volume.

These visions are not dated. They remain quite relevant because they tap deeply rooted political and philosophical traditions that have competed tenaciously over several centuries, their respective popularity ebbing and flowing with events. Dramatic as all that has happened since the Cold War is, events have not rendered a final verdict on the future. Different events of recent years imply different long-term developments. Observers who look at the evidence selectively can make strong predictions for international politics in either direction—conflict or cooperation. A thorough grasp of the question, however, cannot afford to ignore any of the arguments in this section.

These visions comport with different readings of history. War keeps coming back, but by some measures peace keeps getting better and better. Optimists can take comfort from research by Steven Pinker and Joshua Goldstein showing the consistent decline of war and violence over time in both frequency and scale.[1] Pessimists can look to questions about the data behind that conclusion.[2] Moreover, Pinker presents disastrous exceptions that punctuate the downward curve as aberrations (such as the World Wars of the twentieth century), horrific blips in the long-term march away from war. The possibility of another such huge blip, especially in the age of weapons of mass destruction or potential awesome empowerment of malign small groups through technological advances (see the selection by Fred C. Iklé), is a sobering qualification to where his data point.

Two of the following selections bracket more moderate and conditional versions of liberal and realist predictions. Francis Fukuyama argues that the developed world has evolved toward a liberal consensus that is close to ending the bases for violent contention of the past.[3] Fukuyama's argument is particularly remarkable because it was first written before the opening of the Berlin Wall and was prescient in anticipating the global collapse of Marxism. Contrary to critics who believe that widespread violence and continued authoritarianism since he wrote discredit his vision, Fukuyama recognized that the Third World was still "mired in history" and that the spread of the West's victorious model might take time. At the other extreme, John J. Mearsheimer challenges optimistic conventional wisdom with a pure distillation of the realist tradition represented in the readings that follow in Part II.[4] To him, the intellectual developments that Fukuyama sees as decisive forces actually matter very little. When push comes to shove, ideas give way to interests. Mearsheimer asserted not only that the new era of peace is a mirage, but that the future will be worse than the Cold War. That period, not the new world, represents the most stable and peaceful order we are likely to see. Some critics believe that the persistence of the North Atlantic Treaty Organization (NATO), indeed its expansion and activism, discredited Mearsheimer's pessimism. Recent challenges to European unity, however, and doubts about the alliance's readiness to handle resurgent Russia, keep prospects for renewed conflict in Europe on the table.

Samuel P. Huntington's essay, which was extremely controversial when it appeared in the early post–Cold War period, struck many as more compelling after September 11th. Like liberals, he accords greater importance to motives and values as sources of conflict than do realists. Unlike liberals, he does not see Westernization as an irresistible tide that overwhelms world politics. Like realists, he sees conflict as natural rather than aberrant, and though not inevitable in the future, quite probable. Unlike realists, he places less emphasis on states as the sources of war in the future, and more on cleavages between major culture areas. Those who focus on the pessimistic aspect of Huntington's argument should be sure not to miss his essay (drawn from his more thoroughly developed book) that ends this volume, since it charts a course for preventing a clash of civilizations from becoming a war of civilizations. Like Huntington, Fareed Zakaria accords much more significance than other commentators to the rise of the "rest" as alternative sources of power to the West, emphasizing the economic growth and dynamism of Asian countries. Unlike Huntington, Zakaria sees most of this shift in world power as compatible with Western norms and interests. More than the others, he gets out of the shadow of the twentieth century and sees economic change dominating cultural differences. Fred C. Iklé, on the other hand, worries that revolutionary technological changes combined with intensified cultural conflict may empower malign individuals or small groups to a degree unprecedented in history.

All of these arguments are arresting, but most observers, even if they gravitate toward one, will have more conditional diagnoses and predictions.[5]

Fukuyama, Mearsheimer, and others who argue in the same vein reflect philosophical assumptions rooted in earlier and well-developed schools of thought. Huntington reflects a respect for the causal importance of identity and culture that anthropologists, or constructivists in political science, have long recognized. (Many of them would be shocked to find themselves placed in the same boat with Huntington, who does not share the tendency of many constructivists to see liberal values as ascendant.) Zakaria does not superimpose any single theory on the rise of the non-Western world that he sees as characteristic of the new century, but his assessment applies insights that come out of the development of Western capitalism. Iklé points to the dark side of technological progress, the dangers in disjoined development of science and culture, and especially the potential for unanticipated discontinuities in the control of mass destruction that have escaped the attention of most strategists.[6] Roots of all these approaches to argument about war and peace are traced in more detail in the subsequent selections.

—RKB

NOTES

1 Steven Pinker, *The Better Angels of Our Nature: Why Violence Has Declined* (New York: Viking, 2011); Joshua S. Goldstein, *Winning the War on War: The Decline of Armed Conflict Worldwide* (New York: Dutton, 2011).
2 For example, Tanisha M. Fazal, "Dead Wrong? Battle Deaths, Military Medicine, and Exaggerated Reports of War's Demise," *International Security* 39, no. 1 (Summer 2014).
3 For the full-length version of these arguments see Francis Fukuyama, *The End of History and the Last Man* (New York: Free Press, 1992).
4 A more academic and detailed version of the argument can be found in John J. Mearsheimer, "Back to the Future: Instability in Europe After the Cold War," *International Security* 15, no. 4 (Spring 1990).
5 See Richard K. Betts, "Conflict of Cooperation? Three Visions Revisited," *Foreign Affairs* 89, no. 6 (November/December 2010).
6 Another similarly alarming discussion of potential catastrophic threats, from nature as well as political intent, is the scientist Sir Martin Rees's *Our Final Hour* (New York: Basic Books, 2003).

Reading 1.1

The End of History? FRANCIS FUKUYAMA

In watching the flow of events over the past decade or so, it is hard to avoid the feeling that something very fundamental has happened in world history. The past year has seen a flood of articles commemorating the end of the Cold War, and the fact that "peace" seems to be breaking out in many regions of the world. Most of these analyses lack any larger conceptual framework for distinguishing between what is essential and what is contingent or accidental in world history, and are predictably superficial. If Mr. Gorbachev were ousted from the Kremlin or a new Ayatollah proclaimed the millennium from a desolate Middle Eastern capital, these same commentators would scramble to announce the rebirth of a new era of conflict.

And yet, all of these people sense dimly that there is some larger process at work, a process that gives coherence and order to the daily headlines. The twentieth century saw the developed world descend into a paroxysm of ideological violence, as liberalism contended first with the remnants of absolutism, then bolshevism and fascism, and finally an updated Marxism that threatened to lead to the ultimate apocalypse of nuclear war. But the century that began full of self-confidence in the ultimate triumph of Western liberal democracy seems at its close to be returning full circle to where it started: not to an "end of ideology" or a convergence between capitalism and socialism, as earlier predicted, but to an unabashed victory of economic and political liberalism.

The triumph of the West, of the Western *idea*, is evident first of all in the total exhaustion of viable systematic alternatives to Western liberalism. In the past decade, there have been unmistakable changes in the intellectual climate of the world's two largest communist countries, and the beginnings of significant reform movements in both. But this phenomenon extends beyond high politics and it can be seen also in the ineluctable spread of consumerist Western culture in such diverse contexts as the peasants' markets and color television sets now omnipresent throughout China, the cooperative restaurants and clothing stores opened in the past year in Moscow, the Beethoven piped into Japanese department stores, and the rock music enjoyed alike in Prague, Rangoon, and Tehran.

What we may be witnessing is not just the end of the Cold War, or the passing of a particular period of postwar history, but the end of history as such: that is, the end point of mankind's ideological evolution and the universalization of Western liberal democracy as the final form of human government. This is not to say that there will no longer be events to fill the pages of *Foreign Affairs'* yearly summaries of international relations, for the victory of

---

Source: Francis Fukuyama, "The End of History?" The National Interest, No. 16 (Summer 1989).

liberalism has occurred primarily in the realm of ideas or consciousness and is as yet incomplete in the real or material world. But there are powerful reasons for believing that it is the ideal that will govern the material world *in the long run*. To understand how this is so, we must first consider some theoretical issues concerning the nature of historical change.

I

The notion of the end of history is not an original one. Its best known propagator was Karl Marx, who believed that the direction of historical development was a purposeful one determined by the interplay of material forces, and would come to an end only with the achievement of a communist utopia that would finally resolve all prior contradictions. But the concept of history as a dialectical process with a beginning, a middle, and an end was borrowed by Marx from his great German predecessor, Georg Wilhelm Friedrich Hegel.

For better or worse, much of Hegel's historicism has become part of our contemporary intellectual baggage. The notion that mankind has progressed through a series of primitive stages of consciousness on his path to the present, and that these stages corresponded to concrete forms of social organization, such as tribal, slave-owning, theocratic, and finally democratic-egalitarian societies, has become inseparable from the modern understanding of man. Hegel was the first philosopher to speak the language of modern social science, insofar as man for him was the product of his concrete historical and social environment and not, as earlier natural right theorists would have it, a collection of more or less fixed "natural" attributes. The mastery and transformation of man's natural environment through the application of science and technology was originally not a Marxist concept, but a Hegelian one. Unlike later historicists whose historical relativism degenerated into relativism *tout court*, however, Hegel believed that history culminated in an absolute moment—a moment in which a final, rational form of society and state became victorious.

It is Hegel's misfortune to be known now primarily as Marx's precursor, and it is our misfortune that few of us are familiar with Hegel's work from direct study, but only as it has been filtered through the distorting lens of Marxism. In France, however, there has been an effort to save Hegel from his Marxist interpreters and to resurrect him as the philosopher who most correctly speaks to our time. Among those modern French interpreters of Hegel, the greatest was certainly Alexandre Kojève, a brilliant Russian emigre who taught a highly influential series of seminars in Paris in the 1930s at the *Ecole Practique des Hautes Etudes*.[1] While largely unknown in the United States, Kojève had a major impact on the intellectual life of the continent. Among his students ranged such future luminaries as Jean-Paul Sartre on the Left and Raymond Aron on the Right; postwar existentialism borrowed many of its basic categories from Hegel via Kojève.

Kojève sought to resurrect the Hegel of the *Phenomenology of Mind*, the Hegel who proclaimed history to be at an end in 1806. For as early as this Hegel saw in Napoleon's defeat of the Prussian monarchy at the Battle of Jena the victory of the ideals of the French Revolution, and the imminent universalization of the state incorporating the principles of liberty and equality. Kojève, far from rejecting Hegel in light of the turbulent events of the next century and a half, insisted that the latter had been essentially correct. The Battle of Jena marked the end of history because it was at that point that the *vanguard* of humanity (a term quite familiar to Marxists) actualized the principles of the French Revolution. While there was considerable work to be done after 1806—abolishing slavery and the slave trade, extending the franchise to workers, women, blacks, and other racial minorities, etc.—the basic *principles* of the liberal democratic state could not be improved upon. The two world wars in this century and their attendant revolutions and upheavals simply had the effect of extending those principles spatially, such that the various provinces of human civilization were brought up to the level of its most advanced outposts, and of forcing those societies in Europe and North America at the vanguard of civilization to implement their liberalism more fully. . . .

II

For Hegel, the contradictions that drive history exist first of all in the realm of human consciousness, i.e., on the level of ideas—not the trivial election year proposals of American politicians, but ideas in the sense of large unifying world views that might best be understood under the rubric of ideology. Ideology in this sense is not restricted to the secular and explicit political doctrines we usually associate with the term, but can include religion, culture, and the complex of moral values underlying any society as well.

Hegel's view of the relationship between the ideal and the real or material worlds was an extremely complicated one, beginning with the fact that for him the distinction between the two was only apparent. He did not believe that the real world conformed or could be made to conform to ideological preconceptions of philosophy professors in any simple-minded way, or that the "material" world could not impinge on the ideal. Indeed, Hegel the professor was temporarily thrown out of work as a result of a very material event, the Battle of Jena. But while Hegel's writing and thinking could be stopped by a bullet from the material world, the hand on the trigger of the gun was motivated in turn by the ideas of liberty and equality that had driven the French Revolution.

For Hegel, all human behavior in the material world, and hence all human history, is rooted in a prior state of consciousness—an idea similar to the one expressed by John Maynard Keynes when he said that the views of men of affairs were usually derived from defunct economists and academic scribblers of earlier generations. This consciousness may not be explicit and self-aware, as are modern political doctrines, but may rather take the form of religion or simple cultural or moral habits. And yet this realm of consciousness *in the long run* necessarily becomes manifest in the material world, indeed creates the material world in its own image. Consciousness is cause and not effect, and can develop autonomously from the material world; hence the real subtext underlying the apparent jumble of current events is the history of ideology.

Hegel's idealism has fared poorly at the hands of later thinkers. Marx reversed the priority of the real and the ideal completely, relegating the entire realm of consciousness—religion, art, culture, philosophy itself—to a "superstructure" that was determined entirely by the prevailing material mode of production. Yet another unfortunate legacy of Marxism is our tendency to retreat into materialist or utilitarian explanations of political or-historical phenomena, and our disinclination to believe in the autonomous power of ideas. A recent example of this is Paul Kennedy's hugely successful *The Rise and Fall of the Great Powers*, which ascribes the decline of great powers to simple economic overextension. Obviously, this is true on some level: an empire whose economy is barely above the level of subsistence cannot bankrupt its treasury indefinitely. But whether a highly productive modern industrial society chooses to spend 3 or 7 percent of its GNP on defense rather than consumption is entirely a matter of that society's political priorities, which are in turn determined in the realm of consciousness.

The materialist bias of modern thought is characteristic not only of people on the Left who may be sympathetic to Marxism, but of many passionate anti-Marxists as well. Indeed, there is on the Right what one might label the *Wall Street Journal* school of deterministic materialism that discounts the importance of ideology and culture and sees man as essentially a rational, profit-maximizing individual. It is precisely this kind of individual and his pursuit of material incentives that is posited as the basis for economic life as such in economic textbooks. One small example will illustrate the problematic character of such materialist views.

Max Weber begins his famous book, *The Protestant Ethic and the Spirit of Capitalism*, by noting the different economic performance of Protestant and Catholic communities throughout Europe and America, summed up in the proverb that Protestants eat well while Catholics sleep well. Weber notes that according to any economic theory that posited man as a rational profit-maximizer, raising the piece-work rate should increase labor productivity. But in fact, in many traditional peasant communities, raising the piece-work rate actually had the opposite effect of *lowering* labor productivity: at the higher rate, a peasant accustomed to earning two and one-half marks per day found he could earn the same amount by working less, and did so because he valued leisure more than income. The choices of leisure over income, or of the militaristic life of the Spartan hoplite over the wealth of the Athenian trader, or even the ascetic life of the early capitalist entrepreneur over that of a traditional leisured aristocrat, cannot possibly be explained by the impersonal working of material forces, but come preeminently out of the sphere of consciousness—what we have labeled here broadly as ideology. And indeed, a central theme of Weber's work was to prove that contrary to Marx, the material mode of production, far from being the "base," was itself a "superstructure" with roots in religion and culture, and that to understand the emergence of modern capitalism and the profit motive one had to study their antecedents in the realm of the spirit.

As we look around the contemporary world, the poverty of materialist theories of economic development is all too apparent. The *Wall Street Journal* school of deterministic materialism habitually points to the stunning economic success of Asia in the past few decades as evidence of the viability of free market economics, with the implication that all societies would see similar development were they simply to allow their populations to pursue their material self-interest freely. Surely free markets and stable political systems are a necessary precondition to capitalist economic growth. But just as surely the cultural heritage of those Far Eastern societies, the ethic of work and saving and family, a religious heritage that does not, like Islam, place restrictions on certain forms of economic behavior, and other deeply ingrained moral qualities, are equally important in explaining their economic performance.[2] And yet the intellectual weight of materialism is such that not a single respectable contemporary theory of economic development addresses consciousness and culture seriously as the matrix within which economic behavior is formed.

Failure to understand that the roots of economic behavior lie in the realm of consciousness and culture leads to the common mistake of attributing material causes to phenomena that are essentially ideal in nature. For example, it is commonplace in the West to interpret the reform movements first in China and most recently in the Soviet Union as the victory of the material over the ideal— that is, a recognition that ideological incentives could not replace material ones in stimulating a highly productive modern economy, and that if one wanted to prosper one had to appeal to baser forms of self-interest. But the deep defects of socialist economies were evident thirty or forty years ago to anyone who chose to look. Why was it that these countries moved away from central planning only in the 1980s? The answer must be found in the consciousness of the elites and leaders ruling them, who decided to opt for the "Protestant" life of wealth and risk over the "Catholic" path of poverty and security. That change was in no way made inevitable by the material conditions in which either country found itself on the eve of the reform, but instead came about as the result of the victory of one idea over another. . . .

III

. . . In the past century, there have been two major challenges to liberalism, those of fascism and of communism. The former[3] saw the political weakness, materialism, anomie, and lack of community of the West as fundamental contradictions in liberal societies that could only be resolved by a strong state that forged a new "people" on the basis of national exclusiveness. Fascism was destroyed as a living ideology by World War II. This was a defeat, of course, on a very material level, but it amounted to a defeat of the idea as well. What destroyed fascism as an idea was not universal moral revulsion against it, since plenty of people were willing to endorse the idea as long as it seemed the wave of the future, but its lack of success. After the war, it seemed to most people that German fascism as well as its other European and Asian variants were bound to self-destruct. There was no material reason why new fascist movements could not have sprung up again after the war in other locales, but for the fact that expansionist ultranationalism, with its promise of unending conflict leading to disastrous military defeat, had completely lost its appeal. The ruins of the Reich chancellory as well as the atomic bombs dropped on Hiroshima and Nagasaki killed this ideology on the level of consciousness as well as materially, and all of the proto-fascist movements spawned by the German and Japanese examples like the Peronist movement in Argentina or Sub-has Chandra Bose's Indian National Army withered after the war.

The ideological challenge mounted by the other great alternative to liberalism, communism, was far more serious. Marx, speaking Hegel's language, asserted that liberal society contained a fundamental contradiction that could not be resolved within its context, that between capital and labor, and this contradiction has constituted the chief accusation against liberalism ever since. But surely, the class issue has actually been successfully resolved in the West. . . .

But the power of the liberal idea would seem much less impressive if it had not infected the largest and oldest culture in Asia, China. The simple existence of communist China created an alternative pole of ideological attraction, and as such constituted a threat to liberalism. But the past fifteen years have seen an almost total discrediting of Marxism-Leninism as an economic system. Beginning with the famous third plenum of the Tenth Central Committee in 1978, the Chinese Communist party set about decollectivizing agriculture for the 800 million Chinese who still lived in the countryside. The role of the state in agriculture was reduced to that of a tax collector, while production of consumer goods was sharply increased in order to give peasants a taste of the universal homogenous state and thereby an incentive to work. The reform doubled Chinese grain output in only five years, and in the process created for Deng Xiao-ping a solid political base from which he was able to extend the reform to other parts of the economy. Economic statistics do not begin to describe the dynamism, initiative, and openness, evident in China since the reform began.

China could not now be described in any way as a liberal democracy. At present, no more than 20 percent of its economy has been marketized, and most importantly it continues to be ruled by a self-appointed Communist party which has given no hint of wanting to devolve power. Deng has made none of Gorbachev's promises regarding democratization of the political system and there is no Chinese equivalent of *glasnost*. The Chinese leadership has in fact been much more circumspect in criticizing Mao and Maoism than Gorbachev with respect to Brezhnev and Stalin, and the regime continues to pay lip service to Marxism-Leninism as its ideological underpinning. But anyone familiar with the outlook and behavior of the new technocratic elite now governing China knows that Marxism and ideological principle have become virtually irrelevant as guides to policy, and that bourgeois consumerism has a real meaning in that country for the first time since the revolution. The various slowdowns in the pace of reform, the campaigns against "spiritual pollution" and crackdowns on political dissent are more properly seen as tactical adjustments made in the process of managing what is an extraordinarily difficult political transition. By ducking the question of political reform while putting the economy on a new footing, Deng has managed to avoid the breakdown of authority that has accompanied Gorbachev's *perestroika*. Yet the pull of the liberal idea continues to be very strong as economic power devolves and the economy becomes more open to the outside world. There are currently over 20,000 Chinese students studying in the U.S. and other Western countries, almost all of them the children of the Chinese elite. It is hard to believe that when they return home to run the country they will be content for China to be the only country in Asia unaffected by the larger democratizing trend. The student demonstrations in Beijing that broke out first in December 1986 and recurred recently on the occasion of Hu Yao-bang's death were only the beginning of what will inevitably be mounting pressure for change in the political system as well.

What is important about China from the standpoint of world history is not the present state of the reform or even its future prospects. The central issue is the fact that the People's Republic of China can no longer act as a beacon for illiberal forces around the world, whether they be guerrillas in some Asian jungle or middle class students in Paris. Maoism, rather than being the pattern for Asia's future, became an anachronism. . . .

If we admit for the moment that the fascist and communist challenges to liberalism are dead, are there any other ideological competitors left? Or put another way, are there contradictions in liberal society beyond that of class that are not resolvable? Two possibilities suggest themselves, those of religion and nationalism.

The rise of religious fundamentalism in recent years within the Christian, Jewish, and Muslim traditions has been widely noted. One is inclined to say that the revival of religion in some way attests to a broad unhappiness with the impersonality and spiritual vacuity of liberal consumerist societies. Yet while the emptiness at the core of liberalism is most certainly a defect in the ideology—indeed, a flaw that one does not need the perspective of religion to recognize—it is not at all clear that it is remediable through politics. Modern liberalism itself was historically a consequence of the weakness of religiously-based societies which, failing to agree on the nature of the good life, could not provide even the minimal preconditions of peace and stability. In the contemporary world only Islam has offered a theocratic state as a political alternative to both liberalism and communism. But the doctrine has little appeal for non-Muslims, and it is hard to believe that the movement will take on any universal significance. Other less organized religious impulses have been successfully satisfied within the sphere of personal life that is permitted in liberal societies.

The other major "contradiction" potentially unresolvable by liberalism is the one posed by nationalism and other forms of racial and ethnic consciousness. It is certainly true that a very large degree of conflict since the Battle of Jena has had its roots in nationalism. Two cataclysmic world wars in this century have been spawned by the nationalism of the developed world in various guises, and if those passions have been muted to a certain extent in postwar Europe, they are still extremely powerful in the Third World. Nationalism has been a threat to liberalism historically in Germany, and continues to be one in isolated parts of "post-historical" Europe like Northern Ireland.

But it is not clear that nationalism represents an irreconcilable contradiction in the heart of liberalism. In the first place, nationalism is not one single phenomenon but several, ranging from mild cultural nostalgia to the highly organized and elaborately articulated doctrine of National Socialism. Only systematic nationalisms of the latter sort can qualify as a formal ideology on the level of liberalism or communism. The vast majority of the world's nationalist movements do not have a political program beyond the negative desire of independence *from* some other group or people, and do not offer anything like a comprehensive agenda for socio-economic organization. As such, they are compatible with doctrines and ideologies that do offer such agendas. While they may constitute a source of conflict for liberal societies, this conflict does not arise from liberalism itself so much as from the fact that the liberalism in question is incomplete. Certainly a great deal of the world's ethnic and nationalist tension can be explained in terms of peoples who are forced to live in unrepresentative political systems that they have not chosen.

While it is impossible to rule out the sudden appearance of new ideologies or previously unrecognized contradictions in liberal societies, then, the present world seems to confirm that the fundamental principles of socio-political organization have not advanced terribly far since 1806. Many of the wars and revolutions fought since that time have been undertaken in the name of ideologies which claimed to be more advanced than liberalism, but whose pretensions were ultimately unmasked by history. In the meantime, they have helped to spread the universal homogenous state to the point where it could have a significant effect on the overall character of international relations.

IV

What are the implications of the end of history for international relations? Clearly, the vast bulk of the Third World remains very much mired in history, and will be a terrain of conflict for many years to come. But let us focus for the time being on the larger and more developed states of the world who after all account for the greater part of world politics. Russia and China are not likely to join the developed nations of the West as liberal societies any time in the foreseeable future, but suppose for a moment that Marxism-Leninism ceases to be a factor driving the foreign policies of these states—a prospect which, if not yet here, the last few years have made a real possibility. How will the overall characteristics of a de-ideologized world differ from those of the one with which we are familiar at such a hypothetical juncture?

The most common answer is—not very much. For there is a very widespread belief among many observers of international relations that underneath the skin of ideology is a hard core of great power national interest that guarantees a fairly high level of competition and conflict between nations. Indeed, according to one academically popular school of international relations theory, conflict inheres in the international system as such, and to understand the prospects for conflict one must look at the shape of the system—for example, whether it is bipolar or multipolar—rather than at the specific character of the nations and regimes that constitute it. This school in effect applies a Hobbesian view of politics to international relations, and assumes that aggression and insecurity are universal characteristics of human societies rather than the product of specific historical circumstances.

Believers in this line of thought take the relations that existed between the participants in the classical nineteenth-century European balance of power as a model for what a de-ideologized contemporary world would look like. Charles Krauthammer, for example, recently explained that if as a result of Gorbachev's reforms the USSR is shorn of Marxist-Leninist ideology, its behavior will revert to that of nineteenth-century imperial Russia.[4] While he finds this more reassuring than the threat posed by a communist Russia, he implies that there will still be a substantial degree of competition and conflict in the international system, just as there was say between Russia and Britain or Wilhelmine Germany in the last century. This is, of course, a convenient point of view for people who want to admit that something major is changing in the Soviet Union, but do not want to accept responsibility for recommending the radical policy redirection implicit in such a view. But is it true?

In fact, the notion that ideology is a superstructure imposed on a substratum of permanent great power interest is a highly questionable proposition. For the way in which any state defines its national interest is not universal but rests on some kind of prior ideological basis, just as we saw that economic behavior is determined by a prior state of consciousness. In this century, states have adopted highly articulated doctrines with explicit foreign policy agendas legitimizing expansionism, like Marxism-Leninism or National Socialism.

The expansionist and competitive behavior of nineteenth-century European states rested on no less ideal a basis; it just so happened that the ideology driving it was less explicit than the doctrines of the twentieth century. For one thing, most "liberal" European societies were illiberal insofar as they believed in the legitimacy of imperialism, that is, the right of one nation to rule over other nations without regard for the wishes of the ruled. The justifications for imperialism varied from nation to nation, from a crude belief in the legitimacy of force, particularly when applied to non-Europeans, to the White Man's Burden and Europe's Christianizing mission, to the desire to give people of color access to the culture of Rabelais and Molière. But whatever the particular ideological basis, every "developed" country believed in the acceptability of higher civilizations ruling lower ones—including, incidentally, the United States with regard to the Philippines. This led to a drive for pure territorial aggrandizement in the latter half of the century and played no small role in causing the Great War.

The radical and deformed outgrowth of nineteenth-century imperialism was German fascism, an ideology which justified Germany's right not only to rule over non-European peoples, but over *all* non-German ones. But in retrospect it seems that Hitler represented a diseased bypath in the general course of European development, and since his fiery defeat, the legitimacy of any kind of territorial aggrandizement has been thoroughly discredited.[5] Since the Second World War, European nationalism has been defanged and shorn of any real relevance to foreign policy, with the consequence that the nineteenth-century model of great power behavior has become a serious anachronism. The most extreme form of nationalism that any Western European state has mustered since 1945 has been Gaullism, whose self-assertion has been confined largely to the realm of nuisance politics and culture. International life for the part of the world that has reached the end of history is far more preoccupied with economics than with politics or strategy.

The developed states of the West do maintain defense establishments and in the postwar period have competed vigorously for influence to meet a worldwide communist threat. This behavior has been driven, however, by an external threat from states that possess overtly expansionist ideologies, and would not exist in their absence. To take the "neo-realist" theory seriously, one would have to believe that "natural" competitive behavior would reassert itself among the OECD states were Russia and China to disappear from the face of the earth. That is, West Germany and France would arm themselves against each other as they did in the 1930s, Australia and New Zealand would send military advisers to block each other's advances in Africa, and the U.S.-Canadian border would become fortified. Such a prospect is, of course, ludicrous: minus Marxist-Leninist ideology, we are far more likely to see the "Common Marketization" of world politics than the disintegration of the EEC into nineteenth-century competitiveness. Indeed, as our experience in dealing with Europe on matters such as terrorism or Libya prove, they are much further gone than we down the road that denies the legitimacy of the use of force in international politics, even in self-defense.

The automatic assumption that Russia shorn of its expansionist communist ideology should pick up where the czars left off just prior to the Bolshevik Revolution is therefore a curious one. It assumes that the evolution of human consciousness has stood still in the meantime, and that the Soviets, while picking up currently fashionable ideas in the realm of economics, will return to foreign policy views a century out of date in the rest of Europe. This is certainly not what happened to China after it began its reform process. Chinese competitiveness and expansionism on the world scene have virtually disappeared: Beijing no longer sponsors Maoist insurgencies or tries to cultivate influence in distant African countries as it did in the 1960s. This is not to say that there are not troublesome aspects to contemporary Chinese foreign policy, such as the reckless sale of ballistic missile technology in the Middle East; and the PRC continues to manifest traditional great power behavior in its sponsorship of the Khmer Rouge against Vietnam. But the former is explained by commercial motives and the latter is a vestige of earlier ideologically-based rivalries. The new China far more resembles Gaullist France than pre–World War I Germany.

The real question for the future, however, is the degree to which Soviet elites have assimilated the consciousness of the universal homogenous state that is post-Hitler Europe. From their writings and from my own personal contacts with them, there is no question in my mind that the liberal Soviet intelligentsia rallying around Gorbachev has arrived at the end-of-history view in a remarkably short time, due in no small measure to the contacts they have had since the Brezhnev era with the larger European civilization around them.

"New political thinking," the general rubric for their views, describes a world dominated by economic concerns, in which there are no ideological grounds for major conflict between nations, and in which, consequently, the use of military force becomes less legitimate. As Foreign Minister Shevardnadze put it in mid-1988:

> The struggle between two opposing systems is no longer a determining tendency of the present-day era. At the modern stage, the ability to build up material wealth at an accelerated rate on the basis of front-ranking science and high-level techniques and technology, and to distribute it fairly, and through joint efforts to restore and protect the resources necessary for mankind's survival acquires decisive importance.

The post-historical consciousness represented by "new thinking" is only one possible future for the Soviet Union, however. There has always been a very strong current of great Russian chauvinism in the Soviet Union, which has found freer expression since the advent of *glasnost*. It may be possible to return to traditional Marxism-Leninism for a while as a simple rallying point for those who want to restore the authority that Gorbachev has dissipated. But as in Poland, Marxism-Leninism is dead as a mobilizing ideology: under its banner people cannot be made to work harder, and its adherents have lost confidence in themselves. Unlike the propagators of traditional Marxism-Leninism, however, ultranationalists in the USSR believe in their Slavophile cause passionately, and one gets the sense that the fascist alternative is not one that has played itself out entirely there.

The Soviet Union, then, is at a fork in the road: it can start down the path that was staked out by Western Europe forty-five years ago, a path that most of Asia has followed, or it can realize its own uniqueness and remain stuck in history. The choice it makes will be highly important for us, given the Soviet Union's size and military strength, for that power will continue to preoccupy us and slow our realization that we have already emerged on the other side of history.

V

The passing of Marxism-Leninism first from China and then from the Soviet Union will mean its death as a living ideology of world historical significance. For while there may be some isolated true believers left in places like Managua, Pyongyang, or Cambridge, Massachusetts, the fact that there is not a single large state in which it is a going concern undermines completely its pretensions to being in the vanguard of human history. And the death of this ideology means the growing "Common Marketization" of international relations, and the diminution of the likelihood of large-scale conflict between states.

This does not by any means imply the end of international conflict *per se*. For the world at that point would be divided between a part that was historical and a part that was post-historical. Conflict between states still in history, and between those states and those at the end of history, would still be possible.

There would still be a high and perhaps rising level of ethnic and nationalist violence, since those are impulses incompletely played out, even in parts of the post-historical world. Palestinians and Kurds, Sikhs and Tamils, Irish Catholics and Walloons, Armenians and Azeris, will continue to have their unresolved grievances. This implies that terrorism and wars of national liberation will continue to be an important item on the international agenda. But large-scale conflict must involve large states still caught in the grip of history, and they are what appear to be passing from the scene.

The end of history will be a very sad time. The struggle for recognition, the willingness to risk one's life for a purely abstract goal, the worldwide ideological struggle that called forth daring, courage, imagination, and idealism, will be replaced by economic calculation, the endless solving of technical problems, environmental concerns, and the satisfaction of sophisticated consumer demands. In the post-historical period there will be neither art nor philosophy, just the perpetual caretaking of the museum of human history. I can feel in myself, and see in others around me, a powerful nostalgia for the time when history existed. Such nostalgia, in fact, will continue to fuel competition and conflict even in the post-historical world for some time to come. Even though I recognize its inevitability, I have the most ambivalent feelings for the civilization that has been created in Europe since 1945, with its North Atlantic and Asian offshoots. Perhaps this very prospect of centuries of boredom at the end of history will serve to get history started once again.

NOTES

1 Kojève's best-known work is his *Introduction à la lecture de Hegel* (Paris: Editions Gallimard, 1947), which is a transcript of the Ecole Practique lectures from the 1930s. This book is available in English entitled *Introduction to the Reading of Hegel* arranged by Raymond Queneau, edited by Allan Bloom, and translated by James Nichols (New York: Basic Books, 1969).

2 One need look no further than the recent performance of Vietnamese immigrants in the U.S. school system when compared to their black or Hispanic classmates to realize that culture and consciousness are absolutely crucial to explain not only economic behavior but virtually every other important aspect of life as well.

3 I am not using the term "fascism" here in its most precise sense, fully aware of the frequent misuse of this term to denounce anyone to the right of the user. "Fascism" here denotes any organized ultranationalist movement with universalistic pretensions— not universalistic with regard to its nationalism, of course, since the latter is exclusive by definition, but with regard to the movement's belief in its right to rule other people. Hence Imperial Japan would qualify as fascist while former strongman Stoessner's Paraguay or Pinochet's Chile would not. Obviously fascist ideologies cannot be universalistic in the sense of Marxism or liberalism, but the structure of the doctrine can be transferred from country to country.

4 See his article, "Beyond the Cold War," *New Republic*, December 19, 1988.

5 It took European colonial powers like France several years after the war to admit the illegitimacy of their empires, but decolonization was an inevitable consequence of the Allied victory which had been based on the promise of a restoration of democratic freedoms.

Reading 1.2

Why We Will Soon Miss the Cold War
JOHN J. MEARSHEIMER

Peace: It's wonderful. I like it as much as the next man, and have no wish to be willfully gloomy at a moment when optimism about the future shape of the world abounds. Nevertheless, my thesis in this essay is that we are likely soon to regret the passing of the Cold War.

To be sure, no one will miss such by-products of the Cold War as the Korean and Vietnam conflicts. No one will want to replay the U–2 affair, the Cuban missile crisis, or the building of the Berlin Wall. And no one will want to revisit the domestic Cold War, with its purges and loyalty oaths, its xenophobia and stifling of dissent. We will not wake up one day to discover fresh wisdom in the collected fulminations of John Foster Dulles.

We may, however, wake up one day lamenting the loss of the order that the Cold War gave to the anarchy of international relations. For untamed anarchy is what Europe knew in the forty-five years of this century before the Cold War, and untamed anarchy—Hobbes's war of all against all—is a prime cause of armed conflict. Those who think that armed conflicts among the European states are now out of the question, that the two world wars burned all the war out of Europe, are projecting unwarranted optimism onto the future. The theories of peace that implicitly undergird this optimism are notably shallow constructs. They stand up to neither logical nor historical analysis. You would not want to bet the farm on their prophetic accuracy.

The world is about to conduct a vast test of the theories of war and peace put forward by social scientists, who never dreamed that their ideas would be tested by the world-historic events announced almost daily in newspaper headlines. This social scientist is willing to put his theoretical cards on the table as he ventures predictions about the future of Europe. In the process, I hope to put alternative theories of war and peace under as much intellectual pressure as I can muster. My argument is that the prospect of major crises, even wars, in Europe is likely to increase dramatically now that the Cold War is receding into history. The next forty-five years in Europe are not likely to be so violent as the forty-five years before the Cold War, but they are likely to be substantially more violent than the past forty-five years, the era that we may someday look back upon not as the Cold War but as the Long Peace, in John Lewis Gaddis's phrase.

This pessimistic conclusion rests on the general argument that the distribution and character of military power among states are the root causes of war and peace. Specifically, the peace in Europe since 1945—precarious at first, but increasingly robust over time—has flowed from three factors: the bipolar distribution of military power on the Continent; the rough military equality between the polar powers, the United States and the Soviet Union; and the ritualistically deplored fact that each of these superpowers is armed with a large nuclear arsenal.

We don't yet know the entire shape of the new Europe. But we do know some things. We know, for example, that the new Europe will involve a return to the multipolar distribution of power that characterized the European state system from its founding, with the Peace of Westphalia, in 1648, until 1945. We know that this multipolar European state system was plagued by war from first to last. We know that from 1900 to 1945 some 50 million Europeans were killed in wars that were caused in great part by the instability of this state system. We also know that since 1945 only some 15,000 Europeans have been killed in wars; roughly 10,000 Hungarians and Russians, in what we might call the Russo-Hungarian War of October and November, 1956, and somewhere between 1,500 and 5,000 Greeks and Turks, in the July and August, 1974, war on Cyprus.

The point is clear: Europe is reverting to a state system that created powerful incentives for aggression in the past. If you believe (as the Realist school of international-relations theory, to which I belong, believes) that the prospects of international peace are not markedly influenced by the domestic political character of states—that it is the character of the state system, not the character of the individual units composing it, that drives states toward war—then it is difficult to share in the widespread elation of the moment about the future of Europe. Last year was repeatedly compared to 1789, the year the French Revolution began, as the Year of Freedom, and so it was. Forgotten in the general exaltation was that the hope-filled events of 1789 signaled the start of an era of war and conquest.

A "HARD" THEORY OF PEACE

What caused the era of violence in Europe before 1945, and why has the postwar era, the period of the Cold War, been so much more peaceful? The two world wars before 1945 had myriad particular and unrepeatable causes, but to the student of international relations seeking to establish generalizations about the behavior of states in the past which might illuminate their behavior in the future, two fundamental causes stand out. These are the multipolar distribution of power in Europe, and the imbalances of strength that often developed among the great powers as they jostled for supremacy or advantage.

There is something elementary about the geometry of power in international relations, and so its importance is easy to overlook. "Bipolarity" and "multipolarity" are ungainly but necessary coinages. The Cold War, with two superpowers serving to anchor rival alliances of clearly inferior powers, is our model of bipolarity. Europe in 1914, with France, Germany, Great Britain, Austria-Hungary, and Russia positioned as great powers, is our model of multipolarity.

If the example of 1914 is convincing enough evidence that multipolar systems are the more dangerous geometry of power, then perhaps I should rest my case. Alas for theoretical elegance, there are no empirical studies providing conclusive support for this proposition. From its beginnings until 1945 the European state system was multipolar, so this history is barren of comparisons that would reveal the differing effects of the two systems. Earlier history, to be sure, does furnish scattered examples of bipolar systems, including some—Athens and Sparta, Rome and Carthage—that were warlike. But this history is inconclusive, because it is incomplete. Lacking a comprehensive survey of history, we can't do much more than offer examples—now on this, now on that side of the debate. As a result, the case made here rests chiefly on deduction.

Deductively, a bipolar system is more peaceful for the simple reason that under it only two major powers are in contention. Moreover, those great powers generally demand allegiance from minor powers in the system, which is likely to produce rigid alliance structures. The smaller states are then secure from each other as well as from attack by the rival great power. Consequently (to make a Dick-and-Jane point with a well-worn social-science term), a bipolar system has only one dyad across which war might break out. A multipolar system is much more fluid and has many such dyads. Therefore, other things being equal, war is statistically more likely in a multipolar system than it is in a bipolar one. Admittedly, wars in a multipolar world that involve only minor powers or only one major power are not likely to be as devastating as a conflict between two major powers. But small wars always have the potential to widen into big wars.

Also, deterrence is difficult to maintain in a multipolar state system, because power imbalances are common-place, and when power asymmetries develop, the strong become hard to deter. Two great powers can join together to attack a third state, as Germany and the Soviet Union did in 1939, when they ganged up on Poland. Furthermore, a major power might simply bully a weaker power in a one-on-one encounter, using its superior strength to coerce or defeat the minor state. Germany's actions against Czechoslovakia in the late 1930s provide a good example of this sort of behavior. Ganging up and bullying are largely unknown in a bipolar system, since with only two great powers dominating center stage, it is impossible to produce the power asymmetries that result in ganging up and bullying.

There is a second reason that deterrence is more problematic under multipolarity. The resolve of opposing states and also the size and strength of opposing coalitions are hard to calculate in this geometry of power, because the shape of the international order tends to remain in flux, owing to the tendency of coalitions to gain and lose partners. This can lead aggressors to conclude falsely that they can coerce others by bluffing war, or even achieve outright victory on the battlefield. For example, Germany was not certain before 1914 that Britain would oppose it if it reached for Continental hegemony, and Germany completely failed to foresee that the United States would eventually move to contain it. In 1939 Germany hoped that France and Britain would stand aside as it conquered Poland, and again failed to foresee the eventual American entry into the war. As a result, Germany exaggerated its prospects for success, which undermined deterrence by encouraging German adventurism.

The prospects for peace, however, are not simply a function of the number of great powers in the system. They are also affected by the relative military strength of those major states. Bipolar and multipolar systems both are likely to be more peaceful when power is distributed equally in them. Power inequalities invite war, because they increase an aggressor's prospects for victory on the battlefield. Most of the general wars that have tormented Europe over the past five centuries have involved one particularly powerful state against the other major powers in the system. This pattern characterized the wars that grew from the attempts at hegemony by Charles V, Philip II, Louis XIV, Revolutionary and Napoleonic France, Wilhelmine Germany, and Nazi Germany. Hence the size of the gap in military power between the two leading states in the system is a key determinant of stability. Small gaps foster peace; larger gaps promote war.

Nuclear weapons seem to be in almost everybody's bad book, but the fact is that they are a powerful force for peace. Deterrence is most likely to hold when the costs and risks of going to war are unambiguously stark. The more horrible the prospect of war, the less likely war is. Deterrence is also more robust when conquest is more difficult. Potential aggressor states are given pause by the patent futility of attempts at expansion.

Nuclear weapons favor peace on both counts. They are weapons of mass destruction, and would produce horrendous devastation if used in any numbers. Moreover, they are more useful for self-defense than for aggression. If both sides' nuclear arsenals are secure from attack, creating an arrangement of mutual assured destruction, neither side can employ these weapons to gain a meaningful military advantage. International conflicts then become tests of pure will. Who would dare to use these weapons of unimaginable destructive power? Defenders have the advantage here, because defenders usually value their freedom more than aggressors value new conquests.

Nuclear weapons further bolster peace by moving power relations among states toward equality. States that possess nuclear deterrents can stand up to one another, even if their nuclear arsenals vary greatly in size, as long as both sides have an assured destruction capability. In addition, mutual assured destruction helps alleviate the vexed problem of miscalculation by leaving little doubt about the relative power of states.

No discussion of the causes of peace in the twentieth century would be complete without a word on nationalism. With "nationalism" as a synonym for "love of country" I have no quarrel. But hypernationalism, the belief that other nations or nation-states are both inferior and threatening, is perhaps the single greatest domestic threat to peace, although it is still not a leading force in world politics. Hypernationalism arose in the past among European states because most of them were nation-states—states composed mainly of people from a single ethnic group—that existed in an anarchic world, under constant threat from other states. In such a system people who love their own nation can easily come to be contemptuous of the nationalities inhabiting opposing states. The problem is worsened when domestic elites demonize a rival nation to drum up support for national-security policy.

Hypernationalism finds its most fertile soil under military systems relying on mass armies. These require sacrifices to sustain, and the state is tempted to appeal to nationalist sentiments to mobilize its citizens to make them. The quickening of hypernationalism is least likely when states can rely on small professional armies, or on complex high-technology military organizations that operate without vast manpower. For this reason, nuclear weapons work to dampen nationalism, because they shift the basis of military power away from mass armies and toward smaller, high-technology organizations.

Hypernationalism declined sharply in Europe after 1945, not only because of the nuclear revolution but also because the postwar occupation forces kept it down. Moreover, the European states, no longer providing their own security, lacked an incentive to whip up nationalism to bolster public support for national defense. But the decisive change came in the shift of the prime locus of European politics to the United States and the Soviet Union—two states made up of peoples of many different ethnic origins which had not exhibited nationalism of the virulent type found in Europe. This welcome absence of hypernationalism has been further helped by the greater stability of the postwar order. With less expectation of war, neither superpower felt compelled to mobilize its citizens for war.

Bipolarity, an equal balance of military power, and nuclear weapons—these, then, are the key elements of my explanation for the Long Peace.

Many thoughtful people have found the bipolar system in Europe odious and have sought to end it by dismantling the Soviet empire in Eastern Europe and diminishing Soviet military power. Many have also lamented the military equality obtaining between the superpowers; some have decried the indecisive stalemate it produced, recommending instead a search for military superiority; others have lamented the investment of hundreds of billions of dollars to deter a war that never happened, proving not that the investment, though expensive, paid off, but rather that it was wasted. As for nuclear weapons, well, they are a certifiable Bad Thing. The odium attached to these props of the postwar order has kept many in the West from recognizing a hard truth: they have kept the peace.

But so much for the past. What will keep the peace in the future? Specifically, what new order is likely to emerge if NATO and the Warsaw Pact dissolve, which they will do if the Cold War is really over, and the Soviets withdraw from Eastern Europe and the Americans quit Western Europe, taking their nuclear weapons with them—and should we welcome or fear it?

One dimension of the new European order is certain: it will be multipolar. Germany, France, Britain, and perhaps Italy will assume major-power status. The Soviet Union will decline from superpower status, not only because its military is sure to shrink in size but also because moving forces out of Eastern Europe will make it more difficult for the Soviets to project power onto the Continent. They will, of course, remain a major European power. The resulting four- or five-power system will suffer the problems endemic to multipolar systems—and will therefore be prone to instability. The other two dimensions—the distribution of power among the major states and the distribution of nuclear weapons—are less certain. Indeed, who gets nuclear weapons is likely to be the most problematic question facing the new Europe. Three scenarios of the nuclear future in Europe are possible.

THE "EUROPE WITHOUT NUCLEAR WEAPONS" SCENARIO

Many Europeans (and some Americans) seek to eliminate nuclear weapons from Europe altogether. Fashioning this nuclear-free Europe would require that Britain, France, and the Soviet Union rid themselves of these talismans of their sovereignty—an improbable eventuality, to say the least. Those who wish for it nevertheless believe that it would be the most peaceful arrangement possible. In fact a nuclear-free Europe has the distinction of being the most dangerous among the envisionable post–Cold War orders. The pacifying effects of nuclear weapons—the caution they generate, the security they provide, the rough equality they impose, and the clarity of the relative power they create—would be lost. Peace would then depend on the other dimensions of the new order—the number of poles and the distribution of power among them. The geometry of power in Europe would look much as it did between the world wars—a design for tension, crisis, and possibly even war.

The Soviet Union and a unified Germany would likely be the most powerful states in a nuclear-free Europe. A band of small independent states in Eastern Europe would lie between them. These minor Eastern European powers would be likely to fear the Soviets as much as the Germans, and thus would probably not be disposed to cooperate with the Soviets to deter possible German aggression. In fact, this very problem arose in the 1930s, and the past forty-five years of Soviet occupation have surely done little to mitigate Eastern European fears of a Soviet military presence. Thus scenarios in which Germany uses force against Poland, Czechoslovakia, or even Austria enter the realm of the possible in a nuclear-free Europe.

Then, too, the Soviet withdrawal from Eastern Europe hardly guarantees a permanent exit. Indeed, the Russian presence in Eastern Europe has surged and ebbed repeatedly over the past few centuries. In a grave warning, a member of President Mikhail Gorbachev's negotiating team at the recent Washington summit said, "You have the same explosive mixture you had in Germany in the 1930s. The humiliation of a great power. Economic troubles. The rise of nationalism. You should not underestimate the danger."

Conflicts between Eastern European states might also threaten the stability of the new European order. Serious tensions already exist between Hungary and Romania over Romania's treatment of the Hungarian minority in Transylvania, a formerly Hungarian region that still contains roughly two million ethnic Hungarians. Absent the Soviet occupation of Eastern Europe, Romania and Hungary might have gone to war over this issue by now, and it might bring them to war in the future. This is not the only potential danger spot in Eastern Europe as the Soviet empire crumbles. The Polish-German border could be a source of trouble. Poland and Czechoslovakia have a border dispute. If the Soviets allow some of their republics to achieve independence, the Poles and the Romanians may lay claim to territory now in Soviet hands which once belonged to them. Looking farther south, civil war in Yugoslavia is a distinct possibility. Yugoslavia and Albania might come to blows over Kosovo, a region of Yugoslavia harboring a nationalistic Albanian majority. Bulgaria has its own quarrel with Yugoslavia over Macedonia, while Turkey resents Bulgaria's treatment of its Turkish minority. The danger that these bitter ethnic and border disputes will erupt into war in a supposedly Edenic nuclear-free Europe is enough to make one nostalgic for the Cold War.

Warfare in Eastern Europe would cause great suffering to Eastern Europeans. It also might widen to include the major powers, especially if disorder created fluid politics that offered opportunities for expanded influence, or threatened defeat for states friendly to one or another of the major powers. During the Cold War both superpowers were drawn into Third World conflicts across the globe, often in distant areas of little strategic importance. Eastern Europe is directly adjacent to both the Soviet Union and Germany, and it has considerable economic and strategic importance. Thus trouble in Eastern Europe would offer even greater temptations to these powers than past conflicts in the Third World offered to the superpowers. Furthermore, Eastern European states would have a strong incentive to drag the major powers into their local conflicts, because the results of such conflicts would be largely determined by the relative success of each party in finding external allies.

It is difficult to predict the precise balance of conventional military power that will emerge in post–Cold War Europe. The Soviet Union might recover its strength soon after withdrawing from Eastern Europe. In that case Soviet power would outmatch German power. But centrifugal national forces might pull the Soviet Union apart, leaving no remnant state that is the equal of a unified Germany. Finally, and probably most likely, Germany and the Soviet Union might emerge as powers of roughly equal strength. The first two geometries of power, with their marked military inequality between the two leading countries, would be especially worrisome, although there would be cause for concern even if Soviet and German power were balanced.

A non-nuclear Europe, to round out this catalogue of dangers, would likely be especially disturbed by hypernationalism, since security in such an order would rest on mass armies, which, as we have seen, often cannot be maintained without a mobilized public. The problem would probably be most acute in Eastern Europe, with its uncertain borders and irredentist minority groups. But there is also potential for trouble in Germany. The Germans have generally done an admirable job of combating hypernationalism over the past forty-five years, and of confronting the dark side of their past. Nevertheless, a portent like the recent call of some prominent Germans for a return to greater nationalism in historical education is disquieting.

For all these reasons, it is perhaps just as well that a nuclear-free Europe, much as it may be longed for by so many Europeans, does not appear to be in the cards.

THE "CURRENT OWNERSHIP" SCENARIO

Under this scenario Britain, France, and the Soviet Union retain their nuclear weapons, but no new nuclear powers emerge in Europe. This vision of a nuclear-free zone in Central Europe, with nuclear weapons remaining on the flanks of the Continent, is also popular in Europe, but it, too, has doubtful prospects.

Germany will prevent it over the long run. The Germans are not likely to be willing to rely on the Poles or the Czechs to provide their forward defense against a possible direct Soviet conventional attack on their homeland. Nor are the Germans likely to trust the Soviet Union to refrain for all time from nuclear blackmail against a non-nuclear Germany. Hence they will eventually look to nuclear weapons as the surest means of security, just as NATO has done.

The small states of Eastern Europe will also have strong incentives to acquire nuclear weapons. Without them they would be open to nuclear blackmail by the Soviet Union, or by Germany if proliferation stopped there. Even if those major powers did not have nuclear arsenals, no Eastern European state could match German or Soviet conventional strength.

Clearly, then, a scenario in which current ownership continues, without proliferation, seems very unlikely.

THE "NUCLEAR PROLIFERATION" SCENARIO

The most probable scenario in the wake of the Cold War is further nuclear proliferation in Europe. This outcome is laden with dangers, but it also might just provide the best hope for maintaining stability on the Continent. Everything depends on how proliferation is managed. Mismanaged proliferation could produce disaster; well-managed proliferation could produce an order nearly as stable as that of the Long Peace.

The dangers that could arise from mismanaged proliferation are both profound and numerous. There is the danger that the proliferation process itself could give one of the existing nuclear powers a strong incentive to stop a non-nuclear neighbor from joining the club, much as Israel used force to stop Iraq from acquiring a nuclear capability. There is the danger that an unstable nuclear competition would emerge among the new nuclear states. They might lack the resources to make their nuclear forces invulnerable, which could create first-strike fears and incentives—a recipe for disaster in a crisis. Finally, there is the danger that by increasing the number of fingers on the nuclear trigger, proliferation would increase the risk that nuclear weapons would be fired by accident or captured by terrorists or used by madmen.

These and other dangers of proliferation can be lessened if the current nuclear powers take the right steps. To forestall preventive attacks, they can extend security guarantees. To help the new nuclear powers secure their deterrents, they can provide technical assistance. And they can help to socialize nascent nuclear societies to understand the lethal character of the forces they are acquiring. This kind of well-managed proliferation could help bolster peace.

Proliferation should ideally stop with Germany. It has a large economic base, and so could afford to sustain a secure nuclear force. Moreover, Germany would no doubt feel insecure without nuclear weapons, and if it felt insecure its impressive conventional strength would give it a significant capacity to disturb the tranquility of Europe. But if the broader spread of nuclear weapons proves impossible to prevent without taking extreme steps, the current nuclear powers should let proliferation occur in Eastern Europe while doing all they can to channel it in safe directions.

However, I am pessimistic that proliferation can be well managed. The members of the nuclear club are likely to resist proliferation, but they cannot easily manage this tricky process while at the same time resisting it—and they will have several motives to resist. The established nuclear powers will be exceedingly chary of helping the new nuclear powers build secure deterrents, simply because it goes against the grain of state behavior to share military secrets with other states. After all, knowledge of sensitive military technology could be turned against the donor state if that technology were passed on to adversaries. Furthermore, proliferation in Europe will undermine the legitimacy of the 1968 Nuclear Non-Proliferation Treaty, and this could open the floodgates of proliferation worldwide. The current nuclear powers will not want that to happen, and so they will probably spend their energy trying to thwart proliferation, rather than seeking to manage it.

The best time for proliferation to occur would be during a period of relative international calm. Proliferation in the midst of a crisis would obviously be dangerous, since states in conflict with an emerging nuclear power would then have a powerful incentive to interrupt the process by force. However, the opposition to proliferation by citizens of the potential nuclear powers would be so vociferous, and the external resistance from the nuclear club would be so great, that it might take a crisis to make those powers willing to pay the domestic and international costs of building a nuclear force. All of which means that proliferation is likely to occur under international conditions that virtually ensure it will be mismanaged.

IS WAR OBSOLETE?

Many students of European politics will reject my pessimistic analysis of post–Cold War Europe. They will say that a multipolar Europe, with or without nuclear weapons, will be no less peaceful than the present order. Three specific scenarios for a peaceful future have been advanced, each of which rests on a well-known theory of international relations. However, each of these "soft" theories of peace is flawed.

Under the first optimistic scenario, a non-nuclear Europe would remain peaceful because Europeans recognize that even a conventional war would be horrific. Sobered by history, national leaders will take care to avoid war. This scenario rests on the "obsolescence of war" theory, which posits that modern conventional war had become so deadly by 1945 as to be unthinkable as an instrument of statecraft. War is yesterday's nightmare.

The fact that the Second World War occurred casts doubt on this theory: if any war could have persuaded Europeans to forswear conventional war, it should have been the First World War, with its vast casualties. The key flaw in this theory is the assumption that all conventional wars will be long and bloody wars of attrition. Proponents ignore the evidence of several wars since 1945, as well as several campaign-ending battles of the Second World War, that it is still possible to gain a quick and decisive victory on the conventional battlefield and avoid the devastation of a protracted conflict. Conventional wars can be won rather cheaply; nuclear war cannot be, because neither side can escape devastation by the other, regardless of what happens on the battlefield. Thus the incentives to avoid war are of another order of intensity in a nuclear world than they are in a conventional world.

There are several other flaws in this scenario. There is no systematic evidence demonstrating that Europeans believe war is obsolete. The Romanians and the Hungarians don't seem to have gotten the message. However, even if it were widely believed in Europe that war is no longer thinkable, attitudes could change. Public opinion on national-security issues is notoriously fickle and responsive to manipulation by elites as well as to changes in the international environment. An end to the Cold War, as we have seen, will be accompanied by a sea change in the geometry of power in Europe, which will surely alter European thinking about questions of war and peace. Is it not possible, for example, that German thinking about the benefits of controlling Eastern Europe will change markedly once American forces are withdrawn from Central Europe and the Germans are left to provide for their own-security? Is it not possible that they would countenance a conventional war against a substantially weaker Eastern European state to enhance their position vis-à-vis the Soviet Union? Finally, only one country need decide that war is thinkable to make war possible.

IS PROSPERITY THE PATH TO PEACE?

Proponents of the second optimistic scenario base their optimism about the future of Europe on the unified European market coming in 1992—the realization of the dream of the European Community. A strong EC, they argue, ensures that the European economy will remain open and prosperous, which will keep the European states cooperating with one another. Prosperity will make for peace. The threat of an aggressive Germany will be removed by enclosing the newly unified German state in the benign embrace of the EC. Even Eastern Europe and the Soviet Union can eventually be brought into the EC. Peace and prosperity will then extend their sway from the Atlantic to the Urals.

This scenario is based on the theory of economic liberalism, which assumes that states are primarily motivated by the desire to achieve prosperity and that leaders place the material welfare of their publics above all other considerations, including security. Stability flows not from military power but from the creation of a liberal economic order.

A liberal economic order works in several ways to enhance peace and dampen conflict. In the first place, it requires significant political cooperation to make the trading system work—make states richer. The more prosperous states grow, the greater their incentive for further political cooperation. A benevolent spiral relationship sets in between political cooperation and prosperity. Second, a liberal economic order fosters economic interdependence, a situation in which states are mutually vulnerable in the economic realm. When interdependence is high, the theory holds, there is less temptation to cheat or behave aggressively toward other states, because all states can retaliate economically. Finally, some theorists argue, an international institution like the EC will, with ever-increasing political cooperation, become so powerful that it will take on a life of its own, eventually evolving into a superstate. In short, Mrs. Thatcher's presentiments about the EC are absolutely right.

This theory has one grave flaw: the main assumption underpinning it is wrong. States are not primarily motivated by the desire to achieve prosperity. Although economic calculations are hardly trivial to them, states operate in both an international political and an international economic environment, and the former dominates the latter when the two systems come into conflict. Survival in an anarchic international political system is the highest goal a state can have.

Proponents of economic liberalism largely ignore the effects of anarchy on state behavior and concentrate instead on economic motives. When this omission is corrected, however, their arguments collapse for two reasons.

Competition for security makes it difficult for states to cooperate, which, according to the theory of economic liberalism, they must do. When security is scarce, states become more concerned about relative than about absolute gains. They ask of an exchange not "Will both of us gain?" but "Who will gain more?" They reject even cooperation that will yield an absolute economic gain if the other state will gain more, from fear that the other might convert its gain to military strength, and then use this strength to win by coercion in later rounds. Cooperation is much easier to achieve if states worry only about absolute gains. The goal, then, is simply to ensure that the overall economic pie is expanding and that each state is getting at least some part of the increase. However, anarchy guarantees that security will often be scarce; this heightens states' concerns about relative gains, which makes cooperation difficult unless the pie can be finely sliced to reflect, and thus not disturb, the current balance of power.

Interdependence, moreover, is as likely to lead to conflict as to cooperation, because states will struggle to escape the vulnerability that interdependence creates, in order to bolster their national security. In time of crisis or war, states that depend on others for critical economic supplies will fear cutoff or blackmail; they may well respond by trying to seize the source of supply by force of arms. There are numerous historical examples of states' pursuing aggressive military policies for the purpose of achieving economic autarky. One thinks of both Japan and Germany during the interwar period. And one recalls that during the Arab oil embargo of the early 1970s there was much talk in America about using military force to seize Arab oil fields.

In twentieth-century Europe two periods saw a liberal economic order with high levels of interdependence. According to the theory of economic liberalism, stability should have obtained during those periods. It did not.

The first case clearly contradicts the economic liberals. The years from 1890 to 1914 were probably the time of greatest economic interdependence in Europe's history. Yet those years of prosperity were all the time making hideously for the First World War.

The second case covers the Cold War years, during which there has been much interdependence among the EC states, and relations among them have been very peaceful. This case, not surprisingly, is the centerpiece of the economic liberals' argument.

We certainly see a correlation in this period between interdependence and stability, but that does not mean that interdependence has caused cooperation among the Western democracies. More likely the Cold War was the prime cause of cooperation among the Western democracies, and the main reason that intra-EC relations have flourished.

A powerful and potentially dangerous Soviet Union forced the Western democracies to band together to meet a common threat. This threat muted concerns about relative gains arising from economic cooperation among the EC states by giving each Western democracy a vested interest in seeing its alliance partners grow powerful. Each increment of power helped deter the Soviets. Moreover, they all had a powerful incentive to avoid conflict with one another while the Soviet Union loomed to the East, ready to harvest the grain of Western quarrels.

In addition, America's hegemonic position in NATO, the military counterpart to the EC, mitigated the effects of anarchy on the Western democracies and induced cooperation among them. America not only provided protection against the Soviet threat; it also guaranteed that no EC state would aggress against another. For example, France did not have to fear Germany as it re-armed, because the American presence in Germany meant that the Germans were contained. With the United States serving as a night watchman, fears about relative gains among the Western European states were mitigated, and furthermore, those states were willing to allow their economies to become tightly interdependent.

Take away the present Soviet threat to Western Europe, send the American forces home, and relations among the EC states will be fundamentally altered. Without a common Soviet threat or an American night watchman, Western European states will do what they did for centuries before the onset of the Cold War—look upon one another with abiding suspicion. Consequently, they will worry about imbalances in gains and about the loss of autonomy that results from cooperation. Cooperation in this new order will be more difficult than it was during the Cold War. Conflict will be more likely.

In sum, there are good reasons for being skeptical about the claim that a more powerful EC can provide the basis for peace in a multipolar Europe.

DO DEMOCRACIES REALLY LOVE PEACE?

Under the third scenario war is avoided because many European states have become democratic since the early twentieth century, and liberal democracies simply do not fight one another. At a minimum, the presence of liberal democracies in Western Europe renders that half of Europe free from armed conflict. At a maximum, democracy spreads to Eastern Europe and the Soviet Union, bolstering peace. The idea that peace is cognate with democracy is a vision of international relations shared by both liberals and neoconservatives.

This scenario rests on the "peace-loving democracies" theory. Two arguments are made for it.

First, some claim that authoritarian leaders are more likely to go to war than leaders of democracies, because authoritarian leaders are not accountable to their publics, which carry the main burdens of war. In a democracy the citizenry, which pays the price of war, has a greater say in what the government does. The people, so the argument goes, are more hesitant to start trouble, because it is they who must pay the bloody price; hence the greater their power, the fewer wars.

The second argument rests on the claim that the citizens of liberal democracies respect popular democratic rights—those of their countrymen, and those of people in other states. They view democratic governments as more legitimate than others, and so are loath to impose a foreign regime on a democratic state by force. Thus an inhibition on war missing from other international relationships is introduced when two democracies face each other.

The first of these arguments is flawed because it is not possible to sustain the claim that the people in a democracy are especially sensitive to the costs of war and therefore less willing than authoritarian leaders to fight wars. In fact the historical record shows that democracies are every bit as likely to fight wars as are authoritarian states, though admittedly, thus far, not with other democracies.

Furthermore, mass publics, whether in a democracy or not, can become deeply imbued with nationalistic or religious fervor, making them prone to support aggression and quite indifferent to costs. The widespread public support in post-Revolutionary France for Napoleon's wars is just one example of this phenomenon. At the same time, authoritarian leaders are often fearful of going to war, because war tends to unleash democratic forces that can undermine the regime. In short, war can impose high costs on authoritarian leaders as well as on their citizenry.

The second argument, which emphasizes the transnational respect for democratic rights among democracies, rests on a secondary factor that is generally overridden by other factors such as nationalism and religious fundamentalism. Moreover, there is another problem with the argument. The possibility always exists that a democracy, especially the kind of fledgling democracy emerging in Eastern Europe, will revert to an authoritarian state. This threat of backsliding means that one democratic state can never be sure that another democratic state will not turn on it sometime in the future. Liberal democracies must therefore worry about relative power among themselves, which is tantamount to saying that each has an incentive to consider aggression against another to forestall trouble. Lamentably, it is not possible for even liberal democracies to transcend anarchy.

Problems with the deductive logic aside, at first glance the historical record seems to offer strong support for the theory of peace-loving democracies. It appears that no liberal democracies have ever fought against each other. Evidentiary problems, however, leave the issue in doubt.

First, democracies have been few in number over the past two centuries, and thus there have not been many cases in which two democracies were in a position to fight with each other. Three prominent cases are usually cited: Britain and the United States (1832 to the present); Britain and France (1832–1849; 1871–1940); and the Western democracies since 1945.

Second, there are other persuasive explanations for why war did not occur in those three cases, and these competing explanations must be ruled out before the theory of peace-loving democracies can be accepted. Whereas relations between the British and the Americans during the nineteenth century were hardly blissful, in the twentieth century they have been quite harmonious, and thus fit closely with the theory's expectations. That harmony, however, can easily be explained by common threats that forced Britain and the United States to work together—a serious German threat in the first part of the century, and later a Soviet threat. The same basic argument applies to relations between France and Britain. Although they were not on the best of terms during most of the nineteenth century, their relations improved significantly around the turn of the century, with the rise of Germany. Finally, as noted above, the Soviet threat goes far in explaining the absence of war among the Western democracies since 1945.

Third, several democracies have come close to fighting each other, suggesting that the absence of war may be due simply to chance. France and Britain approached war during the Fashoda crisis of 1898. France and Weimar Germany might have come to blows over the Rhineland during the 1920s. The United States has clashed with a number of elected governments in the Third World during the Cold War, including the Allende regime in Chile and the Arbenz regime in Guatemala.

Last, some would classify Wilhelmine Germany as a democracy, or at least a quasi-democracy; if so, the First World War becomes a war among democracies.

While the spread of democracy across Europe has great potential benefits for human rights, it will not guarantee peaceful relations among the states of post–Cold War Europe. Most Americans will find this argument counterintuitive. They see the United States as fundamentally peace-loving, and they ascribe this peacefulness to its democratic character. From this they generalize that democracies are more peaceful than authoritarian states, which leads them to conclude that the complete democratization of Europe would largely eliminate the threat of war. This view of international politics is likely to be repudiated by the events of coming years.

MISSING THE COLD WAR

The implications of my analysis are straightforward, if paradoxical. Developments that threaten to end the Cold War are dangerous. The West has an interest in maintaining peace in Europe. It therefore has an interest in maintaining the Cold War order, and hence has an interest in continuing the Cold War confrontation. The Cold War antagonism could be continued at lower levels of East-West tension than have prevailed in the past, but a complete end to the Cold War would create more problems than it would solve.

The fate of the Cold War is mainly in the hands of the Soviet Union. The Soviet Union is the only superpower that can seriously threaten to overrun Europe, and the Soviet threat provides the glue that holds NATO together. Take away that offensive threat and the United States is likely to abandon the Continent; the defensive alliance it has headed for forty years may well then disintegrate, bringing an end to the bipolar order that has kept the peace of Europe for the past forty-five years.

There is little the Americans or the West Europeans can do to perpetuate the Cold War.

For one thing, domestic politics preclude it. Western leaders obviously cannot base national-security policy on the need to maintain forces in Central Europe simply to keep the Soviets there. The idea of deploying large numbers of troops in order to bait the Soviets into an order-keeping competition would be dismissed as bizarre, and contrary to the general belief that ending the Cold War and removing the Soviet yoke from Eastern Europe would make the world safer and better.

For another, the idea of propping up a declining rival runs counter to the basic behavior of states. States are principally concerned about their relative power in the system—hence they look for opportunities to take advantage of one another. If anything, they prefer to see adversaries decline, and invariably do whatever they can to speed up the process and maximize the distance of the fall. States, in other words, do not ask which distribution of power best facilitates stability and then do everything possible to build or maintain such an order. Instead, each pursues the narrower aim of maximizing its power advantage over potential adversaries. The particular international order that-results is simply a by-product of that competition.

Consider, for example, the origins of the Cold War order in Europe. No state intended to create it. In fact the United States and the Soviet Union each worked hard in the early years of the Cold War to undermine the other's position in Europe, which would have needed the bipolar order on the Continent. The remarkably stable system that emerged in Europe in the late 1940s was the unintended consequence of an intense competition between the superpowers.

Moreover, even if the Americans and the West Europeans wanted to help the Soviets maintain their status as a superpower, it is not apparent that they could do so. The Soviet Union is leaving Eastern Europe and cutting its military forces largely because its economy is floundering badly. The Soviets don't know how to fix their economy themselves, and there is little that Western governments can do to help them. The West can and should avoid doing malicious mischief to the Soviet economy, but at this juncture it is difficult to see how the West can have a significant positive influence.

The fact that the West cannot sustain the Cold War does not mean that the United States should make no attempt to preserve the current order. It should do what it can to avert a complete mutual withdrawal from Europe. For instance, the American negotiating position at the conventional-arms-control talks should aim toward large mutual force reductions but should not contemplate complete mutual withdrawal. The Soviets may opt to withdraw all their forces unilaterally anyway; if so, there is little the United States can do to stop them.

Should complete Soviet withdrawal from Eastern Europe prove unavoidable, the West would confront the question of how to maintain peace in a multipolar Europe. Three policy prescriptions are in order.

First, the United States should encourage the limited and carefully managed proliferation of nuclear weapons in Europe. The best hope for avoiding war in post–Cold War Europe is nuclear deterrence; hence some nuclear proliferation is necessary, to compensate for the withdrawal of the Soviet and American nuclear arsenals from Central Europe. Ideally, as I have argued, nuclear weapons would spread to Germany but to no other state.

Second, Britain and the United States, as well as the Continental states, will have to counter any emerging aggressor actively and efficiently, in order to offset the ganging up and bullying that are sure to arise in post–Cold War Europe. Balancing in a multipolar system, however, is usually a problem-ridden enterprise, because of either geography or the problems of coordination. Britain and the United States, physically separated from the Continent, may conclude that they have little interest in what happens there. That would be abandoning their responsibilities and, more important, their interests. Both states failed to counter Germany before the two world wars, making war more likely. It is essential for peace in Europe that they not repeat their past mistakes.

Both states must maintain military forces that can be deployed against Continental states that threaten to start a war. To do this they must persuade their citizens to support a policy of continued Continental commitment. This will be more difficult than it once was, because its principal purpose will be to preserve peace, rather than to prevent an imminent hegemony, and the prevention of hegemony is a simpler goal to explain publicly. Furthermore, this prescription asks both countries to take on an unaccustomed task, given that it is the basic nature of states to focus on maximizing relative power, not on bolstering stability. Nevertheless, the British and the Americans have a real stake in peace, especially since there is the risk that a European war might involve the large-scale use of nuclear weapons. Therefore, it should be possible for their governments to lead their publics to recognize this interest and support policies that protect it.

The Soviet Union may eventually return to its past expansionism and threaten to upset the status quo. If so, we are back to the Cold War. However, if the Soviets adhere to status-quo policies, Soviet power could play a key role in countering Germany and in maintaining order in Eastern Europe. It is important in those cases where the Soviets are acting in a balancing capacity that the United States cooperate with its former adversary and not let residual distrust from the Cold War obtrude.

Third, a concerted effort should be made to keep hypernationalism at bay, especially in Eastern Europe. Nationalism has been contained during the Cold War, but it is likely to re-emerge once Soviet and American forces leave the heart of Europe. It will be a force for trouble unless curbed. The teaching of honest national history is especially important, since the teaching of false, chauvinist history is the main vehicle for spreading hypernationalism. States that teach a dishonestly self-exculpating or self-glorifying history should be publicly criticized and sanctioned.

None of these tasks will be easy. In fact, I expect that the bulk of my prescriptions will not be followed; most run contrary to important strains of domestic American and European opinion, and to the basic nature of state behavior. And even if they are followed, peace in Europe will not be guaranteed. If the Cold War is truly behind us, therefore, the stability of the past forty-five years is not likely to be seen again in the coming decades.

Reading 1.3

The Clash of Civilizations?

SAMUEL P. HUNTINGTON

THE NEXT PATTERN OF CONFLICT

World politics is entering a new phase, and intellectuals have not hesitated to proliferate visions of what it will be—the end of history, the return of traditional rivalries between nation states, and the decline of the nation state from the conflicting pulls of tribalism and globalism, among others. Each of these visions catches aspects of the emerging reality. Yet they all miss a crucial, indeed a central, aspect of what global politics is likely to be in the coming years.

It is my hypothesis that the fundamental source of conflict in this new world will not be primarily ideological or primarily economic. The great divisions among humankind and the dominating source of conflict will be cultural. Nation states will remain the most powerful actors in world affairs, but the principal conflicts of global politics will occur between nations and groups of different civilizations. The clash of civilizations will dominate global politics. The fault lines between civilizations will be the battle lines of the future.

Source: Samuel P. Huntington, "The Clash of Civilizations?" Reprinted by permission of Foreign Affairs, *Vol. 72, No. 3 (Summer 1993). Copyright 1993 by the Council on Foreign Relations, Inc.*

Conflict between civilizations will be the latest phase in the evolution of conflict in the modern world. For a century and a half after the emergence of the modern international system with the Peace of Westphalia, the conflicts of the Western world were largely among princes—emperors, absolute monarchs and constitutional monarchs attempting to expand their bureaucracies, their armies, their mercantilist economic strength and, most important, the territory they ruled. In the process they created nation states, and beginning with the French Revolution the principal lines of conflict were between nations rather than princes. In 1793, as R. R. Palmer put it, "The wars of kings were over; the wars of peoples had begun." This nineteenth-century pattern lasted until the end of World War I. Then, as a result of the Russian Revolution and the reaction against it, the conflict of nations yielded to the conflict of ideologies, first among communism, fascism-Nazism and liberal democracy, and then between communism and liberal democracy. During the Cold War, this latter conflict became embodied in the struggle between the two superpowers, neither of which was a nation state in the classical European sense and each of which defined its identity in terms of its ideology.

These conflicts between princes, nation states and ideologies were primarily conflicts within Western civilization, "Western civil wars," as William Lind has labeled them. This was as true of the Cold War as it was of the world wars and the earlier wars of the seventeenth, eighteenth and nineteenth centuries. With the end of the Cold War, international politics moves out of its Western phase, and its centerpiece becomes the interaction between the West and non-Western civilizations and among non-Western civilizations. In the politics of civilizations, the peoples and governments of non-Western civilizations no longer remain the objects of history as targets of Western colonialism but join the West as movers and shapers of history.

THE NATURE OF CIVILIZATIONS

During the Cold War the world was divided into the First, Second and Third Worlds. Those divisions are no longer relevant. It is far more meaningful now to group countries not in terms of their political or economic systems or in terms of their level of economic development but rather in terms of their culture and civilization.

What do we mean when we talk of a civilization? A civilization is a cultural entity. Villages, regions, ethnic groups, nationalities, religious groups, all have distinct cultures at different levels of cultural heterogeneity. The culture of a village in southern Italy may be different from that of a village in northern Italy, but both will share in a common Italian culture that distinguishes them from German villages. European communities, in turn, will share cultural features that distinguish them from Arab or Chinese communities. Arabs, Chinese and Westerners, however, are not part of any broader cultural entity. They constitute civilizations. A civilization is thus the highest cultural grouping of people and the broadest level of cultural identity people have short of that which distinguishes humans from other species. It is defined both by common objective elements, such as language, history, religion, customs, institutions, and by the subjective self-identification of people. People have levels of identity: a resident of Rome may define himself with varying degrees of intensity as a Roman, an Italian, a Catholic, a Christian, a European, a Westerner. The civilization to which he belongs is the broadest level of identification with which he intensely identifies. People can and do redefine their identities and, as a result, the composition and boundaries of civilizations change.

Civilizations may involve a large number of people, as with China ("a civilization pretending to be a state," as Lucian Pye put it), or a very small number of people, such as the Anglophone Caribbean. A civilization may include several nation states, as is the case with Western, Latin American and Arab civilizations, or only one, as is the case with Japanese civilization. Civilizations obviously blend and overlap, and may include subcivilizations. Western civilization has two major variants, European and North American, and Islam has its Arab, Turkic and Malay subdivisions. Civilizations are nonetheless meaningful entities, and while the lines between them are seldom sharp, they are real. Civilizations are dynamic; they rise and fall; they divide and merge. And, as any student of history knows, civilizations disappear and are buried in the sands of time.

Westerners tend to think of nation states as the principal actors in global affairs. They have been that, however, for only a few centuries. The broader reaches of human history have been the history of civilizations. In *A Study of History*, Arnold Toynbee identified 21 major civilizations; only six of them exist in the contemporary world.

WHY CIVILIZATIONS WILL CLASH

Civilization identity will be increasingly important in the future, and the world will be shaped in large measure by the interactions among seven or eight major civilizations. These include Western, Confucian, Japanese, Islamic, Hindu, Slavic-Orthodox, Latin American and possibly African civilization. The most important conflicts of the future will occur along the cultural fault lines separating these civilizations from one another.

Why will this be the case?

First, differences among civilizations are not only real; they are basic. Civilizations are differentiated from each other by history, language, culture, tradition and, most important, religion. The people of different civilizations have different views on the relations between God and man, the individual and the group, the citizen and the state, parents and children, husband and wife, as well as differing views of the relative importance of rights and responsibilities, liberty and authority, equality and hierarchy. These differences are the product of centuries. They will not soon disappear. They are far more fundamental than differences among political ideologies and political regimes. Differences do not necessarily mean conflict, and conflict does not necessarily mean violence. Over the centuries, however, differences among civilizations have generated the most prolonged and the most violent conflicts.

Second, the world is becoming a smaller place. The interactions between peoples of different civilizations are increasing; these increasing interactions intensify civilization consciousness and awareness of differences between civilizations and commonalities within civilizations. North African immigration to France generates hostility among Frenchmen and at the same time increased receptivity to immigration by "good" European Catholic Poles. Americans react far more negatively to Japanese investment than to larger investments from Canada and European countries. Similarly, as Donald Horowitz has pointed out, "An Ibo may be . . . an Owerri Ibo or an Onitsha Ibo in what was the Eastern region of Nigeria. In Lagos, he is simply an Ibo. In London, he is a Nigerian. In New York, he is an African." The interactions among peoples of different civilizations enhance the civilization-consciousness of people that, in turn, invigorates differences and animosities stretching or thought to stretch back deep into history.

Third, the processes of economic modernization and social change throughout the world are separating people from longstanding local identities. They also weaken the nation state as a source of identity. In much of the world religion has moved in to fill this gap, often in the form of movements that are labeled "fundamentalist." Such movements are found in Western Christianity, Judaism, Buddhism and Hinduism, as well as in Islam. In most countries and most religions the people active in fundamentalist movements are young, college-educated, middle-class technicians, professionals and business persons. The "unsecularization of the world," George Weigel has remarked, "is one of the dominant social facts of life in the late twentieth century." The revival of religion, "la-revanche de Dieu," as Gilles Kepel labeled it, provides a basis for identity and commitment that transcends national boundaries and unites civilizations.

Fourth, the growth of civilization-consciousness is enhanced by the dual role of the West. On the one hand, the West is at a peak of power. At the same time, however, and perhaps as a result, a return to the roots phenomenon is occurring among non-Western civilizations. Increasingly one hears references to trends toward a turning inward and "Asianization" in Japan, the end of the Nehru legacy and the "Hinduization" of India, the failure of Western ideas of socialism and nationalism and hence "re-Islamization" of the Middle East, and now a debate over Westernization versus Russianization in Boris Yeltsin's country. A West at the peak of its power confronts non-Wests that increasingly have the desire, the will and the resources to shape the world in non-Western ways.

In the past, the elites of non-Western societies were usually the people who were most involved with the West, had been educated at Oxford, the Sorbonne or Sandhurst, and had absorbed Western attitudes and values. At the same time, the populace in non-Western countries often remained deeply imbued with the indigenous culture. Now, however, these relationships are being reversed. A de-Westernization and indigenization of elites is occurring in many non-Western countries at the same time that Western, usually American, cultures, styles and habits become more popular among the mass of the people.

Fifth, cultural characteristics and differences are less mutable and hence less easily compromised and resolved than political and economic ones. In the former Soviet Union, communists can become democrats, the rich can become poor and the poor rich, but Russians cannot become Estonians and Azeris cannot become Armenians. In class and ideological conflicts, the key question was "Which side are you on?" and people could and did choose sides and change sides. In conflicts between civilizations, the question is "What are you?" That is a given that cannot be changed. And as we know, from Bosnia to the Caucasus to the Sudan, the wrong answer to that question can mean a bullet in the head. Even more than ethnicity, religion discriminates sharply and exclusively among people. A person can be half-French and half-Arab and simultaneously even a citizen of two countries. It is more difficult to be half-Catholic and half-Muslim.

Finally, economic regionalism is increasing. The proportions of total trade that were intraregional rose between 1980 and 1989 from 51 percent to 59 percent in Europe, 33 percent to 37 percent in East Asia, and 32 percent to 36 percent in North America. The importance of regional economic blocs is likely to continue to increase in the future. On the one hand, successful economic regionalism will reinforce civilization-consciousness. On the other hand, economic regionalism may succeed only when it is rooted in a common civilization. The European Community rests on the shared foundation of European culture and Western Christianity. The success of the North American Free Trade Area depends on the convergence now underway of Mexican, Canadian and American cultures. Japan, in contrast, faces difficulties in creating a comparable economic entity in East Asia because Japan is a society and civilization unique to itself. However strong the trade and investment links Japan may develop with other East Asian countries, its cultural differences with those countries inhibit and perhaps preclude its promoting regional economic integration like that in Europe and North America.

Common culture, in contrast, is clearly facilitating the rapid expansion of the economic relations between the People's Republic of China and Hong Kong, Taiwan, Singapore and the overseas Chinese communities in other Asian countries. With the Cold War over, cultural commonalities increasingly overcome ideological differences, and mainland China and Taiwan move closer together. If cultural commonality is a prerequisite for economic integration, the principal East Asian economic bloc of the future is likely to be centered on China. This bloc is, in fact, already coming into existence. As Murray Weidenbaum has observed,

> Despite the current Japanese dominance of the region, the Chinese-based economy of Asia is rapidly emerging as a new epicenter for industry, commerce and finance. This strategic area contains substantial amounts of technology and manufacturing capability (Taiwan), outstanding entrepreneurial, marketing and services acumen (Hong Kong), a fine communications network (Singapore), a tremendous pool of financial capital (all three), and very large endowments of land, resources and labor (mainland China). . . .

From Guangzhou to Singapore, from Kuala Lumpur to Manila, this influential network—often based on extensions of the traditional clans—has been described as the backbone of the East Asian economy.[1]

Culture and religion also form the basis of the Economic Cooperation Organization, which brings together ten non-Arab Muslim countries: Iran, Pakistan, Turkey, Azerbaijan, Kazakhstan, Kyrgyzstan, Turkmenistan, Tadjikistan, Uzbekistan and Afghanistan. One impetus to the revival and expansion of this organization, founded originally in the 1960s by Turkey, Pakistan and Iran, is the realization by the leaders of several of these countries that they had no chance of admission to the European Community. Similarly, Caricom, the Central American Common Market and Mercosur rest on common cultural foundations. Efforts to build a broader Caribbean-Central American economic entity bridging the Anglo-Latin divide, however, have to date failed.

As people define their identity in ethnic and religious terms, they are likely to see an "us" versus "them" relation existing between themselves and people of different ethnicity or religion. The end of ideologically defined states in Eastern Europe and the former Soviet Union permits traditional ethnic identities and animosities to come to the fore. Differences in culture and religion create differences over policy issues, ranging from human rights to immigration to trade and commerce to the environment. Geographical propinquity gives rise to conflicting territorial claims from Bosnia to Mindanao. Most important, the efforts of the West to promote its values of democracy and liberalism as universal values, to maintain its military predominance and to advance its economic interests engender countering responses from other civilizations. Decreasingly able to mobilize support and form coalitions on the basis of ideology, governments and groups will increasingly attempt to mobilize support by appealing to common religion and civilization identity.

The clash of civilizations thus occurs at two levels. At the microlevel, adjacent groups along the fault lines between civilizations struggle, often violently, over the control of territory and each other. At the macro-level, states from different civilizations compete for relative military and economic power, struggle over the control of international institutions and third parties, and competitively promote their particular political and religious values.

THE FAULT LINES BETWEEN CIVILIZATIONS

The fault lines between civilizations are replacing the political and ideological boundaries of the Cold War as the flash points for crisis and bloodshed. The Cold War began when the Iron Curtain divided Europe politically and ideologically. The Cold War ended with the end of the Iron Curtain. As the ideological division of Europe has disappeared, the cultural division of Europe between Western Christianity, on the one hand, and Orthodox Christianity and Islam, on the other, has reemerged. The most significant dividing line in Europe, as William Wallace has suggested, may well be the eastern boundary of Western Christianity in the year 1500. This line runs along what are now the boundaries between Finland and Russia and between the Baltic states and Russia, cuts through Belarus and Ukraine separating the more Catholic western Ukraine from Orthodox eastern Ukraine, swings westward separating Transylvania from the rest of Romania, and then goes through Yugoslavia almost exactly along the line now separating Croatia and Slovenia from the rest of Yugoslavia. In the Balkans this line, of course, coincides with the historic boundary between the Hapsburg and Ottoman empires. The peoples to the north and west of this line are Protestant or Catholic; they shared the common experiences of European history—feudalism, the Renaissance, the Reformation, the Enlightenment, the French Revolution, the Industrial Revolution; they are generally economically better off than the peoples to the east; and they may now look forward to increasing involvement in a common European economy and to the consolidation of democratic political systems. The peoples to the east and south of this line are Orthodox or Muslim; they historically belonged to the Ottoman or Tsarist empires and were only lightly touched by the shaping events in the rest of Europe; they are generally less advanced economically; they seem much less likely to develop stable democratic political systems. The Velvet Curtain of-culture has replaced the Iron Curtain of ideology as the most significant dividing line in Europe. As the events in Yugoslavia show, it is not only a line of difference; it is also at times a line of bloody conflict.

Conflict along the fault line between Western and Islamic civilizations has been going on for 1,300 years. After the founding of Islam, the Arab and Moorish surge west and north only ended at Tours in 732. From the eleventh to the thirteenth century the Crusaders attempted with temporary success to bring Christianity and Christian rule to the Holy Land. From the fourteenth to the seventeenth century, the Ottoman Turks reversed the balance, extended their sway over the Middle East and the Balkans, captured Constantinople, and twice laid siege to Vienna. In the nineteenth and early twentieth centuries as Ottoman power declined Britain, France, and Italy established Western control over most of North Africa and the Middle East.

After World War II, the West, in turn, began to retreat; the colonial empires disappeared; first Arab nationalism and then Islamic fundamentalism manifested themselves; the West became heavily dependent on the Persian Gulf countries for its energy; the oil-rich Muslim countries became money-rich and, when they wished to, weapons-rich. Several wars occurred between Arabs and Israel (created by the West). France fought a bloody and ruthless war in Algeria for most of the 1950s; British and French forces invaded Egypt in 1956; American forces went into Lebanon in 1958; subsequently American forces returned to Lebanon, attacked Libya, and engaged in various military encounters with Iran; Arab and Islamic terrorists, supported by at least three Middle Eastern governments, employed the weapon of the weak and bombed Western planes and installations and seized Western hostages. This warfare between Arabs and the West culminated in 1990, when the United States sent a massive army to the Persian Gulf to defend some Arab countries against aggression by another. In its aftermath NATO planning is increasingly directed to potential threats and instability along its "southern tier."

This centuries-old military interaction between the West and Islam is unlikely to decline. It could become more virulent. The Gulf War left some Arabs feeling proud that Saddam Hussein had attacked Israel and stood up to the West. It also left many feeling humiliated and resentful of the West's military presence in the Persian Gulf, the West's overwhelming military dominance, and their apparent inability to shape their own destiny. Many Arab countries, in addition to the oil exporters, are reaching levels of economic and social development where autocratic forms of government become inappropriate and efforts to introduce democracy become stronger. Some openings in Arab political systems have already occurred. The principal beneficiaries of these openings have been Islamist movements. In the Arab world, in short, Western democracy strengthens anti-Western political forces. This may be a passing phenomenon, but it surely complicates relations between Islamic countries and the West.

Those relations are also complicated by demography. The spectacular population growth in Arab countries, particularly in North Africa, has led to increased migration to Western Europe. The movement within Western Europe toward minimizing internal boundaries has sharpened political sensitivities with respect to this development. In Italy, France and Germany, racism is increasingly open, and political reactions and violence against Arab and Turkish migrants have become more intense and more widespread since 1990.

On both sides the interaction between Islam and the West is seen as a clash of civilizations. The West's "next confrontation," observes M. J. Akbar, an Indian Muslim author, "is definitely going to come from the Muslim world. It is in the sweep of the Islamic nations from the Maghreb to Pakistan that the struggle for a new world order will begin." Bernard Lewis comes to a similar conclusion:

> We are facing a mood and a movement far transcending the level of issues and policies and the governments that pursue them. This is no less than a clash of civilizations—the perhaps irrational but surely historic reaction of an ancient rival against our Judeo-Christian heritage, our secular present, and the worldwide expansion of both.[2]

Historically, the other great antagonistic interaction of Arab Islamic civilization has been with the pagan, animist, and now increasingly Christian black peoples to the south. In the past, this antagonism was epitomized in the image of Arab slave dealers and black slaves. It has been reflected in the on-going civil war in the Sudan between Arabs and blacks, the fighting in Chad between Libyan-supported insurgents and the government, the tensions between Orthodox Christians and Muslims in the Horn of Africa, and the political conflicts, recurring riots and communal violence between Muslims and Christians in Nigeria. The modernization of Africa and the spread of Christianity are likely to enhance the probability of violence along this fault line. Symptomatic of the intensification of this conflict was the Pope John Paul II's speech in Khartoum in February 1993 attacking the actions of the Sudan's Islamist government against the Christian minority there.

On the northern border of Islam, conflict has increasingly erupted between Orthodox and Muslim peoples, including the carnage of Bosnia and Sarajevo, the simmering violence between Serb and Albanian, the tenuous relations between Bulgarians and their Turkish minority, the violence between Ossetians and Ingush, the unremitting slaughter of each other by Armenians and Azeris, the tense relations between Russians and Muslims in Central Asia, and the deployment of Russian troops to protect Russian interests in the Caucasus and Central Asia. Religion reinforces the revival of ethnic identities and restimulates Russian fears about the security of their southern borders. This concern is well captured by Archie Roosevelt:

> Much of Russian history concerns the struggle between the Slavs and the Turkic peoples on their borders, which dates back to the foundation of the Russian state more than a thousand years ago. In the Slavs' millennium-long confrontation with their eastern neighbors lies the key to an understanding not only of Russian history, but Russian character. To understand Russian realities today one has to have a concept of the great Turkic ethnic group that has preoccupied Russians through the centuries.[3]

The conflict of civilizations is deeply rooted elsewhere in Asia. The historic clash between Muslim and Hindu in the subcontinent manifests itself now not only in the rivalry between Pakistan and India but also in intensifying religious strife within India between increasingly militant Hindu groups and India's substantial Muslim minority. The destruction of the Ayodhya mosque in December 1992 brought to the fore the issue of whether India will remain a secular democratic state or become a Hindu one. In East Asia, China has outstanding territorial disputes with most of its neighbors. It has pursued a ruthless policy toward the Buddhist people of Tibet, and it is pursuing an increasingly ruthless policy toward its Turkic-Muslim minority. With the Cold War over, the underlying differences between China and the United States have reasserted themselves in areas such as human rights, trade and weapons proliferation. These differences are unlikely to moderate. A "new cold war," Deng Xaioping reportedly asserted in 1991, is under way between China and America.

The same phrase has been applied to the increasingly difficult relations between Japan and the United States. Here cultural difference exacerbates economic conflict. People on each side allege racism on the other, but at least on the American side the antipathies are not racial but cultural. The basic values, attitudes, behavioral patterns of the two societies could hardly be more different. The economic issues between the United States and Europe are no less serious than those between the United States and Japan, but they do not have the same political salience and emotional intensity because the differences between American culture and European culture are so much less than those between American civilization and Japanese civilization.

The interactions between civilizations vary greatly in the extent to which they are likely to be characterized by violence. Economic competition clearly predominates between the American and European subcivilizations of the West and between both of them and Japan. On the Eurasian continent, however, the proliferation of ethnic conflict, epitomized at the extreme in "ethnic cleansing," has not been totally random. It has been most frequent and most violent between groups belonging to different civilizations. In Eurasia the great historic fault lines between civilizations are once more aflame. This is particularly true along the boundaries of the crescent-shaped Islamic bloc of nations from the bulge of Africa to central Asia. Violence also occurs between Muslims, on the one hand, and Orthodox Serbs in the Balkans, Jews in Israel, Hindus in India, Buddhists in Burma and Catholics in the Philippines. Islam has bloody borders.

CIVILIZATION RALLYING: THE KIN-COUNTRY SYNDROME

Groups or states belonging to one civilization that become involved in war with people from a different civilization naturally try to rally support from other members of their own civilization. As the post–Cold War world evolves, civilization commonality, what H. D. S. Greenway has termed the "kin-country" syndrome, is replacing political ideology and traditional balance of power considerations as the principal basis for cooperation and coalitions. It can be seen gradually emerging in the post–Cold War conflicts in the Persian Gulf, the Caucasus and Bosnia. None of these was a full-scale war between civilizations, but each involved some elements of civilizational rallying, which seemed to become more important as the conflict continued and which may provide a foretaste of the future.

First, in the Gulf War one Arab state invaded another and then fought a coalition of Arab, Western and other states. While only a few Muslim governments overtly supported Saddam Hussein, many Arab elites privately cheered him on, and he was highly popular among large sections of the Arab publics. Islamic fundamentalist movements universally supported Iraq rather than the Western-backed governments of Kuwait and Saudi Arabia. Forswearing Arab nationalism, Saddam Hussein explicitly invoked an Islamic appeal. He and his supporters attempted to define the war as a war between civilizations. "It is not the world against Iraq," as Safar Al-Hawali, dean of Islamic Studies at the Umm Al-Qura University in Mecca, put it in a widely circulated tape. "It is the West against Islam." Ignoring the rivalry between Iran and Iraq, the chief Iranian religious leader, Ayatollah Ali Khamenei, called for a holy war against the West: "The struggle against American aggression, greed, plans and policies will be counted as a jihad, and anybody who is killed on that path is a martyr." "This is a war," King Hussein of Jordan argued, "against all Arabs and all Muslims and not against Iraq alone."

The rallying of substantial sections of Arab elites and publics behind Saddam Hussein caused those Arab governments in the anti-Iraq coalition to moderate their activities and temper their public statements. Arab governments opposed or distanced themselves from subsequent Western efforts to apply pressure on Iraq, including enforcement of a no-fly zone in the summer of 1992 and the bombing of Iraq in January 1993. The Western-Soviet Turkish-Arab anti-Iraq coalition of 1990 had by 1993 become a coalition of almost only the West and Kuwait against Iraq.

Muslims contrasted Western actions against Iraq with the West's failure to protect Bosnians against Serbs and to impose sanctions on Israel for violating U.N. resolutions. The West, they alleged, was using a double standard. A world of clashing civilizations, however, is inevitably a world of double standards: people apply one standard to their kin-countries and a different standard to others.

Second, the kin-country syndrome also appeared in conflicts in the former Soviet Union. Armenian military successes in 1992 and 1993 stimulated Turkey to become increasingly supportive of its religious, ethnic and linguistic brethren in Azerbaijan. "We have a Turkish nation feeling the same sentiments as the Azerbaijanis," said one Turkish official in 1992. "We are under pressure. Our newspapers are full of the photos of atrocities and are asking us if we are still serious about pursuing our neutral policy. Maybe we should show Armenia that there's a big Turkey in the region." President Turgut Özal agreed, remarking that Turkey should at least "scare the Armenians a little bit." Turkey, Özal threatened again in 1993, would "show its fangs." Turkish Air Force jets flew reconnaissance flights along the Armenian border; Turkey suspended food shipments and air flights to Armenia; and Turkey and Iran announced they would not accept dismemberment of Azerbaijan. In the last years of its existence, the Soviet government supported Azerbaijan because its government was dominated by former communists. With the end of the Soviet Union, however, political considerations gave way to religious ones. Russian troops fought on the side of the Armenians, and Azerbaijan accused the "Russian government of turning 180 degrees" toward support for Christian Armenia.

Third, with respect to the fighting in the former Yugoslavia, Western publics manifested sympathy and support for the Bosnian Muslims and the horrors they suffered at the hands of the Serbs. Relatively little concern was expressed, however, over Croatian attacks on Muslims and participation in the dismemberment of Bosnia-Herzegovina. In the early stages of the Yugoslav breakup, Germany, in an unusual display of diplomatic initiative and muscle, induced the other 11 members of the European Community to follow its lead in recognizing Slovenia and Croatia. As a result of the pope's determination to provide strong backing to the two Catholic countries, the Vatican extended recognition even before the Community did. The United States followed the European lead. Thus the leading actors in Western civilization rallied behind their coreligionists. Subsequently Croatia was reported to be receiving substantial quantities of arms from Central European and other Western countries. Boris Yeltsin's government, on the other hand, attempted to pursue a middle course that would be sympathetic to the Orthodox Serbs but not alienate Russia from the West. Russian conservative and nationalist groups, however, including many legislators, attacked the government for not being more forthcoming in its support for the Serbs. By early 1993 several hundred Russians apparently were serving with the Serbian forces, and reports circulated of Russian arms being supplied to Serbia.

Islamic governments and groups, on the other hand, castigated the West for not coming to the defense of the Bosnians. Iranian leaders urged Muslims from all countries to provide help to Bosnia; in violation of the U.N. arms embargo, Iran supplied weapons and men for the Bosnians; Iranian-supported Lebanese groups sent guerrillas to train and organize the Bosnian forces. In 1993 up to 4,000 Muslims from over two dozen Islamic countries were reported to be fighting in Bosnia. The governments of Saudi Arabia and other countries felt under increasing pressure from fundamentalist groups in their own societies to provide more vigorous support for the Bosnians. By the end of 1992, Saudi Arabia had reportedly supplied substantial funding for weapons and supplies for the Bosnians, which significantly increased their military capabilities vis-à-vis the Serbs.

In the 1930s the Spanish Civil War provoked intervention from countries that politically were fascist, communist and democratic. In the 1990s the Yugo-slav conflict is provoking intervention from countries that are Muslim, Orthodox and Western Christian. The parallel has not gone unnoticed. "The war in Bosnia-Herzegovina has become the emotional equivalent of the fight against fascism in the Spanish Civil War," one Saudi editor observed. "Those who died there are regarded as martyrs who tried to save their fellow Muslims."

Conflicts and violence will also occur between states and groups within the same civilization. Such conflicts, however, are likely to be less intense and less likely to expand than conflicts between civilizations. Common membership in a civilization reduces the probability of violence in situations where it might otherwise occur. In 1991 and 1992 many people were alarmed by the possibility of violent conflict between Russia and Ukraine over territory, particularly Crimea, the Black Sea fleet, nuclear weapons and economic issues. If civilization is what counts, however, the likelihood of violence between Ukrainians and Russians should be low. They are two Slavic, primarily Orthodox peoples who have had close relationships with each other for centuries. As of early 1993, despite all the reasons for conflict, the leaders of the two countries were effectively negotiating and defusing the issues between the two countries. While there has been serious fighting between Muslims and Christians elsewhere in the former Soviet Union and much tension and some fighting between Western and Orthodox Christians in the Baltic states, there has been virtually no violence between Russians and Ukrainians.

Civilization rallying to date has been limited, but it has been growing, and it clearly has the potential to spread much further. As the conflicts in the Persian Gulf, the Caucasus and Bosnia continued, the positions of nations and the cleavages between them increasingly were along civilizational lines. Populist politicians, religious leaders and the media have found it a potent means of arousing mass support and of pressuring hesitant governments. In the coming years, the local conflicts most likely to escalate into major wars will be those, as in Bosnia and the Caucasus, along the fault lines between civilizations. The next world war, if there is one, will be a war between civilizations.

THE WEST VERSUS THE REST

The West is now at an extraordinary peak of power in relation to other civilizations. Its superpower opponent has disappeared from the map. Military conflict among Western states is unthinkable, and Western military power is unrivaled. Apart from Japan, the West faces no economic challenge. It dominates international political and security institutions and with Japan international economic institutions. Global political and security issues are effectively settled by a directorate of the United States, Britain and France, world economic issues by a directorate of the United States, Germany and Japan, all of which maintain extraordinarily close relations with each other to the exclusion of lesser and largely non-Western countries. Decisions made at the U.N. Security Council or in the International Monetary Fund that reflect the interests of the West are presented to the world as reflecting the desires of the world community. The very phrase "the world community" has become the euphemistic collective noun (replacing "the Free World") to give global legitimacy to actions reflecting the interests of the United States and other Western powers.[4] Through the IMF and other international economic institutions, the West promotes its economic interests and imposes on other nations the economic policies it thinks appropriate. In any poll of non-Western peoples, the IMF undoubtedly would win the support of finance ministers and a few others, but get an overwhelmingly unfavorable rating from just about everyone else, who would agree with Georgy Arbatov's characterization of IMF officials as "neo-Bolsheviks who love expropriating other people's money, imposing undemocratic and alien rules of economic and political conduct and stifling economic freedom."

Western domination of the U.N. Security Council and its decisions, tempered only by occasional abstention by China, produced U.N. legitimation of the West's use of force to drive Iraq out of Kuwait and its elimination of Iraq's sophisticated weapons and capacity to produce such weapons. It also produced the quite unprecedented action by the United States, Britain and France in getting the Security Council to demand that Libya hand over the Pan Am 103 bombing suspects and then to impose sanctions when Libya refused. After defeating the largest Arab army, the West did not hesitate to throw its weight around in the Arab world. The West in effect is using international institutions, military power and economic resources to run the world in ways that will maintain Western predominance, protect Western interests and promote Western political and economic values.

That at least is the way in which non-Westerners see the new world, and there is a significant element of truth in their view. Differences in power and struggles for military, economic and institutional power are thus one source of conflict between the West and other civilizations. Differences in culture, that is basic values and beliefs, are a second source of conflict. V. S. Naipaul has argued that Western civilization is the "universal civilization" that "fits all men." At a superficial level much of Western culture has indeed permeated the rest of the world. At a more basic level, however, Western concepts differ fundamentally from those prevalent in other civilizations. Western ideas of individualism, liberalism, constitutionalism, human rights, equality, liberty, the rule of law, democracy, free markets, the separation of church and state, often have little resonance in Islamic, Confucian, Japanese, Hindu, Buddhist or Orthodox cultures. Western efforts to propagate such ideas produce instead a reaction against "human rights imperialism" and a reaffirmation of indigenous values, as can be seen in the support for religious fundamentalism by the younger generation in non-Western cultures. The very notion that there could be a "universal civilization" is a Western idea, directly at odds with the particularism of most Asian societies and their emphasis on what distinguishes one people from another. Indeed, the author of a review of 100 comparative studies of values in different societies concluded that "the values that are most important in the West are least important worldwide."[5] In the political realm, of course, these differences are most manifest in the efforts of the United States and other Western powers to induce other peoples to adopt Western ideas concerning democracy and human rights. Modern democratic government originated in the West. When it has developed in non-Western societies it has usually been the product of Western colonialism or imposition.

The central axis of world politics in the future is likely to be, in Kishore Mahbubani's phrase, the conflict between "the West and the Rest" and the responses of non-Western civilizations to Western power and values.[6] Those responses generally take one or a combination of three forms. At one extreme, non-Western states can, like Burma and North Korea, attempt to pursue a course of isolation, to insulate their societies from penetration or "corruption" by the West, and, in effect, to opt out of participation in the Western-dominated global community. The costs of this course, however, are high, and few states have pursued it exclusively. A second alternative, the equivalent of "bandwagoning" in international relations theory, is to attempt to join the West and accept its values and institutions. The third alternative is to attempt to "balance" the West by developing economic and military power and cooperating with other non-Western societies against the West, while preserving indigenous values and institutions; in short, to modernize but not to Westernize.

THE TORN COUNTRIES

In the future, as people differentiate themselves by civilization, countries with large numbers of peoples of different civilizations, such as the Soviet Union and Yugoslavia, are candidates for dismemberment. Some other countries have a fair degree of cultural homogeneity but are divided over whether their society belongs to one civilization or another. These are torn countries. Their leaders typically wish to pursue a bandwagoning strategy and to make their countries members of the West, but the history, culture and traditions of their countries are non-Western. The most obvious and prototypical torn country is Turkey. The late twentieth-century leaders of Turkey have followed in the Attatürk tradition and defined Turkey as a modern, secular, Western nation state. They allied Turkey with the West in NATO and in the Gulf War; they applied for membership in the European Community. At the same time, however, elements in Turkish society have supported an Islamic revival and have argued that Turkey is basically a Middle Eastern Muslim society. In addition, while the elite of Turkey has defined Turkey as a Western society, the elite of the West refuses to accept Turkey as such. Turkey will not become a member of the European Community, and the real reason, as President Özal said, "is that we are Muslim and they are Christian and they don't say that." Having rejected Mecca, and then being rejected by Brussels, where does Turkey look? Tashkent may be the answer. The end of the Soviet Union gives Turkey the opportunity to become the leader of a revived Turkic civilization involving seven countries from the borders of Greece to those of China. Encouraged by the West, Turkey is making strenuous efforts to carve out this new identity for itself.

During the past decade Mexico has assumed a position somewhat similar to that of Turkey. Just as Turkey abandoned its historic opposition to Europe and attempted to join Europe, Mexico has stopped defining itself by its opposition to the United States and is instead attempting to imitate the United States and to join it in the North American Free Trade Area. Mexican leaders are engaged in the great task of redefining Mexican identity and have introduced fundamental economic reforms that eventually will lead to fundamental political change. In 1991 a top adviser to President Carlos Salinas de Gortari described at length to me all the changes the Salinas government was making. When he finished, I remarked: "That's most impressive. It seems to me that basically you want to change Mexico from a Latin American country into a North American country." He looked at me with surprise and exclaimed: " Exactly! That's precisely what we are trying to do, but of course we could never say so publicly." As his remark indicates, in Mexico as in Turkey, significant elements in society resist the redefinition of their country's identity. In Turkey, European-oriented leaders have to make gestures to Islam (Özal's pilgrimage to Mecca); so also Mexico's North American—oriented leaders have to make gestures to those who hold Mexico to be a Latin American country (Salinas' Ibero-American Guadalajara summit).

Historically Turkey has been the most profoundly torn country. For the United States, Mexico is the most immediate torn country. Globally the most important torn country is Russia. The question of whether Russia is part of the West or the leader of a distinct Slavic-Orthodox civilization has been a recurring one in Russian history. That issue was obscured by the communist victory in Russia, which imported a Western ideology, adapted it to Russian conditions and then challenged the West in the name of that ideology. The dominance of communism shut off the historic debate over Westernization versus Russification. With communism discredited Russians once again face that question.

President Yeltsin is adopting Western principles and goals and seeking to make Russia a "normal" country and a part of the West. Yet both the Russian elite and the Russian public are divided on this issue. Among the more moderate dissenters, Sergei Stankevich argues that Russia should reject the "Atlanticist" course, which would lead it "to become European, to become a part of the world economy in rapid and organized fashion, to become the eighth member of the Seven, and to put particular emphasis on Germany and the United States as the two dominant members of the Atlantic alliance." While also rejecting an exclusively Eurasian policy, Stankevich nonetheless argues that Russia should give priority to the protection of Russians in other countries, emphasize its Turkic and Muslim connections, and promote "an appreciable redistribution of our resources, our options, our ties, and our interests in favor of Asia, of the eastern direction." People of this persuasion criticize Yeltsin for subordinating Russia's interests to those of the West, for reducing Russian military strength, for failing to support traditional friends such as Serbia, and for pushing economic and political reform in ways injurious to the Russian people. Indicative of this trend is the new popularity of the ideas of Petr Savitsky, who in the 1920s argued that Russia was a unique Eurasian civilization.[7] More extreme dissidents voice much more blatantly nationalist, anti-Western and anti-Semitic views, and urge Russia to redevelop its military strength and to establish closer ties with China and Muslim countries. The people of Russia are as divided as the elite. An opinion survey in European Russia in the spring of 1992 revealed that 40 percent of the public had positive attitudes toward the West and 36 percent had negative attitudes. As it has been for much of its history, Russia in the early 1990s is truly a torn country.

To redefine its civilization identity, a torn country must meet three requirements. First, its political and economic elite has to be generally supportive of and enthusiastic about this move. Second, its public has to be willing to acquiesce in the redefinition. Third, the dominant groups in the recipient civilization have to be willing to embrace the convert. All three requirements in large part exist with respect to Mexico. The first two in large part exist with respect to Turkey. It is not clear that any of them exist with respect to Russia's joining the West. The conflict between liberal democracy and Marxism-Leninism was between ideologies which, despite their major differences, ostensibly shared ultimate goals of freedom, equality and prosperity. A traditional, authoritarian, nationalist Russia could have quite different goals. A Western democrat could carry on an intellectual debate with a Soviet Marxist. It would be virtually impossible for him to do that with a Russian traditionalist. If, as the Russians stop behaving like Marxists, they reject liberal democracy and begin behaving like Russians but not like Westerners, the relations between Russia and the West could again become distant and conflictual.[8]

THE CONFUCIAN-ISLAMIC CONNECTION

The obstacles to non-Western countries joining the West vary considerably. They are least for Latin American and East European countries. They are greater for the Orthodox countries of the former Soviet Union. They are still greater for Muslim, Confucian, Hindu and Buddhist societies. Japan has established a unique position for itself as an associate member of the West: it is in the West in some respects but clearly not of the West in important dimensions. Those countries that for reason of culture and power do not wish to, or cannot, join the West compete with the West by developing their own economic, military and political power. They do this by promoting their internal development and by cooperating with other non-Western countries. The most prominent form of this cooperation is the Confucian-Islamic connection that has emerged to challenge Western interests, values and power.

Almost without exception, Western countries are reducing their military power; under Yeltsin's leadership so also is Russia. China, North Korea and several Middle Eastern states, however, are significantly expanding their military capabilities. They are doing this by the import of arms from Western and non-Western sources and by the development of indigenous arms industries. One result is the emergence of what Charles Krauthammer has called "Weapon States," and the Weapon States are not Western states. Another result is the redefinition of arms control, which is a Western concept and a Western goal. During the Cold War the primary purpose of arms control was to establish a stable military balance between the United States and its allies and the Soviet Union and its allies. In the post–Cold War world the primary objective of arms control is to prevent the development by non-Western societies of military capabilities that could threaten Western interests. The West attempts to do this through international agreements, economic pressure and controls on the transfer of arms and weapons technologies.

The conflict between the West and the Confucian-Islamic states focuses largely, although not exclusively, on nuclear, chemical and biological weapons, ballistic missiles and other sophisticated means for delivering them, and the guidance, intelligence and other electronic capabilities for achieving that goal. The West promotes nonproliferation as a universal norm and nonproliferation treaties and inspections as means of realizing that norm. It also threatens a variety of sanctions against those who promote the spread of sophisticated weapons and proposes some benefits for those who do not. The attention of the West focuses, naturally, on nations that are actually or potentially hostile to the West.

The non-Western nations, on the other hand, assert their right to acquire and to deploy whatever weapons they think necessary for their security. They also have absorbed, to the full, the truth of the response of the Indian defense minister when asked what lesson he learned from the Gulf War: "Don't fight the United States unless you have nuclear weapons." Nuclear weapons, chemical weapons and missiles are viewed, probably erroneously, as the potential equalizer of superior Western conventional power. China, of course, already has nuclear weapons; Pakistan and India have the capability to deploy them. North Korea, Iran, Iraq, Libya and Algeria appear to be attempting to acquire them. A top Iranian official has declared that all Muslim states should acquire nuclear weapons, and in 1988 the president of Iran reportedly issued a directive calling for development of "offensive and defensive chemical, biological and radiological weapons."

Centrally important to the development of counter-West military capabilities is the sustained expansion of China's military power and its means to create military power. Buoyed by spectacular economic development, China is rapidly increasing its military spending and vigorously moving forward with the modernization of its armed forces. It is purchasing weapons from the former Soviet states; it is developing long-range missiles; in 1992 it tested a one-megaton nuclear device. It is developing power-projection capabilities, acquiring aerial refueling technology, and trying to purchase an aircraft carrier. Its military buildup and assertion of sovereignty over the South China Sea are provoking a multilateral regional arms race in East Asia. China is also a major exporter of arms and weapons technology. It has exported materials to Libya and Iraq that could be used to manufacture nuclear weapons and nerve gas. It has helped Algeria build a reactor suitable for nuclear weapons research and production. China has sold to Iran nuclear technology that American officials believe could only be used to create weapons and apparently has shipped components of 300-mile-range missiles to Pakistan. North Korea has had a nuclear weapons program under way for some while and has sold advanced missiles and missile technology to Syria and Iran. The flow of weapons and weapons technology is generally from East Asia to the Middle East. There is, however, some movement in the reverse direction; China has received Stinger missiles from Pakistan.

A Confucian-Islamic military connection has thus come into being, designed to promote acquisition by its members of the weapons and weapons technologies needed to counter the military power of the West. It may or may not last. At present, however, it is, as Dave McCurdy has said, "a renegades' mutual support pact, run by the proliferators and their backers." A new form of arms competition is thus occurring between Islamic-Confucian states and the West. In an old-fashioned arms race, each side developed its own arms to balance or to achieve superiority against the other side. In this new form of arms competition, one side is developing its arms and the other side is attempting not to balance but to limit and prevent that arms build-up while at the same time reducing its own military capabilities.

IMPLICATIONS FOR THE WEST

This article does not argue that civilization identities will replace all other identities, that nation states will disappear, that each civilization will become a single coherent political entity, that groups within a civilization will not conflict with and even fight each other. This paper does set forth the hypotheses that differences between civilizations are real and important; civilization-consciousness is increasing; conflict between civilizations will supplant ideological and other forms of conflict as the dominant global form of conflict; international relations, historically a game played out within Western civilization, will increasingly be de-Westernized and become a game in which non-Western civilizations are actors and not simply objects; successful political, security and economic international institutions are more likely to develop within civilizations than across civilizations; conflicts between groups in different civilizations will be more frequent, more sustained and more violent than conflicts between groups in the same civilization; violent conflicts between groups in different civilizations are the most likely and most dangerous source of escalation that could lead to global wars; the paramount axis of world politics will be the relations between "the West and the Rest"; the elites in some torn non-Western countries will try to make their countries part of the West, but in most cases face major obstacles to accomplishing this; a central focus of conflict for the immediate future will be between the West and several Islamic-Confucian states.

This is not to advocate the desirability of conflicts between civilizations. It is to set forth descriptive hypotheses as to what the future may be like. If these are plausible hypotheses, however, it is necessary to consider their implications for Western policy. These implications should be divided between short-term advantage and long-term accommodation. In the short term it is clearly in the interest of the West to promote greater cooperation and unity within its own civilization, particularly between its European and North American components; to incorporate into the West societies in Eastern Europe and Latin America whose cultures are close to those of the West; to promote and maintain cooperative relations with Russia and Japan; to prevent escalation of local inter-civilization conflicts into major inter-civilization wars; to limit the expansion of the military strength of Confucian and Islamic states; to moderate the reduction of Western military capabilities and maintain military superiority in East and Southwest Asia; to exploit differences and conflicts among Confucian and Islamic states; to support in other civilizations groups sympathetic to Western values and interests; to strengthen international institutions that reflect and legitimate Western interests and values and to promote the involvement of non-Western states in those institutions.

In the longer term other measures would be called for. Western civilization is both Western and modern. Non-Western civilizations have attempted to become modern without becoming Western. To date only Japan has fully succeeded in this quest. Non-Western civilizations will continue to attempt to acquire the wealth, technology, skills, machines and weapons that are part of being modern. They will also attempt to reconcile this modernity with their traditional culture and values. Their economic and military strength relative to the West will increase. Hence the West will increasingly have to accommodate these non-Western modern civilizations whose power approaches that of the West but whose values and interests differ significantly from those of the West. This will require the West to maintain the economic and military power necessary to protect its interests in relation to these civilizations. It will also, however, require the West to develop a more profound understanding of the basic religious and philosophical assumptions underlying other civilizations and the ways in which people in those civilizations see their interests. It will require an effort to identify elements of commonality between Western and other civilizations. For the relevant future, there will be no universal civilization, but instead a world of different civilizations, each of which will have to learn to coexist with the others.

NOTES

1 Murray Weidenbaum, *Greater China: The Next Economic Superpower?* St. Louis: Washington University Center for the Study of American Business, *Contemporary Issues*, Series 57, February 1993, pp. 2–3.

2 Bernard Lewis, "The Roots of Muslim Rage," *The Atlantic Monthly*, vol. 266, September 1990, p. 60; *Time*, June 15, 1992, pp. 24–28.

3 Archie Roosevelt, *For Lust of Knowing*, Boston: Little, Brown, 1988, pp. 332–333.

4 Almost invariably Western leaders claim they are acting on behalf of "the world community." One minor lapse occurred during the run-up to the Gulf War. In an interview on "Good Morning America," December 21, 1990, British Prime Minister John Major referred to the actions "the West" was taking against Saddam Hussein. He quickly corrected himself and subsequently referred to "the world community." He was, however, right when he erred.

5 Harry C. Triandis, *The New York Times*, December 25, 1990, p. 41, and "Cross-Cultural Studies of Individualism and Collectivism," *Nebraska Symposium on Motivation*, vol. 37, 1989, pp. 41–133.

6 Kishore Mahbubani, "The West and the Rest," *The National Interest*, summer 1992, pp. 3–13.

7 Sergei Stankevich, "Russia in Search of Itself," *The National Interest*, summer 1992, pp. 47–51; Daniel Schneider, "A Russian Movement Rejects Western Tilt," *Christian Science Monitor*, February 5, 1993, pp. 5–7.

8 Owen Harries has pointed out that Australia is trying (unwisely in his view) to become a torn country in reverse. Although it has been a full member not only of the West but also of the ABCA military and intelligence core of the West, its current leaders are in effect proposing that it defect from the West, redefine itself as an Asian country and cultivate close ties with its neighbors. Australia's future, they argue, is with the dynamic economies of East Asia. But, as I have suggested, close economic cooperation normally requires a common cultural base. In addition, none of the three conditions necessary for a torn country to join another civilization is likely to exist in Australia's case.

Reading 1.4

Economics Trumps Politics   *FAREED ZAKARIA*

Imagine that it is January 2000, and you ask a fortune-teller to predict the course of the global economy over the next several years. Let's say that you give him some clues, to help him gaze into his crystal ball. The United States will be hit by the worst terrorist attack in history, you explain, and will respond by launching two wars, one of which will go badly awry and keep Iraq—the country with the world's third-largest oil reserves—in chaos for years. Iran will gain strength in the Middle East and move to acquire a nuclear capability.

North Korea will go further, becoming the world's eighth declared nuclear power. Russia will turn hostile and imperious in its dealings with its neighbors and the West. In Latin America, Hugo Chávez of Venezuela will launch the most spirited anti-Western campaign in a generation, winning many allies and fans. Israel and Hezbollah will fight a war in southern Lebanon, destabilizing Beirut's fragile government, drawing in Iran and Syria, and rattling the Israelis. Gaza will become a failed state ruled by Hamas, and peace talks between Israel and the Palestinians will go nowhere. "Given these events," you say to the sage, "how will the global economy fare over the next six years?"

This is not really a hypothetical. We have the forecasts of experts from those years. They were all wrong. The correct prediction would have been that, between 2000 and 2007, the world economy would grow at its fastest pace in nearly four decades. Income per person across the globe would rise at a faster rate (3.2 percent) than in any other period in history.

In the two decades since the end of the Cold War, we have lived through a paradox, one we experience every morning when reading the newspapers. The world's politics seems deeply troubled, with daily reports of bombings, terror plots, rogue states, and civil strife. And yet the global economy forges ahead, not without significant interruptions and crises, but still vigorously upward on the whole. Markets do panic but over economic not political news. The front page of the newspaper seems unconnected to the business section. . . .

What explains this mismatch between a politics that spirals downward and an economy that stays robust? First, it's worth looking more carefully at the cascade of bad news. It seems that we are living in crazily violent times. But don't believe everything you see on television. Our anecdotal impression turns out to be wrong. War and organized violence have declined dramatically over the last two decades. Ted Robert Gurr and a team of scholars at the University of Maryland's Center for International Development and Conflict Management tracked the data carefully and came to the following conclusion: "the general magnitude of global warfare has decreased by over sixty percent [since the mid-1980s], falling by the end of 2004 to its lowest level since the late 1950s." Violence increased steadily throughout the Cold War—increasing sixfold between the 1950s and early 1990s—but the trend peaked just before the collapse of the Soviet Union in 1991 and "the extent of warfare among and within states lessened by nearly half in the first decade after the Cold War." Harvard's polymath professor Steven Pinker argues "that today we are probably living in the most peaceful time in our species' existence. . . ."

It *feels* like a very dangerous world. But it isn't. Your chances of dying as a consequence of organized violence of any kind are low and getting lower. The data reveal a broad trend away from wars among major countries, the kind of conflict that produces massive casualties. . . .

THE ISLAMIC THREAT

Islamic terror, which makes the headlines daily, is a large and persistent problem, but one involving small numbers of fanatics. It feeds on the dysfunctions of the Muslim world, the sense (real and imagined) of humiliation at the hands of the West, and easy access to technologies of violence. And yet, does it rank as a threat on the order of Germany's drive for world domination in the first half of the twentieth century? Or Soviet expansionism in the second half? Or Mao's efforts to foment war and revolution across the Third World in the 1950s and 1960s? These were all challenges backed by the power and purpose of major countries, often with serious allies, and by an ideology that was seen as a plausible alternative to liberal democracy. By comparison, consider the jihadist threat. Before 9/11, when groups like Al Qaeda operated under the radar, governments treated them as minor annoyances, and they roamed freely, built some strength, and hit symbolic, often military targets, killing Americans and other foreigners. Even so, the damage was fairly limited. Since 2001, governments everywhere have been aggressive in busting terrorists' networks, following their money, and tracking their recruits—with almost immediate results. In Indonesia, the largest Muslim nation in the world, the government captured both the chief and the military leader of Jemaah Islamiah, the country's deadliest jihadist group and the one that carried out the Bali bombings in 2002. With American help, the Filipino army battered the Qaeda-style terrorist outfit Abu Sayyaf. The group's leader was killed by Filipino troops in January 2007, and its membership has declined from as many as two thousand guerrillas six years ago to a few hundred today. In Egypt and Saudi Arabia—Al Qaeda's original bases and targets of attack—terrorist cells have been rounded up, and those still at large have been unable to launch any new attacks in three years. Finance ministries—especially the U.S. Department of the Treasury—have made life far more difficult for terrorists. Global organizations cannot thrive without being able to move money around, and so the more terrorists' funds are tracked and targeted, the more they have to resort to small-scale and hastily improvised operations. This struggle, between governments and terrorists, will persist, but it is the former who have the upper hand. . . .

Here is the bottom line. In the six years since 9/11, Al Qaeda Central—the group led by Osama bin Laden and Ayman Zawahiri—has been unable to launch a major attack anywhere. It was a terrorist organization; it has become a communications company, producing the occasional videotape rather than actual terrorism. Jihad continues, but the jihadists have had to scatter, make do with smaller targets, and operate on a local level—usually through groups with almost no connection to Al Qaeda Central. And this improvised strategy has a crippling weakness: it kills locals, thus alienating ordinary Muslims—a process that is well underway in countries as diverse as Indonesia, Iraq, and Saudi Arabia. Over the last six years, support for bin Laden and his goals has fallen steadily throughout the Muslim world. Between 2002 and 2007, approval of suicide bombing as a tactic—a figure that was always low—has dropped by over 50 percent in most Muslim countries that have been tracked. There have been more denunciations of violence and fatwas against bin Laden than ever before, including from prominent clerics in Saudi Arabia. Much more must happen to modernize the Muslim world, but the modernizers are no longer so scared. They have finally realized that, for all the rhetoric of the madrassas and mosques, few people want to live under the writ of Al Qaeda. Those who have, whether in Afghanistan or Iraq, have become its most dedicated opponents. In contrast to Soviet socialism or even fascism in the 1930s, no society looks with admiration and envy on the fundamentalist Islamic model. On an ideological level, it presents no competition to the Western-originated model of modernity that countries across the world are embracing. . . .

The ideological watchdogs have spent so much time with the documents of jihad that they have lost sight of actual Muslim societies. Were they to step back, they would see a frustration with the fundamentalists, a desire for modernity (with some dignity and cultural pride for sure), and a search for practical solutions—not a mass quest for immortality through death. When Muslims travel, they flock by the millions to see the razzle-dazzle of Dubai, not the seminaries of Iran. The minority that wants jihad is real, but it operates within societies where such activities are increasingly unpopular and irrelevant. . . .

The challenges from rogue states are also real, but we should consider them in context. The GDP of Iran is 1/68 that of the United States, its military spending 1/110 that of the Pentagon. If this is 1938, as many conservatives argue, then Iran is Romania, not Germany North Korea is even more bankrupt and dysfunctional. Its chief threat—the one that keeps the Chinese government awake at night—is that it will implode, flooding the region with refugees. That's power? These countries can cause trouble in their neighborhood and must be checked and contained, but we need to keep in mind the larger world of which they are a relatively small part. Look at Latin America. Venezuela is a troublemaker, but what has that meant on the ground? The broad trend in the region—exemplified by the policies of the major countries like Brazil, Mexico, and Chile—has been toward open markets, trade, democratic governance, and an outward orientation. And that trend, not Hugo Chávez's insane rants, represents the direction of history.

THE GREAT EXPANSION

Today's relative calm has a deep structural basis. Across the world, economics is trumping politics. What Wall Street analysts call "political risk" has been almost nonexistent. Wars, coups, and terrorism have lost much of their ability to derail markets more than temporarily. Again, this may not last (it has not historically), but it has been the world we have lived in for at least a decade.

This is not the first time that political tumult and economic growth have come together. Two earlier periods seem much like ours: the turn-of-the-century boom of the 1890s and 1900s, and the postwar boom of the 1950s and early 1960s. In both, politics was turbulent and yet growth was robust. These two periods had one feature in common: large countries were entering the world economy, increasing its size and changing its shape. The expansion of the pie was so big that it overwhelmed day-to-day dislocations. . . .

We are living through the third such expansion of the global economy, and by far the largest. Over the last two decades, about two billion people have entered the world of markets and trade—a world that was, until recently, the province of a small club of Western countries. The expansion was spurred by the movement of Western capital to Asia and across the globe. As a result, between 1990 and 2007, the global economy grew from $22.8 trillion to $53.3 trillion, and global trade increased 133 percent. The so-called emerging markets have accounted for over half of this global growth, and they now account for over 40 percent of the world economy measured at purchasing power parity (or over 30 percent at market exchange rates). Increasingly, the growth of newcomers is being powered by their own markets, not simply by exports to the West—which means that this is not an ephemeral phenomenon.

Some people dismiss such trends by pointing to the rise of Japan in the 1980s, when Westerners were scared that the Japanese would come to dominate the world economy. That turned out to be a phantom fear: Japan in fact went into a fifteen-year slump. But the analogy is misleading. In 1985, Japan was already the second-largest economy in the world. Many experts believed it was on track to unseat the United States as the largest, but because Japan's economy, institutions, and politics were still not fully modernized, the country could not make that final leap. China, by contrast, is still a poor country. It has a per capita GDP of $2,500. It will certainly face many problems as and when it becomes a first-world country. But, for the foreseeable future, it will surely manage to double the size of its economy just by continuing to make toys and shirts and cell phones. India, starting at an even lower base income, will also be able to grow for several decades before hitting the kinds of challenges that derailed Japan. Even if India and China never get past middle-income status, they are likely to be the second- and third-largest economies in the world for much of the twenty-first century. . . .

THE THREE FORCES: POLITICS, ECONOMICS, AND TECHNOLOGY

How did all this come to be? To answer that question, we have to go back a few decades, to the 1970s, and recall the way most countries ran their economies at the time. I remember the atmosphere vividly because I was growing up in India, a country that really didn't think it was playing on the same field as the United States. In the minds of India's policy and intellectual elites, there was a U.S.-led capitalist model on one end of the spectrum and a Soviet-led socialist model on the other. New Delhi was trying to carve a middle way between them. In this respect, India was not unusual. Brazil, Egypt, and Indonesia—and in fact, the majority of the world—were on this middle path. But it turned out to be a road to nowhere, and this was becoming apparent to many people in these countries by the late 1970s. As they stagnated, Japan and a few other East Asian economies that had charted a quasi-capitalist course succeeded conspicuously, and the lesson started to sink in.

But the earthquake that shook everything was the collapse of the Soviet Union in the late 1980s. With central planning totally discredited and one end of the political spectrum in ruins, the entire debate shifted. Suddenly there was only one basic approach to organizing a country's economy. This is why Alan Greenspan has described the fall of the Soviet Union as the seminal *economic* event of our time. Since then, despite all the unease about various liberalization and marketization plans, the general direction has not changed. As Margaret Thatcher famously put it in the years when she was reviving the British economy, "There is no alternative."

The ideological shift in economics had been building over the 1970s and 1980s even before the fall of the Berlin Wall. Conventional economic wisdom, embodied in organizations such as the International Monetary Fund and the World Bank, had become far more critical of the quasi-socialist path of countries like India. Academic experts like Jeffrey Sachs traveled around the world advising governments to liberalize, liberalize, liberalize. Graduates of Western economics programs, such as Chile's "Chicago Boys," went home and implemented market-friendly policies. Some developing countries worried about becoming rapacious capitalists, and Sachs recalls explaining to them that they should debate long and hard whether they wanted to end up more like Sweden, France, or the United States. But, he would add, they didn't have to worry about that decision for a while: most of them were still much closer to the Soviet Union.

The financial force that has powered the new era is the free movement of capital. This, too, is a relatively recent phenomenon. The post–World War II period was one of fixed exchange rates. Most Western countries, including France and Italy, had capital controls restricting the movement of currency in and out of their borders. The dollar was pegged to gold. But as global trade grew, fixed rates created frictions and inefficiencies and prevented capital from being put to its best use. Most Western countries removed controls during the 1970s and 1980s. The result: a vast and ever-growing supply of capital that could move freely from one place to the next. Today, when people think about globalization, they still think of it mostly in terms of the huge amount of cash—currency traders swap about $2 trillion *a day*—that sloshes around the globe, rewarding some countries and punishing others. It is globalization's celestial mechanism for discipline. . . .

THE PROBLEMS OF PLENTY

For the last two decades, we have spent much time, energy, and attention worrying about crises and breakdown in the global economy and terrorism, nuclear blackmail, and war in geopolitics. This is natural—preparing for the worst can help avert it. And we have indeed had bad news—from wars in the Balkans and Africa, to terrorism around the world, to economic crises in East Asia, Russia, and—most dangerously—the United States. But focusing on the gloom has also left us unprepared for many of the largest problems we face: *which are the product not of failure but of success.* The fact that we are living in a world of synchronous global growth is good news, for the most part, but it is also raising a series of complex and potentially lethal dilemmas. . . .

It's not just oil that has become more expensive. Commodity prices are at a 200-year high. Raw materials of all kinds are increasingly dear. Agricultural produce is now so expensive that developing countries face a growing political problem of how to respond to food inflation. The cost of construction has exploded from New York to Dubai to Shanghai. Even the humble gas, helium, which is used not merely in party balloons but also in MRI machines and microchip factories, is in short supply globally—and it's the second-most-abundant element in the universe. These pressures will surely at some point end the era of low inflation that has undergirded global prosperity.

Meanwhile, robust growth has also produced a number of anomalies. Within an increasingly globalized and disciplined world, certain countries—those endowed with natural resources, especially petroleum and natural gas—are getting free rides. They are surfing the wave of global growth, getting rich without having to play by most of the rules that govern the global economy. This phenomenon is the strange but inevitable outgrowth of the success of everyone else. These countries are the nonmarket parasites on a market world.

Consider the principal political challenges to the United States and to Western ideas of international order. In the Middle East they come from Iran, in Latin America from Venezuela, and in Eurasia from Russia. All have newfound strength built on oil. Sudan's ability to defy the world over Darfur is difficult to imagine absent its oil reserves. Petroleum brings in eye-popping amounts of cash. Iran's take from oil in 2006 amounted to $50 billion—enough to dispense patronage to interest groups, bribe the army, and stay in power while still having piles left over to foment trouble abroad. This situation is unlikely to change. Resource-rich countries will thrive as long as the others are growing. It's the yin and yang of today's globalization. . . .

The most acute problem of plenty is the impact of global growth on natural resources and the environment. It is not an exaggeration to say that the world is running out of clean air, potable water, agricultural produce, and many vital commodities. Some of these problems can be fixed—by improving efficiency and developing new sources of supply—but progress has been far too slow. Agricultural productivity, for example, is rising. But feeding a global population of eight billion, which we will get to by 2025, will require crop yields to reach four tons per hectare from only three tons today. Similarly, our ability to manage and conserve water is not growing nearly as fast as our consumption of it. World population tripled in the twentieth century, but water consumption increased sixfold. Americans use more than four hundred liters of water a day to drink, cook, and clean themselves. People in poorer countries today are lucky to get forty, but as they get richer, their rising demands will cause greater stress. Violent clashes over water have already broken out in Africa and the Middle East. Historically, populations have moved to find water; if water sources dry up in the future, tens of millions of people will be forced to start moving.

Over the last decade, many predictions about the effects of climate change have proven to be underestimates because global growth has exceeded all projections. The most recent assessment of the Intergovernmental Panel on Climate

Change was released in mid-2007. By the year's end, scientists had shown that the polar ice caps are melting twice as fast as the report expected. There is greater demand for electricity, more cars, and more planes than anyone imagined fifteen years ago. And it keeps growing. The McKinsey Global Institute projects that, from 2003 to 2020, the number of vehicles in China will rise from 26 million to 120 million. And then there's India, Russia, the Middle East . . .

THE RISE OF NATIONALISM

In a globalized world, almost all problems spill over borders. Whether it's terrorism, nuclear proliferation, disease, environmental degradation, economic crisis, or water scarcity, no issue can be addressed without significant coordination and cooperation among many countries. But while economics, information, and even culture might have become globalized, formal political power remains firmly tethered to the nation-state, even as the nation-state has become less able to solve most of these problems unilaterally. And increasingly, nation-states are becoming less willing to come together to solve common problems. As the number of players—governmental and nongovernmental—increases and each one's power and confidence grows, the prospects for agreement and common action diminish. This is the central challenge of the rise of the rest—to stop the forces of global growth from turning into the forces of global disorder and disintegration.

The rise of pride and confidence among other nations, particularly the largest and most successful ones, is readily apparent. For me, it was vividly illustrated a few years ago in an Internet café in Shanghai, where I was chatting with a young Chinese executive. He was describing the extraordinary growth that was taking place in his country and a future in which China would be modern and prosperous. He was thoroughly Westernized in dress and demeanor, spoke excellent English, and could comfortably discuss the latest business trends or gossip about American pop culture. He seemed the consummate product of globalization, the person who bridges cultures and makes the world a smaller, more cosmopolitan place. But when we began talking about Taiwan, Japan, and the United States, his responses were filled with bile. He explained in furious tones that were Taiwan to dare to declare independence, China should instantly invade it. He said that Japan was an aggressor nation that could never be trusted. He was sure that the United States deliberately bombed the Chinese embassy during the Kosovo war in 1999, to terrify the Chinese people with its military might. And so on. I felt as if I were in Berlin in 1910, speaking to a young German professional, who in those days would have also been both thoroughly modern and thoroughly nationalist.

As economic fortunes rise, so does nationalism. This is understandable. Imagine that you lived in a country that had been poor and unstable for centuries. And then, finally, things turn and your nation is on the rise. You would be proud and anxious to be seen. This desire for recognition and respect is surging throughout the world. It may seem paradoxical that globalization and economic modernization are breeding political nationalism, but that is so only if we view nationalism as a backward ideology, certain to be erased by the onward march of progress.

Nationalism has always perplexed Americans. When the United States involves itself abroad, it always believes that it is genuinely trying to help other countries better themselves. From the Philippines and Haiti to Vietnam and Iraq, the natives' reaction to U.S. efforts has taken Americans by surprise. Americans take justified pride in their own country—we call it patriotism—and yet are genuinely startled when other people are proud and possessive of theirs.

In the waning days of Britain's rule in India, its last viceroy, Lord Louis Mountbatten, turned to the great Indian leader Mahatma Gandhi and said in exasperation, "If we just leave, there will be chaos." Gandhi replied, "Yes, but it will be *our* chaos." That sense of being governed by one's "own," without interference, is a powerful feeling in emerging countries, especially those that were once colonies or quasi-colonies of the West.

Zbigniew Brzezinski recently called attention to what he terms a "global political awakening." He pointed to rising mass passions, fueled by various forces—economic success, national pride, higher levels of education, greater information and transparency, and memories of the past. Brzezinski noted the disruptive aspects of this new force. "The population of much of the developing world is politically stirring and in many places seething with unrest," he wrote. "It is acutely conscious of social injustice to an unprecedented degree . . . [and this] is creating a community of shared perceptions and envy that can be galvanized and channeled by demagogic political or religious passions. These energies transcend sovereign borders and pose a challenge both to existing states as well as to the existing global hierarchy, on top of which America still perches."

In many countries outside the Western world, there is pent-up frustration with having had to accept an entirely Western or American narrative of world history—one in which they either are miscast or remain bit players. . . .

Such divergent national perspectives have always existed, but today, thanks to greater education, information, and confidence, they are widely disseminated on new news networks, cable channels, and Internet sites of the emerging world. Many of the "rest" are dissecting the narratives, arguments, and assumptions of the West and countering them with a different view of the world. "When you tell us that we support a dictatorship in Sudan to have access to its oil," a young Chinese official told me in 2006, "what I want to say is, 'And how is that different from your support for a medieval monarchy in Saudi Arabia?' We see the hypocrisy, we just don't say anything, yet."

After the Cold War ended, there was a general hope and expectation that China and Russia would move inexorably into the post–World War II Western political and economic system. When George H. W Bush spoke of "a new world order," he meant simply that the old Western one would be extended worldwide. Perhaps this view stemmed from the postwar experience with Japan and Germany, both of which rose to the heights of economic power and yet were accommodating, cooperative, and largely silent members of the existing order. But perhaps those were special circumstances. The two countries had unique histories, having waged aggressive wars and become pariahs as a consequence, and they faced a new threat from Soviet communism and relied on American military power for their protection. The next round of rising powers might not be so eager to "fit in."

We still think of a world in which a rising power must choose between two stark options: integrate into the Western order, or reject it, becoming a rogue nation and facing the penalties of excommunication. In fact, rising powers appear to be following a third way: entering the Western order but doing so on their own terms—thus reshaping the system itself. As the political scientists Naazneen Barma, Ely Ratner, and Steven Weber point out, in a world where everyone feels empowered, countries can choose to bypass this Western "center" entirely and forge their own ties with one another. In a post-American world, there may be no center to integrate into. U.S. Secretary of State James Baker suggested in 1991 that the world was moving toward a hub-and-spoke system, with every country going through the United States to get to its destination. The twenty-first-century world might be better described as one of point-to-point routes, with new flight patterns being mapped every day. (This is true even in a physical sense: in just ten years, the number of Russian visitors to China increased more than fourfold, from 489,000 in 1995 to 2.2 million in 2005.) The focus has shifted. Countries are increasingly interested in themselves—the story of their rise—and pay less attention to the West and the United States. As a result, the urgent discussions on the presidential campaign trail throughout 2007 about the need to lessen anti-Americanism are somewhat off-point. The world is moving from anger to indifference, from anti-Americanism to post-Americanism. . . .

The traditional mechanisms of international cooperation are relics of another era. The United Nations system represents an outdated configuration of power. The permanent members of the un Security Council are the victors of a war that ended sixty years ago. The body does not include Japan or Germany the world's second- and third-largest economies (at market exchange rates), or India, the world's largest democracy, or any Latin American or African country. The Security Council exemplifies the antique structure of global governance more broadly. The G-8 does not include China, already the world's fourth-largest economy, or India and South Korea, the twelfth and thirteenth. By tradition, the IMF is always headed by a European and the World Bank by an American. This "tradition," like the customs of an old segregated country club, may be charming and amusing to insiders, but to outsiders it is bigoted and outrageous.

A further complication: when I write of the rise of nationalism, I am describing a broader phenomenon—the assertion of identity. The nation-state is a relatively new invention, often no more than a hundred years old. Much older are the religious, ethnic, and linguistic groups that live within nation-states. And these bonds have stayed strong, in fact grown, as economic interdependence has deepened. In Europe, the Flemish and French in Belgium remain as distinct as ever. In Britain, the Scots have elected a ruling party that proposes ending the three-hundred-year-old Acts of Union that created the United Kingdom of England, Scotland, and Wales. In India, national parties are losing ground to regional ones. In Kenya, tribal distinctions are becoming more important. In much of the world, these core identities—deeper than the nation-state—remain the defining features of life. It is why people vote, and what they die for. In an open world economy, these groups know that they need the central government less and less. And in a democratic age, they gain greater and greater power if they stay together as a group. This twin ascendancy of identity means that, when relating to the United States or the United Nations or the world at large, Chinese and Indian nationalism grows. But within their own countries, sub-nationalism is also growing. What is happening on the global stage—the rise of identity in the midst of economic growth—is also happening on the local stage. The bottom line: it makes purposeful national action far more difficult. . . .

THE LAST SUPERPOWER

Many observers and commentators have looked at the vitality of this emerging world and concluded that the United States has had its day. Andy Grove, the founder of Intel, puts it bluntly. "America is in danger of following Europe down the tubes," he says, "and the worst part is that nobody knows it. They're all in denial, patting themselves on the back as the *Titanic* heads straight for the iceberg full speed ahead." Thomas Friedman describes watching waves of young Indian professionals get to work for the night shift at Infosys in Bangalore. "Oh, my God, there are so many of them, and they just keep coming, wave after wave. How in the world can it possibly be good for my daughters and millions of other Americans that these Indians can do the same jobs as they can for a fraction of the wages?" "Globalization is striking back," writes Gabor Steingart, an editor at Germany's leading news magazine, *Der Spiegel*, in a bestselling book. As its rivals have prospered, he argues, the United States has lost key industries, its people have stopped saving money, and its government has become increasingly indebted to Asian central banks.

What's puzzling, however, is that these trends have been around for a while—and they have actually helped America's bottom line. Over the past twenty years, as globalization and outsourcing have accelerated dramatically, America's growth rate has averaged just over 3 percent, a full percentage point higher than that of Germany and France. (Japan averaged 2.3 percent over the same period.) Productivity growth, the elixir of modern economics, has been over 2.5 percent for a decade now, again a full percentage point higher than the European average. Even American exports held up, despite a decade-long spike in the value of the dollar that ended recently. In 1980, U.S. exports represented 10 percent of the world total; in 2007, that figure was still almost 9 percent. According to the World Economic Forum, the United States remains the most competitive economy in the world and ranks first in innovation, ninth in technological readiness, second in company spending for research and technology, and second in the quality of its research institutions. China does not come within thirty countries of the United States in any of these, and India breaks the top ten on only one count: market size. In virtually every sector that advanced industrial countries participate in, U.S. firms lead the world in productivity and profits.

The United States' share of the global economy has been remarkably steady through wars, depressions, and a slew of other powers rising. With 5 percent of the world's population, the United States has generated between 20 and 30 percent of world output for 125 years. There will surely be some slippage of America's position over the next few decades. This is not a political statement but a mathematical one. As other countries grow faster, America's relative economic weight will fall. But the decline need not be large-scale, rapid, or consequential, as long as the United States can adapt to new challenges as well as it adapted to those it confronted over the last century. In the next few decades, the rise of the emerging nations is likely to come mostly at the expense of Western Europe and Japan, which are locked in a slow, demographically determined decline.

America will face the most intense economic competition it has ever faced. The American economic and social system knows how to respond and adjust to such pressures. The reforms needed are obvious but because they mean some pain now for long-term gain, the political system cannot make them. The more difficult challenge that the United States faces is international. It will confront a global order quite different from the one it is used to operating in. For now, the United States remains the most powerful player. But every year the balance shifts.

For the roughly two decades since 1989, the power of the United States has defined the international order. All roads have led to Washington, and American ideas about politics, economics, and foreign policy have been the starting points for global action. Washington has been the most powerful outside actor on every continent in the world, dominating the Western Hemisphere, remaining the crucial outside balancer in Europe and East Asia, expanding its role in the Middle East and Central and South Asia, and everywhere remaining the only country that can provide the muscle for any serious global military operation. For every country—from Russia and China to South Africa and India—its most important relationship in the world has been the relationship with the United States.

That influence reached its apogee with Iraq. Despite the reluctance, opposition, or active hostility of much of the world, the United States was able to launch an unprovoked attack on a sovereign country and to enlist dozens of countries and international agencies to assist it during and after the invasion. It is not just the complications of Iraq that have unwound this order. Even had Iraq been a glorious success, the method of its execution would have made utterly clear the unchallenged power of the United States—and it is this exercise of unipolarity that has provoked a reaction around the world. The unipolar order of the last two decades is waning not because of Iraq but because of the broader diffusion of power across the world. . . .

Reading 1.5

The Dark Side of Progress

FRED C. IKLÉ

The storyline of this book is at once forward-looking and historical. The prospect ahead features revolutionary new threats to national security and could end in demolition of the existing world order. Looking backward, the story traces this coming upheaval to historic forces that have been centuries in the making. Today's menaces—jihadist terrorism, rogue nations producing nuclear bombs—may be viewed as mere symptoms of these forces, as the rustling wind that foretells the gathering storm. Few military strategists and political experts have grasped the dimensions of the storm awaiting us. Fewer still are mindful of its historic evolution.

The emerging crisis is the outgrowth of technological progress. It reflects the dark side of progress. Globalization guarantees the ceaseless spread of new technologies, whether beneficial or destructive. The nuclear age offers the clearest lesson of this problem. Until the end of the Cold War, it appeared that we were somehow managing the nuclear threat. Over a span of half a century, the political and military leaders of the nuclear powers were able to pursue strategies that averted the use of nuclear weapons. Their long-run success in maintaining the regime of "non-use" is one of the greatest achievements in the history of military strategy.

Alas, the world is now different. After our stressful journey through the Cold War—a journey with a happy ending—we now face a ghastly new predicament. One nation after another is starting up nuclear programs, allegedly for peaceful purposes, but often and obviously as a stratagem for getting to an arsenal of nuclear weapons. And the proliferation problem does not end there. A cascade of frightening news reports tells us that the control of national governments over nuclear materials and bombs is far from secure. The inescapable subtext of these reports is that, all too soon, we must expect these weapons to be acquired by doomsday cults, anarchists, and terrorist gangs.

Other technologies, not yet on the radar screens of the world's media, will be even more resistant to political control. It is well known that immensely beneficial advances in the life sciences can be misused to develop biological weapons. But the most revolutionary impact of the life sciences might be the most difficult to control: the conquest of the human mind by brain science. A vast enhancement in intelligent decision-making might be just decades away. Some powerful nations have already built elaborate command and decision centers that exploit the capabilities of the latest computer systems. As day follows night, these projects will gradually take advantage of the rapid advances

---

Source: Fred Charles Iklé, Annihilation from Within *(New York: Columbia University Press, 2006), pp. vi–xiii. Reprinted by permission.*

in brain science to complement the strengths of computers with the unique capabilities of the human brain. If these projects are successful, they will achieve a superhuman intelligence able to trump the performance of first-rate human experts and the latest super-computers. Any such leap forward in intelligent decision-making would be a change comparable to the evolution from primates to *Homo sapiens*. The transition would pose the most fundamental challenge to all religions. It would upend human civilization. It would instantly obliterate all previous notions about relative national power. And in light of our experience with nuclear proliferation, it would be absurd to expect the United Nations to "control" this new intelligence. Today, the United States uses computerized command centers for its military leaders, while China is experimenting with computerized decision centers that can serve both the military and its political leadership. If China moved ahead of America in the race to develop superhuman intelligence systems, would the U.S. Government wait for UN approval to catch up?

Today, our policymakers and analysts are preoccupied with terrorist attacks by militant Islamists. These attacks, often by suicide bombers, have been painful and enormously costly for the victims, but they cannot defeat established democracies or indeed any nation that is not already a failed state. The fact is that contemporary Islamic terrorism does not have a strategy for victory. It is swayed by impulses animated by a fervidness for revenge and religious utopias. It is as if these jihadist terrorists—enraged by their impotence—seek gratification from bloodshed and self-immolation. While these murderous assaults hurt us, they also spur us to increase our military power and to strengthen the defense of our homeland. What does not kill us makes us stronger.

Yet terrorists, anarchists, and other evildoers seek to acquire weapons of mass destruction, and some of them are bound to succeed. Most of them will merely want to use these weapons to inflict immense damage without knowing how to achieve a lasting victory. But keep in mind that, throughout history, mankind had to suffer the depredations of leaders who can rally throngs of followers and intimidate the masses. The twentieth century offers vivid examples. Among such historic evildoers, the most relevant in this context are Lenin and Hitler. The greatest threat to the world order in this century will be the next Hitler or Lenin, a charismatic leader who combines utter ruthlessness with a brilliant strategic sense, cunning, and boundless ambition—and who gains control over just a few weapons of mass destruction.

This new threat, still offstage, now awaits us. Any such evil but charismatic leader will be able to attack a major nation from within even if that nation possesses enormous military strength and capable police forces. If this new tyrant turns out to be strategically intelligent, he could prepare to launch a couple of mass destruction weapons against carefully chosen targets—without training camps in another nation, without help from a foreign terrorist organization, without a military campaign across the nation's borders. He would thus offer no targets for retaliation and render useless a nation's most powerful deterrent forces. By contrast, an expanding caliphate—the utopia that jihadists dream about—would offer the leading democracies plenty of easy targets for retaliation.

The purpose of this new tyrant would not be to destroy landmark buildings, highjack airplanes, attack railroad stations and religious shrines. His aim would be to paralyze the national leadership and spread nationwide panic, to ensure that the center could not hold. He would be well prepared to exploit this chaos by seizing complete control of the nation's government and imposing his dictatorship. Success in any such endeavor would be a shattering event, signifying to democracies everywhere that their world, their basic institutions, their national security strategies, their citizens' everyday lives—that all this was now up for grabs. Living comfortably on borrowed time, most democratic societies lack the will and foresight needed to defend against any such calamity.

Non-democratic governments will also be vulnerable—indeed, more vulnerable—to annihilation from within. In those Central Asian republics, for example, where authoritarian rulers confront large Muslim populations who want a fundamentalist Islamic state, the detonation of a single nuclear bomb in the capital would create a political vacuum. This could enable a religious leader (perhaps a cleric like Iraq's Muqtada al-Sadr) to mobilize his throngs of followers and seize control of the country.

Today's military planners have not given much thought to averting annihilation from within. The conventional wisdom about the world's future holds that it is steadily becoming more democratic and therefore more peaceful. Technological progress is said to make all countries interdependent—to push us toward a unified world in which distance is no longer an impediment to travel and trade and, thanks to the Internet, has been erased entirely as an obstacle to communications. The appealing vision of a new "flat world" has left many commentators blind to the dark side of technological progress. . . .

If we hope to navigate our way past the deadly threats confronting us, it will help to understand the roots and evolution of the historic forces that have unleashed them. They originated some 250 years ago in Western Europe, in a schism in mankind's culture. Science was rather suddenly freed from political and religious controls. The ascendance of Enlightenment thinking diminished the influence of religious beliefs, a development in which the Protestant Reformation also played a role. And government policies that increasingly promoted a free market served to promote, and handsomely reward, technological advances.

Since then, technological progress has brought immense improvements in the human condition. These gains seemed to outweigh all the potential applications of technology that would be destructive or harmful. But surprisingly, already at the very beginning of the Industrial Revolution, many thinkers had a foreboding of technology's dark side. And today we begin to understand the dangerous dynamic of the cultural schism.

As a result of this schism, two modes of human thought and activity split apart. One mode is animated by religious faiths, ethnic and national traditions, and societal customs. This mode remained essentially the same as it had been before the schism. It shapes the basic structure of society and nourishes the sense of patriotism and loyalty that enables nations to function. But the other mode of thinking is guided by science, which seeks to understand the workings of nature by relying on empirical verification, not on a definition of "truth" handed down through generations. Our growing knowledge of the physical universe has enabled us to transform our environment progressively and to alter the human condition. Following the initial cultural schism, the accelerating scientific and technological progress gave us the Industrial Revolution, which in turn spread progress to more and more countries and changed the face of our planet.

One might plausibly observe that this story is old hat. But what the standard narrative leaves out is the most important part of the saga, namely that the cultural schism is *still* widening—and dangerously so. Technological progress and the global political order march to different drummers.

Science makes cumulative discoveries and hence can advance at an accelerating pace. It has acquired an inner dynamic of progress that is nearly self-sustaining. But the sphere of government and international affairs is marked by alternating periods of advance and decline, of gains and losses. Individual liberty expands and is suppressed again. Peace is followed by war and war by a new peace. Religious tolerance is followed by theocratic repression, to be replaced by a more secular regime. Periods of free trade are followed by protectionism and again by new efforts to spread free trade. In sum, the political, social, and religious sphere moves in a zigzag course, while science makes cumulative advances.

The two modes of human thought and activity that split apart some 250 years ago are destined to drift farther apart because disparate aspirations of the two modes aggravate the widening schism. Science and technology do not have a final goal. They pursue a continuing conquest of nature in which disproved theories are replaced by new knowledge. But political endeavors have finite goals. Marxism did not aspire to be followed by capitalism, Islam does not seek to be replaced by Christianity, America's propagation of democracy does not strive to be succeeded by autocratic governments.

This widening divergence in human culture might overwhelm the political order of the world in a way that endangers the survival of all nations. And, bear in mind, only sovereign nations can marshal troops and rally political support to defeat terrorist organizations, deter aggression, enforce UN decisions. When push comes to shove, only nations can keep some order in the world.

Annihilation from within is not a temporary peril, but the end point and ultimate impact of this elemental historic force that has gained ever more strength over two centuries. Military history offers no lessons that tell nations how to cope with a continuing global dispersion of cataclysmic means for destruction. Because of the cultural split some 250 years ago, the threat of annihilation from within is now woven into the fabric of our era.

Let us admit it: mankind became entrapped in a Faustian bargain. In the famous medieval legend, Faust sells his soul to the devil in exchange for the magical powers of science (or rather the imagined powers of alchemy in those days). There is much that we can do to avert the worst disaster. But as we begin to discern the trials that lie ahead, our exuberance about unending progress is tempered by a premonition that our "bargain with the devil" might end badly.

International Realism: Anarchy and Power

Outside of the ivory tower theory is often disdained as naïve and impractical, and inside the ivory tower students are often impatient with it. All people, however, statesmen as well as intellectuals, use theory, whether they realize it or not. If only unconsciously, nearly everyone has assumptions about how the world works that underlie their conscious views of what foreign policies should and can be, and that tilt the balance in their perceptions of ambiguous evidence. At least in the West, those assumptions about international relations are usually variants of realism or liberalism. (Most "constructivist" views tend to overlap with liberalism in their predictions or prescriptions.)

The appeal of these contrasting schools of thought tends to vary with developments in the real world. Perhaps because the twentieth century was one of unprecedented catastrophe, the dominant tradition has been what is known colloquially as "power politics." In academic circles this family of ideas is known as "realism." The main themes in this school of thought are that in order to survive and prosper, states are driven to seek power, that moral or legal principles that can govern relations among citizens within states cannot control the relations among states, and that wars occur because there is no sovereign in the international system to settle disputes peacefully and enforce judgments. States have no one but themselves to rely on for protection, or to obtain what they believe they are entitled to by right.

Thucydides's *Peloponnesian War*, the history of the conflict between Athens and Sparta two and a half millennia ago, is the classic statement of these ideas. The selection included here—the Melian Dialogue—is perhaps the most extreme and frank discussion of power politics, unclouded by diplomatic niceties, ever recorded. Taken alone, the dialogue can appear a caricature, so readers are encouraged to delve into more of the original work, which is rich in commentary on various aspects of balance of power politics, strategy, and the role of ideology and domestic conflict in international relations.[1]

The tradition of realism can be traced in various forms through Machiavelli, Hobbes, the German schools of *Realpolitik* and *Machtpolitik*, to E.H. Carr, Reinhold Niebuhr, Hans Morgenthau, Kenneth N. Waltz, and others in the twentieth century. The selections from Machiavelli's *The Prince* and Hobbes's *Leviathan* that follow capsulize their views of the roots of political ruthlessness, the similarity of diplomacy and political competition to the state of nature, and the need for leaders who seek to secure their regimes to do things in public life that are condemned in traditional codes of morality.

Readers should avoid the popular misinterpretation of these thinkers as amoral. Rather they should be understood as moral relativists, concerned with the need to secure the prerequisite (power) for achievement of anything moral, a need that may require behavior inconsistent with absolute norms or religious ethics. As Machiavelli argues in the following excerpt, a prince must "not deviate from what is good, if possible, but be able to do evil if constrained."

In the past century, Morgenthau's *Politics Among Nations*[2] was the most prominent textbook of realism in the United States. Carr's *Twenty Years Crisis*, on the other hand, is distinguished by its pungency, which helps to convey the essence of realism in brief selections. Before pigeon-holing Carr as a strident realist, however, note his eloquent discussion of the serious deficiencies of the theory in the middle of the excerpts that follow.

The most prominent recent writings in the realist school have been dubbed "neo" or "structural" realism to distinguish their more rigorously scientific formulation of the theory. Neorealists focus less on the questions of human motivation or the nature of political regimes than on the security incentives posed by the structure of the international system. The following selection by Kenneth N. Waltz, the dean of neorealism, is close to a summary of his masterwork, *Theory of International Politics*.[3] Mearsheimer's hyper-realist argument in favor of the Cold War, in Part I and in his magnum opus on realism, *The Tragedy of Great Power Politics*,[4] derives directly from Waltz's reasoning about the stability of a bipolar world (discussed in this selection) and the pacifying effect of nuclear weapons (discussed in the selection by Waltz in Part VII).

The favorable view of bipolarity among neorealists, however, contradicts traditional balance of power theory. In considering whether a world of only two major powers, as opposed to a world of many, should be less likely to lead to war, compare Waltz and Mearsheimer with Thucydides, Blainey, and Gilpin. The competitions between Athens and Sparta or Rome and Carthage, for example, unlike that between the United States and the Soviet Union, ended in disaster. Where Waltz sees bipolarity as imposing clarity and stability on the competition, others see it as inherently unstable—a delicate balance between contenders ever striving for primacy. Robert Gilpin sees history as a succession of struggles for hegemony between declining and rising powers, with the struggles normally resolved by a major war. Geoffrey Blainey considers a hierarchical system, in which differences in power are clear, as most stable. When there is no doubt about who would prevail if disagreements were to lead to combat, there is little chance that the strong will need to resort to combat or that the weak will dare. Blainey sees a world of rough parity, in contrast, as unstable, because it is easier for states to miscalculate the balance of power and their chances of being able to impose their will by either initiating or resisting the use of force. This view is consistent with Gilpin's, since the challenger in a hegemonic transition is usually one whose power is approaching that of the leading state, and it directly contradicts the view of Waltz and Mearsheimer.

How much do the structure of the international balance of power and competition for primacy determine the actions of states? We might ask how one could have predicted the end of the Cold War from realist theories. Was the Soviet Union's voluntary surrender of control over Eastern Europe in 1989, indeed its entire withdrawal from the power struggle with the West, consistent with such explanations of state behavior? Realists understand that statesmen do not always act in accord with realist norms, but the enormity of the Gorbachev revolution is an uncomfortable exception for the theory to have to bear. Nevertheless, realist scholars offer arguments for why the end of the Cold War should confirm their theories rather than revise them.[5]

If readers are not fully convinced that realist theories adequately explain the end of the Cold War, they might consider another possibility. The greatest irony might be that the end came from the adoption of liberal ideas about international cooperation by the leadership of the Soviet Union, the superpower that had so tenaciously opposed Western liberalism as a model for the world.[6] The readings in Part III will present some tenets of the liberal tradition that offer a very different view of the possibilities of peace from the one presented in this section.

—RKB

NOTES

1 Thucydides also presents examples that differ markedly from the Melian dialogue, such as the Mytilene debate. See Michael Walzer's comparison in *Just and Unjust Wars* (New York: Basic Books, 1977), pp. 5–11.

2 Hans Morgenthau, *Politics Among Nations*, Fifth edition (New York: Knopf, 1973).

3 Kenneth N. Waltz, *Theory of International Politics* (Reading, Mass.: Addison-Wesley, 1979). See also Waltz, *Man, the State, and War* (New York: Columbia University Press, 1959).

4 John J. Mearsheimer, *The Tragedy of Great Power Politics*, Second Edition (New York: W. W. Norton, 2014).

5 Kenneth N. Waltz, "Structural Realism After the Cold War," *International Security* 25, no. 1 (Summer 2000); William C. Wohlforth, "Realism and the End of the Cold War," *International Security* 19, no. 3 (Winter 1994/95); Richard K. Betts, "Not with My Thucydides You Don't," *The American Interest* 2, no. 4 (March/April 2007). See also Richard K. Betts, "The Realist Persuasion," *The National Interest* no. 139 (September/October 2015).

6 A further irony would be that if the liberal explanation for Soviet foreign policy at the end of the Cold War is convincing, the results in terms of international politics are still consistent with realism. The Gorbachev revolution contributed to the destruction of the Soviet Union, even if it did not fully cause it. It was not necessarily inevitable that a more ruthless Soviet leadership would have failed to preserve the empire, at least into the twenty-first century. In Waltz's terms, the Soviet Union certainly did "fall by the wayside."

Reading 2.1

The Melian Dialogue   THUCYDIDES

The Melians are a colony of Lacedaemon [Sparta] that would not submit to the Athenians like the other islanders, and at first remained neutral and took no part in the struggle, but afterwards upon the Athenians using violence and plundering their territory, assumed an attitude of open hostility. Cleomedes, son of Lycomedes, and Tisias, son of Tisimachus, the generals, encamping in their territory with the above armament, before doing any harm to their land, sent envoys to negotiate. These the Melians did not bring before the people, but bade them state the object of their mission to the magistrates and the few; upon which the Athenian envoys spoke as follows:—

Athenians: 'Since the negotiations are not to go on before the people, in order that we may not be able to speak straight on without interruption, and deceive the ears of the multitude by seductive arguments which would pass without refutation (for we know that this is the meaning of our being brought before the few), what if you who sit there were to pursue a method more cautious still! Make no set speech yourselves, but take us up at whatever you do not like, and settle that before going any farther. And first tell us if this proposition of ours suits you.'

The Melian commissioners answered:—

Melians: 'To the fairness of quietly instructing each other as you propose there is nothing to object; but your military preparations are too far advanced to agree with what you say, as we see you are come to be judges in your own cause, and that all we can reasonably expect from this negotiation is war, if we prove to have right on our side and refuse to submit, and in the contrary case, slavery.'

Athenians: 'If you have met to reason about presentiments of the future, or for anything else than to consult for the safety of your state upon the facts that you see before you, we will give over; otherwise we will go on.'

Melians: 'It is natural and excusable for men in our position to turn more ways than one both in thought and utterance. However, the question in this conference is, as you say, the safety of our country; and the discussion, if you please, can proceed in the way which you propose.'

Athenians: 'For ourselves, we shall not trouble you with specious pretences—either of how we have a right to our empire because we overthrew the Mede, or are now attacking you because of wrong that you have done

Source: Thucydides, The Peloponnesian War, *Richard Crawley, trans. (New York: The Modern Library, 1934), Book V.*

us—and make a long speech which would not be believed; and in return we hope that you, instead of thinking to influence us by saying that you did not join the Lacedaemonians, although their colonists, or that you have done us no wrong, will aim at what is feasible, holding in view the real sentiments of us both; since you know as well as we do that right, as the world goes, is only in question between equals in power, while the strong do what they can and the weak suffer what they must.'

Melians: 'As we think, at any rate, it is expedient—we speak as we are obliged, since you enjoin us to let right alone and talk only of interest—that you should not destroy what is our common protection, the privilege of being allowed in danger to invoke what is fair and right, and even to profit by arguments not strictly valid if they can be got to pass current. And you are as much interested in this as any, as your fall would be a signal for the heaviest vengeance and an example for the world to meditate upon.'

Athenians: 'The end of our empire, if end it should, does not frighten us: a rival empire like Lacedaemon, even if Lacedaemon was our real antagonist, is not so terrible to the vanquished as subjects who by themselves attack and overpower their rulers. This, however, is a risk that we are content to take. We will now proceed to show you that we are come here in the interest of our empire, and that we shall say what we are now going to say, for the preservation of your country; as we would fain exercise that empire over you without trouble, and see you preserved for the good of us both.'

Melians: 'And how, pray, could it turn out as good for us to serve as for you to rule?'

Athenians: 'Because you would have the advantage of submitting before suffering the worst, and we should gain by not destroying you.'

Melians: 'So that you would not consent to our being neutral, friends instead of enemies, but allies of neither side.'

Athenians: 'No; for your hostility cannot so much hurt us as your friendship will be an argument to our subjects of our weakness, and your enmity of our power.'

Melians: 'Is that your subjects' idea of equity, to put those who have nothing to do with you in the same category with peoples that are most of them your own colonists, and some conquered rebels?'

Athenians: 'As far as right goes they think one has as much of it as the other, and that if any maintain their independence it is because they are strong, and that if we do not molest them it is because we are afraid; so that besides extending our empire we should gain in security by your subjection; the fact that you are islanders and weaker than others rendering it all the more important that you should not succeed in baffling the masters of the sea.'

Melians: 'But do you consider that there is no security in the policy which we indicate? For here again if you debar us from talking about justice and invite us to obey your interest, we also must explain ours, and try to persuade you, if the two happen to coincide. How can you avoid making enemies of all existing neutrals who shall look at our case and conclude from it that one day or another you will attack them? And what is this but to make greater the enemies that you have already, and to force others to become so who would otherwise have never thought of it?'

Athenians: 'Why, the fact is that continentals generally give us but little alarm; the liberty which they enjoy will long prevent their taking precautions against us; it is rather islanders like yourselves, outside our empire, and subjects smarting under the yoke, who would be the most likely to take a rash step and lead themselves and us into obvious danger.'

Melians: 'Well then, if you risk so much to retain your empire, and your subjects to get rid of it, it were surely great baseness and cowardice in us who are still free not to try everything that can be tried, before submitting to your yoke.'

Athenians: 'Not if you are well advised, the contest not being an equal one, with honour as the prize and shame as the penalty, but a question of self-preservation and of not resisting those who are far stronger than you are.'

Melians: 'But we know that the fortune of war is sometimes more impartial than the disproportion of numbers might lead one to suppose; to submit is to give ourselves over to despair, while action still preserves for us a hope that we may stand erect.'

Athenians: 'Hope, danger's comforter, may be indulged in by those who have abundant resources, if not without loss at all events without ruin; but its nature is to be extravagant, and those who go so far as to put their all upon the venture see it in its true colours only when they are ruined; but so long as the discovery would enable them to guard against it, it is never found wanting. Let not this be the case with you, who are weak and hang on a single turn of the scale; nor be like the vulgar, who, abandoning such security as human means may still afford, when visible hopes fail them in extremity, turn to invisible, to prophecies and oracles, and other such inventions that delude men with hopes to their destruction.'

Melians: 'You may be sure that we are as well aware as you of the difficulty of contending against your power and fortune, unless the terms be equal. But we trust that the gods may grant us fortune as good as yours, since we are just men fighting against unjust, and that what we want in power will be made up by the alliance of the Lacedaemonians, who are bound if only for very shame, to come to the aid of their kindred. Our confidence, therefore, after all is not so utterly irrational.'

Athenians: 'When you speak of the favour of the gods, we may as fairly hope for that as yourselves; neither our pretensions nor our conduct being in any way contrary to what men believe of the gods, or practise among themselves. Of the gods we believe, and of men we know, that by a necessary law of their nature they rule wherever they can. And it is not as if we were the first to make this law, or to act upon it when made: we found it existing before us, and shall leave it to exist for ever after us; all we do is to make use of it, knowing that you and everybody else, having the same power as we have, would do the same as we do. Thus, as far as the gods are concerned, we have no fear and no reason to fear that we shall be at a disadvantage. But when we come to your notion about the Lacedaemonians, which leads you to believe that shame will make them help you, here we bless your simplicity but do not envy your folly. The Lacedaemonians, when their own interests of their country's laws are in question, are the worthiest men alive; of their conduct towards others much might be said, but no clearer idea of it could be given than by shortly saying that of all the men we know they are most conspicuous in considering what is agreeable honourable, and what is expedient just. Such a way of thinking does not promise much for the safety which you now unreasonably count upon.'

Melians: 'But it is for this very reason that we now trust to their respect for expediency to prevent them from betraying the Melians, their colonists, and thereby losing the confidence of their friends in Hellas and helping their enemies.'

Athenians: 'Then you do not adopt the view that expediency goes with security, while justice and honour cannot be followed without danger; and danger the Lacedaemonians generally court as little as possible.'

Melians: 'But we believe that they would be more likely to face even danger for our sake, and with more confidence than for others, as our nearness to Peloponnese makes it easier for them to act, and our common blood insures our fidelity.'

Athenians: 'Yes, but what an intending ally trusts to, is not the goodwill of those who ask his aid, but a decided superiority of power for action; and the Lacedaemonians look to this even more than others. At least, such is their distrust of their home resources that it is only with numerous allies that they attack a neighbour; now is it likely that while we are masters of the sea they will cross over to an island?'

Melians: 'But they would have others to send. The Cretan sea is a wide one, and it is more difficult for those who command it to intercept others, than for those who wish to elude them to do so safely. And should the Lacedaemonians miscarry in this, they would fall upon your land, and upon those left of your allies whom Brasidas did not reach; and instead of places which are not yours, you will have to fight for your own country and your own confederacy.'

Athenians: 'Some diversion of the kind you speak of you may one day experience, only to learn, as others have done, that the Athenians never once yet withdrew from a siege for fear of any. But we are struck by the fact, that after saying you would consult for the safety of your country, in all this discussion you have mentioned nothing which men might trust in and think to be saved by. Your strongest arguments depend upon hope and the future, and your actual resources are too scanty, as compared with those arrayed against you, for you to come out victorious. You will therefore show great blindness of judgment, unless, after allowing us to retire, you can find some counsel more prudent than this. You will surely not be caught by that idea of disgrace, which in dangers that are disgraceful, and at the same time too plain to be mistaken, proves so fatal to mankind; since in too many cases the very men that have their eyes perfectly open to what they are rushing into, let the thing called disgrace, by the mere influence of a seductive name, lead them on to a point at which they become so enslaved by the phrase as in fact to fall wilfully into hopeless disaster, and incur disgrace more disgraceful as the companion of error, than when it comes as the result of misfortune. This, if you are well advised, you will guard against; and you will not think it dishonourable to submit to the greatest city in Hellas, when it makes you the moderate offer of becoming its tributary ally, without ceasing to enjoy the country that belongs to you; nor when you have the choice given you between war and security, will you be so blinded as to choose the worse. And it is certain that those who do not yield to their equals, who keep terms with their superiors, and are moderate towards their inferiors, on the whole succeed best. Think over the matter, therefore, after our withdrawal, and reflect once and again that it is for your country that you are consulting, that you have not more than one, and that upon this one deliberation depends its prosperity or ruin.'

The Athenians now withdrew from the conference; and the Melians, left to themselves, came to a decision corresponding with what they had maintained in the discussion, and answered, 'Our resolution, Athenians, is the same as it was at first. We will not in a moment deprive of freedom a city that has been inhabited these seven hundred years; but we put our trust in the fortune by which the gods have preserved it until now, and in the help of men, that is, of the Lacedaemonians; and so we will try and save ourselves. Meanwhile we invite you to allow us to be friends to you and foes to neither party, and to retire from our country after making such a treaty as shall seem fit to us both.'

Such was the answer of the Melians. The Athenians now departing from the conference said, 'Well, you alone, as it seems to us, judging from these resolutions, regard what is future as more certain than what is before your eyes, and what is out of sight, in your eagerness, as already coming to pass; and as you have staked most on, and trusted most in, the Lacedaemonians, your fortune, and your hopes, so will you be most completely deceived.'

The Athenian envoys now returned to the army; and the Melians showing no signs of yielding, the generals at once betook themselves to hostilities, and drew a line of circumvallation round the Melians, dividing the work among the different states. Subsequently the Athenians returned with most of their army, leaving behind them a certain number of their own citizens and of the allies to keep guard by land and sea. The force thus left stayed on and besieged the place. . . .

Summer was now over. The next winter the Lacedaemonians intended to invade the Argive territory, but arriving at the frontier found the sacrifices for crossing unfavourable, and went back again. This intention of theirs gave the Argives suspicions of certain of their fellow-citizens, some of whom they arrested; others, however, escaped them. About the same time the Melians again took another part of the Athenian lines which were but feebly garrisoned. Reinforcements afterwards arriving from Athens in consequence, under the command of Philocrates, son of Demeas, the siege was now pressed vigorously; and some treachery taking place inside, the Melians surrendered at discretion to the Athenians, who put to death all the grown men whom they took, and sold the women and children for slaves, and subsequently sent out five hundred colonists and inhabited the place themselves.

Reading 2.2

Doing Evil in Order to Do Good

NICCOLÒ MACHIAVELLI

OF THE THINGS FOR WHICH MEN, AND ESPECIALLY PRINCES, ARE PRAISED OR BLAMED

It now remains to be seen what are the methods and rules for a prince as regards his subjects and friends. And as I know that many have written of this, I fear that my writing about it may be deemed presumptuous, differing as I do, especially in this matter, from the opinions of others. But my intention being to write something of use to those who understand, it appears to me more proper to go to the real truth of the matter than to its imagination; and many have imagined republics and principalities which have never been seen or known to exist in reality; for how we live is so far removed from how we ought to live, that he who abandons what is done for what ought to be done, will rather learn to bring about his own ruin than his preservation. A man who wishes to make a profession of goodness in everything must necessarily come to grief among so many who are not good. Therefore it is necessary for a prince, who wishes to maintain himself, to learn how not to be good, and to use this knowledge and not use it, according to the necessity of the case.

Source: Niccolò Machiavelli, The Prince, *Luigi Ricci and E. R. P. Vincent, trans. (Modern Library, 1950), Chapters 15, 17, 18.*

Leaving on one side, then, those things which concern only an imaginary prince, and speaking of those that are real, I state that all men, and especially princes, who are placed at a greater height, are reputed for certain qualities which bring them either praise or blame. Thus one is considered liberal, another *misero* or miserly (using a Tuscan term, seeing that *avaro* with us still means one who is rapaciously acquisitive and *misero* one who makes grudging use of his own); one a free giver, another rapacious; one cruel, another merciful; one a breaker of his word, another trustworthy; one effeminate and pusillanimous, another fierce and high-spirited; one humane, another haughty; one lascivious, another chaste; one frank, another astute; one hard, another easy; one serious, another frivolous; one religious, another an unbeliever, and so on. I know that every one will admit that it would be highly praiseworthy in a prince to possess all the above-named qualities that are reputed good, but as they cannot all be possessed or observed, human conditions not permitting of it, it is necessary that he should be prudent enough to avoid the scandal of those vices which would lose him the state, and guard himself if possible against those which will not lose it him, but if not able to, he can indulge them with less scruple. And yet he must not mind incurring the scandal of those vices, without which it would be difficult to save the state, for if one considers well, it will be found that some things which seem virtues would, if followed, lead to one's ruin, and some others which appear vices result in one's greater security and well-being. . . .

OF CRUELTY AND CLEMENCY, AND WHETHER IT IS BETTER TO BE LOVED OR FEARED

Proceeding to the other qualities before named, I say that every prince must desire to be considered merciful and not cruel. He must, however, take care not to misuse this mercifulness. Cesare Borgia was considered cruel, but his cruelty had brought order to the Romagna, united it, and reduced it to peace and fealty. If this is considered well, it will be seen that he was really much more merciful than the Florentine people, who, to avoid the name of cruelty, allowed Pistoia to be destroyed. A prince, therefore, must not mind incurring the charge of cruelty for the purpose of keeping his subjects united and faithful; for, with a very few examples, he will be more merciful than those who, from excess of tenderness, allow disorders to arise, from whence spring bloodshed and rapine; for these as a rule injure the whole community, while the executions carried out by the prince injure only individuals. And of all princes, it is impossible for a new prince to escape the reputation of cruelty, new states being always full of dangers. Wherefore Virgil through the mouth of Dido says:

> Res dura, et regni novitas me talia cogunt
> Moliri, et late fines custode tueri.

Nevertheless, he must be cautious in believing and acting, and must not be afraid of his own shadow, and must proceed in a temperate manner with prudence and humanity, so that too much confidence does not render him incautious, and too much diffidence does not render him intolerant.

From this arises the question whether it is better to be loved more than feared, or feared more than loved. The reply is, that one ought to be both feared and loved, but as it is difficult for the two to go together, it is much safer to be feared than loved, if one of the two has to be wanting. For it may be said of men in general that they are ungrateful, voluble, dissemblers, anxious to avoid danger, and covetous of gain; as long as you benefit them, they are entirely yours; they offer you their blood, their goods, their life, and their children, as I have before said, when the necessity is remote; but when it approaches, they revolt. And the prince who has relied solely on their words, without making other preparations, is ruined; for the friendship which is gained by purchase and not through grandeur and nobility of spirit is bought but not secured, and at a pinch is not to be expended in your service. And men have less scruple in offending one who makes himself loved than one who makes himself feared; for love is held by a chain of obligation which, men being selfish, is broken whenever it serves their purpose; but fear is maintained by a dread of punishment which never fails.

Still, a prince should make himself feared in such a way that if he does not gain love, he at any rate avoids hatred; for fear and the absence of hatred may well go together, and will be always attained by one who abstains from interfering with the property of his citizens and subjects or with their women. And when he is obliged to take the life of any one, let him do so when there is a proper justification and manifest reason for it; but above all he must abstain from taking the property of others, for men forget more easily the death of their father than the loss of their patrimony. Then also pretexts for seizing property are never wanting, and one who begins to live by rapine will always find some reason for taking the goods of others, whereas causes for taking life are rarer and more fleeting.

But when the prince is with his army and has a large number of soldiers under his control, then it is extremely necessary that he should not mind being thought cruel; for without this reputation he could not keep an army united or disposed to any duty. Among the noteworthy actions of Hannibal is numbered this, that although he had an enormous army, composed of men of all nations and fighting in foreign countries, there never arose any dissension either among them or against the prince, either in good fortune or in bad. This could not be due to anything but his inhuman cruelty, which together with his infinite other virtues, made him always venerated and terrible in the sight of his soldiers, and without it his other virtues would not have sufficed to produce that effect. Thoughtless writers admire on the one hand his actions, and on the other blame the principal cause of them.

And that it is true that his other virtues would not have sufficed may be seen from the case of Scipio (famous not only in regard to his own times, but all times of which memory remains), whose armies rebelled against him in Spain, which arose from nothing but his excessive kindness, which allowed more licence to the soldiers than was consonant with military discipline. He was reproached with this in the senate by Fabius Maximus, who called him a corrupter of the Roman militia. Locri having been destroyed by one of Scipio's officers was not revenged by him, nor was the insolence of that officer punished, simply by reason of his easy nature; so much so, that someone wishing to—excuse him in the senate, said that there were many men who knew rather how not to err, than how to correct the errors of others. This disposition would in time have tarnished the fame and glory of Scipio had he persevered in it under the empire, but living under the rule of the senate this harmful quality was not only concealed but became a glory to him.

I conclude, therefore, with regard to being feared and loved, that men love at their own free will, but fear at the will of the prince, and that a wise prince must rely on what is in his power and not on what is in the power of others, and he must only contrive to avoid incurring hatred, as has been explained.

IN WHAT WAY PRINCES MUST KEEP FAITH

How laudable it is for a prince to keep good faith and live with integrity, and not with astuteness, everyone knows. Still the experience of our times shows those princes to have done great things who have had little regard for good faith, and have been able by astuteness to confuse men's brains, and who have ultimately overcome those who have made loyalty their foundation.

You must know, then, that there are two methods of fighting, the one by law, the other by force: the first method is that of men, the second of beasts; but as the first method is often insufficient, one must have recourse to the second. It is therefore necessary for a prince to know well how to use both the beast and the man. This was covertly taught to rulers by ancient writers, who relate how Achilles and many others of those ancient princes were given to Chiron the centaur to be brought up and educated under his discipline. The parable of this semi-animal, semi-human teacher is meant to indicate that a prince must know how to use both natures, and that the one without the other is not durable.

A prince being thus obliged to know well how to act as a beast must imitate the fox and the lion, for the lion cannot protect himself from traps, and the fox cannot defend himself from wolves. One must therefore be a fox to recognise traps, and a lion to frighten wolves. Those that wish to be only lions do not understand this. Therefore, a prudent ruler ought not to keep faith when by so doing it would be against his interest, and when the reasons which made him bind himself no longer exist. If men were all good, this precept would not be a good one; but as they are bad, and would not observe their faith with you, so you are not bound to keep faith with them. Nor have legitimate grounds ever failed a prince who wished to show colourable

excuse for the non-fulfilment of his promise. Of this one could furnish an infinite number of modern examples, and show how many times peace has been
broken, and how many promises rendered worthless, by the faithlessness of
princes, and those that have been best able to imitate the fox have succeeded
best. But it is necessary to be able to disguise this character well, and to be
a great feigner and dissembler; and men are so simple and so ready to obey
present necessities, that one who deceives will always find those who allow
themselves to be deceived.

I will only mention one modern instance. Alexander VI did nothing else
but deceive men, he thought of nothing else, and found the occasion for it; no
man was ever more able to give assurances, or affirmed things with stronger
oaths, and no man observed them less; however, he always succeeded in his
deceptions, as he well knew this aspect of things.

It is not, therefore, necessary for a prince to have all the above-named
qualities, but it is very necessary to seem to have them. I would even be
bold to say that to possess them and always to observe them is dangerous,
but to appear to possess them is useful. Thus it is well to seem merciful,
faithful, humane, sincere, religious, and also to be so; but you must have
the mind so disposed that when it is needful to be otherwise you may
be able to change to the opposite qualities. And it must be understood
that a prince, and especially a new prince, cannot observe all those things
which are considered good in men, being often obliged, in order to maintain the state, to act against faith, against charity, against humanity, and
against religion. And, therefore, he must have a mind disposed to adapt
itself according to the wind, and as the variations of fortune dictate, and,
as I said before, not deviate from what is good, if possible, but be able to
do evil if constrained.

A prince must take great care that nothing goes out of his mouth which is
not full of the above-named five qualities, and, to see and hear him, he should
seem to be all mercy, faith, integrity, humanity, and religion. And nothing is
more necessary than to seem to have this last quality, for men in general judge
more by the eyes than by the hands, for everyone can see, but very few have to
feel. Everybody sees what you appear to be, few feel what you are, and those
few will not dare to oppose themselves to the many, who have the majesty of the
state to defend them; and in the actions of men, and especially of princes, from
which there is no appeal, the end justifies the means. Let a prince therefore aim
at conquering and maintaining the state, and the means will always be judged
honourable and praised by everyone, for the vulgar is always taken by appear-
ances and the issue of the event; and the world consists only of the vulgar, and
the few who are not vulgar are isolated when the many have a rallying point in
the prince. A certain prince of the present time, whom it is well not to name,
never does anything but preach peace and good faith, but he is really a great
enemy to both, and either of them, had he observed them, would have lost him
state or reputation on many occasions.

Reading 2.3

The State of Nature and the State of War

THOMAS HOBBES

OF THE NATURAL CONDITION OF MANKIND AS CONCERNING THEIR FELICITY AND MISERY

Men by Nature Equal

Nature hath made men so equal, in the faculties of the body, and mind; as that though there be found one man sometimes manifestly stronger in body, or of quicker mind than another; yet when all is reckoned together, the difference between man, and man, is not so considerable, as that one man can thereupon claim to himself any benefit, to which another may not pretend, as well as he. For as to the strength of body, the weakest has strength enough to kill the strongest, either by secret machination, or by confederacy with others, that are in the same danger with himself.

And as to the faculties of the mind, setting aside the arts grounded upon words, and especially that skill of proceeding upon general, and infallible rules, called science; which very few have, and but in few things; as being not a native faculty, born with us; nor attained, as prudence, while we look after somewhat else, I find yet a greater equality amongst men, than that of strength. For prudence, is but experience; which equal time, equally bestows on all men, in those things they equally apply themselves unto. That which may perhaps make such equality incredible, is but a vain conceit of one's own wisdom, which almost all men think they have in a greater degree, than the vulgar; that is, than all men but themselves, and a few others, whom by fame, or for concurring with themselves, they approve. For such is the nature of men, that howsoever they may acknowledge many others to be more witty, or more eloquent, or more learned; yet they will hardly believe there be many so wise as themselves; for they see their own wit at hand, and other men's at a distance. But this proveth rather that men are in that point equal, than unequal. For there is not ordinarily a greater sign of the equal distribution of any thing, than that every man is contented with his share.

From Equality Proceeds Diffidence

From this equality of ability, ariseth equality of hope in the attaining of our ends. And therefore if any two men desire the same thing, which nevertheless

---

Source: Thomas Hobbes, Leviathan, *ed. Michael Oakeshott. Macmillan Publishing Company, 1962. Originally published in 1651.*

they cannot both enjoy, they become enemies; and in the way to their end, which is principally their own conservation, and sometimes their delectation only, endeavour to destroy, or subdue one another. And from hence it comes to pass, that where an invader hath no more to fear, than another man's single power; if one plant, sow, build, or possess a convenient seat, others may probably be expected to come prepared with forces united, to dispossess, and deprive him, not only of the fruit of his labour, but also of his life, or liberty. And the invader again is in the like danger of another.

From Diffidence War

And from this diffidence of one another, there is no way for any man to secure himself, so reasonable, as anticipation; that is, by force, or wiles, to master the persons of all men he can, so long, till he see no other power great enough to endanger him: and this is no more than his own conservation requireth, and is generally allowed. Also because there be some, that taking pleasure in contemplating their own power in the acts of conquest, which they pursue farther than their security requires; if others, that otherwise would be glad to be at ease within modest bounds, should not by invasion increase their power, they would not be able, long time, by standing only on their defence, to subsist. And by consequence, such augmentation of dominion over men being necessary to a man's conservation, it ought to be allowed him.

Again, men have no pleasure, but on the contrary a great deal of grief, in keeping company, where there is no power able to over-awe them all. For every man looketh that his companion should value him, at the same rate he sets upon himself: and upon all signs of contempt, or undervaluing, naturally endeavours, as far as he dares, (which amongst them that have no common power to keep them in quiet, is far enough to make them destroy each other), to extort a greater value from his contemners, by damage; and from others, by the example.

So that in the nature of man, we find three principal causes of quarrel. First, competition; secondly, diffidence; thirdly, glory.

The first, maketh men invade for gain; the second, for safety; and the third, for reputation. The first use violence, to make themselves masters of other men's persons, wives, children, and cattle; the second, to defend them; the third, for trifles, as a word, a smile, a different opinion, and any other sign of undervalue, either direct in their persons, or by reflection in their kindred, their friends, their nation, their profession, or their name.

Out of Civil States, There Is Always War of Every One Against Every One

Hereby it is manifest, that during the time men live without a common power to keep them all in awe, they are in that condition which is called war; and such a war, as is of every man, against every man. For WAR, consisteth not in battle only, or the act of fighting; but in a tract of time, wherein the will to contend by battle is sufficiently known: and therefore the notion of *time*, is to be considered in the nature of war; as it is in the nature of weather. For as the nature of foul weather, lieth not in a shower or two of rain; but in an inclination thereto of many days together: so the nature of war, consisteth not in actual fighting; but in the known disposition thereto, during all the time there is no assurance to the contrary. All other time is PEACE.

The Incommodities of Such a War

Whatsoever therefore is consequent to a time of war, where every man is enemy to every man; the same is consequent to the time, wherein men live without other security, than what their own strength, and their own invention shall furnish them withal. In such condition, there is no place for industry; because the fruit thereof is uncertain: and consequently no culture of the earth; no navigation, nor use of the commodities that may be imported by sea; no commodious building; no instruments of moving, and removing, such things as require much force; no knowledge of the face of the earth; no account of time; no arts; no letters; no society; and which is worst of all, continual fear, and danger of violent death; and the life of man, solitary, poor, nasty, brutish, and short.

It may seem strange to some man, that has not well weighed these things; that nature should thus dissociate, and render men apt to invade, and destroy one another: and he may therefore, not trusting to this inference, made from the passions, desire perhaps to have the same confirmed by experience. Let him therefore consider with himself, when taking a journey, he arms himself, and seeks to go well accompanied; when going to sleep, he locks his doors; when even in his house he locks his chests; and this when he knows there be laws, and public officers, armed, to revenge all injuries shall be done him; what opinion he has of his fellow-subjects, when he rides armed; of his fellow citizens, when he locks his doors; and of his children, and servants, when he locks his chests. Does he not there as much accuse mankind by his actions, as I do by my words? But neither of us accuse man's nature in it. The desires, and other passions of man, are in themselves no sin. No more are the actions, that proceed from those passions, till they know a law that forbids them: which till laws be made they cannot know: nor can any law be made, till they have agreed upon the person that shall make it.

It may peradventure be thought, there was never such a time, nor condition of war as this; and I believe it was never generally so, over all the world: but there are many places, where they live so now. For the savage people in many places of America, except the government of small families, the concord whereof dependeth on natural lust, have no government at all; and live at this day in that brutish manner, as I said before. Howsoever, it may be perceived what manner of life there would be, where there were no common power to fear, by the manner of life, which men that have formerly lived under a peaceful government, use to degenerate into, in a civil war.

But though there had never been any time, wherein particular men were in a condition of war one against another; yet in all times, kings, and persons of sovereign authority, because of their independency, are in continual jealousies, and in the state and posture of gladiators; having their weapons pointing, and their eyes fixed on one another; that is, their forts, garrisons, and guns upon the frontiers of their kingdoms; and continual spies upon their neighbours; which is a posture of war. But because they uphold thereby, the industry of their subjects; there does not follow from it, that misery, which accompanies the liberty of particular men.

In Such a War Nothing Is Unjust

To this war of every man, against every man, this also is consequent; that nothing can be unjust. The notions of right and wrong, justice and injustice have there no place. Where there is no common power, there is no law: where no law, no injustice. Force, and fraud, are in war the two cardinal virtues. Justice, and injustice are none of the faculties neither of the body, nor mind. If they were, they might be in a man that were alone in the world, as well as his senses, and passions. They are qualities, that relate to men in society, not in solitude. It is consequent also to the same condition, that there be no propriety, no dominion, no *mine* and *thine* distinct; but only that to be every man's, that he can get: and for so long, as he can keep it. And thus much for the ill condition, which man by mere nature is actually placed in; though with a possibility to come out of it, consisting partly in the passions, partly in his reason.

The Passions That Incline Men to Peace

The passions that incline men to peace, are fear of death; desire of such things as are necessary to commodious living; and a hope by their industry to obtain them. And reason suggesteth convenient articles of peace, upon which men may be drawn to agreement. These articles, are they, which otherwise are called the Laws of Nature: whereof I shall speak more particularly, in the two following chapters. . . .

OF OTHER LAWS OF NATURE

The Third Law of Nature, Justice

From that law of nature, by which we are obliged to transfer to another, such rights, as being retained, hinder the peace of mankind, there followeth a third; which is this, *that men perform their covenants made*: without which, covenants are in vain, and but empty words; and the right of all men to all things remaining, we are still in the condition of war.

Justice and Injustice What

And in this law of nature, consisteth the fountain and original of JUSTICE. For where no covenant hath preceded, there hath no right been transferred, and every man has right to everything; and consequently, no action can be unjust. But when a covenant is made, then to break it is *unjust*: and the definition of INJUSTICE, is no other than *the not performance of covenant*. And whatsoever is not unjust, is *just*.

Justice and Propriety Begin With the Constitution of Commonwealth

But because covenants of mutual trust, where there is a fear of not performance on either part, as hath been said in the former chapter, are invalid; though the original of justice be the making of covenants; yet injustice actually there can be none, till the cause of such fear be taken away; which while men are in the natural condition of war, cannot be done. Therefore before the names of just, and unjust can have place, there must be some coercive power, to compel men equally to the performance of their covenants, by the terror of some punishment, greater than the benefit they expect by the breach of their covenant; and to make good that propriety, which by mutual contract men acquire, in recompense of the universal right they abandon: and such power there is none before the erection of a commonwealth. And this is also to be gathered out of the ordinary definition of justice in the Schools: for they say, that *justice is the constant will of giving to every man his own.* And therefore where there is no own, that is no propriety, there is no injustice; and where there is no coercive power erected, that is, where there is no commonwealth, there is no propriety; all men having right to all things: therefore where there is no commonwealth, there nothing is unjust. So that the nature of justice, consisteth in keeping of valid covenants: but the validity of covenants begins not but with the constitution of a civil power, sufficient to compel men to keep them: and then it is also that propriety begins.

Reading 2.4

Realism and Idealism   *Edward Hallett Carr*

. . . In Europe after 1919, planned economy, which rests on the assumption that no natural harmony of interests exists and that interests must be artificially harmonised by state action, became the practice, if not the theory, of almost every state. In the United States, the persistence of an expanding

Source: *Edward Hallett Carr, The Twenty Years' Crisis, 1919–1939, published 1960, Palgrave. Reproduced with permission of Palgrave Macmillan.*

domestic market staved off this development till after 1929. The natural harmony of interests remained an integral part of the American view of life; and in this as in other respects, current theories of international politics were deeply imbued with the American tradition. Moreover, there was a special reason for the ready acceptance of the doctrine in the international sphere. In domestic affairs it is clearly the business of the state to create harmony if no natural harmony exists. In international politics, there is no organized power charged with the task of creating harmony; and the temptation to assume a natural harmony is therefore particularly strong. But this is no excuse for burking the issue. To make the harmonisation of interests the goal of political action is not the same thing as to postulate that a natural harmony of interests exist; and it is this latter postulate which has caused so much confusion in international thinking.

Politically, the doctrine of the identity of interests has commonly taken the form of an assumption that every nation has an identical interest in peace, and that any nation which desires to disturb the peace is therefore both irrational and immoral. This view bears clear marks of its Anglo-Saxon origin. It was easy after 1918 to convince that part of mankind which lives in English-speaking countries that war profits nobody. The argument did not seem particularly convincing to Germans, who had profited largely from the wars of 1866 and 1870, and attributed their more recent sufferings, not to the war of 1914, but to the fact that they had lost it; or to Italians, who blamed not the war, but the treachery of allies who defrauded them in the peace settlement; or to Poles or Czecho-Slovaks who, far from deploring the war, owed their national existence to it; or to Frenchmen, who could not unreservedly regret a war which had restored Alsace-Lorraine to France; or to people of other nationalities who remembered profitable wars waged by Great Britain and the United States in the past. But these people had fortunately little influence over the formation of current theories of international relations, which emanated almost exclusively from the English-speaking countries. British and American writers continued to assume that the uselessness of war had been irrefutably demonstrated by the experience of 1914–18, and that an intellectual grasp of this fact was all that was necessary to induce the nations to keep the peace in the future; and they were sincerely puzzled as well as disappointed at the failure of other countries to share this view.

The confusion was increased by the ostentatious readiness of other countries to flatter the Anglo-Saxon world by repeating its slogans. In the fifteen years after the first world war, every Great Power (except, perhaps, Italy) repeatedly did lip-service to the doctrine by declaring peace to be one of the main objects of its policy.[1] But as Lenin observed long ago, peace in itself is a meaningless aim. "Absolutely everybody is in favour of peace in general," he wrote in 1915, "including Kitchener, Joffre, Hindenburg and Nicholas the Bloody, for every one of them wishes to end the war."[2] The common interest in peace masks the fact that some nations desire to maintain the *status quo* without having to fight for it, and others to change the *status quo* without having to fight in order to do so. . . .

INTERNATIONAL ECONOMIC HARMONY

. . . We find in the modern period an extraordinary divergence between the theories of economic experts and the practice of those responsible for the economic policies of their respective countries. Analysis will show that this divergence springs from a simple fact. The economic expert, dominated in the main by *laissez-faire* doctrine, considers the hypothetical economic interest of the world as a whole, and is content to assume that this is identical with the interest of each individual country. The politician pursues the concrete interest of his country, and assumes (if he makes any assumption at all) that the interest of the world as a whole is identical with it. Nearly every pronouncement of every international economic conference held between the two world wars was vitiated by this assumption that there was some "solution" or "plan" which, by a judicious balancing of interests, would be equally favourable to all and prejudicial to none. . . .

In the nineteenth century, Germany and the United States, by pursuing a "strictly nationalistic policy," had placed themselves in a position to challenge Great Britain's virtual monopoly of world trade. No conference of economic experts, meeting in 1880, could have evolved a "general plan" for "parallel or concerted action" which would have allayed the economic rivalries of the time in a manner equally advantageous to Great Britain, Germany and the United States. It was not less presumptuous to suppose that a conference meeting in 1927 could allay the economic rivalries of the later period by a "plan" beneficial to the interests of everyone. Even the economic crisis of 1930–33 failed to bring home to the economists the true nature of the problem which they had to face. The experts who prepared the "Draft Annotated Agenda" for the World Economic Conference of 1933—condemned the "world-wide adoption of ideals of national self-sufficiency which cut unmistakably athwart the lines of economic development."[3] They did not apparently pause to reflect that those so-called "lines of economic development," which might be beneficial to some countries and even to the world as a whole, would inevitably be detrimental to other countries, which were using weapons of economic nationalism in self-defence. . . . *Laissez-faire*, in international relations as in those between capital and labour, is the paradise of the economically strong. State control, whether in the form of protective legislation or of protective tariffs, is the weapon of self-defence invoked by the economically weak. The clash of interests is real and inevitable; and the whole nature of the problem is distorted by an attempt to disguise it.

THE FOUNDATIONS OF REALISM

. . . The three essential tenets implicit in Machiavelli's doctrine are the foundation-stones of the realist philosophy. In the first place, history is a sequence of cause and effect, whose course can be analysed and understood by intellectual effort, but not (as the utopians believe) directed by "imagination." Secondly, theory does not (as the utopians assume) create practice, but practice theory. In

Machiavelli's words, "good counsels, whencesoever they come, are born of the wisdom of the prince, and not the wisdom of the prince from good counsels." Thirdly, politics are not (as the utopians pretend) a function of ethics, but ethics of politics. Men "are kept honest by constraint." Machiavelli recognised the importance of morality, but thought that there could be no effective morality where there was no effective authority. Morality is the product of power.[4]

The extraordinary vigour and vitality of Machiavelli's challenge to orthodoxy may be attested by the fact that, more than four centuries after he wrote, the most conclusive way of discrediting a political opponent is still to describe him as a disciple of Machiavelli. . . .

. . . Theories of social morality are always the product of a dominant group which identifies itself with the community as a whole, and which possesses facilities denied to subordinate groups or individuals for imposing its view of life on the community. Theories of international morality are, for the same reason and in virtue of the same process, the product of dominant nations or groups of nations. For the past hundred years, and more especially since 1918, the English-speaking peoples have formed the dominant group in the world; and current theories of international morality have been designed to perpetuate their supremacy and expressed in the idiom peculiar to them. France, retaining something of her eighteenth-century tradition and restored to a position of dominance for a short period after 1918, has played a minor part in the creation of current international morality, mainly through her insistence on the role of law in the moral order. Germany, never a dominant Power and reduced to helplessness after 1918, has remained for these reasons outside the charmed circle of creators of international morality. Both the view that the English-speaking peoples are monopolists of international morality and the view that they are consummate international hypocrites may be reduced to the plain fact that the current canons of international virtue have, by a natural and—inevitable process, been mainly created by them.

THE REALIST CRITIQUE OF THE HARMONY OF INTERESTS

The doctrine of the harmony of interests yields readily to analysis in terms of this principle. It is the natural assumption of a prosperous and privileged class, whose members have a dominant voice in the community and are therefore naturally prone to identify its interest with their own. In virtue of this identification, any assailant of the interests of the dominant group is made to incur the odium of assailing the alleged common interest of the whole community, and is told that in making this assault he is attacking his own higher interests. The doctrine of the harmony of interests thus serves as an ingenious moral device invoked, in perfect sincerity, by privileged groups in order to justify and maintain their dominant position. But a further point requires notice. The supremacy within the community of the privileged group may be, and often is, so overwhelming that there is, in fact, a sense in which its interests are those of the community, since its well-being necessarily carries with it some measure of well-being for other members of the community, and its collapse would entail the collapse of the community as a whole. In so far, therefore, as the alleged natural harmony of interests has any reality, it is created by the overwhelming power of the privileged group, and is an excellent illustration of the Machiavellian maxim that morality is the product of power.

. . . British nineteenth-century statesmen, having discovered that free trade promoted British prosperity, were sincerely convinced that, in doing so, it also promoted the prosperity of the world as a whole. British predominance in world trade was at that time so overwhelming that there was a certain undeniable harmony between British interests and the interests of the world. British prosperity flowed over into other countries, and a British economic collapse would have meant world-wide ruin. British free traders could and did argue that protectionist countries were not only egotistically damaging the prosperity of the world as a whole, but were stupidly damaging their own, so that their behaviour was both immoral and muddle headed. In British eyes, it was irrefutably proved that international trade was a single whole, and flourished or slumped together. Nevertheless, this alleged international harmony of interests seemed a mockery to those under-privileged nations whose inferior status and insignificant stake in international trade were consecrated by it. The revolt against it destroyed that overwhelming British preponderance which had provided a plausible basis for the theory. Economically, Great Britain in the nineteenth century was dominant enough to make a bold bid to impose on the world her own conception of international economic morality. When competition of all against all replaced the domination of the world market by a single Power, conceptions of international economic morality necessarily became chaotic.

Politically, the alleged community of interest in the maintenance of peace, whose ambiguous character has already been discussed, is capitalised in the same way by a dominant nation or group of nations. Just as the ruling class in a community prays for domestic peace, which guarantees its own security and predominance, and denounces class-war, which might threaten them, so international peace becomes a special vested interest of predominant Powers. In the past, Roman and British imperialism were commended to the world in the guise of the *pax Romana* and the *pax Britannica*. Today, when no single Power is strong enough to dominate the world, and supremacy is vested in a group of nations, slogans like "collective security" and "resistance to aggression" serve the same purpose of proclaiming an identity of interest between the dominant group and the world as a whole in the maintenance of peace.

. . . It is a familiar tactic of the privileged to throw moral discredit on the under-privileged by depicting them as disturbers of the peace; and this tactic is as readily applied internationally as within the national community. "International law and order," writes Professor Toynbee of a recent crisis, "were in the true interests of the whole of mankind . . . whereas the desire to perpetuate the region of violence in international affairs was an anti-social desire which was not even in the ultimate interests of the citizens of the handful of states that officially professed this benighted and anachronistic creed."[5] This is precisely the argument, compounded of platitude and falsehood in about equal parts, which did duty in every strike in the early days of the British and American Labour movements. It was common form for employers, supported by the whole capitalist press, to denounce the "anti-social" attitude of trade union leaders, to accuse them of attacking law and order and of introducing "the reign of violence," and to declare that "true" and "ultimate" interests of the workers lay in peaceful cooperation with the employers.[6] In the field of social relations, the disingenuous character of this argument has long been recognised. But just as the threat of class-war by the proletarian is "a natural cynical reaction to the sentimental and dishonest efforts of the privileged classes to obscure the conflict of interest between classes by a constant emphasis on the minimum interests which they have in common,"[7] so the war-mongering of the dissatisfied Powers was the "natural, cynical reaction" to the sentimental and dishonest platitudinising of the satisfied Powers on the common interest in peace. When Hitler refused to believe "that God has permitted some nations first to acquire a world by force and then to defend this robbery with moralising theories"[8] he was merely echoing in another context the Marxist denial of a community of interest between "haves" and "have-nots," the Marxist exposure of the interested character of "*bourgeois* morality," and the Marxist demand for the expropriation of the expropriators. . . .

THE LIMITATIONS OF REALISM

The exposure by realist criticism of the hollowness of the utopian edifice is the first task of the political thinker. It is only when the sham has been demolished that there can be any hope of raising a more solid structure in its place. But we cannot ultimately find a resting place in pure realism; for realism, though logically overwhelming, does not provide us with the springs of action which are necessary even to the pursuit of thought. Indeed, realism itself, if we attack it with its own weapons, often turns out in practice to be just as much conditioned as any other mode of thought. In politics, the belief that certain facts are unalterable or certain trends irresistible commonly reflects a lack of desire or lack of interest to change or resist them. The impossibility of being a consistent and thorough-going realist is one of the most certain and most curious lessons of political science. Consistent realism excludes four things which appear to be essential ingredients of all effective political thinking: a finite goal, an emotional appeal, a right of moral judgment and a ground for action. . . .

Consistent realism, as has already been noted, involves acceptance of the whole historical process and precludes moral judgments on it. As we have seen, men are generally prepared to accept the judgment of history on the past, praising success and condemning failure. This test is also widely applied to contemporary politics. Such institutions as the League of Nations, or the Soviet or Fascist regimes, are to a considerable extent judged by their capacity to achieve what they profess to achieve; and the legitimacy of this test is implicitly admitted by their own propaganda, which constantly seeks to exaggerate their successes and minimise their failures. Yet it is clear that mankind as a whole is not prepared to accept this rational test as a universally valid basis of political judgment. The belief that whatever succeeds is right, and has only to be understood to be approved, must, if consistently held, empty thought of purpose, and thereby sterilise and ultimately destroy it. Nor do those whose philosophy appears to exclude the possibility of moral judgments in fact refrain from pronouncing them. Frederick the Great, having explained that treaties should be observed for the reason that "one can trick only once," goes on to call the breaking of treaties "a bad and knavish policy," though there is nothing in his thesis to justify the moral epithet. Marx, whose philosophy appeared to demonstrate that capitalists could only act in a certain way, spends many pages—some of the most effective in *Capital*—in denouncing the wickedness of capitalists for behaving in precisely that way. The necessity, recognised by all politicians, both in domestic and in international affairs, for cloaking—interests in a guise of moral principles is in itself a symptom of the inadequacy of realism. Every age claims the right to create its own values, and to pass judgments in the light of them; and even if it uses realist weapons to dissolve other values, it still believes in the absolute character of its own. It refuses to accept the implication of realism that the word "ought" is meaningless.

Most of all, consistent realism breaks down because it fails to provide any ground for purposive or meaningful action. If the sequence of cause and effect is sufficiently rigid to permit of the "scientific prediction" of events, if our thought is irrevocably conditioned by our status and our interests, then both action and thought become devoid of purpose. If, as Schopenhauer maintains, "the true philosophy of history consists of the insight that, throughout the jumble of all these ceaseless changes, we have ever before our eyes the same unchanging being, pursuing the same course today, yesterday and for ever," then passive contemplation is all that remains to the individual. Such a conclusion is plainly repugnant to the most deep-seated belief of man about himself. That human affairs can be directed and modified by human action and human thought is a postulate so fundamental that its rejection seems scarcely compatible with existence as a human being. Nor is it in fact rejected by those realists who have left their mark on history. Machiavelli, when he exhorted his compatriots to be good Italians, clearly assumed that they were free to follow or ignore his advice. Marx, by birth and training a *bourgeois*, believed himself free to think and act like a proletarian, and regarded it as his mission to persuade others, whom he assumed to be equally free, to think and act likewise. Lenin, who wrote of the imminence of world revolution as a "scientific prediction," admitted elsewhere that "no situations exist from which there is absolutely no way out." In moments of crisis, Lenin appealed to his followers in terms which might equally well have been used by so thorough-going a believer in the power of the human will as Mussolini or by any other leader of any period: "At the decisive moment and in the decisive place, you *must prove* the stronger, you must *be victorious*." Every realist, whatever his professions, is ultimately compelled to believe not only that there is something which man ought to think and do, but that there is something which he can think and do, and that his thought and action are neither mechanical nor meaningless.

We return therefore to the conclusion that any sound political thought must be based on elements of both utopia and reality. Where utopianism has become a hollow and intolerable sham, which serves merely as a disguise for the interests of the privileged, the realist performs an indispensable service in unmasking it. But pure realism can offer nothing but a naked struggle for power which makes any kind of international society impossible. Having demolished the current utopia with the weapons of realism, we still need to build a new utopia of our own, which will one day fall to the same weapons. The human will continue to seek and escape from the logical consequences of realism in the vision of an international order which, as soon as it crystallizes itself into concrete political form, becomes tainted with self-interest and hypocrisy, and must once more be attacked with the instruments of realism.

Here, then, is the complexity, the fascination and the tragedy of all political life. Politics are made up of two elements—utopia and reality—belonging to two different planes which can never meet. There is no greater barrier to clear political thinking than failure to distinguish between ideals, which are utopia, and institutions, which are reality. The communist who set communism against democracy was usually thinking of communism as a pure ideal of equality and brotherhood, and of democracy as an institution which existed in Great Britain, France or the United States and which exhibited the vested interests, the inequalities and the oppression inherent in all political institutions. The democrat who made the same comparison was in fact comparing an ideal pattern of democracy laid up in heaven with communism as an institution existing in Soviet Russia with its class-divisions, its heresy-hunts and its concentration camps. The comparison, made in each case between an ideal and an institution, is irrelevant and makes no sense. The ideal, once it is embodied in an institution, ceases to be an ideal and becomes the expression of a selfish interest, which must be destroyed in the name of a new ideal. This constant interaction of irreconcilable forces is the stuff of politics. Every political situation contains mutually incompatible elements of utopia and reality, of morality and power. . . .

Military Power

The supreme importance of the military instrument lies in the fact that the *ultima ratio* of power in international relations is war. Every act of the state, in its power aspect, is directed to war, not as a desirable weapon, but as a weapon which it may require in the last resort to use. Clausewitz's famous aphorism that "war is nothing but the continuation of political relations by other means" has been repeated with approval both by Lenin and by the Communist International[9] and Hitler meant much the same thing when he said that "an alliance whose object does not include the intention to fight is meaningless and useless."[10] In the same sense, Mr. Hawtrey defines diplomacy as "potential war."[11] These are half-truths. But the important thing is to recognise that they are true. War lurks in the background of international politics just as revolution lurks in the background of domestic politics. There are few European countries where, at some time during the past thirty years, potential revolution has not been an important factor in politics;[12] and the international community has in this respect the closest analogy to those states where the possibility of revolution is most frequently and most conspicuously present to the mind.

Potential war being thus a dominant factor in international politics, military strength becomes a recognised standard of political values. Every great civilisation of the past has enjoyed in its day a superiority of military power. . . .

Military power, being an essential element in the life of the state, becomes not only an instrument, but an end in itself. Few of the important wars of the last hundred years seem to have been waged for the deliberate and conscious purpose of increasing either trade or territory. The most serious wars are fought in order to make one's own country militarily stronger or, more often, to prevent another country from becoming militarily stronger, so that there is much justification for the epigram that "the principal cause of war is war itself."[13] Every stage in the Napoleonic Wars was devised to prepare the way for the next stage: the invasion of Russia was undertaken in order to make Napoleon strong enough to defeat Great Britain. The Crimean War was waged by Great Britain and France in order to prevent Russia from becoming strong enough to attack their Near Eastern possessions and interests at some future time. The origin of the Russo-Japanese War of 1904–5 is described as follows in a note addressed to the League of Nations by the Soviet Government in 1924: "When the Japanese torpedo-boats attacked the Russian fleet at Port Arthur in 1904, it was clearly an act of aggression from a technical point of view, but, politically speaking, it was an act caused by the aggressive policy of the Tsarist Government towards Japan, who, in order to forestall the danger, struck the first blow at her adversary."[14] In 1914, Austria sent an ultimatum to Servia because she believed that Servians were planning the downfall of the Dual Monarchy; Russia feared that Austria-Hungary, if she defeated Servia, would be strong enough to menace her; Germany feared that Russia, if she defeated Austria-Hungary, would be strong enough to menace her; France had long believed that Germany, if she defeated Russia, would be strong enough to menace her, and had therefore concluded the Franco-Russian alliance; and Great Britain feared that Germany, if she defeated France and occupied Belgium, would be strong enough to menace her. Finally, the United States came to fear that Germany, if she won the war would be strong enough to menace them. Thus the war, in the minds of all the principal combatants, had a defensive or preventive character. They fought in order that they might not find themselves in a more unfavourable position in some future war. Even colonial acquisitions have often been prompted by the same motive. The consolidation and formal annexation of the original British settlements in Australia were inspired by fear of Napoleon's alleged design to establish French colonies there. Military, rather than economic, reasons dictated the capture of German colonies during the war of 1914 and afterwards precluded their return to Germany.

It is perhaps for this reason that the exercise of power always appears to beget the appetite for more power. There is, as Dr. Niebuhr says, "no possibility of drawing a sharp line between the will-to-live and the will-to-power."[15] Nationalism, having attained its first objective in the form of national unity and independence, develops almost automatically into imperialism. International politics amply confirm the aphorisms of Machiavelli that "men never appear to themselves to possess securely what they have unless they acquire something further from another,"[16] and of Hobbes that man "cannot assure the power and means to live well which he hath present, without the acquisition of more."[17] Wars, begun for motives of security, quickly become wars of aggression and self-seeking. President McKinley invited the United States to intervene in Cuba against Spain in order "to secure a full and final termination of hostilities between the Government of Spain and the people of Cuba and to secure on the island the establishment of a stable government."[18] But by the time the war was over the temptation to self-aggrandisement by the annexation of the Philippines had become irresistible. Nearly every country participating in the first world war regarded it initially as a war of self-defence; and this belief was particularly strong on the Allied side. Yet during the course of the war, every Allied Government in Europe announced war aims which included the acquisition of territory from the enemy Powers. In modern conditions, wars of limited objective have become almost as impossible as wars of limited liability. It is one of the fallacies of the theory of collective security that war can be waged for the specific and disinterested purpose of "resisting aggression." Had the League of Nations in the autumn of 1935, under the leadership of Great Britain, embarked on "military sanctions" against Italy, it would have been impossible to restrict the campaign to the expulsion of Italian troops from Abyssinia. Operations would in all probability have led to the occupation of Italy's East African colonies by Great Britain and France, of Trieste, Fiume and Albania by Yugoslavia, and of the islands of the Dodecanese by Greece or Turkey or both; and war aims would have been announced, precluding on various specious grounds the restoration of these territories to Italy. Territorial ambitions are just as likely to be the product as the cause of war.

Economic Power

Economic strength has always been an instrument of political power, if only through its association with the military instrument. Only the most primitive kinds of warfare are altogether independent of the economic factor. The wealthiest prince or the wealthiest city-state could hire the largest and most efficient army of mercenaries; and every government was therefore compelled to pursue a policy designed to further the acquisition of wealth. The whole progress of civilisation has been so closely bound up with economic development that we are not surprised to trace, throughout modern history, an increasingly intimate association between military and economic power. In the prolonged conflicts which marked the close of the Middle Ages in Western Europe, the merchants of the towns, relying on organised economic power, defeated the feudal barons, who put their trust in individual military prowess. The rise of modern nations has everywhere been marked by the emergence of a new middle class economically based on industry and trade. Trade and finance were the foundation of the short-lived political supremacy of the Italian cities of the Renaissance and later of the Dutch. The principal international wars of the period from the Renaissance to the middle of the eighteenth century were trade wars (some of them were actually so named). Throughout this period, it was universally held that, since wealth is a source of political power, the state should seek actively to promote the acquisition of wealth; and it was believed that the right way to make a country powerful was to stimulate production at home, to buy as little as possible from abroad, and to accumulate wealth in the convenient form of precious metals. Those who argued in this way afterwards came to be known as mercantilists. Mercantilism was a system of economic policy based on the hitherto unquestioned assumption that to promote the acquisition of wealth was part of the normal function of the state.

THE SEPARATION OF ECONOMICS FROM POLITICS

The *laissez-faire* doctrine of the classical economists made a frontal attack on this assumption. The principal implications of *laissez-faire* have already been discussed. Its significance in the present context is that it brought about a complete theoretical divorce between economics and politics. The classical economists conceived a natural economic order with laws of its own, independent of politics and functioning to the greatest profit of all concerned when political authority interfered least in is automatic operation. This doctrine dominated the economic thought, and to some extent the economic practice (though far more in Great Britain than elsewhere), of the nineteenth century. . . .

Marx was overwhelmingly right when he insisted on the increasing importance of the role played by economic forces in politics; and since Marx, history can never be written again exactly as it was written before him. But Marx believed, just as firmly as did the *laissez-faire* liberal, in an economic system with laws of its own working independently of the state, which was its adjunct and its instrument. In writing as if economics and politics were separate domains, one subordinate to the other, Marx was dominated by nineteenth-century presuppositions in much the same way as his more recent opponents who are equally sure that "the primary laws of history are political laws, economic laws are secondary."[19] Economic forces are in fact political forces. Economics can be treated neither as a minor accessory of history, nor as an independent science in the light of which history can be interpreted. Much confusion would be saved by a general return to the term "political economy," which was given the new science by Adam Smith himself and not abandoned in favour of the abstract "economics," even in Great Britain itself, till the closing years of the nineteenth century.[20] The science of economics presupposes a given political order, and cannot be profitably studied in isolation from politics.

SOME FALLACIES OF THE SEPARATION OF ECONOMICS FROM POLITICS

. . . The most conspicuous practical failure caused by the persistence of this nineteenth-century illusion was the breakdown of League sanctions in 1936. Careful reading of the text of Article 16 of the Covenant acquits its framers of responsibility for the mistake. Paragraph 1 prescribes the economic weapons, paragraph 2 the military weapons, to be employed against the violator of the Covenant. Paragraph 2 is clearly complementary to paragraph 1, and assumes as a matter of course that, in the event of an application of sanctions, "armed forces" would be required "to protect the Covenants of the League." The only difference between the two paragraphs is that, whereas all members of the League would have to apply the economic weapons, it would be natural to draw the necessary armed forces from those members which possessed them in sufficient strength and in reasonable geographical proximity to the offender.[21] Subsequent commentators, obsessed with the assumption that economics and politics were separate and separable things, evolved the doctrine that paragraphs 1 and 2 of Article 16 were not complementary, but alternative, the difference being that "economic sanctions" were obligatory and "military sanctions" optional. This doctrine was eagerly seized on by the many who felt that the League might conceivably be worth a few million pounds worth of trade, but not a few million human lives; and in the famous 1934 Peace Ballot in Great Britain, some two million deluded voters expressed simultaneously their approval of economic, and their disapproval of military, sanctions. "One of the many conclusions to which I have been drawn," said Lord Baldwin at this time, "is that there is no such thing as a sanction which will work, which does not mean war."[22] But the bitter lesson of 1935–36 was needed to drive home the truth that in sanctions, as in war, the only motto is "all or nothing," and that economic power is impotent if the military weapon is not held in readiness to support it.[23] Power is indivisible; and the military and economic weapons are merely different instruments of power.[24]

A different, and equally serious, form in which this illusory separation of politics and economics can be traced is the popular phraseology which distinguishes between "power" and "welfare," between "guns" and "butter." "Welfare arguments are 'economic,'" remarks an American writer, "power arguments are 'political.'"[25] This fallacy is particularly difficult to expose because it appears to be deducible from a familiar fact. Every modern government and every parliament is continually faced with the dilemma of spending money on armaments or social services; and this encourages the illusion that the choice really lies between "power" and "welfare," between political guns and economic butter. Reflexion shows, however, that this is not the case. The question asked never takes the form, Do you prefer guns or butter? For everyone (except a handful of pacifists in those Anglo-Saxon countries which have inherited a long tradition of uncontested security) agrees that, in case of need, guns must come before butter. The question asked is always either, Have we already sufficient guns to enable us to afford some butter? or, Granted that we need x

guns, can we increase revenue sufficiently to afford more butter as well? But the neatest exposure of this fallacy comes from the pen of Professor Zimmern; and the exposure is none the less effective for being unconscious. Having divided existing states on popular lines into those which pursue "welfare" and those which pursue "power," Professor Zimmern revealingly adds that "the welfare states, taken together, enjoy a preponderance of power and resources over the power states"[26] thereby leading us infallibly to the correct conclusion that "welfare states" are states which, already enjoying a preponderance of power, are not primarily concerned to increase it, and can therefore afford butter, and "power states" those which, being inferior in power, are primarily concerned to increase it, and devote the major part of their resources to this end. In this popular terminology, "welfare states" are those which possess preponderant power, and "power states" those which do not. Nor is this classification as illogical as it may seem. Every Great Power takes the view that the minimum number of guns necessary to assert the degree of power which it considers requisite takes precedence over butter, and that it can only pursue "welfare" when this minimum has been achieved. For many years prior to 1933, Great Britain, being satisfied with her power, was a "welfare state." After 1935, feeling her power contested and inadequate, she became a "power state"; and even the Opposition ceased to press with any insistence the prior claim of the social services. The contrast is not one between "power" and "welfare," and still less between "politics" and "economics," but between different degrees of power. In the pursuit of power, military and economic instruments will both be used. . . .

THE NATURE OF INTERNATIONAL LAW

International law differs from the municipal law of modern states in being the law of an undeveloped and not fully integrated community. It lacks three institutions which are essential parts of any developed system of municipal law: a judicature, an executive and a legislature.

(1) International law recognises no court competent to give on any issue of law or fact decisions recognised as binding by the community as a whole. It has long been the habit of some states to make special agreements to submit particular disputes to an international court for judicial settlement. The Permanent Court of International Justice, set up under the Covenant of the League, represents an attempt to extend and generalise this habit. But the institution of the court has not changed international law: it has merely created certain special obligations for states willing to accept them.

(2) International law has no agents competent to enforce observance of the law. In certain cases, it does indeed recognise the right of an aggrieved party, where a breach of the law has occurred, to take reprisals against the offender. But this is the recognition of a right of self-help, not the enforcement of a penalty by an agent of the law. The measures contemplated in Article 16 of the Covenant of the League, in so far as they can be regarded as punitive and not merely preventive, fall within this category.

(3) Of the two main sources of law—custom and legislation—international law knows only the former, resembling in this respect the law of all primitive communities. To trace the stages by which a certain kind of action or behaviour, from being customary, comes to be recognised as obligatory on all members of the community is the task of the social psychologist rather than of the jurist. But it is by some such process that international law has come into being. In advanced communities, the other source of law—direct legislation—is more prolific, and could not possibly be dispensed with in any modern state. So serious does this lack of international legislation appear that, in the view of some authorities, states do on certain occasions constitute themselves a legislative body, and many multilateral agreements between states are in fact "law-making treaties" *(traités-lois)*.[27] This view is open to grave objections. A treaty, whatever its scope and content, lacks the essential quality of law: it is not automatically and unconditionally applicable to all members of the community whether they assent to it or not. Attempts have been made from time to time to embody customary international law in multilateral treaties between states. But the value of such attempts has been largely nullified by the fact that no treaty can bind a state which has not accepted it. The Hague Conventions of 1907 on the rules of war are sometimes treated as an example of international legislation. But these conventions were not only not binding on states which were not parties to them, but were not binding on the parties *vis-à-vis* states which were not parties. The Briand-Kellogg Pact is not, as is sometimes loosely said, a legislative act prohibiting war. It is an agreement between a large number of states "to renounce war as an instrument of national policy in their relations with one another." International agreements are contracts concluded by states with one another in their capacity as subjects of international law, and not laws created by states in the capacity of international legislators. International legislation does not yet exist. . . .

In June 1933, the British Government ceased to pay the regular installments due under its war debt agreement, substituting minor "token payments"; and a year later these token payments came to an end. Yet in 1935 Great Britain and France once more joined in a solemn condemnation of Germany for unilaterally repudiating her obligations under the disarmament clauses of the Versailles Treaty. Such inconsistencies are so common that the realist finds little difficulty in reducing them to a simple rule. The element of power is inherent in every political treaty. The contents of such a treaty reflect in some degree the relative strength of the contracting parties. Stronger states will insist on the sanctity of the treaties concluded by them with weaker states. Weaker states will renounce treaties concluded by them with stronger states so soon as the power position alters and the weaker state feels itself strong enough to reject or modify the obligation. Since 1918, the United States have concluded no treaty with a stronger state, and have therefore unreservedly upheld the sanctity of treaties. Great Britain concluded the war debt agreement with a country financially stronger than herself, and defaulted. She concluded no other important treaty with a stronger Power and, with this single exception, upheld the sanctity of treaties. The countries which had concluded the largest number of treaties with states stronger than themselves, and subsequently strengthened their position, were Germany, Italy and Japan; and these are the countries which renounced or violated the largest number of treaties. But it would be rash to assume any *moral* distinction between these different attitudes. There is no reason to assume that these countries would insist any less strongly than Great Britain or the United States on the sanctity of treaties favourable to themselves concluded by them with weaker states.

The case is convincing as far as it goes. The rule *pacta sunt servanda* is not a moral principle, and its application cannot always be justified on ethical grounds. It is a rule of international law; and as such it not only is, but is universally recognised to be, necessary to the existence of an international society. But law does not purport to solve every political problem; and where it fails, the fault often lies with those who seek to put it to uses for which it was never intended. It is no reproach to law to describe it as a bulwark of the existing order. The essence of law is to promote stability and maintain the existing framework of society; and it is perfectly natural everywhere for conservatives to describe themselves as the party of law and order, and to denounce radicals as disturbers of the peace and enemies of the law. The history of every society reveals a strong tendency on the part of those who want important changes in the existing order to commit acts which are illegal and which can plausibly be denounced as such by conservatives. It is true that in highly organised societies, where legally constituted machinery exists for bringing about changes in the law, this tendency to illegal action is mitigated. But it is never removed altogether. Radicals are always more likely than conservatives to come into conflict with the law.

Before 1914, international law did not condemn as illegal resort to war for the purpose of changing the existing international order; and no legally constituted machinery existed for bringing about changes in any other way. After 1918 opinion condemning "aggressive" war became almost universal, and nearly all the nations of the world signed a pact renouncing resort to war as an instrument of policy. While therefore resort to war for the purpose of altering the *status quo* now usually involves the breach of a treaty obligation and is accordingly illegal in international law, no effective international machinery has been constituted for bringing about changes by pacific means. The rude nineteenth-century system, or lack of system, was logical in recognising as legal the one effective method of changing the *status quo*. The rejection of the traditional method as illegal and the failure to provide any effective alternative have made contemporary international law a bulwark of the existing order to an extent unknown in previous international law or in the municipal law of any civilised country. This is the most fundamental cause of the recent decline of respect for international law; and those who, in deploring the phenomenon, fail to recognise its origin, not unnaturally expose themselves to the charge of hypocrisy or of obtuseness.

Of all the considerations which render unlikely the general observance of the legal rule of the sanctity of treaties, and which provide a plausible moral justification for the repudiation of treaties, this last is by far the most important. Respect for international law and for the sanctity of treaties will not be increased by the sermons of those who, having most to gain from the maintenance of the existing order, insist most firmly on the morally binding character of the law. Respect for law and treaties will be maintained only in so far as the law recognises effective political machinery through which it can itself be modified and superseded. There must be a clear recognition of that play of political forces which is antecedent to all law. Only when these forces are in stable equilibrium can the law perform its social function without becoming a tool in the hands of the defenders of the *status quo*. The achievement of this equilibrium is not a legal, but a political task. . . .

Peaceful Change

. . . The attempt to make a moral distinction between wars of "aggression" and wars of "defence" is misguided. If a change is necessary and desirable, the use or threatened use of force to maintain the *status quo* may be morally more culpable than the use or threatened use of force to alter it. Few people now believe that the action of the American colonists who attacked the *status quo* by force in 1776, or of the Irish who attacked the *status quo* by force between 1916 and 1920, was necessarily less moral than that of the British who defended it by force. The moral criterion must be not the "aggressive" or "defensive" character of the war, but the nature of the change which is being sought and resisted. . . .

. . . When the change is effected by legislation, the compulsion is that of the state. But where the change is effected by the bargaining procedure, the *force majeure* can only be that of the stronger party. The employer who concedes the strikers' demands pleads inability to resist. The trade union leader who calls off an unsuccessful strike pleads that the union was too weak to continue. "Yielding to threats of force," which is sometimes used as a term of reproach, is therefore a normal part of the process. . . .

The defence of the *status quo* is not a policy which can be lastingly successful. It will end in war as surely as rigid conservatism will end in revolution. "Resistance to aggression," however necessary as a momentary device of national policy, is no solution; for readiness to fight to prevent change is just as unmoral as readiness to fight to enforce it. To establish methods of peaceful change is therefore the fundamental problem of international morality and of international politics. We can discard as purely utopian and muddle-headed plans for a procedure of peaceful change dictated by a world legislature or a world court. We can describe as utopian in the right sense (i.e. performing the proper function of a utopia in proclaiming an ideal to be aimed at, though not wholly attainable) the desire to eliminate the element of power and to base the bargaining process of peaceful change on a common feeling of what is just and reasonable. But we shall also keep in mind the realist view of peaceful change as an adjustment to the changed relations of power; and since the party which is able to bring most power to bear normally emerges successful from operations of peaceful change, we shall do our best to make ourselves as powerful as we can. In practice, we know that peaceful change can only be achieved through a compromise between the utopian conception of a common feeling of right and the realist conception of a mechanical adjustment to a changed equilibrium of forces. That is why a successful foreign policy must oscillate between the apparently opposite poles of force and appeasement. . . .

NOTES

1 "Peace must prevail, must come before all" (Briand, *League of Nations: Ninth Assembly*, p. 83). "The maintenance of peace is the first objective of British foreign policy" (Eden, *League of Nations: Sixteenth Assembly*, p. 106). "Peace is our dearest treasure" (Hitler, in a speech in the German Reichstag on January 30, 1937, reported in *The Times*, February 1, 1937). "The principal aim of the international policy of the Soviet Union is the preservation of peace" (Chicherin in *The Soviet Union and Peace* [1929], p. 249). "The object of Japan, despite propaganda to the contrary, is peace" (Matsuoka, *League of Nations: Special Assembly 1932–33*, iii, p. 73). The paucity of Italian pronouncements in favour of peace was probably explained by the poor reputation of Italian troops as fighters: Mussolini feared that any emphatic expression of preference for peace would be construed as an admission that Italy had no stomach for war.

2 Lenin, *Collected Works* (Engl. transl.), xviii. p. 264. Compare Spenser Wilkinson's dictum: "It is not peace but preponderance that is in each case the real object. The truth cannot be too often repeated that peace is never the object of policy: you cannot define peace except by reference to war, which is a means and never an end" (Government and the War, p. 121).

3 *League of Nations:* C.48, M.18, 1933, ii. p. 6.

4 Machiavelli, *The Prince*, chs. 15 and 23 (Engl. transl., Everyman's Library, pp. 121, 193).

5 Toynbee, *Survey of International Affairs, 1935*, ii. p. 46.

6 "Pray earnestly that right may triumph," said the representative of the Philadelphia coal-owners in an early strike organised by the United Mine Workers, "remembering that the Lord God Omnipotent still reigns, and that His reign is one of law and order, and not of violence and crime" (H. F. Pringle, *Theodore Roosevelt*, p. 267).

7 R. Niebuhr, *Moral Man and Immoral Society*, p. 153.

8 *Speech in the Reichstag*, January 30, 1939.

9 Lenin, *Collected Works* (English transl.), xviii. p. 97; Theses of the Sixth Congress of Comintern quoted in Taracouzio, *The Soviet Union and International Law*, p. 436.

10 Hitler, *Mein Kampf*, p. 749.

11 R. G. Hawtrey, *Economic Aspects of Sovereignty*, p. 107.

12 It is perhaps necessary to recall the part played in British politics in 1914 by the threat of the Conservative Party to support revolutionary action in Ulster.

13 R. G. Hawtrey, *Economic Aspects of Sovereignty*, p. 105.

14 *League of Nations: Official Journal*, May 1924, p. 578.

15 R. Niebuhr, *Moral Man and Immoral Society*, p. 42.

16 Machiavelli, *Discorsi*, I. i. ch. v.

17 Hobbes, *Leviathan*, ch. xi.

18 *British and Foreign State Papers*, ed. Hertslet, xc. p. 811.

19 Moeller van den Bruck, *Germany's Third Empire*, p. 50. The idea is a commonplace of National Socialist and Fascist writers.

20 In Germany, "political economy" was at first translated *Nationalökonomie*, which was tentatively replaced in the present century by *Sozialökonomie*.

21 This interpretation is confirmed by the report of the Phillimore Committee, on whose proposals the text of Article 16 was based. The Committee "considered financial and economic sanctions as being simply the contribution to the work of preventing aggression which might properly be made by countries which were not in a position to furnish actual military aid" (*International Sanctions: Report by a Group of Members of the Royal Institute of International Affairs*, p. 115 where the relevant texts are examined).

22 House of Commons, May 18, 1934; *Official Report*, col. 2139.

23 It is not, of course, suggested that the military weapon must always be used. The British Grand Fleet was little used in the first world war. But it would be rash to assume that the result would have been much the same if the British Government had not been prepared to use it. What paralyzed sanctions in 1935–36 was the common knowledge that the League Powers were not prepared to use the military weapon.

24 It is worth noting that Stresemann was fully alive to this point when Germany entered the League of Nations. When the Secretary-General argued that Germany, if she contracted out of military sanctions, could still participate in economic sanctions, Stresemann replied: "We cannot do that either; if we take part in an economic boycott of a powerful neighbour, a declaration of war against Germany might be the consequence, since the exclusion of another country from intercourse with a nation of sixty million citizens would be a hostile act" (*Stresemann's Diaries and Papers* [Engl. Transl.], ii. p. 69).

25 F. L. Schuman, *International Politics*, p. 356.

26 Zimmern, *Quo Vadimus?* p. 41.

27 The Carnegie Endowment has, for example, given the title *International Legislation* to a collection published under its auspices of "multipartite instruments of general interest."

Reading 2.5

The Origins of War in Neorealist Theory
KENNETH N. WALTZ

L ike most historians, many students of international politics have been skeptical about the possibility of creating a theory that might help one to understand and explain the international events that interest us. Thus Morgenthau, foremost among traditional realists, was fond of repeating Blaise Pascal's remark that "the history of the world would have been different had

Source: Kenneth N. Waltz, "The Origins of War in Neorealist Theory." Reprinted from The Journal of Interdisciplinary History, XVIII (1988), 615–628, *with the permission of the editors of* The Journal of Interdisciplinary History *and the MIT Press, Cambridge, Massachusetts.* © 1988 by the Massachusetts Institute of Technology and The Journal of Interdisciplinary History, Inc.

Cleopatra's nose been a bit shorter" and then asking "How do you systemize that?"[1] His appreciation of the role of the accidental and the occurrence of the unexpected in politics dampened his theoretical ambition.

The response of neorealists is that, although difficulties abound, some of the obstacles that seem most daunting lie in misapprehensions about theory. Theory obviously cannot explain the accidental or account for unexpected events; it deals in regularities and repetitions and is possible only if these can be identified. A further difficulty is found in the failure of realists to conceive of international politics as a distinct domain about which theories can be fashioned. Morgenthau, for example, insisted on "the autonomy of politics," but he failed to apply the concept to international politics. A theory is a depiction of the organization of a domain and of the connections among its parts. A theory indicates that some factors are more important than others and specifies relations among them. In reality, everything is related to everything else, and one domain cannot be separated from others. But theory isolates one realm from all others in order to deal with it intellectually. By defining the structure of international political systems, neorealism establishes the autonomy of international politics and thus makes a theory about it possible.[2]

In developing a theory of international politics, neorealism retains the main tenets of *realpolitik*, but means and ends are viewed differently, as are causes and effects. Morgenthau, for example, thought of the "rational" statesman as ever striving to accumulate more and more power. He viewed power as an end in itself. Although he acknowledged that nations at times act out of considerations other than power, Morgenthau insisted that, when they do so, their actions are not "of a political nature."[3] In contrast, neorealism sees power as a possibly useful means, with states running risks if they have either too little or too much of it. Excessive weakness may invite an attack that greater strength would have dissuaded an adversary from launching. Excessive strength may prompt other states to increase their arms and pool their efforts against the dominant state. Because power is a possibly useful means, sensible statesmen try to have an appropriate amount of it. In crucial situations, however, the ultimate concern of states is not for power but for security. This revision is an important one.

An even more important revision is found in a shift of causal relations. The infinite materials of any realm can be organized in endlessly different ways. Realism thinks of causes as moving in only one direction, from the interactions of individuals and states to the outcomes that their acts and interactions produce. Morgenthau recognized that, when there is competition for scarce goods and no one to serve as arbiter, a struggle for power will ensue among the competitors and that consequently the struggle for power can be explained without reference to the evil born in men. The struggle for power arises simply because men want things, not because of the evil in their desires. He labeled man's desire for scarce goods as one of the two roots of conflict, but, even while discussing it, he seemed to pull toward the "other root of conflict and concomitant evil"—"the *animus dominandi*, the desire for power." He often considered that man's drive for power is more basic than the chance conditions under which struggles for power occur. This attitude is seen in his statement that "in a world where power counts, no nation pursuing a rational policy has a choice between renouncing and wanting power; *and, if it could,* the lust for power for the individual's sake would still confront us with its less spectacular yet no less pressing moral defects."[4]

Students of international politics have typically inferred outcomes from salient attributes of the actors producing them. Thus Marxists, like liberals, have linked the outbreak of war or the prevalence of peace to the internal qualities of states. Governmental forms, economic systems, social institutions, political ideologies—these are but a few examples of where the causes of war have been found. Yet, although causes are specifically assigned, we know that states with widely divergent economic institutions, social customs, and political ideologies have all fought wars. More striking still, many different sorts of organizations fight wars, whether those organizations be tribes, petty principalities, empires, nations, or street gangs. If an identified condition seems to have caused a given war, one must wonder why wars occur repeatedly even though their causes vary. Variations in the characteristics of the states are not linked directly to the outcomes that their behaviors produce, nor are variations in their patterns of interaction. Many historians, for example, have claimed that World War I was caused by the interaction of two opposed and closely balanced coalitions. But then many have claimed that World War II was caused by the failure of some states to combine forces in an effort to right an imbalance of power created by an existing alliance.

Neorealism contends that international politics can be understood only if the effects of structure are added to the unit-level explanations of traditional realism. By emphasizing how structures affect actions and outcomes, neorealism rejects the assumption that man's innate lust for power constitutes a sufficient cause of war in the absence of any other. It reconceives the causal link between interacting units and international outcomes. According to the logic of international politics, one must believe that some causes of international outcomes are the result of interactions at the unit level, and, since variations in presumed causes do not correspond very closely to variations in observed outcomes, one must also assume that others are located at the structural level. Causes at the level of units interact with those at the level of structure, and, because they do so, explanation at the unit level alone is bound to be misleading. If an approach allows the consideration of both unit-level and structural-level causes, then it can cope with both the changes and the continuities that occur in a system.

Structural realism presents a systemic portrait of international politics depicting component units according to the manner of their arrangement. For the purpose of developing a theory, states are cast as unitary actors wanting at least to survive, and are taken to be the system's constituent units. The essential structural quality of the system is anarchy—the absence of a central monopoly of legitimate force. Changes of structure and hence of system occur with variations in the number of great powers. The range of expected outcomes is inferred from the assumed motivation of the units and the structure of the system in which they act.

A systems theory of international politics deals with forces at the international, and not at the national, level. With both systems-level and unit-level forces in play, how can one construct a theory of international politics without simultaneously constructing a theory of foreign policy? An international-political theory does not imply or require a theory of foreign policy any more than a market theory implies or requires a theory of the firm. Systems theories, whether political or economic, are theories that explain how the organization of a realm acts as a constraining and disposing force on the interacting units within it. Such theories tell us about the forces to which the units are subjected. From them, we can draw some inferences about the expected behavior and fate of the units: namely, how they will have to compete with and adjust to one another if they are to survive and flourish. To the extent that the dynamics of a system limit the freedom of its units, their behavior and the outcomes of their behavior become predictable. How do we expect firms to respond to differently structured markets, and states to differently structured international-political systems? These theoretical questions require us to take firms as firms, and states as states, without paying attention to differences among them. The questions are then answered by reference to the placement of the units in their system and not by reference to the internal qualities of the units. Systems theories explain why different units behave similarly and, despite their variations, produce outcomes that fall within expected ranges. Conversely, theories at the unit level tell us why different units behave differently despite their similar placement in a system. A theory about foreign policy is a theory at the national level. It leads to expectations about the responses that dissimilar polities will make to external pressures. A theory of international politics bears on the foreign policies of nations although it claims to explain only certain aspects of them. It can tell us what international conditions national policies have to cope with.

From the vantage point of neorealist theory, competition and conflict among states stem directly from the twin facts of life under conditions of anarchy: States in an anarchic order must provide for their own security, and threats or seeming threats to their security abound. Preoccupation with identifying dangers and counteracting them become a way of life. Relations remain tense; the actors are usually suspicious and often hostile even though by nature they may not be given to suspicion and hostility. Individually, states may only be doing what they can to bolster their security. Their individual intentions aside, collectively their actions yield arms races and alliances. The uneasy state of affairs is exacerbated by the familiar "security dilemma," wherein measures that enhance one state's security typically diminish that of others.[5] In an anarchic domain, the source of one's own comfort is the source of another's worry. Hence a state that is amassing instruments of war, even for its own defensive, is cast by others as a threat requiring response. The response itself then serves to confirm the first state's belief that it had reason to worry. Similarly, an alliance that in the interest of defense moves to increase cohesion among its members and add to its ranks inadvertently imperils an opposing alliance and provokes countermeasures.

Some states may hunger for power for power's sake. Neorealist theory, however, shows that it is not necessary to assume an innate lust for power in order to account for the sometimes fierce competition that marks the international arena. In an anarchic domain, a state of war exists if all parties lust for power. But so too will a state of war exist if all states seek only to ensure their own safety.

Although neorealist theory does not explain why particular wars are fought, it does explain war's dismal recurrence through the millennia. Neorealists point not to the ambitions or the intrigues that punctuate the outbreak of individual conflicts but instead to the existing structure within which events, whether by design or accident, can precipitate open clashes of arms. The origins of hot wars lie in cold wars, and the origins of cold wars are found in the anarchic ordering of the international arena.

The recurrence of war is explained by the structure of the international system. Theorists explain what historians know: War is normal. Any given war is explained not by looking at the structure of the international-political system but by looking at the particularities within it: the situations, the characters, and the interactions of states. Although particular explanations are found at the unit level, general explanations are also needed. Wars vary in frequency, and in other ways as well. A central question for a structural theory is this: How do changes of the system affect the expected frequency of war?

KEEPING WARS COLD: THE STRUCTURAL LEVEL

In an anarchic realm, peace is fragile. The prolongation of peace requires that potentially destabilizing developments elicit the interest and the calculated response of some or all of the system's principal actors. In the anarchy of states, the price of inattention or miscalculation is often paid in blood. An important issue for a structural theory to address is whether destabilizing conditions and events are managed better in multipolar or bipolar systems.

In a system of, say, five great powers, the politics of power turns on the diplomacy by which alliances are made, maintained, and disrupted. Flexibility of alignment means both that the country one is wooing may prefer another suitor and that one's present alliance partner may defect. Flexibility of alignment limits a state's options because, ideally, its strategy must please potential allies and satisfy present partners. Alliances are made by states that have some but not all of their interests in common. The common interest is ordinarily a negative one: fear of other states. Divergence comes when positive interests are at issue. In alliances among near equals, strategies are always the product of compromise since the interests of allies and their notions of how to secure them are never identical.

If competing blocs are seen to be closely balanced, and if competition turns on important matters, then to let one's side down risks one's own destruction. In a moment of crisis the weaker or the more adventurous party is likely to determine its side's policy. Its partners can afford neither to let the weaker member be defeated nor to advertise their disunity by failing to back a venture even while deploring its risks.

The prelude to World War I provides striking examples of such a situation. The approximate equality of partners in both the Triple Alliance and Triple

Entente made them closely interdependent. This interdependence, combined with the keen competition between the two camps, meant that, although any country could commit its associates, no one country on either side could exercise control. If Austria-Hungary marched, Germany had to follow; the dissolution of the Austro-Hungarian Empire would have left Germany alone in the middle of Europe. If France marched, Russia had to follow; a German victory over France would be a defeat for Russia. And so the vicious circle continued. Because the defeat or the defection of a major ally would have shaken the balance, each state was constrained to adjust its strategy and the use of its forces to the aims and fears of its partners.

In alliances among equals, the defection of one member threatens the security of the others. In alliances among unequals, the contributions of the lesser members are at once wanted and of relatively small importance. In alliances among unequals, alliance leaders need worry little about the faithfulness of their followers, who usually have little choice anyway. Contrast the situation in 1914 with that of the United States and Britain and France in 1956. The United States could dissociate itself from the Suez adventure of its two principal allies and subject one of them to heavy financial pressure. Like Austria-Hungary in 1914, Britain and France tried to commit or at least immobilize their ally by presenting a fait accompli. Enjoying a position of predominance, the United States could continue to focus its attention on the major adversary while disciplining its two allies. Opposing Britain and France endangered neither the United States nor the alliance because the security of Britain and France depended much more heavily on us than our security depended on them. The ability of the United States, and the inability of Germany, to pay a price measured in intra-alliance terms is striking.

In balance-of-power politics old style, flexibility of alignment led to rigidity of strategy or the limitation of freedom of decision. In balance-of-power politics new style, the obverse is true: Rigidity of alignment in a two-power world results in more flexibility of strategy and greater freedom of decision. In a multipolar world, roughly equal parties engaged in cooperative endeavors must look for the common denominator of their policies. They risk finding the lowest one and easily end up in the worst of all possible worlds. In a bipolar world, alliance leaders can design strategies primarily to advance their own interests and to cope with their main adversary and less to satisfy their own allies.

Neither the United States nor the Soviet Union has to seek the approval of other states, but each has to cope with the other. In the great-power politics of a multipolar world, who is a danger to whom and who can be expected to deal with threats and problems are matters of uncertainty. In the great-power politics of a bipolar world, who is a danger to whom is never in doubt. Any event in the world that involves the fortunes of either of the great powers automatically elicits the interest of the other. President Harry S. Truman, at the time of the Korean invasion, could not very well echo Neville Chamberlain's words in the Czechoslovakian crisis by claiming that the Americans knew nothing about the Koreans, a people living far away in the east of Asia. We had to know about them or quickly find out.

In a two-power competition, a loss for one is easily taken to be a gain for the other. As a result, the powers in a bipolar world promptly respond to unsettling events. In a multipolar world, dangers are diffused, responsibilities unclear, and definitions of vital interests easily obscured. Where a number of states are in balance, the skillful foreign policy of a forward power is designed to gain an advantage without antagonizing other states and frightening them into united action. At times in modern Europe, the benefits of possible gains have seemed to outweigh the risks of likely losses. Statesmen have hoped to push an issue to the limit without causing all of the potential opponents to unite. When there are several possible enemies, unity of action among them is difficult to achieve. National leaders could therefore think—or desperately hope, as did Theobald Von Bethmann Hollweg and Adolf Hitler before two world wars—that a united opposition would not form.

If interests and ambitions conflict, the absence of crises is more worrisome than their presence. Crises are produced by the determination of a state to resist a change that another state tries to make. As the leaders in a bipolar system, the United States and the Soviet Union are disposed to do the resisting, for in important matters they cannot hope that their allies will do it for them. Political action in the postwar world has reflected this condition. Communist guerrillas operating in Greece prompted the Truman Doctrine. The tightening of Soviet control over the states of Eastern Europe led to the Marshall Plan and the Atlantic Defense Treaty, and these in turn gave rise to the Cominform and the Warsaw Pact. The plan to create a West German government produced the Berlin blockade. During the past four decades, our responses have been geared to the Soviet Union's actions, and theirs to ours.

Miscalculation by some or all of the great powers is a source of danger in a multipolar world; overreaction by either or both of the great powers is a source of danger in a bipolar world. Which is worse: miscalculation or overreaction? Miscalculation is the greater evil because it is more likely to permit an unfolding of events that finally threatens the status quo and brings the powers to war. Overreaction is the lesser evil because at worst it costs only money for unnecessary arms and possibly the fighting of limited wars. The dynamics of a bipolar system, moreover, provide a measure of correction. In a world in which two states united in their mutual antagonism overshadow any others, the benefits of a calculated response stand out most clearly, and the sanctions against irresponsible behavior achieve their greatest force. Thus two states, isolationist by tradition, untutored in the ways of international politics, and famed for impulsive behavior, have shown themselves—not always and everywhere, but always in crucial cases—to be wary, alert, cautious, flexible, and forbearing. . . .

WARS, HOT AND COLD

Wars, hot and cold, originate in the structure of the international political system. Most Americans blame the Soviet Union for creating the Cold War, by the actions that follow necessarily from the nature of its society and government. Revisionist historians, attacking the dominant view, assign blame to the United

States. Some American error, or sinister interest, or faulty assumption about Soviet aims, they argue, is what started the Cold War. Either way, the main point is lost. In a bipolar world, each of the two great powers is bound to focus its fears on the other, to distrust its motives, and to impute offensive intentions to defensive measures. The proper question is what, not who, started the Cold War. Although its content and virulence vary as unit-level forces change and interact, the Cold War continues. It is firmly rooted in the structure of postwar international politics, and will last as long as that structure endures.

NOTES

1 Hans J. Morgenthau, "International Relations: Quantitative and Qualitative Approaches," in Norman D. Palmer (ed.), *A Design for International Relations Research: Scope, Theory, Methods, and Relevance* (Philadelphia, 1970), 78.

2 Morgenthau, *Politics among Nations* (New York, 1973; 5th ed.), 11. Ludwig Boltzman (trans. Rudolf Weingartner), "Theories as Representations," excerpted in Arthur Danto and Sidney Morgenbesser (eds.), *Philosophy of Science* (Cleveland, 1960), 245–252. Neorealism is sometimes dubbed structural realism. I use the terms interchangeably and, throughout this article, refer to my own formulation of neorealist theory. See Waltz, *Theory of International Politics* (Reading, Mass., 1979); Robert Keohane (ed.), *Neorealism and Its Critics* (New York, 1986).

3 Morgenthau, *Politics among Nations*, 27.

4 Idem, *Scientific Man vs. Power Politics* (Chicago, 1946), 192, 200. Italics added.

5 See John H. Herz, "Idealist Internationalism and the Security Dilemma," *World Politics*, II (1950), 157–180.

Reading 2.6

Hegemonic War and International Change

ROBERT GILPIN

Because of the redistribution of power, the costs to the traditional dominant state of maintaining the international system increase relative to its capacity to pay; this, in turn, produces the severe fiscal crisis. . . . By the same token, the costs to the rising state of changing the system decrease; it begins to appreciate that it can increase its own gains by forcing changes in the nature of the system. Its enhanced power position means that the relative costs of changing the system and securing its interests have decreased. Thus, in accordance with the law of demand, the rising state, as its power increases, will seek to change the status quo as the perceived potential benefits begin to exceed the perceived costs of undertaking a change in the system.

As its relative power increases, a rising state attempts to change the rules governing the international system, the division of the spheres of influence, and, most important of all, the international distribution of territory. In response, the dominant power counters this challenge through changes in its policies that attempt to restore equilibrium in the system. The historical record reveals that if it fails in this attempt, the disequilibrium will be resolved by war. Shepard Clough, in his book *The Rise and Fall of Civilization*, drew on a distinguished career in historical scholarship to make the point: "At least in all the cases which we have passed . . . in review in these pages, cultures with inferior civilization but with growing economic power have always attacked the most civilized cultures during the latters' economic decline" (1970, p. 263). The fundamental task of the challenged dominant state is to solve what Walter Lippmann once characterized as the fundamental problem of foreign policy—the balancing of commitments and resources (Lippmann, 1943, p. 7). An imperial, hegemonic, or great power has essentially two courses of action open to it as it attempts to restore equilibrium in the system. The first and preferred solution is that the challenged power can seek to increase the resources devoted to maintaining its commitments and position in the international system. The second is that it can attempt to reduce its existing commitments (and associated costs) in a way that does not ultimately jeopardize its international position. Although neither response will be followed to the exclusion of the other, they may be considered analytically as separate policies. The logic and the pitfalls of each policy will be considered in turn.

Historically, the most frequently employed devices to generate new resources to meet the increasing costs of dominance and to forestall decline have been to increase domestic taxation and to exact tribute from other states. Both of these courses of action have inherent dangers in that they can provoke resistance and rebellion. The French Revolution was triggered in part by the effort of the monarchy to levy the higher taxes required to meet the British challenge (von Ranke, 1950, p. 211). Athens's "allies" revolted against Athenian demands for increased tribute. Because higher taxes (or tribute) mean decreased productive investment and a lowered standard of living, in most instances such expedients can be employed for only relatively short periods of time, such as during a war.

The powerful resistance within a society to higher taxes or tribute encourages the government to employ more indirect methods of generating additional resources to meet a fiscal crisis. Most frequently, a government will resort to inflationary policies or seek to manipulate the terms of trade with other countries. As Carlo Cipolla observed (1970, p. 13), the invariable symptoms of a society's decline are excessive taxation, inflation, and balance-of-payments difficulties as government and society spend beyond their means. But these indirect devices also bring hardship and encounter strong resistance over the long run.

The most satisfactory solution to the problem of increasing costs is increased efficiency in the use of existing resources. Through organizational, technological, and other types of innovations, a state can either economize with respect to the resources at its disposal or increase the total amount of disposable resources. Thus, as Mark Elvin explained, the fundamental reason that imperial China survived intact for so long was its unusually high rate of economic and technological innovation; over long periods China was able to generate sufficient resources to finance the costs of protection against successive invaders (Elvin, 1973). Conversely, the Roman economy stagnated and failed to innovate. Among the reasons for the decline and destruction of Rome was its inability to generate resources sufficient to stave off barbarian invaders. More recently, the calls for greater industrial productivity in contemporary America derive from the realization that technological innovation and more efficient use of existing resources are needed to meet the increasing demands of consumption, investment, and protection.

This innovative solution involves rejuvenation of the society's military, economic, and political institutions. In the case of declining Rome, for example, a recasting of its increasingly inefficient system of agricultural production and a revised system of taxation were required. Unfortunately, social reform and institutional rejuvenation become increasingly difficult as a society ages, because this implies more general changes in customs, attitudes, motivation, and sets of values that constitute a cultural heritage (Cipolla, 1970, p. 11). Vested interests resist the loss of their privileges. Institutional rigidities frustrate abandonment of "tried and true" methods (Downs, 1967, pp. 158–66). One could hardly expect it to be otherwise: "Innovations are important not for their immediate, actual results but for their potential for future development, and potential is very difficult to assess" (Cipolla, 1970, pp. 9–10).

A declining society experiences a vicious cycle of decay and immobility, much as a rising society enjoys a virtuous cycle of growth and expansion. On the one hand, decline is accompanied by lack of social cooperation, by emphasis on rights rather than emphasis on duty, and by decreasing productivity. On the other hand, the frustration and pessimism generated by this gloomy atmosphere inhibit renewal and innovation. The failure to innovate accentuates the decline and its psychologically debilitating consequences. Once caught up in this cycle, it is difficult for the society to break out (Cipolla, 1970, p. 11). For this reason, a more rational and more efficient use of existing resources to meet increasing military and productive needs is seldom achieved.

There have been societies that have managed their resources with great skill for hundreds of years and have rejuvenated themselves in response to external challenges, and this resilience has enabled them to survive for centuries in a hostile environment. In fact, those states that have been notable for their longevity have been the ones most successful in allocating their scarce resources in an optimal fashion in order to balance, over a period of centuries, the conflicting demands of consumption, protection, and investment. An outstanding example was the Venetian city-state. Within this aristocratic republic the governing elite moderated consumption and shifted resources back and forth between protection and investment as need required over the centuries (Lane, 1973). The Chinese Empire was even more significant. Its longevity and unity were due to the fact that the Chinese were able to increase their production more rapidly than the rise in the costs of protection (Elvin, 1973, pp. 92–3, 317). The progressive nature of the imperial Chinese economy meant that sufficient resources were in most cases available to meet external threats and preserve the integrity of the empire for centuries. In contrast to the Romans, who were eventually inundated and destroyed by the barbarians, the Chinese "on the whole . . . managed to keep one step ahead of their neighbours in the relevant technical skills, military, economic and organizational" (Elvin, 1973, p. 20).

An example of social rejuvenation intended to meet an external challenge was that of revolutionary France. The point has already been made that European aristocracies were reluctant to place firearms in the hands of the lower social orders, preferring to rely on small professional armies. The French Revolution and the innovation of nationalism made it possible for the French state to tap the energies of the masses of French citizens. The so-called *levée en masse* greatly increased the human resources available to the republic and, later, to Napoleon. Although this imperial venture was ultimately unsuccessful, it does illustrate the potentiality for domestic rejuvenation of a society in response to decline.

The second type of response to declining fortunes is to bring costs and resources into balance by reducing costs. This can be attempted in three general ways. The first is to eliminate the reason for the increasing costs (i.e., to weaken or destroy the rising challenger). The second is to expand to a more secure and less costly defensive perimeter. The third is to reduce international commitments. Each of these alternative strategies has its attractions and its dangers.

The first and most attractive response to a society's decline is to eliminate the source of the problem. By launching a preventive war the declining power destroys or weakens the rising challenger while the military advantage is still with the declining power. Thus, as Thucydides explained, the Spartans initiated the Peloponnesian War in an attempt to crush the rising Athenian challenger while Sparta still had the power to do so. When the choice ahead has appeared to be to decline or to fight, statesmen have most generally fought. However, besides causing unnecessary loss of life, the greatest danger inherent in preventive war is that it sets in motion a course of events over which statesmen soon lose control (see the subsequent discussion of hegemonic war).

Second, a state may seek to reduce the costs of maintaining its position by means of further expansion.[1] In effect, the state hopes to reduce its long-term costs by acquiring less costly defensive positions. As Edward Luttwak (1976) demonstrated in his brilliant study of Roman grand strategy, Roman expansion in its later phases was an attempt to find more secure and less costly defensive positions and to eliminate potential challengers. Although this response to declining fortunes can be effective, it can also lead to further overextension of commitments, to increasing costs, and thereby to acceleration of the decline.

It is difficult for a successful and expanding state to break the habit of expansion, and it is all too easy to believe that "expand or die" is the imperative of international survival. Perhaps the greatest danger for every imperial or hegemonic power, as it proved eventually to be for Rome, is overextension of commitments that gradually begin to sap its strength (Grant, 1968, p. 246).[2]

The third means of bringing costs and resources into balance is, of course, to reduce foreign-policy commitments. Through political, territorial, or economic retrenchment, a society can reduce the costs of maintaining its international position. However, this strategy is politically difficult, and carrying it out is a delicate matter. Its success is highly uncertain and strongly dependent on timing and circumstances. The problem of retrenchment will be considered first in general terms; then a case of relatively successful retrenchment by a great power will be discussed.

The most direct method of retrenchment is unilateral abandonment of certain of a state's economic, political, or military commitments. For example, a state may withdraw from exposed and costly strategic positions. Venice, as was pointed out, pursued for centuries a conscious policy of alternating advance and retreat. The longevity of the later Roman Empire or Byzantine Empire may be partially explained by its withdrawal from its exposed and difficult-to-defend western provinces and consolidation of its position on a less costly basis in its eastern provinces; its survival for a thousand years was due to the fact that it brought the scale of empire and resources into balance (Cipolla, 1970, p. 82; Rader, 1971, p. 54). In our own time, the so-called Nixon doctrine may be interpreted as an effort on the part of the United States to disengage from vulnerable commitments and to shift part of the burden of defending the international status quo to other powers (Hoffmann, 1978, pp. 46–7).

A second standard technique of retrenchment is to enter into alliances with or seek rapprochement with less threatening powers. In effect, the dominant but declining power makes concessions to another state and agrees to share the benefits of the status quo with that other state in exchange for sharing the costs of preserving the status quo. Thus the Romans brought the Goths into the empire (much to their later regret) in exchange for their assistance in defending the frontiers of the empire. As will be pointed out in a moment, the policy of entente or rapprochement was pursued by the British prior to World War I as they sought to meet the rising German challenge. The American rapprochement with Communist China is a late-twentieth-century example. In exchange for weakening the American commitment to Taiwan, the Americans seek Chinese assistance in containing the expanding power of the Soviet Union.

Unfortunately, there are several dangers associated with this response to decline. First, in an alliance between a great power and a lesser power there is a tendency for the former to overpay in the long run, as has occurred with the United States and the North Atlantic Treaty Organization (NATO); the great power increases its commitments without a commensurate increase in the resources devoted by its allies to finance those commitments. Further, the ally is benefited materially by the alliance, and as its capabilities increase, it may turn against the declining power. Thus the Romans educated the Goths in their military techniques only to have the latter turn these techniques against them. Second, the utility of alliances is limited by Riker's theory of coalitions: An increase in the number of allies decreases the benefits to each. Therefore, as an alliance increases in number, the probability of defection increases (Riker, 1962). Third, the minor ally may involve the major ally in disputes of its own from which the latter cannot disengage itself without heavy costs to its prestige. For these reasons, the utility of an alliance as a response to decline and a means to decrease costs is severely restricted.

The third and most difficult method of retrenchment is to make concessions to the rising power and thereby seek to appease its ambitions. Since the Munich conference in 1938, "appeasement" as a policy has been in disrepute and has been regarded as inappropriate under every conceivable set of circumstances. This is unfortunate, because there are historical examples in which appeasement has succeeded. Contending states have not only avoided conflict but also achieved a relationship satisfactory to both. A notable example was British appeasement of the rising United States in the decades prior to World War I (Perkins, 1968). The two countries ended a century-long hostility and laid the basis for what has come to be known as the "special relationship" of the two Anglo-Saxon powers.

The fundamental problem with a policy of appeasement and accommodation is to find a way to pursue it that does not lead to continuing deterioration in a state's prestige and international position. Retrenchment by its very nature is an indication of relative weakness and declining power, and thus retrenchment can have a deteriorating effect on relations with allies and rivals. Sensing the decline of their protector, allies try to obtain the best deal they can from the rising master of the system. Rivals are stimulated to "close in," and frequently they precipitate a conflict in the process. Thus World War I began as a conflict between Russia and Austria over the disposition of the remnants of the retreating Ottoman Empire (Hawtrey, 1952, pp. 75–81).

Because retrenchment signals waning power, a state seldom retrenches or makes concessions on its own initiative. Yet, not to retrench voluntarily and then to retrench in response to threats or military defeat means an even more severe loss of prestige and weakening of one's diplomatic standing. As a consequence of such defeats, allies defect to the victorious party, opponents press their advantage, and the retrenching society itself becomes demoralized. Moreover, if the forced retrenchment involves the loss of a "vital interest," then the security and integrity of the state are placed in jeopardy. For these reasons, retrenchment is a hazardous course for a state; it is a course seldom pursued by a declining power. However, there have been cases of a retrenchment policy being carried out rather successfully.

An excellent example of a declining hegemon that successfully brought its resources and commitments into balance is provided by Great Britain in the decades just prior to World War I. Following its victory over France in the Napoleonic wars, Great Britain had become the world's most powerful and most prestigious state. It gave its name to a century of relative peace, the Pax Britannica. British naval power was supreme on the high seas, and British industry and commerce were unchallengeable in world markets. An equilibrium had been established on the European continent by the Congress of Vienna (1814), and no military or industrial rivals then existed outside of Europe. By the last decades of the century, however, a profound transformation had taken place. Naval and industrial rivals had risen to challenge British supremacy both on the Continent and overseas. France, Germany, the United States, Japan, and Russia, to various degrees, had become expanding imperial powers. The unification of Germany by Prussia had destroyed the protective Continental equilibrium, and Germany's growing naval might threatened Britain's command of the seas.

As a consequence of these commercial, naval, and imperial challenges, Great Britain began to encounter the problems that face every mature or declining power. On the one hand, external demands were placing steadily increasing strains on the economy; on the other hand, the capacity of the economy to meet these demands had deteriorated. Thus, at the same time that the costs of protection were escalating, both private consumption and public consumption were also increasing because of greater affluence. Superficially the economy appeared strong, but the rates of industrial expansion, technological innovation, and domestic investment had slowed. Thus the rise of foreign challenges and the climacteric of the economy had brought on disequilibrium between British global commitments and British resources.

As the disequilibrium between its global hegemony and its limited resources intensified, Britain faced the dilemma of increasing its resources or reducing its commitments or both. In the national debate on this critical issue the proponents of increasing the available resources proposed two general courses of action. First, they proposed a drawing together of the empire and drawing on these combined resources, as well as the creation of what John Seeley (1905) called Greater Britain, especially the white dominions. This idea, however, did not have sufficient appeal at home or abroad. Second, reformers advocated measures to rejuvenate the declining British economy and to achieve greater efficiency. Unfortunately, as W. Arthur Lewis argued, all the roads that would have led to industrial innovation and a higher rate of economic growth were closed to the British for social, political, or ideological reasons (Lewis, 1978, p. 133). The primary solution to the problem of decline and disequilibrium, therefore, necessarily lay in the reduction of overseas diplomatic and strategic commitments.

The specific diplomatic and strategic issue that faced British leadership was whether to maintain the global position identified with the Pax Britannica or to bring about a retrenchment of its global commitments. By the last decade of the century, Great Britain was confronted by rival land and sea powers on every continent and every sea. European rivals were everywhere: Russia in the Far East, south Asia, and the Middle East; France in Asia, the Middle East, and north Africa; Germany in the Far East, the Middle East, and Africa. Furthermore, in the Far East, Japan had suddenly emerged as a great power; the United States also was becoming a naval power of consequence and was challenging Great Britain in the Western Hemisphere and the Pacific Ocean.

At the turn of the century, however, the predominant problem was perceived to be the challenge of German naval expansionism. Whereas all the other challenges posed limited and long-term threats, the danger embodied in Germany's decision to build a battle fleet was immediate and portentous. Despite intense negotiations, no compromise of this naval armaments race could be reached. The only course open to the British was retrenchment of their power and commitments around the globe in order to concentrate their total efforts on the German challenge.

Great Britain settled its differences with its other foreign rivals one after another. In the 1890s came the settlement of the Venezuela-British Guiana border dispute in accordance with American desires; in effect, Britain acquiesced in America's primacy in the Caribbean Sea. A century of American-British uneasiness came to an end, and the foundation was laid for the Anglo-American alliance that would prevail in two world wars. Next, in the Anglo-Japanese alliance of 1902, Great Britain gave up its policy of going it alone and took Japan as its partner in the Far East. Accepting Japanese supremacy in the northwestern Pacific as a counterweight to Russia, Great Britain withdrew to the south. This was immediately followed in 1904 by the *entente cordiale*, which settled the Mediterranean and colonial confrontation between France and Great Britain and ended centuries of conflict. In 1907 the Anglo-Russian agreement resolved the British-Russian confrontation in the Far East, turned Russia's interest toward the Balkans, and eventually aligned Russia, Great Britain, and France against Germany and Austria. Thus, by the eve of World War I, British commitments had been retrenched to a point that Britain could employ whatever power it possessed to arrest further decline in the face of expanding German power.

Thus far we have described two alternative sets of strategies that a great power may pursue in order to arrest its decline: to increase resources or to decrease costs. Each of these policies has succeeded to some degree at one time or another. Most frequently, however, the dominant state is unable to generate sufficient additional resources to defend its vital commitments; alternatively, it may be unable to reduce its cost and commitments to some manageable size. In these situations, the disequilibrium in the system becomes increasingly acute as the declining power tries to maintain its position and the rising power attempts to transform the system in ways that will advance its interests. As a consequence of this persisting disequilibrium, the international system is beset by tensions, uncertainties, and crises. However, such a stalemate in the system seldom persists for a long period of time.

Throughout history the primary means of resolving the disequilibrium between the structure of the international system and the redistribution of power has been war, more particularly, what we shall call a hegemonic war. In the words of Raymond Aron, describing World War I, a hegemonic war "is characterized less by its immediate causes or its explicit purposes than by its extent and the stakes involved. It affected all the political units inside one system of relations between sovereign states. Let us call it, for want of a better term, a war of hegemony, hegemony being, if not conscious motive, at any rate the inevitable consequence of the victory of at least one of the states or groups" (Aron, 1964, p. 359). Thus, a hegemonic war is the ultimate test of change in the relative standings of the powers in the existing system.

Every international system that the world has known has been a consequence of the territorial, economic, and diplomatic realignments that have followed such hegemonic struggles. The most important consequence of a hegemonic war is that it changes the system in accordance with the new international distribution of power; it brings about a reordering of the basic components of the system. Victory and defeat reestablish an unambiguous hierarchy of prestige congruent with the new distribution of power in the system. The war determines who will govern the international system and whose interests will be primarily served by the new international order. The war leads to a redistribution of territory among the states in the system, a new set of rules of the system, a revised international division of labor, etc. As a consequence of these changes, a relatively more stable international order and effective governance of the international system are created based on the new realities of the international distribution of power. In short, hegemonic wars have (unfortunately) been functional and integral parts of the evolution and dynamics of international systems.

It is not inevitable, of course, that a hegemonic struggle will give rise immediately to a new hegemonic power and a renovated international order. As has frequently occurred, the combatants may exhaust themselves, and the "victorious" power may be unable to reorder the international system. The destruction of Rome by barbarian hordes led to the chaos of the Dark Ages. The Pax Britannica was not immediately replaced by the Pax Americana; there was a twenty year interregnum, what E. H. Carr called the "twenty years' crisis." Eventually, however, a new power or set of powers emerges to give governance to the international system.

What, then, are the defining characteristics of a hegemonic war? How does it differ from more limited conflicts among states? In the first place, such a war involves a direct contest between the dominant power or powers in an international system and the rising challenger or challengers. The conflict becomes total and in time is characterized by participation of all the major states and most of the minor states in the system. The tendency, in fact, is for every state in the system to be drawn into one or another of the opposing camps. Inflexible bipolar configurations of power (the Delian League versus the Peloponnesian League, the Triple Alliance versus the Triple Entente) frequently presage the outbreak of hegemonic conflict.

Second, the fundamental issue at stake is the nature and governance of the system. The legitimacy of the system may be said to be challenged. For this reason, hegemonic wars are unlimited conflicts; they are at once political, economic, and ideological in terms of significance and consequences. They become directed at the destruction of the offending social, political, or economic system and are usually followed by religious, political, or social transformation of the defeated society. The leveling of Carthage by Rome, the conversion of the Middle East to Islam by the Arabs, and the democratization of contemporary Japan and West Germany by the United States are salient examples. . . .

Third, a hegemonic war is characterized by the unlimited means employed and by the general scope of the warfare. Because all parties are drawn into the war and the stakes involved are high, few limitations, if any, are observed with respect to the means employed; the limitations on violence and treachery tend to be only those necessarily imposed by the state of technology, the available resources, and the fear of retaliation. Similarly, the geographic scope of the war tends to expand to encompass the entire international system; these are "world" wars. Thus, hegemonic wars are characterized by their intensity, scope, and duration.

From the premodern world, the Peloponnesian War between Athens and Sparta and the Second Punic War between Carthage and Rome meet these criteria of hegemonic war. In the modern era, several wars have been hegemonic struggles: the Thirty Years' War (1618–48); the wars of Louis XIV (1667–1713); the wars of the French Revolution and Napoleon (1792–1814); World Wars I and II (1914–18, 1939–45) (Mowat, 1928, pp. 1–2). At issue in each of these great conflicts was the governance of the international system.

In addition to the preceding criteria that define hegemonic war, three preconditions generally appear to be associated with the outbreak of hegemonic war. In the first place, the intensification of conflicts among states is a consequence of the "closing in" of space and opportunities. With the aging of an international system and the expansion of states, the distance between states decreases, thereby causing them increasingly to come into conflict with one another. The once-empty space around the centers of power in the system is appropriated. The exploitable resources begin to be used up, and opportunities for economic growth decline. The system begins to encounter limits to the growth and expansion of member states; states increasingly come into conflict with one another. Interstate relations become more and more a zero-sum game in which one state's gain is another's loss.

Marxists and realists share a sense of the importance of contracting frontiers and their significance for the stability and peace of the system. As long as expansion is possible, the law of uneven growth (or development) can operate with little disturbing effect on the overall stability of the system. In time, however, limits are reached, and the international system enters a period of crisis. The clashes among states for territory, resources, and markets increase in frequency and magnitude and eventually culminate in hegemonic war. Thus, as E. H. Carr told us, the relative peace of nineteenth-century Europe and the belief that a harmony of interest was providing a basis for increasing economic interdependence were due to the existence of "continuously expanding territories and markets" (1951, p. 224). The closing in of political and economic space led to the intensification of conflict and the final collapse of the system in the two world wars.

The second condition preceding hegemonic war is temporal and psychological rather than spatial; it is the perception that a fundamental historical change is taking place and the gnawing fear of one or more of the great powers that time is somehow beginning to work against it and that one should settle matters through preemptive war while the advantage is still on one's side. It was anxiety of this nature that Thucydides had in mind when he wrote that the growth of Athenian power inspired fear on the part of the Lacedaemonians and was the unseen cause of the war. The alternatives open to a state whose relative power is being eclipsed are seldom those of waging war versus promoting peace, but rather waging war while the balance is still in that state's favor or waging war later when the tide may have turned against it. Thus the motive for hegemonic war, at least from the perspective of the dominant power, is to minimize one's losses rather than to maximize one's gains. In effect, a precondition for hegemonic war is the realization that the law of uneven growth has begun to operate to one's disadvantage.

The third precondition of hegemonic war is that the course of events begins to escape human control. Thus far, the argument of this study has proceeded as if mankind controlled its own destiny. The propositions presented and explored in an attempt to understand international political change have been phrased in terms of rational cost/benefit calculations. Up to a point, rationality does appear to apply; statesmen do explicitly or implicitly make rational calculations and then attempt to set the course of the ship of state accordingly. But it is equally true that events, especially those associated with the passions of war, can easily escape from human control.

"What is the force that moves nations?" Tolstoy inquires in the concluding part of *War and Peace*, and he answers that ultimately it is the masses in motion (1961, Vol. II, p. 1404). Leadership, calculation, control over events—these are merely the illusions of statesmen and scholars. The passions of men and the momentum of events take over and propel societies in novel and unanticipated directions. This is especially true during times of war. As the Athenians counseled the Peloponnesians in seeking to forestall war, "consider the vast influence of accident in war, before you engage in it. As it continues, it generally becomes an affair of chances, chances from which neither of us is exempt, and whose event we must risk in the dark. It is a common mistake in going to war to—begin at the wrong end, to act first, and wait for disaster to discuss the matter" (Thucydides, 1951, p. 45).

Indeed, men seldom determine or even anticipate the consequences of hegemonic war. Although in going to war they desire to increase their gains or minimize their losses, they do not get the war they want or expect; they fail to recognize the pent-up forces they are unleashing or the larger historical significance of the decisions they are taking. They underestimate the eventual scope and intensity of the conflict on which they are embarking and its implications for their civilization. Hegemonic war arises from the structural conditions and disequilibrium of an international system, but its consequences are seldom predicted by statesmen. As Toynbee suggested, the law governing such conflicts would appear to favor rising states on the periphery of an international system rather than the contending states in the system itself. States directly engaged in hegemonic conflict, by weakening themselves, frequently actually eliminate obstacles to conquest by a peripheral power.

The great turning points in world history have been provided by these hegemonic struggles among political rivals; these periodic conflicts have reordered the international system and propelled history in new and uncharted directions. They resolve the question of which state will govern the system, as well as what ideas and values will predominate, thereby determining the ethos of succeeding ages. The outcomes of these wars affect the economic, social, and ideological structures of individual societies as well as the structure of the larger international system.

In contrast to the emphasis placed here on the role of hegemonic war in changing the international system, it might be argued that domestic revolution can change the international system. This is partially correct. It would be foolish to suggest, for example, that the great revolutions of the twentieth century (the Russian, Chinese, and perhaps Iranian) have not had a profound impact on world politics. However, the primary consequence of these social and political upheavals (at least of the first two) has been to facilitate the mobilization of the society's resources for purposes of national power. In other words, the significance of these revolutions for world politics is that they have served to strengthen (or weaken) their respective states and thereby cause a redistribution of power in the system.

As the distinguished French historian Elie Halévy put it, "all great convulsions in the history of the world, and more particularly in modern Europe, have been at the same time wars and revolutions" (1965, p. 212). Thus the Thirty Years' War was both an international war among Sweden, France, and the Hapsburg Empire and a series of domestic conflicts among Protestant and Catholic parties. The wars of the French Revolution and the Napoleonic period that pitted France against the rest of Europe triggered political upheavals of class and national revolutions throughout Europe. World Wars I and II represented not only the decay of the European international political order but also an onslaught against political liberalism and economic laissez-faire. The triumph of American power in these wars meant not only American governance of the system but also reestablishment of a liberal world order.

NOTES

1 This cause of expansion is frequently explained by the "turbulent-frontier" thesis. A classic example was Britain's steady and incremental conquest of India in order to eliminate threatening political disturbances on the frontier of the empire. Two recent examples are the American invasion of Cambodia during the Vietnam War and the Soviet invasion of Afghanistan.

2 As Raymond Aron argued (1974), defeat in Vietnam may, in the long run, save the United States from the corrupting and ultimately weakening vice of overexpansion of commitments.

REFERENCES

Aron, Raymond. "War and Industrial Society." In *War—Studies from Psychology, Sociology, Anthropology*, edited by Leon Bramson and George W. Goethals, pp. 351–394. New York: Basic Books, 1964.

———. *Peace and War—A Theory of International Relations*. Garden City, N.Y.: Doubleday, 1966.

———. *The Imperial Republic*. Englewood Cliffs, N.J.: Prentice-Hall, 1974.

Beer, Francis A. *Peace Against War—The Ecology of International Violence.* San Francisco: W. H. Freeman, 1981.

Carr, Edward Hallett, *The Twenty Years' Crisis, 1919–1939. An Introduction to the Study of International Relations.* London: Macmillan, 1951.

Cipolla, Carlo M. *Guns, Sails and Empires—Technological Innovation and the Early Phases of European Expansion 1400–1700.* New York: Minerva Press, 1965.

———. ed. *The Economic Decline of Empires.* London: Methuen, 1970.

Clark, George. *War and Society in the Seventeenth Century.* Cambridge University Press, 1958.

Clough, Shepard B. *The Rise and Fall of Civilization.* New York: Columbia University Press, 1970.

Downs, Anthony. *An Economic Theory of Democracy.* New York: Harper & Row, 1957.

———. *Inside Bureaucracy.* Boston: Little, Brown, 1967.

Elvin, Mark. *The Pattern of the Chinese Past.* Stanford: Stanford University Press, 1973.

Grant, Michael. *The Climax of Rome, the Final Achievements of the Ancient World.* London: Weidenfeld and Nicolson, 1968.

Halévy, Elie. *The Era of Tyrannies.* New York: Doubleday, 1965.

Hawtrey, Ralph G. *Economic Aspects of Sovereignty.* London: Longmans, Green, 1952.

Hoffmann, Stanley, ed. *Contemporary Theory in International Relations.* Englewood Cliffs, N.J.: Prentice-Hall, 1960.

———. "International Systems and International Law." In *The State of War—Essays on the Theory and Practice of International Politics*, edited by Stanley Hoffmann, pp. 88–122. New York: Praeger, 1965.

———. "Choices." *Foreign Policy* 12 (1973): 3–42.

———. "An American Social Science: International Relations." *Daedalus* 1 (1977): 41–60.

———. *Primacy or World Order—American Foreign Policy since the Cold War.* New York: McGraw-Hill, 1978.

Lane, Frederic C. "The Economic Meaning of War and Protection." *Journal of Social Philosophy and Jurisprudence* 7 (1942): 254–70.

———. "Economic Consequences of Organized Violence." *The Journal of Economic History* 18 (1958): 401–17.

———. *Venice and History: The Collected Papers of Frederic C. Lane.* Baltimore: Johns Hopkins University Press, 1966.

———. *Venice—A Maritime Republic.* Baltimore: Johns Hopkins University Press, 1973.

Lewis, W. Arthur. *The Theory of Economic Growth.* New York: Harper & Row, 1970.

———. *Growth and Fluctuations 1870–1913.* London: George Allen and Unwin, 1978.

Lippmann, Walter. *U.S. Foreign Policy: Shield of the Republic.* Boston: Little, Brown, 1943.

Luttwak, Edward. *The Grand Strategy of the Roman Empire—From the First Century A.D. to the Third.* Baltimore: Johns Hopkins University Press, 1976.

Mensch, Gerhard. *Stalemate in Technology—Innovations Overcome the Depression.* Cambridge, Mass.: Ballinger Publishing, 1979.

Modelski, George. "Agraria and Industria: Two Models of the International System." *World Politics* 14 (1961): 118–43.

———. *Principles of World Politics.* New York: Free Press, 1972.

———. "The Long Cycle of Global Politics and the Nation-State." *Comparative Studies in Society and History* 20 (1978): 214–35.

Mowat, R. B. *A History of European Diplomacy 1451–1789.* New York: Longmans, Green, 1928.

Perkins, Bradford. *The Great Rapprochement—England and the United States, 1895–1914*. New York: Atheneum, 1968.

Rader, Trout. *The Economics of Feudalism*. New York: Gordon & Breach, 1971.

Riker, William H. *The Theory of Political Coalitions*. New Haven: Yale University Press, 1962.

Rostow, W. W. *Politics and the Stages of Growth*. Cambridge University Press, 1971.

———. *Getting from Here to There*. New York: McGraw-Hill, 1978.

———. *Why the Poor Get Richer and the Rich Slow Down: Essays in the Marshallian Long Period*. Austin: University of Texas Press, 1980.

Seeley, John. *The Expansion of England—Two Courses of Lectures*. Boston: Little, Brown, 1905.

Thucydides. *The Peloponnesian War*. New York: Modern Library, 1951.

Tolstoy, L. N. *War and Peace*. 2 vols. Baltimore: Penguin Books, 1961.

Toynbee, Arnold J. *Survey of International Affairs 1930*. London: Oxford University Press, 1931.

———. *A Study of History*. Vols. 3 and 12. London: Oxford University Press, 1961.

von Ranke, Leopold. "The Great Powers." In *Leopold Ranke—The Formative Years*, edited by Theodore H. von Laue, pp. 181–218. Princeton University Press, 1950.

Walbank, F. W. *The Awful Revolution: The Decline of the Roman Empire in the West*. Liverpool: Liverpool University Press, 1969.

Wright, Quincy. *A Study of War*. 2 vols. Chicago: University of Chicago Press, 1942.

Reading 2.7

Power, Culprits, and Arms   GEOFFREY BLAINEY

THE ABACUS OF POWER

I

The Prussian soldier, Carl von Clausewitz, died of cholera in 1831, while leading an army against Polish rebels. He left behind sealed packets containing manuscripts which his widow published in the following year. The massive dishevelled books, entitled *On War*, could have been called *On War and Peace*, for Clausewitz implied that war and peace had much in common. In his opinion the leisurely siege of the eighteenth century was not much more than a forceful diplomatic note; that kind of war was 'only diplomacy somewhat intensified.'[1] In essence diplomatic despatches breathed deference, but their courtesy was less effective than the silent threats which underwrote them. The threat might not be mentioned, but it was understood. The blunt words of Frederick the Great had similarly summed up the way in which military power influenced diplomacy: 'Diplomacy without armaments is like music without instruments.'[2]

Clausewitz had fought for Prussia in many campaigns against the French but he had more influence on wars in which he did not fight. He is said to have been the talisman of the German general who planned the invasions of France in 1870 and 1914. His books were translated into French just before the Crimean War and into English just after the Franco-Prussian War, and in military academies in many lands the name of this man who had won no great battles became more famous than most of those names inseparably linked with victorious battles. His writings however had less influence outside military circles. He was seen as a ruthless analyst who believed that war should sometimes be 'waged with the whole might of national power.'[3] His views therefore seemed tainted to most civilians; he appeared to be the sinister propagandist of militarism. Those who studied a war's causes, as distinct from its course, ignored him. And yet one of the most dangerous fallacies in the study of war is the belief that the causes of a war and the events of a war belong to separate compartments and reflect completely different principles. This fallacy, translated into medicine, would require the causes and course of an illness to be diagnosed on quite different principles.

Clausewitz's tumble of words was overwhelmingly on warfare, and the index of the three English volumes of his work points to only one sentence on peace. Nevertheless some of his views on peace can be inferred from lonely sentences. He believed that a clear ladder of international power tended to promote peace. 'A conqueror is always a lover of peace,' he wrote.[4] His statement at first sight seems preposterous, but at second sight it commands respect.[5]

II

Power is the crux of many explanations of war and peace, but its effects are not agreed upon. Most observers argue that a nation which is too powerful endangers the peace. A few hint, like Clausewitz, that a dominant nation can preserve the peace simply by its ability to keep inferior nations in order. There must be an answer to the disagreement. The last three centuries are studded with examples of how nations behaved in the face of every extremity of military and economic power.

That a lopsided balance of power will promote war is probably the most popular theory of international relations. It has the merit that it can be turned upside down to serve as an explanation of peace. It is also attractive because it can be applied to wars of many centuries, from the Carthaginian wars to the Second World War. The very phrase, 'balance of power,' has the soothing sound of the panacea: it resembles the balance of nature and the balance of trade and other respectable concepts. It therefore suggests that an even balance of power is somehow desirable. The word 'balance,' unfortunately, is confusing. Whereas at one time it usually signified a set of weighing scales—in short it formerly signified either equality or inequality—it now usually signifies equality and equilibrium. In modern language the assertion that 'Germany had a favourable balance of power' is not completely clear. It is rather like a teacher who, finding no equality of opportunity in a school, proceeded to denounce the 'unfavourable equality of opportunity.' The verbal confusion may be partly responsible for the million vague and unpersuasive words which have been written around the concept of the balance of power.

The advantages of an even balance of power in Europe have been stressed by scores of historians and specialists in strategy. The grand old theory of international relations, it is still respected though no longer so venerated. According to Hedley Bull, who was a director of a research unit on arms control in the British foreign office before becoming professor of international relations at the Australian National University, 'The alternative to a stable balance of military power is a preponderance of power, which is very much more dangerous.'[6] Likewise, Alastair Buchan, director of London's Institute for Strategic Studies, suggested in his excellent book *War in Modern Society*: 'certainly we know from our experience of the 1930s that the lack of such a balance creates a clear temptation to aggression.'[7] Many writers of history have culled a similar lesson from past wars.

Most believers in the balance of power think that a world of many powerful states tends to be more peaceful. There an aggressive state can be counterbalanced by a combination of other strong states. Quincy Wright, in his massive book, *A Study of War*, suggested with some reservations that 'the probability of war will decrease in proportion as the number of states in the system increases.'[8] Arnold Toynbee,[9] observing that the world contained eight major powers on the eve of the First World War and only two—the United States and the Soviet Union—at the close of the Second World War, thought the decline was ominous. A chair with only two legs, he argued, had less balance. As the years passed, and the two great powers avoided major war, some specialists on international affairs argued that a balance of terror had replaced the balance of power. In the nuclear age, they argued, two great powers were preferable to eight. The danger of a crisis that slipped from control was diminished if two powers dominated the world.[10] Nevertheless even those who preferred to see two powers dominant in the nuclear age still believed, for the most part, that in the pre-nuclear era a world of many strong powers was safer.[11]

To my knowledge no historian or political scientist produced evidence to confirm that a power system of seven strong states was more conducive to peace than a system of two strong states. The idea relies much on analogies. Sometimes it resembles the kind of argument which old men invoked in European cities when the two-wheeled bicycle began to supersede the tricycle. At other times it resembles a belief in the virtues of free competition within an economic system. It parallels the idea that in business many strong competitors will so function that none can win a preponderance of power; if one seems likely to become predominant, others will temporarily combine to subdue him. It is possibly significant that this doctrine of flexible competition in economic affairs was brilliantly systematised at the time when a similar doctrine was refined in international affairs. While Adam Smith praised the virtues of the free market in economic affairs, the Swiss jurist Emerich de Vattel praised it in international affairs. In one sense both theories were reactions against a Europe in which powerful monarchs hampered economic life with meddlesome regulations and disturbed political life with frequent wars.

It is axiomatic that a world possessing seven nations of comparable strength, each of which values its independence, will be a substantial safeguard against the rise of one world-dominating power. Even two nations of comparable strength will be a useful safeguard. When all this has been said we possess not an axiom for peace but an axiom for national independence. And that in fact was the main virtue of a balance of power in the eyes of those who originally practiced it. It was not primarily a formula for peace: it was a formula for national independence. Edward Gulick,[12] Massachusetts historian, was adamant that its clearest theorists and practitioners—the Metternichs and Castlereaghs—'all thought of war as an instrument to preserve or restore a balance of power.' In essence a balance of power was simply a formula designed to prevent the rise of a nation to world dominance. It merely masqueraded as a formula for peace.

III

The idea that an even distribution of power promotes peace has gained strength partly because it has never been accompanied by tangible evidence. Like a ghost it has not been captured and examined for pallor and pulse-beat. And yet there is a point of time when the ghost can be captured. The actual distribution of power can be measured at the end of the war.

The military power of rival European alliances was most imbalanced, was distributed most unevenly, at the end of a decisive war. And decisive wars tended to lead to longer periods of international peace. Indecisive wars, in contrast, tended to produce shorter periods of peace. Thus the eighteenth century was characterised by inconclusive wars and by short periods of peace. During the long wars one alliance had great difficulty in defeating the other. Many of the wars ended in virtual deadlock: military power obviously was evenly balanced. Such wars tended to lead to short periods of peace. The War of the Polish Succession—basically an ineffectual war between France and—Austria—was followed within five years by the War of the Austrian Succession. That war after eight years was so inconclusive on most fronts that the peace treaty signed in 1748 mainly affirmed the status quo. That ineffectual war was followed only eight years later by another general war, the Seven Years War, which ended with Britain the clear victor in the war at sea and beyond the seas, though on European soil the war was a stalemate. But even the Anglo-French peace which followed the Treaty of Paris in 1763 was not long; it ended after fifteen years. It ended when the revolt of the American colonies against Britain removed Britain's preponderance of power over France.

The French Revolutionary Wars which, beginning in 1792, raged across Europe and over the sea for a decade were more decisive than any major war for more than a century. They ended with France dominant on the continent and with England dominant at sea and in America and the East. They thus failed to solve the crucial question: was England or France the stronger power? The Peace of Amiens, which England and France signed in 1802, lasted little more than a year. So began the Napoleonic Wars which at last produced undisputed victors.

This is not to suggest that a general war which ended in decisive victory was the sole cause of a long period of peace. A decisive general war did not always lead to a long period of peace. This survey of the major wars of the period 1700 to 1815 does suggest however that the traditional theory which equates an even balance of power with peace should be reversed. Instead a clear preponderance of power tended to promote peace.

Of the general wars fought in Europe in the last three centuries those with the most decisive outcome were the Napoleonic (1815), Franco-Prussian (1871), First World War (1918), and Second World War (1945). The last days of those wars and the early years of the following periods of peace marked the height of the imbalance of power in Europe. At the end of those wars the scales of power were so tilted against the losers that Napoleon Bonaparte was sent as a captive to an island in the South Atlantic, Napoleon III was captured and permitted to live in exile in England, Kaiser Wilhelm II went into exile in Holland and Adolf Hitler committed suicide. Years after the end of those wars, the scales of power were still strongly tilted against the losers. And yet those years of extreme—imbalance marked the first stages of perhaps the most pronounced periods of peace known to Europe in the last three or more centuries.

Exponents of the virtues of an even distribution of military power have concentrated entirely on the outbreak of war. They have ignored however the conditions surrounding the outbreak of peace. By ignoring the outbreak of peace they seem to have ignored the very period when the distribution of military power between warring nations can be accurately measured. For warfare is the one convincing way of measuring the distribution of power. The end of a war produces a neat ledger of power which has been duly audited and signed. According to that ledger an agreed preponderance of power tends to foster peace. In contrast the exponents of the orthodox theory examine closely the prelude to a war, but that is a period when power is muffled and much more difficult to measure. It is a period characterised by conflicting estimates of which nation or alliance is the most powerful. Indeed one can almost suggest that war is usually the outcome of a diplomatic crisis which cannot be solved because both sides have conflicting estimates of their bargaining power.

The link between a diplomatic crisis and the outbreak of war seems central to the understanding of war. That link however seems to be misunderstood. Thus many historians, in explaining the outbreak of war, argue that 'the breakdown in diplomacy led to war.' This explanation is rather like the argument that the end of winter led to spring: it is a description masquerading as an explanation. In fact that main influence which led to the breakdown of diplomacy—a contradictory sense of bargaining power—also prompted the nations to fight. At the end of a war the situation was reversed. Although I have not come across the parallel statement—'so the breakdown of war led to diplomacy'—it can be explained in a similar way. In essence the very factor which made the enemies reluctant to continue fighting also persuaded them to negotiate. That factor was their agreement about their relative bargaining position.

It is not the actual distribution or balance of power which is vital: it is rather the way in which national leaders *think* that power is distributed. In contrast orthodox theory assumes that the power of nations can be measured with some objectivity. It assumes that, in the pre-nuclear era, a statesman's knowledge of the balance of international power rested mainly on an 'objective comparison of military capabilities.'[13] I find it difficult however to accept the idea that power could ever be measured with such objectivity. The clear exception was at the end of wars—the points of time which theorists ignore. Indeed, it is the problem of accurately measuring the relative power of nations which goes far to explain why wars occur. War is a dispute about the measurement of power. War marks the choice of a new set of weights and measures.

IV

In peace time the relations between two diplomats are like relations between two merchants. While the merchants trade in copper or transistors, the diplomats' transactions involve boundaries, spheres of influence, commercial concessions and a variety of other issues which they have in common. A foreign minister or diplomat is a merchant who bargains on behalf of his country. He is both buyer and seller, though he buys and sells privileges and obligations rather than commodities. The treaties he signs are simply more courteous versions of commercial contracts.

The difficulty in diplomacy, as in commerce, is to find an acceptable price for the transaction. Just as the price of merchandise such as copper roughly represents the point where the supply of copper balances the demand for it, the price of a transaction in diplomacy roughly marks the point at which one nation's willingness to pay matches the price demanded by the other. The diplomatic market however is not as sophisticated as the mercantile market. Political currency is not so easily measured as economic currency. Buying and selling in the diplomatic market is much closer to barter, and so resembles an ancient bazaar in which the traders have no accepted medium of exchange. In diplomacy each nation has the rough equivalent of a selling price—a price which it accepts when it sells a concession—and the equivalent of a buying price. Sometimes these prices are so far apart that a transaction vital to both nations cannot be completed peacefully; they cannot agree on the price of the transaction. The history of diplomacy is full of such crises. The ministers and diplomats of Russia and Japan could not agree in 1904, on the eve of the Russo-Japanese War; the Germans could not find acceptable terms with British and French ministers on the eve of the Second World War.

A diplomatic crisis is like a crisis in international payments; like a crisis in the English pound or the French franc. In a diplomatic crisis the currency of one nation or alliance is out of alignment with that of the others. These currencies are simply the estimates which each nation nourishes about its relative bargaining power. These estimates are not easy for an outsider to assess or to measure; and yet these estimates exist clearly in the minds of the ministers and diplomats who bargain.

For a crisis in international payments there are ultimate solutions which all nations recognise. If the English pound is the object of the crisis, and if its value is endangered because England is importing too much, the English government usually has to admit that it is living beyond its present means. As a remedy it may try to discourage imports and encourage exports. It may even have to declare that the value of the English pound is too high in relation to the French franc, the German mark and all other currencies, and accordingly it may fix the pound at a lower rate. Whichever solution it follows is not pleasant for the national pride and the people's purse. Fortunately there is less shame and humiliation for a nation which has to confess that its monetary currency is overvalued than for a country which has to confess that its diplomatic currency is overvalued. It is almost as if the detailed statistics which record the currency crisis make it seem anonymous and unemotional. In contrast a diplomatic crisis is personal and emotional. The opponent is not a sheet of statistics representing the sum of payments to and from all nations: the opponent is an armed nation to which aggressive intentions can be attributed and towards whom hatred can be felt.

A nation facing a payments crisis can *measure* the extent to which it is living beyond its means. As the months pass by, moreover, it can measure whether its remedies have been effective, for the statistics of its balance of payments are an accurate guide to the approach of a crisis and the passing of crisis. On the other hand a deficit in international power is not so easy to detect. A nation with an increasing deficit in international power may not even recognise its weaknesses. A nation may so mistake its bargaining power that it may make the ultimate appeal to war, and then learn through defeat in warfare to accept a humbler assessment of its bargaining position.

The death-watch wars of the eighteenth century exemplified such crises. A kingdom which was temporarily weakened by the accession of a new ruler or by the outbreak of civil unrest refused to believe that it was weaker. It usually behaved as if its bargaining position were unaltered. But its position, in the eyes of rival nations, was often drastically weaker. Negotiations were therefore frustrated because each nation demanded far more than the other was prepared to yield. Likewise the appeal to war was favoured because each side believed that it would win.

In diplomacy some nations for a longer period can live far beyond their means: to live beyond their means is to concede much less than they would have to concede if the issue was resolved by force. A government may be unyielding in negotiations because it predicts that its adversary does not want war. It may be unyielding because it has an inflated idea of its own military power. Or it may be unyielding because to yield to an enemy may weaken its standing and grip within its own land. Whereas an endangered nation facing a currency crisis cannot escape some punishment, in a diplomatic crisis it can completely escape punishment so long as the rival nation or alliance does not insist on war. Thus diplomacy may become more unrealistic, crises may become more frequent, and ultimately the tension and confusion may end in war. . . .

War itself provides the most reliable and most objective test of which nation or alliance is the most powerful. After a war which ended decisively, the warring nations agreed on their respective strength. The losers and the winners might have disagreed about the exact margin of superiority; they did agree however that decisive superiority existed. A decisive war was therefore usually followed by an orderly market in political power, or in other words peace. Indeed one vital difference between the eighteenth and nineteenth centuries was that wars tended to become more decisive. This is part of the explanation for the war-studded history of one century and the relative peacefulness of the following century. Whereas the eighteenth century more often had long and inconclusive wars followed by short periods of peace, the century after 1815 more often had short and decisive wars and long periods of peace.

Nevertheless, during both centuries, the agreement about nations' bargaining power rarely lasted as long as one generation. Even when a war had ended decisively the hierarchy of power could not last indefinitely. It was blurred by the fading of memories of the previous war, by the accession of new leaders who blamed the old leaders for the defeat, and by the legends and folklore which glossed over past defeats. It was blurred by the weakening effects of internal unrest or the strengthening effects of military reorganisation, by economic and technical change, by shifts in alliances, and by a variety of other influences. So the defeated nation regained confidence. When important issues arose, war became a possibility. The rival nations believed that each could gain more by fighting than by negotiating. Those contradictory hopes are characteristic of the outbreak of war. . . .

VII

Wars usually end when the fighting nations *agree* on their relative strength, and wars usually begin when fighting nations *disagree* on their relative strength. Agreement or disagreement is shaped by the same set of factors. Thus each factor that is a prominent cause of war can at times be a prominent cause of peace. Each factor can oscillate between war and peace, and the oscillation is most vivid in the history of nations which decided to fight because virtually everything was in their favour and decided to cease fighting because everything was pitted against them. . . .

AIMS AND ARMS

I

A culprit stands in the centre of most generalised explanations of war. While there may be dispute in naming the culprit, it is widely believed that the culprit exists.

In the eighteenth century many philosophers thought that the ambitions of absolute monarchs were the main cause of war: pull down the mighty, and wars would become rare. Another theory contended that many wars came from the Anglo-French rivalry for colonies and commerce: restrain that quest, and peace would be more easily preserved. The wars following the French Revolution fostered an idea that popular revolutions were becoming the main cause of international war. In the nineteenth century, monarchs who sought to unite their troubled country by a glorious foreign war were widely seen as culprits. At the end of that century the capitalists' chase for markets or investment outlets became a popular villain. The First World War convinced many writers that armaments races and arms salesmen had become the villains, and both world wars fostered the idea that militarist regimes were the main disturbers of the peace.

Most of these theories of war have flourished, then fallen away, only to appear again in new dress. The eighteenth-century belief that mercantilism was the main cause of war was re-clothed by the Englishman, J. A. Hobson, and the Russian exile, V. I. Lenin, in the Boer War and in the First World War; and the theme that manufacturers of armaments were the chief plotters of war was revived to explain the widening of the war in Vietnam. The resilience of this type of explanation is probably aided by the fact that it carries its own solution to war. Since it points to a particular culprit, we only have to eliminate the culprit in order to abolish war. By abolishing dictators, capitalists, militarists, manufacturers of armaments or one of the other villains, peace would be preserved. Indeed it is often the passion for the antidote—whether democracy, socialism or free trade—rather than an analysis of the illness that popularises many of these theories of war.

These theories assume that ambitions and motives are the dominant cause of wars. As war is increasingly denounced as the scarlet sin of civilisation, it is understandable that the search for the causes of war should often become a search for villains. The search is aided by the surviving records of war. So many of the documents surrounding the outbreak of every war—whether the War of Spanish Succession or the recent War of the Saigon Succession—are attempts to blame the other side. The surviving records of wars are infected with insinuations and accusations of guilt, and some of that infection is transmitted to the writings of those who, generations or centuries later, study those wars. Since so much research into war is a search for villains, and since the evidence itself is dominated by attempts to apportion blame, it is not surprising that many theories of war and explanations of individual wars are centred on the aims of 'aggressors.'

Most controversies about the causes of particular wars also hinge on the aims of nations. What did France and England hope to gain by aiding the Turks against the Russians in the Crimean War? What were the ambitions of Bismarck and Napoleon III on the eve of the Franco-Prussian War of 1870? Who deserves most blame for the outbreak of the First World War? The evergreen examination-question at schools and universities—were the main causes of a certain war political or economic or religious—reflects the strong tradition that ambitions are the key to understanding war.

The running debate on the causes of the Vietnam War is therefore in a rich tradition. Measured by the mileage of words unrolled it must be the most voluminous which any war has aroused, but it is mainly the traditional debate about ambitions and motives. The war in Vietnam is variously said to have been caused by the desire of United States' capitalists for markets and investment outlets, by the pressures of American military suppliers, by the American hostility to communism, by the crusading ambitions of Moscow and Peking, the aggressive nationalism or communism of Hanoi, the corruption or aggression of Saigon, or the headlong clash of other aims. The kernel of the debate is the assumption that pressures or ambitions are the main causes of the war.

II

The idea that war is caused simply by a clash of aims is intrinsically satisfying. It is easy to believe that historians will ultimately understand the causes of war if only they can unravel the ambitions held on the eve of a war by the relevant monarchs, prime ministers, presidents, chiefs of staff, archbishops, editors, intellectuals and cheering or silent crowds. Explanations based on ambitions however have a hidden weakness. They portray ambitions which were so strong that war was inevitable. It is almost a hallmark of such interpretations to describe ambitions—whether for prestige, ideology, markets or empire—as the fundamental causes, the basic causes, the deepseated, underlying or longterm causes. Such causes merely need the provocation of minor events to produce war. The minor events are usually referred to as the occasion for war as distinct from the causes of war. Sometimes the incidents which immediately precede the war are called the short-term causes: the assumption is that longterm causes are more powerful.

This idea of causation has a distinctive shape. Its exponents see conflict as a volcano which, seeming to slumber, is really approaching the day of terror. They see conflict as water which slowly gathers heat and at last comes to the boil. The events which happen on the eve of a war add the last few degrees of heat to the volcano or kettle. It is a linear kind of argument: the causes of war are like a graph of temperatures and the last upward movement on the graph marks the transition from peace to war. If in fact such a graph were a valid way of depicting the coming of war, one would also expect to see the temperature curve move downwards in the last days of a war. One would also expect that if, on the eve of a war, minor incidents could convert the long-term causes of conflict into war, similar incidents could activate the transition from war to peace. No such explanations however are offered for the end of a war. If one believes that the framework of an explanation of war should also be valid for an explanation of peace, the volcano or kettle theories are suspect.

For any explanation the framework is crucial. In every field of knowledge the accepted explanations depend less on the marshalling of evidence than on preconceptions of what serves as a logical framework for the evidence. The framework dominates the evidence, because it dictates what evidence should be sought or ignored. Our idea of a logical framework is often unconscious, and this elusiveness enhances its grip. One may suggest that the explanations of war which stress ambitions are resting on a persuasive but rickety framework.

The policies of a Frederick the Great, a Napoleon and a President Lincoln were clearly important in understanding wars. So too were the hopes of the inner circles of power in which they moved and the hopes of the people whom they led. Likewise the aims of all the surrounding nations—irrespective of their eagerness or reluctance to fight—were important. It is doubtful however whether a study of the aims of many wars will yield useful patterns. There is scant evidence to suggest that century after century the main aims of nations which went to war could be packaged into a simple economic, religious or political formula. There is no evidence that, over a long period, the desire for territory or markets or the desire to spread an ideology tended to dominate all other war aims. It is even difficult to argue that certain kinds of aims were dominant in one generation. Admittedly it is often said that the main 'causes'—meaning the main aims—of war were religious in the sixteenth century, dynastic or mercantile in various phases of the eighteenth century and nationalist or economic in the nineteenth century. It seems more likely, however, that those who share in a decision to wage war pursued a variety of aims which even fluctuated during the same week and certainly altered during the course of the war.

One generalisation about war aims can be offered with confidence. The aims are simply varieties of power. The vanity of nationalism, the will to spread an ideology, the protection of kinsmen in an adjacent land, the desire for more territory or commerce, the avenging of a defeat or insult, the craving for greater national strength or independence, the wish to impress or cement alliances—all these represent power in different wrappings. The conflicting aims of rival nations are always conflicts of power. Not only is power the issue at stake, but the decision to resolve that issue by peaceful or warlike methods is largely determined by assessments of relative power.

III

The explanations that stress aims are theories of rivalry and animosity and not theories of war. They help to explain increasing rivalry between nations but they do not explain why the rivalry led to war. For a serious rift between nations does not necessarily end in war. It may take other forms: the severing of diplomatic relations; the peaceful intervention of a powerful outside nation; an economic blockade; heavy spending on armaments; the imposing of tariffs; an invasion accomplished without bloodshed; the enlisting of allies; or even the relaxing of tension through a successful conference. Of course these varieties of conflict may merely postpone the coming of war but serious rivalry and animosity can exist for a century without involving warfare. France and Britain were serious rivals who experienced dangerous crises between 1815 and 1900, but the war so often feared did not eventuate.

One may suggest that this kind of interpretation is hazy about the causes of peace as well as war. Its exponents usually ignore the question of why a war came to an end. They thus ignore the event which would force them to revise their analysis of the causes of war. Consider for instance the popular but dubious belief that the main cause of the First World War was Berlin's desire to dominate Europe. Now if such an explanation is valid, what were the main causes of the peace which ensued in 1918? It would be consistent with this interpretation to reply that the crumbling of German ambitions led to peace. And why had those ambitions crumbled? Because by October 1918 Germany's military power—and morale is a vital ingredient of power—was no longer adequate. As the emphasis on aims cannot explain Germany's desire for peace in 1918, it would be surprising if the emphasis on aims could explain Germany's decision for war in 1914. Indeed Germany's aims would not have been high in 1914 if her leaders then had believed that Germany lacked adequate power. Bethmann Hollweg, chancellor of Germany at the outbreak of war, confessed later that Germany in 1914 had overvalued her strength. 'Our people', he said, 'had developed so amazingly in the last twenty years that wide circles succumbed to the temptation of overestimating our enormous forces in relation to those of the rest of the world.'[14]

One conclusion seems clear. It is dangerous to accept any explanation of war which concentrates on ambitions and ignores the means of carrying out those ambitions. A government's aims are strongly influenced by this assessment of whether it has sufficient strength to achieve these aims. Indeed the two factors interact quietly and swiftly. When Hitler won power in 1933 and had long-term hopes of reviving German greatness, his ambitions could not alone produce a forceful foreign policy. Hitler's foreign policy in 1933 was no more forceful than his means, in his judgment, permitted. His military and diplomatic weapons, in his opinion, did not at first permit a bold foreign policy. A. J. P. Taylor's *The Origins of the Second World War*, one of the most masterly books on a particular war, reveals Hitler as an alert opportunist who tempered his objectives to the available means of achieving them. When Hitler began to rearm Germany he was guided not only by ambitions but by his sense of Germany's bargaining position in Europe. He would not have rearmed if he had believed that France or Russia would forcefully prevent him from building aircraft, submarines and tanks. In the main decisions which Hitler made between 1933 and the beginning of war in 1939, his short-term objectives and his sense of Germany's bargaining position marched so neatly in step that it is impossible to tell whether his aims or his oscillating sense of Germany's strength beat the drum. Opportunity and ambition—or aims and arms—so acted upon one another that they were virtually inseparable. The interaction was not confined to Berlin; it occurred in the 1930s in London, Paris, Warsaw, Moscow, Rome, Prague and all the cities of power. . . .

NOTES

1 A siege likened to diplomacy: Clausewitz, III 97.
2 Diplomacy without armaments': Gooch, *Studies in Diplomacy*, p. 226.
3 'Waged with the whole might': Leonard, p. 25.

4 'A conqueror': Clausewitz, II 155.

5 Clausewitz on peace: On first reading Clausewitz I noticed no comment on peace. Later, realizing that he must have commented by implication, I skimmed through his work again. As his references to peace seem sparse, I cannot be sure that I have interpreted his views correctly.

6 Bull: cited in Buchan, p. 34.

7 Buchan, p. 177.

8 Wright, abridged edn., p. 122.

9 Toynbee, *A Study of History*, IX 244.

10 The preference for a bi-polar system often seems to hinge on the idea that wars are often the result of situations which go further than either nation intended.

11 Scholars' preference for a multi-polar system before 1945 and bi-polar system thereafter: G.H. Snyder in Pruitt and Snyder, p. 124.

12 Gulick, p. 36.

13 'The objective comparison of military capabilities': G.H. Snyder in Pruitt and Snyder, p. 117. According to Wright, p. 116, the term 'balance of power' implies that fluctuations in power 'can be observed and measured'.

14 'Our people,' Fischer, p. 637.

REFERENCES

Buchan, Alastair. *War in Modern Society: An Introduction* (London, 1968).

Clausewitz, Carl von. *On War*, ed. by F. N. Maude, tr. from German, 3 vols. (London, 1940).

Fischer, Fritz. *Germany's Aims in the First World War*, tr. from German (London, 1967).

Gooch, G. P. *Studies in Diplomacy and Statecraft* (London, 1942).

———. *Louis XV: The Monarchy in Decline* (London, 1956).

Gulick, E. V. *Europe's Classical Balance of Power* (New York, 1967).

Leonard, Roger A., ed. *A Short Guide to Clausewitz on War* (London, 1967).

Pruitt, Dean G. and Snyder, R. C., eds. *Theory and Research on the Causes of War* (Englewood Cliffs, N.J., 1969).

Toynbee, Arnold. *Experiences* (London, 1969).

———. *A Study of History*, 12 vols. (London, 1934–61).

Wright, Quincy. *A Study of War*, 2 vols. (Chicago, 1942).

———. *A Study of War*, abridged by Louis L. Wright (Chicago, 1965).

International Liberalism: Institutions and Cooperation

.

For much of the West, and certainly for most Americans, liberalism is the conventional wisdom about politics, both national and international. "Liberal" in the sense used here does not mean left-of-center, the colloquial meaning of the word in the United States. Rather it means the broad philosophical tradition that enshrines the values of individual political and economic liberty, the free market of ideas and enterprise—the basic values that *unite* what passes for left and right in American politics. The United States has been so fundamentally liberal a country in this general sense that most Americans take the basic principles utterly for granted, and are not even conscious of their liberalism as a distinct ideology. Debates occur only among varieties of liberalism.[1] Although they can overlap realist perspectives for some purposes, liberal ideas compete with realism as guides to foreign policy.

Realist theories sometimes dominate both popular and academic thinking about international relations, but this is most often true in periods when the world finds itself locked in conflict. Realist attitudes have never been popular in periods of optimism because they seem so fatalistic and unhopeful, and so unimpressed by the power of values, cooperative institutions, and logical alternatives to destructive competition.

In the previous section E. H. Carr presented *idealism* as the alternative to realism. Many sorts of ideals can drive people toward war or away from it: for example, religious militance (the Crusades, the Thirty Years War, Al Qaeda, Islamic State), religious pacifism (Quakers, most Buddhists), racist ideology (German Nazism), or militarist moral codes (Japanese Bushido). At the moment, however, liberalism—the idealism of the contemporary Western world—is the only globe-spanning challenge to realism. (Radical Islamism is such a transnational ideological challenger, but only in parts of the world where the religion is already rooted. It remains primarily a varied collection of insurgent movements, in control of few countries.) Many theorists also believe that liberal ideas about international life are no less grounded in reality than is realism—that liberalism is not just idealism, nor wishful thinking about the "harmony of interests," as Carr presented it, but a description of how the world can and sometimes does work as well as how it should.

Three general points distinguish liberal views of international conflict from realism or, in some respects, Marxism:

First, ideas matter. The pen is mightier than the sword, and a society's political and economic values will make it more or less prone to peace, no matter what the structure of the international balance of power may be. "Good" states—liberal republics—are likely to use force only in what they believe to be self-defense, not for the purpose of ruling or exploiting others. Societies devoted to free trade will seek profit through exchange and comparative advantage in production rather than through conquest and plunder.

Second, history is *progress*, a process of development in which the right ideas steadily drive out the wrong, not a cycle in which the fate of nations is to repeat the same follies. With allowances for exceptions and occasional backsliding, the world has been developing from primitive, parochial, short-sighted, and destructive behavior toward modern, cosmopolitan, efficient interchange. This is the conviction that animates Fukuyama's "The End of History" earlier in this volume and Kant's "Perpetual Peace" in this section.

Third, the fact that the international system is anarchic does not bar civility among nations. Under certain conditions, norms of cooperation can help keep countries from each others' throats because governments can recognize their mutual interest in avoiding conflict.[2] To realists, insecurity and the possibility of war are inherent in a system of autonomous states without an overarching authority. To liberals, anarchy may be a necessary cause of war but not a sufficient one. The proximate cause of war is usually that people who are bad, backward, or deluded decide to start it. The causes can be exposed as unnecessary, inimical to selfish material interests as well as moral ones, and thus can be overcome by the spread of liberal values and institutions.

Kant's "Perpetual Peace" is as classic a statement of some aspects of the liberal paradigm as Thucydides's *Peloponnesian War* is of the realist.[3] Kant claims that the tendency to progress is inherent in nature, and that as men and republics improve themselves they will create permanent peace. Michael W. Doyle supplements Kant's theory with empirical evidence that democratic states do not go to war with each other. True, they have fought many wars eagerly, but not against each other. If the authoritarian states that democracies tend to fight are disappearing, there should soon be fewer occasions for war. The "democratic peace" theory, which has burgeoned since Doyle revived it, has become the most influential idea to be adopted by U.S. foreign policy from academic political science. The Clinton administration proclaimed it as a warrant for enlarging the international community of democracies, and a reason that activism otherwise seen as humanitarian should be considered to serve the material interest of the United States; the administration of George W. Bush cited it as justification for liberating Iraq from the regime of Saddam Hussein; and the Obama administration honored the idea in rhetoric and projects like support for rebels against the Qaddaffi regime in Libya.

Faith in the pacifying effects of liberal practices and institutions animates the thinking of Western political leaders with a frequency that should discredit some hyper-realists' claim that domestic politics have little impact on foreign policy. This is illustrated in the speeches of British parliamentarian Richard Cobden and American President Woodrow Wilson, excerpted in this section. Both reflect the conviction that international order can be modeled on the domestic legal norms and practices of liberal societies. Keohane and Nye present the case for why modern interdependence among states reduced the utility of force in relations among them, even before the end of the Cold War.[4] John Mueller argues for the possibility that liberal values can decisively overcome age-old practices—and thus that war is not an inevitable part of the human condition—by citing the abolition of dueling and slavery as analogous epochal changes.

Liberal arguments of various sorts about the obsolescence of war, declining significance of the nation state, and growing import of cooperative supranational institutions have been popular periodically in the past. One instance was the resurgence of such ideas in the 1970s, just after the Vietnam War soured many observers on the utility of force and before the collapse of the U.S.–Soviet détente made optimism about basic changes in international relations seem premature. With the reinvigoration of the Cold War at the end of the 1970s, realism became the dominant school of thought again. Then as the end of the Cold War was celebrated and widely seen as a fundamentally new departure in world development, the liberal paradigm again became ascendant in the 1990s. September 11, 2001, shook the confidence many had in the ineluctable triumph of international liberalism and the pacifying effects of globalization. The record of the past two centuries suggests, however, that as long as Western societies remain strong and vigorous, liberalism will be a resilient and durable source of thinking about the causes of peace.

—RKB

NOTES

1 See Louis Hartz, *The Liberal Tradition in America* (New York: Harcourt, Brace, 1955). The deep roots of liberal assumptions lie behind much of the American behavior that realists criticize as legalistic and moralistic. See George F. Kennan, *American Diplomacy, 1900–1950* (Chicago: University of Chicago Press, 1951).
2 See Kenneth A. Oye, ed., *Cooperation Under Anarchy* (Princeton, N.J.: Princeton University Press, 1986) and Robert Axelrod, *The Evolution of Cooperation* (New York: Basic Books, 1984).

3 For an argument that reconciles Kant with realism see Kenneth N. Waltz, "Kant, Liberalism, and War," *American Political Science Review* 56, no. 2 (June 1962).

4 For an earlier argument in this vein see Klaus Knorr, *On the Utility of Force in the Nuclear Age* (Princeton, N.J.: Princeton University Press, 1966). Knorr later had second thoughts about how far the argument was being taken in literature of the early 1970s, and qualified his views. See Knorr, "Is International Coercion Waning or Rising?" *International Security* 1, no. 4 (Spring 1977) and "On the International Uses of Force in the Contemporary World," *Orbis* 21, no. 1 (Spring 1977).

Reading 3.1

Perpetual Peace

IMMANUEL KANT

SECTION II: CONTAINING THE DEFINITIVE ARTICLES FOR PERPETUAL PEACE AMONG STATES

The state of peace among men living side by side is not the natural state *(status naturalis)*; the natural state is one of war. This does not always mean open hostilities, but at least an unceasing threat of war. A state of peace, therefore, must be *established*, for in order to be secured against hostility it is not sufficient that hostilities simply be not committed; and, unless this security is pledged to each by his neighbor (a thing that can occur only in a civil state), each may treat his neighbor, from whom he demands this security, as an enemy.

First Definitive Article for Perpetual Peace

"The Civil Constitution of Every State Should Be Republican" The only constitution which derives from the idea of the original compact, and on which all juridical legislation of a people must be based, is the republican.

. . . The republican constitution, besides the purity of its origin (having sprung from the pure source of the concept of law), also gives a favorable prospect for the desired consequence, i.e., perpetual peace. The reason is this: if the consent of the citizens is required in order to decide that war should be declared (and in this constitution it cannot but be the case), nothing is more natural than that they would be very cautious in commencing such a poor game, decreeing for themselves all the calamities of war. Among the latter would be: having to fight, having to pay the costs of war from their own resources, having painfully to repair the devastation war leaves behind, and, to fill up the measure of evils, load themselves with a heavy national debt that would embitter peace itself and that can never be liquidated on account of constant wars in the future. But, on the other hand, in a constitution which is not republican, and under which the subjects are not citizens, a declaration of war is the easiest thing in the world to decide upon, because war does not require of the ruler, who is the proprietor and not a member of the state, the least sacrifice of the pleasures of his table, the chase, his country houses, his court functions, and the like. He may, therefore, resolve on war as on a pleasure party for the

---

Source: Immanuel Kant, "Perpetual Peace," in Immanuel Kant: On History, Lewis White Beck, *ed. and trans. Copyright © 1964. Reprinted by permission of Prentice Hall, Inc., Upper Saddle River, NJ. Originally published in 1795.*

most trivial reasons, and with perfect indifference leave the justification which decency requires to the diplomatic corps who are ready to provide it. . . .

Second Definitive Article for a Perpetual Peace

"The Law of Nations Shall Be Founded on a Federation of Free States" Peoples, as states, like individuals, may be judged to injure one another merely by their coexistence in the state of nature (i.e., while independent of external laws). Each of them may and should for the sake of its own security demand that the others enter with it into a constitution similar to the civil constitution, for under such a constitution each can be secure in his right. This would be a league of nations, but it would not have to be a state consisting of nations. That would be contradictory, since a state implies the relation of a superior (legislating) to an inferior (obeying) i.e., the people, and many nations in one state would then constitute only one nation. This contradicts the presupposition, for here we have to weigh the rights of nations against each other so far as they are distinct states and not amalgamated into one.

When we see the attachment of savages to their lawless freedom, preferring ceaseless combat to subjection to a lawful constraint which they might establish, and thus preferring senseless freedom to rational freedom, we regard it with deep contempt as barbarity, rudeness, and a brutish degradation of humanity. Accordingly, one would think that civilized people (each united in a state) would hasten all the more to escape, the sooner the better, from such a depraved condition. But, instead, each state places its majesty (for it is absurd to speak of the majesty of the people) in being subject to no external juridical restraint, and the splendor of its sovereign consists in the fact that many thousands stand at his command to sacrifice themselves for something that does not concern them and without his needing to place himself in the least danger. The chief difference between European and American savages lies in the fact that many tribes of the latter have been eaten by their enemies, while the former know how to make better use of their conquered enemies than to dine off them; they know better how to use them to increase the number of their subjects and thus the quantity of instruments for even more extensive wars.

When we consider the perverseness of human nature which is nakedly revealed in the uncontrolled relations between nations (this perverseness being veiled in the state of civil law by the constraint exercised by government), we may well be astonished that the word "law" has not yet been banished from war politics as pedantic, and that no state has yet been bold enough to advocate this point of view. Up to the present, Hugo Grotius, Pufendorf, Vattel, and many other irritating comforters have been cited in justification of war, though their code, philosophically or diplomatically formulated, has not and cannot have the least legal force, because states as such do not stand under a common external power. There is no instance on record that a state has ever been moved to desist from its purpose because of arguments backed up by the testimony of such great men. But the homage which each state pays (at least in words) to the concept of law proves that there is slumbering in man an even greater moral disposition to become master of the evil principle in himself (which he cannot disclaim) and to hope for the same from others. Otherwise the word "law" would never be pronounced by states which wish to war upon one another; it would be used only ironically, as a Gallic prince interpreted it when he said, "It is the prerogative which nature has given the stronger that the weaker should obey him."

States do not plead their cause before a tribunal; war alone is their way of bringing suit. But by war and its favorable issue in victory, right is not decided, and though by treaty of peace this particular war is brought to an end, the state of war, of always finding a new pretext to hostilities, is not terminated. Nor can this be declared wrong, considering the fact that in this state each is the judge of his own case. Notwithstanding, the obligation which men in a lawless condition have under the natural law, and which requires them to abandon the state of nature, does not quite apply to states under the law of nations, for as states they already have an internal juridical constitution and have thus outgrown compulsion from others to submit to a more extended lawful constitution according to their ideas of right. This is true in spite of the fact that reason, from its throne of supreme moral legislating authority, absolutely condemns war as a legal recourse and makes a state of peace a direct duty, even though peace cannot be established or secured except by a compact among nations.

For these reasons there must be a league of a particular kind, which can be called a league of peace *(foedus pacificum)*, and which would be distinguished from a treaty of peace *(pactum pacis)* by the fact that the latter terminates only one war, while the former seeks to make an end of all wars forever. This league does not tend to any dominion over the power of the state but only to the maintenance and security of the freedom of the state itself and of other states in league with it, without there being any need for them to submit to civil laws and their compulsion, as men in a state of nature must submit.

The practicability (objective reality) of this idea of federation, which should gradually spread to all states and thus lead to perpetual peace, can be proved. For if fortune directs that a powerful and enlightened people can make itself a republic, which by its nature must be inclined to perpetual peace, this gives a fulcrum to the federation with other states so that they may adhere to it and thus secure freedom under the idea of the law of nations. By more and more such associations, the federation may be gradually extended.

We may readily conceive that a people should say, "There ought to be no war among us, for we want to make ourselves into a state; that is, we want to establish a supreme legislative, executive, and judiciary power which will reconcile our differences peaceably." But when this state says, "There ought to be no war between myself and other states, even though I acknowledge no supreme legislative power by which our rights are mutually guaranteed," it is not at all clear on what I can base my confidence in my own rights unless it is the free federation, the surrogate of the civil social order, which reason necessarily associates with the concept of the law of nations—assuming that something is really meant by the latter.

The concept of a law of nations as a right to make war does not really mean anything, because it is then a law of deciding what is right by unilateral maxims through force and not by universally valid public laws which restrict the freedom of each one. The only conceivable meaning of such a law of nations might be that it serves men right who are so inclined that they should destroy each other and thus find perpetual peace in the vast grave that swallows both the atrocities and their perpetrators. For states in their relation to each other, there cannot be any reasonable way out of the lawless condition which entails only war except that they, like individual men, should give up their savage (lawless) freedom, adjust themselves to the constraints of public law, and thus establish a continuously growing state consisting of various nations *(civitas gentium)*, which will ultimately include all the nations of the world. But under the idea of the law of nations they do not wish this, and reject in practice what is correct in theory. If all is not to be lost, there can be, then, in place of the positive idea of a world republic, only the negative surrogate of an alliance which averts war, endures, spreads, and holds back the stream of those hostile passions which fear the law though such an alliance is in constant peril of their breaking loose again. *Furor impius intus . . . fremit horridus ore cruento* (Virgil). . . .

First Supplement: Of the Guarantee for Perpetual Peace

The guarantee of perpetual peace is nothing less than that great artist, nature *(natura daedala rerum)*. In her mechanical course we see that her aim is to produce a harmony among men, against their will and indeed through their discord. As a necessity working according to laws we do not know, we call it destiny. But considering its design in world history, we call it "providence," inasmuch as we discern in it the profound wisdom of a higher cause which predetermines the course of nature and directs it to the objective final end of the human race.

. . . Before we more narrowly define the guarantee which nature gives, it is necessary to examine the situation in which she has placed her actors on her vast stage, a situation which finally assures peace among them. Then we shall see how she accomplishes the latter. Her preparatory arrangements are:

1. In every region of the world she has made it possible for men to live.
2. By war she has driven them even into the most inhospitable regions in order to populate them.
3. By the same means, she has forced them into more or less lawful relations with each other. . . .

The first instrument of war among the animals which man learned to tame and to domesticate was the horse (for the elephant belongs to later times, to the luxury of already established states). The art of cultivating certain types of plants (grain) whose original characteristics we do not know, and the increase and improvement of fruits by transplantation and grafting (in Europe perhaps only the crab apple and the wild pear), could arise only under conditions prevailing in already established states where property was secure. Before this could take place, it was necessary that men who had first subsisted in anarchic freedom by hunting, fishing, and sheepherding should have been forced into an agricultural life. Then salt and iron were discovered. These were perhaps the first articles of commerce for the various peoples and were sought far and wide; in this way a peaceful traffic among nations was established, and thus understanding, conventions, and peaceable relations were established among the most distant peoples.

As nature saw to it that men *could* live everywhere in the world, she also despotically willed that they *should* do so, even against their inclination and without this *ought* being based on a concept of duty to which they were bound by a moral law. She chose war as the means to this end. So we see peoples whose common language shows that they have a common origin. For instance, the Samoyeds on the Arctic Ocean and a people with a similar language a thousand miles away in the Altaian Mountains are separated by a Mongolian people adept at horsemanship and hence at war; the latter drove the former into the most inhospitable arctic regions where they certainly would not have spread of their own accord. Again, it is the same with the Finns who in the most northerly part of Europe are called Lapps; Goths and Sarmatians have separated them from the Hungarians to whom they are related in language. What can have driven the Eskimos, a race entirely distinct from all others in America and perhaps descended from primeval European adventurers, so far into the North, or the Pescherais as far south as Tierra del Fuego, if it were not war which nature uses to populate the whole earth? War itself requires no special motive but appears to be engrafted on human nature; it passes even for something noble, to which the love of glory impels men quite apart from any selfish urges. Thus among the American savages, just as much as among those of Europe during the age of chivalry, military valor is held to be of great worth in itself, not only during war (which is natural) but in order that there should be war. Often war is waged only in order to show valor; thus an inner dignity is ascribed to war itself, and even some philosophers have praised it as an ennoblement of humanity, forgetting the pronouncement of the Greek who said, "War is an evil inasmuch as it produces more wicked men than it takes away." So much for the measures nature takes to lead the human race, considered as a class of animals, to her own end.

Now we come to the question concerning that which is most essential in the design of perpetual peace: What has nature done with regard to this end which man's own reason makes his duty? That is, what has nature done to favor man's moral purpose, and how has she guaranteed (by compulsion but without prejudice to his freedom) that he shall do that which he ought to but does not do under the laws of freedom? This question refers to all three phases of public law, namely, civil law, the law of nations, and the law of citizenship. If I say of nature that she wills that this or that occur, I do not mean that she imposes a duty on us to do it, for this can be done only by free practical reason; rather I mean that she herself does it, whether we will or not (*fata volentem ducunt, nolentem trahunt*).

(1) Even if a people were not forced by internal discord to submit to public laws, war would compel them to do so, for we have already seen that nature has placed each people near another which presses upon it, and against this it must form itself into a state in order to defend itself. Now the republican constitution is the only one entirely fitting to the rights of man. But it is the most difficult to establish and even harder to preserve, so that many say a republic would have to be a nation of angels, because men with their selfish inclinations are not capable of a constitution of such sublime form. But precisely with these inclinations nature comes to the aid of the general will established on reason, which is revered even though impotent in practice. Thus it is only a question of a good organization of the state (which does lie in man's power), whereby the powers of each selfish inclination are so arranged in opposition that one moderates or destroys the ruinous effect of the other. The consequence for reason is the same as if none of them existed, and man is forced to be a good citizen even if not a morally good person.

The problem of organizing a state, however hard it may seem, can be solved even for a race of devils, if only they are intelligent. The problem is: "Given a multitude of rational beings requiring universal laws for their preservation, but each of whom is secretly inclined to exempt himself from them, to establish a constitution in such a way that, although their private intentions conflict, they check each other, with the result that their public conduct is the same as if they had no such intentions."

A problem like this must be capable of solution; it does not require that we know how to attain the moral improvement of men but only that we should know the mechanism of nature in order to use it on men, organizing the conflict of the hostile intentions present in a people in such a way that they must compel themselves to submit to coercive laws. Thus a state of peace is established in which laws have force. We can see, even in actual states, which are far from perfectly organized, that in their foreign relations they approach that which the idea of right prescribes. This is so in spite of the fact that the intrinsic element of morality is certainly not the cause of it. (A good constitution is not to be expected from morality, but, conversely, a good moral condition of a people is to be expected only under a good constitution.) Instead of genuine morality, the mechanism of nature brings it to pass through selfish inclinations, which naturally conflict outwardly but which can be used by reason as a means for its own end, the sovereignty of law, and, as concerns the state, for promoting and securing internal and external peace.

This, then, is the truth of the matter: Nature inexorably wills that the right should finally triumph. What we neglect to do comes about by itself, though with great inconveniences to us. "If you bend the reed too much, you break it; and he who attempts too much attempts nothing" (Bouterwek).

(2) The idea of international law presupposes the separate existence of many independent but neighboring states. Although this condition is itself a state of war (unless a federative union prevents the outbreak of hostilities), this is rationally preferable to the amalgamation of states under one superior power, as this would end in one universal monarchy, and laws always lose in vigor what government gains in extent; hence a soulless despotism falls into anarchy after stifling the seeds of the good. Nevertheless, every state, or its ruler, desires to establish lasting peace in this way, aspiring if possible to rule the whole world. But nature wills otherwise. She employs two means to separate peoples and to prevent them from mixing: differences of language and of religion. These differences involve a tendency to mutual hatred and pretexts for war, but the progress of civilization and men's gradual approach to greater harmony in their principles finally leads to peaceful agreement. This is not like that peace which despotism (in the burial ground of freedom) produces through a weakening of all powers; it is, on the contrary, produced and maintained by their equilibrium in liveliest competition.

(3) Just as nature wisely separates nations, which the will of every state, sanctioned by the principles of international law, would gladly unite by artifice or force, nations which could not have secured themselves against violence and war by means of the law of world citizenship unite because of mutual interest. The spirit of commerce, which is incompatible with war, sooner or later gains the upper hand in every state. As the power of money is perhaps the most dependable of all the powers (means) included under the state power, states see themselves forced, without any moral urge, to promote honorable peace and by mediation to prevent war wherever it threatens to break out. They do so exactly as if they stood in perpetual alliances, for great offensive alliances are in the nature of the case rare and even less often successful.

In this manner nature guarantees perpetual peace by the mechanism of human passions. Certainly she does not do so with sufficient certainty for us to predict the future in any theoretical sense, but adequately from a practical point of view, making it our duty to work toward this end, which is not just a chimerical one.

Reading 3.2

Peace Through Arbitration   RICHARD COBDEN

. . . I assume that every one in this House would only sanction war, in case it was imperatively demanded on our part, in defence of our honour, or our just interest. I take it that every one here would repudiate war, unless it were called for by such motives. I assume, moreover, that there is not a man in this House who would not repudiate war, if those objects—the just interests and honour of the country—could be preserved by any other means. My object is to see if we cannot devise some better method than war for attaining those ends; and my plan is, simply and solely, that we should resort to that mode of settling disputes in communities, which individuals resort to in private life. I only want you to go one step farther, to carry out in another instance the principle which you recognize in other cases—that the intercourse between communities is nothing more than the intercourse of individuals in the aggregate. I want to know why there may not be an agreement between this country and France, or between this country and America, by which the nations should respectively bind themselves, in case of any misunderstanding arising which could not be settled by mutual representation or diplomacy, to refer the dispute to the decision of arbitrators. . . .

I should prefer to see these disputes referred to individuals, whether designated commissioners, or plenipotentiaries, or arbitrators, appointed from one country to meet men appointed from another country, to inquire into the matter and decide upon it; or, if they cannot do so, to have the power of calling in an umpire, as is done in all arbitrations. I propose that these individuals should have absolute power to dispose of the question submitted to them.

I want to show that I am practical on this occasion, and, therefore, I will cite some cases in which this method of arranging difficulties has already been resorted to. In 1794 we had a Treaty with America, for the settlement of certain British claims on the American Government. Those claims were referred to four commissioners, two appointed on each side, with the proviso that they should elect unanimously, an arbitrator; in case they should not agree in the choice of an arbitrator, it was provided that the representatives of each country should put the names of certain arbitrators into an urn, one to be drawn out by lot; and this arbitrator and the four commissioners decided by a majority all the cases brought before them. Again, in the Treaty of 1814 with the United States, provision was made for settling most important matters, precisely in the

Source: *Speech in the House of Commons, June 12, 1849, in John Bright and James E. Thorold Rogers, eds.,* Speeches on Questions of Public Policy *by Richard Cobden, M. P., Vol. II (London: Macmillan and Co., 1870).*

way I now propose. Provision was made for settling the boundary between the United States and Canada, for some thousands of miles; also for defining the right to certain islands lying on the coast; and for settling the boundary between Maine and New Brunswick. The plan was this: each country named a commissioner; the commissioners were to endeavour to agree on these disputed points; and the matters on which they could not agree were referred to some neutral state. All the matters referred to them—and most important they were—were arranged by mutual conference and mutual concessions, except the question of the Maine boundary, which was accordingly referred to the King of the Netherlands. Afterwards, exception was taken to his decision by the United States; the matter remained open till the time of Lord Ashburton's mission; and it was finally settled by him. But in no case has any such reference ever been followed by war. In 1818 there was a Convention with America, for settling the claims made by that country for captured negroes during the war. It was agreed to refer that matter to the Emperor of Russia; and he decided in favour of the principle of compensation. He was then appealed to by both the Governments to define a mode by which this compensation should be adjudged; and his plan was this: he said, Let each party name a commissioner and an arbitrator; let the commissioners meet, and, if they can agree, well and good; if not, let the names of the arbitrators be put into an urn, and one drawn out by lot; and that arbitrator and the two commissioners shall decide the question by a majority. This method was adopted, and compensation to the extent of 1,200,000 dollars was given, without any difficulty. Hence, it appears that what I propose is no novelty, no innovation; it has been practised, and practised with success; I only want you to carry the principle a little farther, and resort to it, in anticipation, as a mode of arranging all quarrels.

For this reason, I propose an address to the Crown, praying that Her Majesty will instruct her Foreign Secretary to propose to foreign Powers to enter into treaties, providing that, in case of any future misunderstanding, which cannot be settled by amicable negotiation, an arbitration, such as I have described, shall be resorted to. There is no difficulty in fixing the means of arbitration, and providing the details; for arbitration is so much used in private life, and is, indeed, made parts of so many statutes and Acts of Parliament, that there is no difficulty whatever in carrying out the plan, provided you are agreed as to the policy of doing so. Now, I shall be met with this objection—I have heard it already—and I know there are Members of this House who purpose to vote against the motion on this ground: they say, 'What is the use of a treaty of this sort, between France and England, for instance; the parties would not observe the treaty; it would be a piece of waste paper; they would go to war, as before, in spite of any treaty.' It would be a sufficient answer to this objection to say, 'What is the use of any treaty? What is the use of the Foreign Office? What is the use of your diplomacy?' You might shut up the one and cashier the other. I maintain, that a treaty binding two countries to refer their disputes to arbitration, is just as likely to be observed as any other treaty. Nay, I question very much whether it is not more likely to be observed; because, I think there is no object which other countries will be less likely to seek than that of having a war with a country so powerful as England. Therefore, if any provision were made by which you might honourably avoid a war, that provision would be as gladly sought by your opponents as by yourselves. But I deny that, as a rule, treaties are violated; as a rule, they are respected and observed. I do not find that wars, generally, arise out of the violation of any specific treaty—they more commonly arise out of accidental collisions; and, as a rule, treaties are observed by powerful States against the weak, just as well as by weak States against the powerful. I, therefore, see no difficulty specially applying to a treaty of this kind, greater than exists with other treaties. There would be this advantage, at all events, in having a treaty binding another country to refer all disputes to arbitration. If that country did not fulfil its engagement, it would enter into war with the brand of infamy stamped upon its banners. It could not proclaim to the world that it was engaged in a just and necessary war. On the contrary, all the world would point to that nation as violating a treaty, by going to war with a country with whom they had engaged to enter into arbitration. I anticipate another objection which I have heard made: they say, 'You cannot entrust the great interests of England to individuals or commissioners.' That difficulty springs out of the assumption, that the quarrels with foreign countries are about questions involving the whole existence of the empire. On the contrary, whenever these quarrels take place, it is generally upon the most minute and absurd pretexts—so trivial that it is almost impossible, on looking back for the last hundred years, to tell precisely what any war was about. I heard the other day of a boy going to see a model of the battle of Waterloo, and when he asked what the battle was about, neither the old soldier who had charge of the exhibition, nor any one in the room, could answer the question. . . .

Now, I would ask, in the face of these facts, where is the argument you can use against the reasonable proposition which I now put forward? I may be told that, even if you make treaties of this kind, you cannot enforce the award. I admit it. I am no party to the plan which some advocate—no doubt with the best intentions—of having a Congress of nations, with a code of laws—a supreme court of appeal, with an army to support its decisions. I am no party to any such plan. I believe it might lead to more armed interference than takes place at present. The hon. Gentleman opposite, who is to move an amendment to my motion (Mr. Urquhart), has evidently mistaken my object. The hon. Gentleman is exceedingly attentive in tacking on amendments to other persons' motions. My justification for alluding to him, on the present occasion, is, that he has founded his amendment on a misapprehension of what my motion is. He has evidently conceived the idea that I have a grand project for putting the whole world under some court of justice. I have no such plan in view at all; and, therefore, neither the hon. Gentleman, nor any other person, will answer my arguments, if he has prepared a speech assuming that I contemplate anything of the kind. I have no plan for compelling the fulfillment of treaties of arbitration. I have no idea of enforcing treaties in any other way than that now resorted to. I do not, myself, advocate an appeal to arms; but that which follows the violation of a treaty, under the present system, may follow the violation of a treaty of arbitration, if adopted. What I say, however, is, if you make a treaty with another country, binding it to refer any dispute to arbitration, and if that country violates that treaty, when the dispute arises, then you will place it in a worse position before the world—you will place it in so infamous a position, that I doubt if any country would enter into war on such bad grounds as that country must occupy. . . .

Reading 3.3

Community of Power vs. Balance of Power
WOODROW WILSON

. . . The question upon which the whole future peace and policy of the world depends is this: Is the present war a struggle for a just and secure peace, or only for a new balance of power? If it be only a struggle for a new balance of power, who will guarantee, who can be guaranteed, the stable equilibrium of the new arrangement? Only a tranquil Europe can be a stable Europe. There must be, not a balance of power, but a community of power; not organized rivalries, but an organized common peace.

Fortunately we have received very explicit assurances on this point. The statesmen of both of the groups of nations now arrayed against one another have said, in terms that could not be misinterpreted, that it was no part of the purpose they had in mind to crush their antagonists. But the implications of these assurances may not be equally clear to all,—may not be the same on both sides of the water. I think it will be serviceable if I attempt to set forth what we understand them to be.

They imply, first of all, that it must be a peace without victory. It is not pleasant to say this. I beg that I may be permitted to put my own interpretation upon it and that it may be understood that no other interpretation was in my thought. I am seeking only to face realities and to face them without soft concealments. Victory would mean peace forced upon the loser, a victor's terms imposed upon the vanquished. It would be accepted in humiliation, under duress, at an intolerable sacrifice, and would leave a sting, a resentment, a bitter memory upon which terms of peace would rest, not permanently, but only as upon quicksand. Only a peace between equals can last. Only a peace the very principle of which is equality and a common participation in a common benefit. The right state of mind, the right feeling between nations, is as necessary for a lasting peace as is the just settlement of vexed questions of territory or of racial and national allegiance.

Source: Address of the President of the United States to the U.S. Senate, January 22, 1917, Congressional Record: Senate, Vol. 54, 64th Congress, 2nd session.

The equality of nations upon which peace must be founded if it is to last must be an equality of rights; the guarantees exchanged must neither recognize nor imply a difference between the big nations and small, between those that are powerful and those that are weak. Right must be based upon the common strength, not upon the individual strength, of the nations upon whose concert peace will depend. Equality of territory or of resources there of course cannot be; nor any other sort of equality not gained in the ordinary peaceful and legitimate development of the people themselves. But no one asks or expects anything more than an equality of rights. Mankind is looking now for freedom of life, not for equipoises of power.

And there is a deeper thing involved than even equality of right among organized nations. No peace can last, or ought to last, which does not recognize and accept the principle that governments derive all their just powers from the consent of the governed, and that no right anywhere exists to hand peoples about from sovereignty to sovereignty as if they were property. I take it for granted, for instance, if I may venture upon a single example, that statesmen everywhere are agreed that there should be a united, independent, and autonomous Poland, and that henceforth inviolable security of life, of worship, and of industrial and social development should be guaranteed to all peoples who have lived hitherto under the power of governments devoted to a faith and purpose hostile to their own.

I speak of this, not because of any desire to exalt an abstract political principle which has always been held very dear by those who have sought to build up liberty in America, but for the same reasons that I have spoken of the other conditions of peace which seem to me clearly indispensable,—because I wish frankly to uncover realities. Any peace which does not recognize and accept this principle will inevitably be upset. It will not rest upon the affections or the convictions of mankind. The ferment of spirit of whole populations will fight subtly and constantly against it, and all the world will sympathize. The world can be at peace only if its life is stable, and there can be no stability where the will is in rebellion, where there is not tranquility of spirit and a sense of justice, of freedom, and of right.

So far as practicable, moreover, every great people now struggling towards a full development of its resources and of its powers should be assured a direct outlet to the great highways of the sea. Where this cannot be done by the cession of territory, it can no doubt be done by the neutralization of direct rights of way under the general guarantee which will assure the peace itself. With a right comity of arrangement no nation need be shut away from free access to the open paths of the world's commerce.

And the paths of the sea must alike in law and in fact be free. The freedom of the seas is the *sine qua non* of peace, equality, and cooperation. No doubt a somewhat radical reconsideration of many of the rules of international practice hitherto thought to be established may be necessary in order to make the seas indeed free and common in practically all circumstances for the use of mankind, but the motive for such changes is convincing and compelling. There can be no trust or intimacy between the peoples of the world without them.

The free, constant, unthreatened intercourse of nations is an essential part of the process of peace and of development. It need not be difficult either to define or to secure the freedom of the seas if the governments of the world sincerely desire to come to an agreement concerning it.

It is a problem closely connected with the limitation of naval armaments and the cooperation of the navies of the world in keeping the seas at once free and safe. And the question of limiting naval armaments opens the wider and perhaps more difficult question of the limitation of armies and of all programmes of military preparation. Difficult and delicate as these questions are, they must be faced with the utmost candour and decided in a spirit of real accommodation if peace is to come with healing in its wings, and come to stay. Peace cannot be had without concession and sacrifice. There can be no sense of safety and equality among the nations if great preponderating armaments are henceforth to continue here and there to be built up and maintained. The statesmen of the world must plan for peace and nations must adjust and accommodate their policy to it as they have planned for war and made ready for pitiless contest and rivalry. The question of armaments, whether on land or sea, is the most immediately and intensely practical question connected with the future fortunes of nations and of mankind.

I have spoken upon these great matters without reserve and with the utmost explicitness because it has seemed to me to be necessary if the world's yearning desire for peace was anywhere to find free voice and utterance. Perhaps I am the only person in high authority amongst all the peoples of the world who is at liberty to speak and hold nothing back. I am speaking as an individual, and yet I am speaking also, of course, as the responsible head of a great government, and I feel confident that I have said what the people of the United States would wish me to say. May I not add that I hope and believe that I am in effect speaking for liberals and friends of humanity in every nation and of every programme of liberty? I would fain believe that I am speaking for the silent mass of mankind everywhere who have as yet had no place or opportunity to speak their real hearts out concerning the death and ruin they see to have come already upon the persons and the homes they hold most dear.

And in holding out the expectation that the people and Government of the United States will join the other civilized nations of the world in guaranteeing the permanence of peace upon such terms as I have named I speak with the greater boldness and confidence because it is clear to every man who can think that there is in this promise no breach in either our traditions or our policy as a nation, but a fulfillment, rather, of all that we have professed or striven for.

I am proposing, as it were, that the nations should with one accord adopt the doctrine of President Monroe as the doctrine of the world: that no nation should seek to extend its polity over any other nation or people, but that every people should be left free to determine its own policy, its own way of development, unhindered, unthreatened, unafraid, the little along with the great and powerful.

I am proposing that all nations henceforth avoid entangling alliances which would draw them into competitions of power, catch them in a net of intrigue and selfish rivalry, and disturb their own affairs with influences intruded from without. There is no entangling alliance in a concert of power. When all unite to act in the same sense and with the same purpose all act in the common interest and are free to live their own lives under a common protection.

I am proposing government by the consent of the governed; that freedom of the seas which in international conference after conference representatives of the United States have urged with the eloquence of those who are the convinced disciples of liberty; and that moderation of armaments which makes of armies and navies a power for order merely, not an instrument of aggression or of selfish violence.

These are American principles, American policies. We could stand for no others. And they are also the principles and policies of forward looking men and women everywhere, of every modern nation, of every enlightened community. They are the principles of mankind and must prevail.

Reading 3.4

Liberalism and World Politics

MICHAEL W. DOYLE

Promoting freedom will produce peace, we have often been told. In a speech before the British Parliament in June of 1982, President Reagan proclaimed that governments founded on a respect for individual liberty exercise "restraint" and "peaceful intentions" in their foreign policy. He then announced a "crusade for freedom" and a "campaign for democratic development" (Reagan, June 9, 1982).

In making these claims the president joined a long list of liberal theorists (and propagandists) and echoed an old argument: the aggressive instincts of authoritarian leaders and totalitarian ruling parties make for war. Liberal states, founded on such individual rights as equality before the law, free speech and other civil liberties, private property, and elected representation, are fundamentally against war, this argument asserts. When the citizens who bear the burdens of war elect their governments, wars become impossible. Furthermore, citizens appreciate that the benefits of trade can be enjoyed only under conditions of peace. Thus the very existence of liberal states, such as the U.S., Japan, and our European allies, makes for peace.

Building on a growing literature in an international political science, I reexamine the liberal claim President Reagan reiterated for us. I look at

Source: Michael W. Doyle, "Liberalism and World Politics," The American Political Science Review, Vol. 80, No. 4 (December 1986). Reprinted with permission of Michael W. Doyle and the American Political Science Association.

three distinct theoretical traditions of liberalism, attributable to three theorists: Schumpeter, a brilliant explicator of the liberal pacifism the president invoked; Machiavelli, a classical republican whose glory is an imperialism we often practice; and Kant.

Despite the contradictions of liberal pacifism and liberal imperialism, I find, with Kant and other liberal republicans, that liberalism does leave a coherent legacy on foreign affairs. Liberal states are different. They are indeed peaceful, yet they are also prone to make war, as the U.S. and our "freedom fighters" are now doing, not so covertly, against Nicaragua. Liberal states have created a separate peace, as Kant argued they would, and have also discovered liberal reasons for aggression, as he feared they might. I conclude by arguing that the differences among liberal pacifism, liberal imperialism, and Kant's liberal internationalism are not arbitrary but rooted in differing conceptions of the citizen and the state.

LIBERAL PACIFISM

There is no canonical description of liberalism. What we tend to call liberal resembles a family portrait of principles and institutions, recognizable by certain characteristics—for example, individual freedom, political participation, private property, and equality of opportunity—that most liberal states share, although none has perfected them all. Joseph Schumpeter clearly fits within this family when he considers the international effects of capitalism and democracy. . . .

Democratic capitalism leads to peace. As evidence, Schumpeter claims that throughout the capitalist world an opposition has arisen to "war, expansion, cabinet diplomacy"; that contemporary capitalism is associated with peace parties; and that the industrial worker of capitalism is "vigorously anti-imperialist." In addition, he points out that the capitalist world has developed means of preventing war, such as the Hague Court and that the least feudal, most capitalist society—the United States—has demonstrated the least imperialistic tendencies (Schumpeter, 1955, pp. 95–96). An example of the lack of imperialistic tendencies in the U.S., Schumpeter thought, was our leaving over half of Mexico unconquered in the war of 1846–48.

Schumpeter's explanation for liberal pacifism is quite simple: Only war profiteers and military aristocrats gain from wars. No democracy would pursue a minority interest and tolerate the high costs of imperialism. When free trade prevails, "no class" gains from forcible expansion because

> foreign raw materials and food stuffs are as accessible to each nation as though they were in its own territory. Where the cultural backwardness of a region makes normal economic intercourse dependent on colonization it does not matter, assuming free trade, which of the "civilized" nations undertakes the task of colonization.

> (Schumpeter, 1955, pp. 75–76)

Schumpeter's arguments are difficult to evaluate. In partial tests of quasi-Schumpeterian propositions, Michael Haas (1974, pp. 464–65) discovered a cluster that associates democracy, development, and sustained modernization with peaceful conditions. However, M. Small and J. D. Singer (1976) have discovered that there is no clearly negative correlation between democracy and war in the period 1816–1965—the period that would be central to Schumpeter's argument (see also Wilkenfeld, 1968; Wright, 1942, p. 841).

Later in his career, in *Capitalism, Socialism, and Democracy*, Schumpeter (1950, pp. 127–28) acknowledged that "almost purely bourgeois commonwealths were often aggressive when it seemed to pay—like the Athenian or the Venetian commonwealths." Yet he stuck to his pacifistic guns, restating the view that capitalist democracy "steadily tells . . . against the use of military force and for peaceful arrangements, even when the balance of pecuniary advantage is clearly on the side of war which, under modern circumstances, is not in general very likely" (Schumpeter, 1950, p. 128). A recent study by R. J. Rummel (1983) of "libertarianism" and international violence is the closest test Schumpeterian pacifism has received. "Free" states (those enjoying political and economic freedom) were shown to have considerably less conflict at or above the level of economic sanctions than "nonfree" states. The free states, the partly free states (including the democratic socialist countries such as Sweden), and the nonfree states accounted for 24%, 26%, and 61%, respectively, of the international violence during the period examined.

These effects are impressive but not conclusive for the Schumpeterian thesis. The data are limited, in this test, to the period 1976 to 1980. It includes, for example, the Russo-Afghan War, the Vietnamese invasion of Cambodia, China's invasion of Vietnam, and Tanzania's invasion of Uganda but just misses the U.S., quasi-covert intervention in Angola (1975) and our not so covert war against Nicaragua (1981–). More importantly, it excludes the cold war period, with its numerous interventions, and the long history of colonial wars (the Boer War, the Spanish-American War, the Mexican Intervention, etc.) that marked the history of liberal, including democratic capitalist, states (Doyle, 1983b; Chan, 1984; Weede, 1984).

The discrepancy between the warlike history of liberal states and Schumpeter's pacifistic expectations highlights three extreme assumptions. First, his "materialistic monism" leaves little room for noneconomic objectives, whether espoused by states or individuals. Neither glory, nor prestige, nor ideological justification, nor the pure power of ruling shapes policy. These nonmaterial goals leave little room for positive-sum gains, such as the comparative advantages of trade. Second, and relatedly, the same is true for his states. The political life of individuals seems to have been homogenized at the same time as the individuals were "rationalized, individualized, and democratized." Citizens—capitalists and workers, rural and urban—seek material welfare. Schumpeter seems to presume that ruling makes no difference. He also presumes that no one is prepared to take those measures (such as stirring up foreign quarrels to preserve a domestic ruling coalition) that enhance one's political power, despite detrimental effects on mass welfare. Third, like domestic politics, world politics are homogenized. Materially monistic and democratically capitalist, all states evolve toward free trade and liberty together. Countries differently constituted seem to disappear from Schumpeter's analysis. "Civilized" nations govern "culturally backward" *regions*. These assumptions are not shared by Machiavelli's theory of liberalism.

LIBERAL IMPERIALISM

Machiavelli argues, not only that republics are not pacifistic, but that they are the best form of state for imperial expansion. Establishing a republic fit for imperial expansion is, moreover, the best way to guarantee the survival of a state.

Machiavelli's republic is a classical mixed republic. It is not a democracy—which he thought would quickly degenerate into a tyranny—but is characterized by social equality, popular liberty, and political participation (Machiavelli, 1950, bk. 1, chap. 2, p. 112; see also Huliung, 1983, chap. 2; Mansfield, 1970; Pocock, 1975, pp. 198–99; Skinner, 1981, chap. 3). The consuls serve as "kings," the senate as an aristocracy managing the state, and the people in the assembly as the source of strength.

Liberty results from "disunion"—the competition and necessity for compromise required by the division of powers among senate, consuls, and tribunes (the last representing the common people). Liberty also results from the popular veto. The powerful few threaten the rest with tyranny, Machiavelli says, because they seek to dominate. The mass demands not to be dominated, and their veto thus preserves the liberties of the state (Machiavelli, 1950, bk. 1, chap. 5, p. 122). However, since the people and the rulers have different social characters, the people need to be "managed" by the few to avoid having their recklessness overturn or their fecklessness undermine the ability of the state to expand (Machiavelli, 1950, bk. 1, chap. 53, pp. 249–50). Thus the senate and the consuls plan expansion, consult oracles, and employ religion to manage the resources that the energy of the people supplies.

Strength, and then imperial expansion, results from the way liberty encourages increased population and property, which grow when the citizens know their lives and goods are secure from arbitrary seizure. Free citizens equip large armies and provide soldiers who fight for public glory and the common good because these are, in fact, their own (Machiavelli, 1950, bk. 2, chap. 2, pp. 287–90). If you seek the honor of having your state expand, Machiavelli advises, you should organize it as a free and popular republic like Rome, rather than as an aristocratic republic like Sparta or Venice. Expansion thus calls for a free republic.

"Necessity"—political survival—calls for expansion. If a stable aristocratic republic is forced by foreign conflict "to extend her territory, in such a case we shall see her foundations give way and herself quickly brought to ruin"; if, on the other hand, domestic security prevails, "the continued tranquility would enervate her, or provoke internal dissensions, which together, or either of them separately, will apt to prove her ruin" (Machiavelli, 1950, bk. 1, chap. 6, p. 129). Machiavelli therefore believes it is necessary to take the constitution of Rome, rather than that of Sparta or Venice, as our model.

Hence, this belief leads to liberal imperialism. We are lovers of glory, Machiavelli announces. We seek to rule or, at least, to avoid being oppressed. In either case, we want more for ourselves and our states than just material welfare (materialistic monism). Because other states with similar aims thereby threaten us, we prepare ourselves for expansion. Because our fellow citizens threaten us if we do not allow them either to satisfy their ambition or to release their political energies through imperial expansion, we expand.

There is considerable historical evidence for liberal imperialism. Machiavelli's (Polybius's) Rome and Thucydides' Athens both were imperial republics in the Machiavellian sense (Thucydides, 1954, bk. 6). The historical record of numerous U.S. interventions in the postwar period supports Machiavelli's argument (Aron, 1974, chaps. 3–4; Barnet, 1968, chap. 11), but the current record of liberal pacifism, weak as it is, calls some of his insights into question. To the extent that the modern populace actually controls (and thus unbalances) the mixed republic, its diffidence may outweigh elite ("senatorial") aggressiveness.

We can conclude either that (1) liberal pacifism has at least taken over with the further development of capitalist democracy, as Schumpeter predicted it would or that (2) the mixed record of liberalism—pacifism and imperialism—indicates that some liberal states are Schumpeterian democracies while others are Machiavellian republics. Before we accept either conclusion, however, we must consider a third apparent regularity of modern world politics.

LIBERAL INTERNATIONALISM

Modern liberalism carries with it two legacies. They do not affect liberal states separately, according to whether they are pacifistic or imperialistic, but simultaneously.

The first of these legacies is the pacification of foreign relations among liberal states. During the nineteenth century, the United States and Great Britain engaged in nearly continual strife; however, after the Reform Act of 1832 defined actual representation as the formal source of the sovereignty of the British parliament, Britain and the United States negotiated their disputes. They negotiated despite, for example, British grievances during the Civil War against the North's blockade of the South, with which Britain had close economic ties. Despite several Anglo-French colonial rivalries, liberal France and liberal Britain formed an entente against illiberal Germany before World War I. And from 1914 to 1915, Italy, the liberal member of the Triple Alliance with Germany and Austria, chose not to fulfill its obligations under that treaty to support its allies. Instead, Italy joined in an alliance with Britain and France, which prevented it from having to fight other liberal states and then declared war on Germany and Austria. Despite generations of Anglo-American tension and Britain's wartime restrictions on American trade with Germany, the United States leaned toward Britain and France from 1914 to 1917 before entering World War I on their side.

Beginning in the eighteenth century and slowly growing since then, a zone of peace, which Kant called the "pacific federation" or "pacific union," has begun to be established among liberal societies. More than 40 liberal states currently make up the union. Most are in Europe and North America, but they can be found on every continent, as Appendix 1 indicates.

Here the predictions of liberal pacifists (and President Reagan) are borne out: liberal states do exercise peaceful restraint, and a separate peace exists among them. This separate peace provides a solid foundation for the United States' crucial alliances with the liberal powers, e.g., the North Atlantic Treaty Organization and our Japanese alliance. This foundation appears to be impervious to the quarrels with our allies that bedeviled the Carter and Reagan administrations. It also offers the promise of a continuing peace among liberal states, and as the number of liberal states increases, it announces the possibility of global peace this side of the grave or world conquest.

Of course, the probability of the outbreak of war in any given year between any two given states is low. The occurrence of a war between any two adjacent states, considered over a long period of time, would be more probable. The apparent absence of war between liberal states, whether adjacent or not, for almost 200 years thus may have significance. Similar claims cannot be made for feudal, fascist, communist, authoritarian, or totalitarian forms of rule (Doyle, 1983a, p. 222), nor for pluralistic or merely similar societies. More significant perhaps is that when states are forced to decide on which side of an impending world war they will fight, liberal states all wind up on the same side despite the complexity of the paths that take them there. These characteristics do not prove that the peace among liberals is statistically significant nor that liberalism is the sole valid explanation for the peace. They do suggest that we consider the possibility that liberals have indeed established a separate peace— but only among themselves.

Liberalism also carries with it a second legacy: international "imprudence" (Hume, 1963, pp. 346–47). Peaceful restraint only seems to work in liberals' relations with other liberals. Liberal states have fought numerous wars with nonliberal states. (For a list of international wars since 1816 see Appendix 2.)

Many of these wars have been defensive and thus prudent by necessity. Liberal states have been attacked and threatened by nonliberal states that do not exercise any special restraint in their dealings with the liberal states. Authoritarian rulers both stimulate and respond to an international political environment in which conflicts of prestige, interest, and pure fear of what other states might do all lead states toward war. War and conquest have thus characterized the careers of many authoritarian rulers and ruling parties, from Louis XIV and Napoleon to Mussolini's fascists, Hitler's Nazis, and Stalin's communists.

Yet we cannot simply blame warfare on the authoritarians or totalitarians, as many of our more enthusiastic politicians would have us do. Most wars arise out of calculations and miscalculations of interest, misunderstandings, and mutual suspicions, such as those that characterized the origins of World War I. However, aggression by the liberal state has also characterized a large number of wars. Both France and Britain fought expansionist colonial wars throughout the nineteenth century. The United States fought a similar war with Mexico from 1846 to 1848, waged a war of annihilation against the American

Indians, and intervened militarily against sovereign states many times before and after World War II. Liberal states invade weak nonliberal states and display striking distrust in dealings with powerful nonliberal states (Doyle, 1983b).

Neither realist (statist) nor Marxist theory accounts well for these two legacies. While they can account for aspects of certain periods of international stability (Aron, 1966, pp. 151–54; Russett, 1985), neither the logic of the balance of power nor the logic of international hegemony explains the separate peace maintained for more than 150 years among states sharing one particular form of governance—liberal principles and institutions. Balance-of-power theory expects—indeed is premised upon—flexible arrangements of geostrategic rivalry that include preventive war. Hegemonies wax and wane, but the liberal peace holds. Marxist "ultra-imperialists" expect a form of peaceful rivalry among capitalists, but only liberal capitalists maintain peace. Leninists expect liberal capitalists to be aggressive toward nonliberal states, but they also (and especially) expect them to be imperialistic toward fellow liberal capitalists.

Kant's theory of liberal internationalism helps us understand these two legacies. . . .

[*See the selection by Kant in this Part.* (Ed.)]

Liberal republics will progressively establish peace among themselves by means of the pacific federation, or union (foedus pacificum), described in Kant's Second Definitive Article. The pacific union will establish peace within a federation of free states and securely maintain the rights of each state. The world will not have achieved the "perpetual peace" that provides the ultimate guarantor of republican freedom until "a late stage and after many unsuccessful attempts" (Kant, *UH*, p. 47). At that time, all nations will have learned the lessons of peace through right conceptions of the appropriate constitution, great and sad experience, and good will. Only then will individuals enjoy perfect republican rights or the full guarantee of a global and just peace. In the meantime, the "pacific federation" of liberal republics—"an enduring and gradually expanding federation likely to prevent war"—brings within it more and more republics—despite republican collapses, backsliding, and disastrous wars—creating an ever-expanding separate peace (Kant, *PP*, p. 105). Kant emphasizes that

> it can be shown that this idea of federalism, extending gradually to encompass all states and thus leading to perpetual peace, is practicable and has objective reality. For if by good fortune one powerful and enlightened nation can form a republic (which is by nature inclined to seek peace), this will provide a focal point for federal association among other states. These will join up with the first one, thus securing the freedom of each state in accordance with the idea of international right, and the whole will gradually spread further and further by a series of alliances of this kind.
>
> (Kant, *PP*, p. 104)

The pacific union is not a single peace treaty ending one war, a world state, nor a state of nations. Kant finds the first insufficient. The second and third are impossible or potentially tyrannical. National sovereignty precludes reliable subservience to a state of nations; a world state destroys the civic freedom on which the development of human capacities rests (Kant, *UH*, p. 50). Although Kant obliquely refers to various classical interstate confederations and modern diplomatic congresses, he develops no systematic organizational embodiment of this treaty and presumably does not find institutionalization necessary (Riley, 1983, chap. 5; Schwarz, 1962, p. 77). He appears to have in mind a mutual nonaggression pact, perhaps a collective security agreement, and the cosmopolitan law set forth in the Third Definitive Article. . . .

Perpetual peace, for Kant, is an epistemology, a condition for ethical action, and, most importantly, an explanation of how the "mechanical process of nature visibly exhibits the purposive plan of producing concord among men, even against their will and indeed by means of their very discord" (Kant, *PP*, p. 108; *UH*, pp. 44–45). Understanding history requires an epistemological foundation, for without a teleology, such as the promise of perpetual peace, the complexity of history would overwhelm human understanding (Kant, *UH*, pp. 51–53). Perpetual peace, however, is not merely a heuristic device with which to interpret history. It is guaranteed, Kant explains in the "First Addition" to *Perpetual Peace* ("On the Guarantee of Perpetual Peace"), to result from men fulfilling their ethical duty or, failing that, from a hidden plan. Peace is an ethical duty because it is only under conditions of peace that all men can treat each other as ends, rather than means to an end (Kant, *UH*, p. 50; Murphy, 1970, chap. 3). In order for this duty to be practical, Kant needs, of course, to show that peace is in fact possible. The widespread sentiment of approbation that he saw aroused by the early success of the French revolutionaries showed him that we can indeed be moved by ethical sentiments with a cosmopolitan reach (Kant, *CF*, pp. 181–82; Yovel, 1980, pp. 153–54). This does not mean, however, that perpetual peace is certain ("prophesiable"). Even the scientifically regular course of the planets could be changed by a wayward comet striking them out of orbit. Human freedom requires that we allow for much greater reversals in the course of history. We must, in fact, anticipate the possibility of backsliding and destructive wars—though these will serve to educate nations to the importance of peace (Kant, *UH*, pp. 47–48).

In the end, however, our guarantee of perpetual peace does not rest on ethical conduct. As Kant emphasizes,

> we now come to the essential question regarding the prospect of perpetual peace. What does nature do in relation to the end which man's own reason prescribes to him as a duty, i.e. how does nature help to promote his *moral purpose*? And how does nature guarantee that what man *ought* to do by the laws of his freedom (but does not do) will in fact be done through nature's compulsion, without prejudice to the free agency of man? . . . This does not mean that nature imposes on us a *duty* to do it, for duties can only be imposed by practical reason. On the contrary, nature does it herself, whether we are willing or not: *facta volentem ducunt, nolentem tradunt.*

> (*PP*, p. 112)

The guarantee thus rests, Kant argues, not on the probable behavior of moral angels, but on that of "devils, so long as they possess understanding" (*PP*, p. 112). In explaining the sources of each of the three definitive articles of the perpetual peace, Kant then tells us how we (as free and intelligent devils) could be motivated by fear, force, and calculated advantage to undertake a course of action whose outcome we could reasonably anticipate to be perpetual peace. Yet while it is possible to conceive of the Kantian road to peace in these terms, Kant himself recognizes and argues that social evolution also makes the conditions of moral behavior less onerous and hence more likely (*CF*, pp. 187–89; Kelly, 1969, pp. 106–13). In tracing the effects of both political and moral development, he builds an account of why liberal states do maintain peace among themselves and of how it will (by implication, has) come about that the pacific union will expand. He also explains how these republics would engage in wars with nonrepublics and therefore suffer the "sad experience" of wars that an ethical policy might have avoided. . . .

Kant shows how republics, once established, lead to peaceful relations. He argues that once the aggressive interests of absolutist monarchies are tamed and the habit of respect for individual rights engrained by republican government, wars would appear as the disaster to the people's welfare that he and the other liberals thought them to be. . . . Yet these domestic republican restraints do not end war. If they did, liberal states would not be warlike, which is far from the case. They do introduce republican caution—Kant's "hesitation"—in place of monarchical caprice. Liberal wars are only fought for popular, liberal purposes. The historical liberal legacy is laden with popular wars fought to promote freedom, to protect private property, or to support liberal allies against nonliberal enemies. Kant's position is ambiguous. He regards these wars as unjust and warns liberals of their susceptibility to them (Kant, *PP*, p. 106). At the same time, Kant argues that each nation "can and ought to" demand that its neighboring nations enter into the pacific union of liberal states (*PP*, p. 102). . . .

A further cosmopolitan source of liberal peace is the international market's removal of difficult decisions of production and distribution from the direct sphere of state policy. A foreign state thus does not appear directly responsible for these outcomes, and states can stand aside from, and to some degree above, these contentious market rivalries and be ready to step in to resolve crises. The interdependence of commerce and the international contacts of state officials help create crosscutting transnational ties that serve as lobbies for mutual accommodation. According to modern liberal scholars, international financiers and transnational and transgovernmental organizations create interests in favor of accommodation. Moreover, their variety has ensured that no single conflict sours an entire relationship by setting off a spiral of reciprocated retaliation (Brzezinski and Huntington, 1963, chap. 9; Keohane and Nye, 1977, chap. 7; Neustadt, 1970; Polanyi, 1944, chaps. 1–2). Conversely, a sense of suspicion, such as that characterizing relations between liberal and nonliberal governments, can lead to restrictions on the range of contacts between societies, and this can increase the prospect that a single conflict will determine an entire relationship.

No single constitutional, international, or cosmopolitan source is alone sufficient, but together (and only together) they plausibly connect the characteristics of liberal polities and economies with sustained liberal peace. Alliances founded on mutual strategic interest among liberal and nonliberal states have been broken; economic ties between liberal and nonliberal states have proven fragile; but the political bonds of liberal rights and interests have proven a remarkably firm foundation for mutual nonaggression. A separate peace exists among liberal states.

In their relations with nonliberal states, however, liberal states have not escaped from the insecurity caused by anarchy in the world political system considered as a whole. Moreover, the very constitutional restraint, international respect for individual rights, and shared commercial interests that establish grounds for peace among liberal states establish grounds for additional conflict in relations between liberal and nonliberal societies.

CONCLUSION

. . . Unlike Machiavelli's republics, Kant's republics are capable of achieving peace among themselves because they exercise democratic caution and are capable of appreciating the international rights of foreign republics. These international rights of republics derive from the representation of foreign individuals, who are our moral equals. Unlike Schumpeter's capitalist democracies, Kant's republics—including our own—remain in a state of war with nonrepublics. Liberal republics see themselves as threatened by aggression from nonrepublics that are not constrained by representation. Even though wars often cost more than the economic return they generate, liberal republics also are prepared to protect and promote—sometimes forcibly—democracy, private property, and the rights of individuals overseas against nonrepublics, which, because they do not authentically represent the rights of individuals, have no rights to noninterference. These wars may liberate oppressed individuals overseas; they also can generate enormous suffering.

Preserving the legacy of the liberal peace without succumbing to the legacy of liberal imprudence is both a moral and a strategic challenge. The bipolar stability of the international system, and the near certainty of mutual devastation resulting from a nuclear war between the superpowers, have created a "crystal ball effect" that has helped to constrain the tendency toward miscalculation present at the outbreak of so many wars in the past (Carnesale, Doty, Hoffmann, Huntington, Nye, and Sagan, 1983, p. 44; Waltz, 1964). However, this "nuclear peace" appears to be limited to the superpowers. It has not curbed military interventions in the Third World. Moreover, it is subject to a desperate technological race designed to overcome its constraints and to crises that have pushed even the superpowers to the brink of war. We must still reckon with the war fevers and moods of appeasement that have almost alternately swept liberal democracies.

Yet restraining liberal imprudence, whether aggressive or passive, may not be possible without threatening liberal pacification. Improving the strategic acumen of our foreign policy calls for introducing steadier strategic calculations of the national interest in the long run and more flexible responses to changes in the international political environment. Constraining the indiscriminate meddling of our foreign interventions calls for a deeper appreciation of the "particularism of history, culture, and membership" (Walzer, 1983, p. 5), but both the improvement in strategy and the constraint on intervention seem, in turn, to require an executive freed from the restraints of a representative legislature in the management of foreign policy and a political culture indifferent to the universal rights of individuals. These conditions, in their turn, could break the chain of constitutional guarantees, the respect for representative government, and the web of transnational contact that have sustained the pacific union of liberal states.

Perpetual peace, Kant says, is the end point of the hard journey his republics will take. The promise of perpetual peace, the violent lessons of war, and the experience of a partial peace are proof of the need for and the possibility of world peace. They are also the grounds for moral citizens and statesmen to assume the duty of striving for peace.

This list excludes covert interventions, some of which have been directed by liberal regimes against other liberal regimes—for example, the United States' effort to destabilize the Chilean election and Allende's government. Nonetheless, it is significant that such interventions are not pursued publicly as acknowledged policy. The covert destabilization campaign against Chile is recounted by the Senate Select Committee to Study Governmental Operations with Respect to Intelligence Activities (1975, *Covert Action in Chile, 1963–73*).

Following the argument of this article, this list also excludes civil wars. Civil wars differ from international wars, not in the ferocity of combat, but in the issues that engender them. Two nations that could abide one another as independent neighbors separated by a border might well be the fiercest of enemies if forced to live together in one state, jointly deciding how to raise and spend taxes, choose leaders, and legislate fundamental questions of value. Notwithstanding these differences, no civil wars that I recall upset the argument of liberal pacification.

APPENDIX 1

Liberal Regimes and the Pacific Union, 1700–1982

Period	Period	Period
18th Century	1800–1850	1850–1900
Swiss Cantons[a]	Belgium, 1830–	Belgium
French Republic, 1790–1795	Great Britain, Netherlands, 1848–	1832–Great Britain Netherlands
United States,[a] 1776–	Piedmont, 1848–	Piedmont, –1861
Total = 3	Denmark, 1849–	Italy, –1861
	Total = 8	Denmark, –1866
		Sweden, 1864–

(Continued)

APPENDIX 1

Liberal Regimes and the Pacific Union, 1700–1982

Period	Period	Period
1850–1900 (cont.)	**1850–1900**	**1945 (cont.)**
Swiss Confederation	Switzerland	Greece, 1864–
United States	United States	Canada, 1867–
France, 1830–1849	Mexico, 1928–	France, 1871–
Argentina, 1880–	Lebanon, 1944–	Sri Lanka, 1948–1961;
Chile, 1891–	Total = 29	1963–1971; 1978–
Total = 14		Ecuador, 1948–1963;
	1945–[b]	1979–
1900–1945	Switzerland	Israel, 1949–
Switzerland	United States	West Germany, 1949–
United States	Great Britain	Greece, 1950–1967;
Great Britain	Sweden	1975–
Sweden	Canada	Peru, 1950–1962;
Canada	Australia	1963–1968; 1980–
Greece, –1911;	New Zealand	El Salvador, 1950–1961
1928–1936	Finland	Turkey, 1950–1960;
Italy, –1922	Ireland	1966–1971
Belgium, –1940	Mexico	Japan, 1951–
Netherlands, –1940	Uruguay, –1973	Bolivia 1956–1969;
	Chile, –1973	1982–
1900–1945	Lebanon, –1975	Colombia, 1958–
Argentina, –1943	Costa Rica, –1948;	Venezuela, 1959–
France, –1940	1953–	Nigeria, 1961–1964;
Chile, –1924, 1932–	Iceland, 1944–	1979–1984
Australia, 1901	France, 1945–	Jamaica, 1962–
Norway, 1905–1940	Denmark, 1945	Trinidad and Tobago,
New Zealand, 1907–	Norway, 1945	1962–
Colombia, 1910–1949	Austria, 1945–	Senegal, 1963–
Denmark, 1914–1940		Malaysia, 1963–
Poland, 1917–1935	**1945**	Botswana, 1966–
Latvia, 1922–1934	Brazil, 1945–1954,	Singapore, 1965–
Germany, 1918–1932	1955–1964	Portugal, 1976–
Austria, 1918–1934	Belgium, 1946–	Spain, 1978–
Estonia, 1919–1934	Luxemburg, 1946–	Dominican Republic,
Finland, 1919–	Netherlands, 1946–	1978–
Uruguay, 1919–	Italy, 1946–	Honduras, 1981–
Costa Rica, 1919–	Philippines, 1946–	Papua New Guinea,
Czechoslovakia, 1920–	1972	1982–
1939	India, 1947–1975,	Total = 50
Ireland, 1920–	1977–	

NOTE: I have drawn up this approximate list of "Liberal Regimes" according to the four institutions Kant described as essential: market and private property economies; polities that are

(Continued)

APPENDIX 1

Liberal Regimes and the Pacific Union, 1700–1982

externally sovereign; citizens who possess juridical rights; and "republican" (whether republican or parliamentary monarchy), representative government. This latter includes the requirement that the legislative branch have an effective role in public policy and be formally and competitively (either inter- or intra-party) elected. Furthermore, I have taken into account whether male suffrage is wide (i.e., 30%) or, as Kant (*MM*, p. 139) would have had it, open by "achievement" to inhabitants of the national or metropolitan territory (e.g., to poll-tax payers or householders). This list of liberal regimes is thus more inclusive than a list of democratic regimes, or polyarchies (Powell, 1982, p. 5). Other conditions taken into account here are that female suffrage is granted within a generation of its being demanded by an extensive female suffrage movement and that representative government is internally sovereign (e.g., including, and especially over military and foreign affairs) as well as stable (in existence for at least three years). Sources for these data are Banks and Overstreet (1983), Gastil (1985), *The Europa Yearbook, 1985* (1985), Langer (1968), U.K. Foreign and Commonwealth Office (1980), and U.S. Department of State (1981). Finally, these lists exclude ancient and medieval "republics," since none appears to fit Kant's commitment to liberal individualism (Holmes, 1979).

[a]There are domestic variations within these liberal regimes: Switzerland was liberal only in certain cantons; the United States was liberal only north of the Mason-Dixon line until 1865, when it became liberal throughout.

[b]Selected list, excludes liberal regimes with populations less than one million. These include all states categorized as "free" by Gastil and those "partly free" (four-fifths or more free) states with a more pronounced capitalist orientation.

APPENDIX 2

International Wars Listed Chronologically

British-Maharattan (1817–1818)	Italo-Roman (1860)
Greek (1821–1828)	Italo-Sicilian (1860–1861)
Franco-Spanish (1823)	Franco-Mexican (1862–1867)
First Anglo-Burmese (1823–1826)	Ecuadorian-Colombian (1863)
Javanese (1825–1830)	Second Polish (1863–1864)
Russo-Persian (1826–1828)	Spanish-Santo Dominican (1863–1865)
Russo-Turkish (1828–1829)	Second Schleswig-Holstein (1864)
First Polish (1831)	Lopez (1864–1870)
First Syrian (1831–1832)	Spanish-Chilean (1865–1866)
Texas (1835–1836)	Seven Weeks (1866)
First British-Afghan (1838–1842)	Ten Years (1868–1878)
Second Syrian (1839–1940)	Franco-Prussian (1870–1871)
Franco-Algerian (1839–1847)	Dutch-Achinese (1873–1878)
Peruvian-Bolivian (1841)	Balkan (1875–1877)
First British-Sikh (1845–1846)	Russo-Turkish (1877–1878)
Mexican-American (1846–1848)	Bosnian (1878)
Austro-Sardinian (1848–1849)	Second British-Afghan (1878–1880)

(Continued)

APPENDIX 2

International Wars Listed Chronologically

First Schleswig-Holstein (1848–1849)

Hungarian (1848–1849)

Second British-Sikh (1848–1849)

Roman Republic (1849)

La Plata (1851–1852)

First Turco-Montenegran (1852–1853)

Crimean (1853–1856)

Anglo-Persian (1856–1857)

Sepoy (1857–1859)

Second Turco-Montenegran (1858–1859)

Italian Unification (1859)

Spanish-Moroccan (1859–1860)

Greco-Turkish (1897)

Spanish-American (1898)

Second Philippine (1899–1902)

Boer (1899–1902)

Boxer Rebellion (1900)

Ilinden (1903)

Russo-Japanese (1904–1905)

Central American (1906)

Central American (1907)

Spanish-Moroccan (1909–1910)

Italo-Turkish (1911–1912)

First Balkan (1912–1913)

Second Balkan (1913)

World War I (1914–1918)

Russian Nationalities (1917–1921)

Russo-Polish (1919–1920)

Hungarian-Allies (1919)

Greco-Turkish (1919–1922)

Riffian (1921–1926)

Druze (1925–1927)

Sino-Soviet (1929)

Manchurian (1931–1933)

Chaco (1932–1935)

Italo-Ethiopian (1935–1936)

Pacific (1879–1883)

British-Zulu (1879)

Franco-Indochinese (1882–1884)

Mahdist (1882–1885)

Sino-French (1884–1885)

Central American (1885)

Serbo-Bulgarian (1885)

Sino-Japanese (1894–1895)

Franco-Madagascan (1894–1895)

Cuban (1895–1898)

Italo-Ethiopian (1895–1896)

First Philippine (1896–1898)

Indonesian (1945–1946)

Indochinese (1945–1954)

Madagascan (1947–1948)

First Kashmir (1947–1949)

Palestine (1948–1949)

Hyderabad (1948)

Korean (1950–1953)

Algerian (1954–1962)

Russo-Hungarian (1956)

Sinai (1956)

Tibetan (1956–1959)

Sino-Indian (1962)

Vietnamese (1965–1975)

Second Kashmir (1965)

Six Day (1967)

Israeli-Egyptian (1969–1970)

Football (1969)

Bangladesh (1971)

Philippine-MNLF (1972–)

Yom Kippur (1973)

Turco-Cypriot (1974)

Ethiopian-Eritrean (1974–)

Vietnamese-Cambodian (1975–)

Timor (1975–)

APPENDIX 2

International Wars Listed Chronologically

Sino-Japanese (1937–1941)	Saharan (1975–)
Changkufeng (1938)	Ogaden (1976–)
Nomohan (1939)	Ugandan-Tanzanian (1978–1979)
World War II (1939–1945)	Sino-Vietnamese (1979)
Russo-Finnish (1939–1940)	Russo-Afghan (1979–)
Franco-Thai (1940–1941)	Iran-Iraqi (1980–)

NOTE: This table is taken from Melvin Small and J. David Singer (1982, pp. 79–80). This is a partial list of international wars fought between 1816 and 1980. In Appendices A and B, Small and Singer identify a total of 575 wars during this period, but approximately 159 of them appear to be largely domestic, or civil wars.

REFERENCES

Aron, Raymond. 1966. *Peace and War: A Theory of International Relations*. Richard Howard and Annette Baker Fox, trans. Garden City, NY: Doubleday.

———. 1974. *The Imperial Republic*. Frank Jellinek, trans. Englewood Cliffs, NJ: Prentice Hall.

Banks, Arthur, and William Overstreet, eds. 1983. A *Political Handbook of the World; 1982–1983*. New York: McGraw-Hill.

Barnet, Richard. 1968. *Intervention and Revolution*. Cleveland: World Publishing Co.

Brzezinski, Zbigniew, and Samuel Huntington. 1963. *Political Power: USA/USSR*. New York: Viking Press.

Carnesale, Albert, Paul Doty, Stanley Hoffmann, Samuel Huntington, Joseph Nye, and Scott Sagan. 1983. *Living with Nuclear Weapons*. New York: Bantam.

Chan, Steve. 1984. Mirror, Mirror on the Wall . . . : Are Freer Countries More Pacific? *Journal of Conflict Resolution*, 28:617–48.

Doyle, Michael W. 1983a. Kant, Liberal Legacies, and Foreign Affairs: Part 1. *Philosophy and Public Affairs*, 12:205–35.

———. 1983b. Kant, Liberal Legacies, and Foreign Affairs: Part 2. *Philosophy and Public Affairs*, 12:323–53.

———. 1986. *Empires*. Ithaca, NY: Cornell University Press.

The Europa Yearbook for 1985. 1985. 2 vols. London: Europa Publications.

Friedrich, Karl. 1948. *Inevitable Peace*. Cambridge, MA: Harvard University Press.

Gastil, Raymond. 1985. The Comparative Survey of Freedom 1985. *Freedom at Issue*, 82:3–16.

Haas, Michael. 1974. *International Conflict*. New York: Bobbs-Merrill.

Hermens, Ferdinand A. 1944. *The Tyrants' War and the People's Peace*. Chicago: University of Chicago Press.

Holmes, Stephen. 1979. Aristippus in and out of Athens. *American Political Science Review*, 73:113–28.

Huliung, Mark. 1983. *Citizen Machiavelli*. Princeton, NJ: Princeton University Press.

Hume, David. 1963. *Of the Balance of Power. Essays: Moral, Political and Literary*. Oxford: Oxford University Press.

Kant, Immanuel. 1970. *Kant's Political Writings*. Hans Reiss, ed. H. B. Nisbet, trans. Cambridge: Cambridge University Press.

Kelly, George A. 1969. *Idealism, Politics, and History*. Cambridge: Cambridge University Press.

Keohane, Robert, and Joseph Nye. 1977. *Power and Interdependence*. Boston: Little Brown.

Langer, William L., ed. 1968. *The Encyclopedia of World History*. Boston: Houghton Mifflin.

Machiavelli, Niccolò. 1950. *The Prince and the Discourses*. Max Lerner, ed. Luigi Ricci and Christian Detmold, trans. New York: Modern Library.

Mansfield, Harvey C. 1970. Machiavelli's New Regime. *Italian Quarterly*, 13:63–95.

Murphy, Jeffrie. 1970. *Kant: The Philosophy of Right*. New York: St. Martin's.

Neustadt, Richard. 1970. *Alliance Politics*. New York: Columbia University Press.

Pocock, J. G. A. 1975. *The Machiavellian Moment*. Princeton, NJ: Princeton University Press.

Polanyi, Karl. 1944. *The Great Transformation*. Boston: Beacon Press.

Posen, Barry, and Stephen Van Evera. 1980. Over-arming and Underwhelming. *Foreign Policy*, 40:99–118.

Powell, G. Bingham. 1982. *Contemporary Democracies*. Cambridge, MA: Harvard University Press.

Riley, Patrick. 1983. *Kant's Political Philosophy*. Totowa, NJ: Rowman and Littlefield.

Rummel, Rudolph J. 1979. *Understanding Conflict and War*, 5 vols. Beverly Hills: Sage Publications.

Rummel, Rudolph J. 1983. Libertarianism and International Violence. *Journal of Conflict Resolution*, 27:27–71.

Russett, Bruce. 1985. The Mysterious Case of Vanishing Hegemony. *International Organization*, 39:207–31.

Schumpeter, Joseph. 1950. *Capitalism, Socialism, and Democracy*. New York: Harper Torchbooks.

———. 1955. The Sociology of Imperialism. In *Imperialism and Social Classes*. Cleveland: World Publishing Co. (Essay originally published in 1919.)

Schwarz, Wolfgang. 1962. Kant's Philosophy of Law and International Peace. *Philosophy and Phenomenological Research*, 23:71–80.

Shell, Susan. 1980. *The Rights of Reason*. Toronto: University of Toronto Press.

Skinner, Quentin. 1981. *Machiavelli*. New York: Hill and Wang.

Small, Melvin, and J. David Singer. 1976. The War-Proneness of Democratic Regimes. *The Jerusalem Journal of International Relations*, 1 (4):50–69.

———. 1982. *Resort to Arms*. Beverly Hills, CA: Sage Publications.

Thucydides. 1954. *The Peloponnesian War*. Rex Warner, ed. and trans. Baltimore: Penguin.

U.K. Foreign and Commonwealth Office. 1980. *A Yearbook of the Commonwealth 1980*. London: HMSO.

U.S. Congress, Senate. Select Committee to Study Governmental Operations with Respect to Intelligence Activities. 1975. *Covert Action in Chile, 1963–74*. 94th Cong., 1st sess., Washington, D.C.: U.S. Government Printing Office.

U.S. Department of State. 1981. *Country Reports on Human Rights Practices*. Washington, D.C.: U.S. Government Printing Office.

Waltz, Kenneth. 1964. The Stability of a Bipolar World. *Daedalus*, 93:881–909.

Walzer, Michael. 1983. *Spheres of Justice*. New York: Basic Books.

Weede, Erich. 1984. Democracy and War Involvement. *Journal of Conflict Resolution*, 28:649–64.

Wilkenfeld, Jonathan. 1968. Domestic and Foreign Conflict Behavior of Nations. *Journal of Peace Research*, 5:56–69.

Wright, Quincy. 1942. *A Study of History*. Chicago: Chicago University Press.

Yovel, Yirmiahu. 1980. *Kant and the Philosophy of History*. Princeton, NJ: Princeton University Press.

Reading 3.5

Power and Interdependence

ROBERT O. KEOHANE AND JOSEPH S. NYE

. . . For political realists, international politics, like all other politics, is a struggle for power but, unlike domestic politics, a struggle dominated by organized violence. In the words of the most influential postwar textbook, "All history shows that nations active in international politics are continuously preparing for, actively involved in, or recovering from organized violence in the form of war."[1] Three assumptions are integral to the realist vision. First, states as coherent units are the dominant actors in world politics. This is a double assumption: states are predominant; and they act as coherent units. Second, realists assume that force is a usable and effective instrument of policy. Other instruments may also be employed, but using or threatening force is the most effective means of wielding power. Third, partly because of their second assumption, realists assume a hierarchy of issues in world politics, headed by questions of military security: the "high politics" of military security dominates the "low politics" of economic and social affairs.

These realist assumptions define an ideal type of world politics. They allow us to imagine a world in which politics is continually characterized by active or potential conflict among states, with the use of force possible at any time. Each state attempts to defend its territory and interests from real or perceived threats. Political integration among states is slight and lasts only as long as it serves the national interests of the most powerful states. Transnational actors either do not exist or are politically unimportant. Only the adept exercise of force or the threat of force permits states to survive, and only while statesmen succeed in adjusting their interests, as in a well-functioning balance of power, is the system stable.

Each of the realist assumptions can be challenged. If we challenge them all simultaneously, we can imagine a world in which actors other than states participate directly in world politics, in which a clear hierarchy of issues does not exist, and in which force is an ineffective instrument of policy. Under these conditions—which we call the characteristics of complex interdependence—one would expect world politics to be very different than under realist conditions. . . .

We do not argue, however, that complex interdependence faithfully reflects world political reality. Quite the contrary: both it and the realist portrait are ideal types. Most situations will fall somewhere between these two extremes.

Source: From Robert O. Keohane and Joseph S. Nye, Power and Interdependence: World Politics in Transition, *3rd ed. New York: Longman, 2001, pp. 20–28. Copyright © 1989 by Robert O. Keohane and Joseph S. Nye. Reprinted by permission of Pearson Education, Inc., Glenview, IL.*

Sometimes, realist assumptions will be accurate, or largely accurate, but frequently complex interdependence will provide a better portrayal of reality. Before one decides what explanatory model to apply to a situation or problem, one will need to understand the degree to which realist or complex interdependence assumptions correspond to the situation.

THE CHARACTERISTICS OF COMPLEX INTERDEPENDENCE

Complex interdependence has three main characteristics:

(1) *Multiple channels* connect societies, including: informal ties between governmental elites as well as formal foreign office arrangements; informal ties among non-governmental elites (face-to-face and through telecommunications); and transnational organizations (such as multinational banks or corporations). These channels can be summarized as interstate, transgovernmental, and transnational relations. *Interstate* relations are the normal channels assumed by realists. *Transgovernmental* applies when we relax the realist assumption that states act coherently as units; *transnational* applies when we relax the assumption that states are the only units.

(2) The agenda of interstate relationships consists of multiple issues that are not arranged in a clear or consistent hierarchy. This *absence of hierarchy among issues* means, among other things, that military security does not consistently dominate the agenda. Many issues arise from what used to be considered domestic policy, and the distinction between domestic and foreign issues becomes blurred. These issues are considered in several government departments (not just foreign offices), and at several levels. Inadequate policy coordination on these issues involves significant costs. Different issues generate different coalitions, both within governments and across them, and involve different degrees of conflict. Politics does not stop at the waters' edge.

(3) Military force is not used by governments toward other governments within the region, or on the issues, when complex interdependence prevails. It may, however, be important in these governments' relations with governments outside that region, or on other issues. Military force could, for instance, be irrelevant to resolving disagreements on economic issues among members of an alliance, yet at the same time be very important for that alliance's political and military relations with a rival bloc. For the former relationships this condition of complex interdependence would be met; for the latter, it would not. . . .

MINOR ROLE OF MILITARY FORCE

Political scientists have traditionally emphasized the role of military force in international politics. . . . Force dominates other means of power: *if* there are no constraints on one's choice of instruments (a hypothetical situation that has only been approximated in the two world wars), the state with superior military force will prevail. If the security dilemma for all states were extremely acute, military force, supported by economic and other resources, would clearly be the dominant source of power. Survival is the primary goal of all states, and in the worst situations, force is ultimately necessary to guarantee survival. Thus military force is always a central component of national power.

Yet particularly among industrialized, pluralist countries, the perceived margin of safety has widened: fears of attack in general have declined, and fears of attack *by one another* are virtually nonexistent. France has abandoned the *tous azimuts* (defense in all directions) strategy that President de Gaulle advocated (it was not taken entirely seriously even at the time). Canada's last war plans for fighting the United States were abandoned half a century ago. Britain and Germany no longer feel threatened by each other. Intense relationships of mutual influence exist between these countries, but in most of them force is irrelevant or unimportant as an instrument of policy.

Moreover, force is often not an appropriate way of achieving other goals (such as economic and ecological welfare) that are becoming more important. It is not impossible to imagine dramatic conflict or revolutionary change in which the use or threat of military force over an economic issue or among advanced industrial countries might become plausible. Then realist assumptions would again be a reliable guide to events. But in most situations, the effects of military force are both costly and uncertain.[2]

Even when the direct use of force is barred among a group of countries, however, military power can still be used politically. Each superpower continues to use the threat of force to deter attacks by other superpowers on itself or its allies; its deterrence ability thus serves an indirect, protective role, which it can use in bargaining on other issues with its allies. This bargaining tool is particularly important for the United States, whose allies are concerned about potential Soviet threats and which has fewer other means of influence over its allies than does the Soviet Union over its Eastern European partners. The United States has, accordingly, taken advantage of the Europeans' (particularly the Germans') desire for its protection and linked the issue of troop levels in Europe to trade and monetary negotiations. Thus, although the first-order effect of deterrent force is essentially negative—to deny effective offensive power to a superpower opponent—a state can use that force positively—to gain political influence.

Thus, even for countries whose relations approximate complex interdependence, two serious qualifications remain: (1) drastic social and political change could cause force again to become an important direct instrument of policy; and (2) even when elites' interests are complementary, a country that uses military force to protect another may have significant political influence over the other country.

In North-South relations, or relations among Third World countries, as well as in East-West relations, force is often important. Military power helps the Soviet Union to dominate Eastern Europe economically as well as politically. The threat of open or covert American military intervention has helped to limit revolutionary changes in the Caribbean, especially in Guatemala in 1954 and in the Dominican Republic in 1965. Secretary of State Kissinger, in January 1975, issued a veiled warning to members of the Organization of Petroleum Exporting Countries (OPEC) that the United States might use force against them "where there is some actual strangulation of the industrialized world."[3]

Even in these rather conflictual situations, however, the recourse to force seems less likely now than at most times during the century before 1945. The destructiveness of nuclear weapons makes any attack against a nuclear power dangerous. Nuclear weapons are mostly used as a deterrent. Threats of nuclear action against much weaker countries may occasionally be efficacious, but they are equally or more likely to solidify relations between one's adversaries. The limited usefulness of conventional force to control socially mobilized populations has been shown by the United States failure in Vietnam as well as by the rapid decline of colonialism in Africa. Furthermore, employing force on one issue against an independent state with which one has a variety of relationships is likely to rupture mutually profitable relations on other issues. In other words, the use of force often has costly effects on non-security goals. And finally, in Western democracies, popular opposition to prolonged military conflicts is very high.[4]

It is clear that these constraints bear unequally on various countries, or on the same countries in different situations. Risks of nuclear escalation affect everyone, but domestic opinion is far less constraining for communist states, or for authoritarian regional powers, than for the United States, Europe, or Japan. Even authoritarian countries may be reluctant to use force to obtain economic objectives when such use might be ineffective and disrupt other relationships. Both the difficulty of controlling socially mobilized populations with foreign troops and the changing technology of weaponry may actually enhance the ability of certain countries, or nonstate groups, to use terrorism as a political weapon without effective fear of reprisal.

The fact that the changing role of force has uneven effects does not make the change less important, but it does make matters more complex. This complexity is compounded by differences in the usability of force among issue areas. When an issue arouses little interest or passion, force may be unthinkable. In such instances, complex interdependence may be a valuable concept for analyzing the political process. But if that issue becomes a matter of life and death—as some people thought oil might become—the use or threat of force could become decisive again. Realist assumptions would then be more relevant.

It is thus important to determine the applicability of realism or of complex interdependence to each situation. Without this determination further analysis is likely to be confused. Our purpose in developing an alternative to the realist description of world politics is to encourage a differentiated approach that distinguishes among dimensions and areas of world politics—not (as some modernist observers do) to replace one oversimplification with another.

THE POLITICAL PROCESSES OF COMPLEX INTERDEPENDENCE

Three main characteristics of complex interdependence give rise to distinctive political processes, which translate power resources into power as control of outcomes. As we argued earlier, something is usually lost or added in the translation. Under conditions of complex interdependence the translation will be different than under realist conditions, and our predictions about outcomes will need to be adjusted accordingly.

In the realist world, military security will be the dominant goal of states. It will even affect issues that are not directly involved with military power or territorial defense. Nonmilitary problems will not only be subordinated to military ones; they will be studied for their politico-military implications. Balance of payments issues, for instance, will be considered at least as much in the light of their implications for world power generally as for their purely financial ramifications. McGeorge Bundy conformed to realist expectations when he argued in 1964 that devaluation of the dollar should be seriously considered if necessary to fight the war in Vietnam.[5] To some extent, so did former Treasury Secretary Henry Fowler when he contended in 1971 that the United States needed a trade surplus of $4 billion to $6 billion in order to lead in Western defense.[6]

In a world of complex interdependence, however, one expects some officials, particularly at lower levels, to emphasize the *variety* of state goals that must be pursued. In the absence of a clear hierarchy of issues, goals will vary by issue, and may not be closely related. Each bureaucracy will pursue its own concerns; and although several agencies may reach compromises on issues that affect them all, they will find that a consistent pattern of policy is difficult to maintain. Moreover, transnational actors will introduce different goals into various groups of issues.

LINKAGE STRATEGIES

Goals will therefore vary by issue area under complex interdependence, but so will the distribution of power and the typical political processes. Traditional analysis focuses on *the* international system, and leads us to anticipate similar political processes on a variety of issues. Militarily and economically strong states will dominate a variety of organizations and a variety of issues, by linking their own policies on some issues to other states' policies on other issues. By using their overall dominance to prevail on their weak issues, the strongest states will, in the traditional model, ensure a congruence between the overall structure of military and economic power and the pattern of outcomes on any one issue area. Thus world politics can be treated as a seamless web.

Under complex interdependence, such congruence is less likely to occur. As military force is devalued, militarily strong states will find it more difficult to use their overall dominance to control outcomes on issues in which they are weak. And since the distribution of power resources in trade, shipping, or oil, for example, may be quite different, patterns of outcomes and distinctive political processes are likely to vary from one set of issues to another. If force were readily applicable, and military security were the highest foreign policy goal, these variations in the issue structures of power would not matter very much. The linkages drawn from them to military issues would ensure consistent dominance by the overall strongest states. But when military force is largely immobilized, strong states will find that linkage is less effective. They may still attempt such links, but in the absence of a hierarchy of issues, their success will be problematic.

Dominant states may try to secure much the same result by using overall economic power to affect results on other issues. If only economic objectives are at stake, they may succeed: money, after all, is fungible. But economic objectives have political implications, and economic linkage by the strong is limited by domestic, transnational, and transgovernmental actors who resist having their interests traded off. Furthermore, the international actors may be different on different issues, and the international organizations in which negotiations take place are often quite separate. Thus it is difficult, for example, to imagine a militarily or economically strong state linking concessions on monetary policy to reciprocal concessions in oceans policy. On the other hand, poor weak states are not similarly inhibited from linking unrelated issues, partly because their domestic interests are less complex. Linkage of unrelated issues is often a means of extracting concessions or side payments from rich and powerful states. And unlike powerful states whose instrument for linkage (military force) is often too costly to use, the linkage instrument used by poor, weak states—international organization—is available and inexpensive.

Thus as the utility of force declines, and as issues become more equal in importance, the distribution of power within each issue will become more important. If linkages become less effective on the whole, outcomes of political bargaining will increasingly vary by issue area.

The differentiation among issue areas in complex interdependence means that linkages among issues will become more problematic and will tend to reduce rather than reinforce international hierarchy. Linkage strategies, and defense against them, will pose critical strategic choices for states. Should issues be considered separately or as a package? If linkages are to be drawn, which issues should be linked, and on which of the linked issues should concessions be made? How far can one push a linkage before it becomes counterproductive? For instance, should one seek formal agreements or informal, but less politically sensitive, understandings? The fact that world politics under complex interdependence is not a seamless web leads us to expect that efforts to stitch seams together advantageously, as reflected in linkage strategies, will, very often, determine the shape of the fabric.

The negligible role of force leads us to expect states to rely more on other instruments in order to wield power. For the reasons we have already discussed, less vulnerable states will try to use asymmetrical interdependence in particular groups of issues as a source of power; they will also try to use international organizations and transnational actors and flows. States will approach economic interdependence in terms of power as well as its effects on citizens' welfare, although welfare considerations will limit their attempts to maximize power. Most economic and ecological interdependence involves the possibility of joint gains, or joint losses. Mutual awareness of potential gains and losses and the danger of worsening each actor's position through overly rigorous struggles over the distribution of the gains can limit the use of asymmetrical interdependence.

AGENDA SETTING

Our second assumption of complex interdependence, the lack of clear hierarchy among multiple issues, leads us to expect that the politics of agenda formation and control will become more important. Traditional analyses lead statesmen to focus on politico-military issues and to pay little attention to the broader politics of agenda formation. Statesmen assume that the agenda will be set by shifts in the balance of power, actual or anticipated, and by perceived threats to the security of states. Other issues will only be very important when they seem to affect security and military power. In these cases, agendas will be influenced strongly by considerations of the overall balance of power.

Yet, today, some nonmilitary issues are emphasized in interstate relations at one time, whereas others of seemingly equal importance are neglected or quietly handled at a technical level. International monetary politics, problems of commodity terms of trade, oil, food, and multinational corporations have all been important during the last decade; but not all have been high on interstate agendas throughout that period.

Traditional analysts of international politics have paid little attention to agenda formation: to how issues come to receive sustained attention by high officials. The traditional orientation toward military and security affairs implies that the crucial problems of foreign policy are imposed on states by the actions or threats of other states. These are high politics as opposed to the low politics of economic affairs. Yet, as the complexity of actors and issues in world politics increases, the utility of force declines and the line between domestic policy and foreign policy becomes blurred: as the conditions of complex interdependence are more closely approximated, the politics of agenda formation becomes more subtle and differentiated.

NOTES

1 Hans J. Morgenthau, *Politics among Nations: The Struggle for Power and Peace*, 4th ed. (New York: Knopf, 1967), p. 36.
2 For a valuable discussion, see Klaus Knorr, *The Power of Nations: The Political Economy of International Relations* (New York: Basic Books, 1975).
3 *Business Week*, January 13, 1975.
4 Stanley Hoffmann, "The Acceptability of Military Force," and Laurence Martin, "The Utility of Military Force," in *Force in Modern Societies: Its Place in International*

Politics (Adelphi Paper, International Institute for Strategic Studies, 1973). See also Knorr, *The Power of Nations.*

5 Henry Brandon, *The Retreat of American Power* (New York: Doubleday, 1974), p. 218.

6 *International Implications of the New Economic Policy*, U.S. Congress, House of Representatives, Committee on Foreign Affairs, Subcommittee on Foreign Economic Policy, Hearings, September 16, 1971.

Reading 3.6

The Obsolescence of Major War

JOHN MUELLER

O n May 15, 1984, the major countries of the developed world had managed to remain at peace with each other for the longest continuous
stretch of time since the days of the Roman Empire. If a significant
battle in a war had been fought on that day, the press would have bristled with
it. As usual, however, a landmark crossing in the history of peace caused no
stir: the most prominent story in the *New York Times* that day concerned the
saga of a manicurist, a machinist, and a cleaning woman who had just won a
big Lotto contest. . . .

For decades now, two massively armed countries, the United States and
the Soviet Union, have dominated international politics, and during that time
they have engaged in an intense, sometimes even desperate, rivalry over political, military, and ideological issues. Yet despite this enormous mutual hostility,
they have never gone to war with each other. Furthermore, although they have
occasionally engaged in confrontational crises, there have been only a few of
these—and virtually none at all in the last two-thirds of the period. Rather
than gradually drawing closer to armed conflict, as often happened after earlier
wars, the two major countries seem to be drifting farther away from it.

Insofar as it is discussed at all, there appear to be two schools of thought
to explain what John Lewis Gaddis has called the "long peace."[1]

One school concludes that we have simply been lucky. Since 1947, the
Bulletin of Atomic Scientists has decorated its cover with a "doomsday" clock
set ominously at a few minutes before midnight. From time to time the editors
push the clock's big hand forward or backward a bit to demonstrate their pleasure with an arms control measure or their disapproval of what they perceive
to be rising tension; but they never nudge it very far away from the fatal hour,
and the message they wish to convey is clear. They believe we live perpetually

on the brink, teetering on a fragile balance; if our luck turns a bit sour, we are likely at any moment to topple helplessly in cataclysmic war.[2] As time goes by, however, this point of view begins to lose some of its persuasiveness. When a clock remains poised at a few minutes to midnight for decades, one may gradually come to suspect that it isn't telling us very much.

The other school stresses paradox: It is the very existence of unprecedentedly destructive weapons that has worked, so far, to our benefit—in Winston Churchill's memorable phrase, safety has been the "sturdy child of [nuclear] terror."[3] This widely held (if minimally examined) view is, to say the least, less than fully comforting, because the very weapons that have been so necessary for peace according to this argument, also possess the capability of cataclysmic destruction, should they somehow be released. For many, this perpetual threat is simply too much to bear, and to them the weapons' continued existence seals our ultimate doom even as it perpetuates our current peace. In his influential best-seller, *The Fate of the Earth*, Jonathan Schell dramatically prophesies that if we do not "rise up and cleanse the earth of nuclear weapons," we will soon "sink into the final coma and end it all."[4]

This book develops a third explanation: The long peace since World War II is less a product of recent weaponry than the culmination of a substantial historical process. For the last two or three centuries major war—war among developed countries—has gradually moved toward terminal disrepute because of its perceived repulsiveness and futility.

The book also concludes that nuclear weapons have not had an important impact on this remarkable trend—they have not crucially defined postwar stability, and they do not threaten to disturb it severely. They have affected rhetoric (we live, we are continually assured, in the atomic age, the nuclear epoch), and they certainly have influenced defense budgets and planning. However, they do not seem to have been necessary to deter major war, to cause the leaders of major countries to behave cautiously, or to determine the alliances that have been formed. Rather, it seems that things would have turned out much the same had nuclear weapons never been invented.

That something other than nuclear terror explains the long peace is suggested in part by the fact that there have been numerous nonwars since 1945 besides the nonwar that is currently being waged by the United States and the Soviet Union. With only one minor and fleeting exception (the Soviet invasion of Hungary in 1956), there have been no wars among the forty-four wealthiest (per capita) countries during that time.[5] Although there have been many wars since World War II, some of them enormously costly by any standard, these have taken place almost entirely within the third—or really the fourth—world. The developed countries have sometimes participated in these wars on distant turf, but not directly against each other.

Several specific nonwars are in their own way even more extraordinary than the one that has taken place between the United States and the Soviet Union. France and Germany are important countries which had previously spent decades—centuries even—either fighting each other or planning to do so. For this ages-old antagonism World War II indeed served as the war to end war: like Greece and Turkey, they have retained the creative ability to discover a motivation for war even under an overarching nuclear umbrella if they really wanted to, yet they have now lived side by side for decades, perhaps with some bitterness and recrimination, but without even a glimmer of war fever. The case of Japan is also striking: this formerly aggressive major country seems now to have fully embraced the virtues (and profits) of peace.

In fact, within the first and second worlds warfare of *all* sorts seems generally to have lost its appeal. Not only have there been virtually no international wars among the major and not-so-major countries, but the developed world has experienced virtually no civil war either. The only exception is the 1944–49 Greek civil war—more an unsettled residue of World War II than an autonomous event. The sporadic violence in Northern Ireland or the Basque region of Spain has not really been sustained enough to be considered civil war, nor have the spurts of terrorism carried out by tiny bands of self-styled revolutionaries elsewhere in Western Europe that have never coalesced into anything bigger. Except for the fleeting case of Hungary in 1956, Europeans under Soviet rule have so far accepted their fate, no matter how desperate their disaffection, rather than take arms to oppose it—though some sort of civil uprising there is certainly not out of the question.[6]

Because it is so quiet, peace often is allowed to carry on unremarked. We tend to delimit epochs by wars and denote periods of peace not for their own character, but for the wars they separate. As Geoffrey Blainey has observed, "For every thousand pages published on the causes of wars there is less than one page directly on the causes of peace."[7] But now, surely, with so much peace at hand in so much of the world, some effort ought to be made to explain the unprecedented cornucopia. Never before in history have so many well-armed, important countries spent so much time not using their arms against each other. . . .

THE RISING COSTS OF WAR

War is merely an idea. It is not a trick of fate, a thunderbolt from hell, a natural calamity, or a desperate plot contrivance dreamed up by some sadistic puppeteer on high. And if war begins in the minds of men, as the UNESCO charter insists, it can end there as well. Over the centuries war opponents have been trying to bring this about by discrediting war as an idea. In part, their message . . . stresses that war is unacceptably costly, and they have pointed to two kinds of costs: (1) psychic ones—war, they argue, is repulsive, immoral, and uncivilized; and (2) physical ones—war is bloody, destructive, and expensive.

It is often observed that war's physical costs have risen. World War II was the most destructive in history, and World War I was also terrible. World War III, even if nuclear weapons were not used, could easily be worse; and a thermonuclear war might, as Schell would have it, "end it all."

Rising physical costs do seem to have helped to discredit war. But there are good reasons to believe that this cannot be the whole story.

In 1889, Baroness Bertha von Suttner of Austria published a sentimental antiwar novel, *Die Waffen Nieder!*, that swiftly became an international bestseller—the *Uncle Tom's Cabin* of the nineteenth-century peace movement. In it she describes the travails of a young Austrian woman who turns against war when her husband is killed in the Franco-Austrian War of 1859. Now, in historical perspective, that brief war was one of the least memorable in modern history, and its physical costs were minor in comparison with many other wars of that, or any other, era. But Suttner's fictional young widow was repelled not by the war's size, but by its existence and by the devastating personal consequences to her. Opposition to war has been growing in the developed world because more and more people have come to find war repulsive for what it *is*, not simply for the extent of the devastation it causes.

Furthermore, it is simply not true that cataclysmic war is an invention of the 20th century.[8] To annihilate ancient Carthage in 146 b.c., the Romans used weaponry that was primitive by today's standard, but even nuclear weapons could not have been more thorough. And, as Thucydides recounts with shattering calm, when the Athenians invaded Melos in 416 b.c., they "put to death all the grown men whom they took and sold the women and children for slaves, and subsequently sent out five hundred colonists and inhabited the place for themselves."[9]

During the Thirty Years War of 1618–48 the wealthy city of Magdeburg, together with its 20,000 inhabitants, was annihilated. According to standard estimates accepted as late as the 1930s, Germany's population in that war declined from 21 million to under 13.5 million—absolute losses far larger than it suffered in either world war of the twentieth century. Moreover, and more importantly, most people apparently *thought* things were even worse: for centuries a legend prevailed that Germany had suffered a 75 percent decline in population, from 16 million to 4 million.[10] Yet the belief that war could cause devastation of such enormous proportions did not lead to its abandonment. After the Thirty Years War, conflict remained endemic in Europe, and in 1756 Prussia fought the Seven Years War, which, in the estimate of its king and generalissimo, Frederick the Great, cost it 500,000 lives—one-ninth of its population, a proportion higher than almost any suffered by any combatant in the wars of the nineteenth or twentieth centuries.[11]

Wars in the past have often caused revolts and economic devastation as well. Historians have been debating for a century whether the Thirty Years War destroyed a vibrant economy in Germany or whether it merely administered the final blow to an economy that was already in decline—but destruction was the consequence in either case. The Seven Years War brought Austria to virtual bankruptcy, and it so weakened France that the conditions for revolution were established. When the economic costs of war are measured as a percentage of the gross national product of the combatants, observes Alan Milward, war "has not shown any discernible long-term trend towards greater costliness."[12]

And in sheer pain and suffering wars used to be far worse than ones fought by developed countries today. In 1840 or 1640 or 1240 a wounded or diseased soldier often died slowly and in intense agony. Medical aid was inadequate, and since physicians had few remedies and were unaware of the germ theory, they often only made things worse. War, indeed, was hell. By contrast, an American soldier wounded in the Vietnam jungle could be in a sophisticated, sanitized hospital within a half hour.

Consequently, if the revulsion toward war has grown in the developed world, this development cannot be due entirely to a supposed rise in its physical costs. Also needed is an appreciation for war's increased psychic costs. Over the last century or two, war in the developed world has come widely to be regarded as repulsive, immoral, and uncivilized. There may also be something of an interactive effect between psychic and physical costs here: If for moral reasons we come to place a higher value on human life—even to have a sort of reverence for it—the physical costs of war or any other life-taking enterprise will effectively rise as cost tolerance declines.

It may not be obvious that an accepted, time-honored institution that serves an urgent social purpose can become obsolescent and then die out because a lot of people come to find it obnoxious. But this book will argue that something like that has been happening to war in the developed world. To illustrate the dynamic and to set up a framework for future discussion, it will be helpful briefly to assess two analogies: the processes through which the once-perennial institutions of dueling and slavery have been virtually expunged from the earth.

DUELING CEASES TO BE A "PECULIAR NECESSITY"

In some important respects war in the developed world may be following the example of another violent method for settling disputes, dueling, which up until a century ago was common practice in Europe and America among a certain class of young and youngish men who liked to classify themselves as gentlemen. When one man concluded that he had been insulted by another and therefore that his honor had been besmirched, he might well engage the insulter in a short, private, and potentially deadly battle. The duel was taken somehow to settle the matter, even if someone was killed in the process—or even if someone wasn't.[13]

At base, dueling was a matter of attitude more than of cosmology or technology; it was something someone might want to do, and in some respects was even expected to do, from time to time. The night before his famous fatal duel with Aaron Burr in 1804, the methodical Alexander Hamilton wrote out his evaluation of the situation. He could find many reasons to reject Burr's challenge—he really felt no ill will toward his challenger, he wrote, and dueling was against his religious and moral principles, as well as against the laws of New York (where he lived) and New Jersey (where the duel was to be held); furthermore, his death would endanger the livelihood of his wife, children, and creditors. In sum, "I shall hazard much, and can possibly gain nothing." Nevertheless, he still concluded he must fight. All these concerns were overwhelmed because he felt that "what men of the world denominate honor" imposed upon him a "peculiar necessity": his refusal to duel would reduce his political effectiveness by subjecting him to contempt and derision in the circles he considered important. Therefore, he felt that he had to conform with "public prejudice in this particular."[14] Although there were solid economic, legal, moral, and religious reasons to turn down the challenge of Vice President Burr, the prick of honor and the attendant fear of immobilizing ridicule—Hamilton's peculiar necessities—impelled him to venture out that summer morning to meet his fate, and his maker, at Weehawken, N.J.

Dueling died out as a general practice eighty years later in the United States after enjoying quite a vogue, especially in the South and in California. It finally faded, not so much because it was outlawed (like liquor—and war—in the 1920s), but because the "public prejudice" Hamilton was so fatally concerned about changed in this particular. Since dueling was an activity carried out by consenting adults in private, laws prohibiting it were difficult to enforce when the climate of opinion accepted the institution. But gradually a consensus emerged that dueling was contemptible and stupid, and it came to be duelers, not nonduelers, who suffered ridicule. As one student of the subject has concluded, "It began to be clear that pistols at ten paces did not settle anything except who was the better shot. . . . Dueling had long been condemned by both statute book and church decree. But these could make no headway against public opinion." However, when it came to pass that "solemn gentlemen went to the field of honor only to be laughed at by the younger generation, that was more than any custom, no matter how sanctified by tradition, could endure. And so the code of honor in America finally died." One of the last duels was in 1877. After the battle (at which no blood was spilled), the combatants found themselves the butt of public hilarity, causing one of them to flee to Paris, where he remained in self-exile for several years.[15]

The American experience was reflected elsewhere. Although dueling's decline in country after country was due in part to enforced legislation against it, the "most effective weapon" against it, one study concludes, "has undoubtedly been ridicule."[16] The ultimate physical cost of dueling—death—did not, and could not rise. But the psychic costs did.

Men of Hamilton's social set still exist, they still get insulted, and they still are concerned about their self-respect and their standing among their peers. But they don't duel. However, they do not avoid dueling today because they evaluate the option and reject it on cost-benefit grounds—to use the jargon of a later chapter, they do not avoid it because it has become rationally unthinkable. Rather, the option never percolates into their consciousness as something that is available—that is, it has become subrationally unthinkable. Dueling under the right conditions—with boxing gloves, for example—would not violate current norms or laws. And, of course, in other social classes duel-like combat, such as the street fight or gang war, persists. But the romantic, ludicrous institution of formal dueling has faded from the scene. Insults of the sort that led to the Hamilton-Burr duel often are simply ignored or, if applicable, they are settled with peaceful methods like litigation.[17]

A dueling manual from 1847 states that "dueling, like war, is the necessary consequence of offense."[18] By now, however, dueling, a form of violence famed and fabled for centuries, is avoided not merely because it has ceased to seem "necessary," but because it has sunk from thought as a viable, conscious possibility. You can't fight a duel if the idea of doing so never occurs to you or your opponent.

The Prussian strategist Carl von Clausewitz opens his famous 1832 book, *On War*, by observing that "war is nothing but a duel on a larger scale."[19] If war, like dueling, comes to be viewed as a thoroughly undesirable, even ridiculous, policy, and if it can no longer promise gains or if potential combatants no longer value the things it can gain for them, then war could fade away first as a "peculiar necessity" and then as a coherent possibility, even if a truly viable substitute or "moral equivalent" for it were never formulated. Like dueling, it could become unfashionable and then obsolete.

SLAVERY ABRUPTLY BECOMES A "PECULIAR INSTITUTION"

From the dawn of prehistory until about 1788 it had occurred to almost no one that there was anything the least bit peculiar about the institution of slavery. Like war, it could be found just about everywhere in one form or another, and it flourished in every age.[20] Here and there, some people expressed concern about excessive cruelty, and a few found slavery an unfortunate necessity. But the abolitionist movement that broke out at the end of the eighteenth century in Britain and the United States was something new, not the culmination of a substantial historical process.

Like war opponents, the antislavery forces had come to believe that the institution that concerned them was unacceptable because of both its psychic and its physical costs. For some time a small but socially active religious sect in England and the United States, the Quakers, had been arguing that slavery, like war, was repulsive, immoral, and uncivilized, and this sentiment gradually picked up adherents.

Slavery's physical costs, opponents argued, stemmed from its inefficiency. In 1776, Adam Smith concluded that the "work done by slaves . . . is in the end the dearest of any" because "a person who can acquire no property, can have no other interest but to eat as much and to labor as little as possible." Smith's view garnered adherents, but not, as it happens, among slaveowners. That is, either Smith was wrong, or slaveholders were bad businessmen. Clearly, if the economic argument had been correct, slavery would have eventually died of its own inefficiency. Although some have argued that this process was indeed under way, Stanley Engerman observes that in "the history of slave emancipation in the Americas, it is difficult to find any cases of slavery declining economically prior to the imposition of emancipation." Rather, he says, "it took political and military action to bring it to a halt," and "political, cultural, and ideological factors" played crucial roles. In fact, at exactly the time that the antislavery movement was taking flight, the Atlantic slave economy, as Seymour Drescher notes, "was entering what was probably the most dynamic and profitable period in its existence."[21]

Thus, the abolitionists were up against an institution that was viable, profitable, and expanding, and one that had been uncritically accepted for thousands—perhaps millions—of years as a natural and inevitable part of human existence. To counter this time-honored institution, the abolitionists' principal weapon was a novel argument: it had recently occurred to them, they said, that slavery was no longer the way people ought to do things.

As it happened, it was an idea whose time had come. The abolition of slavery required legislative battles, international pressures, economic travail, and, in the United States, a cataclysmic war (but, notably, it did *not* require the fabrication of a functional equivalent or the formation of an effective supranational authority). Within a century slavery, and most similar institutions like serfdom, had been all but eradicated from the face of the globe. Slavery became controversial, then peculiar, and then obsolete.

WAR

Dueling and slavery no longer exist as effective institutions and have faded from human experience except as something one reads about in books. Although their reestablishment is not impossible, they show after a century of neglect no signs of revival. Other once-popular, even once admirable, institutions in the developed world have been, or are being, eliminated because at some point they began to seem repulsive, immoral, and uncivilized: bear-baiting, bareknuckle fighting, freak shows, casual torture, wanton cruelty to animals, the burning of heretics, Jim Crow laws, human sacrifice, family feuding, public and intentionally painful methods of execution, deforming corseting, infanticide, laughing at the insane, executions for minor crimes, eunuchism, flogging, public cigarette smoking. . . . War is not, of course, the same as dueling or slavery. Like war, dueling is an institution for settling disputes; but it usually involved only matters of "honor," not ones of physical gain. Like war, slavery was nearly universal and an apparently inevitable part of human existence, but it could be eliminated area by area: a country that abolished slavery did not have to worry about what other countries were doing. A country that would like to abolish war, however, must continue to be concerned about those that have kept it in their repertoire.

On the other hand, war has against it not only substantial psychic costs but also very obvious and widespread physical ones. Dueling brought death and injury, but only to a few people who, like Hamilton, had specifically volunteered to participate. And although slavery may have brought moral destruction, it generally was a considerable economic success in the view of those who ran the system, if not to every ivory-tower economist.

In some respects, then, the fact that war has outlived dueling and slavery is curious. But there are signs that, at least in the developed world, it has begun, like them, to succumb to obsolescence. Like dueling and slavery, war does not appear to be one of life's necessities—it is not an unpleasant fact of existence that is somehow required by human nature or by the grand scheme of things. One can live without it, quite well in fact. War may be a social affliction, but in important respects it is also a social affectation that can be shrugged off.

NOTES

1 Gaddis 1987b. The calculations about eras of peace are by Paul Schroeder (1985, p. 88). The previous record, he notes, was chalked up during the period from the end of the Napoleonic Wars in 1815 to the effective beginning of the Crimean War in 1854. The period between the conclusion of the Franco-Prussian War in 1871 and the outbreak of World War I in 1914 marred by a major war in Asia between Russia and Japan in 1904—was an even longer era of peace among major European countries. That record was broken on November 8, 1988. On some of these issues, see also Nye 1987; Hinsley 1963, ch. 17; Luard 1986, pp. 395–99; Russett and Starr 1981, ch. 15.

2 Said Herman Kahn in 1960: "I have a firm belief that unless we have more serious and sober thought on various aspects of the strategic problem . . . we are not going to reach the year 2000—and maybe not even the year 1965—without a cataclysm" (1960, p. x). Hans J. Morgenthau stated in 1979, "In my opinion the world is moving ineluctably towards a third world war—a strategic nuclear war. I do not believe that anything can be done to prevent it. The international system is too unstable to survive for long" (quoted, Boyle 1985, p. 73). And astronomer Carl Sagan commented in 1983: "I do not think our luck can hold out forever" (quoted, Schroeder 1985, p. 87). On the history of the doomsday clock, see Feld 1978.

3 Churchill: Bartlett 1977, p. 104. Edward Luttwak says, "We have lived since 1945 without another world war precisely because rational minds . . . extracted a durable peace from the very terror of nuclear weapons" (1983b, p. 82). Kenneth N. Waltz: "Nuclear weapons have banished war from the center of international politics" (1988, p. 627). See also Knorr 1985, p. 79; Mearsheimer 1984/85, pp. 25–26; Art and Waltz 1983, p. 28; Gilpin 1981, pp. 213–19; Betts 1987, pp. 1–2; Joffe 1987, p. 37; F. Lewis 1987.

4 Schell 1982, p. 231. For a discussion of expert opinion concluding that the chances of nuclear war by the year 2000 were at least fifty-fifty, see Russett 1983, pp. 3–4.

5 Wealth is calculated using 1978 data when Iran and Iraq were at their financial peak (World Bank 1980). If later data are used, the figure of forty-four would be greater. Countries like Monaco that have no independent foreign policy are not included in the count. The Soviet invasion of Hungary was in some sense requested by ruling politicians in Hungary and for that reason is sometimes not classified as an international war. On classification issues, see Small and Singer 1982, pp. 55, 305; Luard 1986, pp. 5–7. Small and Singer consider Saudi Arabia to have been a participant in the Yom Kippur War of 1973 because it committed 1,000 troops to the anti-Israeli conflict (p. 306); if one accepts their procedure here, that war would form another example of war among the top forty-four. Some might also include the bloodless "war" between the USSR and Czechoslovakia in 1968.

6 Even as dedicated a foe of the Soviet regime as Aleksandr Solzhenitsyn has said, "I have never advocated physical general revolution. That would entail such destruction of our people's life as would not merit the victory obtained" (quoted, S. Cohen 1985, p. 214).

7 Blainey, 1973, p. 3.

8 To put things in somewhat broader perspective, it may be useful to note that war is not the century's greatest killer. Although there have been a large number of extremely destructive wars, totalitarian and extreme authoritarian governments have put more of their own people to death—three times more according to one calculation—than have died in all the century's international and civil wars combined (Rummel 1986). For example, the man-made famine in China between 1958 and 1962 apparently caused the deaths of 30 million people (see p. 165), far more than died during World War I. Governments at peace can also surpass war in their economic destruction as well; largely because of government mismanagement and corruption, the average Zairian's wages in 1988, after adjusting for inflation, were 10 percent of what they had been in 1960 (Greenhouse 1988).

9 Thucydides 1934, p. 337.

10 Wedgwood 1938, p. 516. German civilian and military deaths have been estimated at 3,160,000 in World War I and 6,221,000 in World War II (Sivard 1987, p. 29). For the latter-day argument that the losses in the Thirty Years War have been grossly overestimated, see Steinberg 1966, ch. 3. A recent estimate suggests a population decline from 20 million to 16 or 17 million (Parker 1984, p. 211).

11 Luard 1986, p. 51. Small and Singer 1982, pp. 82–99. About 180,000 of the half-million were soldiers (Kennedy 1987, p. 115), giving a battle death rate of about 4 percent.

12 Thirty Years War: Robb 1962. Seven Years War: Kennedy 1987, p. 114; Brodie 1973, pp. 248–49; Milward 1977, p. 3.

13 For other observations of the analogy between war and dueling, see Brodie 1973, p. 275; Angell 1914, pp. 202–3; Gooch 1911, p. 249; Cairnes 1865, p. 650n.

14 Seitz 1929, pp. 98–101; Freeman 1884, pp. 345–48.

15 Stevens 1940, pp. 280–83. See also Cochran 1963, p. 287.

16 Baldick 1965, p. 199.

17 It is sometimes held that dueling died out because improved access to the legal system provided a nonviolent alternative. But most duels were fought over matters of "honor," not legality. Furthermore, lawyers, hardly a group alienated or disenfranchised from the legal system, were frequent duelists—in Tennessee 90 percent of all duels were fought between attorneys (Seitz 1929, p. 30).

18 Stowe 1987, p. 15.

19 Clausewitz 1976, p. 75.

20 See Patterson 1982; Engerman 1986, pp. 318–19.

21 Smith 1976, p. 387 (book 3, ch. 2). Engerman 1986, pp. 322–33, 339. Drescher 1987, p. 4; see also Eltis 1987.

REFERENCES

Angell, Norman. 1914. *The Great Illusion: A Study of the Relation of Military Power to National Advantage.* London: Heinemann.

———. 1933. *The Great Illusion 1933.* New York: Putnam's.

———. 1951. *After All: An Autobiography.* New York: Farrar, Straus and Young.

Art, Robert J., and Kenneth N. Waltz. 1983. Technology, Strategy, and the Uses of Force. In Robert J. Art and Kenneth N. Waltz (eds.), *The Use of Force.* Lanham, MD: University Press of America.

Baldick, Robert. 1965. *The Duel: A History of Dueling.* New York: Potter.

Bartlett, C. J. 1977. *A History of Postwar Britain, 1945–1974.* London: Longman.

Betts, Richard K. 1987. *Nuclear Blackmail and Nuclear Balance.* Washington: Brookings.

Boyle, Francis Anthony. 1985. *World Politics and International Law.* Durham, NC: Duke University Press.

Brodie, Bernard. 1946. The Weapon. In Bernard Brodie (ed.), *The Absolute Weapon.* New York: Harcourt, Brace, pp. 21–107.

———. 1959. *Strategy in the Missile Age.* Princeton, NJ: Princeton University Press.

———. 1966. *Escalation and the Nuclear Option.* Princeton, NJ: Princeton University Press.

———. 1973. *War and Politics.* New York: Macmillan.

———. 1976a. The Continuing Relevance of *On War*, and A Guide to the Reading of *On War*. In Carl von Clausewitz, *On War.* Princeton, NJ: Princeton University Press, pp. 45–58, 641–711.

———. 1976b. On the Objectives of Arms Control. *International Security*, vol. 1, no. 1 (summer), pp. 17–36.

Cairnes, J. E. 1865. International Law. *Fortnightly Review*, vol. 2 (November 1), pp. 641–50.

Clausewitz, Carl von. 1976. *On War* (edited and translated by Michael Howard and Peter Paret).

Cochran, Hamilton. 1963. *Noted American Duels and Hostile Encounters.* Philadelphia: Chilton.

Drescher, Seymour. 1987. *Capitalism and Antislavery: British Mobilization in Comparative Perspective.* New York: Oxford University Press.

———. 1988. Brazilian Abolition in Comparative Perspective. *Hispanic American Historical Review*, vol. 68, no. 3 (August), pp. 429–60.

Eltis, David. 1987. *Economic Growth and the Ending of the Transatlantic Slave Trade.* New York: Oxford University Press.

Engerman, Stanley L. 1986. Slavery and Emancipation in Comparative Perspective: A Look at Some Recent Debates. *Journal of Economic History*, vol. 46, no. 2 (June), pp. 317–39.

Feld, Bernard T. 1978. To Move or Not to Move the Clock. *Bulletin of Atomic Scientists*, January, pp. 8–9.

Freeman, Major Ben C. 1884. *The Field of Honor: Being a Complete and Comprehensive History of Dueling in All Countries.* New York: Fords, Howard, and Hulbert.

Gaddis, John Lewis. 1972. *The United States and the Origins of the Cold War, 1941–1947.* New York: Columbia University Press.

———. 1974. Was the Truman Doctrine a Real Turning Point? *Foreign Affairs*, vol. 52, no. 2 (January), pp. 386–401.

———. 1982. *Strategies of Containment: A Critical Appraisal of Postwar American National Security Policy.* New York: Oxford University Press.

———. 1987a. Expanding the Data Base: Historians, Political Scientists, and the Enrichment of Security Studies. *International Security*, vol. 12, no. 1 (summer), pp. 3–21.

———. 1987b. *The Long Peace: Inquiries into the History of the Cold War.* New York: Oxford University Press.

Gilpin, Robert. 1981. *War and Change in World Politics.* Cambridge: Cambridge University Press.

Gooch, B. P. 1911. *History of Our Time, 1885–1911.* London: Williams and Norgate.

Greenhouse, Steven. 1988. Zaire, The Manager's Nightmare, So Much Potential, So Poorly Harnessed. *New York Times*, May 23, p. 48. See also correction, May 26, p. A3.

Hinsley, F. H. 1963. *Power and the Pursuit of Peace: Theory and Practice in the History of Relations between States*. London: Cambridge University Press.

Joffe, Josef. 1987. Peace and Populism: Why the European Anti-Nuclear Movement Failed. *International Security*, vol. 11, no. 4 (spring), pp. 3–40.

Kahn, Herman. 1960. *On Thermonuclear War*. Princeton, NJ: Princeton University Press.

———. 1970. Issues of Thermonuclear War Termination. *Annals of the American Academy of Political and Social Science*, vol. 390 (November), pp. 133–72.

Kennedy, Paul. 1987. *The Rise and Fall of the Great Powers*. New York: Random House.

Knorr, Klaus. 1966. *On the Uses of Military Power in the Nuclear Age*. Princeton, NJ: Princeton University Press.

———. 1985. Controlling Nuclear War. *International Security*, vol. 9, no. 4 (spring), pp. 79–98.

Lewis, Flora. 1986. Step Back from Folly. *New York Times*, November 7, p. A35.

———. 1987. Don't Be Afraid of 'Da'. *New York Times*, April 17, p. A31.

Luard, Evan. 1986. *War in International Society: A Study in International Sociology*. New Haven, CT: Yale University Press.

Luttwak, Edward N. 1983a. *The Grand Strategy of the Soviet Union*. New York: St. Martin's.

———. 1983b. Of Bombs and Men. *Commentary*, August, pp. 77–82.

———. 1988. An Emerging Postnuclear Era? *Washington Quarterly*, vol. 11, no. 1 (winter), pp. 5–15.

Mearsheimer, John J. 1983. *Conventional Deterrence*. Ithaca, NY: Cornell University Press.

———. 1984/85. Nuclear Weapons and Deterrence in Europe. *International Security*, vol. 9, no. 3 (winter), pp. 19–47.

Milward, Alan S. 1977. *War, Economy and Society, 1939–1945*. Berkeley, CA. University of California Press.

Morgenthau, Hans J. 1948. *Politics among Nations: The Struggle for Power and Peace*. New York: Knopf.

Nye, Joseph S., Jr. 1987. Nuclear Learning and U.S.—Soviet Security Regimes. *International Organization*, vol. 41, no. 3 (summer), pp. 371–402.

Parker, Geoffrey. 1984. *The Thirty Years War*. London: Routledge and Kegan Paul.

Patterson, Orlando. 1982. *Slavery and Social Death: A Comparative Study*. Cambridge, MA: Harvard University Press.

Robb, Theodore K. 1962. The Effects of the Thirty Years' War. *Journal of Modern History*, vol. 34 (March), pp. 40–51.

Rummel, Rudolph J. 1983. Libertarianism and International Violence. *Journal of Conflict Resolution*, vol. 27, no. 1 (March), pp. 27–71.

———. 1986. War Isn't This Century's Biggest Killer. *Wall Street Journal*, July 7, p. 12.

Russett, Bruce. 1963. The Calculus of Deterrence. *Journal of Conflict Resolution*, vol. 7 (June), pp. 97–109.

———. 1972. *No Clear and Present Danger: A Skeptical View of the United States' Entry into World War II*. New York: Harper and Row.

———. 1983. *The Prisoners of Insecurity: Nuclear Deterrence, the Arms Race, and Arms Control*. San Francisco: Freeman.

Russett, Bruce, and Harvey Starr. 1981. *World Politics: The Menu for Choice*. San Francisco: Freeman.

Sagan, Carl. 1983/84. Nuclear War and Climatic Catastrophe: Some Policy Implications. *Foreign Affairs*, vol. 62, no. 2 (winter), pp. 257–92.

Schell, Jonathan. 1982. *The Fate of the Earth*. New York: Knopf.

Schroeder, Paul. 1985. Does Murphy's Law Apply to History? *Wilson Quarterly*, vol. 9, no. 1 (New Year's), pp. 84–93.

Seitz, Don C. 1929. *Famous American Duels*. New York: Crowell.

Sivard, Ruth Leger. 1985. *World Military and Social Expenditures 1985*. Washington: World Priorities.

———. 1987. *World Military and Social Expenditures 1987/88*. Washington: World Priorities.

Small, Melvin, and J. David Singer. 1982. *Resort to Arms: International Civil Wars, 1816–1980*. Beverly Hills, CA: Sage.

Smith, Adam. 1976. *An Inquiry into the Nature and Causes of the Wealth of Nations*. New York: Oxford University Press.

Steinberg, S. H. 1966. *The Thirty Years War and the Conflict for European Hegemony 1600–1660*. New York: Norton.

Stevens, William Oliver. 1940. *Pistols at Ten Paces: The Story of the Code of Honor in America*. Boston: Houghton Mifflin.

Stowe, Steven M. 1987. *Intimacy and Power in the Old South: Ritual in the Lives of the Planters*. Baltimore, MD: Johns Hopkins University Press.

Thucydides. 1934. *The Peloponnesian War*. New York: Modern Library.

Waltz, Kenneth. 1959. *Man, the State, and War*. New York: Columbia University Press.

———. 1979. *Theory of International Politics*. Reading, MA: Addison-Wesley.

———. 1988. The Origins of War in Neorealist Theory. *Journal of Interdisciplinary History*, vol. 18, no. 4 (spring), pp. 615–28.

Wedgwood, C. V. 1938. *The Thirty Years War*. London: Jonathan Cape.

———. 1961. *The Thirty Years War*. Garden City, NY: Anchor.

Psychology and Culture: The Human Mind, Norms, and Learning

Historically, many theorists of war, peace, and strategy were keenly aware of the impact of subjective factors on policymakers. They assumed that emotion, tradition, personal honor or shame, and other such concerns could determine decisions and control events. In recent times analysts have tended to favor the perspective of economists who see choices in terms of the material value of stakes and the balance of benefits and costs of strategies to gain or guard them.

The thinkers sampled so far also view war or peace as products of explicitly political incentives and constraints. These pressures may be external or domestic, but for the most part, both realist and liberal schools see politics as a rational process of adaptation to the environment or application of conscious value systems to policy. Views of human nature and social competition play a large role in the ideas of classical realists such as Machiavelli and Hobbes, and more recent ones such as Hans Morgenthau and Reinhold Niebuhr, but most of the theories in the approaches to international relations that have dominated political science in recent times do not dwell on the sources of motivation, emotion, inhibition, or risk-propensity of the actors who make policy, or how the physical limitations of human cognition affect judgments and decisions in foreign policy.[1]

Observers outside political science have focused more often on unconscious roots of conflict and cooperation. Explanations from psychology challenge the economic model of political calculation that had dominated much of recent international relations theory in both realist and liberal schools of thought. Psychological approaches present political behavior, including foreign policy initiatives, as manifestations of individual impulses, irrational urges, physiologically limited perceptual mechanisms, and unrecognized driving forces. To deal with the problem of war requires not only explicitly political solutions—stabilization of how power is distributed among countries, or promulgation of liberal principles—but the taming or channeling of emotional and subliminal drives, and compensation for common forms of misperception.

Sigmund Freud's letter to Albert Einstein—written only months before Hitler's accession to power in Germany—presents his view of how aggressive and destructive instincts compete with erotic and constructive ones, and how cultural development works through the superego to suppress the urges conducive to war. Freudian psychology, highly influential through most of the twentieth century, has gone out of favor in recent decades. Indeed, Freud's writing excerpted here looks rather naïve to a student of international relations, and implies an assumption that politics is simply derivative of individual psychic urges. Nevertheless, Freud's thoughts reflect views still popular among many intellectuals outside of political science, particularly the notion that people are driven by subconscious fears of unreal threats.[2]

For war to be possible, the human as well as technical instruments for prosecuting it must be usable. Governments or groups must be able to get large numbers of citizens to kill and to participate in terrible destruction, activities that, in the context of normal daily life, they would assume to be abominable and criminal. Stanley Milgram's entry graphically summarizes the findings of his famous experiments showing the willingness of normal, decent, intelligent people to inflict suffering on innocent victims in a situation where apparently legitimate authorities direct them to do so. Mobilizing populations for even aggressive and brutal wars, thus, does not require extraordinary coercion. (The validity of Milgram's experiments has been challenged, particularly by Gina Perry, but others have convincingly upheld the essence of his conclusions.[3]) The selection "War and Misperception" by Robert Jervis focuses on how cognitive biases and limitations of communication can increase the risk of war from miscalculation or misreading of the motives or intentions of adversaries.

Paying attention to unconscious motivations or the physical limitations of conscious calculation implies optimism about the future of war if one assumes that better understanding of causes will prompt their cure. If paranoid statesmen can be put in the care of effective and humane psychotherapists, or cognitively impaired leaders can be shown how their thought processes fall short of rigorous logic, would-be aggressors might become reasonable cooperators. If aggression is as deeply rooted in human nature as some psychologists believe, however, or if physiological constraints on cognition cannot be transcended, it will be difficult to eliminate conflictual impulses or misjudgments from foreign policies.[4]

Beyond individual psychology, culture is a collective source of subjective influences on governments' or groups' judgments and decisions about conflict. The concept of culture is a slippery one, and some social scientists are more at home with it than others. Anthropologists have focused on primitive social functions of war more than on its effects on modern international political order, the aspect that preoccupies historians and political scientists.[5] A loose definition suffices for our purposes: cultural causes of war and peace are ones that involve assumptions, attitudes, values, or norms that are not universal, but that are pervasive within a particular country or national group, and whose validity is taken for granted by its people and leaders, usually without reflection, as the natural order of things.

Margaret Mead's article in this section asserts that war is not a universal phenomenon, but simply a custom common to many cultures, and thus not an inevitable part of human relations.[6] Her argument goes well with John Mueller's in Part III of this volume that major war has become obsolete because it has been recognized as an unnecessary, uncivilized anachronism, like dueling and slavery—in short, that it has been culturally delegitimated. J. Ann Tickner's application of feminist ideas to the question argues that the entire frame of reference within which theories of international conflict are debated has been determined by the attitudes and assumptions characteristic of only half of the human population—males—and that perspectives more common to women can have a different effect on international political interaction when given the chance.

The selection by Richard Ned Lebow represents a "constructivist" approach to international relations.[7] He rejects the fixation of most theorists on rationalist and materialist explanations for warlike behavior and looks instead to the subjective, spiritual, and emotional factors on which the ancients focused. Constructivist ideas such as Lebow's should be considered in the context of the alternative to realist and liberal paradigms given by Samuel P. Huntington in Part I. Recall also how Huntington poses major civilizational culture areas as the bases of international cleavage in the post–Cold War world (and see his reflections in Part X on why these cleavages are a reason for both Western cohesion and nonintervention in other civilizations' conflicts).

Huntington's particular twist on the importance and implications of identity evokes discomfort or opposition from many constructivists, who tend toward liberal constructions of their own personal identities. This is a reminder that although many who see culture as important hope that cultures will evolve in ways consistent with liberal norms and values, constructivist theory is logically one of cultural and intellectual relativism. As such, there is nothing in the causal logic of the theory that ordains that one set of norms or identities must triumph over others, or that good ones will drive out bad ones, or even defend themselves successfully against them. There is nothing intrinsic in a cultural approach that makes construction of liberal-friendly identity more likely than identities consistent with racism, fascism, militarism, or religious fanaticism.[8] The most telling reminder of this is how members of Al Qaeda or Islamic State construct their identity. In academic debate, interpretations that emphasize the importance of individual, sociological, or domestic factors emphasized in this part of the volume are usually seen as incompatible with structural realism. This is true only if Waltz's theory is used in a way that he says it should not be—to predict particular policy decisions. Waltz argues that his emphasis on the international system (anarchy and the distribution of capabilities) as the prime level of analysis is due to his mission of presenting a theory of international politics as distinct from a theory of foreign policy. The two are distinct in the same way that, in economics, a theory of the market is distinct from a theory of the firm. Theories of international politics (the market) are about typical outcomes from the system over time; theories of foreign policy (the firm) are about particular actions of units in the market. Anarchy in the external environment is the permissive cause of war, but motives and calculations of policymakers are efficient causes. To understand particular wars, we need to look at foreign policy decisions and their sources.[9] Psychology, anthropology, sociology, and intellectual history can all illuminate the motives of those who make policy, and thus can be relevant to understanding the efficient causes of war. A structural realist in Waltz's mold will simply argue that whatever the motives behind decisions for wars made by individuals in governments, if they do not heed the imperative of self-help posed by the international system, their states will fall by the wayside.[10] In short, policymakers may sometimes act for the reasons asserted in this section, but if they do so in ways that contradict adaptation to the external distribution of power, they will fail.

—RKB

NOTES

1 Exceptions include Robert Jervis, *Perception and Misperception in International Politics* (Princeton, N.J.: Princeton University Press, 1976); Jervis, *The Logic of Images in International Relations* (Princeton, N.J.: Princeton University Press, 1970); Irving Janis, *Groupthink* (Boston: Houghton Mifflin, 1982); John D. Steinbruner, *The Cybernbetic Theory of Decision* (Princeton, N.J.: Princeton University Press, 1974); Barbara Rearden Farnham, *Roosevelt and the Munich Crisis* (Princeton, N.J.: Princeton University Press, 1997); Alexander and Juliette George, *Woodrow Wilson and Colonel House* (New York: Dover, 1964); Deborah Larson, *Origins of Containment* (Princeton, N.J.: Princeton University Press, 1985).

2 See for example Barbara Ehrenreich, *Blood Rites: Origins and History of the Passions of War* (New York: Henry Holt, 1997), and especially Franco Fornari, *The Psychoanalysis of War*, Alenka Pfeifer, trans. (Bloomington: Indiana University Press, 1975). Fornari's extreme theory is practically a caricature of the Freudian approach, but it is significant because he was not a fringe figure but a president of the Italian Psychoanalytic Society. For criticism of psychoanalytic explanations for war see Richard K. Betts, *American Force: Dangers, Delusions, and Dilemmas in National Security* (New York: Columbia University Press, 2012), chapter 10. For discussions of the effect of emotions on thought processes and policies see Stephen Peter Rosen, *War and Human Nature* (Princeton, N.J.: Princeton University Press, 2005); Neta Crawford, "The Passion of World Politics: Propositions on Emotion and Emotional Relationships," *International Security* 24, no. 4 (Spring 2000); and Jonathan Mercer, "Emotional Beliefs," *International Organization* 64, no. 1 (Winter 2010).

3 Gina Perry, *Behind the Shock Machine* (New York: New Press, 2013). For criticism of Perry see the review by Carol Tavris, "The Experiments That Still Shock," *Wall Street Journal*, September 7–8, 2013, pp. C5, C7. See also Jerry Burger, "Replicating Milgram," *Observer* 20, no. 10 (December 2007).

4 See Konrad Lorenz, *On Aggression*, Marjorie Kerr Wilson, trans. (New York: Harcourt, Brace & World, 1966); Anthony Storr, *Human Aggression* (New York: Atheneum, 1968).

5   Bronislaw Malinowski, "An Anthropological Analysis of War," and Robert E. Park, "The Social Function of War," both in *American Journal of Sociology* 46, no. 4 (January 1941); Harry Holbert Turney-High, *Primitive War: Its Practice and Concepts*, Second edition (Columbia: University of South Carolina Press, 1971).

6   For arguments against reliance on psychological and anthropological explanations of war, see Kenneth N. Waltz, *Man, the State, and War* (New York: Columbia University Press, 1959), chaps. 2–3.

7   For more see Richard Ned Lebow, *A Cultural Theory of International Relations* (New York: Cambridge University Press, 2008) and Alexander Wendt, *Social Theory of International Politics* (New York: Cambridge University Press, 1999).

8   See John J. Mearsheimer, "The False Promise of International Institutions," *International Security* 19, no. 3 (Winter 1994/95), pp. 41–44. See rebuttals by Robert O. Keohane and Lisa Martin, Charles and Clifford Kupchan, John Ruggie, and Alexander Wendt, and Mearsheimer's reply, in *International Security* 20, no. 1 (Summer 1995).

9   Many critics forget that Waltz wrote a whole book on domestic sources of policy: *Foreign Policy and Democratic Politics* (Boston: Little, Brown, 1967).

10 Some critics deny Waltz's analogy and argue that the international system is one of oligopoly (several great powers) rather than pure market competition, and that a theory of international politics therefore cannot be separated from a theory of foreign policy. Graham Allison and Philip Zelikow, *Essence of Decision: Explaining the Cuban Missile Crisis*, Second edition (New York: Longman, 1999), p. 405.

Reading 4.1

Why War?   SIGMUND FREUD

VIENNA
SEPTEMBER 1932.

DEAR PROFESSOR EINSTEIN,

When I learnt of your intention to invite me to a mutual exchange of views upon a subject which not only interested you personally but seemed deserving, too, of public interest, I cordially assented. I expected you to choose a problem lying on the borderland of the knowable, as it stands today, a theme which each of us, physicist and psychologist, might approach from his own angle, to meet at last on common ground, though setting out from different premises. Thus the question which you put me—what is to be done to rid mankind of the war-menace?—took me by surprise. And, next, I was dumbfounded by the thought of my (of *our*, I almost wrote) incompetence; for this struck me as being a matter of practical politics, the statesman's proper study. But then I realized that you did not raise the question in your capacity of scientist or physicist, but as a lover of his fellow-men, who responded to the call of the League of Nations much as Fridtjof Nansen, the Polar explorer, took on himself the task of succouring homeless and starving victims of the World War. And, next, I reminded myself that I was not being called on to formulate practical proposals, but, rather, to explain how this question of preventing wars strikes a psychologist.

But here, too, you have stated the gist of the matter in your letter—and taken the wind out of my sails! Still, I will gladly follow in your wake and content myself with endorsing your conclusions, which, however, I propose to amplify to the best of my knowledge or surmise.

You begin with the relations between Might and Right, and this is assuredly the proper starting-point for our inquiry. But, for the term 'might', I would substitute a tougher and more telling word: 'violence'. In right and violence we have today an obvious antinomy. It is easy to prove that one has evolved from the other and, when we go back to origins and examine primitive conditions, the solution of the problem follows easily enough. I must crave your indulgence if in what follows I speak of well-known, admitted facts as though they were new data; the context necessitates this method.

Conflicts of interest between man and man are resolved, in principle, by the recourse to violence. It is the same in the animal kingdom, from which man cannot claim exclusion; nevertheless men are also prone to conflicts of opinion, touching, on occasion, the loftiest peaks of abstract thought, which seem to call for settlement by quite another method. This refinement is, however, a late development. To start with, brute force was the factor which, in small communities, decided points of ownership and the question which man's will was to prevail. Very soon physical force was implemented, then replaced, by the use of various adjuncts; he proved the victor whose weapon was the better, or handled the more skilfully. Now, for the first time, with the coming of weapons, superior brains began to oust brute force, but the object of the conflict remained the same: one party was to be constrained, by the injury done him or impairment of his strength, to retract a claim or a refusal. This end is most effectively gained when the opponent is definitively put out of action—in other words, is killed. This procedure has two advantages; the enemy cannot renew hostilities, and, secondly, his fate deters others from following his example. Moreover, the slaughter of a foe gratifies an instinctive craving—a point to which we shall revert hereafter. However, another consideration may be set off against this will to kill: the possibility of using an enemy for servile tasks if his spirit be broken and his life spared. Here violence finds an outlet not in slaughter but in subjugation. Hence springs the practice of giving quarter; but the victor, having from now on to reckon with the craving for revenge that rankles in his victim, forfeits to some extent his personal security.

Thus, under primitive conditions, it is superior force—brute violence, or violence backed by arms—that lords it everywhere. We know that in the course of evolution this state of things was modified, a path was traced that led away from violence to law. But what was this path? Surely it issued from a single verity; that the superiority of one strong man can be overborne by an alliance of many weaklings, that *l'union fait la force*. Brute force is overcome by union, the allied might of scattered units makes good its right against the isolated giant. Thus we may define 'right' (i.e. law) as the might of a community. Yet it, too, is nothing else than violence, quick to attack whatever individual stands in its path, and it employs the selfsame methods, follows like ends, with but one difference; it is the communal, not individual, violence that has its way. But, for the transition from crude violence to the reign of law, a certain psychological condition must first obtain. The union of the majority must be stable and enduring. If its sole *raison d'être* be the discomfiture of some overweening individual and, after his downfall, it be dissolved, it leads to nothing. Some other man, trusting to his superior power, will seek to reinstate the rule of violence and the cycle will repeat itself unendingly. Thus the union of the people must be permanent and well organised; it must enact rules to meet the risk of possible revolts; must set up machinery ensuring that its rules—the laws—are observed and that such acts of violence as the laws demand are duly carried out. This recognition of a community of interests engenders among the members of the group a sentiment of unity and fraternal solidarity which constitutes its real strength.

So far I have set out what seems to me the kernel of the matter: the suppression of brute force by the transfer of power to a larger combination, founded on the community of sentiments linking up its members. All the rest is mere tautology and glosses. Now the position is simple enough so long as the community consists of a number of equipollent individuals. The laws of such a group can determine to what extent the individual must forfeit his personal freedom, the right of using personal force as an instrument of violence, to ensure the safety of the group. But such a combination is only theoretically possible; in practice the situation is always complicated by the fact that, from the outset, the group includes elements of unequal power, men and women, elders and children, and, very soon, as a result of war and conquest, victors and the vanquished—i.e. masters and slaves—as well. From this time on the common law takes notice of these inequalities of power, laws are made by and for the rulers, giving the servile classes fewer rights. Thenceforward there exist within the state two factors making for legal instability, but legislative evolution, too: first, the attempts by members of the ruling class to set themselves above the law's restrictions and, secondly, the constant struggle of the ruled to extend their rights and see each gain embodied in the code, replacing legal disabilities by equal laws for all. The second of these tendencies will be particularly marked when there takes place a positive mutation of the balance of power within the community, the frequent outcome of certain historical conditions. In such cases the laws may gradually be adjusted to the changed conditions or (as more usually ensues) the ruling class is loath to reckon with the new developments, the result being insurrections and civil wars, a period when law is in abeyance and force once more the arbiter, followed by a new regime of law. There is another factor of constitutional change, which operates in a wholly pacific manner, namely: the cultural evolution of the mass of the community; this factor, however, is of a different order and can only be dealt with later.

Thus we see that, even within the group itself, the exercise of violence cannot be avoided when conflicting interests are at stake. But the common needs and habits of men who live in fellowship under the same sky favour a speedy issue of such conflicts and, this being so, the possibilities of peaceful solutions make steady progress. Yet the most casual glance at world-history will show an unending series of conflicts between one community and another or a group of others, between large and smaller units, between cities, countries, races, tribes and kingdoms, almost all of which were settled by the ordeal of war. Such wars end either in pillage or in conquest and its fruits, the downfall of the loser. No single all-embracing judgment can be passed on these wars of aggrandizement. Some, like the war between the Mongols and the Turks, have led to unmitigated misery; others, however, have furthered the transition from violence to law, since they brought larger units into being, within whose limits a recourse to violence was banned and a new régime determined all disputes. Thus the Roman conquests brought that boon, the *pax romana*, to the Mediterranean lands. The French kings' lust for aggrandizement created a new France, flourishing in peace and unity. Paradoxical as it sounds, we must admit that warfare well might serve to pave the way to that unbroken peace we so desire, for it is war that brings vast empires into being, within whose frontiers all warfare is proscribed by a strong central power. In practice, however, this end is not attained, for as a rule the fruits of victory are but short-lived, the new-created unit falls as under once again, generally because there can be no true cohesion between the parts that violence has welded. Hitherto, moreover, such conquests have only led to aggregations which, for all their magnitude, had limits, and disputes between these units could be resolved only by recourse to arms. For humanity at large the sole result of all these military enterprises was that, instead of frequent not to say incessant little wars, they had now to face great wars which, for all they came less often, were so much the more destructive.

Regarding the world of today the same conclusion holds good, and you, too, have reached it, though by a shorter path. There is but one sure way of ending war and that is the establishment, by common consent, of a central control which shall have the last word in every conflict of interests. For this, two things are needed: first, the creation of such a supreme court of judicature; secondly, its investment with adequate executive force. Unless this second requirement be fulfilled, the first is unavailing. Obviously the League of Nations, acting as a Supreme Court, fulfils the first condition; it does not fulfil the second. It has no force at its disposal and can only get it if the members of the new body, its constituent nations, furnish it. And, as things are, this is a forlorn hope. Still we should be taking a very short-sighted view of the League of Nations were we to ignore the fact that here is an experiment the like of which has rarely—never before, perhaps, on such a scale—been attempted in the course of history. It is an attempt to acquire the authority (in other words, coercive influence), which hitherto reposed exclusively on the possession of power, by calling into play certain idealistic attitudes of mind. We have seen that there are two factors of cohesion in a community: violent compulsion and ties of sentiment ('identifications', in technical parlance) between the members of the group. If one of these factors becomes inoperative, the other may still suffice to hold the group together. Obviously such notions as these can only be significant when they are the expression of a deeply rooted sense of unity, shared by all. It is necessary, therefore, to gauge the efficacy of such sentiments. History tells us that, on occasion, they have been effective. For example, the Panhellenic conception, the Greeks' awareness of superiority over their barbarian neighbours, which found expression in the Amphictyonies, the Oracles and Games, was strong enough to humanize the methods of warfare as between Greeks, though inevitably it failed to prevent conflicts between different elements of the Hellenic race or even to deter a city or group of cities from joining forces with their racial foe, the Persians, for the discomfiture of a rival. The solidarity of Christendom in the Renaissance age was no more effective, despite its vast authority, in hindering Christian nations, large and small alike, from calling in the Sultan to their aid. And, in our times, we look in vain for some such unifying notion whose authority would be unquestioned. It is all too clear that the nationalistic ideas, paramount today in every country, operate in quite a contrary direction. There are some who hold that the Bolshevist conceptions may make an end of war, but, as things are, that goal lies very far away and, perhaps, could only be attained after a spell of brutal internecine warfare. Thus it would seem that any effort to replace brute force by the might of an ideal is, under present conditions, doomed to fail. Our logic is at fault if we ignore the fact that right is founded on brute force and even today needs violence to maintain it.

I now can comment on another of your statements. You are amazed that it is so easy to infect men with the war-fever, and you surmise that man has in him an active instinct for hatred and destruction, amenable to such stimulations. I entirely agree with you. I believe in the existence of this instinct and have been recently at pains to study its manifestations. In this connection may I set out a fragment of that knowledge of the instincts, which we psychoanalysts, after so many tentative essays and gropings in the dark, have compassed? We assume that human instincts are of two kinds: those that conserve and unify, which we call 'erotic' (in the meaning Plato gives to *Eros* in his *Symposium*), or else 'sexual' (explicitly extending the popular connotation of 'sex'), and, secondly, the instincts to destroy and kill, which we assimilate as the aggressive or destructive instincts. These are, as you perceive, the well-known opposites, Love and Hate, transformed into theoretical entities; they are, perhaps, another aspect of those eternal polarities, attraction and repulsion, which fall within your province. But we must be chary of passing over-hastily to the notions of good and evil. Each of these instincts is every whit as indispensable as its opposite and all the phenomena of life derive from their activity, whether they work in concert or in opposition. It seems that an instinct of either category can operate but rarely in isolation; it is always blended ('alloyed', as we say) with a certain dosage of its opposite, which modifies its aim or even, in certain circumstances, is a prime condition of its attainment. Thus the instinct of self-preservation is certainly of an erotic nature, but to gain its ends this very instinct necessitates aggressive action. In the same way the love-instinct, when directed to a specific object, calls for an admixture of the acquisitive instinct if it is to enter into effective possession of that object. It is the difficulty of isolating the two kinds of instinct in their manifestations that has so long prevented us from recognizing them.

If you travel with me a little further on this road, you will find that human affairs are complicated in yet another way. Only exceptionally does an action follow on the stimulus of a single instinct, which is *per se* a blend of Eros and destructiveness. As a rule several motives of similar composition concur to bring about the act. This fact was duly noted by a colleague of yours, Professor G. C. Lichtenberg, sometime Professor of Physics at Göttingen; he was perhaps even more eminent as a psychologist than as a physical scientist. He evolved the notion of a 'Compass-card of Motives' and wrote: 'The efficient motives impelling man to act can be classified like the 32 Winds, and described in the same manner; for example, *Food-Food-Fame* or *Fame-Fame-Food*.' Thus, when a nation is summoned to engage in war, a whole gamut of human motives may respond to this appeal; high and low motives, some openly avowed, others slurred over. The lust for aggression and destruction is certainly included; the innumerable cruelties of history and man's daily life confirm its prevalence and strength. The stimulation of these destructive impulses by appeals to idealism and the erotic instinct naturally facilitates their release. Musing on the atrocities recorded on history's page, we feel that the ideal motive has often served as a camouflage for the lust of destruction; sometimes, as with the cruelties of the Inquisition, it seems that, while the ideal motives occupied the foreground of consciousness, they drew their strength from the destructive instincts submerged in the unconscious. Both interpretations are feasible.

You are interested, I know, in the prevention of war, not in our theories, and I keep this fact in mind. Yet I would like to dwell a little longer on this destructive instinct which is seldom given the attention that its importance warrants. With the least of speculative efforts we are led to conclude that this instinct functions in every living being, striving to work its ruin and reduce life to its primal state of inert matter. Indeed it might well be called the 'death-instinct'; whereas the erotic instincts vouch for the struggle to live on. The death instinct becomes an impulse to destruction when, with the aid of certain organs, it directs its action outwards, against external objects. The living being, that is to say, defends its own existence by destroying foreign bodies. But, in one of its activities, the death instinct is operative *within* the living being and we have sought to trace back a number of normal and pathological phenomena to this *introversion* of the destructive instinct. We have even committed the heresy of explaining the origin of human conscience by some such 'turning inward' of the aggressive impulse. Obviously when this internal tendency operates on too large a scale, it is no trivial matter, rather a positively morbid state of things; whereas the diversion of the destructive impulse towards the external world must have beneficial effects. Here is then the biological justification for all those vile, pernicious propensities which we now are combating. We can but own that they are really more akin to nature than this our stand against them, which, in fact, remains to be accounted for.

All this may give you the impression that our theories amount to a species of mythology and a gloomy one at that! But does not every natural science lead ultimately to this—a sort of mythology? Is it otherwise today with your physical science?

The upshot of these observations, as bearing on the subject in hand, is that there is no likelihood of our being able to suppress humanity's aggressive tendencies. In some happy corners of the earth, they say, where nature brings forth abundantly whatever man desires, there flourish races whose lives go gently by, unknowing of aggression or constraint. This I can hardly credit; I would like further details about these happy folk. The Bolshevists, too, aspire to do away with human aggressiveness by ensuring the satisfaction of material needs and enforcing equality between man and man. To me this hope seems vain. Meanwhile they busily perfect their armaments, and their hatred of outsiders is not the least of the factors of cohesion amongst themselves. In any case, as you too have observed, complete suppression of man's aggressive tendencies is not an issue; what we may try is to divert it into a channel other than that of warfare.

From our 'mythology' of the instincts we may easily deduce a formula for an indirect method of eliminating war. If the propensity for war be due to the destructive instinct, we have always its counter-agent, Eros, to our hand. All that produces ties of sentiment between man and man must serve us as war's antidote. These ties are of two kinds. First, such relations as those towards a beloved object, void though they be of sexual intent. The psychoanalyst need feel no compunction in mentioning 'love' in this connection; religion uses the same language: Love thy neighbour as thyself. A pious injunction easy to enounce, but hard to carry out! The other bond of sentiment is by way of identification. All that brings out the significant resemblances between men calls into play this feeling of community, identification, whereon is founded, in large measure, the whole edifice of human society.

In your strictures on the abuse of authority I find another suggestion for an indirect attack on the war-impulse. That men are divided into leaders and the led is but another manifestation of their inborn and irremediable inequality. The second class constitutes the vast majority; they need a high command to make decisions for them, to which decisions they usually bow without demur. In this context we would point out that men should be at greater pains than heretofore to form a superior class of independent thinkers, unamenable to intimidation and fervent in the quest of truth, whose function it would be to guide the masses dependent on their lead. There is no need to point out how little the rule of politicians and the Church's ban on liberty of thought encourage such a new creation. The ideal conditions would obviously be found in a community where every man subordinated his instinctive life to the dictates of reason. Nothing less than this could bring about so thorough and so durable a union between men, even if this involved the severance of mutual ties of sentiment. But surely such a hope is utterly utopian, as things are. The other indirect methods of preventing war are certainly more feasible, but entail no quick results. They conjure up an ugly picture of mills which grind so slowly that, before the flour is ready, men are dead of hunger.

As you see, little good comes of consulting a theoretician, aloof from worldly contacts, on practical and urgent problems! Better it were to tackle each successive crisis with means that we have ready to our hands. However, I would like to deal with a question which, though it is not mooted in your letter, interests me greatly. Why do we, you and I and many another, protest so vehemently against war, instead of just accepting it as another of life's odious importunities? For it seems a natural thing enough, biologically sound and practically unavoidable. I trust you will not be shocked by my raising such a question. For the better conduct of an inquiry it may be well to don a mask of feigned aloofness. The answer to my query may run as follows: Because every man has a right over his own life and war destroys lives that were full of promise; it forces the individual into situations that shame his manhood, obliging him to murder fellow-men, against his will; it ravages material amenities, the fruits of human toil, and much besides. Moreover wars, as now conducted, afford no scope for acts of heroism according to the old ideals and, given the high perfection of modern arms, war today would mean the sheer extermination of one of the combatants, if not of both. This is so true, so obvious, that we can but wonder why the conduct of war is not banned by general consent. Doubtless either of the points I have just made is open to debate. It may be asked if the community, in its turn, cannot claim a right over the individual lives of its members. Moreover, all forms of war cannot be indiscriminately condemned; so long as there are nations and empires, each prepared callously to exterminate its rival, all alike must be equipped for war. But we will not dwell on any of these problems; they lie outside the debate to which you have invited me. I pass on to another point, the basis, as it strikes me, of our common hatred of war. It is this: we cannot do otherwise than hate it. Pacifists we are, since our organic nature wills us thus to be. Hence it comes easy to us to find arguments that justify our standpoint.

This point, however, calls for elucidation. Here is the way in which I see it. The cultural development of mankind (some, I know, prefer to call it civilization) has been in progress since immemorial antiquity. To this processus we owe all that is best in our composition, but also much that makes for human suffering. Its origins and causes are obscure, its issue is uncertain, but some of its characteristics are easy to perceive. It well may lead to the extinction of mankind, for it impairs the sexual function in more than one respect, and even today the uncivilized races and the backward classes of all nations are multiplying more rapidly than the cultured elements. This process may, perhaps, be likened to the effect of domestication on certain animals—it clearly involves physical changes of structure—but the view that cultural development is an organic process of this order has not yet become generally familiar. The psychic changes which accompany this process of cultural change are striking, and not to be gainsaid. They consist in the progressive rejection of instinctive ends and a scaling down of instinctive reactions. Sensations which delighted our forefathers have become neutral or unbearable to us; and, if our ethical and æsthetic ideals have undergone a change, the causes of this are ultimately organic. On the psychological side two of the most important phenomena of culture are, firstly, a strengthening of the intellect, which tends to master our instinctive life, and, secondly, an introversion of the aggressive impulse, with all its consequent benefits and perils. Now war runs most emphatically counter to the psychic disposition imposed on us by the growth of culture; we are therefore bound to resent war, to find it utterly intolerable. With pacifists like us it is not merely an intellectual and affective repulsion, but a constitutional intolerance, an idiosyncrasy in its most drastic form. And it would seem that the æsthetic ignominies of warfare play almost as large a part in this repugnance as war's atrocities.

How long have we to wait before the rest of men turn pacifist? Impossible to say, and yet perhaps our hope that these two factors—man's cultural disposition and a well-founded dread of the form that future wars will take—may serve to put an end to war in the near future, is not chimerical. But by what ways or by-ways this will come about, we cannot guess. Meanwhile we may rest on the assurance that whatever makes for cultural development is working also against war.

With kindest regards and, should this *exposé* prove a disappointment to you, my sincere regrets,

Yours,
SIGMUND FREUD.

Reading 4.2

How Good People Do Bad Things

STANLEY MILGRAM

O bedience is as basic an element in the structure of social life as one can point to. Some system of authority is a requirement of all communal living, and it is only the man dwelling in isolation who is not forced to respond, through defiance or submission, to the commands of others. Obedience, as a determinant of behavior, is of particular relevance to our time. It has been reliably established that from 1933 to 1945 millions of innocent people were systematically slaughtered on command. Gas chambers were built, death camps were guarded, daily quotas of corpses were produced with the same efficiency as the manufacture of appliances. These inhumane policies may have originated in the mind of a single person, but they could only have been carried out on a massive scale if a very large number of people obeyed orders.

Obedience is the psychological mechanism that links individual action to political purpose. It is the dispositional cement that binds men to systems of authority. Facts of recent history and observation in daily life suggest that for many people obedience may be a deeply ingrained behavior tendency, indeed, a prepotent impulse overriding training in ethics, sympathy, and moral conduct. C. P. Snow (1961) points to its importance when he writes:

> When you think of the long and gloomy history of man, you will find more hideous crimes have been committed in the name of obedience than have ever been committed in the name of rebellion. If you doubt that, read William Shirer's 'Rise and Fall of the Third Reich.' The German Officer Corps were brought up in the most rigorous code of obedience . . . in the name of obedience they were party to, and assisted in, the most wicked large scale actions in the history of the world.

(p. 24)

The Nazi extermination of European Jews is the most extreme instance of abhorrent immoral acts carried out by thousands of people in the name of obedience. Yet in lesser degree this type of thing is constantly recurring: ordinary citizens are ordered to destroy other people, and they do so because they consider it their duty to obey orders. Thus, obedience to authority, long praised as a virtue, takes on a new aspect when it serves a malevolent cause; far from appearing as a virtue, it is transformed into a heinous sin. Or is it?

The moral question of whether one should obey when commands conflict with conscience was argued by Plato, dramatized in *Antigone*, and treated

Source: Chapter 1 "The Dilemma of Obedience," pp. 1–12 from Obedience to Authority: An Experimental View *by Stanley Milgram. Copyright © 1974 by Stanley Milgram. Reprinted by permission of HarperCollins Publishers.*

to philosophic analysis in every historical epoch. Conservative philosophers argue that the very fabric of society is threatened by disobedience, and even when the act prescribed by an authority is an evil one, it is better to carry out the act than to wrench at the structure of authority. Hobbes stated further that an act so executed is in no sense the responsibility of the person who carries it out but only of the authority that orders it. But humanists argue for the primacy of individual conscience in such matters, insisting that the moral judgments of the individual must override authority when the two are in conflict.

The legal and philosophic aspects of obedience are of enormous import, but an empirically grounded scientist eventually comes to the point where he wishes to move from abstract discourse to the careful observation of concrete instances. In order to take a close look at the act of obeying, I set up a simple experiment at Yale University. Eventually, the experiment was to involve more than a thousand participants and would be repeated at several universities, but at the beginning, the conception was simple. A person comes to a psychological laboratory and is told to carry out a series of acts that come increasingly into conflict with conscience. The main question is how far the participant will comply with the experimenter's instructions before refusing to carry out the actions required of him.

But the reader needs to know a little more detail about the experiment. Two people come to a psychology laboratory to take part in a study of memory and learning. One of them is designated as a "teacher" and the other a "learner." The experimenter explains that the study is concerned with the effects of punishment on learning. The learner is conducted into a room, seated in a chair, his arms strapped to prevent excessive movement, and an electrode attached to his wrist. He is told that he is to learn a list of word pairs; whenever he makes an error, he will receive electric shocks of increasing intensity.

The real focus of the experiment is the teacher. After watching the learner being strapped into place, he is taken into the main experimental room and seated before an impressive shock generator. Its main feature is a horizontal line of thirty switches, ranging from 15 volts to 450 volts, in 15-volt increments. There are also verbal designations which range from slight shock to danger—severe shock. The teacher is told that he is to administer the learning test to the man in the other room. When the learner responds correctly, the teacher moves on to the next item; when the other man gives an incorrect answer, the teacher is to give him an electric shock. He is to start at the lowest shock level (15 volts) and to increase the level each time the man makes an error, going through 30 volts, 45 volts, and so on.

The "teacher" is a genuinely naïve subject who has come to the laboratory to participate in an experiment. The learner, or victim, is an actor who actually receives no shock at all. The point of the experiment is to see how far a person will proceed in a concrete and measurable situation in which he is ordered to inflict increasing pain on a protesting victim. At what point will the subject refuse to obey the experimenter?

Conflict arises when the man receiving the shock begins to indicate that he is experiencing discomfort. At 75 volts, the "learner" grunts. At 120 volts he complains verbally; at 150 he demands to be released from the experiment. His protests continue as the shocks escalate, growing increasingly vehement and emotional. At 285 volts his response can only be described as an agonized scream.

Observers of the experiment agree that its gripping quality is somewhat obscured in print. For the subject, the situation is not a game; conflict is intense and obvious. On one hand, the manifest suffering of the learner presses him to quit. On the other, the experimenter, a legitimate authority to whom the subject feels some commitment, enjoins him to continue. Each time the subject hesitates to administer shock, the experimenter orders him to continue. To extricate himself from the situation, the subject must make a clear break with authority. The aim of this investigation was to find when and how people would defy authority in the face of a clear moral imperative.

There are, of course, enormous differences between carrying out the orders of a commanding officer during times of war and carrying out the orders of an experimenter. Yet the essence of certain relationships remain, for one may ask in a general way: How does a man behave when he is told by a legitimate authority to act against a third individual? If anything, we may expect the experimenter's power to be considerably less than that of the general, since he has no power to enforce his imperatives, and participation in a psychological experiment scarcely evokes the sense of urgency and dedication engendered by participation in war. Despite these limitations, I thought it worthwhile to start careful observation of obedience even in this modest situation, in the hope that it would stimulate insights and yield general propositions applicable to a variety of circumstances.

A reader's initial reaction to the experiment may be to wonder why anyone in his right mind would administer even the first shocks. Would he not simply refuse and walk out of the laboratory? But the fact is that no one ever does. Since the subject has come to the laboratory to aid the experimenter, he is quite willing to start off with the procedure. There is nothing very extraordinary in this, particularly since the person who is to receive the shocks seems initially cooperative, if somewhat apprehensive. What is surprising is how far ordinary individuals will go in complying with the experimenter's instructions. Indeed, the results of the experiment are both surprising and dismaying. Despite the fact that many subjects experience stress, despite the fact that many protest to the experimenter, a substantial proportion continue to the last shock on the generator.

Many subjects will obey the experimenter no matter how vehement the pleading of the person being shocked, no matter how painful the shocks seem to be, and no matter how much the victim pleads to be let out. This was seen time and again in our studies and has been observed in several universities where the experiment was repeated. It is the extreme willingness of adults to go to almost any lengths on the command of an authority that constitutes the chief finding of the study and the fact most urgently demanding explanation.

A commonly offered explanation is that those who shocked the victim at the most severe level were monsters, the sadistic fringe of society. But if one considers that almost two-thirds of the participants fall into the category of "obedient" subjects, and that they represented ordinary people drawn from working, managerial, and professional classes, the argument becomes very shaky. Indeed, it is highly reminiscent of the issue that arose in connection with Hannah Arendt's 1963 book, *Eichmann in Jerusalem*. Arendt contended that the prosecution's effort to depict Eichmann as a sadistic monster was fundamentally wrong, that he came closer to being an uninspired bureaucrat who simply sat at his desk and did his job. For asserting these views, Arendt became the object of considerable scorn, even calumny. Somehow, it was felt that the monstrous deeds carried out by Eichmann required a brutal, twisted, and sadistic personality, evil incarnate. After witnessing hundreds of ordinary people submit to the authority in our own experiments, I must conclude that Arendt's conception of the *banality of evil* comes closer to the truth than one might dare imagine. The ordinary person who shocked the victim did so out of a sense of obligation—a conception of his duties as a subject—and not from any peculiarly aggressive tendencies.

This is, perhaps, the most fundamental lesson of our study: ordinary people, simply doing their jobs, and without any particular hostility on their part, can become agents in a terrible destructive process. Moreover, even when the destructive effects of their work become patently clear, and they are asked to carry out actions incompatible with fundamental standards of morality, relatively few people have the resources needed to resist authority. A variety of inhibitions against disobeying authority come into play and successfully keep the person in his place.

Sitting back in one's armchair, it is easy to condemn the actions of the obedient subjects. But those who condemn the subjects measure them against the standard of their own ability to formulate high-minded moral prescriptions. That is hardly a fair standard. Many of the subjects, at the level of stated opinion, feel quite as strongly as any of us about the moral requirement of refraining from action against a helpless victim. They, too, in general terms know what ought to be done and can state their values when the occasion arises. This has little, if anything, to do with their actual behavior under the pressure of circumstances.

If people are asked to render a moral judgment on what constitutes appropriate behavior in this situation, they unfailingly see disobedience as proper. But values are not the only forces at work in an actual, ongoing situation. They are but one narrow band of causes in the total spectrum of forces impinging on a person. Many people were unable to realize their values in action and found themselves continuing in the experiment even though they disagreed with what they were doing.

The force exerted by the moral sense of the individual is less effective than social myth would have us believe. Though such prescriptions as "Thou shalt not kill" occupy a pre-eminent place in the moral order, they do not occupy a correspondingly intractable position in human psychic structure. A few changes in newspaper headlines, a call from the draft board, orders from a man with epaulets, and men are led to kill with little difficulty. Even the forces mustered in a psychology experiment will go a long way toward removing the individual from moral controls. Moral factors can be shunted aside with relative ease by a calculated restructuring of the informational and social field.

What, then, keeps the person obeying the experimenter? First, there is a set of "binding factors" that lock the subject into the situation. They include such factors as politeness on his part, his desire to uphold his initial promise of aid to the experimenter, and the awkwardness of withdrawal. Second, a number of adjustments in the subject's thinking occur that undermine his resolve to break with the authority. The adjustments help the subject maintain his relationship with the experimenter, while at the same time reducing the strain brought about by the experimental conflict. They are typical of thinking that comes about in obedient persons when they are instructed by authority to act against helpless individuals.

One such mechanism is the tendency of the individual to become so absorbed in the narrow technical aspects of the task that he loses sight of its broader consequences. The film *Dr. Strangelove* brilliantly satirized the absorption of a bomber crew in the exacting technical procedure of dropping nuclear weapons on a country. Similarly, in this experiment, subjects become immersed in the procedures, reading the word pairs with exquisite articulation and pressing the switches with great care. They want to put on a competent performance, but they show an accompanying narrowing of moral concern. The subject entrusts the broader tasks of setting goals and assessing morality to the experimental authority he is serving.

The most common adjustment of thought in the obedient subject is for him to see himself as not responsible for his own actions. He divests himself of responsibility by attributing all initiative to the experimenter, a legitimate authority. He sees himself not as a person acting in a morally accountable way but as the agent of external authority. In the postexperimental interview, when subjects were asked why they had gone on, a typical reply was: "I wouldn't have done it by myself. I was just doing what I was told." Unable to defy the authority of the experimenter, they attribute all responsibility to him. It is the old story of "just doing one's duty" that was heard time and time again in the defense statements of those accused at Nuremberg. But it would be wrong to think of it as a thin alibi concocted for the occasion. Rather, it is a fundamental mode of thinking for a great many people once they are locked into a subordinate position in a structure of authority. The disappearance of a sense of responsibility is the most far-reaching consequence of submission to authority.

Although a person acting under authority performs actions that seem to violate standards of conscience, it would not be true to say that he loses his moral sense. Instead, it acquires a radically different focus. He does not respond with a moral sentiment to the actions he performs. Rather, his moral concern now shifts to a consideration of how well he is living up to the expectations that the authority has of him. In wartime, a soldier does not ask whether it is good or bad to bomb a hamlet; he does not experience shame or guilt in the destruction of a village: rather he feels pride or shame depending on how well he has performed the mission assigned to him.

Another psychological force at work in this situation may be termed "counteranthropomorphism." For decades psychologists have discussed the primitive tendency among men to attribute to inanimate objects and forces the qualities of the human species. A countervailing tendency, however, is that of attributing an impersonal quality to forces that are essentially human in origin and maintenance. Some people treat systems of human origin as if they existed above and beyond any human agent, beyond the control of whim or human feeling. The human element behind agencies and institutions is denied. Thus, when the experimenter says, "The experiment *requires* that you continue," the subject feels this to be an imperative that goes beyond any merely human command. He does not ask the seemingly obvious question, "Whose experiment? Why should the designer be served while the victim suffers?" The wishes of a man— the designer of the experiment—have become part of a schema which exerts on the subject's mind a force that transcends the personal. "It's *got* to go on. It's *got* to go on," repeated one subject. He failed to realize that a man like himself wanted it to go on. For him the human agent had faded from the picture, and "The Experiment" had acquired an impersonal momentum of its own.

No action of itself has an unchangeable psychological quality. Its meaning can be altered by placing it in particular contexts. An American newspaper recently quoted a pilot who conceded that Americans were bombing Vietnamese men, women, and children but felt that the bombing was for a "noble cause" and thus was justified. Similarly, most subjects in the experiment see their behavior in a larger context that is benevolent and useful to society—the pursuit of scientific truth. The psychological laboratory has a strong claim to legitimacy and evokes trust and confidence in those who come to perform there. An action such as shocking a victim, which in isolation appears evil, acquires a totally different meaning when placed in this setting. But allowing an act to be dominated by its context, while neglecting its human consequences, can be dangerous in the extreme.

At least one essential feature of the situation in Germany was not studied here—namely, the intense devaluation of the victim prior to action against him. For a decade and more, vehement anti-Jewish propaganda systematically prepared the German population to accept the destruction of the Jews. Step by step the Jews were excluded from the category of citizen and national, and finally were denied the status of human beings. Systematic devaluation of the victim provides a measure of psychological justification for brutal treatment of the victim and has been the constant accompaniment of massacres, pogroms, and wars. In all likelihood, our subjects would have experienced greater ease in shocking the victim had he been convincingly portrayed as a brutal criminal or a pervert.

Of considerable interest, however, is the fact that many subjects harshly devalue the victim *as a consequence* of acting against him. Such comments as, "He was so stupid and stubborn he deserved to get shocked," were common. Once having acted against the victim, these subjects found it necessary to view him as an unworthy individual, whose punishment was made inevitable by his own deficiencies of intellect and character.

Many of the people studied in the experiment were in some sense against what they did to the learner, and many protested even while they obeyed. But between thoughts, words, and the critical step of disobeying a malevolent authority lies another ingredient, the capacity for transforming beliefs and values into action. Some subjects were totally convinced of the wrongness of what they were doing but could not bring themselves to make an open break with authority. Some derived satisfaction from their thoughts and felt that—within themselves, at least—they had been on the side of the angels. What they failed to realize is that subjective feelings are largely irrelevant to the moral issue at hand so long as they are not transformed into action. Political control is effected through action. The attitudes of the guards at a concentration camp are of no consequence when in fact they are allowing the slaughter of innocent men to take place before them. Similarly, so-called "intellectual resistance" in occupied Europe—in which persons by a twist of thought felt that they had defied the invader—was merely indulgence in a consoling psychological mechanism. Tyrannies are perpetuated by diffident men who do not possess the courage to act out their beliefs. Time and again in the experiment people disvalued what they were doing but could not muster the inner resources to translate their values into action.

A variation of the basic experiment depicts a dilemma more common than the one outlined above: the subject was not ordered to push the trigger that shocked the victim, but merely to perform a subsidiary act (administering the word-pair test) before another subject actually delivered the shock. In this situation, 37 of 40 adults from the New Haven area continued to the highest shock level on the generator. Predictably, subjects excused their behavior by saying that the responsibility belonged to the man who actually pulled the switch. This may illustrate a dangerously typical situation in complex society: it is psychologically easy to ignore responsibility when one is only an intermediate link in a chain of evil action but is far from the final consequences of the action. Even Eichmann was sickened when he toured the concentration camps, but to participate in mass murder he had only to sit at a desk and shuffle papers. At the same time the man in the camp who actually dropped Cyclon-B into the gas chambers was able to justify *his* behavior on the grounds that he was only following orders from above. Thus there is a fragmentation of the total human act; no one man decides to carry out the evil act and is confronted with its consequences. The person who assumes full responsibility for the act has evaporated. Perhaps this is the most common characteristic of socially organized evil in modern society.

The problem of obedience, therefore, is not wholly psychological. The form and shape of society and the way it is developing have much to do with it. There was a time, perhaps, when men were able to give a fully human response to any situation because they were fully absorbed in it as human beings. But as soon as there was a division of labor among men, things changed. Beyond a certain point, the breaking up of society into people carrying out narrow and very special jobs takes away from the human quality of work and life. A person does not get to see the whole situation but only a small part of it, and is thus unable to act without some kind of over-all direction. He yields to authority but in doing so is alienated from his own actions.

George Orwell caught the essence of the situation when he wrote:

> As I write, highly civilized human beings are flying overhead, trying to kill me. They do not feel any enmity against me as an individual, nor I against them. They are only "doing their duty," as the saying goes. Most of them, I have no doubt, are kind-hearted law abiding men who would never dream of committing murder in private life. On the other hand, if one of them succeeds in blowing me to pieces with a well-placed bomb, he will never sleep any the worse for it.

Reading 4.3

War and Misperception ROBERT JERVIS

War has so many causes—in part because there are so many kinds of wars—and misperception has so many effects—again in part because there are so many kinds of misperceptions—that it is not possible to draw any definitive conclusions about the impact of misperception on war.[1] But we can address some conceptual and methodological problems, note several patterns, and try to see how misperceptions might lead to World War III. In this article, I use the term misperception broadly, to include inaccurate inferences, miscalculations of consequences, and misjudgments about how others will react to one's policies.

Although war can occur even when both sides see each other accurately, misperception often plays a large role. Particularly interesting are judgments and misjudgments of another state's intentions. Both overestimates and underestimates of hostility have led to war in the past, and much of the current debate about policy toward the Soviet Union revolves around different judgments about how that country would respond to American policies that were either firm or conciliatory. Since statesmen know that a war between the United States and the Soviet Union would be incredibly destructive, however, it is hard to see how errors of judgment, even errors like those that have led to past wars, could have the same effect today. But perceptual dynamics could cause statesmen to see policies as safe when they actually were very dangerous or, in the final stages of deep conflict, to see war as inevitable and therefore to see striking first as the only way to limit destruction.

Source: Robert Jervis, "War and Misperception," Reprinted from The Journal of Interdisciplinary History, *XVIII (1988), 675–690, 692–693, 696–698, with permission of the editors of* The Journal of Interdisciplinary History *and the MIT Press, Cambridge, Massachusetts.* © 1988 by the Massachusetts Institute of Technology and The Journal of Interdisciplinary History, Inc.

Possible Areas of Misperception Although this article will concentrate on misperceptions of intentions of potential adversaries, many other objects can be misperceived as well. Capabilities of course can be misperceived; indeed, as Blainey stresses, excessive military optimism is frequently associated with the outbreak of war.[2] Military optimism is especially dangerous when coupled with political and diplomatic pessimism. A country is especially likely to strike if it feels that, although it can win a war immediately, the chances of a favorable diplomatic settlement are slight and the military situation is likely to deteriorate. Furthermore, these estimates, which are logically independent, may be psychologically linked. Pessimism about current diplomatic and long run military prospects may lead statesmen to exaggerate the possibility of current military victory as a way of convincing themselves that there is, in fact, a solution to what otherwise would be an intolerable dilemma.

Less remarked on is the fact that the anticipated consequences of events may also be incorrect. For example, America's avowed motive for fighting in Vietnam was not the direct goal of saving that country, but rather the need to forestall the expected repercussions of defeat. What it feared was a "domino effect" leading to a great increase in Communist influence in Southeast Asia and the perception that the United States lacked the resolve to protect its interests elsewhere in the world. In retrospect, it seems clear that neither of these possibilities materialized. This case is not unique; states are prone to fight when they believe that "band-wagoning" rather than "balancing" dynamics are at work—that is, when they believe that relatively small losses or gains will set off a self-perpetuating cycle. In fact, such beliefs are often incorrect. Although countries will sometimes side with a state which is gaining power, especially if they are small and can do little to counteract such a menace, the strength and resilience of balancing incentives are often underestimated by the leading powers. Statesmen are rarely fatalistic; they usually resist the growth of dominant powers.[3] A striking feature of the Cold War is how little each side has suffered when it has had to make what it perceived as costly and dangerous retreats.

At times we may need to distinguish between misperceptions of a state's predispositions—that is, its motives and goals—and misperceptions of the realities faced by the state. Either can lead to incorrect predictions, and, after the fact, it is often difficult to determine which kind of error was made. When the unexpected behavior is undesired, decision-makers usually think that they have misread the other state's motives, not the situation it faced.[4] Likewise, scholars generally focus on misjudgments of intentions rather than misjudgments of situations. We, too, shall follow this pattern, although it would be very useful to explore the proposition that incorrect explanations and predictions concerning other states' behaviors are caused more often by misperceptions concerning their situations than by misperceptions about their predispositions.

War Without Misperception It has often been argued that, by definition, the proposition is true that every war involves at least one serious misperception. If every war has a loser, it would seem to stand to reason that the defeated state made serious miscalculations when it decided to fight. But, whereas empirical investigations reveal that decisions to go to war are riddled with misperceptions, it is not correct that such a proposition follows by definition.

A country could rationally go to war even though it was certain it would lose. First, the country could value fighting itself, either as an ultimate goal or as a means for improving man and society. Second, faced with the choice of giving up territory to a stronger rival or losing it through a war, the state might choose war because of considerations of honor, domestic politics, or international reputation. Honor is self-explanatory, although, like the extreme form of Social Darwinism alluded to earlier, it sounds strange to modern ears. Domestic politics, however, are likely to remain with us and may have been responsible for at least some modern wars. It is a commonplace that leaders may seek "a quick and victorious war" in order to unify the country (this sentiment is supposed to have been voiced by Vyacheslav Plehve, the Russian minister of the interior on the eve of the Russo-Japanese War), but statesmen might also think that a short, unsuccessful war might serve the same function.

Although examples seem rare, international considerations could also lead a statesman to fight a war he knows he will lose. The object would be to impress third countries. Such a decision might appear particularly perverse because a loss would seem to show that the country is weak. But more important than the display of its lack of military capability could be the display of its resolve, if not foolhardiness. Other nations which had quarrels with the state might infer that it is willing to fight even when its position is weak, and such an inference might strengthen the state's bargaining position.[5]

Only rarely can statesmen be certain of a war's outcome, and once we take the probabilistic nature of judgments into consideration, it is even more clear that one can have wars without misperception. A state may believe that the chances of victory are small and yet rationally decide to fight if the gains of victory are large and the costs of losing are not much greater than those of making the concessions necessary to avoid war.

Although a state could start a war that it had little prospect of winning solely because of the attractions of victory, psychology and politics both conspire to make it much more likely that states go to war because of their gloomy prognostications of what will happen if they do not fight. Psychologically, losses hurt more than gains gratify. Both domestic and international politics produce a similar effect. Public opinion and partisan opposition is more easily turned against a government which seems to be sacrificing existing values than one which is not expanding the country's influence rapidly enough. Analyses of international politics reinforce these pressures. Statesmen are generally slower to believe that the domino effect will work for them than against them. They realize that other states will often respond to their gains by attempting to block further advances; by contrast, they also believe that any loss of their influence will lead to a further erosion of their power.

Because a state which finds the status quo intolerable or thinks it can be preserved only by fighting can be driven to act despite an unfavorable assessment of the balance of forces, it is neither surprising nor evidence of misperception that those who start wars often lose them. For example, Austria and

Germany attacked in 1914 largely because they believed that the status quo was unstable and that the tide of events was moving against them. As Sagan shows, the Japanese made a similar calculation in 1941.[6] Although they overestimated the chance of victory because they incorrectly believed that the United States would be willing to fight—and lose—a limited war, the expectation of victory was not a necessary condition for their decision to strike. According to their values, giving up domination of China—which would have been required in order to avoid war—was tantamount to sacrificing their national survival. Victory, furthermore, would have placed them in the first rank of nations and preserved their domestic values. The incentives were somewhat similar in 1904, when they attacked Russia even though "the Emperor's most trusted advisers expressed no confidence as to the outcome of the war. . . . The army calculated that Japan had a fifty-fifty chance to win a war. The Navy expected that half its forces would be lost, but it hoped the enemy's naval forces would be annihilated with the remaining half."[7] Fighting was justified in light of Japan's deteriorating military position combined with the possibility of increasing its influence over its neighbors.

Methodological Problems   The most obvious way to determine the influence of misperception on war would be to employ the comparative method and contrast the effects of accurate and inaccurate perceptions. But several methodological problems stand in the way. First is the question of whether perceptions should be judged in terms of outcomes or processes—that is, whether we should compare them to what was later revealed to have been reality or whether we should ask how reasonable were the statesmen's inferences, given the information available at the time. The two criteria call for different kinds of evidence and often yield different conclusions.[8] People are often right for the wrong reasons and, conversely, good analyses may produce answers which later will be shown to have been incorrect. Shortly after Adolf Hitler took power, Robert Vansittart, the permanent undersecretary of the British Foreign Office, concluded that the Germans would increase their military power as rapidly as possible in order to overturn the status quo. In criticizing military officials, who generally disagreed with him, he said: "Prophecy is largely a matter of insight. I do not think the Service Departments have enough. On the other hand they might say I have too much. The answer is that I knew the Germans better."[9] His image of Hitler was quite accurate, but it is not clear that he reached it by better reasoning or supported it with more evidence than did those who held a different view.

A second difficulty is that historians and political scientists are drawn to the study of conflict more often than to the analysis of peaceful interactions. As a result, we know little about the degree to which harmonious relationships are characterized by accurate perceptions. I suspect, however, that they are the product of routinized and highly constrained patterns of interaction more often than the result of accurate perceptions.

A third problem lies in determining whether perceptions were accurate, which involves two subproblems. First, it is often difficult to determine what a statesman's—let alone a country's—perceptions are. We usually have to tease the person's views out of confused and conflicting evidence and try to separate his true beliefs from those he merely wants others to believe he holds.

Indeed, in some cases the person initially may not have well-defined perceptions but may develop them to conform to the actions he has taken.[10] Second, even greater difficulties arise when the perceptions are compared with "reality." The true state of the military balance can be determined only by war; states' intentions may be impossible to determine, even after the fact and with all the relevant records open for inspection.

Our ability to determine whether statesmen's assessments are accurate is further reduced by the probabilistic nature of these assessments. Statesmen often believe that a given image is the one most likely to be correct or that a given outcome is the one most likely to occur. But the validity of such judgments is extremely hard to determine unless we have a large number of cases. If someone thinks that something will happen nine out of ten times, the fact that it does not happen once does not mean that the judgment was wrong. Thus if a statesman thinks that another country probably is aggressive and we later can establish that it was not, we cannot be sure that his probabilistic judgment was incorrect.[11]

Misperceptions and the Origins of World Wars I and II Tracing the impact of beliefs and perceptions in any given case might seem easy compared to the problems just presented. But it is not, although even a brief list of the misperceptions preceding the major conflicts of this century is impressive. Before World War I, all of the participants thought that the war would be short. They also seem to have been optimistic about its outcome, but there is conflicting evidence. (For example, both Edward Grey and Theobald von Bethmann Hollweg made well-known gloomy predictions, but it is unclear whether these statements accurately reflected their considered judgments. In addition, quantitative analysis of the available internal memoranda indicates pessimism, although there are problems concerning the methodology employed.[12])

May argues that the analyses of the intentions of the adversaries during this period were more accurate than the analyses of their capabilities, but even the former were questionable.[13] Some of the judgments of July 1914 were proven incorrect—for example, the German expectation that Britain would remain neutral and Germany's grander hopes of keeping France and even Russia out of the war. Furthermore, the broader assumptions underlying the diplomacy of the period may also have been in error. Most important on the German side was not an image of a particular country as the enemy, but its basic belief that the ensuing events would lead to either "world power or decline." For the members of the Triple Entente, and particularly Great Britain, the central question was German intentions, so brilliantly debated in Eyre Crowe's memorandum and Thomas Sanderson's rebuttal to it. We still cannot be sure whether the answer which guided British policy was correct.[14]

The list of misperceptions preceding World War II is also impressive. Capabilities again were misjudged, although not as badly as in the previous era.[15] Few people expected the blitzkrieg to bring France down; the power of strategic bombardment was greatly overestimated; the British exaggerated the vulnerability of the German economy, partly because they thought that it was stretched taut at the start of the war. Judgments of intention were even less accurate. The appeasers completely misread Hitler; the anti-appeasers failed to see that he could not be stopped without a war. For his part, Hitler underestimated his adversaries' determination. During the summer of 1939 he doubted whether Britain would fight and, in the spring of 1940, expected her to make peace.[16]

It might also be noted that in both cases the combatants paid insufficient attention to and made incorrect judgments about the behavior of neutrals. To a large extent, World War I was decided by the American entry and World War II by the involvement of the Soviet Union and the United States.[17] But we cannot generalize from these two examples to say that states are prone to make optimistic estimates concerning the role of neutrals; it may be equally true that pessimistic judgments may lead states to remain at peace, and we would have no way of determining the validity of such assessments.

Did the Misperceptions Matter?   But did these misperceptions cause the wars? Which if any of them, had they been corrected, would have led to a peaceful outcome? In attempting to respond to such questions, we should keep in mind that they are hypothetical and so do not permit conclusive answers. As Stein has noted, not all misperceptions have significant consequences.[18]

If Britain and France had understood Hitler, they would have fought much earlier, when the balance was in their favor and victory could have been relatively quick and easy. (Managing the postwar world might have been difficult, however, especially if others—including the Germans—held a more benign image of Hitler.) If Hitler had understood his adversaries, the situation would have been much more dangerous since he might have devised tactics that would have allowed him to fight on more favorable terms. But on either of these assumptions, war still would have been inevitable; both sides preferred to fight rather than make the concessions that would have been necessary to maintain peace.[19]

The case of 1914 is not as clear. I suspect that the misperceptions of intentions in July, although fascinating, were not crucial. The Germans probably would have gone to war even if they had known that they would have had to fight all of the members of the Triple Entente. The British misjudgment of Germany—if it were a misjudgment—was more consequential, but even on this point the counterfactual question is hard to answer. Even if Germany did not seek domination, the combination of her great power, restlessness, and paranoia made her a menace. Perhaps a British policy based on a different image of Germany might have successfully appeased the Germans—to use the term in the older sense—but Britain could not have afforded to see Germany win another war in Europe, no matter what goals it sought.

Capabilities were badly misjudged, but even a correct appreciation of the power of the defense might not have changed the outcome of the July crisis. The "crisis instability" created by the belief that whoever struck first would gain a major advantage made the war hard to avoid once the crisis was severe, but may not have been either a necessary or a sufficient condition for the outbreak of the fighting. The Germans' belief that time was not on their side and that a quick victory would soon be beyond their reach was linked in part to the mistaken belief in the power of the offensive, but was not entirely driven by it. Thus, a preventive war might have occurred in the absence of the pressures for preemption.

Had the participants realized not only that the first offensive would not end the war, but also that the fighting would last for four punishing years, they might well have held back. Had they known what the war would bring, the kaiser, the emperor, and the czar presumably might have bluffed or sought a limited war, but they would have preferred making concessions to joining a general struggle. The same was probably true for the leaders of Britain and France, and certainly would have been true had they known the long-term consequences of the war. In at least one sense, then, World War I was caused by misperception.

Models of Conflict   Two possible misperceptions of an adversary are largely the opposites of each other, and each is linked to an important argument about the causes of conflict. On the one hand, wars can occur if aggressors underestimate the willingness of status quo powers to fight (the World War II model); on the other hand, wars can also result if two states exaggerate each other's hostility when their differences are in fact bridgeable (the spiral or World War I model). These models only approximate the cases that inspired them. As noted earlier, World War II would have occurred even without this perceptual error, and the judgments of intentions before 1914 may have been generally accurate and, even if they were not, may not have been necessary for the conflict to have erupted. Nevertheless, the models are useful for summarizing two important sets of dynamics.

The World War II model in large part underlies deterrence theory. The main danger which is foreseen is that of an aggressive state which underestimates the resolve of the status quo powers. The latter may inadvertently encourage this misperception by errors of their own—for example, they may underestimate the aggressor's hostility and propose compromises that are taken as evidence of weakness. In the spiral model, by contrast, the danger is that each side will incorrectly see the other as a menace to its vital interests and will inadvertently encourage this belief by relying on threats to prevent war, thereby neglecting the pursuit of agreement and conciliation.

As I have stated elsewhere, the heated argument between the proponents of the two models is not so much a dispute between two rival theories as it is a dispute about the states' intentions.[20] The nature of the difference of opinion then points up both the importance and the difficulty of determining what states' motives and goals are, what costs and risks they are willing to run in order to expand, and the likely way in which they will respond to threats and conciliation. Determining others' intentions is so difficult that states have resorted to an approach that, were it suggested by an academic, would be seen as an example of how out of touch scholars are with international realities. On several occasions, states directly ask their adversaries what it is they want.

The British frequently discussed directing such an inquiry to Hitler, and the United States did so to Joseph Stalin shortly after the end of World War II. Statesmen might be disabused of their misperceptions if they could listen in on their adversary's deliberations. Thus in his analysis of the Eastern crisis of 1887/88, Seton-Watson argues that Benjamin Disraeli's government greatly exaggerated the Russian ambitions, and points out that "it is difficult to believe that even the most confirmed Russophobe in the British Cabinet of those days could have failed to be reassured if it had been possible for him to [read the czar's telegrams to his ambassador in London]."[21] But of course were such access possible, it could be used for deception, and the information would therefore not be credible.

It is clear that states can either underestimate or overestimate the aggressiveness of their adversaries and that either error can lead to war. Although one issue raised by these twin dangers is not central to our discussion here, it is so important that it should at least be noted. If the uncertainty about others' intentions cannot be eliminated, states should design policies that will not fail disastrously even if they are based on incorrect assumptions. States should try to construct a policy of deterrence which will not set off spirals of hostility if existing political differences are in fact bridgeable; the policy should also be designed to conciliate without running the risk that the other side, if it is aggressive, will be emboldened to attack. Such a policy requires the state to combine firmness, threats, and an apparent willingness to fight with reassurances, promises, and a credible willingness to consider the other side's interests. But the task is difficult, and neither decision-makers nor academics have fully come to grips with it.[22]

The existence of a spiral process does not prove the applicability of the spiral model, for increasing tension, hostility, and violence can be a reflection of the underlying conflict, not a cause of it. For example, conflict between the United States and Japan increased steadily throughout the 1930s, culminating in the American oil embargo in 1941 and the Japanese attack on Pearl Harbor four months later. Misperceptions were common, but the spiral model should not be used to explain these events because the escalating exchange of threats and actions largely revealed rather than created the incompatibility of goals. Japan preferred to risk defeat rather than forego dominance of China; the United States preferred to fight rather than see Japan reach its goal.

Blainey advances similar arguments in his rebuttal of Higonnet's views on the origins of the Seven Years' War. Higonnet claims that "no one wanted to fight this war. It would never have occurred if, in their sincere efforts to resolve it, the French and English governments had not inadvertently magnified its insignificant original cause into a wide conflict."[23] Hostilities escalated as Britain and France attempted to counteract (and surpass) each other's moves. They became increasingly suspicious of their adversary's motives, and felt that the stakes were higher than originally had been believed. The cycle of action and threat perception eventually led both sides to believe that they had to fight a major war in order to protect themselves. Blainey's rebuttal is simple: what was at stake from the beginning was "mastery in North America." The initial moves were at a low level of violence because each side, having underestimated the other's willingness to fight, thought it was possible to prevail quickly and cheaply.[24] Resolving such differences would require detailed research and responses to a number of hypothetical questions. But it should be kept in mind that the existence of increasing and reciprocal hostility does not always mean that the participants have come to overestimate the extent to which the other threatens its vital interests.

Furthermore, even if the initial conflict of interest does not justify a war and it is the process of conflict itself which generates the impulse to fight, misperception may not be the crucial factor. The very fact that states contest an issue raises the stakes because influence and reputation are involved. To retreat after having expended prestige and treasure, if not blood, is psychologically more painful than retreating at the start; it is also more likely to have much stronger domestic and international repercussions.[25] The dilemmas which are created were outlined in 1953 by the American intelligence community in a paper which tried to estimate how the Russians and Chinese would react to various forms of American military pressure designed to produce an armistice in Korea:

> If prior to the onset of any UN/U.S. military course of action, the Communists recognized that they were faced with a clear choice between making the concessions necessary to reach an armistice, or accepting the likelihood that UN/U.S. military operations would endanger the security of the Manchurian and Soviet borders, destroy the Manchurian industrial complex, or destroy the Chinese Communist armed forces, the Communists would probably agree to an armistice. However, it would be extremely difficult to present them with a clear choice of alternatives before such action was begun. Moreover, once such UN/U.S. action was begun, Communist power and prestige would become further involved, thereby greatly increasing the difficulties of making the choice between agreeing to [an] armistice or continuing the war.[26]

Assessing Hostile Intent   On balance, it seems that states are more likely to overestimate the hostility of others than to underestimate it. States are prone to exaggerate the reasonableness of their own positions and the hostile intent of others; indeed, the former process feeds the latter. Statesmen, wanting to think well of themselves and their decisions, often fail to appreciate others' perspectives, and so greatly underestimate the extent to which their actions can be seen as threats.

When their intentions are peaceful, statesmen think that others will understand their motives and therefore will not be threatened by the measures that they are taking in their own self-defense. Richard Perle, former assistant secretary of defense, once said that if we are in doubt about Soviet intentions, we should build up our arms. He explained that if the Russians are aggressive, the buildup will be needed, and, if they are not, the only consequence will be wasted money. Similarly, when United States troops were moving toward the Yalu River, Secretary of State Dean Acheson said that there was no danger that the Chinese would intervene in an effort to defend themselves because they understood that we were not a threat to them. Exceptions, such as the British belief in the 1930s that German hostility was based largely on fear of encirclement and the Israeli view before the 1973 war that Egypt feared attack, are rare.[27] (The British and the Israeli perceptions were partly generated by the lessons they derived from their previous wars.)

This bias also operates in retrospect, when states interpret the other side's behavior after the fact. Thus American leaders, believing that China had no reason to be alarmed by the movement of troops toward the Yalu, assumed the only explanation for Chinese intervention in the Korean War was its unremitting hostility to the United States. India, although clearly seeing the Chinese point of view in 1950, saw the Chinese attack on her in 1962 as unprovoked, and so concluded that future cooperation was impossible. Similarly, although all Westerners, even those who could empathize with the Soviet Union, understand how the invasion of Afghanistan called up a strong reaction, Soviet leaders apparently did not and instead saw the Western response as "part of a hostile design that would have led to the same actions under any circumstances."[28]

This problem is compounded by a second and better known bias—states tend to infer threatening motives from actions that a disinterested observer would record as at least partly cooperative. John Foster Dulles' view of Nikita Khrushchev's arms cuts in the mid-1950s is one such example and President Ronald Reagan's view of most Soviet arms proposals may be another.[29]

These two biases often operate simultaneously, with the result that both sides are likely to believe that they are cooperating and that others are responding with hostility. For example, when Leonid Brezhnev visited President Richard Nixon in San Clemente during 1973 and argued that the status quo in the Middle East was unacceptable, and when Andrei Gromyko later said that "the fire of war [in the Mid-East] could break out onto the surface at any time," they may well have thought that they were fulfilling their obligations under the Basic Principles Agreement to consult in the event of a threat to peace. The Americans, however, felt that the Soviets were making threats in the spring and violating the spirit of detente by not giving warning in the fall.[30]

People also tend to overperceive hostility because they pay closest attention to dramatic events. Threatening acts often achieve high visibility because they consist of instances like crises, occupation of foreign territory, and the deployment of new weapons. Cooperative actions, by contrast, often call less attention to themselves because they are not dramatic and can even be viewed as nonevents. Thus Larson notes how few inferences American statesmen drew from the Soviet's willingness to sign the Austrian State Treaty of 1955.[31] Similarly, their withdrawal of troops from Finland after World War II made little impact, and over the past few years few decision-makers or analysts have commented on the fact that the Soviets have *not* engaged in a strategic buildup. . . .

Whether a commitment—and indeed any message—is perceived as intended (or perceived at all) depends not only on its clarity and plausibility, but also on how it fits with the recipient's cognitive predispositions. Messages which are inconsistent with a person's beliefs about international politics and other actors are not likely to be perceived the way the sender intended. For example, shortly before the Spanish-American War President William McKinley issued what he thought was a strong warning to Spain to make major concessions over Cuba or face American military intervention. But the Spanish were worried primarily not about an American declaration of war, but about American aid for the Cuban rebels, and so they scanned the president's speech with this problem in mind. They therefore focused on sections of the speech that McKinley regarded as relatively unimportant and passed quickly over the paragraphs that he thought were vital.[32]

Furthermore, the state sending the message of commitment is likely to assume that it has been received. Thus one reason the United States was taken by surprise when the Soviet Union put missiles into Cuba was that it had assumed that the Soviets understood that such action was unacceptable. Statesmen, like people in their everyday lives, find it difficult to realize that their own intentions, which seem clear to them, can be obscure to others. The problem is magnified because the belief that the message has been received and understood as it was intended will predispose the state to interpret ambiguous information as indicating that the other side does indeed understand its commitment.

Psychological Commitment and Misperception Misperception can lead to war not only through mistaken beliefs about the impact of the state's policy of commitment on others, but also through the impact of commitment on the state. We should not forget the older definition of the term commitment, which is more psychological than tactical. People and states become committed to policies not only by staking their bargaining reputations on them, but by coming to believe that their policies are morally justified and politically necessary. For example, the process of deciding that a piece of territory warrants a major international dispute and the effort that is involved in acting on this policy can lead a person to see the territory as even more valuable than he had originally thought. Furthermore, other members of the elite and the general public may become aroused, with the result that a post-commitment retreat will not only feel more costly to the statesman; it may actually be more costly in terms of its effect on his domestic power.

Commitment can also create misperceptions. As the decision-maker comes to see his policy as necessary, he is likely to believe that the policy can succeed, even if such a conclusion requires the distortion of information about what others will do. He is likely to come to believe that his threats will be credible and effective and that his opponents will ultimately cooperate and permit him to reach his objectives. Facing sharp value trade-offs is painful; no statesman wants to acknowledge that he may have to abandon an important foreign policy goal in order to avoid war or that he may have to engage in a bloody struggle if he is to reach his foreign policy goals. Of course, he will not embark on the policy in the first place if he thinks that the other will fight. Quite often, the commitment develops incrementally, without a careful and disinterested analysis of how others are likely to react. When commitments develop in this way, decision-makers can find themselves supporting untenable policies that others can and will challenge. The result could be war because the state behaves more recklessly than the chicken context would warrant. . . .[33]

If war is believed to be very likely but not inevitable, launching a first strike would be an incredible gamble. As noted at the start of this article, such gambles can be rational, but, even when they are not, psychological factors can lead people to take them. Although most people are risk-averse for gains, they are risk-acceptant for losses.[34] For example, given the choice between a 100 percent chance of winning $10 and a 20 percent chance of winning $55, most people will choose the former. But if the choice is between the certainty of losing $10 and a 20 percent chance of losing $55, they will gamble and opt for the latter. In order to increase the chance of avoiding any loss at all, people are willing to accept the danger of an even greater sacrifice. Such behavior is consistent with the tendency for people to be influenced by "sunk costs" which rationally should be disregarded and to continue to pursue losing ventures in the hope of recovering their initial investment when they would be better off simply cutting their losses.

This psychology of choice has several implications concerning crisis stability. First, because the status quo forms people's point of reference, they are willing to take unusual risks to recoup recent losses. Although a setback might be minor when compared to the total value of a person's holdings, he will see his new status in terms of where he was shortly before and therefore may risk an even greater loss in the hope of reestablishing his position. In a crisis, then, a decision-maker who had suffered a significant, but limited, loss might risk world war if he thought such a war held out the possibility of reversing the recent defeat. Where fully rational analysis would lead a person to cut his losses, the use of the status quo as the benchmark against which other results are measured could lead the statesman to persevere even at high risk. The danger would be especially great if both sides were to feel that they were losing, which could easily happen because they probably would have different perspectives and use different baselines. Indeed, if the Russians consider the status quo to be constant movement in their favor, they might be prone to take high risks when the United States thought that it was maintaining the status quo. Furthermore, it could prove dangerous to follow a strategy of making gains by fait accompli.[35] Unless the state which has been victimized quickly adjusts to and accepts the new situation, it may be willing to run unusually high risks to regain its previous position. The other side, expecting the first to be "rational," will in turn be taken by surprise by this resistance, with obvious possibilities for increased conflict.

A second consequence is that if a statesman thinks that war—and therefore enormous loss—is almost certain if he does not strike and that attacking provides a small chance of escaping unscathed, he may decide to strike even though a standard probability-utility calculus would call for restraint. Focusing on the losses that will certainly occur if his state is attacked can lead a decision-maker to pursue any course of action that holds out any possibility of no casualties at all. Similar and more likely are the dynamics which could operate in less severe crises, such as the expectation of a hostile coup in an important third-world country or the limited use of force by the adversary in a disputed area. Under such circumstances, the state might take actions which entailed an irrationally high chance of escalation and destruction in order to avoid the certain loss entailed by acquiescing.[36] With his attention riveted on the deterioration which will occur unless he acts strongly to reverse a situation, a statesman may accept the risk of even greater loss, thereby making these crises more dangerous.

The response can also be influenced by how the decision is framed. Although a powerful aversion to losses could lead a decision-maker to strike when the alternatives are posed as they were in the previous example, it also could lead him to hold back. For instance, he might choose restraint if he thought that striking first, although preferable to striking second, would lead to certain retaliation whereas not striking would offer some chance—even if small—of avoiding a war, although he risked much higher casualties if the other side attacked. If a decision-maker takes as his baseline not the existing situation, but the casualties that would be suffered in a war, his choice between the same alternatives might be different. He would then judge the policies according to lives that might be saved, not lost, with the result that he would choose a course of action that he believed would certainly save some lives rather than choose another that might save more, but might not save any. The obvious danger is that a first strike which would significantly reduce the other side's strategic forces would meet the former criterion whereas restraint could not provide the certainty of saving any lives and so would not seem as attractive as standard utility maximization theory implies.

But the picture is not one of unrelieved gloom. First, situations as bleak as those we are positing are extremely rare and probably will never occur. The Cuban missile crisis was probably as close as we have come to the brink of war, and even then President John F. Kennedy rated the chance of war at no more than 50 percent, and he seems to have been referring to the chances or armed conflict, not nuclear war. So American, and presumably Soviet, officials were far from believing that war was inevitable.

Second, the propensity for people to avoid value trade-offs can help to preserve peace. To face the choice between starting World War III and running a very high risk that the other side will strike first would be terribly painful, and decision-makers might avoid it by downplaying the latter danger. Of course to say that a decision-maker will try not to perceive the need for such a sharp value trade-off does not tell us which consideration will guide him, but some evidence indicates that the dominating value may be the one which is most salient and to which the person was committed even before the possibility of conflict with another central value arose. Thus the very fact that decision-makers constantly reiterate the need to avoid war and rarely talk about the need to strike first if war becomes inevitable may contribute to restraint.

Finally, although exaggerating the danger of crisis instability would make a severe confrontation more dangerous than it would otherwise be, it also would serve the useful function of keeping states far from the brink of war. If decision-makers believed that crises could be controlled and manipulated, they would be less inhibited about creating them. The misperception may be useful: fear, even unjustified fear, may make the world a little more tranquil. . . .

NOTES

1 For a good typology of wars caused by misperception, see George H. Quester, "Six Causes of War," *Jerusalem Journal of International Relations*, 6 (1982), 1–23.

2 For a discussion of the concept of intentions in international politics, see Jervis, *Perception and Misperception in International Politics* (Princeton, 1976), 48–57. For a discussion of the meaning of that concept in general, see Gertrude E. M. Anscombe, *Intention* (Ithaca, 1969); Ernest May, "Conclusions: Capabilities and Proclivities," in *idem* (ed.). *Knowing One's Enemies* (Princeton, 1984), 503. A. Geoffrey Blainey, *The Causes of War* (New York, 1973).

3 See Arnold Wolfers, *Discord and Collaboration* (Baltimore, 1962), 122–124; Kenneth N. Waltz, *Theory of International Politics* (Reading, Mass., 1979); Stephen Walt, "Alliance Formation and the Balance of World Power," *International Security*, 9 (1985), 3–43; *idem, The Origins of Alliances* (Ithaca, 1987).

4 For a good review, see Edward Jones, "How Do People Perceive the Causes of Behavior?" *American Scientist*, 44 (1976), 300–305. For an analysis of related phenomena in international politics, see Jervis, *Perception and Misperception*, 343–354.

5 This concept is similar to the economist's notion of the "chain store paradox." It applies in cases in which the state can prevail in the conflict, but only at a cost which exceeds the immediate gains. The reason for fighting in this case is again to impress other potential challengers, and the analogy is the behavior of a large chain store toward small stores which challenge it by cutting prices. The chain store can respond by cutting prices even more, thus losing money but succeeding in driving the competitor out of business. The point of taking such action is to discourage other challengers, but the paradox is that in each particular case the chain store loses money and the tactic will be effective only if others believe it will be repeated. See Reinhard Selten, "The Chain Store Paradox," *Theory and Decision*, 9 (1978), 127–159.

6 Scott D. Sagan, "The Origins of the Pacific War," *Journal of Interdisciplinary History*, 18 (1988), 893–922.

7 Shumpei Okamoto, *The Japanese Oligarchy and the Russo-Japanese War* (New York, 1970), 101.

8 Processes which seem highly rational may yield less accurate perceptions than those which are more intuitive. See Kenneth Hammond, "A Theoretically Based Review of Theory and Research in Judgment and Decision Making," unpub. ms. (Boulder, 1986).

9 Quoted in Donald Watt, "British Intelligence and the Coming of the Second World War in Europe," in May (ed.), *Knowing One's Enemies*, 268.

10 Daryl Bern, "Self-Perception Theory," in Leonard Berkowitz (ed.). *Advances in Experimental Social Psychology* (New York, 1972), VI, 1–62. For an application to foreign policy, see Deborah Larson, *The Origins of Containment* (Princeton, 1985).

11 In politics, not only are situations rarely repeated, but the meaning of probabilistic judgments is not entirely clear. Are these statements merely indications of the degree to which the person feels he lacks important facts or an understanding of significant relationships? Or do they reflect the belief that politics is inherently uncertain and that, if somehow the same situation was repeated in all its details, behavior might be different on different occasions?

12 See Ole Holsti, Robert North, and Richard Brody, "Perception and Action in the 1914 Crisis," in J. David Singer (ed.), *Quantitative International Politics* (New York, 1968), 123–158.

13 May, "Conclusions," 504. For a more detailed discussion of May's argument, see Jervis, "Intelligence and Foreign Policy," *International Security*, 11 (1986/87), 141–161.

14 This continuing debate also underlies the difficulty of determining when perceptions are misperceptions. Indeed, when we contemplate the task of avoiding World War III, it is disheartening to note that we cannot even be sure how the participants could have avoided World War I.

15 See May (ed.), *Knowing One's Enemies*, 237–301, 504–519.

16 This belief may not have been as foolish as it appears in retrospect. While France was falling, the British Cabinet spent two days debating whether to open talks with Germany. See Philip M.H. Bell, *A Certain Eventuality* (Farnborough, England, 1974), 31–54; Martin Gilbert, *Winston Churchill, VI: Finest Hour, 1939–1941* (London, 1983), 402–425. Given the situation Britain faced, seeking peace might have been reasonable. See David Reynolds, "Churchill and the British 'Decision' to Fight on in 1940: Right Policy, Wrong Reason," in Richard Langhorne (ed.), *Diplomacy and Intelligence during the Second World War* (Cambridge, 1985), 147–67.

17 The role of states which are not involved in the first stages of combat is stressed by Blainey, *Causes of War*, 57–67, 228–242; Bruce Bueno de Mesquita, *The War Trap* (New Haven, 1981).

18 Arthur Stein, "When Misperception Matters," *World Politics*, 34 (1982), 505–526.

19 Oddly enough, almost the only view of Hitler which indicates that he could have been deterred is that of Taylor, who paints a picture of the German leader as an opportunist, inadvertently misled by the acquiescence of Western statesmen (Alan J.P. Taylor, *The Origins of the Second World War* [New York, 1961]).

20 Jervis, *Perception and Misperception*, 58–113.

21 Robert W. Seton-Watson, *Disraeli, Gladstone, and the Eastern Question* (New York, 1972), 127, 192. It is interesting to note that during and after World War II the Soviet Union did have high-level spies who had good access to American thinking. The more recent penetrations of the American Embassy in Moscow may have duplicated this feat. The results may not have been entirely deleterious—both the United States and the Soviet Union may gain if the latter has convincing evidence that the former is driven by defensive motivations.

22 For a further discussion, see Jervis, *Perception and Misperception*, 109–113; *idem*, "Deterrence Theory Revisited," *World Politics*, 31 (1979), 289–324; Richard Ned Lebow, "The Deterrence Deadlock: Is There a Way Out?" in Jervis, Lebow, and Janice Stein, *Psychology and Deterrence* (Baltimore, 1985), 180–202; Alexander George, David Hall, and William Simons, *Coercive Diplomacy* (Boston, 1971), 100–103, 238–244; George and Richard Smoke, *Deterrence in American Foreign Policy* (New York, 1974), 588–613; Glenn Snyder and Paul Diesing, *Conflict among Nations* (Princeton, 1977), 489–493.

23 Patrice Louis-René Higonnet, "The Origins of the Seven Years' War," *Journal of Modern History*, 40 (1968), 57–58. See also Smoke, *War* (Cambridge, Mass., 1977), 195–236.

24 Blainey, *Causes of War*, 133–134.

25 One of the psychological mechanisms at work is cognitive dissonance. In order to justify the effort they are expending to reach a goal, people exaggerate its value.

26 Department of State, *Foreign Relations of the United States, 1952–54. XV: Korea* (Washington, D.C., 1984), Pt. 1, 888.

27 Daniel Yergin, "'Scoop' Jackson Goes for Broke," *Atlantic Monthly*, 2 (1974), 82. Perle, then an aide to Sen. Henry Jackson, is describing the latter's views, but what he says seems to apply to his own beliefs as well. Acheson's views are presented in John Spanier, *The Truman-MacArthur Controversy and the Korean War* (New York, 1965), 97; Allen Whiting, *China Crosses the Yalu* (Stanford, 1968), 151.

(Similar examples are discussed in Jervis, *Perception and Misperception*, 67–76.) The case of Israel in 1973 is analyzed in Janice Stein, "Calculation, Miscalculation, and Conventional Deterrence II: The View from Jerusalem," in Jervis, Lebow, and Stein, *Psychology and Deterrence*, 60–88. See also Richard Betts, *Surprise Attack* (Washington, D.C., 1982).

28 Raymond Garthoff, *Detente and Confrontation* (Washington, D.C., 1985), 1076.

29 See the classic essay by Holsti, "Cognitive Dynamics and Images of the Enemy: Dulles and Russia," in David Finlay, Holsti, and Richard Fagen, *Enemies in Politics* (Chicago, 1967), 25–96. Michael Sullivan, *International Relations: Theories and Evidence* (Englewood Cliffs, NJ, 1976), 45–46, questions the links between Dulles' beliefs and American behavior.

30 Gromyko is quoted in Galia Golan, *Yom Kippur and After* (London, 1977), 68. The treatment of the 1973 war is a good litmus test for one's views on detente: compare, for example, the discussions in Harry Gelman, *The Brezhnev Politburo and the Decline of Detente* (Ithaca, 1984), 135–139, 152–156; Garthoff, *Detente and Confrontation*; George, *Managing U.S.-Soviet Rivalry* (Boulder, 1983), 139–154.

31 Larson, "Crisis Prevention and the Austrian State Treaty," *International Organization*, 41 (1987), 27–60.

32 May, *Imperial Democracy* (New York, 1961), 161. For an extended discussion of this problem, see Jervis, *Perception and Misperception*, 203–216; *idem*, "Deterrence Theory Revisited," 305–310. For a discussion of this problem in the context of the limited use of nuclear weapons, see Schelling, "The Role of War Games and Exercises," in Ashton Carter, John Steinbruner, and Charles Zraket (eds.), *Nuclear Operations and Command and Control* (Washington, D.C., 1987), 426–444.

33 The literature on these perceptual processes, which are a subcategory of what are known as "motivated biases" because of the important role played by affect, is large. The best starting place is Irving Janis and Leon Mann, *Decision Making* (New York, 1977). For applications to international politics, see Richard Cottam, *Foreign Policy Motivation* (Pittsburgh, 1977); Lebow, *Between Peace and War* (Baltimore, 1981); Jervis, "Foreign Policy Decision-Making: Recent Developments," *Political Psychology*, 11 (1980), 86–101; *idem*, Lebow, and Stein, *Psychology and Deterrence*. For earlier versions of the argument, see Holsti, North, and Brody, "Perception and Action," 123–158; Snyder, *Deterrence and Defense* (Princeton, 1961), 26–27. For a rebuttal to some points, see Sagan, "Origins of the Pacific War," 893–922. John Orme, "Deterrence Failures: A Second Look," *International Security*, 11 (1987), 96–124. For further discussion of the tendency to avoid trade-offs, see Jervis, *Perception and Misperception*. Quester points to the strategic value of commitment in making the other side retreat (Quester, "Crisis and the Unexpected," *Journal of Interdisciplinary History*, 18 [1988], 701–719). He is correct, but such behavior can still lead to war if the other side does not gauge the situation accurately.

34 This discussion is drawn from Daniel Kahneman and Amos Tversky, "Prospect Theory: An Analysis of Decision Under Risk," *Econometrica*, 57 (1979), 263–291; Tversky and Kahneman, "The Framing of Decisions and the Psychology of Choice," *Science*, 211 (1981), 453–458; Kahneman and Tversky, "Choices, Values, and Frames," *American Psychologist*, 39 (1984), 341–350; Tversky and Kahneman, "Rational Choice and the Framing of Decisions," *Journal of Business*, 59 (1986), S251–S278.

35 See George and Smoke, *Deterrence*, 536–540.

36 States may try to gain the bargaining advantages that come from seeming to be irrational, as Quester reminds us ("Crises and the Unexpected," 703–706).

Reading 4.4

Spirit, Standing, and Honor RICHARD NED LEBOW

Following the ancient Greeks, I contend that appetite, spirit and reason are fundamental drives, each seeking its own ends. Existing paradigms of international relations are nested in appetite (Marxism, liberalism) or fear (realism). The spirit—what the Greeks often called *thumos*—had not until recently generated a paradigm of politics, although Machiavelli and Rousseau recognized its potential to do so. . . .

I limit myself to four underlying motives: appetite, spirit, reason and fear. Modern authorities have offered different descriptions of the psyche and human needs. Freud reduces all fundamental drives to appetite, and understands reason only in its most instrumental sense. Another prominent formulation is Abraham Maslow's hierarchy of needs, developed from his study of great people and what accounted for their accomplishments. More recently, psychologists have sought to subsume all human emotions to seven fundamental ones. Maslow's hierarchy of needs is conceptually confusing and rooted in a distinctly nineteenth-century understanding of human nature. Contemporary psychology's efforts to classify emotions assumes that its typology is universally applicable, which is highly questionable. Even if defensible, this and other typologies include emotions like love, sadness and joy that can hardly be considered central to foreign-policy decisionmaking. Other emotions, like anger, surprise, disgust and contempt, have more relevance but, I contend, can effectively be reduced to one or the other of my four motives.

THE SPIRIT

A spirit-based paradigm starts from the premise that people, individually and collectively, seek self-esteem. Self-esteem is a sense of self-worth that makes people feel good about themselves, happier about life and more confident in their ability to confront its challenges. It is achieved by excelling in activities valued by one's peers or society and gaining respect from those whose opinions matter. By winning the approbation of such people we feel good about ourselves. Self-esteem requires some sense of self but also recognition that self requires society because self-esteem is impossible in the absence of commonly shared values and accepted procedures for demonstrating excellence.

The spirit is fiercely protective of one's autonomy and honor, and for the Greeks the two are closely related. According to Plato, the spirit responds with

Source: Richard Ned Lebow, from "Spirit, Standing, and Honor," in Why Nations Fight: Past and Future Motives for War. *Copyright © 2010 Richard Ned Lebow. Reprinted with the permission of Cambridge University Press.*

anger to any restraint on its self-assertion in private or civic life. It wants to avenge all affronts to its honor, and those against its friends, and seeks immediate satisfaction when aroused. Mature people are restrained by reason and recognize the wisdom of the ancient maxim, as Odysseus did in the *Odyssey*, that revenge is a dish best served cold. . . .

Societies have strong incentives to nurture and channel the spirit. It engenders self-control and sacrifice from which the community as a whole prospers. In warrior societies, the spirit finds expression in bravery and selflessness, from which the society as a whole profits. All societies must restrain, or deflect outwards, the anger aroused when the spirit is challenged or frustrated. The spirit is a human drive; organizations and states do not have psyches and cannot be treated as persons. They can nevertheless respond to the needs of the spirit the same way they do to the appetites of their citizens. People join or support collective enterprises in the expectation of material and emotional rewards. They build self-esteem the same way, through the accomplishments of the groups, sports teams, nations and religions with which they affiliate. Arguably, the most important function of nationalism in the modern world is to provide vicarious satisfaction to the spirit. . . .

Self-esteem is closely connected to honor (*timē*), a status for the Greeks that describes the outward recognition we gain from others in response to our excellence. Honor is a gift, and bestowed upon actors by other actors. It carries with it a set of responsibilities which must be fulfilled properly if honor is to be retained. By the fifth century, honor came to be associated with political rights and offices. It was a means of selecting people for office and of restraining them in their exercise of power. The spirit is best conceived of as an innate human drive, with self-esteem its goal, and honor and standing the means by which it is achieved.

Hierarchy is a rank ordering of statuses. In honor societies, honor determines the nature of the statuses and who fills them. Each status has privileges, but also an associated rule package. The higher the status, the greater the honor and privileges, but also the more demanding the role and elaborate its rules. Kings, formerly at the apex of the social hierarchy, were often expected to mediate between the human and divine worlds and derived authority and status from this responsibility. This holds true for societies as diverse as ancient Assyria, Song China and early modern Europe. Status can be ascribed, as it was in the case of elected kings or German war chiefs. In traditional honor societies, the two are expected to coincide. The king or chief is expected to be the bravest warrior and lead his forces into battle. Other high-ranking individuals must assume high-risk, if subordinate, roles. Service and sacrifice—the means by which honor is won and maintained—have the potential to legitimize hierarchy. In return for honoring and serving those higher up the social ladder, people expect to be looked after in various ways. Protecting and providing for others is invariably one of the key responsibilities of those with high status and office. The Song dynasty carried this system to its logical extreme, integrating all males in the kingdom into a system of social status signified initially by seventeen, and then twenty, ranks. Obligations, including labor and military service, came with rank, as did various economic incentives. As in aristocratic Europe, the severity of punishments for the same crime varied by rank, but in reverse order.

Great powers have had similar responsibilities in the modern era, which have been described by practitioners and theorists alike. The United Nations Security Council is an outgrowth of this tradition. Its purpose, at least in the intent of those who drafted the United Nations Charter, is to coordinate the collective efforts of the community to maintain the peace. Traditional hierarchies justify themselves with reference to the principle of fairness; each actor contributes to the society and to the maintenance of its order to the best of its abilities and receives support depending on its needs. More modern hierarchies invoke the principle of equality. The United Nations attempts to incorporate both in two separate organs: the Security Council and the General Assembly.

Honor is also a mechanism for restraining the powerful and preventing the kind of crass, even brutal exploitation common to hierarchies in modern, interest-based worlds. Honor can maintain hierarchy because challenges to an actor's status, or failure to respect the privileges it confers, arouse anger that can only be appeased by punishing the offender and thereby "putting him in his place." Honor worlds have the potential to degenerate into hierarchies based on power and become vehicles for exploitation when actors at the apex fail to carry out their responsibilities or exercise self-restraint in pursuit of their own interests.

I define hierarchy as a rank order of statuses. Max Weber offers a different understanding of hierarchy: an arrangement of offices and the chain of command linking them together. Weber's formulation reminds us that status and office are not always coterminous, even in ideal-type worlds. In the *Iliad*, the conflict between Agamemnon and Achilles arises from the fact that Agamemnon holds the highest office, making Achilles his subordinate, while Achilles, the bravest and most admired warrior, deeply resents Agamemnon's abuse of his authority. In international relations, great powerdom is both a rank ordering of status and an office. As in the *Iliad*, conflict can become acute when the two diverge, and states—more accurately, the leaders and populations—believe they are denied office commensurate with the status they claim.

Standing and honor are another pair of related concepts. Standing refers to the position an actor occupies in a hierarchy. In an ideal-type spirit world, an actor's standing in a hierarchy is equivalent to its degree of honor. Those toward the apex of the status hierarchy earn the requisite degree of honor by living up to the responsibilities associated with their rank or office, while those who attain honor by virtue of their accomplishments come to occupy appropriate offices. Even in ideal spirit worlds, there is almost always some discrepancy between honor and standing because those who gain honor do not necessarily win the competitions that confer honor. In the *Iliad*, Priam and Hector gain great honor because of their performance on and off the battlefield but lose their lives and city. In fifth-century Greece, Leonidas and his band of Spartan warriors won honor and immortality by dying at Thermopylae. Resigning office for the right reasons can also confer honor. Lucius Quinctius

Cincinnatus was made dictator of Rome in 458 and again in 439 BCE. He resigned his absolute authority and returned to his humble life as a hardscrabble farmer as soon as he saved his city from the threat of the Volscians and Aequi. His humility and lack of ambition made him a legendary figure after whom a city in the wilderness of Ohio was named. George Washington emulated Cincinnatus and retired to his plantation at the end of the Revolutionary War. Later, as first president of the new Republic, he refused a third term on principle and once again returned to Mount Vernon. His self-restraint and commitment to republican principles earned him numerous memorials and a perennial ranking as one of the top three presidents in history.

Honor and standing can diverge for less admirable reasons. Honor worlds are extremely competitive because standing, even more than wealth, is a relational concept. Hobbes compares it to glory, and observes that, "if all men have it, no man hath it." The value placed on honor in spirit-based worlds and the intensity of the competition for it tempt actors to take shortcuts to gain honor. Once actors violate the rules and get away with it, others do the same to avoid being disadvantaged. If the rules governing honor are consistently violated, it becomes a meaningless concept. Competition for honor is transformed into competition for standing, which is more unconstrained and possibly more violent. This is a repetitive pattern in domestic politics and international relations.

The quest for honor generates a proliferation of statuses or ranks. These orderings can keep conflict in check when they are known and respected, and effectively define the relative status of actors. They intensify conflict when they are ambiguous or incapable of establishing precedence. This is most likely to happen when there are multiple ways (ascribed and achieved) of gaining honor and office. Even when this is not a problem, actors not infrequently disagree about who among them deserves a particular status or office. This kind of dispute has particularly threatening consequences in international relations because there are no authorities capable of adjudicating among competing claims.

External honor must be conferred by others and can only be gained through deeds regarded as honorable. It has no meaning until it is acknowledged, and is more valuable still when there is a respectful audience. The Greek word for fame (*kleos*) derives from the verb "to hear" (*kluein*). As Homer knew, fame not only requires heroic deeds, but bards to sing about those deeds and people willing to listen and be impressed, if not inspired to emulate them. For honor to be won and celebrated, there must be a consensus, and preferably one that transcends class or other distinctions, about the nature of honor, how it is won and lost and the distinctions and obligations it confers. This presupposes common values and traditions, even institutions. When society is robust—when its rules are relatively unambiguous and largely followed—the competition for honor and standing instantiates and strengthens the values of the society. As society becomes thinner, as it generally is at the regional and international levels, honor worlds become more difficult to create and sustain. In the absence of common values, there can be no consensus, no rules and no procedures for awarding and celebrating honor. Even in thin societies, honor can often be won within robust sub-cultures. Hamas and other groups that sponsor suicide bombing, publicize the names of successful bombers, sometimes pay stipends to their families and always encourage young people to lionize them. Such activity strengthens the sub-culture and may even give it wider appeal or support.

Honor societies tend to be highly stratified and can be likened to step pyramids. Many, but by no means all, honor societies are sharply divided into two classes: those who are allowed to compete for honor and those who are not. In many traditional honor societies, the principal distinction is between aristocrats, who are expected to seek honor, and commoners, or the low-born, who cannot. This divide is often reinforced by distinctions in wealth, which allow many of the high-born to buy the military equipment, afford the leisure, sponsor the ceremonies and obtain the education and skills necessary to compete. As in ancient Greece, birth and wealth are never fully synonymous, creating another source of social tension. Wealth is generally a necessary, but insufficient condition for gaining honor. Among the egalitarian Sioux, honor and status were achieved by holding various ceremonies, all of which involved providing feasts and gifts to those who attended. Horses and robes, the principal gifts, could only be gained through successful military expeditions against enemy tribes, or as gifts from others because of the high regard in which brave warriors were held.

Recognition into the elite circle where one can compete for honor is the first, and often most difficult, step in honor worlds. The exclusiveness of many honor societies can become a major source of tension, when individuals, classes or political units demand and are refused entry into the circle in which it becomes possible to gain honor. What is honorable, the rules governing its attainment, and the indices used to measure it are all subject to challenge. Historically, challenges of this kind have been resisted, at least initially. Societies that have responded to them positively have evolved, and in some cases gradually moved away from, wholly or partly, their warrior base.

A final caveat is in order. . . . I use the term "recognition" to mean acceptance into the circle where it is possible to compete for honor. Recognition carries with it the possibility of fulfillment of the spirit, and it is not to be confused with the use the term has come to assume in moral philosophy. Hegel made the struggle for recognition (*Kampf um Anerkennung*) a central concept of his *Philosophy of Right*, which is now understood to offer an affirmative account of a just social order that can transcend the inequalities of master-slave relationships. In a seminal essay published in 1992, Charles Taylor applied Hegel's concept to the demands for recognition of minorities and other marginalized groups. He argued that human recognition is a distinctive but largely neglected human good, and that we are profoundly affected by how we are recognized and *mis*recognized by others. The political psychology of recognition has since been extended to international relations, where subordinate states are assumed to have poor self-images and low self-esteem. Axel Honneth stresses the importance of avoiding master-slave relationships among states. Fernando Cornil argues that subaltern states enjoy the trappings of sovereignty but often internalize the negative images of them held by the major powers.

I acknowledge the relationship between status and esteem, but make a different argument. In terms of at least foreign policy, it is powerful states, not weak ones, who often feel most humiliated. My explanation for this phenomenon draws on Aristotle's understanding of anger, which is narrower than our modern Western conception. It is a response to an *oligōria*, which can be translated as a slight, lessening or belittlement. Such a slight can issue from an equal, but provokes even more anger when it comes an actor who lacks the standing to challenge or insult us. Anger is a luxury that can only be felt by those in a position to seek revenge. Slaves and subordinates cannot allow themselves to feel anger, although they may develop many forms of resistance. It is also senseless to feel anger toward those who cannot become aware of our anger. In the realm of international relations, leaders—and often peoples—of powerful states are likely to feel anger of the Aristotelian kind when they are denied entry into the system, refused recognition as a great power or treated in a manner demeaning to their understanding of their status. They will look for some way of asserting their claims and seeking revenge. Subordinate states lack this power and their leaders and populations learn to live with their lower status and more limited autonomy. Great powers will feel enraged if challenged by such states. I believe we can profit from reintroducing the Greek dichotomy between those who were included in and excluded from the circle in which it was possible to achieve honor and Aristotle's definition of anger.

Let us turn to the wider implications of honor as a motive for foreign policy. First and foremost is its effect on the preferences of states and their leaders. Realists and other international-relations scholars insist that survival is the overriding goal of all states, just as domestic politics explanations assert that it is for leaders. This is not true of honor societies, where honor has a higher value. Achilles spurns a long life in favor of an honorable death that brings fame. For Homer and the Greeks, fame allows people to transcend their mortality. Great deeds carry one's name and reputation across the generations where they continue to receive respect and influence other actors. In the real world, not just in Greek and medieval fiction, warriors, leaders, and sometimes entire peoples have opted for honor over survival. We encounter this phenomenon not only in my case studies of ancient and medieval societies but also in nineteenth- and twentieth-century Europe and Japan. Morgenthau and Waltz draw on Hobbes, and Waltz on Rousseau, to argue that survival is the prime directive of individuals and political units alike. Leo Strauss sees Hobbes as an important caesura with the classical tradition and among the first "bourgeois" thinkers because he makes fear of death and the desire for self-preservation the fundamental human end in lieu of aristocratic virtues. A more defensible reading of Hobbes is that he aspired to replace vanity with material interests as a primary human motive because he recognized that it was more effectively controlled by a combination of reason and fear. For Hobbes, the spirit and its drive for standing and honor remained a universal, potent and largely disruptive force.

As Thucydides and Hobbes understand, the quest for honor and willingness to face death to gain or uphold it make honor-based societies extremely war-prone. Several aspects of honor contribute to this phenomenon. Honor has been associated with warrior societies, although not all warrior societies are honor societies, and not all warrior societies are aristocratic. In such societies, war is considered not only a normal activity but a necessary one because without it young men could not demonstrate their mettle and distinguish themselves. More fundamentally, war affirms the identity of warriors and their societies. I have argued elsewhere that Thucydides considered the threat Athenian power posed to Spartan identity, not their security, the fundamental reason why the Spartan assembly voted for war. Erik Ringmar makes a persuasive case that it was the principal motive behind Sweden's intervention in the Thirty Years War, where standing was sought as a means of achieving a national identity. In *A Cultural Theory of International Relations*, I document how such considerations were important for leaders and peoples from post-Westphalian Europe to the post–Cold War world.

In honor societies, status is an actor's most precious possession. Challenges to status or to the privileges it confers are unacceptable when they come from equals or inferiors. In regional and international societies, statuses are uncertain, there may be multiple contenders for them and there are usually no peaceful ways of adjudicating rival claims. Warfare often serves this end, and is a common cause of war in honor societies. It often finds expression in substantive issues such as control over disputed territory, but can also arise from symbolic disputes (e.g. who is to have primacy at certain festivals or processions, or whose ships must honor or be honored by others at sea).

For all three reasons, warfare in honor worlds tends to be frequent, but the ends of warfare and the means by which it is waged tend to be limited. Wars between political units in honor societies often resemble duels. Combat is highly stylized, if still vicious, and governed by a series of rules that are generally followed by participants. Warfare among the Greeks, Aztecs, Plains Indians, and eighteenth-century European states offer variants on this theme. By making a place for violence in community-governed situations, it is partially contained and may be less damaging than it otherwise would be. However, these limitations apply only to warfare between recognized members of the same society. War against outsiders, or against non-elite members of one's own society, often has a no-holds-barred quality. Greek warfare against tribesmen or against the Persians at Marathon, Salamis and Plataea, American warfare against native Americans and colonial wars in general illustrate this nasty truth.

Despite the endemic nature of warfare in warrior-based honor societies, cooperation is not only possible but routine. Cooperation is based on appeals to friendship, common descent and mutual obligation more than it is on mutual interest. The norms of the hierarchy dictate that actors of high status assist those of lower status who are dependent on them, while those of lower status are obliged to honor and serve their protectors or patrons. Friendship usually involves the exchange of gifts and favors and provides additional grounds for asking for and receiving aid. Cooperation in honor societies is most difficult among equals because no actor wants to accept the leadership of another and thereby acknowledge its higher standing. This situation makes cooperation difficult even in situations where there are compelling mutual security concerns.

As honor is more important than survival, the very notion of risk is framed differently. Warrior societies are risk-accepting with respect to both gain and loss. Honor cannot be attained without risk, so leaders and followers alike welcome the opportunity to risk limbs and lives to gain or defend it. Actors will also defend their autonomy at almost any cost because it is so closely linked to their honor, unless they can find some justification for disassociating it from honor that is convincing to their peers. Risk-taking will be extended to the defense of material possessions and territory to the extent that they have become entwined with honor and symbols of them.

To summarize, honor-based societies experience conflict about who is "recognized" and allowed to compete for standing; the rules governing *agon* or competition; the nature of the deeds that confer standing; and the actors who assign honor, determine status and adjudicate competing claims. Tracking the relative intensity of conflict over these issues and the nature of the changes or accommodations to which they lead provide insight into the extent to which honor remains a primary value in a society and its ability to respond to internal and external challenges. It also permits informed speculation about its evolution.

Reading 4.5

Warfare Is Only an Invention—Not a Biological Necessity   MARGARET MEAD

Is war a biological necessity, a sociological inevitability or just a bad invention? Those who argue for the first view endow man with such pugnacious instincts that some outlet in aggressive behavior is necessary if man is to reach full human stature. It was this point of view which lay back of William James's famous essay, "The Moral Equivalent of War," in which he tried to retain the warlike virtues and channel them in new directions. A similar point of view has lain back of the Soviet Union's attempt to make competition between groups rather than between individuals. A basic, competitive, aggressive, warring human nature is assumed, and those who wish to outlaw war or outlaw competitiveness merely try to find new and less socially destructive ways in which these biologically given aspects of man's nature can find expression. Then there are those who take the second view: warfare is the inevitable concomitant of the development of the state, the struggle for land and natural

Source: Margaret Mead, "Warfare Is Only an Invention—Not a Biological Necessity." Reproduced by permission of the American Anthropological Association *from Asia, Vol. 40, Issue 8, pp. 402–405, August 1940. Not for sale or further reproduction.*

resources of class societies springing, not from the nature of man, but from the nature of history. War is nevertheless inevitable unless we change our social system and outlaw classes, the struggle for power, and possessions; and in the event of our success warfare would disappear, as a symptom vanishes when the disease is cured.

One may hold a sort of compromise position between these two extremes; one may claim that all aggression springs from the frustration of man's biologically determined drives and that, since all forms of culture are frustrating, it is certain each new generation will be aggressive and the aggression will find its natural and inevitable expression in race war, class war, nationalistic war and so on. All three of these positions are very popular today among those who think seriously about the problems of war and its possible prevention, but I wish to urge another point of view, less defeatist perhaps than the first and third, and more accurate than the second: that is, that warfare, by which I mean recognized conflict between two groups *as groups*, in which each group puts an army (even if the army is only fifteen pygmies) into the field to fight and kill, if possible, some of the members of the army of the other group—that warfare of this sort is an invention like any other of the inventions in terms of which we order our lives, such as writing, marriage, cooking our food instead of eating it raw, trial by jury or burial of the dead, and so on. Some of this list any one will grant are inventions: trial by jury is confined to very limited portions of the globe; we know that there are tribes that do not bury their dead but instead expose or cremate them; and we know that only part of the human race has had the knowledge of writing as its cultural inheritance. But, whenever a way of doing things is found universally, such as the use of fire or the practice of some form of marriage, we tend to think at once that it is not an invention at all but an attribute of humanity itself. And yet even such universals as marriage and the use of fire are inventions like the rest, very basic ones, inventions which were perhaps necessary if human history was to take the turn that it has taken, but nevertheless inventions. At some point in his social development man was undoubtedly without the institution of marriage or the knowledge of the use of fire.

The case for warfare is much clearer because there are peoples even today who have no warfare. Of these the Eskimo are perhaps the most conspicuous examples, but the Lepchas of Sikkim described by Geoffrey Gorer in *Himalayan Village* are as good. Neither of these peoples understands war, not even defensive warfare. The idea of warfare is lacking, and this idea is as essential to really carrying on war as an alphabet or a syllabary is to writing. But whereas the Lepchas are a gentle, unquarrelsome people, and the advocates of other points of view might argue that they are not full human beings or that they had never been frustrated and so had no aggression to expand in warfare, the Eskimo case gives no such possibility of interpretation. The Eskimo are not a mild and meek people; many of them are turbulent and troublesome. Fights, theft of wives, murder, cannibalism, occur among them—all outbursts of passionate men goaded by desire or intolerable circumstance. Here are men faced with hunger, men faced with loss of their wives, men faced with the threat of extermination by other men, and here are orphan children, growing up miserably with no one to care for them, mocked and neglected by those about them. The personality necessary for war, the circumstances necessary to goad men to desperation are present, but there is no war. When a traveling Eskimo entered a settlement he might have to fight the strongest man in the settlement to establish his position among them, but this was a test of strength and bravery, not war. The idea of warfare, of one *group* organizing against another *group* to maim and wound and kill them, was absent. And without that idea passions might rage but there was no war.

But, it may be argued, isn't this because the Eskimo have such a low and undeveloped form of social organization? They own no land, they move from place to place, camping, it is true, season after season on the same site, but this is not something to fight for as the modern nations of the world fight for land and raw materials. They have no permanent possessions that can be looted, no towns that can be burned. They have no social classes to produce stress and strains within the society which might force it to go to war outside. Doesn't the absence of war among the Eskimo, while disproving the biological necessity of war, just go to confirm the point that it is the state of development of the society which accounts for war, and nothing else?

We find the answer among the pygmy peoples of the Andaman Islands in the Bay of Bengal. The Andamans also represent an exceedingly low level of society; they are a hunting and food-gathering people; they live in tiny hordes without any class stratification; their houses are simpler than the snow houses of the Eskimo. But they knew about warfare. The army might contain only fifteen determined pygmies marching in a straight line, but it was the real thing nonetheless. Tiny army met tiny army in open battle, blows were exchanged, casualties suffered, and the state of warfare could only be concluded by a peace-making ceremony.

Similarly, among the Australian aborigines, who built no permanent dwellings but wandered from water hole to water hole over their almost desert country, warfare—and rules of "international law"—were highly developed. The student of social evolution will seek in vain for his obvious causes of war, struggle for lands, struggle for power of one group over another, expansion of population, need to divert the minds of a populace restive under tyranny, or even the ambition of a successful leader to enhance his own prestige. All are absent, but warfare as a practice remained, and men engaged in it and killed one another in the course of a war because killing is what is done in wars.

From instances like these it becomes apparent that an inquiry into the causes of war misses the fundamental point as completely as does an insistence upon the biological necessity of war. If a people have an idea of going to war and the idea that war is the way in which certain situations, defined within their society, are to be handled, they will sometimes go to war. If they are a mild and unaggressive people, like the Pueblo Indians, they may limit themselves to defensive warfare; but they will be forced to think in terms of war because there are peoples near them who have warfare as a pattern, and offensive, raiding, pillaging warfare at that. When the pattern of warfare is known, people like the Pueblo Indians will defend themselves, taking advantage of their natural defenses, the *mesa* village site, and people like the Lepchas, having no natural defenses and no idea of warfare, will merely submit to the invader. But the essential point remains the same. There is a way of behaving which is known to a given people and labeled as an appropriate form of behavior; a bold and warlike people like the Sioux or the Maori may label warfare as desirable as well as possible; a mild people like the Pueblo Indians may label warfare as undesirable; but to the minds of both peoples the possibility of warfare is present. Their thoughts, their hopes, their plans are oriented about this idea, that warfare may be selected as the way to meet some situation.

So simple peoples and civilized peoples, mild peoples and violent, assertive peoples, will all go to war if they have the invention, just as those peoples who have the custom of dueling will have duels and peoples who have the pattern of vendetta will indulge in vendetta. And, conversely, peoples who do not know of dueling will not fight duels, even though their wives are seduced and their daughters ravished; they may on occasion commit murder but they will not fight duels. Cultures which lack the idea of the vendetta will not meet every quarrel in this way. A people can use only the forms it has. So the Balinese have their special way of dealing with a quarrel between two individuals: if the two feel that the causes of quarrel are heavy they may go and register their quarrel in the temple before the gods, and, making offerings, they may swear never to have anything to do with each other again. Today they register such mutual "not-speaking" with the Dutch government officials. But in other societies, although individuals might feel as full of animosity and as unwilling to have any further contact as do the Balinese, they cannot register their quarrel with the gods and go on quietly about their business because registering quarrels with the gods is not an invention of which they know.

Yet, if it be granted that warfare is after all an invention, it may nevertheless be an invention that lends itself to certain types of personality, to the exigent needs of autocrats, to the expansionist desires of crowded peoples, to the desire for plunder and rape and loot which is engendered by a dull and frustrating life. What, then, can we say of this congruence between warfare and its uses? If it is a form which fits so well, is not this congruence the essential point? But even here the primitive material causes us to wonder, because there are tribes who go to war merely for glory, having no quarrel with the enemy, suffering from no tyrant within their boundaries, anxious neither for land nor loot nor women, but merely anxious to win prestige which within that tribe has been declared obtainable only by war and without which no young man can hope to win his sweetheart's smile of approval. But if, as was the case with the Bush Negroes of Dutch Guiana, it is artistic ability which is necessary to win a girl's approval, the same young man would have to be carving rather than going out on a war party.

In many parts of the world, war is a game in which the individual can win counters—counters which bring him prestige in the eyes of his own sex or of the opposite sex; he plays for these counters as he might, in our society, strive for a tennis championship. Warfare is a frame for such prestige-seeking merely because it calls for the display of certain skills and certain virtues; all of these skills—riding straight, shooting straight, dodging the missiles of the enemy and sending one's own straight to the mark—can be equally well exercised in some other framework and, equally, the virtues—endurance, bravery, loyalty, steadfastness—can be displayed in other contexts. The tie-up between proving oneself a man and proving this by a success in organized killing is due to a definition which many societies have made of manliness. And often, even in those societies which counted success in warfare a proof of human worth, strange turns were given to the idea, as when the plains Indians gave their highest awards to the man who touched a live enemy rather than to the man who brought in a scalp—from a dead enemy—because the latter was less risky. Warfare is just an invention known to the majority of human societies by which they permit their young men either to accumulate prestige or avenge their honor or acquire loot or wives or slaves or sago lands or cattle or appease the blood lust of their gods or the restless souls of the recently dead. It is just an invention, older and more widespread than the jury system, but nonetheless an invention.

But, once we have said this, have we said anything at all? Despite a few instances, dear to the hearts of controversialists, of the loss of the useful arts, once an invention is made which proves congruent with human needs or social forms, it tends to persist. Grant that war is an invention, that it is not a biological necessity nor the outcome of certain special types of social forms, still, once the invention is made, what are we to do about it? The Indian who had been subsisting on the buffalo for generations because with his primitive weapons he could slaughter only a limited number of buffalo did not return to his primitive weapons when he saw that the white man's more efficient weapons were exterminating the buffalo. A desire for the white man's cloth may mortgage the South Sea Islander to the white man's plantation, but he does not return to making bark cloth, which would have left him free. Once an invention is known and accepted, men do not easily relinquish it. The skilled workers may smash the first steam looms which they feel are to be their undoing, but they accept them in the end, and no movement which has insisted upon the mere abandonment of usable inventions has ever had much success. Warfare is here, as part of our thought; the deeds of warriors are immortalized in the words of our poets; the toys of our children are modeled upon the weapons of the soldier; the frame of reference within which our statesmen and our diplomats work always contains war. If we know that it is not inevitable, that it is due to historical accident that warfare is one of the ways in which we think of behaving, are we given any hope by that? What hope is there of persuading nations to abandon war, nations so thoroughly imbued with the idea that resort to war is, if not actually desirable and noble, at least inevitable whenever certain defined circumstances arise?

In answer to this question I think we might turn to the history of other social inventions, and inventions which must once have seemed as firmly entrenched as warfare. Take the methods of trial which preceded the jury system: ordeal and trial by combat. Unfair, capricious, alien as they are to our feeling today, they were once the only methods open to individuals accused of some offense. The invention of trial by jury gradually replaced these methods until only witches, and finally not even witches, had to resort to the ordeal. And for a long time the jury system seemed the one best and finest method of settling legal disputes, but today new inventions, trial before judges only or before commissions, are replacing the jury system. In each case the old method was replaced by a new social invention; the ordeal did not go out because people thought it unjust or wrong, it went out because a method more congruent with the institutions and feelings of the period was invented. And, if we despair over the way in which war seems such an ingrained habit of most of the human race, we can take comfort from the fact that a poor invention will usually give place to a better invention.

For this, two conditions at least are necessary. The people must recognize the defects of the old invention, and someone must make a new one. Propaganda against warfare, documentation of its terrible cost in human suffering and social waste, these prepare the ground by teaching people to feel that warfare is a defective social institution. There is further needed a belief that social invention is possible and the invention of new methods which will render warfare as out-of-date as the tractor is making the plow, or the motor car the horse and buggy. A form of behavior becomes out-of-date only when something else takes its place, and in order to invent forms of behavior which will make war obsolete, it is a first requirement to believe that an invention is possible.

Reading 4.6

Men, Women, and War   *J. ANN TICKNER*

. . . When we think about the provision of national security we enter into what has been, and continues to be, an almost exclusively male domain. While most women support what they take to be legitimate calls for state action in the interests of international security, the task of defining, defending, and advancing the security interests of the state is a man's affair, a task that, through its association with war, has been especially valorized and rewarded in many cultures throughout history. As Simone de Beauvoir's explanation for male superiority suggests, giving one's life for one's country has been considered the highest form of patriotism, but it is an act from which women have been virtually excluded. While men have been associated with defending the state

Source: From "Man, the State, and War: Gendered Perspectives on National Security," in Gender in International Relations: Feminist Perspectives on Achieving Global Security by J. Ann Tickner. Copyright © 1992 Columbia University Press. Reprinted with permission of the publisher.

and advancing its international interests as soldiers and diplomats, women have typically been engaged in the "ordering" and "comforting" roles both in the domestic sphere, as mothers and basic needs providers, and in the caring professions, as teachers, nurses, and social workers.[1] The role of women with respect to national security has been ambiguous: defined as those whom the state and its men are protecting, women have had little control over the conditions of their protection. . . .

In looking for explanations for the causes of war, realists, as well as scholars in other approaches to international relations, have distinguished among three levels of analysis: the individual, the state, and the international system. While realists claim that their theories are "objective" and of universal validity, the assumptions they use when analyzing states and explaining their behavior in the international system are heavily dependent on characteristics that we, in the West, have come to associate with masculinity. The way in which realists describe the individual, the state, and the international system are profoundly gendered; each is constructed in terms of . . . idealized or hegemonic masculinity. . . . In the name of universality, realists have constructed a worldview based on the experiences of certain men: it is therefore a worldview that offers us only a partial view of reality. . . .

"POLITICAL MAN"

In his *Politics Among Nations*, a text rich in historical detail, Morgenthau has constructed a world almost entirely without women. Morgenthau claims that individuals are engaged in a struggle for power whenever they come into contact with one another, for the tendency to dominate exists at all levels of human life: the family, the polity, and the international system; it is modified only by the conditions under which the struggle takes place.[2] Since women rarely occupy positions of power in any of these arenas, we can assume that, when Morgenthau talks about domination, he is talking primarily about men, although not all men.[3] His "political man" is a social construct based on a partial representation of human nature abstracted from the behavior of men in positions of public power.[4] Morgenthau goes on to suggest that, while society condemns the violent behavior that can result from this struggle for power within the polity, it encourages it in the international system in the form of war.

While Morgenthau's "political man" has been criticized by other international relations scholars for its essentializing view of human nature, the social construction of hegemonic masculinity and its opposition to a devalued femininity . . . have been central to the way in which the discourse of international politics has been constructed more generally. In Western political theory from the Greeks to Machiavelli, traditions upon which contemporary realism relies heavily for its analysis, this socially constructed type of masculinity has been projected onto the international behavior of states. The violence with which it is associated has been legitimated through the glorification of war.

The militarized version of citizenship, similar to . . . "manly" behavior . . . can be traced back to the ancient Greek city-states on whose history realists frequently draw in constructing their analysis. For the Greeks, the most honored way to achieve recognition as a citizen was through heroic performance and sacrifice in war. The real test of manly virtue or "arete," a militarized notion of greatness, was victory in battle.[5] The Greek city-state was a community of warriors. Women and slaves involved in the realm of "necessity" in the household or the economy were not included as citizens for they would pollute the higher realm of politics.[6]

This exclusive definition of the citizen-warrior reemerges in sixteenth-century Europe in the writings of Niccolò Machiavelli. Since he associates human excellence with the competitive striving for power, what is a negative but unavoidable characteristic of human nature for Morgenthau is a virtue for Machiavelli. Machiavelli translates this quest for power into the glorification of the warrior-prince whose prowess in battle was necessary for the salvation of his native Florence in the face of powerful external threats.

For feminists, warrior-citizenship is neither a negative, unavoidable characterization of human nature, nor a desirable possibility; it is a revisable, gendered construction of personality and citizenship. Feminist political theorist Wendy Brown suggests that Machiavelli's representation of the political world and its citizenry is profoundly gendered; it is dependent on an image of true manliness that demands qualities that are superior to those that naturally inhere in men.[7] Hannah Pitkin claims that for Machiavelli triumph in war, honor and liberty in civic life, and independent critical thought and manliness in personal relationships are all bound together by a central preoccupation with autonomy, a characteristic associated with masculinity.[8] True manliness, demanded of the ideal citizen-warrior, is encompassed in the concept "virtu," which means, in its literal sense, manly activity. For Machiavelli, virtu is insight, energetic activity, effectiveness, and courage: it demands overcoming a man's self-indulgence and laziness.[9]

Just as the concept of hegemonic masculinity . . . requires for its construction an oppositional relationship to a devalued femininity, Machiavelli's construction of the citizen-warrior required a similarly devalued "other" against which true manhood and autonomy could be set. In Machiavelli's writings this feminine other is "fortuna," originally a Roman goddess associated with capriciousness and unpredictability. Hannah Pitkin claims that in Machiavelli's writings fortuna is presented as the feminine power in men themselves against which they must continually struggle to maintain their autonomy.[10] In the public world, Machiavelli depicts fortuna as chance, situations that could not have been foreseen or that men fail to control. The capriciousness of fortuna cannot be prevented, but it can be prepared against and overcome through the cultivation of manly virtues. According to Brown, fortuna and virtu are in permanent combat: both are supremely gendered constructions that involve a notion of manliness that is tied to the conquest of women.[11] In Machiavelli's own words, "Fortune is a woman, and it is necessary if you wish to master her, to conquer her by force."[12]

Having constructed these explicitly gendered representations of virtu and fortuna, Machiavelli also makes it clear that he considers women to be a threat to the masculinity of the citizen-warrior. Although they scarcely appear in Machiavelli's political writings, when women are discussed, Machiavelli portrays them as both dangerous and inferior.[13] The most dangerous threat to both a man *and* a state is to be like a woman because women are weak, fearful, indecisive, and dependent—stereotypes that . . . still surface when assessing women's suitability for the military and the conduct of foreign policy today.

While contemporary international relations does not employ this explicitly misogynist discourse, the contemporary understanding of citizenship still remains bound up with the Greeks' and Machiavelli's depictions of the citizen-warrior. The most noble sacrifice a citizen can make is to give his life for his country. When the National Organization for Women decided to support the drafting of women into the United States military, it argued its case on the grounds that, if women were barred from participation in the armed forces on an equal footing with men, they would remain second-class citizens denied the unique political responsibility of risking one's life for the state.[14] But in spite of women's increasing numbers in noncombat roles in the armed forces of certain states, the relationship between soldiering, masculinity, and citizenship remains very strong in most societies today.

To be a soldier is to be a man, not a woman; more than any other social institution, the military separates men from women. Soldiering is a role into which boys are socialized in school and on the playing fields. A soldier must be a protector; he must show courage, strength, and responsibility and repress feelings of fear, vulnerability, and compassion. Such feelings are womanly traits, which are liabilities in time of war.[15] War demands manliness; it is an event in which boys become men, for combat is the ultimate test of masculinity. When women become soldiers, this gender identity is called into question; for Americans, this questioning became real during the Persian Gulf war of 1991, the first time that women soldiers were sent into a war zone in large numbers.[16]

To understand the citizen-warrior as a social construction allows us to question the essentialist connection between war and men's natural aggressiveness. Considerable evidence suggests that most men would prefer not to fight; many refuse to do so even when they are put in positions that make it difficult not to. One study shows that in World War II, on the average, only 15 percent of soldiers actually fired their weapons in battle, even when threatened by enemy soldiers.[17] Because military recruiters cannot rely on violent qualities in men, they appeal to manliness and patriotic duty. Judith Stiehm avers that military trainers resort to manipulation of men's anxiety about their sexual identity in order to increase soldiers' willingness to fight. In basic training the term of utmost derision is to be called a girl or a lady.[18] The association between men and violence therefore depends not on men's innate aggressiveness, but on the construction of a gendered identity that places heavy pressure on soldiers to prove themselves as men.

Just as the Greeks gave special respect to citizens who had proved themselves in war, it is still a special mark of respect in many societies to be a war veteran, an honor that is denied to all women as well as to certain men. In the United States, nowhere is this more evident than in the political arena where "political man's" identity is importantly tied to his service in the military. Sheila Tobias suggests that there are risks involved for politicians seeking office who have chosen not to serve in combat or for women who cannot serve. War service is of special value for gaining votes even in political offices not exclusively concerned with foreign policy. In the United States, former generals are looked upon favorably as presidential candidates, and many American presidents have run for office on their war record. In the 1984 vice presidential debates between George Bush and Geraldine Ferraro, Bush talked about his experience as a navy pilot shot down in World War II; while this might seem like a dubious qualification for the office of vice president, it was one that Ferraro—to her detriment—could not counter.[19]

To be a first-class citizen therefore, one must be a warrior. It is an important qualification for the politics of national security for it is to such men that the state entrusts its most vital interests. Characteristics associated with femininity are considered a liability when dealing with the realities of international politics. When realists write about national security, they often do so in abstract and depersonalized terms, yet they are constructing a discourse shaped out of these gendered identities. This notion of manhood, crucial for upholding the interests of the state, is an image that is frequently extended to the way in which we personify the behavior of the state itself. . . .

THE INTERNATIONAL SYSTEM: THE WAR OF EVERYMAN AGAINST EVERYMAN

According to Richard Ashley, realists have privileged a higher reality called "the sovereign state" against which they have posited anarchy understood in a negative way as difference, ambiguity, and contingency—as a space that is external and dangerous.[20] All these characteristics have also been attributed to women. Anarchy is an actual or potential site of war. The most common metaphor that realists employ to describe the anarchical international system is that of the seventeenth-century English philosopher Thomas Hobbes's depiction of the state of nature. Although Hobbes did not write much about international politics, realists have applied his description of individuals' behavior in a hypothetical precontractual state of nature, which Hobbes termed the war of everyman against everyman, to the behavior of states in the international system.[21]

Carole Pateman argues that, in all contemporary discussions of the state of nature, the differentiation between the sexes is generally ignored, even though it was an important consideration for contract theorists themselves.[22] Although Hobbes did suggest that women as well as men could be free and equal individuals in the state of nature, his description of human behavior in this environment refers to that of adult males whose behavior is taken as constitutive of human nature as a whole by contemporary realist analysis. According to Jane

Flax, the individuals that Hobbes described in the state of nature appeared to come to full maturity without any engagement with one another; they were solitary creatures lacking any socialization in interactive behavior. Any interactions they did have led to power struggles that resulted in domination or submission. Suspicion of others' motives led to behavior characterized by aggression, self-interest, and the drive for autonomy.[23] In a similar vein, Christine Di Stephano uses feminist psychoanalytic theory to support her claim that the masculine dimension of atomistic egoism is powerfully underscored in Hobbes's state of nature, which, she asserts, is built on the foundation of denied maternity. "Hobbes' abstract man is a creature who is self-possessed, and radically solitary in a crowded and inhospitable world, whose relations with others are unavoidably contractual and whose freedom consists in the absence of impediments to the attainment of privately generated and understood desires."[24]

As a model of human behavior, Hobbes's depiction of individuals in the state of nature is partial at best; certain feminists have argued that such behavior could be applicable only to adult males, for if life was to go on for more than one generation in the state of nature, women must have been involved in activities such as reproduction and child rearing rather than in warfare. Reproductive activities require an environment that can provide for the survival of infants and behavior that is interactive and nurturing.

An international system that resembles Hobbes's state of nature is a dangerous environment. Driven by competition for scarce resources and mistrust of others' motives in a system that lacks any legitimate authority, states, like men, must rely on their own resources for self-preservation.[25] Machiavelli offers advice to his prince that is based on similar assumptions about the international system. Both Pitkin and Brown note that Machiavelli's portrayal of fortuna is regularly associated with nature, as something outside the political world that must be subdued and controlled. Pitkin refers to "The Golden Ass," a long unfinished poem by Machiavelli, based on the legend of Circe, a female figure who lives in the forest world and turns men into animals.[26] Translated into international politics this depiction of fortuna is similar to the disorder or anarchy of the international system as portrayed by realists. Capturing the essence of Realpolitik, Brown suggests that, for Machiavelli, politics is a continual quest for power and independence; it is dependent on the presence of an enemy at all times, for without spurs to greatness energized by fighting an enemy, the polity would collapse.

Just as the image of waging war against an exterior other figured centrally in Machiavelli's writings, war is central to the way we learn about international relations. Our historical memories of international politics are deeded to us through wars as we mark off time periods in terms of intervals between conflicts. We learn that dramatic changes take place in the international system after major wars when the relative power of states changes. Wars are fought for many reasons; yet, frequently, the rationale for fighting wars is presented in gendered terms such as the necessity of standing up to aggression rather then being pushed around or appearing to be a sissy or a wimp. Support for wars is often garnered through the appeal to masculine characteristics. As Sara Ruddick states, while the masculinity of war may be a myth, it is one that sustains both women and men in their support for violence.[27] War is a time when male and female characteristics become polarized; it is a gendering activity at a time when the discourse of militarism and masculinity permeates the whole fabric of society.[28]

As Jean Elshtain points out, war is an experience to which women are exterior; men have inhabited the world of war in a way that women have not.[29] The history of international politics is therefore a history from which women are, for the most part, absent. Little material can be found on women's roles in wars; generally they are seen as victims, rarely as agents. While war can be a time of advancement for women as they step in to do men's jobs, the battle-front takes precedence, so the hierarchy remains and women are urged to step aside once peace is restored. When women themselves engage in violence, it is often portrayed as a mob or a food riot that is out of control.[30] Movements for peace, which are also part of our history, have not been central to the conventional way in which the evolution of the Western state system has been presented to us. International relations scholars of the early twentieth century, who wrote positively about the possibilities of international law and the collective security system of the League of Nations, were labeled "idealists" and not taken seriously by the more powerful realist tradition.

Metaphors, such as Hobbes's state of nature are primarily concerned with representing conflictual relations between great powers. The images used to describe nineteenth-century imperialist projects and contemporary great power relations with former colonial states are somewhat different. Historically, colonial people were often described in terms that drew on characteristics associated with women in order to place them lower in a hierarchy that put their white male colonizers on top. As the European state system expanded outward to conquer much of the world in the nineteenth century, its "civilizing" mission was frequently described in stereotypically gendered terms. Colonized peoples were often described as being effeminate, masculinity was an attribute of the white man, and colonial order depended on Victorian standards of manliness. Cynthia Enloe suggests that the concept of "ladylike behavior" was one of the mainstays of imperialist civilization. Like sanitation and Christianity, feminine respectability was meant to convince colonizers and colonized alike that foreign conquest was right and necessary. Masculinity denoted protection of the respectable lady; she stood for the civilizing mission that justified the colonization of benighted peoples.[31] Whereas the feminine stood for danger and disorder for Machiavelli, the European female, in contrast to her colonial counterpart, came to represent a stable, civilized order in nineteenth-century representations of British imperialism.

An example of the way in which these gender identities were manipulated to justify Western policy with respect to the rest of the world can also be seen in attitudes toward Latin America prevalent in the United States in the nineteenth century. According to Michael Hunt, nineteenth-century American images of Latin society depicted a (usually black) male who was lazy, dishonest, and corrupt. A contrary image that was more positive—a Latin as redeemable—took the form of a fair-skinned senorita living in a marginalized society, yet escaping its degrading effects. Hunt suggests that Americans entered the twentieth century with three images of Latin America fostered through legends brought back by American merchants and diplomats. These legends, perpetuated through school texts, cartoons, and political rhetoric, were even incorporated into the views of policymakers. The three images pictured the Latin as a half-breed brute, feminized, or infantile. In each case, Americans stood superior; the first image permitted a predatory aggressiveness, the second allowed the United States to assume the role of ardent suitor, and the third justified America's need to provide tutelage and discipline. All these images are profoundly gendered: the United States as a civilizing warrior, a suitor, or a father, and Latin America as a lesser male, a female, or a child.[32]

Such images, although somewhat muted, remain today and are particularly prevalent in the thinking of Western states when they are dealing with the Third World. In the post–World War II era, there was considerable debate in Western capitals about the dangers of premature independence for primitive peoples. In the postindependence era, former colonial states and their leaders have frequently been portrayed as emotional and unpredictable, characteristics also associated with women. C. D. Jackson, an adviser to President Eisenhower and a patron of Western development theorists in the 1950s, evoked these feminine characteristics when he observed that "the Western world has somewhat more experience with the operations of war, peace, and parliamentary procedures than the swirling mess of emotionally super-charged Africans and Asiatics and Arabs that outnumber us."[33] . . .

FEMINIST PERSPECTIVES ON STATES' SECURITY-SEEKING BEHAVIOR

Realists have offered us an instrumental version of states' security-seeking behavior, which, I have argued, depends on a partial representation of human behavior associated with a stereotypical hegemonic masculinity. Feminist redefinitions of citizenship allow us to envisage a less militarized version of states' identities, and feminist theories can also propose alternative models for states' international security-seeking behavior, extrapolated from a more comprehensive view of human behavior.

Realists use state-of-nature stories as metaphors to describe the insecurity of states in an anarchical international system. I shall suggest an alternative story, which could equally be applied to the behavior of individuals in the state of nature. Although frequently unreported in standard historical accounts, it is a true story, not a myth, about a state of nature in early nineteenth-century America. Among those present in the first winter encampment of the 1804–1806 Lewis and Clark expedition into the Northwest territories was Sacajawea, a member of the Shoshone tribe. Sacajawea had joined the expedition as the wife of a French interpreter; her presence was proving invaluable to the security of

the expedition's members, whose task it was to explore unchart
establish contact with the native inhabitants to inform them of
territories by the United States. Although unanticipated by its lea
ence of a woman served to assure the native inhabitants that t.
was peaceful since the Native Americans assumed that war parti
include women: the expedition was therefore safer because it was ᴜᴏᴛ armed.[34]

This story demonstrates that the introduction of women can change the
way humans are assumed to behave in the state of nature. Just as Sacajawea's
presence changed the Native American's expectations about the behavior of
intruders into their territory, the introduction of women into our state-of-
nature myths could change the way we think about the behavior of states in the
international system. The use of the Hobbesian analogy in international relations theory is based on a partial view of human nature that is stereotypically
masculine; a more inclusive perspective would see human nature as both conflictual and cooperative, containing elements of social reproduction and interdependence as well as domination and separation. Generalizing from this more
comprehensive view of human nature, a feminist perspective would assume
that the potential for international community also exists and that an atomistic, conflictual view of the international system is only a partial representation
of reality. Liberal individualism, the instrumental rationality of the marketplace, and the defector's self-help approach in Rousseau's stag hunt are all, in
analogous ways, based on a partial masculine model of human behavior.[35]

These characterizations of human behavior, with their atomistic view of
human society, do not assume the need for interdependence and cooperation.[36]
Yet states frequently exhibit aspects of cooperative behavior when they engage
in diplomatic—negotiations. As Cynthia Enloe states, diplomacy runs smoothly
when there is trust and confidence between officials representing governments
with conflicting interests. She suggests that many agreements are negotiated
informally in the residences of ambassadors where the presence of diplomatic
wives creates an atmosphere in which trust can best be cultivated.[37] As Enloe
concludes, women, often in positions that are unremunerated or undervalued,
remain vital to creating and maintaining trust between men in a hostile world.

Given the interdependent nature of contemporary security threats, new
thinking on security has already assumed that autonomy and self-help, as models
for state behavior in the international system, must be rethought and redefined.
Many feminists would agree with this, but given their assumption that interdependence is as much a human characteristic as autonomy, they would question
whether autonomy is even desirable.[38] Autonomy is associated with masculinity
just as femininity is associated with interdependence: in her discussion of the
birth of modern science in the seventeenth century, Evelyn Keller links the rise
of what she terms a masculine science with a striving for objectivity, autonomy,
and control.[39] Perhaps not coincidentally, the seventeenth century also witnessed
the rise of the modern state system. Since this period, autonomy and separation, importantly associated with the meaning of sovereignty, have determined
our conception of the national interest. Betty Reardon argues that this association of autonomy with the national interest tends to blind us to the realities of

erdependence in the present world situation.[40] Feminist perspectives would thus assume that striving for attachment is also part of human nature, which, while it has been suppressed by both modern scientific thinking and the practices of the Western state system, can be reclaimed and revalued in the future.

Evelyn Keller argues for a form of knowledge that she calls "dynamic objectivity . . . that grants to the world around us its independent integrity, but does so in a way that remains cognizant of, indeed relies on, our connectivity with that world."[41] Keller's view of dynamic objectivity contains parallels with what Sandra Harding calls an African worldview.[42] Harding tells us that the Western liberal notion of instrumentally rational economic man, similar to the notion of rational political man upon which realism has based its theoretical investigations, does not make sense in the African worldview where the individual is seen as part of the social order and as acting within that order rather than upon it. Harding believes that this view of human behavior has much in common with a feminist perspective; such a view of human behavior could help us to begin to think from a more global perspective that appreciates cultural diversity but at the same time recognizes a growing interdependence that makes anachronistic the exclusionary thinking fostered by the state system.

Besides a reconsideration of autonomy, feminist theories also offer us a different definition of power that could be useful for thinking about the achievement of the type of positive-sum security that the women at The Hague and in Halifax and Nairobi described as desirable. Hannah Arendt, frequently cited by feminists writing about power, defines power as the human ability to act in concert or action that is taken with others who share similar concerns.[43] This definition of power is similar to that of psychologist David McClelland's portrayal of female power which he describes as shared rather than assertive.[44] Jane Jaquette argues that, since women have had less access to the instruments of coercion (the way power is usually used in international relations), women have more often used persuasion as a way of gaining power through coalition building.[45] These writers are conceptualizing power as mutual enablement rather than domination. While not denying that the way power is frequently used in international relations comes closer to a coercive mode, thinking about power in these terms is helpful for devising the cooperative solutions necessary for solving the security threats identified in the Halifax women's definitions of security.

These different views of human behavior as models for the international behavior of states point us in the direction of an appreciation of the "other" as a subject whose views are as legitimate as our own, a way of thinking that has been sadly lacking as states go about providing for their own security. Using feminist perspectives that are based on the experiences and behavior of women, I have constructed some models of human behavior that avoid hierarchical dichotomization and that value ambiguity and difference; these alternative models could stand us in good stead as we seek to construct a less gendered vision of global security.

Feminist perspectives on national security take us beyond realism's statist representations. They allow us to see that the realist view of national security is constructed out of a masculinized discourse that, while it is only a partial view of reality, is taken as universal. Women's definitions of security are multilevel and multidimensional. Women have defined security as the absence of violence whether it be military, economic, or sexual. Not until the hierarchical social relations, including gender relations, that have been hidden by realism's frequently depersonalized discourse are brought to light can we begin to construct a language of national security that speaks out of the multiple experiences of both women and men. As I have argued, feminist theory sees all these types of violence as interrelated. I shall turn next to the economic dimension of this multidimensional perspective on security.

NOTES

1 While heads of state, all men, discussed the "important" issues in world politics at the Group of Seven meeting in London in July 1991, Barbara Bush and Princess Diana were pictured on the "CBS Evening News" (July 17, 1991) meeting with British AIDS patients.

2 Morgenthau, *Politics Among Nations*, p. 34.

3 Morgenthau does talk about dominating mothers-in-law, but as feminist research has suggested, it is generally men, legally designated as heads of households in most societies, who hold the real power even in the family and certainly with respect to the family's interaction with the public sphere.

4 For an extended discussion of Morgenthau's "political man," see Tickner, "Hans Morgenthau's Principles of Political Realism." In neorealism's depersonalized structural analysis, Morgenthau's depiction of human nature slips out of sight.

5 Brown, *Manhood and Politics*, pp. 43–59.

6 Jean Elshtain suggests that in Athens and Sparta this notion of heroic sacrifice was extended to women who died in childbirth producing citizens for the state. See Elshtain, "Sovereignty, Identity, Sacrifice," in Peterson, ed., *Gendered States*.

7 Brown, *Manhood and Politics*, ch. 5.

8 Pitkin, *Fortune Is a Woman*, p. 22.

9 Brown, *Manhood and Politics*, p. 82.

10 Pitkin, *Fortune Is a Woman*, ch. 6.

11 Brown, *Manhood and Politics*, pp. 80–88.

12 Machiavelli, *The Prince and the Discourses*, p. 94.

13 For example, he states in the *Art of War*, book 6, that women must not be allowed into a military camp, for they "make soldiers rebellious and useless." Quoted in Pitkin, *Fortune Is a Woman*, p. 72.

14 Kathleen Jones, "Dividing the Ranks: Women and the Draft," ch. 6 in Elshtain and Tobias, eds., *Women, Militarism, and War*, p. 126.

15 Gerzon, *A Choice of Heroes*, p. 31.

16 *A New York Times* interview, January 22, 1991, p. A12, with Sgt. Cheryl Stewart serving in the Gulf, revealed that she was close to divorce because her husband's ego had been bruised by remaining home with the couple's children.

17 Elshtain, *Women and War*, p. 207. Elshtain is citing a study by the military historian S. L. A. Marshall. This figure is, however, disputed by other analysts.

18 Stiehm, "The Protected, the Protector, the Defender," in Stiehm, *Women and Men's Wars*, p. 371.

19 Tobias, "Shifting Heroisms: The Uses of Military Service in Politics," ch. 8 in Elshtain and Tobias, eds., *Women, Militarism, and War*. Tobias uses Daniel Quayle as an

example of a politician who, in the 1988 U.S. election, suffered from the perception that he had avoided military service.

20 Ashley, "Untying the Sovereign State," p. 230.

21 Hobbes, *Leviathan*, part 1, ch. 13, quoted in Vasquez, ed., *Classics of International Relations*, pp. 213–215.

22 Pateman, *The Sexual Contract*, p. 41.

23 Flax, "Political Philosophy and the Patriarchal Unconscious: A Psychoanalytic Perspective on Epistemology and Metaphysics," in Harding and Hintikka, eds., *Discovering Reality*, pp. 245–281.

24 Di Stephano, "Masculinity as Ideology in Political Theory." Carole Pateman has disputed some of Di Stephano's assumptions about Hobbes's characterizations of women and the family in the state of nature. But this does not deny the fact that Di Stephano's characterization of men is the one used by realists in their depiction of the international system. See Pateman, "'God Hath Ordained to Man a Helper': Hobbes, Patriarchy, and Conjugal Right."

25 Critics of realism have questioned whether the Hobbesian analogy fits the international system. See, for example, Beitz, *Political Theory and International Relations*, pp. 35–50.

26 Pitkin, *Fortune Is a Woman*, p. 127.

27 Ruddick, *Maternal Thinking*, p. 152.

28 Higonnet et al., *Behind the Lines*, introduction.

29 Elshtain, *Women and War*, p. 194.

30 Ibid., p. 168.

31 Enloe, *Bananas, Beaches, and Bases*, pp. 48–49.

32 Hunt, *Ideology and U.S. Foreign Policy*, pp. 58–62.

33 Ibid., p. 164.

34 I am grateful to Michael Capps, historian at the Lewis and Clark Museum in St. Louis, Missouri, for this information. The story of Sacajawea is told in one of the museum's exhibits.

35 In *Man, the State, and War*, Waltz argues that "in the stag-hunt example, the will of the rabbit-snatcher was rational and predictable from his own point of view" (p. 183), while "in the early state of nature, men were sufficiently dispersed to make any pattern of cooperation unnecessary" (p. 167). Neorealist revisionists, such as Snidal ["Relative Gains and the Pattern of International Cooperation"] do not question the masculine bias of the stag hunt metaphor. Like Waltz and Rousseau, they also assume the autonomous, adult male (unparented and in an environment without women or children) in their discussion of the stag hunt; they do not question the rationality of the rabbit-snatching defector or the restrictive situational descriptions implied by their payoff matrices. Transformations in the social nature of an interaction are very hard to represent using such a model. Their reformulation of Waltz's position is instead focused on the exploration of different specifications of the game payoff in less conflictual ways (i.e., as an assurance game) and on inferences concerning the likely consequences of relative gain-seeking behavior in a game-like interaction with more than two (equally autonomous and unsocialized) players.

36 For a feminist interpretation that disputes this assumption see Mona Harrington, "What Exactly Is Wrong with the Liberal State as an Agent of Feminist Change?," in Peterson, ed., *Gendered States*.

37 Enloe, *Bananas, Beaches, and Bases*, ch. 5. Enloe points out that women, although very underrepresented in the U.S. State Department, make up half the professional staff of the Office of the U.S. Trade Representative. Trade negotiations are an arena

in which negotiating skills are particularly valuable, and Enloe believes that women are frequently assigned to these positions because the opposing party is more likely to trust them.

38 In her analysis of difference in men's and women's conversational styles, Deborah Tannen describes life from a male perspective as a struggle to preserve independence and avoid failure. In contrast, for women life is a struggle to preserve intimacy and avoid isolation. Tannen claims that all humans need both intimacy and independence but that women tend to focus on the former and men on the latter. Tannen, *You Just Don't Understand*, pp. 25–26.

39 Keller, *Reflections on Gender and Science*, ch. 3.

40 Reardon, *Sexism and the War System*, p. 88.

41 Keller, *Gender and Science*, p. 117.

42 Harding, *The Science Question in Feminism*, ch. 7.

43 Arendt, *On Violence*, p. 44.

44 McClelland, "Power and the Feminine Role," in McClelland, *Power: The Inner Experience*, ch. 3.

45 Jaquette, "Power as Ideology: A Feminist Analysis," in Stiehm, *Women's Views of the Political World of Men*, ch. 2.

REFERENCES

Arendt, Hannah. *On Violence.* New York: Harcourt, Brace and World, 1969.

Ashley, Richard K. "Untying the Sovereign State: A Double Reading of the Anarchy Problematique." *Millennium: Journal of International Studies* 17(2) (1988): 227–262.

Beitz, Charles. *Political Theory and International Relations.* Princeton: Princeton University Press, 1979.

Brown, Wendy. *Manhood and Politics: A Feminist Reading in Political Theory.* Totowa, N.J.: Rowman and Littlefield, 1988.

Di Stephano, Christine. "Masculinity as Ideology in Political Theory: Hobbesian Man Considered." *Women's Studies International Forum* 6(6) (1983): 633–644.

Elshtain, Jean Bethke. *Women and War.* New York: Basic Books, 1987.

Elshtain, Jean Bethke and Sheila Tobias, eds. *Women, Militarism, and War.* Savage, Md.: Rowman and Littlefield, 1990.

Enloe, Cynthia. *Bananas, Beaches, and Bases: Making Feminist Sense of International Politics.* Berkeley: University of California Press, 1990.

Gerzon, Mark. *A Choice of Heroes: The Changing Face of American Manhood.* Boston: Houghton Mifflin, 1984.

Harding, Sandra. *The Science Question in Feminism.* Ithaca, N.Y.: Cornell University Press, 1986.

Harding, Sandra and Merrill B. Hintikka, eds. *Discovering Reality.* Dordrecht, Holland: D. Reidel, 1983.

Higonnet, Margaret Randolph, Jane Jenson, Sonya Michel, and Margaret Collins Weitz, eds. *Behind the Lines: Gender and the Two World Wars.* New Haven: Yale University Press, 1987.

Hunt, Michael H. *Ideology and U.S. Foreign Policy.* New Haven: Yale University Press, 1987.

Keller, Evelyn Fox. *Reflections on Gender and Science.* New Haven: Yale University Press, 1985.

Machiavelli, Niccolò. *The Prince and the Discourses.* New York: Random House, 1940.

McClelland, David. *Power: The Inner Experience.* New York: Wiley, 1975.

Morgenthau, Hans J. *Politics Among Nations: The Struggle for Power and Peace,* 5th ed. New York: Knopf, 1973.

Pateman, Carole. "God Hath Ordained to Man a Helper: Hobbes, Patriarchy, and Conjugal Right." *British Journal of Political Science* 19(4) (October 1989): 445–464.

Pateman, Carole. *The Sexual Contract.* Stanford: Stanford University Press, 1988.

Peterson, V. Spike, ed. *Gendered States: Feminist (Re)visions of International Relations Theory.* Boulder. Lynne Rienner, 1992.

Pitkin, Hanna F. *Fortune Is a Woman: Gender and Politics in the Thought of Niccolò Machiavelli.* Berkeley: University of California Press, 1984.

Reardon, Betty A. *Sexism and the War System.* New York: Teachers College Press, 1985.

Ruddick, Sara. *Maternal Thinking: Toward a Politics of Peace.* New York: Ballantine Books, 1989.

Snidal, Duncan. "Relative Gains and the Pattern of International Cooperation." *American Political Science Review* 85(3) (1991): 701–726.

Stiehm, Judith Hicks. *Women and Men's Wars.* Oxford: Pergamon Press, 1983.

Stiehm, Judith Hicks. *Women's Views of the Political World of Men.* Dobbs Ferry, N.Y.: Transnational Publishers, 1984.

Tannen, Deborah. *You Just Don't Understand: Women and Men in Conversation.* New York: Morrow, 1990.

Tickner, J. Ann. "Hans Morgenthau's Principles of Political Realism: A Feminist Reformulation." *Millennium* 17(3) (Winter 1988): 429–440.

Vasquez, John, ed. *Classics of International Relations,* 2d ed. Englewood Cliffs, N.J.: Prentice Hall, 1990.

Waltz, Kenneth N. *Man, the State, and War.* New York: Columbia University Press, 1959.

Economics: Interests and Interdependence

D o economic interests cause cooperation or conflict in international relations? Economic turbulence such as the Great Recession early in the twenty-first century brought the question back—if it had ever been settled. To many in earlier ages, the answer to the question seemed to be *conflict*. When wealth came from agriculture or mining, the more territory one controlled, the richer one could be, so there was an economic incentive for conquest. To many in the modern era, however, the answer seems to be *cooperation*. When wealth comes primarily from industrial production and information technology, trade is the efficient route to riches, and war simply destroys wealth rather than creating it. If greed led to beliefs that war would be profitable in past eras, does modern understanding of economic logic and globalization of the world economy compel different policies today?

Liberal economic theory opposes mercantilism, imperialism, fascism, and Marxism in seeing war as obsolete not just because it is evil, but because it profits no one. To imperialists of various sorts, however, or to those concerned with dependence on basic commodities such as oil, the liberal view ignores the profits that can be made from simple expropriation, or the threat of monopolies or cartels to free trade, so control of the territory in which resources lie can still be economically advantageous. Thus some today still believe that in certain circumstances, as Machiavelli opined in the following excerpt from *The Discourses*, military power can be the font of wealth. Marxists in turn saw violent conflict as the natural and inevitable result of opposed classes' economic interests. It was not long ago that in the Soviet Union Marxism joined with nationalism and fostered the most serious attempt, apart from fascism, to develop a viable autarky—a state that is economically self-sufficient.

Unabashed mercantilism no longer exists as a serious philosophical challenge to liberal economics or as an overt political movement.[1] To varying degrees, though, it comes alive in other forms of economic nationalism.[2]

Marxism—not long ago a potent challenge to international liberalism and a serious contender for wave of the future—is nearly defunct. Although a few countries remain nominally Communist, most of them have preserved Leninist political forms while moving away from Marxist economic principles. Excerpts from Lenin's theory of imperialism are included here, because it represents a major school of thought in the evolution of ideas on the subject, and makes a specific argument about why the dynamics of capitalism actually push governments toward war and conquest to control foreign markets.

Nonliberal interpretations could become more interesting again if the world economy suffers major or prolonged dislocations. The Asian economic crisis of the late 1990s, the Great Recession that began in 2008, the resurgence of protectionist populism in the West, and faltering Chinese growth are reminders that uninterrupted prosperity and economic contentment are not inevitable. Disillusionment with effects of liberal capitalism and free trade could promote conflictual economic nationalism or Marxist revival. Political developments in South America in recent years, for example, moved in that direction.

Still, the liberal theory of political economy is dominant among Western elites. It holds that free trade in open markets yields the most efficient production and exchange of goods and, ultimately, makes everyone wealthier than if governments interfere. Trade based on specialization and comparative advantage promotes efficient growth and interdependence among nations, which in turn gives them all a stake in each other's security and prosperity. Control of territory does not matter because it does not create wealth, which is only generated by production and exchange. Interdependence makes war counterproductive and wasteful for all, not only because war destroys property but because it deranges the international market and distorts global efficiency.

If peace is the path to profit, greed should discourage war rather than promote it. In this respect liberal theory does not see itself as idealistic, relying on noble motives to suppress war. Just like realism, or mercantilism, or Marxism, the theory focuses on material interest as the driving force, but sees the logic of such interest in a different way. Norman Angell summarizes this view in the selection included here, from one of the most popular tracts of the pre–World War I period. Angell has often gotten an undeservedly harsh rap from realists for foolishly saying that commercial interdependence made war impossible, just before World War I broke out. Angell, however, maintained that he said only that war would be irrational, not impossible.[3] If this logic is valid and persistence of war after the arrival of industrial capitalism can only be irrational, what would account for the irrationality?

Joseph Schumpeter provides a sociological explanation, attributing militarist policies to cultural atavism, the continuing sway of feudal elites and their values in societies where capitalism displaces them. Another source of irrationality, in terms of liberal theory, would be the nationalist ideologies of interwar fascism, which promoted autarky and conquest for direct economic exploitation of subjugated populations. The rationales behind this alternative are discussed in Alan S. Milward's piece. It is not surprising that liberal theories of the pacifying effect of international economic interdependence have the upper hand again today, since fascism and feudal militarism are even further gone than Marxism as a challenge. (The surprises of "Brexit," Donald Trump, and surging populist parties in Europe point back in that direction.)

Realism, however, is not as far gone, and it offers different explanations for the failure of capitalism to prevent wars. Some of these criticisms are noted in the pieces by Blainey and Waltz. Blainey argues that enthusiasts for the view that free trade, cultural exchange, and better communication foster peace mistook the effect for the cause when the phenomena coincided in the nineteenth century. Most notably, Waltz argues that interdependence actually fosters conflict rather than amity because nations fear dependence and seek to overcome it. He cites data indicating that the level of interdependence among the great powers in the Cold War was actually lower than in the earlier part of the century, and counts it a good thing. Richard Rosecrance then argues that the specific *type* of interdependence is what matters, and the type that naturally fosters cooperation and peace (direct investment, as opposed to the portfolio investment of a century ago) has risen substantially in recent times. More recent research, such as Erik Gartzke's, reinforces the case for the pacifying effect of commercial liberalism.[4]

The final item in this section, by G. John Ikenberry, focuses the question by applying it to the current issue at the center of strategists' attention: the rise of China. He endorses the case for why the Western model of commercial liberalism should be pacifying, but notes that China must understand and choose to accept it—an open question—for the effects to take hold.

—RKB

NOTES

1 See Jacob Viner, "Power and Plenty as Objectives of Foreign Policy in the Seventeenth and Eighteenth Centuries," *World Politics* 1, no. 1 (October 1948).
2 See Robert Gilpin with the assistance of Jean M. Gilpin, *The Political Economy of International Relations* (Princeton, N.J.: Princeton University Press, 1987), and James Kurth, "The Pacific Basin versus the Atlantic Alliance: Two Paradigms of International Relations," *Annals of the American Academy of Political and Social Sciences* 505 (September 1989).
3 See Angell's post–World War I revision, *The Great Illusion, 1933* (New York: G.P. Putnam's Sons, 1933), pp. 267–270, and *After All: The Autobiography of Norman Angell* (New York: Farrar, Straus and Young, 1951), pp. 143–161.
4 Erik Gartzke, "The Capitalist Peace," *American Journal of Political Science* 51, no. 1 (January 2007).

Reading 5.1

Money Is Not the Sinews of War, Although It Is Generally So Considered

NICCOLÒ MACHIAVELLI

Every one may begin a war at his pleasure, but cannot so finish it. A prince, therefore, before engaging in any enterprise should well measure his strength, and govern himself accordingly; and he must be very careful not to deceive himself in the estimate of his strength, which he will assuredly do if he measures it by his money, or by the situation of his country, or the good disposition of his people, unless he has at the same time an armed force of his own. For although the above things will increase his strength, yet they will not give it to him, and of themselves are nothing, and will be of no use without a devoted army. Neither abundance of money nor natural strength of the country will suffice, nor will the loyalty and good will of his subjects endure, for these cannot remain faithful to a prince who is incapable of defending them. Neither mountains nor lakes nor inaccessible places will present any difficulties to an enemy where there is a lack of brave defenders. And money alone, so far from being a means of defence, will only render a prince the more liable to being plundered. There cannot, therefore, be a more erroneous opinion than that money is the sinews of war. This was said by Quintus Curtius in the war between Antipater of Macedon and the king of Sparta, when he tells that want of money obliged the king of Sparta to come to battle, and that he was routed; whilst, if he could have delayed the battle a few days, the news of the death of Alexander would have reached Greece, and in that case he would have remained victor without fighting. But lacking money, and fearing the defection of his army, who were unpaid, he was obliged to try the fortune of battle, and was defeated; and in consequence of this, Quintus Curtius affirms money to be the sinews of war. This opinion is constantly quoted, and is acted upon by princes who are unwise enough to follow it; for relying upon it, they believe that plenty of money is all they require for their defence, never thinking that, if treasure were sufficient to insure victory, Darius would have vanquished Alexander, and the Greeks would have triumphed over the Romans; and, in our day, Duke Charles the Bold would have beaten the Swiss; and, quite recently, the Pope and the Florentines together would have had no difficulty in defeating Francesco Maria, nephew of Pope Julius II, in the war of Urbino. All that we have named were vanquished by those who

---

Source: Niccolò Machiavelli, *"Money Is Not the Sinews of War, Although It Is Generally So Considered."* Discourses on the First Ten Books of Titus Livius, *Christian E. Detmold, trans. (Modern Library, 1950).*

regarded good troops, and not money, as the sinews of war. Amongst other objects of interest which Creesus, king of Lydia, showed to Solon of Athens, was his countless treasure; and to the question as to what he thought of his power, Solon replied, "that he did not consider him powerful on that account, because war was made with iron, and not with gold, and that some one might come who had more iron than he, and would take his gold from him." When after the death of Alexander the Great an immense swarm of Gauls descended into Greece, and thence into Asia, they sent ambassadors to the king of Macedon to treat with him for peace. The king, by way of showing his power, and to dazzle them, displayed before them great quantities of gold and silver; whereupon the ambassadors of the Gauls, who had already as good as signed the treaty, broke off all further negotiations, excited by the intense desire to possess themselves of all this gold; and thus the very treasure which the king had accumulated for his defence brought about his spoliation. The Venetians, a few years ago, having also their treasury full, lost their entire state without their money availing them in the least in their defence.

I maintain, then, contrary to the general opinion, that the sinews of war are not gold, but good soldiers; for gold alone will not procure good soldiers, but good soldiers will always procure gold. Had the Romans attempted to make their wars with gold instead of with iron, all the treasure of the world would not have sufficed them, considering the great enterprises they were engaged in, and the difficulties they had to encounter. But by making their wars with iron, they never suffered for the want of gold; for it was brought to them, even into their camp, by those who feared them. And if want of money forced the king of Sparta to try the fortune of battle, it was no more than what often happened from other causes; for we have seen that armies short of provisions, and having to starve or hazard a battle, will always prefer the latter as the more honorable course, and where fortune may yet in some way favor them. It has also often happened that a general, seeing that his opposing enemy is about to receive reinforcements, has preferred to run the risk of a battle at once, rather than wait until his enemy is reinforced and fight him then under greater disadvantage. We have seen also in the case of Asdrubal, when he was attacked upon the river Metaurus by Claudius Nero, together with another Roman Consul, that a general who has to choose between battle or flight will always prefer to fight, as then, even in the most doubtful case, there is still a chance of victory, whilst in flight his loss is certain anyhow.

There are, then, an infinity of reasons that may induce a general to give battle against his will, and the want of money may in some instances be one of them; but that is no reason why money should be deemed the sinews of war, which more than anything else will influence him to that course. I repeat it again, then, that it is not gold, but good soldiers, that insure success in war. Certainly money is a necessity, but a secondary one, which good soldiers will overcome; for it is as impossible that good soldiers should not be able to procure gold, as it is impossible for gold to procure good soldiers. History proves in a thousand cases what I maintain, notwithstanding that Pericles counselled the Athenians to make war with the entire Peloponnesus, demonstrating to them that by perseverance and the power of money they would be successful. And although it is true that the Athenians obtained some successes in that war, yet they succumbed in the end; and good counsels and the good soldiers of Sparta prevailed over the perseverance and money of the Athenians. But the testimony of Titus Livius upon this question is more direct than any other, where, in discussing whether Alexander the Great, had he come into Italy, would have vanquished the Romans, he points out that there are three things pre-eminently necessary to success in war—plenty of good troops, sagacious commanders, and good fortune; and in examining afterwards whether the Romans or Alexander excelled most in these three points, he draws his conclusion without ever mentioning the subject of money. The Campanians, when requested by the Sidicians to take up arms in their behalf against the Samnites, may have measured their strength by their money, and not by their soldiers; for having resolved to grant the required assistance, they were constrained after two defeats to become tributary to the Romans to save themselves.

Reading 5.2

The Great Illusion
NORMAN ANGELL

What are the fundamental motives that explain the present rivalry of armaments in Europe, notably the Anglo-German? Each nation pleads the need for defense; but this implies that someone is likely to attack, and has therefore a presumed interest in so doing. What are the motives which each State thus fears its neighbors may obey?

They are based on the universal assumption that a nation, in order to find outlets for expanding population and increasing industry, or simply to ensure the best conditions possible for its people, is necessarily pushed to territorial expansion and the exercise of political force against others (German naval competition is assumed to be the expression of the growing need of an expanding population for a larger place in the world, a need which will find a realization in the conquest of English Colonies or trade, unless these are defended); it is assumed, therefore, that a nation's relative prosperity is broadly determined by its political power; that nations being competing units, advantage, in the last resort, goes to the possessor of preponderant military force, the weaker going to the wall, as in the other forms of the struggle for life.

The author challenges this whole doctrine. He attempts to show that it belongs to a stage of development out of which we have passed; that the

Source: Norman Angell, The Great Illusion: A Study of the Relation of Military Power to National Advantage, 4th edition (New York: Putnam's, 1913), Synopsis.

commerce and industry of a people no longer depend upon the expansion of its political frontiers; that a nation's political and economic frontiers do not now necessarily coincide; that military power is socially and economically futile, and can have no relation to the prosperity of the people exercising it; that it is impossible for one nation to seize by force the wealth or trade of another—to enrich itself by subjugating, or imposing its will by force on another; that, in short, war, even when victorious, can no longer achieve those aims for which peoples strive.

He establishes this apparent paradox, in so far as the economic problem is concerned, by showing that wealth in the economically civilized world is founded upon credit and commercial contract (these being the outgrowth of an economic interdependence due to the increasing division of labor and greatly developed communication). If credit and commercial contract are tampered with in an attempt at confiscation, the credit-dependent wealth is undermined, and its collapse involves that of the conqueror; so that if conquest is not to be self-injurious it must respect the enemy's property, in which case it becomes economically futile. Thus the wealth of conquered territory remains in the hands of the population of such territory. When Germany annexed Alsatia, no individual German secured a single mark's worth of Alsatian property as the spoils of war. Conquest in the modern world is a process of multiplying by x, and then obtaining the original figure by dividing by x. For a modern nation to add to its territory no more adds to the wealth of the people of such nation than it would add to the wealth of Londoners if the City of London were to annex the county of Hertford.

The author also shows that international finance has become so interdependent and so interwoven with trade and industry that the intangibility of an enemy's property extends to his trade. It results that political and military power can in reality do nothing for trade; the individual merchants and manufacturers of small nations, exercising no such power, compete successfully with those of the great. Swiss and Belgian merchants drive English from the British Colonial market; Norway has, relatively to population, a greater mercantile marine than Great Britain; the public credit (as a rough-and-ready indication, among others, of security and wealth) of small States possessing no political power often stands higher than that of the Great Powers of Europe, Belgian Three per Cents. standing at 96, and German at 82; Norwegian Three and a Half per Cents. at 102, and Russian Three and a Half per Cents. at 81.

The forces which have brought about the economic futility of military power have also rendered it futile as a means of enforcing a nation's moral ideals or imposing social institutions upon a conquered people. Germany could not turn Canada or Australia into German colonies—i.e., stamp out their language, law, literature, traditions, etc.—by "capturing" them. The necessary security in their material possessions enjoyed by the inhabitants of such conquered provinces, quick intercommunication by a cheap press, widely-read literature, enable even small communities to become articulate and effectively to defend their special social or moral possessions, even when military conquest has been complete. The fight for ideals can no longer take the form of fight between nations, because the lines of division on moral questions are within the nations themselves and intersect the political frontiers. There is no modern State which is completely Catholic or Protestant, or liberal or autocratic, or aristocratic or democratic, or socialist or individualist; the moral and spiritual struggles of the modern world go on between citizens of the same State in unconscious intellectual co-operation with corresponding groups in other States, not between the public powers of rival States.

This classification by strata involves necessarily a redirection of human pugnacity, based rather on the rivalry of classes and interests than on State divisions. War has no longer the justification that it makes for the survival of the fittest; it involves the survival of the less fit. The idea that the struggle between nations is a part of the evolutionary law of man's advance involves a profound misreading of the biological analogy.

The warlike nations do not inherit the earth; they represent the decaying human element. The diminishing role of physical force in all spheres of human activity carries with it profound psychological modifications.

These tendencies, mainly the outcome of purely modern conditions (e.g., rapidity of communication), have rendered the problems of modern international politics profoundly and essentially different from the ancient; yet our ideas are still dominated by the principles and axioms, images and terminology of the bygone days.

The author urges that these little-recognized facts may be utilized for the solution of the armament difficulty on at present untried lines—by such modification of opinion in Europe that much of the present motive to aggression will cease to be operative, and by thus diminishing the risk of attack, diminishing to the same extent the need for defense. He shows how such a political reformation is within the scope of practical politics, and the methods which should be employed to bring it about.

Reading 5.3

Paradise Is a Bazaar *GEOFFREY BLAINEY*

The mystery of why the nineteenth century enjoyed unusually long eras of peace did not puzzle some powerful minds. They believed that intellectual and commercial progress were soothing those human misunderstandings and grievances which had caused many earlier wars. The followers of this theory were usually democrats with an optimistic view of human nature.

Though they had emerged earlier in France than in England they became most influential in the English-speaking world and their spiritual home was perhaps the industrial city of Manchester, which exported cotton goods and the philosophy of free trade to every corner of the globe.

Manchester's disciples believed that paradise was an international bazaar.[1] They favored the international flow of goods and ideas and the creation of institutions that channeled that flow and the abolition of institutions that blocked it. Nations, they argued, now grew richer through commerce than through conquest. Their welfare was now enhanced by rational discussion rather than by threats. The fortresses of peace were those institutions and inventions which promoted the exchange of ideas and commodities: parliaments, international conferences, the popular press, compulsory education, the public reading room, the penny postage stamp, railways, submarine telegraphs, three funnelled ocean liners, and the Manchester cotton exchange.

The long peace that followed the Battle of Waterloo was increasingly explained as the result of the international flow of commodities and ideas. 'It is something more than an accident which has turned the attention of mankind to international questions of every description in the same age that established freedom of commerce in the most enlightened nations.'[2] So wrote one of the early biographers of Richard Cobden, merchant of Manchester and citizen of the world. Variations of the same idea were shared by Sir Robert Peel, William Gladstone, John Stuart Mill, scores of economists and poets and men of letters, and by England's Prince Consort, Albert the Good. His sponsorship of the Great Exhibition in the new Crystal Palace in London in 1851 popularised the idea that a festival of peace and trade fair were synonymous. The Crystal Palace was perhaps the world's first peace festival.

In that palace of glass and iron the locomotives and telegraphic equipment were admired not only as mechanical wonders; they were also messengers of peace and instruments of unity. The telegraph cable laid across the English Channel in 1850 had been welcomed as an underwater cord of friendship. The splicing of the cable that snaked beneath the Atlantic in 1858 was another celebration of brotherhood, and the first message tapped across the seabed was a proclamation of peace: 'Europe and America are united by telegraphic communication. Glory to God in the Highest, On Earth Peace, Goodwill towards Men.'[3] That cable of peace was soon snapped, and so was unable to convey the news in the following year that France and Austria were at war, or the news in 1861 that the United States was split by war.

Henry Thomas Buckle was one of many influential prophets of the idea that telegraphs and railways and steamships were powerfully promoting peace. Buckle was a wealthy young London bachelor who in the 1850s studied beneath the skylight of his great London library, writing in powerful prose a vast survey of the influences which, to his mind, were civilising Europe. A brilliant chess player who had competed with Europe's champions at the palace of peace, Buckle thought human affairs obeyed rules that were almost as clear cut as the rules of chess; and those rules permeated his writings. The first volume of the *History of Civilisation in England* appeared in 1857, the second volume in 1861, and they were devoured by thousands of English readers, published in French, Spanish, German, Hungarian and Hebrew editions, and translated four times into Russian.[4]

One of Buckle's themes was the decline of the warlike spirit in western Europe. As a freethinker he attributed that decline not to moral influences but to the progress of knowledge and intellectual activity. The invention of gunpowder had made soldiering the specialist activity of the few rather than the occasional activity of the many, thereby releasing talent for peaceful pursuits. Similarly Adam Smith's *The Wealth of Nations*, 'probably the most important book that has ever been written',[5] had perceived and popularised the idea that a nation gained most when its commercial policy enriched rather than impoverished its neighbours: free trade had replaced war and aggressive mercantilism as the road to commercial prosperity. Buckle argued that the new commercial spirit was making nations depend on one another whereas the old spirit had made them fight one another.

Just as commerce now linked nations, so the steamship and railway linked peoples: 'the greater the contact', argued Buckle, 'the greater the respect'. Frenchmen and Englishmen had curbed their national prejudices because they had done more than railways and steamships to increase their friendship. As he affirmed in his clear rolling prose: 'every new railroad which is laid down, and every fresh steamer which crosses the Channel, are additional guarantees for the preservation of that long and unbroken peace which, during forty years, has knit together the fortunes and the interests of the two most civilised nations of the earth'.[6] Buckle thought foreign travel was the greatest of all educations as well as a spur to peace; and it was while he was travelling near Damascus in 1862 that he caught the typhoid fever which ended his life.

Many readers must have thought that the outbreak of the Crimean War rather dinted Buckle's argument that the warlike spirit was declining in Europe. Buckle was composing that chapter of his book when war was raging in the Crimea, and he foresaw the criticism and met it head on:

> For the peculiarity of the great contest in which we are engaged is, that it was produced, not by the conflicting interests of civilised countries, but by a rupture between Russia and Turkey, the two most barbarous monarchies now remaining in Europe. This is a very significant fact. It is highly characteristic of the actual condition of society, that a peace of unexampled length should have been broken, not, as former peaces were broken, by a quarrel between two civilised nations, but by the encroachments of the uncivilised Russians on the still more uncivilised Turks.[7]

Buckle still had to explain why France and England, his heroes of civilisation, had exultantly joined in the barbarians' war. He explained that simply; the departure of their armies to the distant Crimea was a sign of their civilisation. France and England, he wrote, 'have drawn the sword, not for selfish purposes, but to protect the civilised world against the incursions of a barbarous foe'.

The shattering civil war which began in the United States in the last year of Buckle's life should have been a blow to his theory. On the contrary it seems to have heartened his supporters. They interpreted that war as another crusade against barbarism and the barbaric practice of slavery. At the end of that four-years' war Professor J. E. Cairnes, an Irish economist, wrote a powerful article reaffirming the idea that 'all the leading currents of modern civilisation' were running steadily in the direction of peace.[8] He thought that the way in which the North craved the sympathy of foreign nations during the war was a sign of the increasing force of public opinion in international affairs. He believed that the enlightened public opinion was coming mainly from the expansion of free commerce, the railways and steamships, and the study of modern languages. Henry Thomas Buckle would have sympathized with the emphasis on modern languages; he spoke nineteen.

The idea that ignorance and misunderstanding were the seeds of war inspired the hope that an international language would nourish peace—so long as the chosen language was purged of nationalism. In 1880 a south German priest, J. M. Schleyer, published a neutral language of his own manufacture and called it Volapük. It spread with the speed of rumour to almost every civilised land, claiming one million students within a decade. To Paris in 1889 came the delegates of 283 Volapük societies, and even the waiters at the dining tables of the congress could translate the following manifesto into Volapük:

> I love all my fellow-creatures of the whole world, especially those cultivated ones who believe in Volapük as one of the greatest means of nation-binding.[9]

The rival nation-binding language of Esperanto was then two years old. Its inventor, a Russian physician named Zamenhof, had come from a feuding region where Polish, German, Yiddish, and Russian were all spoken; and he trusted that his Esperanto would ameliorate dissensions between races. Before long, however, many supporters of Esperanto and Volapük were feuding. Even the disciples of Volapük tongue discovered that their universal language did not necessarily lead to harmony. They split after a quarrel about grammar.

In the generation before the First World War there were abundant warnings that the Manchester gospel was not infallible. The very instruments of peace—railways and international canals and steamships and bills of lading—were conspicuous in the background to some wars. The Suez Canal was a marvelous artery of international exchange, but for that reason England and France were intensely interested in controlling it; without the canal it is doubtful if there would have been an Egyptian War in 1882. The Trans-Siberian railway was a great feat of construction and a powerful link between Europe and Asia, but without that railway it is doubtful whether there could have been a Russo-Japanese war in 1904–5. This is not to argue that these new arteries of commerce *caused* those two wars; but certainly they illustrated the hazards of assuming that whatever drew nations together was an instrument of peace. The Manchester creed, to many of its adherents, was a dogma; and so contrary evidence was dismissed. . . .

A war lasting four years and involving nearly all the 'civilised' nations of the world contradicted all the assumptions of the crusaders. Admittedly most had envisaged that the movement towards international peace could meet occasional setbacks. Wars against barbarians and autocrats might have to be fought before the millennium arrived. Indeed, if the First World War had been fought by Britain, France and Germany on the one hand and Russia and Serbia on the other, the belief in the millennium might have been less shaken. Such a war could have seemed a replay of the Crimean or American Civil War and thus been interpreted as a war against the barbarians. It was, however, more difficult for learned Frenchmen, Englishmen and Russians to interpret the war against Germany as simply a war against the ignorant and uncivilised: for Germany in 1914 was the homeland of Albert Einstein, Max Planck, Max Weber and a galaxy of great contemporary intellects. On the other hand German liberals at least had the intellectual satisfaction that the Tsar of Russia was one enemy they were fighting; but another of their enemies was France which in some eyes, was the lamp of civilisation.

There was a peculiar irony in the war which divided Europe. If the length and bitterness of the war had been foreseen, the efforts to preserve the peace in 1914 would have been far more vigorous and might have even succeeded. But one of the reasons why so many national leaders and followers in 1914 could not imagine a long war was their faith in the steady flow of that civilising stream that had seemed to widen during the peaceful nineteenth century. The Great War of 1914 would be short, it was widely believed, partly because civilised opinion would rebel against the war if it began to create chaos. The willingness of hundreds of millions of Europeans to tolerate chaos, slaughter and an atmosphere of hatred was an additional surprise to those who had faith in civilisation.

Despite the shock of a world war, versions of the Manchester creed survived. Indeed that creed may have been partly responsible for the outbreak of another world war only two decades later. The military revival of Germany had complicated causes, but in many of those causes one can detect the mark of Manchester.

Germany could not have revived, militarily, without the willing or reluctant sanction of some of the victors of the First World War. In particular the United States and Britain allowed Germany to revive. As they were themselves protected by ocean they tended to be careless of threats within Europe; as they were democracies they tended to have trouble spending adequately on defense in years of peace, for other calls on revenue were more persuasive. A secure island democracy is of course the haven of the Manchester creed; its optimism about human nature and distrust of excessive force reflect the security of its home environment.

One sign of optimism in England and the United States was the widespread belief that another world war was virtually impossible. The idea of a war to end war had been one of the popular slogans in those democracies from 1914 to 1918, and the idea lived long after the slogan dissolved in the mouths of orators and faded on recruiting billboards. The prediction that the world would not again experience a war of such magnitude aided the neglect of armaments among some of the main victors of the previous war. It was probably in England too that there was the deepest faith that the League of Nations would become an efficient substitute for the use of force in international affairs; this was not surprising, for the League in a sense was a descendant of the House of Commons, the Manchester Cotton Exchange, and the old crusade for free trade. In England public opinion, more than official opinion, tended to expect more of the League of Nations than it was capable of giving. That misplaced faith indirectly helped the Germans to recover their bargaining position in Europe, for in crises the League of Nations proved to be powerless. Likewise in England the widespread mistrust of armaments in the 1920s was more than the normal reaction after a major war; it mirrored the belief that the armaments race had been a major cause of the previous war. The Great War, it was argued, had come through misunderstanding; it had been an unwanted war. This interpretation of 1914, to my mind quite invalid, matched the optimistic tenets of the Manchester creed. And since it was widely believed in England it affected future events. It also was a restraint on the English government's ability to match German re-arming for part of the 1930s: to enter again into an armaments race was to endanger peace, it was believed, even more than to neglect armaments. The ways in which the Manchester creed affected Europe between the two world wars represents only one strand in the rope which raised Germany from her enforced meekness of 1919 to her might of 1939, but it was still an important strand.

In the nineteenth century the Manchester creed in all its hues was favored more by public opinion than by the reigning ministry in England. On the eve of the Second World War, however, it was powerful in Whitehall. Manchester had taken office, even if it was disguised as a former mayor of Birmingham. Neville Chamberlain, England's prime minister from 1937 to 1940, is now often seen as a naïve individualist, an eccentric out of step with British traditions, but he represented one of the most influential traditions of British thought. Though he was re-arming Britain he did not trust primarily in arms. He saw, not an evil world which reacted only to force or threats, but a world of rational men who reacted to goodwill and responded to discussion.[10] He believed that most modern wars were the result of misunderstandings or of grievances. Accordingly there were rational remedies for the causes of war. As he believed that Germany suffered unfairly from the Versailles Peace of 1919, he was prepared to make concessions in the belief that they would preserve the peace. He was eager to hurry to Germany—not summon Germany to England—in the belief that the conference table was the only sane field of battle. He believed Hitler would respond to rational discussion and to appeasement; so did many Englishmen in 1938.

. . . The optimistic theory of peace is still widespread. Within the United States it pervades much of the criticism of the war in Vietnam. Within the western world it is visible in the school of thought which expects quick results from the fostering of friendly contacts with Russia and China. It pervades many of the plans by which richer countries aid poorer countries. It permeates a host of movements and ventures ranging from the Olympic Games, Rotary and Telstar to international tourism and peace organizations. Irrespective of whether the creed rests on sound or false premises of human behaviour, it still influences international relations. In the short term it is a civilising influence. Whether it actually promotes peace or war, however, is open to debate. If it is based on false generalizations about the causes of war and the causes of peace its influence in promoting peace is likely to be limited and indeed haphazard. Moreover, if it is inspired by a strong desire for peace, but gnaws at the skin rather than the core of international relations, the results will be meagre.

Something is missing in that theory of peace which was shaped and popularised by so many gifted men in the nineteenth century. One may suggest that, like many other explanations of war and peace, it relied much on coincidence. Those living in the three generations after Waterloo had wondered at the long peace and sought explanations in events that were happening simultaneously.[11] They noticed that international peace coincided with industrialism, steam engines, foreign travel, freer and stronger commerce and advancing knowledge. As they saw specific ways in which these changes could further peace, they concluded that the coincidence was causal. Their explanation, however, was based on one example or one period of peace. They ignored the earlier if shorter periods of peace experience by a Europe which had no steam trains, few factories, widespread ignorance and restricted commerce. Their explanation of the cluster of European wars in the period 1848–71 was also shaky. These wars were relatively short, and to their mind the shortness of most wars in the century after Waterloo was evidence that Europe's warlike spirit was ebbing. On the contrary one can argue that most of these wars were shortened not by civilising restraints but by unusual political conditions and by new technological factors which the philosophers of peace did not closely investigate. If neglect of war led them into error their attitude was nonetheless a vital reaction to those studies of war which neglected peace.

Most of the changes which were hailed as causes of peace in the nineteenth century were probably more the effects of peace. The ease with which ideas, people and commodities flowed across international borders was very much an effect of peace though in turn the flow may have aided peace. Similarly the optimistic assessment of man's nature and the belief that civilisation was triumphing was aided by the relative peacefulness of the nineteenth century. That optimism would not have been so flourishing if wars had been longer and more devastating. In one sense the Manchester theory of peace was like the mountebank's diagnosis that shepherds were healthy simply because they had ruddy cheeks: therefore the cure for a sick shepherd was to inflame his cheeks.

It is difficult to find evidence that closer contacts between nations promoted peace. Swift communications which drew nations together did not necessarily promote peace: it is indisputable that during the last three centuries most wars have been fought by neighbouring countries—not countries which are far apart. The frequency of civil wars shatters the simple idea that people who have much in common will remain at peace. Even the strain of idealism which characterized most versions of the Manchester creed cannot easily be identified as an influence favoring peace, perhaps because in practice the creed is not idealistic. Thus Neville Chamberlain's concessions to Germany in 1938 were no doubt influenced partly by Germany's increasing strength: moreover his concessions were not so idealistic because they were mainly at the expense of Czechoslovakia's independence.

The conclusion seems unmistakable: the Manchester creed cannot be a vital part of a theory of war and peace. One cannot even be sure whether those influences which it emphasizes actually have promoted peace more than war.

Kenneth Boulding, an Anglo-American economist who brilliantly builds bridges across the chasms that divide regions of knowledge, made one observation which indirectly illuminates the dilemma of the Manchester brotherhood. 'Threat systems', wrote Boulding, 'are the basis of politics as exchange systems are the basis of economics.'[12] The Manchester idealists emphasized exchange and minimized the importance of threats. Believing that mankind contained much more good than evil, they thought that threats were becoming unnecessary in a world which seemed increasingly civilised. Indeed they thought that threats were the tyrannical hallmark of an old order which was crumbling. They despised the open or veiled threat as the weapon of their enemies. Thus they opposed czars and dictators who relied visibly on force and threats. For the same reason they opposed slavery, serfdom, militarism and harsh penal codes. And they mostly opposed the idea of hell, for hell was a threat.

They did not realize, nor perhaps do we, that a democratic country depends on threats and force, even if they are more veiled and more intermittent than in an autocracy. They did not realize that intellectual and commercial liberty were most assured in those two nations—Britain and the United States—which were economically strong and protected by ocean from the threat of foreign invasion. The preference of Anglo-Saxon nations for democratic forms of government had owed much to the military security which the ocean provided. On the rare occasions in the last two centuries when Britain was threatened by a powerful enemy it abandoned temporarily many of its democratic procedures; thus in the Second World War Churchill and the war cabinet probably held as much power as an autocracy of the eighteenth century. Mistakenly the Manchester creed believed that international affairs would soon repeat effortlessly the achievements visible in the internal affairs of a few favored lands. . . .

NOTES

1 The Manchester creed: in selecting this name my main reasons were Manchester's reputation as a symbol of free trade and the popularity of the creed among free-trade economists.
2 'It is something'. Apjohn, p. 234.
3 The Atlantic telegraph: Cruikshank, p. 72.
4 Buckle's career: *D.N.B.*, III 208–11.
5 Praise of Adam Smith: Buckle, I, 214.
6 'Every new railroad': ibid., p. 223.
7 'For the peculiarity of the great contest', ibid., p. 195.
8 'All the leading currents'. Cairnes, p. 123.
9 Volapük: Henry Sweet, *Encyclopaedia Britannica, 1910–11*, XXVIII 178.
10 Chamberlain's faith in rational discussion: Taylor, *The Origins of the Second World War*, pp. 172, 217.

11 Likewise one explanation of the relative peace in Europe since 1945—the influence of nuclear weapons—seems to rely often on coincidence.

12 'Threat systems'. Boulding, *Beyond Economics*, p. 105.

REFERENCES

Apjohn, Lewis, *Richard Cobden and the Free Traders* (London, c. 1880).

Boulding, Kenneth, *Conflict and Defense* (New York, 1962).

———. *Beyond Economics: Essays on Society, Religion and Ethics* (Ann Arbor, MI, 1968).

Buckle, Henry Thomas, *History of Civilization in England*, 3 vols. (London, 1885).

Cairnes, J. E., "International Law." *Fortnightly Review* (November 1865).

Cruikshank, R. J., *Roaring Century* (London, 1946).

Dictionary of National Biography, The, 27 vols. (Oxford, 1968).

Taylor, A. J. P., 'Otto Bismarck', *Encyclopaedia Britannica*, 1962, III 659–668.

———. *The Struggle for Mastery in Europe 1848–1918* (Oxford, 1954).

———. *The Origins of the Second World War* (London, 1964).

Reading 5.4

Imperialism, the Highest Stage of Capitalism
V. I. LENIN

THE EXPORT OF CAPITAL

Under the old capitalism, when free competition prevailed, the export of goods was the most typical feature. Under modern capitalism, when monopolies prevail, the export of capital has become the typical feature.

Capitalism is commodity production at the highest stage of development, when labour power itself becomes a commodity. The growth of internal exchange, and particularly of international exchange, is the characteristic distinguishing feature of capitalism. The uneven and spasmodic character of the development of individual enterprises, of individual branches of industry and individual countries, is inevitable under the capitalist system. England became a capitalist country before any other, and in the middle of the nineteenth century, having adopted free trade, claimed to be the "workshop of the world," the great purveyor of manufactured goods to all countries, which in exchange were to keep her supplied with raw materials. But in the last quarter of the nineteenth century, *this* monopoly was already undermined. Other countries, protecting

Source: V. I. Lenin, Imperialism, the Highest Stage of Capitalism. *Copyright 1939. Reprinted with permission of International Publishers. Chapters 4–7, originally published in 1917.*

themselves by tariff walls, had developed into independent capitalist states. On the threshold of the twentieth century, we see a new type of monopoly coming into existence. Firstly, there are monopolist capitalist combines in all advanced capitalist countries; secondly, a few rich countries, in which the accumulation of capital reaches gigantic proportions, occupy a monopolist position. An enormous "superabundance of capital" has accumulated in the advanced countries.

It goes without saying that if capitalism could develop agriculture, which today lags far behind industry everywhere, if it could raise the standard of living of the masses, who are everywhere still poverty-stricken and underfed, in spite of the amazing advance in technical knowledge, there could be no talk of a superabundance of capital. This "argument" the petty-bourgeois critics of capitalism advance on every occasion. But if capitalism did these things it would not be capitalism; for uneven development and wretched conditions of the masses are fundamental and inevitable conditions and premises of this mode of production. As long as capitalism remains what it is, surplus capital will never be utilized for the purpose of raising the standard of living of the masses in a given country, for this would mean a decline in profits for the capitalists; it will be used for the purpose of increasing those profits by exporting capital abroad to the backward countries. In these backward countries profits are usually high, for capital is scarce, the price of land is relatively low, wages are low, raw materials are cheap. The possibility of exporting capital is created by the fact that numerous backward countries have been drawn into international capitalist intercourse; main railways have either been built or are being built there; the elementary conditions for industrial development have been created, etc. The necessity for exporting capital arises from the fact that in a few countries capitalism has become "over-ripe" and (owing to the backward state of agriculture and the impoverished state of the masses) capital cannot find "profitable" investment. . . .

THE DIVISION OF THE WORLD AMONG CAPITALIST COMBINES

Monopolist capitalist combines—cartels, syndicates, trusts—divide among themselves, first of all, the whole internal market of a country, and impose their control, more or less completely, upon the industry of that country. But under capitalism the home market is inevitably bound up with the foreign market. Capitalism long ago created a world market. As the export of capital increased, and as the foreign and colonial relations and the "spheres of influence" of the big monopolist combines expanded, things "naturally" gravitated towards an international agreement among these combines, and towards the formation of international cartels. . . .

International cartels show to what point capitalist monopolies have developed, and they *reveal the object* of the struggle between the various capitalist groups. This last circumstance is the most important; it alone shows us the historic-economic significance of events; for the *forms* of the struggle may and do constantly change in accordance with varying, relatively particular, and temporary causes, but the *essence* of the struggle, its class *content, cannot* change while classes exist. It is easy to understand, for example, that it is in the interests of the German bourgeoisie, whose theoretical arguments have now been adopted by Kautsky (we will deal with this later), to obscure the *content* of the present economic struggle (the division of the world) and to emphasise this or that *form* of the struggle. Kautsky makes the same mistake. Of course, we have in mind not only the German bourgeoisie, but the bourgeoisie all over the world. The capitalists divide the world, not out of any particular malice, but because the degree of concentration which has been reached forces them to adopt this method in order to get profits. And they divide it in proportion to "capital," in proportion to "strength," because there cannot be any other system of division under commodity production and capitalism. But strength varies with the degree of economic and political development. In order to understand what takes place, it is necessary to know what questions are settled by this change of forces. The question as to whether these changes are "purely" economic or *non*-economic (*e.g.*, military) is a secondary one, which does not in the least affect the fundamental view on the latest epoch of capitalism. To substitute for the question of the *content* of the struggle and agreements between capitalist combines the question of the *form* of these struggles and agreements (today peaceful, tomorrow war-like, the next day war-like again) is to sink to the role of a sophist.

The epoch of modern capitalism shows us that certain relations are established between capitalist alliances, *based* on the economic division of the world; while parallel with this fact and in connection with it, certain relations are established between political alliances, between states, on the basis of the territorial division of the world, of the struggle for colonies, of the "struggle for economic territory."

THE DIVISION OF THE WORLD AMONG THE GREAT POWERS

In his book, *The Territorial Development of the European Colonies*, A. Supan, the geographer, gives the following brief summary of this development at the end of the nineteenth century:

Percentage of Territories Belonging to the European Colonial Powers (Including United States)			
	1876	1900	Increase or Decrease
Africa	10.8	90.4	+79.6
Polynesia	56.8	98.9	+42.1
Asia	51.5	56.6	+15.1
Australia	100.0	100.0	—
America	27.5	27.2	−0.3

"The characteristic feature of this period," he concludes, "is therefore, the division of Africa and Polynesia."

As there are no unoccupied territories—that is, territories that do not belong to any state—in Asia and America, Mr. Supan's conclusion must be carried further, and we must say that the characteristic feature of this period is the final partition of the globe—not in the sense that a *new* partition is impossible—on the contrary, new partitions are possible and inevitable—but in the sense that the colonial policy of the capitalist countries has *completed* the seizure of the unoccupied territories on our planet. For the first time the world is completely divided up, so that in the future *only* redivision is possible; territories can only pass from one "owner" to another, instead of passing as unowned territory to an "owner."

Hence, we are passing through a peculiar period of world colonial policy, which is closely associated with the "latest stage in the development of capitalism," with finance capital. For this reason, it is essential first of all to deal in detail with the facts, in order to ascertain exactly what distinguishes this period from those preceding it, and what the present situation is. In the first place, two questions of fact arise here. Is an intensification of colonial policy, an intensification of the struggle for colonies, observed precisely in this period of finance capital? And how, in this respect, is the world divided at the present time?

The American writer, Morris, in his book on the history of colonization[1] has made an attempt to compile data on the colonial possessions of Great Britain, France and Germany during different periods of the nineteenth century. The following is a brief summary of the results he has obtained:

For Great Britain, the period of the enormous expansion of colonial conquests is that between 1860 and 1880, and it was also very considerable in the last twenty years of the nineteenth century. For France and Germany this period falls precisely in these last twenty years. We saw above that the apex of premonopoly capitalist development, of capitalism in which free competition was predominant, was reached in the 'sixties and 'seventies of the last century. We now see that it is *precisely after that period* that the "boom" in colonial annexations begins, and that the struggle for the territorial division of the world becomes extraordinarily keen. It is beyond doubt, therefore, that capitalism's transition to the stage of monopoly capitalism, to finance capital, is *bound up* with the intensification of the struggle for the partition of the world.

Colonial Possessions (Million square miles and million inhabitants)						
	Great Britain		France		Germany	
	Area	Pop.	Area	Pop.	Area	Pop.
1815–30	?	126.4	0.02	0.5	—	
1860	2.5	145.1	0.2	3.4	—	
1880	7.7	267.9	0.7	7.5	—	
1899	9.3	309.0	3.7	56.4	1.0	14.7

Hobson, in his work on imperialism, marks the years 1884–1900 as the period of the intensification of the colonial "expansion" of the chief European states. According to his estimate, Great Britain during these years acquired 3,700,000 square miles of territory with a population of 57,000,000; France acquired 3,600,000 square miles with a population of 16,700,000; Belgium 900,000 square miles with 30,000,000 inhabitants; Portugal 800,000 square miles with 9,000,000 inhabitants. The quest for colonies by all the capitalist states at the end of the nineteenth century and particularly since the 1880's is a commonly known fact in the history of diplomacy and of foreign affairs.

When free competition in Great Britain was at its zenith, *i.e.*, between 1840 and 1860, the leading British bourgeois politicians were opposed to colonial policy and were of the opinion that the liberation of the colonies and their complete separation from Britain was inevitable and desirable. M. Beer, in an article, "Modern British Imperialism,"[2] published in 1898, shows that in 1852, Disraeli, a statesman generally inclined towards imperialism, declared: "The colonies are millstones round our necks." But at the end of the nineteenth century the heroes of the hour in England were Cecil Rhodes and Joseph Chamberlain, open advocates of imperialism, who applied the imperialist policy in the most cynical manner.

It is not without interest to observe that even at the time these leading British bourgeois politicians fully appreciated the connection between what might be called the purely economic and the politico-social roots of modern imperialism. Chamberlain advocated imperialism by calling it a "true, wise and economical policy," and he pointed particularly to the German, American and Belgian competition which Great Britain was encountering in the world market. Salvation lies in monopolies, said the capitalists as they formed cartels, syndicates and trusts. Salvation lies in monopolies, echoed the political leaders of the bourgeoisie, hastening to appropriate the parts of the world not yet shared out. The journalist, Stead, relates the following remarks uttered by his close friend Cecil Rhodes, in 1895, regarding his imperialist ideas:

> I was in the East End of London yesterday and attended a meeting of the unemployed. I listened to the wild speeches, which were just a cry for 'bread,' 'bread,' 'bread,' and on my way home I pondered over the scene and I became more than ever convinced of the importance of imperialism. . . . My cherished idea is a solution for the social problem, *i.e.*, in order to save the 40,000,000 inhabitants of the United Kingdom from a bloody civil war, we colonial statesmen must acquire new lands to settle the surplus population, to provide new markets for the goods produced by them in the factories and mines. The Empire, as I have always said, is a bread and butter question. If you want to avoid civil war, you must become imperialists. . . .[3]

IMPERIALISM AS A SPECIAL STAGE OF CAPITALISM

We must now try to sum up and put together what has been said above on the subject of imperialism. Imperialism emerged as the development and direct continuation of the fundamental attributes of capitalism in general. But capitalism only became capitalist imperialism at a definite and very high stage of its development, when certain of its fundamental attributes began to be transformed into their opposites, when the features of a period of transition from capitalism to a higher social and economic system began to take shape and reveal themselves all along the line. Economically, the main thing in this process is the substitution of capitalist monopolies for capitalist free competition. Free competition is the fundamental attribute of capitalism, and of commodity production generally. Monopoly is exactly the opposite of free competition; but we have seen the latter being transformed into monopoly before our very eyes, creating large-scale industry and eliminating small industry, replacing large-scale industry by still larger-scale industry, finally leading to such a concentration of production and capital that monopoly has been and is the result: cartels, syndicates and trusts, and merging with them, the capital of a dozen or so banks manipulating thousands of millions. At the same time monopoly, which has grown out of free competition, does not abolish the latter, but exists over it and alongside of it, and thereby gives rise to a number of very acute, intense antagonisms, friction and conflicts. Monopoly is the transition from capitalism to a higher system.

If it were necessary to give the briefest possible definition of imperialism we should have to say that imperialism is the monopoly stage of capitalism. Such a definition would include what is most important, for, on the one hand, finance capital is the bank capital of a few big monopolist banks, merged with the capital of the monopolist combines of manufacturers; and, on the other hand, the division of the world is the transition from a colonial policy which has extended without hindrance to territories unoccupied by any capitalist power, to a colonial policy of monopolistic possession of the territory of the world which has been completely divided up.

But very brief definitions, although convenient, for they sum up the main points, are nevertheless inadequate, because very important features of the phenomenon that has to be defined have to be especially deduced. And so, without forgetting the conditional and relative value of all definitions, which can never include all the concatenations of a phenomenon in its complete development, we must give a definition of imperialism that will embrace the following five essential features:

1. The concentration of production and capital developed to such a high stage that it created monopolies which play a decisive role in economic life.
2. The merging of bank capital with industrial capital, and the creation, on the basis of this "finance capital," of a "financial oligarchy."
3. The export of capital, which has become extremely important, as distinguished from the export of commodities.
4. The formation of international capitalist monopolies which share the world among themselves.
5. The territorial division of the whole world among the greatest capitalist powers is completed. . . .

Finance capital and the trusts are increasing instead of diminishing the differences in the rate of development of the various parts of world economy. When the relation of forces is changed, how else, *under capitalism*, can the solution of contradictions be found, except by resorting to *violence*? Railway statistics provide remarkably exact data on the different rates of development of capitalism and finance capital in world economy. In the last decades of imperialist development, the total length of railways has changed as follows:

Railways (thousand kilometers)			
	1890	1913	Increase
Europe	224	346	122
U.S.A.	268	411	143
Colonies (total)	82 ⎫	210 ⎫	128 ⎫
Independent and semi-dependent states of Asia and America	⎬ 125	⎬ 347	⎬ 222
	43 ⎭	137 ⎭	94 ⎭
Total	617	1,104	

Thus, the development of railways has been more rapid in the colonies and in the independent (and semi-dependent) states of Asia and America. Here, as we know, the finance capital of the four or five biggest capitalist states reigns undisputed. Two hundred thousand kilometres of new railways in the colonies and in the other countries of Asia and America represent more than 40,000,000,000 marks in capital, newly invested on particularly advantageous terms, with special guarantees of a good return and with profitable orders for steel works, etc.

Capitalism is growing with the greatest rapidity in the colonies and in overseas countries. Among the latter, *new* imperialist powers are emerging (*e.g.*, Japan). The struggle of world imperialism is becoming more acute. The tribute levied by finance capital on the most profitable colonial and overseas enterprises is increasing. In sharing out this "booty," an exceptionally large part goes to countries which, as far as the development of productive forces is concerned, do not always stand at the top of the list. In the case of the biggest countries, considered with their colonies, the total length of railways was as follows (in thousands of kilometres):

	1890	1913	Increase
U.S.A.	268	413	145
British Empire	107	208	101
Russia	32	78	46
Germany	43	68	25
France	41	63	22
Total	491	830	339

Thus, about 80 percent of the total existing railways are concentrated in the hands of the five Great Powers. But the concentration of the *ownership* of these railways of finance capital, is much greater still: French and English millionaires, for example, own an enormous amount of stocks and bonds in American, Russian and other railways.

Thanks to her colonies, Great Britain has increased the length of "her" railways by 100,000 kilometres, four times as much as Germany. And yet, it is well known that the development of productive forces in Germany, and especially the development of the coal and iron industries, has been much more rapid during this period than in England—not to mention France and Russia. In 1892, Germany produced 4,900,000 tons of pig iron and Great Britain produced 6,800,000 tons; in 1912 Germany produced 17,600,000 tons and Great Britain 9,000,000 tons. Germany, therefore, had an overwhelming superiority over England in this respect. We ask, is there *under capitalism* any means of removing the disparity between the development of productive forces and the accumulation of capital on the one side, and the division of colonies and "spheres of influence" for finance capital on the other side—other than by resorting to war?

NOTES

1 Henry C. Morris, *The History of Colonization*, New York, 1900, II, p. 88; I, pp. 304, 419.
2 *Die Neue Zeit*, XVI, I, 1898, p. 302.
3 Ibid., p. 304.

Reading 5.5

Imperialism and Capitalism *JOSEPH SCHUMPETER*

Our analysis of the historical evidence has shown, first, the unquestionable fact that "objectless" tendencies toward forcible expansion, without definite, utilitarian limits—that is, non-rational and irrational, purely instinctual inclinations toward war and conquest—play a very large role in the history of mankind. It may sound paradoxical, but numberless wars—perhaps the majority of all wars—have been waged without adequate "reason"—not so much from the moral viewpoint as from that of reasoned and

---

Source: Joseph Schumpeter, "Imperialism and Capitalism," in Imperialism/Social Classes: Two Essays *by Joseph Schumpeter, Heinz Norden, trans. (Cleveland: World, 1968), originally published in 1919.*

reasonable interest. The most herculean efforts of the nations, in other words, have faded into the empty air. Our analysis, in the second place, provides an explanation for this drive to action, this will to war—a theory by no means exhausted by mere references to the "urge" or an "instinct." The explanation lies, instead, in the vital needs of situations that molded peoples and classes into warriors—if they wanted to avoid extinction—and in the fact that psychological dispositions and social structures acquired in the dim past in such situations, once firmly established, tend to maintain themselves and to continue in effect long after they have lost their meaning and their life-preserving function. Our analysis, in the third place, has shown the existence of subsidiary factors that facilitate the survival of such dispositions and structures—factors that may be divided into two groups. The orientation toward war is mainly fostered by the domestic interests of ruling classes, but also by the influence of all those who stand to gain individually from war policy, whether economically or socially. Both groups of factors are generally overgrown by elements of an altogether different character, not only in terms of political phraseology, but also of psychological motivation. Imperialisms differ greatly in detail, but they all have at least these traits in common, turning them into a single phenomenon in the field of sociology, as we noted in the introduction.

Imperialism thus is atavistic in character. It falls into that large group of surviving features from earlier ages that play such an important part in every concrete social situations. In other words, it is an element that stems from the living conditions, not of the present, but of the past—or, put in terms of the economic interpretation of history, from past rather than present relations of production. It is an atavism in the social structure, in individual, psychological habits of emotional reaction. Since the vital needs that created it have passed away for good, it too must gradually disappear, even though every warlike involvement, no matter how non-imperialist in character, tends to revive it. It tends to disappear as a structural element because the structure that brought it to the fore goes into a decline, giving way, in the course of social development, to other structures that have no room for it and eliminate the power factors that supported it. It tends to disappear as an element of habitual emotional reaction, because of the progressive rationalization of life and mind, a process in which old functional needs are absorbed by new tasks, in which heretofore military energies are functionally modified. If our theory is correct, cases of imperialism should decline in intensity the later they occur in the history of a people and of a culture. Our most recent examples of unmistakable, clear-cut imperialism are the absolute monarchies of the eighteenth century. They are unmistakably "more civilized" than their predecessors.

It is from absolute autocracy that the present age has taken over what imperialist tendencies it displays. And the imperialism of absolute autocracy flourished before the Industrial Revolution that created the modern world, or rather, before the consequences of that revolution began to be felt in all their aspects. These two statements are primarily meant in a historical sense, and as such they are no more than self-evident. We shall nevertheless try, within the framework of our theory, to define the significance of capitalism for our phenomenon and to examine the relationship between present-day imperialist tendencies and the autocratic imperialism of the eighteenth century.

The flood tide that burst the dams in the Industrial Revolution had its sources, of course, back in the Middle Ages. But capitalism began to shape society and impress its stamp on every page of social history only with the second half of the eighteenth century. Before that time there had been only islands of capitalist economy imbedded in an ocean of village and urban economy. True, certain political influences emanated from these islands, but they were able to assert themselves only indirectly. Not until the process we term the Industrial Revolution did the working masses, led by the entrepreneur, overcome the bonds of older life-forms—the environment of peasantry, guild, and aristocracy. The causal connection was this: a transformation in the basic economic factors (which need not detain us here) created the objective opportunity for the production of commodities, for large-scale industry, working for a market of customers whose individual identities were unknown, operating solely with a view to maximum financial profit. It was this opportunity that created an economically oriented leadership—personalities whose field of achievement was the organization of such commodity production in the form of capitalist enterprise. Successful enterprises in large numbers represented something new in the economic and social sense. They fought for and won freedom of action. They compelled state policy to adapt itself to their needs. More and more they attracted the most vigorous leaders from other spheres, as well as the manpower of those spheres, causing them and the social strata they represented to languish. Capitalist entrepreneurs fought the former ruling circles for a share in state control, for leadership in the state. The very fact of their success, their position, their resources, their power, raised them in the political and social scale. Their mode of life, their cast of mind became increasingly important elements on the social scene. . . .

A purely capitalist world therefore can offer no fertile soil to imperialist impulses. That does not mean that it cannot still maintain an interest in imperialist expansion. We shall discuss this immediately. The point is that its people are likely to be essentially of an unwarlike disposition. Hence we must expect that anti-imperialist tendencies will show themselves wherever capitalism penetrates the economy and, through the economy, the mind of modern nations—most strongly, of course, where capitalism itself is strongest, where it has advanced furthest, encountered the least resistance, and preeminently where its types and hence democracy—in the "bourgeois" sense—come closest to political dominion. We must further expect that the types formed by capitalism will actually be the carriers of these tendencies. Is such the case? The facts that follow are cited to show that this expectation, which flows from our theory, is in fact justified.

(1) Throughout the world of capitalism, and specifically among the elements formed by capitalism in modern social life, there has arisen a fundamental opposition to war, expansion, cabinet diplomacy, armaments, and socially entrenched professional armies. This opposition had its origin in the country that first turned capitalist—England—and arose coincidentally

with that country's capitalist development. "Philosophical radicalism" was the first politically influential intellectual movement to represent this trend successfully, linking it up, as was to be expected, with economic freedom in general and free trade in particular. Molesworth became a cabinet member, even though he had publicly declared—on the occasion of the Canadian revolution—that he prayed for the defeat of his country's arms. In step with the advance of capitalism, the movement also gained adherents elsewhere— though at first only adherents without influence. It found support in Paris— indeed, in a circle oriented toward capitalist enterprise (for example, Frédéric Passy). True, pacifism as a matter of principle had existed before, though only among a few small religious sects. But modern pacifism, in its political foundations if not its derivation, is unquestionably a phenomenon of the capitalist world.

(2) Wherever capitalism penetrated, peace parties of such strength arose that virtually every war meant a political struggle on the domestic scene. The exceptions are rare—Germany in the Franco-Prussian war of 1870–1871, both belligerents in the Russo-Turkish war of 1877–1878. That is why every war is carefully justified as a defensive war by the governments involved, and by all the political parties, in their official utterances—indicating a realization that a war of a different nature would scarcely be tenable in a political sense. (Here too the Russo-Turkish war is an exception, but a significant one.) In former times this would not have been necessary. Reference to an interest or pretense at moral justification was customary as early as the eighteenth century, but only in the nineteenth century did the assertion of attack, or the threat of attack, become the only avowed occasion for war. In the distant past, imperialism had needed no disguise whatever, and in the absolute autocracies only a very transparent one; but today imperialism is carefully hidden from public view—even though there may still be unofficial appeal to warlike instincts. No people and no ruling class today can openly afford to regard war as a normal state of affairs or a normal element in the life of nations. No one doubts that today it must be characterized as an abnormality and a disaster. True, war is still glorified. But glorification in the style of King Tuglâti-palisharra is rare and unleashes such a storm of indignation that every practical politician carefully dissociates himself from such things. Everywhere there is official acknowledgment that peace is an end in itself—though not necessarily an end overshadowing all purposes that can be realized by means of war. Every expansionist urge must be carefully related to a concrete goal. All this is primarily a matter of political phraseology, to be sure. But the necessity for this phraseology is a symptom of the popular attitude. And that attitude makes a policy of imperialism more and more difficult—indeed, the very word imperialism is applied only to the enemy, in a reproachful sense, being carefully avoided with reference to the speaker's own policies. . . .

Capitalism is by nature anti-imperialist. Hence we cannot readily derive from it such imperialist tendencies as actually exist, but must evidently see them only as alien elements, carried into the world of capitalism from the outside, supported by non-capitalist factors in modern life. The survival of interest in a policy of forcible expansion does not, by itself, alter these facts—not even, it must be steadily emphasized, from the viewpoint of the economic interpretation of history. For objective interests become effective—and, what is important, become powerful political factors—only when they correspond to attitudes of the people or of sufficiently powerful strata.

. . . The national economy as a whole, of course, is impoverished by the tremendous excess in consumption brought on by war. It is, to be sure, conceivable that either the capitalists or the workers might make certain gains as a class, namely, if the volume either of capital or of labor should decline in such a way that the remainder receives a greater share in the social product and that, even from the absolute viewpoint, the total sum of interest or wages becomes greater than it was before. But these advantages cannot be considerable. They are probably, for the most part, more than outweighed by the burdens imposed by war and by losses sustained abroad. Thus the gain of the capitalists as a class cannot be a motive for war—and it is this gain that counts, for any advantage to the working class would be contingent on a large number of workers falling in action or otherwise perishing. There remain the entrepreneurs in the war industries, in the broader sense, possibly also the large landowner—a small but powerful minority. Their war profits are always sure to be an important supporting element. But few will go so far as to assert that this element alone is sufficient to orient the people of the capitalist world along imperialist lines. At most, an interest in expansion may make the capitalist allies of those who stand for imperialist trends.

It may be stated as being beyond controversy that where free trade prevails *no* class has an interest in forcible expansion as such. For in such a case the citizens and goods of every nation can move in foreign countries as freely as though those countries were politically their own—free trade implying far more than mere freedom from tariffs. In a genuine state of free trade, foreign raw materials and foodstuffs are as accessible to each nation as though they were within its own territory. Where the cultural backwardness of a region makes normal economic intercourse dependent on colonization, it does not matter, assuming free trade, which of the "civilized" nations undertakes the task of colonization. . . .

The gain lies in the enlargement of the commodity supply by means of the division of labor among nations, rather than in the profits and wages of the export industry and the carrying trade. For these profits and wages would be reaped even if there were no export, in which case import, the necessary complement, would also vanish. Not even monopoly interests—if they existed—would be disposed toward imperialism in such a case. For under free trade only *international* cartels would be possible. Under a system of free trade there would be conflicts in economic interest neither among different nations nor among the corresponding classes of different nations. And since protectionism is not an essential characteristic of the capitalist economy—otherwise the English national economy would scarcely be capitalist—it is apparent that any economic interest in forcible expansion on the part of a people or a class is not necessarily a product of capitalism. . . .

Consider which strata of the capitalist world are actually economically benefitted by protective tariffs. They do harm to both workers and capitalists—in contrast to entrepreneurs—not only in their role as consumers, but also as producers. The damage to consumers is universal, that to producers almost so. As for entrepreneurs, they have benefitted only by the tariff that happens to be levied on their own product. But this advantage is substantially reduced by the countermeasures adopted by other countries—universally, except in the case of England—and by the effect of the tariff on the prices of other articles, especially those which they require for their own productive process. Why, then, are entrepreneurs so strongly in favor of protective tariffs? The answer is simple. Each industry hopes to score *special* gains in the struggle of political intrigue, thus enabling it to realize a net gain. Moreover, every decline in freight rates, every advance in production abroad, is likely to affect the economic balance, making it necessary for domestic enterprises to adapt themselves, indeed often to turn to other lines of endeavor. This is a difficult task to which not everyone is equal. Within the industrial organism of every nation there survive antiquated methods of doing business that would cause enterprises to succumb to foreign competition—because of poor management rather than lack of capital, for before 1914 the banks were almost forcing capital on the entrepreneurs. If, still, in most countries virtually *all* entrepreneurs are protectionists, this is owing to a reason which we shall presently discuss. Without that reason, their attitude would be different. The fact that all industries today demand tariff protection must not blind us to the fact that even the entrepreneur interest is not unequivocally protectionist. For this demand is only the consequence of a protectionism already in existence, of a protectionist spirit springing from the economic interests of relatively small entrepreneur groups and from non-capitalist elements—a spirit that ultimately carried along all groups, occasionally even the representatives of working-class interests. Today the protective tariff confers its full and immediate benefits—or comes close to conferring them—only on the large landowners. . . .

Trade and industry of the early capitalist period . . . remained strongly pervaded with precapitalist methods, bore the stamp of autocracy, and served its interests, either willingly or by force. With its traditional habits of feeling, thinking, and acting molded along such lines, the bourgeoisie entered the Industrial Revolution. It was shaped, in other words, by the needs and interests of an environment that was essentially non-capitalist, or at least precapitalist—needs stemming not from the nature of the capitalist economy as such but from the fact of the coexistence of early capitalism with another and at first overwhelmingly powerful mode of life and business. Established habits of thought and action tend to persist, and hence the spirit of guild and monopoly at first maintained itself, and was only slowly undermined, even where capitalism did not fully prevail *anywhere* on the Continent. Existing economic interests, "artificially" shaped by the autocratic state, remained dependent on the "protection" of the state. The industrial organism, such as it was, would not have been able to withstand free competition. Even where the old barriers crumbled in the autocratic state, the people did not all at once flock to the clear track. They were creatures of mercantilism and even earlier periods, and many of them huddled together and protested against the affront of being forced to depend on their own ability. They cried for paternalism, for protection, for forcible restraint of strangers, and above all for tariffs. They met with partial success, particularly because capitalism failed to take radical action in the agrarian field. Capitalism did bring about many changes on the land, springing in part from its automatic mechanisms, in part from the political trends it engendered—abolition of serfdom, freeing the soil from feudal entanglements, and so on—but initially it did not alter the basic outlines of the social structure of the countryside. Even less did it affect the spirit of the people, and least of all their political goals. This explains why the features and trends of autocracy—including imperialism—proved so resistant, why they exerted such a powerful influence on capitalist development, why the old export monopolism could live on and merge into the new.

These are facts of fundamental significance to an understanding of the soul of modern Europe. Had the ruling class of the Middle Ages—the war-oriented nobility—changed its profession and function and become the ruling class of the capitalist world; or had developing capitalism swept it away, put it out of business, instead of merely clashing head-on with it in the agrarian sphere—then much would have been different in the life of modern peoples. But as things actually were, neither eventuality occurred; or, more correctly, both are taking place, only at a very slow pace. The two groups of landowners remain social classes clearly distinguishable from the groupings of the capitalist world. The social pyramid of the present age has been formed, not by the substance and laws of capitalism alone, but by two different social substances, and by the laws of two different epochs. Whoever seeks to understand Europe must not forget this and concentrate all attention on the indubitably basic truth that one of these substances tends to be absorbed by the other and thus the sharpest of all class conflicts tends to be eliminated. Whoever seeks to understand Europe must not overlook that even today its life, its ideology, its politics are greatly under the influence of the feudal "substance," that while the bourgeoisie can assert its interests everywhere, it "rules" only in exceptional circumstances, and then only briefly. The bourgeois outside his office and the professional man of capitalism outside his profession cut a very sorry figure. Their spiritual leader is the rootless "intellectual," a slender reed open to every impulse and a prey to unrestrained emotionalism. The "feudal" elements, on the other hand, have both feet on the ground, even psychologically speaking. Their ideology is as stable as their mode of life. They believe certain things to be really true, others to be really false. This quality of possessing a definite character and cast of mind as a class, this simplicity and solidity of social and spiritual position extends their power far beyond their actual bases, gives them the ability to assimilate new elements, to make others serve their purposes—in a word, gives them *prestige*, something to which the bourgeois, as is well known, always looks up, something with which he tends to ally himself, despite all actual conflicts.

The nobility entered the modern world in the form into which it had been shaped by the autocratic state—the same state that had also molded the bourgeoisie. It was the sovereign who disciplined the nobility, instilled loyalty into it, "statized" it, and, as we have shown, imperialized it. He turned its nationalist sentiments—as in the case of the bourgeoisie—into an aggressive nationalism, and then made it a pillar of his organization, particularly his war machine. It had not been that in the immediately preceding period. Rising absolutism had at first availed itself of much more dependent organs. For that very reason in his position as leader of the feudal powers and as warlord, the sovereign survived the onset of the Industrial Revolution, and as a rule—except in France—won victory over political revolution. The bourgeoisie did not simply supplant the sovereign, nor did it make him its leader, as did the nobility. It merely wrested a portion of his power from him and for the rest submitted to him. It did not take over from the sovereign the state as an abstract form of organization. The state remained a special social power, confronting the bourgeoisie. In some countries it has continued to play that role to the present day. It is in the *state* that the bourgeoisie with its interests seeks refuge, protection against external and even domestic enemies. The bourgeoisie seeks to win over the state for itself, and in return serves the state and state interests that are different from its own. Imbued with the spirit of the old autocracy, trained by it, the bourgeoisie often takes over its ideology, even where, as in France, the sovereign is eliminated and the official power of the nobility has been broken. Because the sovereign needed soldiers, the modern bourgeois—at least in his slogans—is an even more vehement advocate of an increasing population. Because the sovereign was in a position to exploit conquests, needed them to be a victorious warlord, the bourgeoisie thirsts for national glory—even in France, worshiping a headless body, as it were. Because the sovereign found a large gold hoard useful, the bourgeoisie even today cannot be swerved from its bullionist prejudices. Because the autocratic state paid attention to the trader and manufacturer chiefly as the most important sources of taxes and credits, today even the intellectual who has not a shred of property looks on international commerce, not from the viewpoint of the consumer, but from that of the trader and exporter. Because pugnacious sovereigns stood in constant fear of attack by their equally pugnacious neighbors, the modern bourgeois attributes aggressive designs to neighboring peoples. All such modes of thought are essentially noncapitalist. Indeed, they vanish most quickly wherever capitalism fully prevails. They are survivals of the autocratic alignment of interests, and they endure wherever the autocratic state endures on the old basis and with the old orientation, even though more and more democratized and otherwise transformed. They bear witness to the extent to which essentially imperialist absolutism has patterned not only the economy of the bourgeoisie but also its mind—in the interests of autocracy and against those of the bourgeoisie itself.

This significant dichotomy in the bourgeois mind—which in part explains its wretched weakness in politics, culture and life generally; earns it the understandable contempt of the Left and the Right; and proves the accuracy of our diagnosis—is best exemplified by two phenomena that are very close to our subject: present-day nationalism and militarism. Nationalism is affirmative awareness of national character, together with an aggressive sense of superiority. It arose from the autocratic state. In conservatives, nationalism in general is understandable as an inherited orientation, as a mutation of the battle instincts of the medieval knights, and finally as a political stalking horse on the domestic scene; and conservatives are fond of reproaching the bourgeois with a lack of nationalism, which from their point of view, is evaluated in a positive sense. Socialists, on the other hand, equally understandably exclude nationalism from their general ideology, because of the essential interests of the proletariat, and by virtue of their domestic opposition to the conservative stalking horse; they, in turn, not only reproach the bourgeoisie with an excess of nationalism (which they, of course, evaluate in a negative sense) but actually identify nationalism and even the very idea of the nation with bourgeois ideology. The curious thing is that both of these groups are right in their criticism of the bourgeoisie. For, as we have seen, the mode of life that flows logically from the nature of capitalism necessarily implies an anti-nationalist orientation in politics and culture. This orientation actually prevails. We find a great many anti-nationalist members of the middle class, and even more who merely parrot the catchwords of nationalism. In the capitalist world it is actually not big business and industry at all that are the carriers of nationalist trends, but the intellectual, and the content of *his* ideology is explained not so much from definite class interests as from chance emotion and individual interest. But the submission of the bourgeoisie to the powers of autocracy, its alliance with them, its economic and psychological patterning by them—all these tend to push the bourgeois in a nationalist direction; and this too we find prevalent, especially among the chief exponents of export monopolism. The relationship between the bourgeoisie and militarism is quite similar. Militarism is not necessarily a foregone conclusion when a nation maintains a large army, but only when high military circles become a political power. The criterion is whether leading generals as such wield political influence and whether the responsible statesmen can act only with their consent. That is possible only when the officer corps is linked to a definite social class, as in Japan, and can assimilate to its position individuals who do not belong to it by birth. Militarism too is rooted in the autocratic state. And again the same reproaches are made against the bourgeois from both sides—quite properly too. According to the "pure" capitalist mode of life, the bourgeois is unwarlike. The alignment of capitalist interests should make him utterly reject military methods, put him in opposition to the professional soldier. Significantly, we see this in the example of England where, first, the struggle against a standing army generally and, next, opposition to its elaboration, furnished bourgeois politicians with their most popular slogan: "retrenchment." Even naval appropriations have encountered resistance. We find similar trends in other countries, though they are less strongly developed. The continental bourgeois, however, was used to the sight of troops. He regarded an army almost as a necessary component of the social order, ever since it had been his terrible taskmaster in the Thirty Years' War. He had no power at all to abolish the army. He might have done so if he had had the power; but not having it, he considered the fact that the army might be useful to him. In his "artificial" economic situation and because of his submission to the sovereign, he thus grew disposed toward militarism, especially where export monopolism flourished. The intellectuals, many of whom still maintained special relationships with feudal elements, were so disposed to an even greater degree.

Just as we once found a dichotomy in the social pyramid, so now we find everywhere, in every aspect of the bourgeois portion of the modern world, a dichotomy of attitudes and interests. Our examples also show in what way the two components work together. Nationalism and militarism, while not creatures of capitalism, become "capitalized" and in the end draw their best energies from capitalism. Capitalism involves them in its workings and thereby keeps them alive, politically as well as economically. And they, in turn, affect capitalism, cause it to deviate from the course it might have followed alone, support many of its interests.

Here we find that we have penetrated to the historical as well as the sociological sources of modern imperialism. It does not *coincide* with nationalism and militarism, though it *fuses* with them by supporting them as it is supported by them. It too is—not only historically, but also sociologically—a heritage of the autocratic state, of its structural elements, organizational forms, interest alignments, and human attitudes, the outcome of precapitalist forces which the autocratic state has reorganized, in part by the methods of early capitalism. It would never have been evolved by the "inner logic" of capitalism itself. This is true even of mere export monopolism. It too has its sources in absolutist policy and the action habits of an essentially precapitalist environment. That it was able to develop to its present dimensions is owing to the momentum of a situation once created, which continued to engender ever new "artificial" economic structures, that is, those which maintain themselves by political power alone. In most of the countries addicted to export monopolism it is also owing to the fact that the old autocratic state and the old attitude of the bourgeoisie toward it were so vigorously maintained. But export monopolism, to go a step further, is not yet imperialism. And even if it had been able to arise without protective tariffs, it would never have developed into imperialism in the hands of an unwarlike bourgeoisie. If this did happen, it was only because the heritage included the war machine, together with its sociopsychological aura and aggressive bent, and because a class oriented toward war maintained itself in a ruling position. This class clung to its domestic interest in war, and the promilitary interests among the bourgeoisie were able to ally themselves with it. This alliance kept alive war instincts and ideas of overlordship, male supremacy, and triumphant glory—ideas that would have otherwise long since died. It led to social conditions that, while they ultimately stem from the conditions of production, cannot be explained from capitalist production methods alone. And it often impresses its mark on present-day politics, threatening Europe with the constant danger of war. . . .

The only point at issue here was to demonstrate, by means of an important example, the ancient truth that the dead always rule the living.

Reading 5.6

War as Policy   ALAN S. MILWARD

For Warre, consisteth not in Battell onely, or the act of fighting; but in a tract of time, wherein the will to contend by Battell is sufficiently known: and therefore the notion of Time, is to be considered in the nature of Warre; as it is in the nature of Weather. For as the nature of Foule weather, lyeth not in a shower or two of rain; but in an inclination thereto of many days together: So the nature of Warre, consisteth not in actual fighting; but in the known disposition thereto, during all the time there is no assurance to the contrary. All other time is Peace.

—*Thomas Hobbes, Leviathan, 1651*

There are two commonly accepted ideas about war which have little foundation in history. One is that war is an abnormality. The other is that with the passage of time warfare has become costlier and deadlier. The first of these ideas established itself in the eighteenth century, when the theory of natural law was used to demonstrate that peace was a logical deduction from the material laws governing the universe or, sometimes, from the psychological laws governing mankind. The second of these ideas came to reinforce the first, which might otherwise have been weakened by the weight of contrary evidence, towards the end of the nineteenth century. The historical record of that century had not been such as to substantiate the logical deductions of eighteenth-century philosophy, for it was a century of unremitting warfare. But after 1850 a large body of economic literature began to reconcile agreeable predictions with unpleasant facts by demonstrating that in spite of the prevalence of warfare it would eventually cease to be a viable economic policy because it would price itself out of the market, a process which, it was agreed, had already begun.

Neither of these ideas has ever been completely accepted by economists but their influence on economic theory has been so powerful as to focus the operation of a substantial body of that theory on to the workings of a peace-time economy only. In spite of the fact that the world has practically never been at peace since the eighteenth century peace has usually been seen as the state of affairs most conducive to the achievement of economic aims and the one which economic theory seeks to analyze and illuminate. In the early nineteenth century, indeed, it was seen as the goal to which economic theory tended.

The frequency of war is in itself the best argument against accepting the idea of its abnormality. The second idea, that war has become more costly, is based less on a refusal to consider history than on a mistaken simplification

Source: Alan S. Milward, "War as Policy" from War, Economy and Society: 1939–1945, *pp. 1–17.*

of it. It was an idea which first gained wide credence with the development of more complicated technologies. War itself was an important stimulus to technological development in many industries in the late nineteenth century such as shipbuilding, the manufacture of steel plate and the development of machine tools. The construction of complex weapons which could only be manufactured by states at a high level of economic development seemed to change the economic possibilities of war. The first heavily armed steel battleships only narrowly preceded the adaptation of the internal combustion engine to military and then to aerial use, and these new armaments coincided with a period of enormous and growing standing armies. The productive capacities which economic development had placed in the hands of developed economies raised prospects of warfare on an absolute scale of cost and deadliness never before conceived. And these prospects in themselves seemed to indicate the economic mechanism by which war would disappear after its rather disappointing persistence in the nineteenth century. These ideas were succinctly expressed by de Molinari, one of the few economists who tried to integrate the existence of war into classical economic theory.

> Can the profits of war still cover its cost? The history of all wars which
> have occurred between civilized peoples for a number of centuries attests
> that these costs have progressively grown, and, finally that any war between
> members of the civilized community today costs the victorious nation more
> than it can possibly yield it.[1]

In the half century after de Molinari so firmly expressed his opinion there were two world wars, each of a far higher absolute cost and each responsible for greater destruction than any previous war. There is, to say the least, circumstantial evidence that de Molinari's judgement was a superficial one and that nations did not continue to go to war merely because they were ignorant of what had become its real economic consequences. War not only continued to meet the social, political and economic circumstances of states but, furthermore, as an instrument of policy, it remained, in some circumstances, economically viable. War remains a policy and investment decision by the state and there seem to be numerous modern examples of its having been a correct and successful decision. The most destructive of modern technologies have not changed this state of affairs. Their deployment by those states sufficiently highly developed economically to possess them is limited by the rarity of satisfactory strategic opportunity. The strategic synthesis by which the Vietnam war was conducted on the American side, for example, is very like the rational decisions frequently taken by all combatants in the First World War against the use of poison gas. The existence of the most costly and murderous armaments does not mean that they will be appropriate or even usable in any particular war, much less that all combinations of combatants will possess them.

The question of the economic cost of war is not one of absolutes. The cost and the effectiveness of a long-range bomber at the present time must be seen in relation to that of a long-range warship in the eighteenth century and both seen in relation to the growth of national product since the eighteenth century. In each case we are dealing with the summation of many different technological developments, and the armament itself is in each of these cases pre-eminently the expression of an extremely high relative level of economic development. The meaningful question is whether the cost of war has absorbed an increasing proportion of the increasing Gross National Products of the combatants. As an economic choice war, measured in this way, has not shown any discernible long-term trend towards greater costliness. As for its deadliness, the loss of human life is but one element in the estimation of cost. There are no humane wars, and where the economic cost of the war can be lowered by substituting labour for capital on the battlefield such a choice would be a rational one. It has been often made. The size of the Russian armies in the First World War reflected the low cost of obtaining and maintaining a Russian soldier and was intended to remedy the Russian deficiencies in more expensive capital equipment. It may be argued that modern technology changes the analysis because it offers the possibility of near-to-total destruction of the complete human and capital stock of the enemy. But numerous societies were so destroyed in the past by sword, fire and pillage and, more appositely, by primitive guns and gunpowder. The possibility of making a deliberate choice of war as economic policy has existed since the late eighteenth century and exists still.

The origins of the Second World War lay in the deliberate choice of warfare as an instrument of policy by two of the most economically developed states. Far from having economic reservations about warfare as policy, both the German and Japanese governments were influenced in their decisions for war by the conviction that war might be an instrument of economic gain. Although economic considerations were in neither case prime reasons in the decision to fight, both governments held a firmly optimistic conviction that war could be used to solve some of their more long-term economic difficulties. Instead of shouldering the economic burden of war with the leaden and apprehensive reluctance of necessity, like their opponents, both governments kept their eyes firmly fixed on the short-term social and economic benefits which might accrue from a successful war while it was being fought, as well as on the long-term benefits of victory. In making such a choice the ruling elites in both countries were governed by the difference between their own political and economic ideas and those of their opponents. The government of Italy had already made a similar choice when it had attacked Ethiopia.

This difference in economic attitudes to warfare was partly attributable to the influence of fascist political ideas. Because these ideas were also of some importance in the formulation of Axis strategy and the economic and social policies pursued by the German occupying forces it is necessary briefly to consider some of their aspects here in so far as they relate to the themes considered in this book. Whether the National Socialist government in Germany and the Italian Fascist party are properly to be bracketed together as fascist governments and indeed whether the word fascist itself has any accurate meaning as a definition of a set of precise political and economic attitudes are complicated questions which cannot be discussed here.[2] Although the Japanese government had few hesitations in using war as an instrument of political and economic policy there is no meaningful definition of the word fascist which can include the ruling elites in Japan. There was a small political group in that country whose political ideas resembled those of the Fascists and the National Socialists but they had practically no influence in the Home Islands although they did influence the policy of the Japanese military government in Manchuria.[3] But for the German and Italian rulers war had a deeper and more positive social purpose and this was related to certain shared ideas. Whether the word fascism is a useful description of the affinities of political outlook between the Italian and German governments is less important than the fact that this affinity existed and extended into many areas of political and economic life. The differences between National Socialism in Germany and Fascism in Italy partly consisted, in fact, of the more unhesitating acceptance of the ideas of Italian Fascism by the National Socialist party and the linking of these ideas to concepts of racial purity.

The basis of Fascist and National Socialist political and economic thought was the rejection of the ideas of the eighteenth-century Enlightenment. In the submergence of the individual will in common instinctive action, which warfare represented, rational doubts and vacillations, which were regarded as a trauma on human society produced by the Enlightenment, could be suppressed. War was seen as an instrument for the healing of this trauma and for the restoration of human society to its pristine state. Both Hitler and Mussolini, whose writings in general not only subscribed to but advanced the political ideas of fascism, referred to war constantly in this vein, seeing it as a powerful instrument for forging a new and more wholesome political society. 'Fascism', wrote Mussolini,

> the more it considers and observes the future and the development of humanity, quite apart from the political considerations of the moment, believes neither in the possibility nor the utility of perpetual peace. . . . War alone brings up to its highest tension all human energy and puts the stamp of nobility upon the peoples who have the courage to meet it.[4]

Hitler similarly wrote and spoke of war and preparation for war as an instrument of the spiritual renewal of the German people, a device for eliminating the corrupting egotistical self-seeking which he saw as the concomitant of false ideas of human liberty, progress and democracy. The basis of existence in Hitler's view was a struggle of the strong for mastery and war was thus an inescapable, necessary aspect of the human condition.[5]

What made this not uncommon viewpoint especially dangerous and what gave to the Second World War its unique characteristic of a war for the political and economic destiny of the whole European continent was the way in which the ideas of fascism were developed by Hitler and the theorists of the National Socialist party. The wound that had been inflicted on European civilization could, they argued, only be healed by a process of spiritual regeneration. That process of regeneration must begin from the small surviving still uncorrupted elite. But politics was not a matter of debate and persuasion but of the instinctive recognition of social obligations, community ideas which were held to be carried not in the brain but in the blood. The elite was also a racial elite and the restoration of the lost European civilization was also a search for a lost racial purity. The nationalist conceptions of race had been derived from the rational mainstream of European politics. What now replaced them was an irrational concept of racial purity as the last hope for the salvation of European society.[6]

Within Germany, the National Socialist party from its earliest days had identified those of Jewish race as the source of corruption and racial pollution. But it was scarcely possible that the 'problem' of the German Jews could be solved as an entirely domestic issue. The spiritual regeneration of Germany and, through Germany, the continent, also required a great extension of Germany's territorial area—*Lebensraum*. This area had to be sufficiently large to enable Germany militarily to play the role of a great power and to impose her will on the rest of the continent and perhaps on an even wider front. This expansion could also take the form of the destruction of what was seen as the last and most dangerous of all the European political heresies, communism and the Soviet state. The need to achieve these goals and the messianic urgency of the political programme of National Socialism meant that war was an unavoidable part of Hitler's plans.

But it was not the intellectual antagonism to communism which determined that the ultimate target of Germany's territorial expansion should be the Ukraine. That choice was more determined by economic considerations. The task of materially and spiritually rearming the German people had meant that Germany after 1933 pursued an economic policy radically different from that of other European states. A high level of state expenditure, of which military expenditure, before 1936, was a minor part, had sharply differentiated the behaviour of the German economy from that of the other major powers. The maintenance of high levels of production and full employment in a depressed international environment had necessitated an extensive battery of economic controls which had increasingly isolated the economy. After 1936 when expenditure for military purposes was increased to still higher levels there was no longer any possibility that the German economy might come back, by means of a devaluation, into a more liberal international payments and trading system. Rather, the political decisions of 1936 made it certain that trade, exchange, price and wage controls would become more drastic and more comprehensive, and the German economy more insulated from the influence of the other major economies. This was particularly so because of the large volume of investment allocated in the Four Year Plan to the production, at prices well above prevailing world prices, of materials of vital strategic importance, such as synthetic fuel, rubber and aluminum.[7]

The National Socialist party did not support the idea of restoring the liberal international order of the gold exchange standard. But neither did they have any clear positive alternative ideas. Economic policy was dictated by political expediency and each successive stage of controls was introduced to cope with crises as they arose. Nevertheless the political ideas of National Socialism favored an autarkic as opposed to a liberal economic order and it was not difficult to justify the apparatus of economic controls as a necessary and beneficial aspect of the National Socialist state. The international aspects of the controlled economy—exchange controls and bilateral trading treaties—could readily be assimilated to an expansionist foreign policy. Indeed Hitler himself regarded a greater degree of self-sufficiency of the German economy as a necessity if he were to have the liberty of strategic action which he desired, and also as a justification of his policy of territorial expansion. The memory of the effectiveness of the Allied naval blockade during the First World War, when Germany had controlled a much larger resource base than was left to her after the Treaty of Versailles, strengthened this line of thought.

National Socialism elaborated its own theory to justify international economic policies which were in fact only the outcome of a set of domestic economic decisions which had been accorded priority over all international aspects. This was the theory of *Grossraumwirtschaft* (the economics of large areas). Although it was only a rhetorical justification after the event of economic necessities, it also played its part in the formulation of strategy and economic policy. On the basis of these economic ideas, it was hoped that the war would bring tangible economic gain, rather than the more spiritual benefits of a transformation of civilization. At an early stage in his political career, Hitler had come to the conclusion that the Ukraine was economically indispensable to Germany if she was to be, in any worthwhile sense, independent of the international economy and thus free to function as a great power. As the insulation of the German economy from the international economy became more complete in the 1930s the economic relationship of Germany to the whole of the continent came to be reconsidered, and National Socialist writers were advocating not merely a political and racial reconstruction of Europe but an economic reconstruction as well.

National Socialist economists argued that the international depression of 1929 to 1933 had brought the 'liberal' phase of economic development, associated with diminishing tariffs and an increasing volume of international trade, to an end. On the other hand, the extent to which the developed economies of Europe still depended on access to raw materials had not diminished. They argued that the epoch of the economic unit of the national state, itself the creation of liberalism, was past, and must be replaced by the concept of large areas (*Grossräume*) which had a classifiable economic and geographical unity. Such areas provided a larger market at a time of failing demand and could also satisfy that demand from their own production and resources. Improving employment levels and increasing *per capita* incomes depended therefore, not on a recovery in international trade, which could only in any case be temporary and inadequate, but on a reordering of the map of the world into larger 'natural' economic areas. The United States and the Soviet Union each represented such an area. Germany too had its own 'larger economic area' which it must claim.[8]

The future economy of this area would be distinguished by its autarkic nature. The international division of labour would be modified into specialization of function within each *Grossraum*. Germany would be the manufacturing heartland of its own area, together with its bordering industrial areas of northeastern France, Belgium and Bohemia. The peripheral areas would supply raw materials and foodstuffs to the developed industrial core.

There were close links between these economic ideas and the political and racial ones. Such large areas were considered to have a racial unity in the sense that central Europe was developed because of the racial superiority of its inhabitants, the 'Aryans'; the periphery would always be the supplier of raw materials because its population was racially unsuitable for any more sophisticated economic activity.[9] For a time it seemed that Germany might create her *Grossraumwirtschaft* and dominate international economic exchanges in Europe through peaceful means; a series of trade agreements was signed between Germany and the underdeveloped countries of southeastern Europe after 1933. Germany was able to get better terms in bilateral trading from these lands than from more developed European economies who were able to threaten, and even, like Britain, to carry out the threat, to sequestrate German balances in order to force Germany to pay at once on her own (import) side of the clearing balance, and German trade with south-eastern Europe increased in relation to the rest of German and world trade in the thirties. But German-Russian trade after 1933 became insignificant and it was clear that a re-ordering of Europe's frontiers to correspond with Germany's economic ambitions would ultimately have to involve large areas of Russian territory. South-eastern Europe, without Russia, could make only a very limited contribution to emancipating Germany from her worldwide network of imports. A war against the Soviet Union seemed to be the necessary vehicle for political and economic gain.

Many scholars, particularly in the Soviet Union and eastern Europe, maintain that there was a further economic dimension to German policy and that the Second World War represented an even more fundamental clash over the economic and social destiny of the continent. Although the definition of fascism in Marxist analysis has varied greatly with time and place it has nevertheless been more consistent than definitions made from other standpoints. The tendency has been to represent it as the political expression of the control of 'state-monopoly capital' over the economy. It is seen as a stage of capitalism in decline, when it can survive only by a brutal and determined imperialism and through a monopolistic control over domestic and foreign markets by the bigger capitalist firms backed by the government. The changes in the German economy after 1933 are explained as following these lines: the readiness to go to war by the bigger profits it might bring and also by the ultimate necessity for an imperialist domination of other economies. Warfare, it is argued, had become an economic necessity for Germany and its ultimate purpose was the preservation of state capitalism, for which both territorial expansion and the destruction of the communist state were essential. The argument is succinctly put by Eichholtz:

> Towards the close of the twenties Germany stood once more in the ranks of the most developed and economically advanced of the imperialist powers. The strength and aggression necessary for expansion grew with the

development of her economic strength. German imperialism was an imperialism which had been deprived of colonies, and imperialism whose development was limited by financial burdens stemming from the war and by the limitations and controls, onerous to the monopolies, which the victorious powers had imposed, especially on armaments, finances, etc. On that account extreme nationalism and chauvinism were characteristic of the development of the fascist movement in Germany from the start; once in power fascism maintained from its first days an overweening purposeful imperialistic aggression—which had been obvious for a long time—towards the outside world. With fascism a ruling form of state monopoly capital had been created which aimed at overcoming the crisis of capitalism by domestic terror and, externally, by dividing the world anew.[10]

Such a theory offers not merely a serious economic explanation of the war but also implies that the most fundamental causes of the war were economic. The major German firms, it is argued, had definite plans to gain from a war of aggression and supported the National Socialist government in many of its economic aims.

Thus the results of research on the period immediately preceding the war, although still fragmentary, already show that German monopoly capital was pursuing a large and complex programme of war aims to extend its domination over Europe and over the world. The kernel of this programme was the destruction of the Soviet Union. Two main aims of war and expansion united the Hitler clique and all important monopolies and monopoly groups from the beginning: the 'dismantling of Versailles' and the 'seizure of a new living space (*Lebensraum*) in the east'. By the 'dismantling of Versailles' the monopolies understood, as they often expressed it later, the 'recapture' of all the economic and political positions which had been lost and the 'restitution' of all the damage to the sources of profit and monopoly situations which the Versailles system had inflicted on them. As an immediate step they planned to overrun the Soviet Union, to liquidate it and appropriate its immeasurable riches to themselves, and to erect a European 'economy of large areas' (*Grossraumwirtschaft*), if possible in conjunction with a huge African colonial empire.[11]

How the *Grossraumwirtschaft* eventually functioned in practice will be examined later. But as far as pre-war plans were concerned it was a concept which attracted sympathy and support from certain business circles in Germany. Some German firms were able to benefit from the government's drive towards a greater level of autarky and hoped to expand their new interests to the limits of the future frontiers of the Reich. This was true, in spite of its extensive extra-European connections, of the large chemical cartel, I. G. Farben. Its profits increasingly came from the massive state investment in synthetic petrol and synthetic rubber production. Several of its important executives had high rank in the Four-Year Plan Organization which was entrusted with these developments, and the company had plans ready in the event of an expansion of German power over other European states.[12] These plans stemmed in part from the German trade drive into south-eastern Europe after 1933 and the consequent penetration of German capital into that region, but there were also unambiguous proposals, some part of which were later put into effect, to recapture the supremacy of the German dyestuffs industry in France, which had been lost as a result of the First World War.[13] Nor was this the only such firm with similar plans prepared.[14] Other firms regarded the expansionist foreign policy as a possible way of securing supplies of raw materials. Such was the case with the non-ferrous metal company, Mansfeld, and with the aluminum companies, who understandably were able to get a very high level of priority because of the great importance of aluminum for aircraft manufacture and the power which the Air Ministry exercised in the German government.[15]

However, the support for the National Socialist party came in large measure from a section of the population whose political sympathies were in many ways antipathetic to the world of big business. It drew its support from a protest against the apparently inexorably increasing power both of organized labour and of organized business. Its urban support came mainly from the lower income groups of the middle classes, such as clerical workers, artisans and shopkeepers, and was combined with massive rural support in Protestant areas after 1931. This support was maintained by a persistent anticapitalist rhetoric but also by a certain amount of legislation which cannot by any shift of argument be explained by a theory which assumes National Socialism to be a stage of state capitalism. Attempts to establish hereditary inalienable peasant tenures, to show favor to artisan enterprises, to restrict the size of retail firms, to restrict the movement of labour out of the agricultural sector, all of which were futile in the face of a massive state investment in reflation which produced a rapid rate of growth of Gross National Product, show the curious ambivalence of National Socialist economic attitudes.[16] On the whole such legislation did little to affect the profits which accrued to the business world in Germany after 1933, some part of which came also from the severe controls on money wages and the destruction of the organized labour movements. But the National Socialist movement kept its inner momentum, which was driving towards a different horizon from that of the business world, a horizon both more distant and more frightening. It was in some ways a movement of protest against modern economic development and became a center of allegiance for all who were displaced and uprooted by the merciless and seemingly ungovernable swings of the German economy after 1918. National Socialism was as much a yearning for a stable utopia of the past as a close alliance between major capital interests and an authoritarian government.

These fundamental economic contradictions and tensions within the movement could only be exacerbated, not resolved, by a war of expansion. The idea—held in some conservative nationalist German business circles—that Germany must eventually dominate the exchanges of the continent if her economy was to find a lasting equilibrium, had a lineage dating from the 1890s and had found some expression in economic policy during the First World War.[17]

The theory of *Grossraumwirtschaft* was only a reformulation of these ideas in terms of National Socialist foreign policy. The much more radical idea of a social and racial reconstruction of European society—accepted by some parts of the National Socialist movement—ran directly counter to it, and raised the possibility of a Europe where the 'business climate' would, to say the least, have been unpropitious.

Although, therefore, the German government in choosing war as an instrument of policy was anticipating an economic gain from that choice, it was by no means clear as to the nature of the anticipated gain. It has been argued that it was the irreconcilable contradictions in the National Socialist economy which finally made a war to acquire more resources (*ein Raubkrieg*) the only way out, and that the invasion of Poland was the last desperate attempt to sustain the Nazi economy.[18] But it is hard to make out a case that the Nazi economy was in a greater state of crisis in the autumn of 1939 than it had been on previous occasions particularly in 1936. Most of the problems which existed in 1939 had existed from the moment full employment had been reached, and some of them, on any calculation, could only be made worse by a war—as indeed they were.

In Italy there were episodes in the 1930s when foreign and economic policy seemed to be directed towards the creation of an Italian *Grossraumwirtschaft* in Europe as a solution to Italy's economic problems. But in the face of the powerful expansion of German trade in the south-east such aspirations were unattainable. In Italy, also, there were attempts at creating by protection and subsidy synthetic industries which might prove strategically necessary in war. But there was little resemblance between these tendencies and the full-scale politico-economic ambitions of Germany. If the Italian government viewed war as a desirable instrument of policy it did not contemplate a serious and prolonged European war and made no adequate preparations for one.

In Japan, however, the choice in favour of war was based on economic considerations which had a certain similarity to those of Germany. It lacked the radical social and racial implications but it was assumed that investment in a war which was strategically well-conceived would bring a substantial accretion to Japan's economic strength. The Japanese government hoped to establish a zone of economic domination which, under the influence of German policy, it dignified by the title 'Co-Prosperity Sphere'. As an economic bloc its trading arrangements would be like those of the *Grossraumwirtschaft*, a manufacturing core supplied by a periphery of raw material suppliers.[19] If the Co-Prosperity Sphere was to be created in the full extent that would guarantee a satisfactory level of economic self-sufficiency, war and conquest would be necessary. Germany's decision for war and early victories over the colonial powers gave Japan the opportunity to establish a zone of domination by military force while her potential opponents were preoccupied with other dangers. After the initial successes the boundaries of the Co-Prosperity Sphere were widened to include a more distant periphery, a decision which had serious strategic consequences, but the original Japanese war aims represented a positive and realistic attempt at the economic reconstruction of her own economic area in her own interests. All the peripheral areas produced raw materials and foodstuffs and semi-manufactures which were imported in large quantities into Japan; rice from Korea, iron ore, coal and foodstuffs from Manchuria, coal and cotton from Jehol, oil and bauxite from the Netherlands East Indies, tin and rubber from Malaya and sugar from Formosa. The variety of commodities and the scope for further developments in the future made the Co-Prosperity Sphere potentially more economically viable and more economically realistic than a European *Grossraumwirtschaft* still heavily dependent on certain vital imports.[20] The Japanese decision for war, like the German, was taken under the persuasion that in Japan's situation, given the correct timing and strategy, war would be economically beneficial.

Of course such plans could only have been formulated where a harshly illiberal outlook on the problems of international economic and political relationships prevailed. But in the government circles of Japan proper the ready acceptance of war had no ideological connotations beyond this generally prevailing political attitude of mind. The major influence on the Japanese decision for war was the strategic conjuncture; with German military successes in Europe, the pressure on the European empires in the Pacific became unbearable and this in turn intensified the strategic dilemma of the United States. If Japan's ambitions were to be achieved it seemed that the opportune moment had arrived.

The probable and possible opponents of the Axis powers viewed this bellicosity with dismay. In these countries the First World War and its aftermath were seen as an economic disaster. Consequently the main problem of a future war, if it had to be fought, was thought to be that of avoiding a similar disaster. The components of that disaster were seen as a heavy loss of human beings and capital, acute and prolonged inflation, profound social unrest, and almost insuperable problems, both domestic and international, of economic readjustment once peace was restored. It was almost universally believed that the unavoidable aftermath of a major war would be a short restocking boom followed by worldwide depression and unemployment. When the *American Economic Review* devoted a special issue in 1940 to a consideration of the economic problems of war the problem of post-war readjustment was regarded by all contributors as the most serious and unavoidable. That the major economies after 1945 would experience a most remarkable period of stability and economic growth was an outcome which was quite unforeseen and unpredicted. The western European powers and the United States were as much the prisoners of their resigned pessimism about the unavoidable economic losses of war as Germany and Japan were the prisoners of their delusions about its possible economic advantages.

In fact the economic experience of the First World War had been for all combatants a chequered one. The First World War had not been a cause of unalloyed economic loss; it had on occasions brought economic and social advantages. What is more it had demonstrated to all the combatant powers that it lay in the hands of government to formulate strategic and economic policies which could to some extent determine whether or not a war would be economically a cause of gain or loss; they were not the hopeless prisoners of circumstance. The extreme importance of what governments had learned of their own potential in this way during the 1914–18 war can be observed in almost every aspect of the Second World War. Nevertheless in most countries this learning process had been thought of as an ingenious economic improvisation to meet a state of emergency, having no connection with peacetime economic activity nor with the 'normal' functioning of government. Although the First World War had left massive files of invaluable administrative experience on the shelves of government, which in 1939 had often only to be reached for and dusted, the influence of wartime events on economic attitudes in the inter-war period had been small.

Faced with a decision for war by two important powers the other major powers accepted the fact reluctantly and with much economic foreboding. The reluctance seems to have been greatest in the Soviet Union, which was in the throes of a violent economic and social transformation, and in the United States, which was less immediately threatened by German policy. The strategic initiative lay with the Axis powers; the strategies of the other powers were only responses to the initial decisions of their enemies. This fact, and the difference in economic attitudes toward warfare, operated decisively to shape each combatant power's strategic plans for fighting the war. By shaping strategy at every turn they also shaped economic policy and economic events. For the combatants the national economy had to be accommodated to a strategic plan and had to play its part in that plan. The economic dimension of the strategy was, however, only one part of the whole strategic synthesis, and the variety of the strategic and economic syntheses which were devised by the combatant powers show how complex and varied the economic experience of warfare can be.

NOTES

1 M. G. de Molinari, *Comment se résoudra la question sociale?*, Guillaumin, Paris, 1896, p. 126.
2 The reader is referred for a recent, short and relatively unbiased discussion of these issues to W. Wippermann, *Faschismustheorien. Zum Stand der gegenwärtigen Diskussion*, Wissenschaftliche Buchgesellschaft, Darmstadt, 1972.
3 G. M. Wilson, 'A New Look at the Problem of "Japanese Fascism"', in *Comparative Studies in Society and History*, no. 10, 1968.
4 Quoted in W. G. Welk, *Fascist Economic Policy. An Analysis of Italy's Economic Experiment* (Harvard Economic Studies, no. 62), Harvard University Press, Cambridge, Mass., 1938, p. 190.

5 The connections between Hitler's political thought and his strategy are developed in an interesting way by E. Jäckel, *Hitlers Weltanschauung. Entwurf einer Herrschaft*, Rainer Wunderlich Verlag Hermann Leins, Tübingen, 1969.

6 The most comprehensive discussion remains A. Kolnai's *The War against the West* (Gollancz, London, 1938), but E. Weber, in *Varieties of Fascism, Doctrines of Revolution in the Twentieth Century* (Van Nostrand, Princeton, 1964), draws out the further implications of these ideas.

7 The best account is D. Petzina's *Autarkiepolitik im Dritten Reich. Der nationalsocxialistische Vierjahresplan* (Schriftenreihe der Vj.f.Z., no. 16, Deutsche Verlags-Anstalt, Stuttgart, 1968).

8 Typical of this line of argument are, F. Fried, *Die Zukunft des Welthandels*, Knorr und Hirth, Munich, 1941; R. W. Krugmann, *Südosteuropa und Grossdeutschland. Entwicklung und Zukunftsmöligchkeiten der Wirtschaftsbeziehungen*, Breslauer Verlag, Breslau, 1939; H. Marschner, ed., *Deutschland in der Wirtschaft der Welt*, Deutscher Verlag für Politik und Wirtschaft, Berlin, 1937; J. Splettstoesser, *Der deutsche Wirtschaftsraum im Osten*, Limpert, Berlin, 1939; H. F. Zeck, *Die deutsche Wirtschaft und Südosteuropa*, Teubner, Leipzig, 1939.

9 W. Daitz, *Der Weg zur völkischen Wirtschaft und zur europäischen Grossraumwirtschaft*, Meinhold, Dresden, 1938.

10 D. Eichholtz, *Geschichte der deutschen Kriegswirtschaft, 1939–1945*, vol. 1, 1939–1941, Akademie-Verlag, Berlin, 1969, p. 1.

11 D. Eichholtz, *Geschichte*, p. 63.

12 D. Eichholtz, *Geschichte*, p. 248 ff.; H. Radandt, 'Die I G Farben-industrie und Südosteuropa 1938 bis zum Ende des zweiten Weltkriegs', in *Jahrbuch für Wirtschaftgeschichte*, no. 1, 1967.

13 A. S. Milward, *The New Order and the French Economy*, Oxford University Press, London, 1970, p. 100 ff.

14 W. Schumann, "Das Kriegsprogramm des Zeiss-Konzerns", in *Zeitschrift für Geschichtswissenschaft*, no. 11, 1963.

15 H. Radandt, *Kriegsverbrecherkonzern Mansfeld. Die Rolle des Mansfeld-Konzerns bei der Vorbereitung und während des zweiten Weltkriegs* (Geschichte der Fabriken und Werke, vol. 3), Akademie-Verlag, Berlin, 1957; A. S. Milward, *The Fascist Economy in Norway*, Clarendon Press, Oxford, 1972, p. 86.

16 They are well described in D. Schoenbaum's *Hitler's Social Revolution: Class and Status in Nazi Germany 1933–1939* (Weidenfeld & Nicolson, London, 1966).

17 The history is traced by J. Freymond, *Le IIIe Reich et la réorganisation économique de l'Europe 1940–1942: origines et projets* (Institut Universitaire de Hautes Etudes, Geneva, Collection de Relations Internationales, 3), Sithoff, Leiden, 1974.

18 T. W. Mason, 'Innere Krise und Angriffskrieg 1938/1939', in F. Forstmeier and H. E. Volkmann (eds.), *Wirtschaft und Rustung am Vorabend des zweiten Weltkrieges*, Droste, Düsseldorf, 1975.

19 F. C. Jones, *Japan's New Order in East Asia: Its Rise and Fall, 1937–45*, Oxford University Press, London, 1954; M. Libal, *Japans Weg in den Krieg. Die Aussenpolitik der Kabinette Konoye 1940–41*, Droste-Verlag, Düsseldorf, 1971.

20 J. R. Cohen, *Japan's Economy in War and Reconstruction*, University of Minnesota Press, Minneapolis, 1949, p. 7.

Reading 5.7

Structural Causes and Economic Effects

KENNETH N. WALTZ

In a self-help system, interdependence tends to loosen as the number of parties declines, and as it does so the system becomes more orderly and peaceful. As with other international political concepts, interdependence looks different when viewed in the light of our theory. Many seem to believe that a growing closeness of interdependence improves the chances of peace. But close interdependence means closeness of contact and raises the prospect of occasional conflict. The fiercest civil wars and the bloodiest international ones are fought within arenas populated by highly similar people whose affairs are closely knit. It is impossible to get a war going unless the potential participants are somehow linked. Interdependent states whose relations remain unregulated must experience conflict and will occasionally fall into violence. If interdependence grows at a pace that exceeds the development of central control, then interdependence hastens the occasion for war. . . .

INTERDEPENDENCE AS SENSITIVITY

. . . As now used, "interdependence" describes a condition in which anything that happens anywhere in the world may affect somebody, or everybody, elsewhere. To say that interdependence is close and rapidly growing closer is to suggest that the impact of developments anywhere on the globe are rapidly registered in a variety of far-flung places. This is essentially an economist's definition. In some ways that is not surprising. Interdependence has been discussed largely in economic terms. The discussion has been led by Americans, whose ranks include nine-tenths of the world's living economists (Strange 1971, p. 223). Economists understandably give meaning to interdependence by defining it in market terms. Producers and consumers may or may not form a market. How does one know when they do? By noticing whether changes in the cost of production, in the price of goods, and in the quality of products in some places respond to similar changes elsewhere. Parties that respond sensitively are closely interdependent. Thus Richard Cooper defines interdependence as "quick responsiveness to differential earning opportunities resulting in a sharp reduction in differences in factor rewards" (1968, p. 152). . . .

In defining interdependence as sensitivity of adjustment rather than as mutuality of dependence, Richard Cooper unwittingly reflects the lesser dependence of today's great powers as compared to those of earlier times. Data excerpted from Appendix Table I graphically show this.

Exports Plus Imports as a Percentage of GNP		
1909–13	U.K., France, Germany, Italy	33–52%
1975	U.S., Soviet Union	8–14%

To say that great powers then depended on one another and on the rest of the world much more than today's great powers do is not to deny that the adjustment of costs across borders is faster and finer now. Interdependence as sensitivity, however, entails little vulnerability. The more automatically, the more quickly, and the more smoothly factor costs adjust, the slighter the political consequences become. Before World War I, as Cooper says, large differences of cost meant that "trade was socially very profitable" but "less sensitive to small changes in costs, prices, and quality" (1968, p. 152). Minor variations of cost mattered little. Dependence on large quantities of imported goods and materials that could be produced at home only with difficulty, if they could be produced at all, mattered much. States that import and export 15 percent or more of their gross national products yearly, as most of the great powers did then and as most of the middle and smaller powers do now, depend heavily on having reliable access to markets outside their borders. Two or more parties involved in such relations are interdependent in the sense of being mutually vulnerable to the disruption of their exchanges. Sensitivity is a different matter.

As Cooper rightly claims, the value of a country's trade is more likely to vary with its magnitude than with its sensitivity. Sensitivity is higher if countries are able to move back and forth from reliance on foreign and on domestic production and investment "in response to relatively small margins of advantage." Under such conditions, the value of trade diminishes. If domestic substitutions for foreign imports cannot be made, or can be made only at high cost, trade becomes of higher value to a country and of first importance to those who conduct its foreign policy. The high value of Japan's trade, to use Cooper's example, "led Japan in 1941 to attack the Philippines and the United States fleet at Pearl Harbor to remove threats to its oil trade with the East Indies." His point is that high sensitivity reduces national vulnerability while creating a different set of problems. The more sensitive countries become, the more internal economic policies have to be brought into accord with external economic conditions. Sensitivity erodes the autonomy of states, but not of all states equally. Cooper's conclusion, and mine, is that even though problems posed by sensitivity are bothersome, they are easier for states to deal with than the interdependence of mutually vulnerable parties, and that the favored position of the United States enhances both its autonomy and the extent of its influence over others (1972, pp. 164, 176–80).

Defining interdependence as sensitivity leads to an economic interpretation of the world. To understand the foreign-policy implications of high or of low interdependence requires concentration on the politics of international economics, not on the economics of international politics. The common conception of interdependence omits inequalities, whether economic or political. And yet inequality is what much of politics is about. The study of politics, theories about politics, and the practice of politics have always turned upon inequalities, whether among interest groups, among religious and ethnic communities, among classes, or among nations. Internally, inequality is more nearly the whole of the political story. Differences of national strength and power and of national capability and competence are what the study and practice of international politics are almost entirely about. This is so not only because international politics lacks the effective laws and the competent institutions found within nations but also because inequalities across nations are greater than inequalities within them (Kuznets 1951). A world of nations marked by great inequalities cannot usefully be taken as the unit of one's analysis.

Most of the confusion about interdependence follows from the failure to understand two points: first, how the difference of structure affects the meaning, the development, and the effects of the interactions of units nationally and internationally; and second, how the interdependence of nations varies with their capabilities. Nations are composed of differentiated parts that become integrated as they interact. The world is composed of like units that become dependent on one another in varying degrees. The parts of a polity are drawn together by their differences; each becomes dependent on goods and services that all specialize in providing. Nations pull apart as each of them tries to take care of itself and to avoid becoming dependent on others. How independent they remain, or how dependent they become, varies with their capabilities. . . . To define interdependence as a sensitivity, then, makes two errors. First, the definition treats the world as a whole, as reflected in the clichés cited earlier. Second, the definition compounds relations and interactions that represent varying degrees of independence for some, and of dependence for others, and lumps them all under the rubric of interdependence.

INTERDEPENDENCE AS MUTUAL VULNERABILITY

A politically more pertinent definition is found in everyday usage. Interdependence suggests reciprocity among parties. Two or more parties are interdependent if they depend on one another about equally for the supply of goods and services. They are interdependent if the costs of breaking their relations or of reducing their exchanges are about equal for each of them. Interdependence means that the parties are mutually dependent. The definition enables one to identify what is politically important about relations of interdependence that are looser or tighter. Quantitatively, interdependence tightens as parties depend on one another for larger supplies of goods and services; qualitatively, interdependence tightens as countries depend on one another for more important goods and services that would be harder to get elsewhere. The definition has two components: the aggregate gains and losses states experience through their interactions and the equality with which those gains and losses are distributed. States that are interdependent at high levels of exchange experience, or are subject to, the common vulnerability that high interdependence entails.

Because states are like units, interdependence among them is low as compared to the close integration of the parts of a domestic order. States do not interact with one another as the parts of a polity do. Instead, some few people and organizations in one state interact in some part of their affairs with people and organizations abroad. Because of their similarity, states are more dangerous than useful to one another. Being functionally undifferentiated, they are distinguished primarily by their greater or lesser capabilities for performing similar tasks. This states formally what students of international politics have long noticed. The great powers of an era have always been marked off from others by both practitioners and theorists.

. . . Many believe that the mere mutualism of international exchange is becoming a true economic-social-political integration. One point can be made in support of this formulation. The common conception of interdependence is appropriate only if the inequalities of nations are fast lessening and losing their political significance. If the inequality of nations is still the dominant political fact of international life, then interdependence remains low. Economic examples in this section, and military examples in the next one, make clear that it is.

In placid times, statement and commentator employ the rich vocabulary of clichés that cluster around the notion of global interdependence. Like a flash of lightning, crises reveal the landscape's real features. What is revealed by the oil crisis following the Arab-Israeli War in October of 1973? Because that crisis is familiar to all of us and will long be remembered, we can concentrate on its lessons without rehearsing the details. Does it reveal states being squeezed by common constraints and limited to applying the remedies they can mutually contrive? Or does it show that the unequal capabilities of states continue to explain their fates and to shape international-political outcomes?

Recall how Kissinger traced the new profile of power. "Economic giants can be militarily weak," he said, "and military strength may not be able to obscure economic weakness. Countries can exert political influence even when they have neither military nor economic strength." . . . Economic, military, and political capabilities can be kept separate in gauging the ability of nations to act. Low politics, concerned with economic and such affairs, has replaced military concerns at the top of the international agenda. Within days the Arab-Israeli War proved that reasoning wrong. Such reasoning had supported references made in the early 1970s to the militarily weak and politically disunited countries of Western Europe as constituting "a great civilian power." Recall the political behavior of the great civilian power in the aftermath of the war. Not Western Europe as any kind of a power, but the separate states of Western Europe, responded to the crisis—in the metaphor of *The Economist*—by behaving at once like hens and ostriches. They ran around aimlessly, clucking loudly while keeping their heads buried deeply in the sand. How does one account for such behavior? Was it a failure of nerve? Is it that the giants of yesteryear—the Attlees and Bevins, the Adenauers and de Gaulles—have been replaced by men of lesser stature? Difference of persons explains some things; difference of situations explains more. In 1973 the countries of Western Europe depended on oil for 60 percent of their energy supply. Much of that oil came from the Middle East. . . . Countries that are highly dependent, countries that get much of what they badly need from a few possibly unreliable suppliers, must do all they can to increase the chances that they will keep getting it. The weak, lacking leverage, can plead their cause or panic. Most of the countries in question unsurprisingly did a little of each.

The behavior of nations in the energy crisis that followed the military one revealed the low political relevance of interdependence defined as sensitivity. Instead, the truth of the propositions I made earlier was clearly shown. Smooth and fine economic adjustments cause little difficulty. Political interventions that bring sharp and sudden changes in prices and supplies cause problems that are economically and politically hard to cope with. The crisis also revealed that, as usual, the political clout of nations correlates closely with their economic power and their military might. In the winter of 1973–74 the policies of West European countries had to accord with economic necessities. The more dependent a state is on others, and the less its leverage over them, the more it must focus on how its decisions affect its access to supplies and markets on which its welfare or survival may depend. This describes the condition of life for states that are no more than the equal of many others. In contrast, the United States was able to make its policy according to political and military calculations. Importing but two percent of its total energy supply from the Middle East, we did not have to appease Arab countries as we would have had to do if our economy had depended heavily on them and if we had lacked economic and other leverage. The United States could manipulate the crisis that others made in order to promote a balance of interests and forces holding some promise of peace. The unequal incidence of shortages led to the possibility of their manipulation. What does it mean then to say that the world is an increasingly interdependent one in which all nations are constrained, a world in which all nations lose control? Very little. To trace the effects that follow from inequalities, one has to unpack the word "interdependent" and identify the varying mixtures of relative dependence for some nations and of relative independence for others. As one should expect in a world of highly unequal nations, some are severely limited while others have wide ranges of choice; some have little ability to affect events outside of their borders while others have immense influence.

The energy crisis should have made this obvious, but it did not. Commentators on public affairs continue to emphasize the world's interdependence and to talk as though all nations are losing control and becoming more closely bound. Transmuting concepts into realities and endowing them with causal force is a habit easily slipped into. Public officials and students of international affairs once wrote of the balance of power causing war or preserving peace. They now attribute a comparable reality to the concept of interdependence and endow it with strong causal effect. Thus Secretary Kissinger, who can well represent both groups, wondered "whether interdependence would foster common progress or common disaster" (January 24, 1975, p. 1). He described American Middle-East policy as being to reduce Europe's and Japan's vulnerability, to engage in dialogue with the producers, and "to give effect to the principle of interdependence on a global basis" (January 16, 1975, p. 3). Interdependence has become a thing in itself: a "challenge" with its own requirements, "a physical and moral imperative" (January 24, 1975, p. 2; April 20, 1974, p. 3).

When he turned to real problems, however, Kissinger emphasized America's special position. The pattern of his many statements on such problems as energy, food, and nuclear proliferation was first to emphasize that our common plight denies all possibility of effective national action and then to place the United States in a separate category. Thus, two paragraphs after declaring our belief in interdependence, we find this query: "In what other country could a leader say, 'We are going to solve energy; we're going to solve food; we're going to solve the problem of nuclear war,' and be taken seriously?" (October 13, 1974, p. 2).

In coupling his many statements about interdependence with words about what we can do to help ourselves and others, was Kissinger not saying that we are much less dependent than most countries are? We are all constrained but, it appears, not equally. Gaining control of international forces that affect nations is a problem for all of them, but some solve the problem better than others. The costs of shortages fall on all of us, but in different proportion. Interdependence, one might think, is a euphemism used to obscure the dependence of most countries (cf. Goodwin 1976, p. 63). Not so, Kissinger says. Like others, we are caught in the web because failure to solve major resource problems would lead to recession in other countries and ruin the international economy. That would hurt all of us. Indeed it would, but again the uneven incidence of injuries inflicted on nations is ignored. Recession in some countries hurts others, but some more and some less so. An unnamed Arab oil minister's grip on economics appeared stronger than Kissinger's. If an oil shortage should drive the American economy into recession, he observed, all of the world would suffer. "Our economies, our regimes, our very survival, depend on a healthy U.S. economy" (*Newsweek*, March 25, 1974, p. 43). How much a country will suffer depends roughly on how much of its business is done abroad. As Chancellor Schmidt said in October of 1975, West Germany's economy depends much more than ours does on a strong international economic recovery because it exports 25 percent of its GNP yearly (October 7, 1975). The comparable figure for the United States was seven percent.

No matter how one turns it, the same answer comes up: We depend somewhat on the external world, and most other countries depend on the external world much more so. Countries that are dependent on others in important respects work to limit or lessen their dependence if they can reasonably hope to do so.[1] From late 1973 onward, in the period of oil embargo and increased prices, Presidents Nixon and Ford, Secretary Kissinger, and an endless number of American leaders proclaimed both a new era of interdependence and the goal of making the United States energy-independent by 1985. This is so much the natural behavior of major states that not only the speakers but seemingly also their audiences failed to notice the humor. Because states are in a self-help system, they try to avoid becoming dependent on others for vital goods and services. To achieve energy independence would be costly. Economists rightly point out that by their definition of interdependence the cost of achieving the goal is a measure of how much international conditions affect us. But that is to think of interdependence merely as sensitivity. Politically the important point is that only the few industrial countries of greatest capability are able to think seriously of becoming independent in energy supply. As Kissinger put it: "We have greater latitude than the others because we can do much on our own. The others can't" (January 13, 1975, p. 76). . . .

When the great powers of the world were small in geographic compass, they did a high proportion of their business abroad. The narrow concentration of power in the present and the fact that the United States and the Soviet Union are little dependent on the rest of the world produce a very different international situation. The difference between the plight of great powers in the new bipolar world and the old multipolar can be seen by contrasting America's condition with that of earlier great powers. When Britain was the world's leading state economically, the portion of her wealth invested abroad far exceeded the portion that now represents America's stake in the world. In 1910 the value of total British investment abroad was one-and-one-half times larger than her national income. In 1973 the value of total American investments abroad was one-fifth as large as her national income. In 1910 Britain's return on investment abroad amounted to eight percent of national income; in 1973 the comparable figure for the United States was 1.6 percent (British figures computed from Imlah 1958, pp. 70–75, and Woytinsky and Woytinsky 1953, p. 791, Table 335; American figures computed from CIEP, March 1976, pp. 160–62, Tables 42, 47, and *US Bureau of the Census*, 1975, p. 384, and *Survey of Current Business*, October 1975, p. 48). Britain in its heyday had a huge stake in the world, and that stake loomed large in relation to her national product. From her immense and far-flung activities, she gained a considerable leverage. Because of the extent to which she depended on the rest of the world, wise and skillful use of that leverage was called for. Great powers in the old days depended on foodstuffs and raw materials imported from abroad much more heavily than the United States and the Soviet Union do now. Their dependence pressed them to make efforts to control the sources of their vital supplies.

Today the myth of interdependence both obscures the realities of international politics and asserts a false belief about the conditions that promote peace, as World War I conclusively showed. "The statistics of the economic interdependence of Germany and her neighbors," John Maynard Keynes remarked, "are overwhelming." Germany was the best customer of six European states, including Russia and Italy; the second best customer of three, including Britain; and the third best customer of France. She was the largest source of supply for ten European states, including Russia, Austria-Hungary, and Italy; and the second largest source of supply for three, including Britain and France (Keynes 1920, p. 17). And trade then was proportionately much higher than now. Then governments were more involved internationally than they were in their national economies. Now governments are more involved in their national economies than they are internationally. This is fortunate.

Economically, the low dependence of the United States means that the costs of, and the odds on, losing our trading partners are low. Other countries depend more on us than we do on them. If links are cut, they suffer more than we do. Given this condition, sustained economic sanctions against us would amount to little more than economic self-mutilation. The United States can get along without the rest of the world better than most of its parts can get along without us. But, someone will hasten to say, if Russia, or anyone, should be able to foreclose American trade and investment in successively more parts of the world, we could be quietly strangled to death. To believe that, one has to think not in terms of politics but in terms of the apocalypse. If some countries want to deal less with us, others will move economically closer to us. More so than any other country, the United States can grant or withhold a variety of favors, in matters of trade, aid, loans, the supply of atomic energy for peaceful purposes, and military security. If peaceful means for persuading other countries to comply with preferred American policies are wanted, the American government does not have to look far to find them. The Soviet Union is even less dependent economically on the outside world than we are, but has less economic and political leverage on it. We are more dependent economically on the outside world than the Soviet Union is, but have more economic and political leverage on it.

The size of the two great powers gives them some capacity for control and at the same time insulates them with some comfort from the effect of other states' behavior. The inequality of nations produces a condition of equilibrium at a low level of interdependence. This is a picture of the world quite different from the one that today's transnationalists and interdependers paint. They cling to an economic version of the domino theory: Anything that happens anywhere in the world may damage us directly or through its repercussions, and therefore we have to react to it. This assertion holds only if the politically important nations are closely coupled. We have seen that they are not. Seldom has the discrepancy been wider between the homogeneity suggested by "interdependence" and the heterogeneity of the world we live in. A world composed of greatly unequal units is scarcely an interdependent one. A world in which a few states can take care of themselves quite well and most states cannot hope to do so is scarcely an interdependent one. A world in which the Soviet Union and China pursue exclusionary policies is scarcely an interdependent one. A world of bristling nationalism is scarcely an interdependent one. The confusion of concepts works against clarity of analysis and obscures both the possibilities and the necessities of action. Logically it is wrong, and politically it is obscurantist, to consider the world a unit and call it "interdependent."

NOTE

1 Notice the implication of the following statement made by Leonid Brezhnev: "Those who think that we need ties and exchanges in the economic and scientific-technical fields more than elsewhere are mistaken. The entire volume of USSR imports from capitalist countries comes to less than 1.5% of our gross social product. It is clear that this does not have decisive importance for the soviet economy's development" (October 5, 1976, p. 3).

REFERENCES

Brezhnev, L. I. (October 5, 1976). "Brezhnev gives interview on French TV." In *The Current Digest of the Soviet Press*, vol. 28. Columbus: Ohio State University, November 3, 1976.

CIEP: Council on International Economic Policy (December 1974). (March 1976). *International Economic Report of the President*. Washington, D.C.: GPO.

———. (January 1977). *International Economic Report of the President*. Washington, D.C.: GPO.

Cooper, Richard N. (1968). *The Economics of Interdependence*. New York: McGraw-Hill.

———. (January 1972). "Economic interdependence and foreign policy in the seventies." *World Politics*, vol. 24.

Finney, John W. (January 18, 1976). "Dreadnought or dinosaur." *New York Times Magazine*.

Goodwin, Geoffrey L. (1976). "International institutions and the limits of interdependence." In Avi Shlaim (ed.), *International Organizations in World Politics Yearbook, 1975*. London: Croom Helm.

Imlah, A. H. (1958). *Economic Elements in the Pax Britannica*. Cambridge: Harvard University Press.

Keynes, John Maynard (1920). *The Economic Consequences of the Peace*. New York: Harcourt, Brace and Howe.

———. (September 1, 1926). "The end of laissez-faire—II." *New Republic*, vol. 48.

———. (n.d.) *The General Theory of Employment, Interest, and Money*. New York: Harcourt, Brace.

Kissinger, Henry A. (1957). *Nuclear Weapons and Foreign Policy*. New York: Harper.

———. (1964). *A World Restored*. New York: Grosset and Dunlap.

———. (1965). *The Troubled Partnership*. New York: McGraw-Hill.

———. (Summer 1968). "The white revolutionary: reflections on Bismarck." *Daedalus*, vol. 97.

———. (April 24, 1973). "Text of Kissinger's talk at A.P. meeting here on U.S. relations with Europe." *New York Times*.

———. (October 10, 1973). "At Pacem in Terris conference." *News Release*. Bureau of Public Affairs: Department of State.

———. (April 20, 1974). "Good partner policy for Americas described by Secretary Kissinger." *New Release*. Bureau of Public Affairs: Department of State.

———. (October 13, 1974). "Interview by James Reston of the *New York Times*." The Secretary of State. Bureau of Public Affairs: Department of State.

———. (January 13, 1975). "Kissinger on oil, food, and trade." *Business Week*.

———. (January 16, 1975). "Interview: for Bill Moyers' Journal." *The Secretary of State*. Bureau of Public Affairs: Department of State.

———. (January 24, 1975). "A new national partnership." *The Secretary of State*. Bureau of Public Affairs: Department of State.

———. (September 13, 1975). "Secretary Henry A. Kissinger interviewed by William F. Buckley, Jr." *The Secretary of State*. Bureau of Public Affairs: Department of State.

———. (December 23, 1975). "Major topics: Angola and detente." *The Secretary of State*. Bureau of Public Affairs: Department of State.

———. (September 30, 1976). "Toward a new understanding of community." *The Secretary of State*. Bureau of Public Affairs: Department of State.

———. (January 10, 1977). "Laying the foundations of a long-term policy." *The Secretary of State*. Bureau of Public Affairs: Department of State.

Kuznets, Simon (Winter 1951). "The state as a unit in study of economic growth." *Journal of Economic History*, vol. 11.

———. (1966). *Modern Economic Growth*. New Haven: Yale University Press.

———. (January 1967). "Quantitative aspects of the economic growth of nations: Paper X." *Economic Development and Cultural Change*, vol. 15.

Marx, Karl, and Frederick Engels (1848). *Communist Manifesto*. Translator unnamed. Chicago: Charles H. Kerr, 1946.

Newsweek (March 25, 1974). "Oil embargo: The Arab's compromise."

Schmidt, Helmut (October 7, 1975). "Schmidt, Ford 'cautiously optimistic' on world's economic recovery." *The Bulletin*. Bonn: Press and Information Office, Government of the Federal Republic of Germany, vol. 23.

Snyder, Glenn H. (1966). *Stockpiling Strategic Materials*. San Francisco: Chandler.

Strange, Susan (January 1971). "The politics of international currencies." *World Politics*, vol. 22.

Survey of Current Business (various issues). U.S. Department of Commerce, Bureau of Economic Analysis. Washington, D.C.: GPO.

UN Department of Economic Affairs (1949). *International Capital Movements During the Inter-War Period*. New York.

———. Department of Economic and Social Affairs (1961). *International Flow of Long Term Capital and Official Donations*. New York.

———. Statistical Office (1957, 1961, 1970, 1974). *Yearbook of National Accounts Statistics*. New York.

———. (1966). *Demographic Yearbook*, 1965, New York.

———. (1976). *Statistical Yearbook*, 1975, vol. 27. New York.

———. (1977). *Statistical Yearbook*, 1976, vol. 28. New York.

US Agency for International Development, Statistics and Reports Divisions (various years). *US Overseas Loans and Grants: July 1, 1945–*. Washington, D.C.: GPO.

———. Bureau of the Census (1975). *Statistical Abstract*, 1974. Washington, D.C.: GPO.

———. Bureau of the Census (1976). *Historical Statistics of the United States: Colonial Times to 1970*. Washington, D.C.: GPO.

———. Department of Commerce, Bureau of Economic Analysis (1975). *Revised Data Series on US Direct Investment Abroad, 1966–1974*. Washington, D.C.: GPO.

———. Department of the Interior (June 1976). *Energy Perspectives 2*. Washington, D.C.: GPO.

———. Senate Committee on Finance (February 1973). *Implications of Multinational Firms for World Trade and Investment and for U.S. Trade and Labor*. Washington, D.C.: GPO.

———. Senate Committee on Government Operations, Permanent Subcommittee on Investigations (August 1974). *Selected Readings on Energy Self-Sufficiency and the Controlled Materials Plan*. Washington, D.C.: GPO.

Woytinsky, W. S., and E. S. Woytinsky (1953). *World Population and Production*. New York: Twentieth Century Fund.

Reading 5.8

Trade and Power
RICHARD ROSECRANCE

In the age of mercantilism—an era in which power and wealth combined—statesmen and stateswomen (for who dares to slight Elizabeth I or Catherine the Great) sought not only territory but also a monopoly of markets of particular goods highly valued in Europe, gold, silver, spices, sugar, indigo, tobacco. Who controlled local production and sales also determined the market in Europe and obtained a monopoly return. Initially, Venice and Genoa vied for dominance of the spice trade from the twelfth to the fourteenth centuries, a struggle that was interrupted by Portuguese navigators, sailors, and soldiers who temporarily established control of the Indies at their source. Later Holland ousted Portugal in the East Indies, and England and France took her place in India. By the seventeenth century, Spain could no longer hold her position in the Caribbean and the New World as Holland, England, and France disputed her monopoly, first by capturing her bullion fleets, then by seizing sugar islands as well as parts of the North American mainland. In the eighteenth century Britain won victory practically everywhere, though Holland was left with the Dutch East Indies, France with her sugar islands in the Caribbean, and Spain with a reduced position in North and South America. As William Pitt the Elder pointed out, "commerce had been made to flourish by war"[1]—English monopolies of colonial produce won her great dividends in trade with the continent. Her near monopoly of overseas empire and tropical products produced a great flow of continuing revenue that supported British military and naval exploits around the world. From either standpoint—territorial or economic—military force could be used to conquer territories or commodity-producing areas that would contribute greater revenue and power in Europe. With a monopoly on goods or territories, one nation or kingdom could forge ahead of others.

Thus we have one basic means by which nations have made their way in the world—by increasing their territories and maintaining them against other states. Sometimes, less cultured or civilized nations have by this means upset ruling empires or centers of civilization. In the past the barbarian invasions disrupted Rome; Attila the Hun and his followers intruded upon Mediterranean civilization; Genghis Khan and his military nomads ranged into Eastern Europe; Islam and the Turks dynamically transformed the culture of the Mediterranean and Southern Europe. In fact, it was not until the relatively recent period that highly developed economic centers could hold their own

---

against military and agrarian peoples. The waging of war and the seizure of territory have been relatively easy tasks for most of Western history. It is not surprising that when territorial states began to take shape in the aftermath of the Reformation, they were organized for the purpose both of waging and of resisting war, and the seventeenth century became the most warlike of epochs. Kings and statesmen could most rapidly enhance their positions through territorial combat.

Associated with the drive for territory is an allied system of international relations which we will here call the "military-political or territorial" system. The more nations choose to conquer territory, the more dominant the allied system of international politics will be. Because territorial expansion has been the dominant mode of national policy since 1648 and the Peace of Westphalia, it is not surprising that the military-political and territorial system has been the prevailing system of international relations since then. In this system, war and the threat of war are the omnipresent features of interstate relationships, and states fear a decisive territorial setback or even extinction. This has not been an idle concern, if one considers that 95 percent of the state-units which existed in Europe in the year 1500 have now been obliterated, subdivided, or combined into other countries.

Whatever else a nation-state does, therefore, it must be concerned with the territorial balance in international politics and no small part of its energies will be absorbed by defense. But defense and territory are not the only concerns of states, nor is territorial expansion the only means by which nations hope to improve their fortunes. If war provides one means of national advancement, peace offers another.

THE OIL CRISIS, 1973–1980

Probably more important in the long-term than the battles of the fourth Arab-Israeli war was the oil crisis and embargo of 1973–74. While the war was being fought, the Organization of Petroleum Exporting Countries (OPEC) announced on October 16, 1973, its first unilateral increase of 70 percent, bringing the cost of a barrel of oil to $5.12. At the end of the year it had been raised to $11.65 (a further 128 percent increase), and by 1980 had risen to almost $40.00 a barrel, about twenty times the price in early 1970. In addition, the Arabs announced oil production cutbacks and on October 20, embargoed all oil exports to the United States and The Netherlands, the two countries closest to Israel.

These decisions stimulated different responses in America and abroad. Most European allies and Japan quickly made it clear that they sympathized with the Arab cause and distanced themselves from the United States. Nixon in response announced "Project Independence" on November 7, which committed the United States to free itself from the need to import oil by 1980. This difficult goal was to be accomplished by conservation and the development of alternative sources of energy. The objective was not achieved, of course, for the United States imported roughly the same 36 to 37 percent of its oil needs in 1980 as it had in 1973. No evolution would allow it to return to the nearly self-sufficient 8.1 percent level of 1947.

There were four ways in which the oil crisis might have been overcome. The first was through the traditional method used by the United States in the Middle East crises of 1956 and 1967. In response to an oil embargo, the United States could simply increase its domestic production of oil, allocating stockpiles to its allies. The United States had had the leverage to do this in previous years because excess domestic capacity more than provided for national requirements, leaving a surplus to be exported abroad, if need arose. In 1956, the United States imported 11 percent of its oil but had a reserve domestic production capacity that could provide for an additional 25 percent of its needs. In 1967, while oil imports had risen to 19 percent of its oil consumption, the United States possessed a similar ability to expand its production by 25 percent, more than replacing imported oil. By 1973, however, the low price of oil and past domestic production had eroded United State reserves. It now imported 35 percent of its needs and could increase production only by an additional 10 percent.[2] When the Arabs embargoed oil shipments to the United States, there was no way for the country to increase domestic production to cover the shortfall. If a solution was to be found, it depended upon reallocating production abroad. As it turned out, the embargo caused no difficulty or shortage in America, because the oil companies simply re-routed production, sending Arab production to compliant European states and Japan, and non-Arab production to the United States and Holland. This measure solved the supply problem, but it did nothing to alleviate the high price. Extra United States production would not be sufficient to create a glut in the world marketplace and thus force a drop in the OPEC price.

A second method of coping with the crisis was to form a cartel of buyers of oil, principally the United States, Europe, and Japan, together with a few developing countries. If all could agree to buy oil at a fixed low price, OPEC would not be able to sell abroad on its terms and would have to reduce the price. Since it was the formation of the producers' cartel (OPEC) which had forced up the price of oil, many thought that only a consumers' cartel could offset its bargaining leverage and bring the price down. Despite American attempts to organize such a consumers' group in 1973 and 1974, the other nations preferred to play an independent role. France, Germany, and Japan negotiated separate oil contracts with individual Arab countries, guaranteeing access to Middle Eastern oil over the long term. They would not cooperate with the United States. When the American-sponsored International Energy Agency was finally set up in 1974, it became an information gathering agency which could allocate supplies of oil only in a crisis and had no monopoly bargaining power.

A third means of overcoming the oil crisis and reducing the real price of oil was through military intervention. This was considered at the end of 1974 and the beginning of 1975 when Secretary of State Kissinger hinted intervention if "actual strangulation of the West" was threatened. Some concluded that the Persian Gulf fields should be seized by United States marines or units of a Rapid Deployment Force. Occupation of such thinly populated areas was possible. The question, however, was whether production could be started up and maintained in the face of determined sabotage by Arab resistance groups, including the Palestine Liberation Organization. Would pipelines be cut or harbors mined? Would oil tankers have free passage through the Gulf? These uncertainties could not be resolved over the long period that would be required to break the Arab embargo and reduce the price of petroleum.

The final and ultimately successful means of overcoming the crisis came through diplomacy and the mechanism of the world market. After the success of the Israeli-Egyptian shuttle negotiations producing a withdrawal of forces on the Sinai front, the very beginning of talks on the Golan with Syria and Israel led the Arabs to end the oil embargo on March 18, 1974.[3] This had no impact on oil prices or supply and therefore did not change the OPEC bargaining position. That awaited complex developments in the world market for oil and for industrial products. In 1973–74, it was generally believed that the market for oil was inelastic, that demand would not decline greatly with an increase in the oil price. If it did not, the Arabs would gain an incredible premium, and a huge surplus of funds. It was estimated that as much as $600 billion might flow to Arab producers over a ten-year period. They would never be able to spend that much importing goods from the industrial and oil-consuming countries; hence, huge Arab surpluses would build up—funds that could have no economic use in the Arab states themselves. The flow of funds from importing countries to OPEC was partly offset when about half the surplus was used to buy Western imports and another large portion was invested in the world financial market, largely in the form of short-term deposits in Western banks. The banks and international financial agencies could then lend funds to the consuming countries, enabling them to finance their oil purchases. At the same time consumers became unwilling or unable to pay the high price. Even in the traditionally energy-extravagant United States, the amount of energy needed to produce one dollar of the gross national product declined 25 percent from 1973 to 1983. The average gas consumption of American-made automobiles almost doubled in the same period to reach 24.6 miles per gallon. Most of the leading industrial corporations instituted energy-conservation programs. The demand for oil dropped.

Between 1973 and 1979 industrial prices in the developed world increased more than oil prices. In the wake of the oil crisis and the ensuing inflation, many governments resorted to freely fluctuating exchange rates for their currencies. No longer under the discipline of gold flows, they could experiment with domestic economic expansion, convinced that their currencies values would not get out of line or their trade balance deteriorate. The result was further inflation of wages, prices, and industrial products. This had two effects on the Arab oil countries. First, it meant that they had to pay a great deal more to buy industrial goods, using up the oil surplus that they were beginning to accumulate. Second, as inflation advanced in the West and Japan, industrial entrepreneurs hesitated to invest, uncertain of their long-run return. Western economies ground to a halt and unemployment mounted. For a decade after 1973, the industrialized world grew at only 2 percent per year, and the number of jobless workers doubled. As a result, Arab investments in the developed countries were threatened by declines in Western profits and wages. Too high oil prices temporarily forced the industrial world into economic stagnation in which it would buy little Middle Eastern oil. The oil price increase, with the exception of the sudden rise of 1979–80, halted and reversed. Even the Iran-Iraq war did not lead to a new jump in prices. Oil consumption of the advanced industrial countries fell by seven million barrels a day between 1979 and 1982. In addition new oil production outside of OPEC increased, and OPEC production declined by twelve million barrels a day. Oil came into surplus, and the price fell back to $28 per barrel by 1983. The oil countries, which also suffered from the worldwide inflation, found they did not have sufficient export surplus to meet their needs in food and industrial imports. In 1982, eight Middle Eastern producers faced a deficit of $23 to $26 billion. Even Ayatollah Ruhollah Khomeini's Iran had to increase its oil production to finance imports and its war with Iraq.

The strange outcome was that the oil and energy crisis abated. The Arabs saw reason for increasing production while holding down the price, but the collapse in international demand for oil was so great, that the price could not be maintained. Consumers emerged in a much better position. The developing countries, which had borrowed to cover oil and industrial imports, found high interest rates imperilling their financial solvency in the first half of the 1980s. Paradoxically, there was then too little Arab money and too small an oil surplus to cover their borrowing needs.

The oil crisis underscored another means of dealing with conflict among nation-states. Instead of defending or fighting over territorial claims, nations found a way to reach a compromise through an international flow of funds, domestic economic adjustments, and world trade. The imbalance in payments threatened by the huge Arab oil surpluses in 1973–74 was reversed by the first years of the 1980s. Despite Kissinger's threats, force was not used to assure Western access to oil, and overarching cooperation was the ruling principle between industrial and oil-producing regions of the world. Each benefitted from the exchange, and consuming countries did not have to adopt policies of national self-sufficiency, reducing income and employment to the point where energy needs could be met on a national basis. Each side, instead, relied upon the other for the products it required.

Territorial gain is not the only means of advancing a nation's interest, and, in the nuclear age, wars of territorial expansion are not only dangerous, they are costly and threatening to both sides. Much more tenable is a policy of economic development and progress sustained by the medium of international trade. If national policies of economic growth depend upon an expanding world market, one country can hardly expect to rely primarily upon territorial aggression and aggrandizement. To attack one's best customers is to undermine the commercial faith and reciprocity in which exchange takes place. Thus, while the territorial and military-political means to national improvement causes inevitable conflict with other nations, the trading method is consistent with international cooperation. No other country's territory is attacked; the benefits that one nation gains from trade can also be realized by others.

If this is true, and two means of national advancement do indeed exist, why is it that Western and world history is mainly a narrative of territorial and military expansion, of unending war, to the detriment of the world's economic and trading system? Louis XIV and Napoleon would easily understand the present concern with territorial frontiers and the military balance, to the degree that one is hard put to explain what has changed in the past three hundred years.

The answer is that states have not until recently had to depend upon one another for the necessities of daily existence. In the past, trade was a tactical endeavor, a method used between wars, and one that could easily be sacrificed when military determinants so decreed. The great outpouring of trade between nations in the latter half of the nineteenth century did not prevent the First World War; it could be stanched as countries resorted to military means to acquire the territory or empire that would make them independent of others. No national leader would sacrifice territory to gain trade, unless the trade constituted a monopoly. Leaders aimed to have all needed resources in their own hands and did not wish to rely upon others.

As long as a state could get bigger and bigger, there was no incentive to regard trade with others as a strategic requirement, and for most of European history since the Renaissance, state units appeared to be growing larger. The five hundred or so units in Europe in 1500 were consolidated into about twenty-five by the year 1900.[4] If this process continued, statesmen and peoples could look forward to the creation of a few huge states like those in Orwell's *1984* which together controlled the globe. The process of imperialism in the late nineteenth century forwarded this conception: ultimately a few empires would become so enormous that they would not have to depend upon anyone else. Thus, the failure of the imperialist drive and the rapid decolonization of recent years have meant a change of direction in world politics. Since 1900, and especially after 1945, the number of nation-states has greatly increased, even more swiftly than the number belonging to the United Nations organizations. Between 170 and 180 states exist, and the number is growing. If contemporary nationalist and ethnic separatist movements succeed, some states in Europe, Africa, Asia, and Oceania may be further subdivided into new independent states or autonomous regions. These small and even weak states will scarcely be self-reliant; increasingly they will come to depend on others for economic and even military necessities, trading or sharing responsibilities with other nations. The age of the independent, self-sufficient state will be at an end. Among such states, the method of international development sustained by trade and exchange will begin to take precedence over the traditional method of territorial expansion and war. . . .

THE TRADING WORLD

. . . The role of Japan and Germany in the trading world is exceedingly interesting because it represents a reversal of past policies in both the nineteenth century and the 1930s. It is correct to say that the two countries experimented with foreign trade because they had been disabused of military expansion by World War II. For a time they were incapable of fighting war on a major scale; their endorsement of the trading system was merely an adoption of the remaining policy alternative. But that endorsement did not change even when the economic strength of the two nations might have sustained a much more nationalistic and militaristic policy. Given the choice between military expansion to achieve self-sufficiency (a choice made more difficult by modern conventional and nuclear weapons in the hands of other powers) and the procurement of necessary markets and raw materials through international commerce, Japan and Germany chose the latter.

It was not until the nineteenth century that this choice became available. During the mercantilist period (1500–1775) commerce was hobbled by restrictions, and any power that relied on it was at the mercy of the tariffs and imperial expansion of other nations. Until the late eighteenth century internal economic development was slow, and there seemed few means of adding to national wealth and power except by conquering territories which contained more peasants and grain. With the Industrial Revolution the link between territory and power was broken; it then became possible to gain economic strength without conquering new lands.[5] New sources of power could be developed within a society, simply by mobilizing them industrially. When combined with peaceful international trade, the Industrial Revolution allowed manufactured goods to find markets in faraway countries. The extra demand would lengthen production runs and increase both industrial efficiency (through economies of scale) and financial return. Such a strategy, if adhered to by all nations, could put an end to war. There was no sense in using military force to acquire power and wealth when they could be obtained more efficiently through peaceful economic development and trade.

The increasing prevalence of the trading option since 1945 raises peaceful possibilities that were neglected during the late nineteenth century and the 1930s. It seems safe to say that an international system composed of more than 160 states cannot continue to exist unless trade remains the primary vocation of most of its members. Were military and territorial orientations to dominate the scene, the trend to greater numbers of smaller states would be reversed, and larger states would conquer small and weak nations.

The possibility of such amalgamations cannot be entirely ruled out. Industrialization had two possible impacts: it allowed a nation to develop its wealth peacefully through internal economic growth, but it also knit new sinews of strength that could coerce other states. Industrialization made territorial expansion easier but also less necessary. In the mid-nineteenth century the Continental states pursued the expansion of their territories while Britain expanded her industry. The industrialization of Prussia and the development of her rail network enabled her armies to defeat Denmark, Austria, and France. Russia also used her new industrial technology to strengthen her military. In the last quarter of the century, even Britain returned to a primarily military and imperialist policy. In his book on imperialism Lenin declared that the drive for colonies was an imminent tendency of the capitalist system. Raw materials would run short and investment capital would pile up at home. The remedy was imperialism with colonies providing new sources for the former and outlets for the latter. But Lenin did not fully understand that an open international economy and intensive economic development at home obviated the need for colonies even under a capitalist, trading system.

The basic effect of World War II was to create much higher world interdependence as the average size of countries declined. The reversal of past trends toward a consolidation of states created instead a multitude of states that could not depend on themselves alone. They needed ties with other nations to prosper and remain viable as small entities. The trading system, as a result, was visible in defense relations as well as international commerce. Nations that could not stand on their own sought alliances or assistance from other powers, and they offered special defense contributions in fighting contingents, regional experience, or particular types of defense hardware. Dutch electronics, French aircraft, German guns and tanks, and British ships all made their independent contribution to an alliance in which no single power might be able to meet its defense needs on a self-sufficient basis. Israel developed a powerful and efficient small arms industry, as well as a great fund of experience combating terrorism. Israeli intelligence added considerably to the information available from Western sources, partly because of its understanding of Soviet weapons systems accumulated in several Arab-Israeli wars.

Defense interdependencies, however, are only one means of sharing the burdens placed upon the modern state. Perhaps more important is economic interdependence among countries. One should not place too much emphasis upon the existence of interdependence per se. European nations in 1913 relied upon the trade and investment between them; that did not prevent the political crisis which led to a breakdown of the international system and to World War I. Interdependence only constrains national policy if leaders accept and agree to work within its limits. In 1914 Lloyds of London had insured the German merchant marine but that did not stop Germany attacking Belgium, a neutral nation, or England from joining the war against Berlin.[6] The United States was Japan's best customer and source of raw materials in the 1930s, but that did not deter the Japanese attack on Pearl Harbor.

At least among the developed and liberal countries, interdependent ties since 1945 have come to be accepted as a fundamental and unchangeable feature of the situation. This recognition dawned gradually, and the United States may perhaps have been the last to acknowledge it, which was not surprising. The most powerful economy is ready to make fewer adjustments, and America tried initially to pursue its domestic economic policies without taking into account the effect on others, on itself, and on the international financial system as a whole. Presidents Kennedy and Lyndon B. Johnson tried to detach American domestic growth strategies from the deteriorating United States balance of payments, but they left a legacy of needed economic change to their successors. Finally, in the 1980s two American administrations accepted lower United States growth in order to control inflation and begin to focus on the international impact of United States policies. The delay in fashioning a strategy of adjustment to international economic realities almost certainly made it more difficult. Smaller countries actively sought to find a niche in the structure of international comparative advantage and in the demand for their goods. Larger countries with large internal markets postponed that reckoning as long as they could. By the 1980s, however, such change could no longer be avoided, and the United States leaders embarked upon new industrial and tax policies designed to increase economic growth and enable America to compete more effectively abroad.

Exports of Goods and Services (as a Percentage of GDP)		
Country	1965	1979
United States	5	9
Japan	11	12
Germany	18	26
United Kingdom	20	29
France	14	22

Note: Michael Stewart, *The Age of Interdependence* (Cambridge, Mass.: MIT Press, 1981). p. 21 (derived from United Nations *Yearbook of National Accounts Statistics*, 1980, vol. 2, table 2A).

The acceptance of new approaches was a reflection of the decline in economic sovereignty. As long as governments could control all the forces impinging upon their economies, welfare states would have no difficulty in implementing domestic planning for social ends. But as trade, investment, corporations, and to some degree labor moved from one national jurisdiction to another, no government could insulate and direct its economy without instituting the extreme protectionist and "beggar thy neighbor" policies of the 1930s. Rather than do this, the flow of goods and capital was allowed to proceed, and in recent years it has become a torrent. In some cases the flow of capital has increased to compensate for barriers or rigidities to the movement of goods.

In both cases the outcome is the result of modern developments in transportation and communications. Railway and high-speed highway networks now allow previously landlocked areas to participate in the international trading network that once depended on rivers and access to the sea. Modern communications and computers allow funds to be instantaneously transferred from one market to another, so that they may earn interest twenty-four hours a day. Transportation costs for a variety of goods have reached a new low, owing to container shipping and handling. For the major industrial countries (member countries of the Organization for Economic Cooperation and Development, which include the European community, Austria, Finland, Iceland, Portugal, Norway, Spain, Sweden, Switzerland, Turkey, Australia, Canada, Japan, New Zealand, and the United States), exports have risen much faster than either industrial production or gross domestic product since 1965, with the growth of GDP (in constant prices) at 4 percent and that of exports at 7.7 percent.[7] Only Japan's domestic growth has been able to keep pace with the increase in exports.

Foreign trade (the sum of exports and imports) percentages were roughly twice as large as these figures in each case. The explosion of foreign trade since 1945 has, if anything, been exceeded by the enormous movement of capital.

In 1950 the value of the stock of direct foreign investment held by U.S. companies was $11.8 billions, compared with $7.2 billions in 1935, $7.6 billions in 1929 and $3.9 billions in 1914. In the following decade, these investments increased by $22.4 billions, and at the end of 1967 their total value stood at $59 billions.[8]

In 1983, it had reached $226 billions.[9] And direct investment (that portion of investment which buys a significant stake in a foreign firm) was only one part of total United States investment overseas. In 1983 United States private assets abroad totaled $774 billion, or about three times as much.

The amounts, although very large, were not significant in themselves. In 1913, England's foreign investments, equaled one and one-half times her GNP as compared to present American totals of one-quarter of United States GNP. England's foreign trade was more than 40 percent of her national income as compared with contemporary American totals of 15–17 percent. England's pre–World War I involvement in international economic activities was greater than America's today.

Part of what must be explained in the evolution of interdependence is not the high level reached post-1945, but how even higher levels in 1913 could have fallen in the interim. Here the role of industrialization is paramount. As Karl Deutsch, following the work of Werner Sombart, has shown, in the early stages of industrial growth nations must import much of their needed machinery: rail and transportation networks are constructed with equipment and materials from abroad. Once new industries have been created, in a variety of fields, ranging from textiles to heavy industry, the national economy can begin to provide the goods that previously were imported.[10] The United States, the Scandinavian countries, and Japan reached this stage only after the turn of the century, and it was then that the gasoline-powered automobile industry and the manufacturing of electric motors and appliances began to develop rapidly and flourish. The further refinement of agricultural technology also rested on these innovations. Thus, even without restrictions and disruptions of trade, the 1920s would not have seen a rehabilitation of the old interdependent world economy of the 1890s. The further barriers erected in the 1930s confirmed and extended this outcome. If new industrial countries had less need for manufacturing imports, the growth and maintenance of general trade would then come to depend upon an increase in some other category of commerce than the traditional exchange of raw materials for finished goods. In the 1920s, as Albert Hirschman shows, the reciprocal exchange of industrial goods increased briefly, but fell again in the 1930s.[11] That decrease was only made up after 1945 when there was a striking and continuing growth in the trade of manufactured goods among industrial countries.[12] Some will say that this trade is distinctly expendable because countries could produce the goods they import on their own. None of the trade that the United States has today with Western Europe or Japan could really be dubbed "critical" in that the United States could not get along without it. American alternatives exist to almost all industrial products from other developed economies. Thus if interdependence means a trading link which "is costly to break,"[13] there is a sense that the sheer physical dependence of one country upon another, or upon international trade as a whole, has declined since the nineteenth century.

But to measure interdependence in this way misses the essence of the concept. Individuals in a state of nature can be quite independent if they are willing to live at a low standard of living and gather herbs, nuts, and fruits. They are not forced to depend on others but decide to do so to increase their total amount of food and security. Countries in an international state of nature (anarchy) can equally decide to depend only on themselves. They can limit what they consume to what they can produce at home, but they will thereby live less well than they might with specialization and extensive trade and interchange with other nations.

There is no shortage of energy in the world, for example, and all energy needs that previously have been satisfied by imported petroleum might be met by a great increase in coal and natural gas production, fission, and hydropower. But coal-generated electric power produces acid rain, and coal liquification (to produce fuel for automobiles) is expensive. Nuclear power leaves radioactive wastes which have to be contained. Importing oil is a cheaper and cleaner alternative. Thus even though a particular country, like the United States, might become energy self-sufficient if it wanted to, there is reason for dependence on the energy supplies of other nations. Does this mean creating a "tie that is costly to break"? Yes, in the sense that we live less well if we break the tie; but that doesn't mean that the tie could not be broken. Any tie can be broken. In this respect, all ties create "vulnerability interdependence" if they are in the interest of those who form them. One could get along without Japanese cars or European fashions, but eliminating them from the market restricts consumer choice and in fact raises opportunity costs. In this manner, trade between industrial countries may be equally important as trade linking industrial and raw material producing countries.

There are other ways in which interdependence has increased since the nineteenth century. Precisely because industrial countries imported agricultural commodities and sold their manufactured goods to less developed states, their dependence upon each other was much less in the nineteenth century and the 1920s than it is today. Toward the end of the nineteenth century Britain increasingly came to depend upon her empire for markets, food, and raw materials or upon countries in the early stages of industrialization. As Continental tariffs increased, Britain turned to her colonies, the United States, and Latin America to find markets for her exports. These markets provided ready receptacles for British goods when other areas became too competitive or unattractive; for example, Australia, India, Brazil and Argentina took the cotton, railways, steel and machinery that could not be sold in European markets. In the same way, whilst British capital exports to the latter dropped from 52 percent in the 1860s to 25 percent in the few years before 1914, those to the empire rose from 36 percent to 46 percent, and those to Latin America from 10.5 percent to 22 percent.[14]

The British foreign trade which totalled 43.5 percent of GNP in 1913 went increasingly to the empire; thus, if one takes Britain and the colonies as a single economic unit, that unit was much less dependent upon the outside world than, say, Britain is today with a smaller (30.4 percent) ratio of trade to GNP. And Britain alone had much less stake in Germany, France, and the Continental countries' economies than she does today as a member of the European Common Market.

In the nineteenth century trade was primarily vertical in character, taking place between countries at different stages of industrial development, and involving an exchange of manufactured goods on the one hand for food and raw materials on the other. But trade was not the only element in vertical interdependence.

British investment was also vertical in that it proceeded from the developed center, London, to less developed capitals in the Western Hemisphere, Oceania, and the Far East. Such ties might contribute to community feeling in the British Empire, later the Commonwealth of Nations, but it would not restrain conflicts among the countries of Western Europe. Three-quarters of foreign investment of all European countries in 1914 was lodged outside of Europe. In 1913, in the British case 66 percent of her foreign investment went to North and South America and Australia, 28 percent to the Middle and Far East, and only 6 percent to Europe.

In addition, about 90 percent of foreign investment in 1913 was portfolio investment, that is, it represented small holdings of foreign shares that could easily be disposed of on the stock exchange. Direct investment, or investment which represented more than a 10 percent share of the total ownership of a foreign firm, was only one-tenth of the total. Today the corresponding figure for the United States is nearly 30 percent. The growth of direct foreign investment since 1945 is a reflection of the greater stake that countries have in each other's well-being in the contemporary period.

In this respect international interdependence has been fostered by a growing interpenetration of economies, in the sense that one economy owns part of another, sends part of its population to live and work in it, and becomes increasingly dependent upon the progress of the latter.[15] The multinational corporation which originates in one national jurisdiction, but operates in others as well, is the primary vehicle for such investment ownership. Stimulated by the demands and incentives of the product life cycle, the multinational corporation invests and produces abroad to make sure of retaining its market share. That market may be in the host country, or it may be in the home country, once the foreign production is imported back into the home economy. Foreign trade has grown enormously since 1945. But its necessary growth has been reduced by the operation of multinational companies in foreign jurisdictions: production abroad reduces the need for exports. In this way an interpenetrative stake has increased between developed economies even when tariffs and other restrictions might appear to have stunted the growth of exports. The application of a common external tariff to the European Economic Community in the 1960s greatly stimulated American foreign investment in Europe, which became such a massive tide that Europeans reacted against the "American challenge," worrying that their prized national economic assets might be preempted by the United States.

They need not have worried. The reverse flow of European and Japanese investment in the United States is reaching such enormous proportions that America has become a net debtor nation: a country that has fewer assets overseas than foreigners have in the United States. The threatened imposition of higher American tariffs and quotas on imports led foreign companies to invest in the United States in gigantic amounts, thereby obviating the need to send exports from their home nation. Such direct investment represents a much more permanent stake in the economic welfare of the host nation than exports to that market could ever be. Foreign production is a more permanent economic commitment than foreign sales, because large shares of a foreign company or subsidiary could not be sold on a stock exchange. The attempt to market such large holdings would only have the effect of depressing the value of the stock. Direct investment is thus illiquid, as opposed to the traditional portfolio investment of the nineteenth century.

After 1945 one country slowly developed a stake in another, but the process was not initially reciprocal. Until the beginning of the 1970s, the trend was largely for Americans to invest abroad, in Europe, Latin America, and East Asia. As the American dollar cheapened after 1973, however, a reverse flow began, with Europeans and Japanese placing large blocs of capital in American firms and acquiring international companies. Third World multinationals, from Hong Kong, the OPEC countries, and East Asia also began to invest in the United States. By the end of the 1970s world investment was much more balanced, with the European stake in the American economy nearly offsetting the American investment in Europe. Japan also moved to diversify her export offensive in the American market by starting to produce in the United States. But Japan did not benefit from a reciprocal stake in her own economy. Since foreign investors have either been kept out of the Japanese market or have been forced to accept cumbersome joint ventures with Japanese firms, few multinationals have a major commitment to the Japanese market. Japan imports the smallest percentage of manufactured goods of any leading industrial nation. Thus when economic policy makers in America and Europe formulate growth strategies, they are not forced to consider the Japanese economy on a par with their own because American and Europeans have little to lose if Japan does not prosper. In her own self-interest Japan will almost certainly have to open her capital market and economy to foreign penetration if she wishes to enjoy corresponding access to economies of other nations. Greater Japanese foreign direct investment will only partly mitigate the pressures on Tokyo in this respect.

NOTES

1 Quoted in Walter L. Dorn, *Competition for Empire* (New York: Harper & Row, 1940), p. 370.
2 See Robert O. Keohane, *After Hegemony* (Princeton: Princeton University Press, 1984), p. 199.
3 Henry A. Kissinger, *Years of Upheaval* (Boston: Little Brown, 1982), pp. 891–95, 939–45, 975–78.

4 Charles Tilly, ed., *The Formation of National States in Western Europe* (Princeton: Princeton University Press, 1975), p. 24.

5 It is true that the greatest imperial edifices were constructed after the start of the Industrial Revolution. It was precisely that revolution, however, which prepared the groundwork for their demise.

6 Paul Kennedy, *Strategy and Diplomacy 1870–1945* (London: Fontana Paperbacks 1984), pp. 95–96.

7 Michael Stewart, *The Age of Interdependence* (Cambridge, Mass.: MIT Press, 1984), p. 20.

8 John H. Dunning, *Studies in International Investment* (London: George Allen and Unwin, 1970), p. 1.

9 "International Investment Position of the United States at Year End" in *Survey of Current Business* (Washington, D.C.: Department of Commerce, June 1984).

10 Karl W. Deutsch and Alexander Eckstein, "National Industrialism and the Declining Share of the International Economic Sector, 1890–1959" in *World Politics*, 13 (January 1961), pp. 267–99.

11 *National Power and the Structure of Foreign Trade* (Berkeley: University of California Press, 1980), pp. 129–43.

12 Richard Rosecrance and Arthur Stein, "Interdependence: Myth or Reality" in *World Politics* (July 1973), pp. 7–9.

13 Kenneth N. Waltz, "The Myth of National Interdependence" in Charles Kindleberger, ed., *The International Corporation* (Cambridge, Mass.: MIT Press, 1970), p. 206.

14 Paul Kennedy, *The Rise and Fall of British Naval Mastery* (London: Allen Lane, 1976), pp. 187–88.

15 Nothing could be more misleading than to equate these interrelations with those of nineteenth-century imperialism. Then imperial dictates went in one direction—military, economic, and social. The metropole dominated the colony. Today, does North America become a colony when Chicanos and Hispanics move to it in increasing numbers or England a tributary of the West Indies? Does Chinese or Korean investment in the United States render it a peripheral member of the system? The point is that influence goes in both directions just as does investment and trade in manufactured goods.

Reading 5.9

China's Choice   *G. John Ikenberry*

The rise of China will undoubtedly be one of the great dramas of the twenty-first century. China's extraordinary economic growth and active diplomacy are already transforming East Asia, and future decades will see even greater increases in Chinese power and influence. But exactly how this

Source: G. John Ikenberry, "The Rise of China and the Future of the West: Can the Liberal System Survive?" Foreign Affairs 87, no. 1 (January/February 2008).

drama will play out is an open question. Will China overthrow the existing order or become a part of it? And what, if anything, can the United States do to maintain its position as China rises?

Some observers believe that the American era is coming to an end, as the Western-oriented world order is replaced by one increasingly dominated by the East. The historian Niall Ferguson has written that the bloody twentieth century witnessed "the descent of the West" and "a reorientation of the world" toward the East. Realists go on to note that as China gets more powerful and the United States' position erodes, two things are likely to happen: China will try to use its growing influence to reshape the rules and institutions of the international system to better serve its interests, and other states in the system—especially the declining hegemon—will start to see China as a growing security threat. The result of these developments, they predict, will be tension, distrust, and conflict, the typical features of a power transition. In this view, the drama of China's rise will feature an increasingly powerful China and a declining United States locked in an epic battle over the rules and leadership of the international system. And as the world's largest country emerges not from within but outside the established post–World War II international order, it is a drama that will end with the grand ascendance of China and the onset of an Asian-centered world order.

That course, however, is not inevitable. The rise of China does not have to trigger a wrenching hegemonic transition. The U.S.–Chinese power transition can be very different from those of the past because China faces an international order that is fundamentally different from those that past rising states confronted. China does not just face the United States; it faces a Western-centered system that is open, integrated, and rule-based, with wide and deep political foundations. The nuclear revolution, meanwhile, has made war among great powers unlikely—eliminating the major tool that rising powers have used to overturn international systems defended by declining hegemonic states. Today's Western order, in short, is hard to overturn and easy to join.

This unusually durable and expansive order is itself the product of far-sighted U.S. leadership. After World War II, the United States did not simply establish itself as the leading world power. It led in the creation of universal institutions that not only invited global membership but also brought democracies and market societies closer together. It built an order that facilitated the participation and integration of both established great powers and newly independent states. (It is often forgotten that this postwar order was designed in large part to reintegrate the defeated Axis states and the beleaguered Allied states into a unified international system.) Today, China can gain full access to and thrive within this system. And if it does, China will rise, but the Western order—if managed properly—will live on.

As it faces an ascendant China, the United States should remember that its leadership of the Western order allows it to shape the environment in which China will make critical strategic choices. If it wants to preserve this leadership, Washington must work to strengthen the rules and institutions that underpin that order—making it even easier to join and harder to overturn. U.S. grand strategy should be built around the motto "The road to the East runs through the West." It must sink the roots of this order as deeply as possible, giving China greater incentives for integration than for opposition and increasing the chances that the system will survive even after U.S. relative power has declined.

The United States' "unipolar moment" will inevitably end. If the defining struggle of the twenty-first century is between China and the United States, China will have the advantage. If the defining struggle is between China and a revived Western system, the West will triumph.

TRANSITIONAL ANXIETIES

China is well on its way to becoming a formidable global power. The size of its economy has quadrupled since the launch of market reforms in the late 1970s and, by some estimates, will double again over the next decade. It has become one of the world's major manufacturing centers and consumes roughly a third of the global supply of iron, steel, and coal. It has accumulated massive foreign reserves, worth more than $1 trillion at the end of 2006. China's military spending has increased at an inflation-adjusted rate of over 18 percent a year, and its diplomacy has extended its reach not just in Asia but also in Africa, Latin America, and the Middle East. Indeed, whereas the Soviet Union rivaled the United States as a military competitor only, China is emerging as both a military and an economic rival—heralding a profound shift in the distribution of global power.

Power transitions are a recurring problem in international relations. As scholars such as Paul Kennedy and Robert Gilpin have described it, world politics has been marked by a succession of powerful states rising up to organize the international system. A powerful state can create and enforce the rules and institutions of a stable global order in which to pursue its interests and security. But nothing lasts forever: long-term changes in the distribution of power give rise to new challenger states, who set off a struggle over the terms of that international order. Rising states want to translate their newly acquired power into greater authority in the global system—to reshape the rules and institutions in accordance with their own interests. Declining states, in turn, fear their loss of control and worry about the security implications of their weakened position.

These moments are fraught with danger. When a state occupies a commanding position in the international system, neither it nor weaker states have an incentive to change the existing order. But when the power of a challenger state grows and the power of the leading state weakens, a strategic rivalry ensues, and conflict—perhaps leading to war—becomes likely. The danger of power transitions is captured most dramatically in the case of late-nineteenth-century Germany. In 1870, the United Kingdom had a three-to-one advantage in economic power over Germany and a significant military advantage as well; by 1903, Germany had pulled ahead in terms of both economic and military power. As Germany unified and grew, so, too, did its dissatisfactions and demands, and as it grew more powerful, it increasingly appeared as a threat to other great powers in Europe, and security competition began. In the strategic realignments that followed, France, Russia, and the United Kingdom, formerly enemies, banded together to confront an emerging Germany. The result was a European war. Many observers see this dynamic emerging in U.S.-Chinese relations. "If China continues its impressive economic growth over the next few decades," the realist scholar John Mearsheimer has written, "the United States and China are likely to engage in an intense security competition with considerable potential for war."

But not all power transitions generate war or overturn the old order. In the early decades of the twentieth century, the United Kingdom ceded authority to the United States without great conflict or even a rupture in relations. From the late 1940s to the early 1990s, Japan's economy grew from the equivalent of five percent of U.S. GDP to the equivalent of over 60 percent of U.S. GDP, and yet Japan never challenged the existing international order.

Clearly, there are different types of power transitions. Some states have seen their economic and geopolitical power grow dramatically and have still accommodated themselves to the existing order. Others have risen up and sought to change it. Some power transitions have led to the breakdown of the old order and the establishment of a new international hierarchy. Others have brought about only limited adjustments in the regional and global system.

A variety of factors determine the way in which power transitions unfold. The nature of the rising state's regime and the degree of its dissatisfaction with the old order are critical: at the end of the nineteenth century, the United States, a liberal country an ocean away from Europe, was better able to embrace the British-centered international order than Germany was. But even more decisive is the character of the international order itself—for it is the nature of the international order that shapes a rising state's choice between challenging that order and integrating into it.

OPEN ORDER

The postwar Western order is historically unique. Any international order dominated by a powerful state is based on a mix of coercion and consent, but the U.S.-led order is distinctive in that it has been more liberal than imperial—and so unusually accessible, legitimate, and durable. Its rules and institutions are rooted in, and thus reinforced by, the evolving global forces of democracy and capitalism. It is expansive, with a wide and widening array of participants and stakeholders. It is capable of generating tremendous economic growth and power while also signaling restraint—all of which make it hard to overturn and easy to join.

It was the explicit intention of the Western order's architects in the 1940s to make that order integrative and expansive. Before the Cold War split the world into competing camps, Franklin Roosevelt sought to create a one-world system managed by cooperative great powers that would rebuild war-ravaged Europe, integrate the defeated states, and establish mechanisms for security cooperation and expansive economic growth. In fact, it was Roosevelt who urged—over the opposition of Winston Churchill—that China be included as a permanent member of the UN Security Council. The then Australian ambassador to the United States wrote in his diary after his first meeting with Roosevelt during the war, "He said that he had numerous discussions with Winston about China and that he felt that Winston was 40 years behind the times on China and he continually referred to the Chinese as 'Chinks' and 'Chinamen' and he felt that this was very dangerous. He wanted to keep China as a friend because in 40 or 50 years' time China might easily become a very powerful military nation."

Over the next half century, the United States used the system of rules and institutions it had built to good effect. West Germany was bound to its democratic Western European neighbors through the European Coal and Steel Community (and, later, the European Community) and to the United States through the Atlantic security pact; Japan was bound to the United States through an alliance partnership and expanding economic ties. The Bretton Woods meeting in 1944 laid down the monetary and trade rules that facilitated the opening and subsequent flourishing of the world economy—an astonishing achievement given the ravages of war and the competing interests of the great powers. Additional agreements between the United States, Western Europe, and Japan solidified the open and multilateral character of the postwar world economy. After the onset of the Cold War, the Marshall Plan in Europe and the 1951 security pact between the United States and Japan further integrated the defeated Axis powers into the Western order.

In the final days of the Cold War, this system once again proved remarkably successful. As the Soviet Union declined, the Western order offered a set of rules and institutions that provided Soviet leaders with both reassurances and points of access—effectively encouraging them to become a part of the system. Moreover, the shared leadership of the order ensured accommodation of the Soviet Union. As the Reagan administration pursued a hard-line policy toward Moscow, the Europeans pursued détente and engagement. For every hard-line "push," there was a moderating "pull," allowing Mikhail Gorbachev to pursue high-risk reforms. On the eve of German unification, the fact that a united Germany would be embedded in European and Atlantic institutions—rather than becoming an independent great power—helped reassure Gorbachev that neither German nor Western intentions were hostile. After the Cold War, the Western order once again managed the integration of a new wave of countries, this time from the formerly communist world. Three particular features of the Western order have been critical to this success and longevity.

First, unlike the imperial systems of the past, the Western order is built around rules and norms of nondiscrimination and market openness, creating conditions for rising states to advance their expanding economic and political goals within it. Across history, international orders have varied widely in terms of whether the material benefits that are generated accrue disproportionately to the leading state or are widely shared. In the Western system, the barriers to economic participation are low, and the potential benefits are high. China has already discovered the massive economic returns that are possible by operating within this open-market system.

Second is the coalition-based character of its leadership. Past orders have tended to be dominated by one state. The stakeholders of the current Western order include a coalition of powers arrayed around the United States—an important distinction. These leading states, most of them advanced liberal democracies, do not always agree, but they are engaged in a continuous process of give-and-take over economics, politics, and security. Power transitions are typically seen as being played out between two countries, a rising state and a declining hegemon, and the order falls as soon as the power balance shifts. But in the current order, the larger aggregation of democratic capitalist states—and the resulting accumulation of geopolitical power—shifts the balance in the order's favor.

Third, the postwar Western order has an unusually dense, encompassing, and broadly endorsed system of rules and institutions. Whatever its shortcomings, it is more open and rule-based than any previous order. State sovereignty and the rule of law are not just norms enshrined in the United Nations Charter. They are part of the deep operating logic of the order. To be sure, these norms are evolving, and the United States itself has historically been ambivalent about binding itself to international law and institutions—and at no time more so than today. But the overall system is dense with multilateral rules and institutions—global and regional, economic, political, and security-related. These represent one of the great breakthroughs of the postwar era. They have laid the basis for unprecedented levels of cooperation and shared authority over the global system.

The incentives these features create for China to integrate into the liberal international order are reinforced by the changed nature of the international economic environment—especially the new interdependence driven by technology. The most farsighted Chinese leaders understand that globalization has changed the game and that China accordingly needs strong, prosperous partners around the world. From the United States' perspective, a healthy Chinese economy is vital to the United States and the rest of the world. Technology and the global economic revolution have created a logic of economic relations that is different from the past—making the political and institutional logic of the current order all the more powerful.

ACCOMMODATING THE RISE

The most important benefit of these features today is that they give the Western order a remarkable capacity to accommodate rising powers. New entrants into the system have ways of gaining status and authority and opportunities to play a role in governing the order. The fact that the United States, China, and other great powers have nuclear weapons also limits the ability of a rising power to overturn the existing order. In the age of nuclear deterrence, great-power war is, thankfully, no longer a mechanism of historical change. War-driven change has been abolished as a historical process.

The Western order's strong framework of rules and institutions is already starting to facilitate Chinese integration. At first, China embraced certain rules and institutions for defensive purposes: protecting its sovereignty and economic interests while seeking to reassure other states of its peaceful intentions by getting involved in regional and global groupings. But as the scholar Marc Lanteigne argues, "What separates China from other states, and indeed previous global powers, is that not only is it 'growing up' within a milieu of international institutions far more developed than ever before, but more importantly, it is doing so while making active use of these institutions to promote the country's development of global power status." China, in short, is increasingly working within, rather than outside of, the Western order.

China is already a permanent member of the UN Security Council, a legacy of Roosevelt's determination to build the universal body around diverse great-power leadership. This gives China the same authority and advantages of "great-power exceptionalism" as the other permanent members. The existing global trading system is also valuable to China, and increasingly so. Chinese economic interests are quite congruent with the current global economic system—a system that is open and loosely institutionalized and that China has enthusiastically embraced and thrived in. State power today is ultimately based on sustained economic growth, and China is well aware that no major state can modernize without integrating into the globalized capitalist system; if a country wants to be a world power, it has no choice but to join the World Trade Organization (WTO). The road to global power, in effect, runs through the Western order and its multilateral economic institutions.

China not only needs continued access to the global capitalist system; it also wants the protections that the system's rules and institutions provide. The WTO's multilateral trade principles and dispute-settlement mechanisms, for example, offer China tools to defend against the threats of discrimination and protectionism that rising economic powers often confront. The evolution of China's policy suggests that Chinese leaders recognize these advantages: as Beijing's growing commitment to economic liberalization has increased the foreign investment and trade China has enjoyed, so has Beijing increasingly embraced global trade rules. It is possible that as China comes to champion the WTO, the support of the more mature Western economies for the WTO will wane. But it is more likely that both the rising and the declining countries will find value in the quasi-legal mechanisms that allow conflicts to be settled or at least diffused.

The existing international economic institutions also offer opportunities for new powers to rise up through their hierarchies. In the International Monetary Fund and the World Bank, governance is based on economic shares, which growing countries can translate into greater institutional voice. To be sure, the process of adjustment has been slow. The United States and Europe still dominate the IMF. Washington has a 17 percent voting share (down from 30 percent)—a controlling amount, because 85 percent approval is needed for action—and the European Union has a major say in the appointment of ten of the 24 members of the board. But there are growing pressures, notably the need for resources and the need to maintain relevance, that will likely persuade the Western states to admit China into the inner circle of these economic governance institutions. The IMF's existing shareholders, for example, see a bigger role for rising developing countries as necessary to renew the institution and get it through its current crisis of mission. At the IMF's meeting in Singapore in September 2006, they agreed on reforms that will give China, Mexico, South Korea, and Turkey a greater voice.

As China sheds its status as a developing country (and therefore as a client of these institutions), it will increasingly be able to act as a patron and stakeholder instead. Leadership in these organizations is not simply a reflection of economic size (the United States has retained its voting share in the IMF even as its economic weight has declined); nonetheless, incremental advancement within them will create important opportunities for China.

POWER SHIFT AND PEACEFUL CHANGE

Seen in this light, the rise of China need not lead to a volcanic struggle with the United States over global rules and leadership. The Western order has the potential to turn the coming power shift into a peaceful change on terms favorable to the United States. But that will only happen if the United States sets about strengthening the existing order. Today, with Washington preoccupied with terrorism and war in the Middle East, rebuilding Western rules and institutions might to some seem to be of only marginal relevance. Many Bush administration officials have been outright hostile to the multilateral, rule-based system that the United States has shaped and led. Such hostility is foolish and dangerous. China will become powerful: it is already on the rise, and the United States' most powerful strategic weapon is the ability to decide what sort of international order will be in place to receive it.

The United States must reinvest in the Western order, reinforcing the features of that order that encourage engagement, integration, and restraint. The more this order binds together capitalist democratic states in deeply rooted institutions; the more open, consensual, and rule-based it is; and the more widely spread its benefits, the more likely it will be that rising powers can and will secure their interests through integration and accommodation rather than through war. And if the Western system offers rules and institutions that benefit the full range of states—rising and falling, weak and strong, emerging and mature—its dominance as an international order is all but certain.

The first thing the United States must do is reestablish itself as the foremost supporter of the global system of governance that underpins the Western order. Doing so will first of all facilitate the kind of collective problem solving that makes all countries better off. At the same time, when other countries see the United States using its power to strengthen existing rules and institutions, that power is rendered more legitimate—and U.S. authority is strengthened. Countries within the West become more inclined to work with, rather than resist, U.S. power, which reinforces the centrality and dominance of the West itself.

Renewing Western rules and institutions will require, among other things, updating the old bargains that underpinned key postwar security pacts. The strategic understanding behind both NATO and Washington's East Asian alliances is that the United States will work with its allies to provide security and bring them in on decisions over the use of force, and U.S. allies, in return, will operate within the U.S.-led Western order. Security cooperation in the West remains extensive today, but with the main security threats less obvious than they were during the Cold War, the purposes and responsibilities of these alliances are under dispute. Accordingly, the United States needs to reaffirm the political value of these alliances—recognizing that they are part of a wider Western institutional architecture that allows states to do business with one another.

The United States should also renew its support for wide-ranging multilateral institutions. On the economic front, this would include building on the agreements and architecture of the WTO, including pursuing efforts to conclude the current Doha Round of trade talks, which seeks to extend market opportunities and trade liberalization to developing countries. The WTO is at a critical stage. The basic standard of nondiscrimination is at risk thanks to the proliferation of bilateral and regional trade agreements. Meanwhile, there are growing doubts over whether the WTO can in fact carry out trade liberalization, particularly in agriculture, that benefits developing countries. These issues may seem narrow, but the fundamental character of the liberal international order—its commitment to universal rules of openness that spread gains widely—is at stake. Similar doubts haunt a host of other multilateral agreements—on global warming and nuclear nonproliferation, among others—and they thus also demand renewed U.S. leadership.

The strategy here is not simply to ensure that the Western order is open and rule-based. It is also to make sure that the order does not fragment into an array of bilateral and "minilateral" arrangements, causing the United States to find itself tied to only a few key states in various regions. Under such a scenario, China would have an opportunity to build its own set of bilateral and "minilateral" pacts. As a result, the world would be broken into competing U.S. and Chinese spheres. The more security and economic relations are multilateral and all-encompassing, the more the global system retains its coherence.

In addition to maintaining the openness and durability of the order, the United States must redouble its efforts to integrate rising developing countries into key global institutions. Bringing emerging countries into the governance of the international order will give it new life. The United States and Europe must find room at the table not only for China but also for countries such as Brazil, India, and South Africa. A Goldman Sachs report on the so-called BRICs (Brazil, Russia, India, and China) noted that by 2050 these countries' economies could together be larger than those of the original G-6 countries (Germany, France, Italy, Japan, the United Kingdom, and the United States) combined. Each international institution presents its own challenges. The UN Security Council is perhaps the hardest to deal with, but its reform would also bring the greatest returns. Less formal bodies—the so-called G-20 and various other intergovernmental networks—can provide alternative avenues for voice and representation.

THE TRIUMPH OF THE LIBERAL ORDER

The key thing for U.S. leaders to remember is that it may be possible for China to overtake the United States alone, but it is much less likely that China will ever manage to overtake the Western order. In terms of economic weight, for example, China will surpass the United States as the largest state in the global system sometime around 2020. (Because of its population, China needs a level of productivity only one-fifth that of the United States to become the world's biggest economy.) But when the economic capacity of the Western system as a whole is considered, China's economic advances look much less significant; the Chinese economy will be much smaller than the combined economies of the Organization for Economic Cooperation and Development far into the future. This is even truer of military might: China cannot hope to come anywhere close to total OECD military expenditures anytime soon. The capitalist democratic world is a powerful constituency for the preservation—and, indeed, extension—of the existing international order. If China intends to rise up and challenge the existing order, it has a much more daunting task than simply confronting the United States.

The "unipolar moment" will eventually pass. U.S. dominance will eventually end. U.S. grand strategy, accordingly, should be driven by one key question: What kind of international order would the United States like to see in place when it is less powerful?

This might be called the neo-Rawlsian question of the current era. The political philosopher John Rawls argued that political institutions should be conceived behind a "veil of ignorance"—that is, the architects should design institutions as if they do not know precisely where they will be within a socioeconomic system. The result would be a system that safeguards a person's interests regardless of whether he is rich or poor, weak or strong. The United States needs to take that approach to its leadership of the international order today. It must put in place institutions and fortify rules that will safeguard its interests regardless of where exactly in the hierarchy it is or how exactly power is distributed in 10, 50, or 100 years.

Fortunately, such an order is in place already. The task now is to make it so expansive and so institutionalized that China has no choice but to become a full-fledged member of it. The United States cannot thwart China's rise, but it can help ensure that China's power is exercised within the rules and institutions that the United States and its partners have crafted over the last century, rules and institutions that can protect the interests of all states in the more crowded world of the future. The United States' global position may be weakening, but the international system the United States leads can remain the dominant order of the twenty-first century.

Politics: Ideology and Identity

War is about who rules, and thus the motives for using force to implant one set of rulers rather than another. Naked material interest may account for motives in some cases, and loftier principles offered as justification may sometimes be no more than false rationalizations for such naked interest. Principles of some sort are almost always invoked, however, when governments or groups decide to spill blood or threaten to do so. A wide range of philosophical principles has been associated with political conflict, including moral rationales for claims of population groups to territory for exclusive living space.

Ideology has played a tremendous role in international interaction, especially since the French Revolution. The twentieth century was dominated by the global clash of secular ideologies—liberalism, communism, and fascism. Ideology has also overlapped with issues of identity, as groups conceived their interests and loyalties in terms of class, ethnicity, religion, or other social attributes. At the end of the twentieth century, identity concerns came to the fore again, as political violence between ethnic groups within many political units escalated in the wake of the Communist collapse, and they continue to play a major role in the twenty-first century, especially in conflicts in the Middle East, South Asia, and Africa.

Assessment of threats even by hard-boiled realists can depend on assumptions about these questions. When E. H. Carr's *Twenty Years Crisis* (excerpted in Part II, this volume) was first published in 1939, its case for realism was also an argument for accommodation with German power. Liberal idealism interfered with sensible policy, as Carr saw it, by placing principle over prudence and by confusing the morality of international relations that coincided with the self-interest of World War I's victorious powers with a disinterested universal morality. In this view, Western liberalism was a visionary philosophy interfering with realist behavior. What Carr failed to see was how Nazi ideology trumped realism as well. The unfolding of World War II made clear that Hitler was not just another opportunistic realist statesman who could be contained or deterred by traditional balance of power politics.[1] Nazi Germany showed the awesome force that idealism of a terrible sort can exert in international politics. It is difficult to appreciate the unlimited nature of Nazi aims without understanding Hitler as an idealist more than a pragmatist.[2] It is also quite doubtful that realism, rather than imprudent idealism and wishful thinking, could have justified Churchill's defiant refusal to make peace, and his stirring insistence on pursuit of victory against all odds, in the desperate days between the fall of France and Hitler's reckless decisions to take on the Soviet Union and United States. Whether or not realists are correct in arguing that ideology *should not* matter in relations between states, it is clear that it often does.

The triumph of liberal political principles in the post-Communist era has so far lagged behind that of liberal economic models. Command economies have given way to the market almost everywhere, yet authoritarian polities have been slower to follow—China is the most obvious and most important example. Nevertheless, the burgeoning of democracy was one of the major world changes after the mid-1980s. If we believe Kant, this trend must be a force for peace. But this burgeoning of democracy coincided with resurgence of strong nationalisms, and the relation between the trends is problematic.

"Democratic peace" theory presented in Part III leaves several questions that may qualify optimism. First, what kind of democracy is necessary? Kant's argument was not that democracies are pacific, but that republics are. If liberalism rather than democracy is the critical ingredient, then the theory depends on a more specific argument. Democracy spread further than liberalism in the post–Cold War world. Democracies that are majoritarian but illiberal—such as post-Communist Yugoslavia, Iran, Iraq, or other states that have elections but not protections for minority rights—may not support democratic peace.[3] Recent populist movements raise this question in the West.

Second, will the post-Communist trend to democratization survive? Or will crushing economic problems prove too much for some new democracies to bear, yielding disillusionment, authoritarian populism, dictatorship, a search for scapegoats, and temptations to project frustration outward? Political liberalism may subvert economic liberalism by empowering people to resist the distribution of pain that goes with tearing down the rickety old economy before a sleek new one is constructed to take its place. The consequent disappointment with economic results may in turn subvert political liberalism. Anxiety arose in the 1990s about the danger of "Weimar Russia," a weakly institutionalized Russian democracy vulnerable to xenophobic nationalist backlash. The process of democratization in that important country was sluggish and incomplete and then suffered further setback under Vladimir Putin.

Third, will democratization unleash violent forms of nationalism, and will national divisions compound a decline of democracy? Mansfield and Snyder's article in this section uses a careful survey of data to demonstrate that although democracy may be conducive to peace, the process of becoming a secure democracy tends toward the reverse—conflict and violence.[4] One thing

Marxism-Leninism did, in institutionalizing regimes based in principle on class solidarity, was delegitimize divisive nationalism and suppress it by force. Now the resurgence of nationalism marks the new world just as much as the proliferation of democratic political forms. Indeed, the norm of self-determination promotes nationalism. Events in the former Yugoslavia and southern parts of the former Soviet Union dramatically highlighted the problem.

Fourth, if ethnic violence, civil war, and regional chaos result from unconstrained nationalist impulses, can such small wars be kept limited, or will they contaminate relations among great powers, creating anxieties about instability, power vacuums, or intervention by others that could catalyze a crisis and escalation to large-scale conflict in a manner similar to 1914? In the 1990s this was a concern in the Balkans, as some liberals argued that outside intervention was necessary to contain local instability, while some realists argued that it was likely to bring the great power patrons of local contenders into confrontation with each other. As the twenty-first century began, the wars in Bosnia and Kosovo were stopped by NATO interventions, a result that appears consistent with the liberal rationale, but at the price of worsened diplomatic relations with Russia and China, which appears consistent with the realist fear.

Nationalism need not contradict liberalism. Indeed, in the nineteenth century the two tidal forces moved together. And if giving each nation its own state prevents civil war in multinational states, the result should favor peace. But the map does not make that solution easy. Should all nations get their own states when we are sometimes unsure what constitutes a "nation"? Or if doing so would truncate other states—for example, a Kurdistan carved from Turkey, Iran, Iraq, and Syria? Or when the intermingling of minorities would produce awkward gerrymandering for South Ossetians in Georgia, Armenians in Azerbaijan, Trans-Dniester Russians in Moldova, or Serbs in Croatia and Bosnia? Or when it could mean endless redivision into tribal mini-states, as in Africa? The selection from Ernest Gellner describes some of the conceptual problems in dealing with nationalism, and differences between benign and malignant forms of it. Can visceral nationalist antipathies annealed in ethnic violence be subordinated to liberal norms, in a reintegrated state, without increasing the risk of reigniting war? Once groups have been at each others' throats, can they live together again in stable peace intermingled, or must they be separated in order to defuse the potential for renewed communal violence? Chaim Kaufmann and Radha Kumar present contrasting arguments on this question.

Neoliberal institutionalism focuses attention on movement in the other direction. Integration rather than independence, through the evolution of organizations such as the European Union, has more often seemed the wave of the future to liberal theorists in recent times. Realists too have often assumed that balance of power imperatives naturally pushed the international system toward consolidation rather than fractionation of states.[5] Which trends will prove to be the wave of the future—integration in the West, or disintegration in the East?

—RKB

NOTES

1 For argument to the contrary, see A.J.P. Taylor, *The Origins of the Second World War* (New York: Atheneum, 1962).

2 See Stanley Kober, "Idealpolitik," *Foreign Policy* No. 79 (Summer 1990).

3 Fareed Zakaria, *The Future of Freedom: Illiberal Democracy at Home and Abroad* (New York: W.W. Norton, 2003).

4 The full version of this analysis is Edward D. Mansfield and Jack Snyder, *Electing to Fight* (Cambridge, Mass.: MIT Press, 2005).

5 E.H. Carr's *Nationalism and After* (New York: Macmillan, 1945) is a fascinating example of reasoning that partakes of both perspectives. It is particularly interesting considering when it was written (the closing days of World War II) and its conviction that the war had made nationalism obsolete—hardly a view that most expect from an author so associated with realism.

Reading 6.1

Democratization and War
EDWARD D. MANSFIELD AND JACK SNYDER

DANGERS OF TRANSITION

The idea that democracies never fight wars against each other has become an axiom for many scholars. It is, as one scholar puts it, "as close as anything we have to an empirical law in international relations." This "law" is invoked by American statesmen to justify a foreign policy that encourages democratization abroad. In his 1994 State of the Union address, President Clinton asserted that no two democracies had ever gone to war with each other, thus explaining why promoting democracy abroad was a pillar of his foreign policy.

It is probably true that a world in which more countries were mature, stable democracies would be safer and preferable for the United States. But countries do not become mature democracies overnight. They usually go through a rocky transition, where mass politics mixes with authoritarian elite politics in a volatile way. Statistical evidence covering the past two centuries shows that in this transitional phase of democratization, countries become more aggressive and war-prone, not less, and they do fight wars with democratic states. In fact, formerly authoritarian states where democratic participation is on the rise are more likely to fight wars than are stable democracies or autocracies. States that make the biggest leap, from total autocracy to extensive mass democracy—like contemporary Russia—are about twice as likely to fight wars in the decade after democratization as are states that remain autocracies.

This historical pattern of democratization, belligerent nationalism, and war is already emerging in some of today's new or partial democracies, especially some formerly communist states. Two pairs of states—Serbia and Croatia, and Armenia and Azerbaijan—have found themselves at war while experimenting with varying degrees of electoral democracy. The electorate of Russia's partial democracy cast nearly a quarter of its votes for the party of radical nationalist Vladimir Zhirinovsky. Even mainstream Russian politicians have adopted an imperial tone in their dealings with neighboring former Soviet republics, and military force has been used ruthlessly in Chechnya.

The following evidence should raise questions about the Clinton administration's policy of promoting peace by promoting democratization. The expectation that the spread of democracy will probably contribute to peace in the long run, once new democracies mature, provides little comfort to those who

Source: Edward D. Mansfield and Jack Snyder, "Democratization and War." Reprinted by permission of Foreign Affairs Vol. 74, No. 3 (May/June 1995). Copyright © 1995 by the Council on Foreign Relations, Inc.

might face a heightened risk of war in the short run. Pushing nuclear-armed great powers like Russia or China toward democratization is like spinning a roulette wheel: many of the outcomes are undesirable. Of course, in most cases the initial steps on the road to democratization will not be produced by any conscious policy of the United States. The roulette wheel is already spinning for Russia and perhaps will be soon for China. Washington and the international community need to think not so much about encouraging or discouraging democratization as about helping to smooth the transition in ways that minimize its risks.

THE EVIDENCE

Our statistical analysis relies on the classifications of regimes and wars from 1811 to 1980 used by most scholars studying the peace among democracies. Starting with these standard data, we classify each state as a democracy, an autocracy, or a mixed regime—that is, a state with features of both democracies and autocracies. This classification is based on several criteria, including the constitutional constraints on the chief executive, the competitiveness of domestic politics, the openness of the process for selecting the chief executive, and the strength of the rules governing participation in politics. Democratizing states are those that made any regime change in a democratic direction—that is, from autocracy to democracy, from a mixed regime to democracy, or from autocracy to a mixed regime. We analyze wars between states as well as wars between a state and a non-state group, such as liberation movements in colonies, but we do not include civil wars.[1]

Because we view democratization as a gradual process, rather than a sudden change, we test whether a transition toward democracy occurring over one, five, and ten years is associated with the subsequent onset of war. To assess the strength of the relationship between democratization and war, we construct a series of contingency tables. Based on those tables, we compare the probability that a

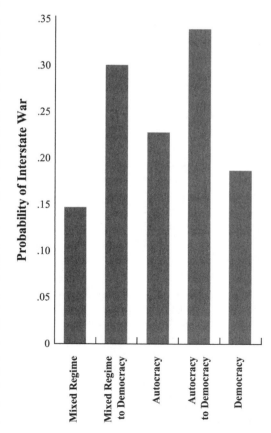

democratizing state subsequently goes to war with the probabilities of war for states in transition toward autocracy and for states undergoing no regime change. The results of all of these tests show that *democratizing states were more likely to fight wars than were states that had undergone no change in regime.* This relationship is weakest one year into democratization and strongest at ten years. During any given ten-year period, a state experiencing no regime change had about one chance in six of fighting a war in the following decade. In the decade following democratization, a state's chance of fighting a war was about one in four. When we analyze the components of our measure of democratization separately, the results are similar. On average, an increase in the openness of the selection process for the chief executive doubled the likelihood of war. Increasing the competitiveness of political participation or increasing the constraints on a country's chief executive (both aspects of democratization) also made war more likely. On average, these changes increased the likelihood of war by about 90 percent and 35 percent respectively.

The statistical results are even more dramatic when we analyze cases in which the process of democratization culminated in very high levels of mass

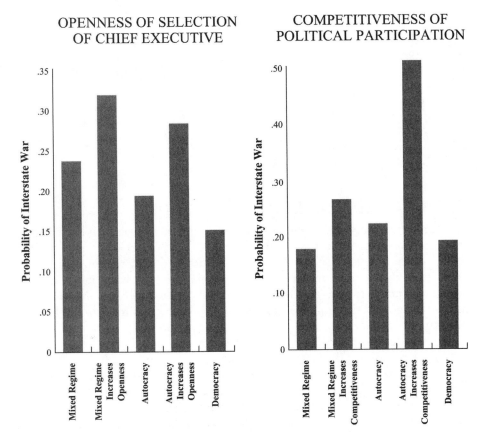

participation in politics. States changing from a mixed regime to democracy were on average about 50 percent more likely to become engaged in war (and about two-thirds more likely to go to war with another nation-state) than states that remained mixed regimes.

The effect was greater still for those states making the largest leap, from full autocracy to high levels of democracy. Such states were on average about two-thirds more likely to become involved in any type of war (and about twice as likely to become involved in an interstate war) than states that remained autocracies. Though this evidence shows that democratization is dangerous, its reversal offers no easy solutions. On average, changes toward autocracy also yielded an increase in the probability of war, though a smaller one than changes toward democracy, compared to states experiencing no regime change.

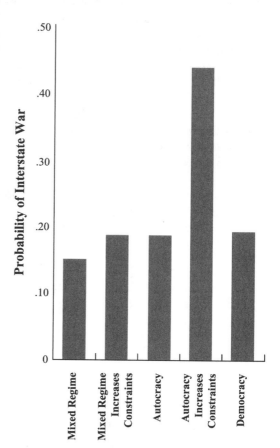

CONSTRAINTS ON THE CHIEF EXECUTIVE

NATIONALISM AND DEMOCRATIZATION

The connection between democratization and nationalism is striking in both the historical record and today's headlines. We did not measure nationalism directly in our statistical tests. Nonetheless, historical and contemporary evidence strongly suggests that rising nationalism often goes hand in hand with rising democracy. It is no accident that the end of the Cold War brought both a wave of democratization and a revival of nationalist sentiment in the former communist states.

In eighteenth-century Britain and France, when nationalism first emerged as an explicit political doctrine, it meant self-rule by the people. It was the rallying cry of commoners and rising commercial classes against rule by aristocratic elites, who were charged with the sin of ruling in their own interests, rather than those of the nation. Indeed, dynastic rulers and imperial courts had hardly been interested in promoting nationalism as a banner of solidarity in their realms. They typically ruled over a linguistically and culturally diverse conglomeration of subjects and claimed to govern by divine right, not in the interest of the nation. Often, these rulers were more closely tied by kinship, language, or culture to elites in other states than to their own subjects. The position of the communist ruling class was strikingly similar: a transnational elite that ruled over an amalgamation of peoples and claimed legitimacy from the communist party's role as the vanguard of history, not from the consent of the governed. Popular forces challenging either traditional dynastic rulers

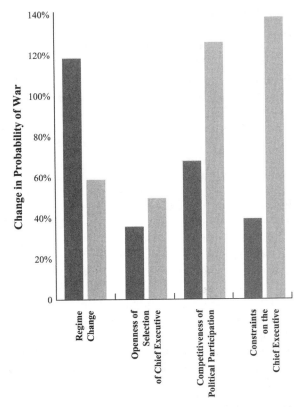

or communist elites naturally tended to combine demands for national self-determination and democratic rule.

This concoction of nationalism and incipient democratization has been an intoxicating brew, leading in case after case to ill-conceived wars of expansion. The earliest instance remains one of the most dramatic. In the French Revolution, the radical Brissotin parliamentary faction polarized politics by harping on the king's slow response to the threat of war with other dynastic states. In the ensuing wars of the French Revolution, citizens flocked to join the revolutionary armies to defend popular self-rule and the French nation. Even after the revolution turned profoundly antidemocratic, Napoleon was able to harness this popular nationalism to the task of conquering Europe, substituting the popularity of empire for the substance of democratic rule.

After this experience, Europe's ruling elites decided to band together in 1815 in the Concert of Europe to contain the twin evils of nationalism and democratization. In this scheme, Europe's crowned heads tried to unite in squelching demands for constitutions, electoral and social democracy, and national self-determination. For a time nationalism and democratization were both held back, and Europe enjoyed a period of relative peace.

But in the long run, the strategy failed in the face of the economic changes strengthening popular forces in Western and Central Europe. British and French politicians soon saw that they would have to rule by co-opting nationalist and democratic demands, rather than suppressing them. Once the specter of revolution returned to Europe in 1848, this reversal of political tactics was complete, and it led quickly to the Crimean War. British Foreign Secretary Palmerston and French Emperor Napoleon III both tried to manage the clamor for a broader political arena by giving democrats what they wanted in foreign affairs—a "liberal" war to free imprisoned nations from autocratic rule and, incidentally, to expand commerce.

But this was just the dress rehearsal for history's most potent combination of mass politics and rising nationalism, which occurred in Germany around the turn of the twentieth century. Chancellor Otto von Bismarck, counting on the conservative votes of a docile peasantry, granted universal suffrage in the newly unified Reich after 1870, but in foreign and military affairs, he kept the elected Reichstag subordinate to the cabinet appointed by the kaiser. Like the sorcerer's apprentice, however, Bismarck underestimated the forces he was unleashing. With the rise of an industrial society, Bismarck's successors could not control this truncated democracy, where over 90 percent of the population voted. Everyone was highly politicized, yet nobody could achieve their aims through the limited powers of the Reichstag. As a result, people organized direct pressure groups outside of electoral party politics. Some of these clamored for economic benefits, but many of them found it tactically useful to cloak their narrow interests in a broader vision of the nation's interests. This mass nationalist sentiment exerted constant pressure on German diplomacy in the Wilhelmine years before 1914 and pushed its vacillating elites toward war.

Democratization and nationalism also became linked in Japan on the eve of the Manchurian invasion in 1931. During the 1920s Japan expanded its suffrage and experimented with two-party electoral competition, though a council of military elder statesmen still made the ultimate decisions about who should govern. These semi-elected governments of the 1920s supported free trade, favored naval arms control, and usually tried to rein in the Japanese army's schemes to undermine the Open Door policy in China. During the 1920s, Young Turks in the army developed a populist, nationalist doctrine featuring a centrally planned economy within an autarkic, industrialized, expanded empire, while scapegoating Japan's alleged internal and external enemies, including leftist workers, rich capitalists, liberals, democrats, Americans, and Russians. After the economic crash of the late 1920s, this nationalist formula became persuasive, and the Japanese military had little trouble gaining popular support for imperial expansion and the emasculation of democracy. As in so many previous cases, nationalism proved to be a way for militarist elite groups to appear populist in a democratizing society while obstructing the advance to full democracy.

The interconnection among nationalism, democratization, and war is even clearer in new states. In today's "Weimar Russia," voters disgruntled by economic distress backed belligerent nationalists like Zhirinovsky, put ostensible liberals like President Boris Yeltsin and Foreign Minister Andrei Kozyrev on the defensive on ethnic and foreign policy issues, and contributed to the climate that led to war in Chechnya. In "Wilhelmine Serbia," the political and military elites of the old regime, facing inexorable pressure for democratization, cynically but successfully created a new basis for legitimacy through nationalist propaganda and military action, and they recently won elections that were only partially manipulated. Until its recent decree suspending the activities of the main opposition party, Armenia had moved quite far toward full democracy while at the same time supporting an invasion of its ethnic foes in Azerbaijan. The Azeris have been less successful in sustaining momentum toward democracy. However, in Azerbaijan's one relatively free and fair presidential election, the winner, Abulfaz Ali Elchibey, attacked the incumbent for being insufficiently nationalist and populist. Elchibey's platform emphasized Turkic identity and the strengthening of the Azeri nation-state to try to mount a counteroffensive against the Armenians. In other ethnically divided societies, where holding an election is like taking a census, democratization has often become an opportunity to exercise the tyranny of the majority.

THE SORCERER'S APPRENTICE

Although democratization in many cases leads to war, that does not mean that the average voter wants war. Public opinion in democratizing states often starts off highly averse to the costs and risks of war. In that sense, the public opinion polls taken in Russia in early 1994 were typical. Respondents said, for example, that Russian policy should make sure the rights of Russians in neighboring states were not infringed, but not at the cost of military intervention. Public opinion often becomes more belligerent, however, as a result of propaganda and military action presented as faits accomplis by elites. This mass opinion, once aroused, may no longer be controllable.

For example, Napoleon III successfully exploited the domestic prestige from France's share of the victory in the Crimean War to consolidate his rule, despite the popular reluctance and war-weariness that had accompanied the war. Having learned this lesson well, Napoleon tried this tactic again in 1859. On the eve of his military intervention in the Italian struggle with Austria, he admitted to his ministers that "on the domestic front, the war will at first awaken great fears; traders and speculators of every stripe will shriek, but national sentiment will [banish] this domestic fright; the nation will be put to the test once more in a struggle that will stir many a heart, recall the memory of heroic times, and bring together under the mantle of glory the parties that are steadily drifting away from one another day after day."[2] Napoleon was trying not just to follow opinion but to make public opinion bellicose, in order to stir a national feeling that would enhance the state's ability to govern a split and stalemated political arena.

Much the same has happened in contemporary Serbia. Despite the memories of Ustashe atrocities in World War II, intermarriage rates between Croats and Serbs living in Croatia were as high as one in three during the 1980s. Opinion has been bellicized by propaganda campaigns in state-controlled media that, for example, carried purely invented reports of rapes of Serbian women in Kosovo, and even more so by the fait accompli of launching the war itself.

In short, democratizing states are war-prone not because war is popular with the mass public, but because domestic pressures create incentives for elites to drum up nationalist sentiment.

THE CAUSES OF DEMOCRATIC WARS

Democratization typically creates a syndrome of weak central authority, unstable domestic coalitions, and high-energy mass politics. It brings new social groups and classes onto the political stage. Political leaders, finding no way to reconcile incompatible interests, resort to shortsighted bargains or reckless gambles in order to maintain their governing coalitions. Elites need to gain mass allies to defend their weakened positions. Both the newly ambitious elites and the embattled old ruling groups often use appeals to nationalism to stay astride their unmanageable political coalitions.

Needing public support, they rouse the masses with nationalist propaganda but find that their mass allies, once mobilized by passionate appeals, are difficult to control. So are the powerful remnants of the old order—the military, for example—which promote militarism because it strengthens them institutionally. This is particularly true because democratization weakens the central government's ability to keep policy coherent and consistent. Governing a society that is democratizing is like driving a car while throwing away the steering wheel, stepping on the gas, and fighting over which passenger will be in the driver's seat. The result, often, is war.

Political Stalemate and Imperialist Coalitions Democratization creates a wider spectrum of politically significant groups with diverse and incompatible interests. In the period when the great powers were first democratizing, kings, aristocrats, peasants, and artisans shared the historical stage with industrialists, an urban working class, and a middle-class intelligentsia. Similarly, in the post-communist world, former party apparatchiks, atavistic heavy industrialists, and downwardly mobile military officers share the stage with populist demagogues, free-market entrepreneurs, disgruntled workers, and newly mobilized ethnic groups. In principle, mature democratic institutions can integrate even the widest spectrum of interests through competition for the favor of the average voter. But where political parties and representative institutions are still in their infancy, the diversity of interests may make political coalitions difficult to maintain. Often the solution is a belligerent nationalist coalition.

In Britain during the period leading up to the Crimean War, neither the Whigs nor Tories could form a lasting governing coalition because so many groups refused to enter stable political alliances. None of the old elites would coalesce with the parliamentary bloc of radicals elected by urban middle-class and Irish voters. Moreover, protectionist Tories would not unite with free-trading Whigs and Peelite Tories. The social and political mid-Victorian equipoise between traditional and modern Britain created a temporary political stalemate. Lord Palmerston's pseudo-liberal imperialism turned out to be the only successful formula for creating a durable ruling coalition during this transitional period of democratization.

The stalemate in Wilhelmine-era electoral politics was even more serious. In principle, coalitions of the left and right might have formed a two-party system to vie for the favor of the average voter, thus moderating policy. In fact, both left and right were too internally divided to mount effective coalitions with internally consistent policies. Progressives dreamed of a bloc extending "from Bassermann to Bebel," from the liberal-democratic middle classes through the Marxist working classes, but the differences between labor and capital chronically barred this development. Conservatives had more success in forging a "marriage of iron and rye," but fundamental differences between military-feudal Junkers and Ruhr industrialists over issues ranging from the distribution of tax burdens to military strategy made their policies incoherent. Germany wound up with plans for a big army and a costly navy, and nobody willing to pay for it.

In more recent times, incipient democratization has likewise caused political impasses by widening the political spectrum to include too many irreconcilable political forces. In the final days of Yugoslavia, efforts by moderates like former Prime Minister Ante Marković to promote a federalist, democratic, economic reformist platform were hindered not only by ethnic divisions but also by the cleavage between market-oriented business interests on the one hand and party bosses and military officers on the other. Similarly, in Russia, the difficulty of reconciling liberal, neo-communist, and nationalist political platforms and the social interests behind them has led to parliamentary stalemate, attempts to break the stalemate by presidential decree, tanks in the streets, and the resort to freelancing by breakaway regions, the military, and spontaneous privatizers of state property. One interpretation of Yeltsin's decision to use force in Chechnya is that he felt it necessary to show that he could act decisively to prevent the unraveling of central authority, with respect not only to ethnic separatists but also to other ungovernable groups in a democratizing society. Chechnya, it was hoped, would allow Yeltsin to demonstrate his ability to coerce Russian society while at the same time exploiting a potentially popular nationalist issue.

Inflexible Interests and Short Time Horizons Groups threatened by social change and democratization, including still-powerful elites, are often compelled to take an inflexible view of their interests, especially when their assets cannot be readily adapted to changing political and economic conditions. In extreme cases, there may be only one solution that will maintain the social position of the group. For Prussian landowners, it was agricultural protection in a nondemocratic state; for the Japanese military, it was organizational autonomy in an autarkic empire; for the Serbian military and party elites, it was a Serbian nationalist state. Since military bureaucracies and imperial interest groups occupied key positions in many authoritarian great powers, whether monarchal or communist, most interests threatened by democratization have been bound up with military programs and the state's international mission. Compromises that may lead down the slippery slope to social extinction or irrelevance have little appeal to such groups. This adds to the difficulty of finding an exit from the domestic political impasse and may make powerful domestic groups impervious to the international risks of their strategies.

Competing for Popular Support The trouble intensifies when elites in a democratizing society try to recruit mass allies to their cause. Threatened elite groups have an overwhelming incentive to mobilize mass backers on the elites' terms, using whatever special resources they might retain. These resources have included monopolies of information (the Wilhelmine navy's unique "expertise" in making strategic assessments), propaganda assets (the Japanese army's public relations blitz justifying the invasion of Manchuria), patronage (Lord Palmerston's gifts of foreign service postings to the sons of cooperative journalists), wealth (the Krupp steel company's bankrolling of mass nationalist and militarist leagues), organizational skills and networks (the Japanese army's exploitation of rural reservist organizations to build a social base), and the ability to use the control of traditional political institutions to shape the political agenda and structure the terms of political bargains (the Wilhelmine ruling elite's agreement to eliminate anti-Catholic legislation in exchange for Catholic support in the Reichstag on the naval budget).

This elite mobilization of mass groups takes place in a highly competitive setting. Elite groups mobilize mass support to neutralize mass threats (for instance, creating patriotic leagues to counter workers' movements) and counter other elite groups' successful efforts at mass mobilization (such as the German Navy League, a political counterweight to the Junker-backed Agrarian League). The elites' resources allow them to influence the direction of mass political participation, but the imperative to compete for mass favor makes it difficult for a single elite group to control the outcome of this process. For example, mass groups that gain access to politics through elite-supported nationalist organizations often try to outbid their erstwhile sponsors. By 1911, German popular nationalist lobbies were in a position to claim that if Germany's foreign foes were really as threatening as the ruling elites had portrayed them, then the government had sold out German interests in reaching a compromise with France over the Moroccan dispute. In this way, elite mobilization of the masses adds to the ungovernability and political impasse of democratizing states.

Ideology takes on particular significance in the competition for mass support. New entrants to the political process, lacking established habits and good information, may be uncertain where their political interests lie. Ideology can yield big payoffs, particularly when there is no efficient free marketplace of ideas to counter false claims with reliable facts. Elites try out all sorts of ideological appeals depending on the social position they are defending, the nature of the mass group they want to recruit, and the kinds of appeals that seem politically plausible. A nearly universal element of these ideological appeals, however, is nationalism, which has the advantage of positing a community of interest uniting elites and masses. This distracts attention from class cleavages that divide elites from the masses they are trying to recruit.

The Weakening of Central Authority The political impasse and recklessness of democratizing states is deepened by the weakening of the state's authority. The autocrat can no longer dictate to elite interest groups or mass groups. Meanwhile, democratic institutions lack the strength to integrate these contending interests and views. Parties are weak and lack mass loyalty. Elections are rigged or intermittent. Institutions of public political participation are distrusted because they are subject to manipulation by elites and arbitrary constraints imposed by the state, which fears the outcome of unfettered competition.

Among the great powers, the problem was not excessive authoritarian power at the center, but the opposite. The Aberdeen coalition that brought Britain into the Crimean War was a makeshift cabinet headed by a weak leader with no substantial constituency. Likewise, on the eve of the Franco-Prussian War, Napoleon III's regime was in the process of caving in to its liberal opponents, who dominated the parliament elected in 1869. As Europe's armies prepared to hurtle from their starting gates in July 1914, Austrian leaders, perplexed by the contradictions between the German chancellor's policy and that of the German military, asked, "Who rules in Berlin?" Similarly, the 1931 Manchurian incident was a fait accompli by the local Japanese military; Tokyo was not even informed. The return to imperial thinking in Moscow today is the result of Yeltsin's weakness, not his strength. As the well-informed Moscow analyst Sergei Karaganov recently argued, the breakdown of the Leninist state "has created an environment where elite interests influence [foreign] policy directly."[3]

In each of these cases, the weak central leadership resorts to the same strategies as do the more parochial elite interests, using nationalist ideological appeals and special-interest payoffs to maintain their short-run viability, despite the long-run risks that these strategies may unleash.

Prestige Strategies One of the simplest but riskiest strategies for a hard-pressed regime in a democratizing country is to shore up its prestige at home by seeking victories abroad. During the Chechen intervention, newspaper commentators in Moscow and the West were reminded of Russian Interior Minister Viacheslav Plehve's fateful remark in 1904, on the eve of the disastrous Russo-Japanese War, that what the tsar needed was "a short, victorious war" to boost his prestige. Though this strategy often backfires, it is a perennial temptation as a means for coping with the political strains of democratization. German Chancellor Johannes Miquel, who revitalized the imperialist-protectionist "coalition of iron and rye" at the turn of the century, told his colleagues that "successes in foreign policy would make a good impression in the Reichstag debates, and political divisions would thus be moderated."[4] The targets of such strategies often share this analysis. Richard Cobden, for example, argued that military victories abroad would confer enough prestige on the military-feudal landed elite to allow them to raise food tariffs and snuff out democracy: "Let John Bull have a great military triumph, and we shall have to take off our hats as we pass the Horse Guards for the rest of our lives."[5]

Prestige strategies make the country vulnerable to slights to its reputation. Napoleon III, for example, was easily goaded into a fateful declaration of war in 1870 by Bismarck's insulting editorial work on a leaked telegram from the kaiser. For those who want to avoid such diplomatic provocations, the lesson is to make sure that compromises forced on the leaders of democratizing states do not take away the fig leaves needed to sustain their domestic prestige.

MANAGING THE DANGERS

Though mature democratic states have virtually never fought wars against each other, promoting democracy may not promote peace because states are especially war-prone during the transition toward democracy. This does not mean, however, that democratization should be squelched in the interests of peace. Many states are now democratizing or on the verge of it, and stemming that turbulent tide, even if it were desirable, may not be possible. Our statistical tests show that movements toward autocracy, including reversals of democratization, are only somewhat less likely to result in war than democratization itself. Consequently, the task is to draw on an understanding of the process of democratization to keep its unwanted side effects to a minimum.

Of course, democratization does not always lead to extreme forms of aggressive nationalism, just as it does not always lead to war. But it makes those outcomes more likely. Cases where states democratized without triggering a nationalist mobilization are particularly interesting, since they may hold clues about how to prevent such unwanted side effects. Among the great powers, the obvious successes were the democratization of Germany and Japan after 1945, due to occupation by liberal democracies and the favorable international setting provided by the Marshall Plan, the Bretton Woods economic system, and the democratic military alliance against the Soviet threat. More recently, numerous Latin American states have democratized without nationalism or war. The recent border skirmishes between Peru and Ecuador, however, coincide with democratizing trends in both states and a nationalist turn in Ecuadorian political discourse. Moreover, all three previous wars between that pair over the past two centuries occurred in periods of partial democratization.

In such cases, however, the cure is probably more democracy, not less. In "Wilhelmine Argentina," the Falkland Islands/Malvinas War came when the military junta needed a nationalist victory to stave off pressure for the return of democracy; the arrival of full democracy has produced more pacific policies. Among the East European states, nationalist politics has been unsuccessful in the most fully democratic ones—Poland, the Czech Republic, and Hungary—as protest votes have gone to former communists. Nationalism has figured more prominently in the politics of the less democratic formerly communist states that are nonetheless partially democratizing. States like Turkmenistan that remain outright autocracies have no nationalist mobilization—indeed no political mobilization of any kind. In those recent cases, in contrast to some of our statistical results, the rule seems to be: go fully democratic, or don't go at all.

In any given case, other factors may override the relative bellicosity of democratizing states. These might include the power of the democratizing state, the strength of the potential deterrent coalition of states constraining it, the attractiveness of more peaceful options available to the democratizing state, and the nature of the groups making up its ruling coalition. What is needed is to identify the conditions that lead to relatively peaceful democratization and try to create those circumstances.

One of the major findings of scholarship on democratization in Latin America is that the process goes most smoothly when elites threatened by the transition—especially the military—are given a golden parachute. Above all, they need a guarantee that they will not wind up in jail if they relinquish power. The history of the democratizing great powers broadens this insight. Democratization was least likely to lead to war when the old elites saw a reasonably bright future for themselves in the new social order. British aristocrats, for example, had more of their wealth invested in commerce and industry than in agriculture, so they had many interests in common with the rising middle classes. They could face democratization with relative equanimity. In contrast, Prussia's capital-starved, small-scale Junker landholders had no choice but to rely on agricultural protection and military careers.

In today's context, finding benign, productive employment for the erstwhile communist nomenklatura, military officer corps, nuclear scientists, and smokestack industrialists ought to rank high on the list of priorities. Policies aimed at giving them a stake in the privatization process and subsidizing the conversion of their skills to new, peaceful tasks in a market economy seem like a step in the right direction. According to some interpretations, Russian Defense Minister Pavel Grachev was eager to use force to solve the Chechen confrontation in order to show that Russian military power was still useful and that increased investment in the Russian army would pay big dividends. Instead of pursuing this reckless path, the Russian military elite needs to be convinced that its prestige, housing, pensions, and technical competence will improve if and only if it transforms itself into a Western-style military, subordinate to civilian authority and resorting to force only in accordance with prevailing international norms. Not only do old elites need to be kept happy, they also need to be kept weak. Pacts should not prop up the remnants of the authoritarian system, but rather create a niche for them in the new system.

Another top priority must be creating a free, competitive, and responsible marketplace of ideas in the newly democratizing states. Most of the war-prone democratizing great powers had pluralistic public debates, but the debates were skewed to favor groups with money, privileged access to the media, and proprietary control over information ranging from archives to intelligence about the military balance. Pluralism is not enough. Without a level playing field, pluralism simply creates the incentive and opportunity for privileged groups to propound self-serving myths, which historically have often taken a nationalist turn. One of the rays of hope in the Chechen affair was the alacrity with which Russian journalists exposed the costs of the fighting and the lies of the government and the military. Though elites should get a golden parachute regarding their pecuniary interests, they should be given no quarter on the battlefield of ideas. Mythmaking should be held up to the utmost scrutiny by aggressive journalists who maintain their credibility by scrupulously distinguishing fact from opinion and tirelessly verifying their sources. Promoting this kind of journalistic infrastructure is probably the most highly leveraged investment the West can make in a peaceful democratic transition.

Finally, the kind of ruling coalition that emerges in the course of democratization depends a great deal on the incentives created by the international environment. Both Germany and Japan started on the path toward liberal, stable democratization in the mid-1920s, encouraged by abundant opportunities for trade with and investment by the advanced democracies and by credible security treaties that defused nationalist scaremongering in domestic politics. When the international supports for free trade and democracy were yanked out in the late 1920s, their liberal coalitions collapsed. For China, whose democratization may occur in the context of expanding economic ties with the West, a steady Western Commercial partnership and security presence is likely to play a major role in shaping the incentives of proto-democratic coalition politics.

In the long run, the enlargement of the zone of stable democracy will probably enhance prospects for peace. In the short run, much work remains to be done to minimize the dangers of the turbulent transition.

NOTES

1 On the definition of war and the data on war used in this analysis, see Melvin Small and J. David Singer, *Resort to Arms: International and Civil Wars, 1816–1980*, Beverly Hills: Sage, 1982.

2 Alain Plessis, *The Rise and Fall of the Second Empire, 1852–1871*, Cambridge: Cambridge University Press, 1985, pp. 146–47.

3 Karaganov, "Russia's Elites," in Robert Blackwill and Sergei Karaganov, *Damage Limitation*, Washington: Brassey's, 1994, p. 42.

4 J.C.G. Rohl, *Germany without Bismarck*, Berkeley: University of California Press, 1967, p. 250.

5 Letter to John Bright, October 1, 1854, quoted in John Morley, *The Life of Richard Cobden*, abridged ed., London: Thomas Nelson, pp. 311–12.

Reading 6.2

Nations and Nationalism ERNEST GELLNER

DEFINITIONS

Nationalism is primarily a political principle, which holds that the political and the national unit should be congruent.

Nationalism as a sentiment, or as a movement, can best be defined in terms of this principle. Nationalist *sentiment* is the feeling of anger aroused by the

Source: Ernest Gellner, Nations and Nationalism. *© 1983 by Ernest Gellner. Reprinted by permission of the publisher, Cornell University Press.*

violation of the principle, or the feeling of satisfaction aroused by its fulfill-ment. A nationalist *movement* is one actuated by a sentiment of this kind.

There is a variety of ways in which the nationalist principle can be vio-lated. The political boundary of a given state can fail to include all the mem-bers of the appropriate nation; or it can include them all but also include some foreigners; or it can fail in both these ways at once, not incorporating all the nationals and yet also including some non-nationals. Or again, a nation may live, unmixed with foreigners, in a multiplicity of states, so that no single state can claim to be *the* national one.

But there is one particular form of the violation of the nationalist principle to which nationalist sentiment is quite particularly sensitive; if the rulers of the political unit belong to a nation other than that of the majority of the ruled, this, for nationalists, constitutes a quite outstandingly intolerable breach of political propriety. This can occur either through the incorporation of the national terri-tory in a larger empire, or by the local domination of an alien group.

In brief, nationalism is a theory of political legitimacy, which requires that ethnic boundaries should not cut across political ones, and, in particular, that ethnic boundaries within a given state—a contingency already formally excluded by the principle in its general formulation—should not separate the power holders from the rest.

The nationalist principle can be asserted in an ethical, 'universalistic' spirit. There could be, and on occasion there have been, nationalists-in-the-abstract, unbiased in favour of any special nationality of their own, and generously preaching the doctrine for all nations alike: let all nations have their own polit-ical roofs, and let all of them also refrain from including non-nationals under it. There is no formal contradiction in asserting such non-egoistic nationalism. As a doctrine it can be supported by some good arguments, such as the desir-ability of preserving cultural diversity, of a pluralistic international political system, and of the diminution of internal strains within states.

In fact, however, nationalism has often not been so sweetly reasonable, nor so rationally symmetrical. It may be that, as Immanuel Kant believed, partial-ity, the tendency to make exceptions on one's own behalf or one's own case, is *the* central human weakness from which all others flow; and that it infects national sentiment as it does all else, engendering what the Italians under Mus-solini called the *sacro egoismo* of nationalism. It may also be that the political effectiveness of national sentiment would be much impaired if nationalists had as fine a sensibility to the wrongs committed by their nation as they have to those committed against it.

But over and above these considerations there are others, tied to the specific nature of the world we happen to live in, which militate against any impartial, general, sweetly reasonable nationalism. To put it in the simplest possible terms: there is a very large number of potential nations on earth. Our planet also contains room for a certain number of independent or autonomous political units. On any reasonable calculation, the former number (of potential nations) is probably much, *much* larger than that of possible viable states. If this argument or calculation is correct, not all nationalisms can be satisfied, at any rate at the same time. The satisfaction of some spells the frustration of others. This argument is further and immeasurably strengthened by the fact that very many of the potential nations of this world live, or until recently have lived, not in compact territorial units but intermixed with each other in complex patterns. It follows that a territorial political unit can only become ethnically homogeneous, in such cases, if it either kills, or expels, or assimilates all non-nationals. Their unwillingness to suffer such fates may make the peaceful implementation of the nationalist principle difficult.

These definitions must, of course, like most definitions, be applied with common sense. The nationalist principle, as defined, is not violated by the presence of *small* numbers of resident foreigners, or even by the presence of the occasional foreigner in, say, a national ruling family. Just how many resident foreigners or foreign members of the ruling class there must be before the principle is effectively violated cannot be stated with precision. There is no sacred percentage figure, below which the foreigner can be benignly tolerated, and above which he becomes offensive and his safety and life are at peril. No doubt the figure will vary with circumstances. The impossibility of providing a generally applicable and precise figure, however, does not undermine the usefulness of the definition.

STATE AND NATION

Our definition of nationalism was parasitic on two as yet undefined terms: state and nation.

Discussion of the state may begin with Max Weber's celebrated definition of it, as that agency within society which possesses the monopoly of legitimate violence. The idea behind this is simple and seductive: in well-ordered societies, such as most of us live in or aspire to live in, private or sectional violence is illegitimate. Conflict as such is not illegitimate, but it cannot rightfully be resolved by private or sectional violence. Violence may be applied only by the central political authority, and those to whom it delegates this right. Among the various sanctions of the maintenance of order, the ultimate one—force—may be applied only by one special, clearly identified, and well centralized, disciplined agency within society. That agency or group of agencies *is* the state.

The idea enshrined in this definition corresponds fairly well with the moral intuitions of many, probably most, members of modern societies. Nevertheless, it is not entirely satisfactory. There are 'states'—or, at any rate, institutions which we would normally be inclined to call by that name—which do not monopolize legitimate violence within the territory which they more or less effectively control. A feudal state does not necessarily object to private wars between its fief-holders, provided they also fulfill their obligations to their overlord; or again, a state counting tribal populations among its subjects does not necessarily object to the institution of the feud, as long as those who indulge in it refrain from endangering neutrals on the public highway or in the market. The Iraqi state, under British tutelage after the First World War, tolerated tribal raids, provided the raiders dutifully reported at the nearest police station before and after the expedition, leaving an orderly bureaucratic record of slain and booty. In brief, there are states which lack either the will or the means to enforce their monopoly of legitimate violence, and which nonetheless remain, in many respects, recognizable 'states'.

Weber's underlying principle does, however, seem valid *now*, however strangely ethnocentric it may be as a general definition, with its tacit assumption of the well-centralized Western state. The state constitutes one highly distinctive and important elaboration of the social division of labour. Where there is no division of labour, one cannot even begin to speak of the state. But not any or every specialism makes a state: the state is the specialization and concentration of order maintenance. The 'state' is that institution or set of institutions specifically concerned with the enforcement of order (whatever else they may also be concerned with). The state exists where specialized order-enforcing agencies, such as police forces and courts, have separated out from the rest of social life. They *are* the state.

Not all societies are state-endowed. It immediately follows that the problem of nationalism does not arise for stateless societies. If there is no state, one obviously cannot ask whether or not its boundaries are congruent with the limits of nations. If there are no rulers, there being no state, one cannot ask whether they are of the same nation as the ruled. When neither state nor rulers exist, one cannot resent their failure to conform to the requirements of the principle of nationalism. One may perhaps deplore statelessness, but that is another matter. Nationalists have generally fulminated against the distribution of political power and the nature of political boundaries, but they have seldom if ever had occasion to deplore the absence of power and of boundaries altogether. The circumstances in which nationalism has generally arisen have not normally been those in which the state itself, as such, was lacking, or when its reality was in any serious doubt. The state was only too conspicuously present. It was its boundaries and/or the distribution of power, and possibly of other advantages, within it which were resented.

This in itself is highly significant. Not only is our definition of nationalism parasitic on a prior and assumed definition of the state: it also seems to be the case that nationalism emerges only in milieux in which the existence of the state is already very much taken for granted. The existence of politically centralized units, and of a moral-political climate in which such centralized units are taken for granted and are treated as normative, is a necessary though by no means a sufficient condition of nationalism.

By way of anticipation, some general historical observations should be made about the state. Mankind has passed through three fundamental stages in its history: the pre-agrarian, the agrarian, and the industrial. Hunting and gathering bands were and are too small to allow the kind of political division of labour which constitutes the state; and so, for them, the question of the state, of a stable specialized order-enforcing institution, does not really arise. By contrast, most, but by no means all, agrarian societies have been state-endowed. Some of these states have been strong and some weak, some have been despotic and others law-abiding. They differ a very great deal in their form. The agrarian phase of human history is the period during which, so to speak, the very existence of the state is an option. Moreover, the form of the state is highly variable. During the hunting-gathering stage, the option was not available.

By contrast, in the post-agrarian, industrial age there is, once again, no option; but now the *presence*, not the absence of the state is inescapable. Paraphrasing Hegel, once none had the state, then some had it, and finally all have it. The form it takes, of course, still remains variable. There are some traditions of social thought—anarchism, Marxism—which hold that even, or especially, in an industrial order the state is dispensable, at least under favourable conditions or under conditions due to be realized in the fullness of time. There are obvious and powerful reasons for doubting this: industrial societies are enormously large, and depend for the standard of living to which they have become accustomed (or to which they ardently wish to become accustomed) on an unbelievably intricate general division of labour and cooperation. Some of this cooperation might under favourable conditions be spontaneous and need no central sanctions. The idea that all of it could perpetually work in this way, that it could exist without any enforcement and control, puts an intolerable strain on one's credulity.

So the problem of nationalism does not arise when there is no state. It does not follow that the problem of nationalism arises for each and every state. On the contrary, it arises only for *some* states. It remains to be seen which ones do face this problem.

THE NATION

The definition of the nation presents difficulties graver than those attendant on the definition of the state. Although modern man tends to take the centralized state (and, more specifically, the centralized national state) for granted, nevertheless he is capable, with relatively little effort, of seeing its contingency, and of imagining a social situation in which the state is absent. He is quite adept at visualizing the 'state of nature'. An anthropologist can explain to him that the tribe is not necessarily a state writ small, and that forms of tribal organization exist which can be described as stateless. By contrast, the idea of a man without a nation seems to impose a far greater strain on the modern imagination. Chamisso, an *emigré* Frenchman in Germany during the Napoleonic period, wrote a powerful proto-Kafkaesque novel about a man who lost his shadow: though no doubt part of the effectiveness of this novel hinges on the intended ambiguity of the parable, it is difficult not to suspect that, for the author, the Man without a Shadow was the Man without a Nation. When his followers and acquaintances detect his aberrant shadowlessness they shun the otherwise well-endowed Peter Schlemiehl. A man without a nation defies the recognized categories and provokes revulsion.

Chamisso's perception—if indeed this is what he intended to convey—was valid enough, but valid only for one kind of human condition, and not for the human condition as such anywhere at any time. A man must have a nationality as he must have a nose and two ears; a deficiency in any of these particulars is not inconceivable and does from time to time occur, but only as a result of some disaster, and it is itself a disaster of a kind. All this seems obviously, though, alas, it is not true. But that it should have come to *seem* so very obviously true is indeed an aspect, or perhaps the very core, of the problem of nationalism. Having a nation is not an inherent attribute of humanity, but it has now come to appear as such.

In fact, nations, like states, are a contingency, and not a universal necessity. Neither nations nor states exist at all times and in all circumstances. Moreover, nations and states are not the *same* contingency. Nationalism holds that they were destined for each other; that either without the other is incomplete, and constitutes a tragedy. But before they could become intended for each other, each of them had to emerge, and their emergence was independent and contingent. The state has certainly emerged without the help of the nation. Some nations have certainly emerged without the blessings of their own state. It is more debatable whether the normative idea of the nation, in its modern sense, did not presuppose the prior existence of the state.

What then is this contingent, but in our age seemingly universal and normative, idea of the nation? Discussion of two very makeshift, temporary definitions will help to pinpoint this elusive concept.

1. Two men are of the same nation if and only if they share the same culture, where culture in turn means a system of ideas and signs and associations and ways of behaving and communicating.
2. Two men are of the same nation if and only if they recognize each other as belonging to the same nation. In other words, *nations make the man*; nations are the artifacts of men's convictions and loyalties and solidarities. A mere category of persons (say, occupants of a given territory, or speakers of a given language, for example) becomes a nation if and when the members of the category firmly recognize certain mutual rights and duties to each other in virtue of their shared membership of it. It is their recognition of each other as fellows of this kind which turns them into a nation, and not the other shared attributes, whatever they might be, which separate that category from nonmembers.

Each of these provisional definitions, the cultural and the voluntaristic, has some merit. Each of them singles out an element which is of real importance in the understanding of nationalism. But neither is adequate. Definitions of culture, presupposed by the first definition, in the anthropological rather than the normative sense, are notoriously difficult and unsatisfactory. It is probably best to approach this problem by using this term without attempting too much in the way of formal definition, and looking at what culture does. . . .

A NOTE ON THE WEAKNESS OF NATIONALISM

It is customary to comment on the strength of nationalism. This is an important mistake, though readily understandable since, whenever nationalism has taken root, it has tended to prevail with ease over other modern ideologies.

Nevertheless, the clue to the understanding of nationalism is its weakness at least as much as its strength. It was the dog who failed to bark who provided the vital clue for Sherlock Holmes. The number of potential nationalisms which failed to bark is far, far larger than those which did, though *they* have captured all our attention.

We have already insisted on the dormant nature of this allegedly powerful monster during the pre-industrial age. But even within the age of nationalism, there is a further important sense in which nationalism remains astonishingly feeble. Nationalism has been defined, in effect, as the striving to make culture and polity congruent, to endow a culture with its own political roof, and not more than one roof at that. Culture, an elusive concept, was deliberately left undefined. But an at least provisionally acceptable criterion of culture might be language, as at least a sufficient, if not a necessary touchstone of it. Allow for a moment a difference of language to entail a difference of culture (though not necessarily the reverse).

If this is granted, at least temporarily, certain consequences follow. I have heard the number of languages on earth estimated at around 8000. The figure can no doubt be increased by counting dialects separately. If we allow the 'precedent' argument, this becomes legitimate: if a kind of differential which in some places defines a nationalism is allowed to engender a 'potential nationalism' wherever else a similar difference is found, then the number of potential nationalisms increases sharply. For instance, diverse Slavonic, Teutonic and Romance languages are in fact often no further apart than are the mere dialects within what are elsewhere conventionally seen as unitary languages. Slav languages, for instance, are probably closer to each other than are the various forms of colloquial Arabic, allegedly a single language.

The 'precedent' argument can also generate potential nationalisms by analogies invoking factors other than language. For instance, Scottish nationalism indisputably exists. (It may indeed be held to contradict my model.) It ignores language (which would condemn some Scots to Irish nationalism, and the rest to English nationalism), invoking instead a shared historical experience. Yet if such additional links be allowed to count (as long as they don't contradict the requirement of my model, that they can serve as a base for an *eventually* homogeneous, internally mobile culture/polity with one educational machine servicing that culture under the surveillance of that polity), then the number of potential nationalisms goes up even higher.

However, let us be content with the figure of 8000, once given to me by a linguist as a rough number of languages based on what was no doubt rather an arbitrary estimate of language alone. The number of states in the world at present is some figure of the order of 200. To this figure one may add all the irredentist nationalisms, which have not yet attained their state (and perhaps never will), but which are struggling in that direction and thus have a legitimate claim to be counted among actual, and not merely potential, nationalisms. On the other hand, one must also subtract all those states which have come into being without the benefit of the blessing of nationalist endorsement, and which do not satisfy the nationalist criteria of political legitimacy, and indeed defy them;

for instance, all the diverse mini-states dotted about the globe as survivals of a pre-nationalist age, and sometimes brought forth as concessions to geographical accident or political compromise. Once all these had been subtracted, the resulting figure would again, presumably, not be too far above 200. But let us, for the sake of charity, pretend that we have four times that number of reasonably effective nationalisms on earth, in other words, 800 of them. I believe this to be considerably larger than the facts would justify, but let it pass.

This rough calculation still gives us only *one* effective nationalism for *ten* potential ones! And this surprising ratio, depressing presumably for any enthusiastic pan-nationalist, if such a person exists, could be made much larger if the 'precedent' argument were applied to the full to determine the number of potential nationalisms, and if the criteria of entry into the class of effective nationalisms were made at all stringent.

What is one to conclude from this? That for every single nationalism which has so far raised its ugly head, nine others are still waiting in the wings? That all the bomb-throwing, martyrdoms, exchange of populations, and worse, which have so far beset humanity, are still to be repeated tenfold?

I think not. For every effective nationalism, there are *n* potential ones, groups defined either by shared culture inherited from the agrarian world or by some other link (on the 'precedent' principle) which *could* give hope of establishing a homogeneous industrial community, but which nevertheless do not bother to struggle, which fail to activate their potential nationalism, which do not even try.

So it seems that the urge to make mutual cultural substitutability the basis of the state is not so powerful after all. The members of *some* groups do indeed feel it, but members of most groups, with analogous claims, evidently do not.

To explain this, we must return to the accusation made against nationalism; that it insists on imposing homogeneity on the populations unfortunate enough to fall under the sway of authorities possessed by the nationalist ideology. The assumption underlying this accusation is that traditional, ideologically uninfected authorities, such as the Ottoman Turks, had kept the peace and extracted taxes, but otherwise tolerated, and been indeed profoundly indifferent to, the diversity of faiths and cultures which they governed. By contrast, their gunman successors seem incapable of resting in peace till they have imposed the nationalist principle of *cuius regio, eius lingua*. They do not want merely a fiscal surplus and obedience. They thirst after the cultural and linguistic souls of their subjects.

This accusation must be stood on its head. It is not the case that nationalism imposes homogeneity out of a wilful cultural *Machtbedürfniss*; it is the objective need for homogeneity which is reflected in nationalism. If it is the case that a modern industrial state can only function with a mobile, literate, culturally standardized, interchangeable population, as we have argued, then the illiterate, half-starved populations sucked from their erstwhile rural cultural ghettoes into the melting pots of shanty-towns yearn for incorporation into some one of those cultural pools which already has, or looks as if it might acquire, a state of its own, with the subsequent promise of full cultural citizenship, access to primary schools, employment, and all. Often, these alienated, uprooted, wandering populations may vacillate between diverse options, and they may often come to a provisional rest at one or another temporary and transitional cultural resting place.

But there are some options which they will refrain from trying to take up. They will hesitate about trying to enter cultural pools within which they know themselves to be spurned; or rather, within which they expect to *continue* to be spurned. Poor newcomers are, of course, almost always spurned. The question is whether they will continue to be slighted, and whether the same fate will await their children. This will depend on whether the newly arrived and hence least privileged stratum possesses traits which its members and their offspring cannot shed, and which will continue to identify them: genetically transmitted or deeply engrained religious cultural habits are impossible or difficult to drop.

The alienated victims of early industrialism are unlikely to be tempted by cultural pools that are very small—a language spoken by a couple of villages offers few prospects—or very diffused or lacking in any literary traditions or personnel capable of carrying skills, and so on. They require cultural pools which are large, and/or have a good historic base, or intellectual personnel well equipped to propagate the culture in question. It is impossible to pick out any single qualification, or set of qualifications, which will either guarantee the success as a nationalist catalyst of the culture endowed with it (or them), or which on the contrary will ensure its failure. Size, historicity, reasonably compact territory, a capable and energetic intellectual class: all these will obviously help; but no single one is necessary, and it is doubtful whether any firm predictive generalization can be established in these terms. That the principle of nationalism will be operative can be predicted; just which groupings will emerge as its carriers can be only loosely indicated, for it depends on too many historic contingencies.

Nationalism as such is fated to prevail, but not any one particular nationalism. We know that reasonably homogeneous cultures, each of them with its own political roof, its own political servicing, are becoming the norm, widely implemented but for few exceptions; but we cannot predict just which cultures, with which political roofs, will be blessed by success. On the contrary, the simple calculations made above, concerning the number of cultures or potential nationalisms and concerning the room available for proper national states, clearly show that most potential nationalisms must either fail, or, more commonly, will refrain from even trying to find political expression.

This is precisely what we do find. Most cultures or potential national groups enter the age of nationalism without even the feeblest effort to benefit from it themselves. The number of groups which in terms of the 'precedent' argument could try to become nations, which could define themselves by the kind of criterion which in some other place does in fact define some real and effective nation, is legion. Yet most of them go meekly to their doom, to see their culture (though not themselves as individuals) slowly disappear, dissolving into the wider culture of some new national state. Most cultures are led to the dust heap of history by industrial civilization without offering any resistance. The linguistic distinctiveness of the Scottish Highlands within Scotland is, of course, incomparably greater than the cultural distinctiveness of Scotland within the UK; but there is no Highland nationalism. Much the same is true of Moroccan Berbers. Dialectal and cultural differences within Germany or Italy are as great as those between recognized Teutonic or Romance languages. Southern Russians differ culturally from Northern Russians, but, unlike Ukrainians, do not translate this into a sense of nationhood.

Does this show that nationalism is, after all, unimportant? Or even that it is an ideological artifact, an invention of febrile thinkers which has mysteriously captured some mysteriously susceptible nations? Not at all. To reach such a conclusion would, ironically, come close to a tacit, oblique acceptance of the nationalist ideologue's most misguided claim: namely, that the 'nations' are there, in the very nature of things, only waiting to be 'awakened' (a favourite nationalist expression and image) from their regrettable slumber, by the nationalist 'awakener'. One would be inferring from the failure of most potential nations ever to 'wake up', from the lack of deep stirrings waiting for reveille, that nationalism was not important after all. Such an inference concedes the social ontology of 'nations', only admitting, with some surprise perhaps, that some of them lack the vigour and vitality needed if they are to fulfill the destiny which history intended for them.

But nationalism is *not* the awakening of an old, latent, dormant force, though that is how it does indeed present itself. It is in reality the consequence of a new form of social organization, based on deeply internalized, education-dependent high cultures, each protected by its own state. It uses some of the pre-existent cultures, generally transforming them in the process, but it cannot possibly use them all. There are too many of them. A viable higher culture-sustaining modern state cannot fall below a certain minimal size (unless in effect parasitic on its neighbours); and there is only room for a limited number of such states on this earth.

The high ratio of determined slumberers, who will not rise and shine and who refuse to be woken, enables us to turn the tables on nationalism-as-seen-by-itself. Nationalism sees itself as a natural and universal ordering of the political life of mankind, only obscured by that long, persistent and mysterious somnolence. As Hegel expressed this vision: 'Nations may have had a long history before they finally reach their destination—that of forming themselves into states'.[1] Hegel immediately goes on to suggest that this pre-state period is really 'pre-historical' *(sic)*: so it would seem that on this view the real history of a nation only begins when it acquires its own state. If we invoke the sleeping-beauty nations, neither possessing a state nor feeling the lack of it, against the nationalist doctrine, we tacitly accept its social metaphysic, which sees nations as the bricks of which mankind is made up. Critics of nationalism who denounce the political movement but tacitly accept the existence of nations, do not go far enough. Nations as a natural, God-given way of classifying men, as an inherent though long-delayed political destiny, are a myth; nationalism, which sometimes takes pre-existing cultures and turns them into nations, sometimes invents them, and often obliterates pre-existing cultures:

that is a reality, for better or worse, and in general an inescapable one. Those who are its historic agents know not what they do, but that is another matter.

But we must not accept the myth. Nations are not inscribed into the nature of things, they do not constitute a political version of the doctrine of natural kinds. Nor were national states the manifest ultimate destiny of ethnic or cultural groups. What do exist are cultures, often subtly grouped, shading into each other, overlapping, intertwined; and there exist, usually but not always, political units of all shapes and sizes. In the past the two did not generally converge. There were good reasons for their failing to do so in many cases. Their rulers established their identity by differentiating themselves downwards, and the ruled micro-communities differentiated themselves laterally from their neighbors grouped in similar units.

But nationalism is not the awakening and assertion of these mythical, supposedly natural and given units. It is, on the contrary, the crystallization of new units, suitable for the conditions now prevailing, though admittedly using as their raw material the cultural, historical and other inheritances from the pre-nationalist world. . . .

TWO TYPES OF NATIONALISM

. . . [In nineteenth-century Europe] most Italians were ruled by foreigners, and in that sense were politically underprivileged. The Germans, most of them, lived in fragmented states, many of them small and weak, at any rate by European great power standards, and thus unable to provide German culture, as a centralized modern medium, with its political roof. (By a further paradox, multi-national great power Austria was endeavoring to do something of that kind, but much to the displeasure of some of its citizens.)

So the political protection of Italian and German culture was visibly and, to the Italians and Germans offensively, inferior to that which was provided for, say, French or English culture. But when it came to access to education, the facilities provided by these two high cultures, to those who were born into dialectal variants of it, were not really in any way inferior. Both Italian and German were literary languages, with an effective centralized standardization of their correct forms and with flourishing literatures, technical vocabularies and manners, educational institutions and academies. There was little if any cultural inferiority. Rates of literacy and standards of education were not significantly lower (if lower at all) among Germans than they were among the French; and they were not significantly low among the Italians, when compared with the dominant Austrians. German in comparison with French, or Italian in comparison with the German used by the Austrians, were not disadvantaged cultures, and their speakers did not need to correct unequal access to the eventual benefits of a modern world. All that needed to be corrected was that inequality of power and the absence of a political roof over a culture (and over an economy), and institutions which would be identified with it and committed to its maintenance. The Risorgimento and the unification of Germany corrected these imbalances.

There is a difference, however, between this kind of unificatory nationalism, on behalf of a fully effective high culture which only needs an improved bit of political roofing, and the classical Habsburg-and-east-and-south type of nationalism. This difference is the subject of a fascinating and rather moving essay by the late Professor John Plamenatz, an essay which might well have been called 'The Sad Reflections of a Montenegrin in Oxford'.[2] Plamenatz called the two kinds of nationalism the Western and the Eastern, the Western type being of the Risorgimento or unificatory kind, typical of the nineteenth century and with deep links to liberal ideas, while the Eastern, though he did not stress it in so many words, was exemplified by the kind of nationalism he knew to exist in his native Balkans. There can be no doubt but that he saw the Western nationalism as relatively benign and nice, and the Eastern kind as nasty, and doomed to nastiness by the conditions which gave rise to it. (It would be an interesting question to ask him whether he would have considered the markedly un-benign forms taken by these once-benign or relatively liberal and moderate Western nationalisms in the twentieth century, as accidental and avoidable aberrations or not.)

The underlying logic of Plamenatz's argument is clear. The relatively benign Western nationalisms were acting on behalf of well-developed high cultures, normatively centralized and endowed with a fairly well-defined folk clientele: all that was required was a bit of adjustment in the political situation and in the international boundaries, so as to ensure for these cultures, and their speakers and practitioners, the same sustained protection as that which was already enjoyed by their rivals. This took a few battles and a good deal of sustained diplomatic activity but, as the making of historical omelettes goes, it did not involve the breaking of a disproportionate or unusual number of eggs, perhaps no more than would have been broken anyway in the course of the normal political game within the general political framework and assumptions of the time.

By way of contrast, consider the nationalism designated as Eastern by Plamenatz. Its implementation did, of course, require battles and diplomacy, to at least the same extent as the realization of Western nationalisms. But the matter did not end there. This kind of Eastern nationalism did not operate on behalf of an already existing, well-defined and codified high culture, which had as it were marked out and linguistically pre-converted its own territory by sustained literary activities ever since the early Renaissance or since the Reformation, as the case might be. Not at all. This nationalism was active on behalf of a high culture as yet not properly crystallized, a merely aspirant or in-the-making high culture. It presided, or strove to preside, in ferocious rivalry with similar competitors, over a chaotic ethnographic map of many dialects, with ambiguous historical or linguo-genetic allegiances, and containing populations which had only just begun to identify with these emergent national high cultures. Objective conditions of the modern world were bound, in due course, to oblige them to identify with one of them. But till this occurred, they lacked the clearly defined cultural basis enjoyed by their German and Italian counterparts.

These populations of eastern Europe were still locked into the complex multiple loyalties of kinship, territory and religion. To make them conform to the nationalist imperative was bound to take more than a few battles and some diplomacy. It was bound to take a great deal of very forceful cultural engineering. In many cases it was also bound to involve population exchanges or expulsions, more or less forcible assimilation, and sometimes liquidation, in order to attain that close relation between state and culture which is the essence of nationalism. And all these consequences flowed, not from some unusual brutality of the nationalists who in the end employed these measures (they were probably no worse and no better than anyone else), but from the inescapable logic of the situation.

NOTES

1 G. W. F. Hegel, *Lectures on the Philosophy of World History*, tr. H. B. Nisbet, Cambridge, 1975, p. 134.
2 John Plamenatz, 'Two Types of Nationalism', in E. Kamenka (ed.), *Nationalism, The Nature and Evolution of an Idea*, London, 1973.

Reading 6.3

Possible and Impossible Solutions to Ethnic Civil Wars
Chaim Kaufmann

Ethnic civil wars are burning in Bosnia, Croatia, Rwanda, Burundi, Angola, Sudan, Turkey, Azerbaijan, Georgia, Chechnya, Tajikistan, Kashmir, Myanmar, and Sri Lanka, and are threatening to break out in dozens of other places throughout the world. Many of these conflicts are so violent, with so much violence directed against unarmed civilians, and are apparently intractable, that they have provoked calls for military intervention to stop them. As yet, however, the international community has done little and achieved less.

Advocates of international action seek to redress the failures of local political institutions and elites by brokering political power-sharing arrangements, by international conservatorship to rebuild a functioning state, or by reconstruction of exclusive ethnic identities into wider, inclusive civic identities. Pessimists doubt these remedies, arguing that ethnic wars express primordial

Source: Chaim Kaufmann, from "Possible and Impossible Solutions to Ethnic Civil Wars," International Security Vol. 20, No. 4 (Spring 1996), pp. 136–175. © 1996 by the President and Fellows of Harvard College and the Massachusetts Institute of Technology. Reprinted by permission.

hatreds which cannot be reduced by outside intervention because they have been ingrained by long histories of intercommunal conflict.

Both sides in the current debate are wrong, because solutions to ethnic wars do not depend on their causes.

This paper offers a theory of how ethnic wars end, and proposes an intervention strategy based on it. The theory rests on two insights: First, in ethnic wars both hypernationalist mobilization rhetoric and real atrocities harden ethnic identities to the point that cross-ethnic political appeals are unlikely to be made and even less likely to be heard. Second, intermingled population settlement patterns create real security dilemmas that intensify violence, motivate ethnic "cleansing," and prevent de-escalation unless the groups are separated. As a result, restoring civil politics in multi-ethnic states shattered by war is impossible because the war itself destroys the possibilities for ethnic cooperation.

Stable resolutions of ethnic civil wars are possible, but only when the opposing groups are demographically separated into defensible enclaves. Separation reduces both incentives and opportunity for further combat, and largely eliminates both reasons and chances for ethnic cleansing of civilians. While ethnic fighting can be stopped by other means, such as peace enforcement by international forces or by a conquering empire, such peaces last only as long as the enforcers remain.

This means that to save lives threatened by genocide, the international community must abandon attempts to restore war-torn multi-ethnic states. Instead, it must facilitate and protect population movements to create true national homelands. Sovereignty is secondary: defensible ethnic enclaves reduce violence with or without independent sovereignty, while partition without separation does nothing to stop mass killing. Once massacres have taken place, ethnic cleansing will occur. The alternative is to let the *interahamwe* and the Chetniks "cleanse" their enemies in their own way. . . .

HOW ETHNIC CIVIL WARS END

Civil wars are not all alike. Ethnic conflicts are disputes between communities which see themselves as having distinct heritages, over the power relationship between the communities, while ideological civil wars are contests between factions within the same community over how that community should be governed. The key difference is the flexibility of individual loyalties, which are quite fluid in ideological conflicts, but almost completely rigid in ethnic wars.

The possible and impossible solutions to ethnic civil wars follow from this fact. War hardens ethnic identities to the point that cross-ethnic political appeals become futile, which means that victory can be assured only by physical control over the territory in dispute. Ethnic wars also generate intense security dilemmas, both because the escalation of each side's mobilization rhetoric presents a real threat to the other, and even more because intermingled population settlement patterns create defensive vulnerabilities and offensive opportunities.

Once this occurs, the war cannot end until the security dilemma is reduced by physical separation of the rival groups. Solutions that aim at restoring multi-ethnic civil politics and at avoiding population transfers—such as power-sharing, state re-building, or identity reconstruction—cannot work because they do nothing to dampen the security dilemma, and because ethnic fears and hatreds hardened by war are extremely resistant to change.

The result is that ethnic wars can end in only three ways: with complete victory of one side; by temporary suppression of the conflict by third party military occupation; or by self-governance of separate communities. The record of the ethnic wars of the last half century bears this out.

The Dynamics of Ethnic War

It is useful to compare characteristics of ethnic conflicts with those of ideological conflicts. The latter are competitions between the government and the rebels for the loyalties of the people. The critical features of these conflicts are that ideological loyalties are changeable and difficult to assess, and the same population serves as the shared mobilization base for both sides. As a result, winning the "hearts and minds" of the population is both possible and necessary for victory. The most important instruments are political, economic, and social reforms that redress popular grievances such as poverty, inequality, corruption, and physical insecurity. Control of access to population is also important, both to allow recruitment and implementation of reform promises, and to block the enemy from these tasks. Population control, however, cannot be guaranteed solely by physical control over territory, but depends on careful intelligence, persuasion, and coercion. Purely military successes are often indecisive as long as the enemy's base of political support is undamaged.

Ethnic wars, however, have nearly the opposite properties. Individual loyalties are both rigid and transparent, while each side's mobilization base is limited to members of its own group in friendly-controlled territory. The result is that ethnic conflicts are primarily military struggles in which victory depends on physical control over the disputed territory, not on appeals to members of the other group.

Identity in Ethnic Wars   Competition to sway individual loyalties does not play an important role in ethnic civil wars, because ethnic identities are fixed by birth.[1] While not everyone may be mobilized as an active fighter for his or her own group, hardly anyone ever fights for the opposing ethnic group.

Different identity categories imply their own membership rules. Ideological identity is relatively soft, as it is a matter of individual belief, or sometimes of political behavior. Religious identities are harder, because while they also depend on belief, change generally requires formal acceptance by the new faith, which may be denied. Ethnic identities are hardest, since they depend on language, culture, and religion, which are hard to change, as well as parentage, which no one can change.

Ethnic identities are hardened further by intense conflict, so that leaders cannot broaden their appeals to include members of opposing groups. As ethnic conflicts escalate, populations come increasingly to hold enemy images of the other group, either because of deliberate efforts by elites to create such images or because of increasing real threats. The intensification of the war in Southeastern Turkey, for example, has led the Turkish public more and more to identify all Kurds with the PKK guerrillas, while even assimilated Kurds increasingly see the war as a struggle for survival. Following riots in Colombo in 1983 in which Sinhalese mobs killed 3,000 Tamils, even formerly liberal-minded Sinhalese came to view all Tamils as separatists: "They all say they are loyal to the government, but scratch a Tamil, any Tamil, and beneath the skin there is an Eelamist." Non-ethnic identity categories, such as neighborhood and friendship, cannot compete: in 1994 much of the hierarchy of the Rwandan Catholic Church split on ethnic lines.

Once the conflict reaches the level of large-scale violence, tales of atrocities—true or invented—perpetuated or planned against members of the group by the ethnic enemy provide hard-liners with an unanswerable argument. In March 1992 a Serb woman in Foča in Eastern Bosnia was convinced that "there were lists of Serbs who were marked for death. My two sons were down on the list to be slaughtered like pigs. I was listed under rape." The fact that neither she nor other townspeople had seen any such lists did not prevent them from believing such tales without question. The Croatian Ustasha in World War II went further, terrorizing Serbs in order to provoke a backlash that could then be used to mobilize Croats for defense against Serb retaliation.

In this environment, cross-ethnic appeals are not likely to attract members of the other group. The Yugoslav Partisans in World War II are often credited with transcending the ethnic conflict between the Croatian Ustasha and the Serbian Chetniks with an anti-German, pan-Yugoslav program. In fact it did not work. Tito was a Croat, but Partisan officers as well as the rank and file were virtually all Serbs and Montenegrins. Only in 1944, when German withdrawal made Partisan victory certain, did Croats begin to join the Partisans in numbers, not because they preferred a multi-ethnic Yugoslavia to a Greater Croatia, but because they preferred a multi-ethnic Yugoslavia to a Yugoslavia cleansed of Croatians.

In both Laos and Thailand in the 1960s, the hill people (Hmong) fought the lowland people (Laos and Thais). The Hmong in Laos called themselves anti-communists, while Hmong on the other side of the Mekong River turned to the Communist Party of Thailand. The ideological affiliations, however, were purely tactical; most Hmong in Laos lived in areas dominated by the communist Pathet Lao and so turned to the United States for support, while most Hmong in Thailand were fighting a U.S.-allied government. Although in both countries both communists and anti-communists offered political reform and economic development, cross-ethnic recruitment bore little fruit, and the outcomes of the rebellions were determined mainly by strictly military operations.

Ethnic war also shrinks scope for individual identity choice. Even those who put little value on their ethnic identity are pressed towards ethnic mobilization for two reasons. First, extremists within each community are likely to impose sanctions on those who do not contribute to the cause. In 1992 the leader of the Croatian Democratic Union in Bosnia was dismissed on the ground that he "was too much Bosnian, too little Croat." Conciliation is easy to denounce as dangerous to group security or as actually traitorous. Such arguments drove nationalist extremists to overthrow President Makarios of Cyprus in 1974, to assassinate Mahatma Gandhi in 1948, to massacre nearly the whole government of Rwanda in 1994, and to kill Yitzhak Rabin in 1995.

Second and more important, identity is often imposed by the opposing group, specifically by its most murderous members. Assimilation or political passivity did no good for German Jews, Rwandan Tutsis, or Azerbaijanis in Nagorno-Karabakh. A Bosnian Muslim schoolteacher recently lamented:

> We never, until the war, thought of ourselves as Muslims. We were Yugoslavs. But when we began to be murdered, because we are Muslims, things changed. The definition of who we are today has been determined by our killers. . . .

The Decisiveness of Territory   Another consequence of the hardness of ethnic identities is that population control depends wholly on territorial control. Since each side can recruit only from its own community and only in friendly-controlled territory, incentives to seize areas populated by co-ethnics are strong, as is the pressure to cleanse friendly-controlled territory of enemy ethnics by relocation to *de facto* concentration camps, expulsion, or massacre.

Because of the decisiveness of territorial control, military strategy in ethnic wars is very different than in ideological conflicts. Unlike ideological insurgents, who often evade rather than risk battle, or a counter-insurgent government, which might forbear to attack rather than risk bombarding civilians, ethnic combatants must fight for every piece of land. By contrast, combatants in ethnic wars are much less free to decline unfavorable battles because they cannot afford to abandon any settlement to an enemy who is likely to "cleanse" it by massacre, expulsion, destruction of homes, and possibly colonization. By the time a town can be retaken, its value will have been lost.

In ethnic civil wars, military operations are decisive. Attrition matters because the side's mobilization pools are separate and can be depleted. Most important, since each side's mobilization base is limited to members of its own community in friendly-controlled territory, conquering the enemy's population centers reduces its mobilization base, while loss of friendly settlements reduces one's own. Military control of the entire territory at issue is tantamount to total victory.

Security Dilemmas in Ethnic Wars

The second problem that must be overcome by any remedy for severe ethnic conflict is the security dilemma. Regardless of the origins of ethnic strife, once violence (or abuse of state power by one group that controls it) reaches the point that ethnic communities cannot rely on the state to protect them, each community must mobilize to take responsibility for its own security.

Under conditions of anarchy, each group's mobilization constitutes a real threat to the security of others for two reasons. First, the nationalist rhetoric that accompanies mobilization often seems to and often does indicate offensive intent. Under these conditions, group identity itself can be seen by other groups as a threat to their safety.[2]

Second, military capability acquired for defense can usually also be used for offense. Further, offense often has an advantage over defense in inter-community conflict, especially when settlement patterns are inter-mingled, because isolated pockets are harder to hold than to take.

The reality of the mutual security threats means that solutions to ethnic conflicts must do more than undo the causes; until or unless the security dilemma can be reduced or eliminated, neither side can afford to demobilize.

Demography and Security Dilemmas   The severity of ethnic security dilemmas is greatest when demography is most intermixed, weakest when community settlements are most separate. The more mixed the opposing groups, the stronger the offense in relation to the defense; the more separated they are, the stronger the defense in relation to offense.[3] When settlement patterns are extremely mixed, both sides are vulnerable to attack not only by organized military forces but also by local militias or gangs from adjacent towns or neighborhoods. Since well-defined fronts are impossible, there is no effective means of defense against such raids. Accordingly, each side has a strong incentive—at both national and local levels—to kill or drive out enemy populations before the enemy does the same to it, as well as to create homogeneous enclaves more practical to defend.

Better, but still bad, are well-defined enclaves with islands of one or both sides' populations behind the other's front. Each side then has an incentive to attack to rescue its surrounded co-ethnics before they are destroyed by the enemy, as well as incentives to wipe out enemy islands behind its own lines, both to pre-empt rescue attempts and to eliminate possible bases for fifth columnists or guerrillas.

The safest pattern is a well-defined demographic front that separates nearly homogeneous regions. Such a front can be defended by organized military forces, so populations are not at risk unless defenses are breached. At the same time the strongest motive for attack disappears, since there are few or no endangered co-ethnics behind enemy lines. . . .

Ethnic Separation and Peace   Once ethnic groups are mobilized for war, the war cannot end until the populations are separated into defensible, mostly homogeneous regions. Even if an international force or an imperial conqueror were to impose peace, the conflict would resume as soon as it left. Even if a national government were somehow re-created despite mutual suspicions, neither group could safely entrust its security to it. Continuing mutual threat also ensures perpetuation of hypernationalist propaganda, both for mobilization and because the plausibility of the threat posed by the enemy gives radical nationalists an unanswerable advantage over moderates in intra-group debates.

Ethnic separation does not guarantee peace, but it allows it. Once populations are separated, both cleansing and rescue imperatives disappear; war is no longer mandatory. At the same time, any attempt to seize more territory requires a major conventional military offensive. Thus the conflict changes from one of mutual pre-emptive ethnic cleansing to something approaching conventional interstate war in which normal deterrence dynamics apply. Mutual deterrence does not guarantee that there will be no further violence, but it reduces the probability of outbreaks, as well as the likely aims and intensity of those that do occur.

There have been no wars among Bulgaria, Greece, and Turkey since their population exchanges of the 1920s. Ethnic violence on Cyprus, which reached crisis on several occasions between 1960 and 1974, has been zero since the partition and population exchange which followed Turkish invasion. The Armenian-Azeri ethnic conflict, sparked by independence demands of the mostly Armenian Nagorno-Karabakh Autonomous Oblast, escalated to full-scale war by 1992. Armenian conquest of all of Karabakh together with the land which formerly separated it from Armenia proper, along with displacement of nearly all members of each group from enemy-controlled territories, created a defensible separation with no minorities to fight over, leading to a cease-fire in April 1994. . . .

Alternatives to Separation

Besides demographic separation, the literature on possible solutions to ethnic conflicts contains four main alternatives: suppression, reconstruction of ethnic identities, power-sharing, and state-building.

Suppression Many ethnic civil wars lead to the complete victory of one side and the forcible suppression of the other. This may reduce violence in some cases, but will never be an aim of outsiders considering humanitarian intervention. Further, remission of violence may be only temporary, as the defeated group usually rebels again at any opportunity. Even the fact that certain conquerors, such as the English in Scotland or the Dutch in Friesland, eventually permitted genuine political assimilation after decades of suppression, does not recommend this as a remedy for endangered peoples today.

Reconstruction of Ethnic Identities The most ambitious program to end ethnic violence would be to reconstruct ethnic identities according to the "Constructivist Model" of nationalism. Constructivists argue that individual and group identities are fluid, continually being made and re-made in social discourse. Further, these identities are manipulable by political entrepreneurs. Violent ethnic conflicts are the result of pernicious group identities created by hypernationalist myth-making; many inter-group conflicts are quite recent, as are the ethnic identities themselves.

The key is elite rivalries within communities, in which aggressive leaders use hypernationalist propaganda to gain and hold power. History does not matter; whether past inter-community relations have in fact been peaceful or conflictual, leaders can redefine, reinterpret, and invent facts to suit their arguments, including alleged atrocities and exaggerated or imagined threats. This process can feed on itself, as nationalists use the self-fulfilling nature of their arguments both to escalate the conflict and to justify their own power, so that intra-community politics becomes a competition in hypernationalist extremism, and inter-community relations enter a descending spiral of violence.

It follows that ethnic conflicts generated by the promotion of pernicious, exclusive identities should be reversible by encouraging individuals and groups to adopt more benign, inclusive identities. Leaders can choose to mobilize support on the basis of broader identities that transcend the ethnic division, such as ideology, class, or civic loyalty to the nation-state. If members of the opposing groups can be persuaded to adopt a larger identity, ethnic antagonisms should fade away. In 1993 David Owen explained why reconciliation in Bosnia was still possible: "I think it's realistic because these people are of the same ethnic stock. . . . Many people there still see themselves as European and even now don't think of themselves as Muslim, Croat, or Serb."

However, even if ethnic hostility can be "constructed," there are strong reasons to believe that violent conflicts cannot be "reconstructed" back to ethnic harmony. Identity reconstruction under conditions of intense conflict is probably impossible because once ethnic groups are mobilized for war, they will have already produced, and will continue reproducing, social institutions and discourses that reinforce their group identity and shut out or shout down competing identities.

Replacement of ethnicity by some other basis for political identification requires that political parties have cross-ethnic appeal, but examples of this in the midst of ethnic violence are virtually impossible to find. In late 1992 Yugoslav Prime Minister Milan Panić attempted to reconstruct Serbian identity in a less nationalist direction. Running for the Serbian presidency against Milošević, Panić promised democratization, economic reform, and ends to the war in Bosnia as well as to un sanctions. Milošević painted him as a tool of foreign interests, and Panić lost with 34 percent of the vote.

In fact, even ethnic tension far short of war often undermines not just political appeals across ethnic lines but also appeals within a single group for cooperation with other groups. In Yugoslavia in the 1920s, Malaya in the 1940s, Ceylon in the 1950s, and in Nigeria in the 1950s and 1960s, parties that advocated cooperation across ethnic lines proved unable to compete with strictly nationalist parties.

Even if constructivists are right that the ancient past does not matter, recent history does. Intense violence creates personal experiences of fear, misery, and loss which lock people into their group identity and their enemy relationship with the other group. Elite as well as mass opinions are affected; more than 5,000 deaths in the 1946 Calcutta riots convinced many previously optimistic Hindu and Muslim leaders that the groups could not live together. The Tutsi-controlled government of Burundi, which had witnessed the partial genocide against Tutsis in Rwanda in 1962–63 and survived Hutu-led coup attempts in 1965 and 1969, regarded the 1972 rebellion as another attempt at geno-cide, and responded by murdering between 100,000 and 200,000 Hutus. Fresh rounds of violence in 1988 and 1993–94 have reinforced the apocalyptic fears of both sides. . . .

Power-Sharing   The best-developed blueprint for civic peace in multi-ethnic states is power-sharing or "consociational democracy," proposed by Arend Lijphart. This approach assumes that ethnicity is somewhat manipulable, but not so freely as constructivists say.[4] Ethnic division, however, need not result in conflict; even if political mobilization is organized on ethnic lines, civil poli-tics can be maintained if ethnic elites adhere to a power-sharing bargain that equitably protects all groups. The key components are: 1) joint exercise of gov-ernmental power; 2) proportional distribution of government funds and jobs; 3) autonomy on ethnic issues (which, if groups are concentrated territorially, may be achieved by regional federation); and 4) a minority veto on issues of vital importance to each group.[5] Even if power-sharing can avert potential ethnic conflicts or dampen mild ones, our concern here is whether it can bring peace under the conditions of intense violence and extreme ethnic mobilization that are likely to motivate intervention.[6]

The answer is no. The indispensable component of any power-sharing deal is a plausible minority veto, one which the strongest side will accept and which the weaker side believes that the stronger will respect. Traditions of stronger loyalties to the state than to parochial groups and histories of inter-ethnic com-promise could provide reason for confidence, but in a civil war these will have been destroyed, if they were ever present, by the fighting itself and accompany-ing ethnic mobilization.

Only a balance of power among the competing groups can provide a "hard" veto—one which the majority must respect. Regional concentration of populations could partially substitute for balanced power if the minority group can credibly threaten to secede if its veto is overridden. In any situation where humanitarian intervention might be considered, however, these conditions too are unlikely to be met. Interventions are likely to be aimed at saving a weak group that cannot defend itself; balanced sides do not need defense. Demo-graphic separation is also unlikely, because if the populations were already separated, the ethnic cleansing and related atrocities which are most likely to provoke intervention would not be occurring.

The core reason why power-sharing cannot resolve ethnic civil wars is that it is inherently voluntaristic; it requires conscious decisions by elites to cooperate to avoid ethnic strife. Under conditions of hypernationalist mobili-zation and real security threats, group leaders are unlikely to be receptive to compromise, and even if they are, they cannot act without being discredited and replaced by harder-line rivals.

Could outside intervention make power-sharing work? One approach would be to adjust the balance of power between the warring sides to a "hurt-ing stalemate" by arming the weaker side, blockading the stronger, or partially disarming the stronger by direct military intervention. When both sides realize that further fighting will bring them costs but no profit, they will negotiate an agreement. This can balance power, although if populations are still intermingled it may actually worsen security dilemmas and increase violence—especially against civilians—as both sides eliminate the threats posed by pockets of the opposing group in their midst. . . .

Ethnic Separation

Regardless of the causes of a particular conflict, once communities are mobilized for violence, the reality of mutual security threats prevents both demobilization and de-escalation of hypernationalist discourse. Thus, lasting peace requires removal of the security dilemma. The most effective and in many cases the only way to do this is to separate the ethnic groups. The more intense the violence, the more likely it is that separation will be the only option. . . .

How Ethnic Wars Have Ended

The most comprehensive data set of recent and current violent ethnic conflicts has been compiled by Ted Robert Gurr. This data set includes 27 ethnic civil wars that have ended. Of these, twelve were ended by complete victory of one side, five by *de jure* or *de facto* partition, and two have been suppressed by military occupation by a third party. Only eight ethnic civil wars have been ended by an agreement that did not partition the country. (See Table 6.1.)

The data supports the argument that separation of groups is the key to ending ethnic civil wars. Every case in which the state was preserved by agreement involved a regionally concentrated minority, and in every case the solution reinforced the ethnic role in politics by allowing the regional minority group to control its own destiny through regional autonomy for the areas where it forms a majority of the population. There is not a single case where non-ethnic civil politics were created or restored by reconstruction of ethnic identities, power-sharing coalitions, or state-building. . . .

INTERVENTION TO RESOLVE ETHNIC CIVIL WARS

International interventions that seek to ensure lasting safety for populations endangered by ethnic war—whether by the United Nations, by major powers with global reach, or by regional powers—must be guided by two principles. First, settlements must aim at physically separating the warring communities and establishing a balance of relative strength that makes it unprofitable for either side to attempt to revise the territorial settlement. Second, although economic or military assistance may suffice in some cases, direct military intervention will be necessary when aid to the weaker side would create a window of opportunity for the stronger, or when there is an immediate need to stop ongoing genocide.

Designing Settlements

Unless outsiders are willing to provide permanent security guarantees, stable resolution of an ethnic civil war requires separation of the groups into defensible regions. The critical variable is demography, not sovereignty. Political partition without ethnic separation leaves incentives for ethnic cleansing unchanged; it actually increases them if it creates new minorities. Conversely, demographic separation dampens ethnic conflicts even without separate sovereignty, although the more intense the previous fighting, the smaller the prospects for preserving a single state, even if loosely federated.

Partition without ethnic separation increases conflict because, while boundaries of sovereign successor states may provide defensible fronts that reduce the vulnerability of the majority group in each state, stay-behind minorities are completely exposed. Significant irredenta are both a call to their ethnic homeland and a danger to their hosts. They create incentives to mount rescue or ethnic cleansing operations before the situation solidifies. Greece's 1920 invasion of Turkey was justified in this way, while the 1947 decision to partition Palestine generated a civil war in advance of implementation, and the inclusion of Muslim-majority Kashmir within India has helped cause three wars. International recognition of Croatian and Bosnian independence did more to cause than to stop Serbian invasion. The war between Armenia and Azerbaijan has the same source, as do concerns over the international security risks of the several Russian diasporas.

Table 6.1 Ethnic Civil Wars Resolved 1944–94

Deaths

Combatants	Dates	(000s)[1]	Outcome
Military victory (12):			
Karens vs. Myanmar	1945–	43	Defeat imminent
Kurds vs. Iran	1945–80s	40	Suppressed
Tibetans vs. China	1959–89	100	Suppressed
Papuans vs. Indonesia	1964–86	19	Suppressed
Ibo vs. Nigeria	1967–70	2000	Suppressed
Timorese vs. Indonesia	1974–80s	200	Suppressed
Aceh vs. Indonesia	1975–80s	15	Suppressed
Tigreans vs. Ethiopia	1975–91	350	Rebels victorious
Uighurs etc. vs. China	1980	2	Suppressed
Bougainville vs. Papua	1988	1	Suppressed
Tutsis vs. Rwanda	1990–94	750	Rebels victorious
Shiites vs. Iraq	1991	35	Suppressed
De facto or *de jure* partition (5):			
Ukrainians vs. USSR	1944–50s	150	Suppressed, independent 1991

Lithuanians vs. USSR	1945–52	40	Suppressed, independent 1991
Eritreans vs. Ethiopia	1961–91	350	Independent 1993
Armenians vs. Azerbaijan	1988–	15	*De facto* partition
Somali clans	1988–	350	*De facto* partition in N., ongoing in S.

Conflict suppressed by ongoing 3rd-party military occupation (2):

Kurds vs. Iraq	1960–	215	*De facto* partition
Lebanese Civil War	1975–90	120	Nominal power sharing, *de facto* partition

Settled by agreements other than partition (8):

Nagas vs. India	1952–75	13	Autonomy 1972
Basques vs. Spain	1959–80s	1	Autonomy 1980
Tripuras vs. India	1967–89	13	Autonomy 1972
Palestinians vs. Israel	1968–93	2	Autonomy 1993, partly implemented
Moros vs. Philippines	1972–87	50	Limited autonomy 1990
Chittagong hill peoples vs. Bangladesh	1975–89	24	Limited autonomy 1989
Miskitos vs. Nicaragua	1981–88	<1	Autonomy 1990
Abkhazians vs. Georgia	1992–93	10	Autonomy 1993

[1]Figures are from Ted Robert Gurr, *Minorities at Risk: A Global View of Ethnopolitical Conflicts* (Washington, D.C.: U.S. Institute of Peace, 1993), and Gurr, "Peoples Against States: Ethnopolitical Conflict and the Changing World System," *International Studies Quarterly*, Vol. 38, No. 3 (September 1994), pp. 347–377.

Inter-ethnic security dilemmas can be nearly or wholly eliminated without partition if three conditions are met: First, there must be enough demographic separation that ethnic regions do not themselves contain militarily significant minorities. Second, there must be enough regional self-defense capability that abrogating the autonomy of any region would be more costly than any possible motive for doing so. Third, local autonomy must be so complete that minority groups can protect their key interests even lacking any influence at the national level. Even after an ethnic war, a single state could offer some advantages, not least of which are the economic benefits of a common market. However, potential interveners should recognize that groups that control distinct territories can insist on the *de facto* partition, and often will.

While peace requires separation of groups into distinct regions, it does not require total ethnic purity. Rather, remaining minorities must be small enough that the host group does not fear them as either a potential military threat or a possible target for irredentist rescue operations. Before the Krajina offensive, for example, President Franjo Tudjman of Croatia is said to have thought that the 12 percent Serb minority in Croatia was too large, but that half as many would be tolerable. The 173,000 Arabs remaining in Israel by 1951 were too few and too disorganized to be seen as a serious threat.

Geographic distribution of minorities is also important; in particular, concentrations near disputed borders or astride strategic communications constitute both a military vulnerability and an irredentist opportunity, and so are likely to spark conflict. It is not surprising that India's portion of Kashmir, with its Muslim majority, has been at the center of three inter-state wars and an ongoing insurgency which continues today, while there has been no international conflict over the hundred million Muslims who live dispersed throughout most of the rest of India, and relatively little violence.

Where possible, inter-group boundaries should be drawn along the best defensive terrain, such as rivers and mountain ranges. Lines should also be as short as possible, to allow the heaviest possible manning of defensive fronts. (Croatian forces were able to overrun Krajina in part because its irregular crescent shape meant that 30,000 Krajina Serb forces had to cover a frontier of more than 725 miles.) Access to the sea or to a friendly neighbor is also important, both for trade and for possible military assistance. Successor state arsenals should be encouraged, by aid to the weaker or sanctions on the stronger, to focus on defensive armaments such as towed artillery and anti-aircraft missiles and rockets, while avoiding instruments that could make blitzkrieg attacks possible, such as tanks, fighter-bombers, and mobile artillery. These conditions would make subsequent offensives exceedingly expensive and likely to fail.

Intervention Strategy

The level of international action required to resolve an ethnic war will depend on the military situation on the ground. If there is an existing stalemate along defensible lines, the international community should simply recognize and strengthen it, providing transportation, protection, and resettlement assistance for refugees. However, where one side has the capacity to go on the offensive against the other, intervention will be necessary.

Interventions should therefore almost always be on behalf of the weaker side; the stronger needs no defense. Moreover, unless the international community can agree on a clear aggressor and a clear victim, there is no moral or political case for intervention. If both sides have behaved so badly that there is little to choose between them, intervention should not and probably will not be undertaken.[7] Almost no one in the West, for instance, has advocated assisting either side in the Croatian-Serb conflict.[8] While the intervention itself could be carried out by any willing actors, un sponsorship is highly desirable, most of all to head off possible external aid to the group identified as the aggressor.

The three available tools are sanctions, military aid, and direct military intervention. Economic sanctions have limited leverage against combatants in ethnic wars, who often see their territorial security requirements as absolute.

Whereas hyperinflation and economic collapse have apparently reduced Serbian government support for the Bosnian Serb rebels and thus limited the latter's material capabilities, Armenians have already suffered five years of extreme privation rather than give up Nagorno-Karabakh. . . .

If the client is too weak to achieve a viable separation with material aid alone, or if either or both sides cannot be trusted to abide by promises of non-retribution against enemy civilians, the international community must designate a separation line and deploy an intervention force to take physical control of the territory on the client's side of the line. We might call this approach "conquer and divide."

The separation campaign is waged as a conventional military operation. The larger the forces committed the better, both to minimize intervenors' casualties and to shorten the campaign by threatening the opponent with overwhelming defeat. Although some argue that any intervention force would become mired in a Vietnam-like quagmire, the fundamentally different nature of ethnic conflict means that the main pitfalls to foreign military interventions in ideological insurgencies are either weaker or absent. Most important, the intervenors' intelligence problems are much simpler, since loyalty intelligence is both less important and easier: outsiders can safely assume that members of the allied group are friends and those of the other are enemies. Even if outsiders cannot tell the groups apart, locals can, and the loyalty of guides provided by the local ally can be counted on. As a result, the main intelligence task shifts from assessing loyalties to locating enemy forces, a task of which major power militaries are very capable. . . .

Bosnia

Early intervention in Bosnia could have saved most of the lives that have been lost, and secured the Muslims a better territorial deal than they are going to get, but only if the international community had been willing to accept that by 1992, restoration of civil politics in a multi-ethnic Bosnia had become impossible, and had been able to overcome its squeamishness about large-scale population transfers.

The Vance-Owen plan did not meet the minimum conditions for stable peace because it aimed at preservation of a multi-ethnic state, not ethnic separation. Each of the ten planned cantons would have contained large minorities, and some would have included enclaves totally surrounded by an opposing ethnic group. The 1994 Contact Group proposal to divide Bosnia 51 percent–49 percent between a Muslim-Croat federation and the Bosnian Serbs would have been better, but incorporated serious instabilities such as the isolated Muslim enclaves of Žepa, Srebrenica, and Goražde, two of which were later overrun with great loss of life.

As the progress of the war has left fewer and fewer unmoved people still to move, more realistic proposals have gradually emerged. The agreement signed at Dayton in November 1995, despite lip service to a unitary Bosnia, ratifies and seeks to strengthen existing territorial divisions. This agreement gives grounds for qualified hope for a stable, relatively peaceful Bosnia.

Future peace in Bosnia depends on resolution of three issues. First and most important, while the military fronts have gradually settled along defensible lines in most areas of the country, serious demographic security dilemmas persist in two places—Serb-held suburbs of Sarajevo which both threaten the city's supply lines and are vulnerable themselves, and the surrounded Muslim enclave of Goražde in the Drina Valley.

Accordingly, the Dayton agreement requires the withdrawal of all Bosnian Serb forces from these Sarajevo suburbs as well as from a corridor stretching from Sarajevo to Goražde, and assigns these areas to the Bosnian government. The Implementation Force (IFOR) is charged with ensuring compliance. The widespread burning of homes by Serbs and others evacuating areas which will pass to control of another group is in a sense encouraging, as it suggests they do not expect to return. More worrisome is the fact that the corridor to Goražde will be only four kilometers wide, leaving the city once again vulnerable after the IFOR departs. A wider corridor here, perhaps in exchange for territory elsewhere, would have been better, even if it meant that more civilians would have to move now.

The second issue is that the agreement, at least nominally, seeks to reconstruct some central government institutions with nationwide authority and a rotating presidency. It also requires all parties to permit the return of refugees. These provisions are undesirable and unenforceable, and should be allowed to die quietly. The procedures provided for compensating refugees for lost property should be followed instead. . . .

OBJECTIONS TO ETHNIC SEPARATION AND PARTITION

There are five important objections to ethnic separation as policy for resolving ethnic conflicts: that it encourages splintering of states, that population exchanges cause human suffering, that it simply transforms civil wars into international ones, that rump states will not be viable, and that, in the end, it does nothing to resolve ethnic antagonisms.

Among most international organizations, western leaders, and scholars, population exchanges and partition are anathema. They contradict cherished western values of social integration, trample on the international legal norm of state sovereignty, and suggest particular policies that have been condemned by most of the world (e.g., Turkey's unilateral partition of Cyprus). The integrity of states and their borders is usually seen as a paramount principle, while self-determination takes second place. In ethnic wars, however, saving lives may require ignoring state-centered legal norms. The legal costs of ethnic separation must be compared to the human consequences, both immediate and long term, if the warring groups are not separated. To paraphrase Winston Churchill: separation is the worst solution, except for all the others.

Partition Encourages Splintering of States

If international interventions for ethnic separation encourage secession attempts elsewhere, they could increase rather than decrease global ethnic violence. However, this is unlikely, because government use of force to suppress them makes almost all secession attempts extremely costly; only groups that see no viable alternative try. What intervention can do is reduce loss of life where states are breaking up anyway. An expectation that the international community will never intervene, however, encourages repression of minorities, as in Turkey or the Sudan, and wars of ethnic conquest, as by Serbia.

Population Transfers Cause Suffering

Separation of intermingled ethnic groups necessarily involves significant refugee flows, usually in both directions. Population transfers during ethnic conflicts have often led to much suffering, so an obvious question is whether foreign intervention to relocate populations would only increase suffering. In fact, however, the biggest cause of suffering in population exchanges is spontaneous refugee movement. Planned population transfers are much safer. When ethnic conflicts turn violent, they generate spontaneous refugee movements as people flee from intense fighting or are kicked out by neighbors, marauding gangs, or a conquering army. Spontaneous refugees frequently suffer direct attack by hostile civilians or armed forces. They often leave precipitately, with inadequate money, transport, or food supplies, and before relief can be organized. They make vulnerable targets for banditry and plunder, and are often so needy as to be likely perpetrators also. Planned population exchanges can address all of these risks by preparing refugee relief and security operations in advance.

In the 1947 India-Pakistan exchange, nearly the entire movement of between 12 and 16 million people took place in a few months. The British were surprised by the speed with which this movement took place, and were not ready to control, support, and protect the refugees. Estimates of deaths go as high as one million. In the first stages of the population exchanges among Greece, Bulgaria, and Turkey in the 1920s, hundreds of thousands of refugees moved spontaneously and many died due to banditry and exposure. When after 1925 the League of Nations deployed capable relief services, the remaining transfers—one million, over 60 percent of the total—were carried out in an organized and planned way, with virtually no losses. . . .

Separation Merely Substitutes International for Civil Wars

Post-separation wars are possible, motivated either by revanchism or by security fears if one side suspects the other of revisionist plans. The frequency and human cost of such wars, however, must be compared to the likely consequences of not separating. When the alternative is intercommunal slaughter, separation is the only defensible choice.

In fact the record of twentieth-century ethnic partitions is fairly good. The partition of Ireland has produced no interstate violence, although intercommunal violence continues in demographically mixed Northern Ireland. India and Pakistan have fought two wars since partition, one in 1965 over ethnically mixed Kashmir, while the second in 1971 resulted not from Indo-Pakistani state rivalry or Hindu-Muslim religious conflict but from ethnic conflict between (West) Pakistanis and Bengalis. Indian intervention resolved the conflict by enabling the independence of Bangladesh. These wars have been much less dangerous, especially to civilians, than the political and possible physical extinction that Muslims feared if the subcontinent were not divided. The worst post-partition history is probably that of the Arab-Israeli conflict. Even here, civilian deaths would almost certainly have been higher without partition. It is difficult even to imagine any alternative; the British could not and would not stay, and neither side would share power or submit to rule by the other.

Rump States Will Not Be Viable

Many analysts of ethnic conflict question the economic and military viability of partitioned states. History, however, records no examples of ethnic partitions which failed for economic reasons. In any case, intervenors have substantial influence over economic outcomes: they can determine partition lines, guarantee trade access and, if necessary, provide significant aid in relation to the economic sizes of likely candidates. Peace itself also enhances recovery prospects.

Thus the more important issue is military viability, particularly since interventions will most often be in favor of the weaker side. If the client has economic strength comparable to the opponent, it can provide for its own defense. If it does not, the intervenors will have to provide military aid and possibly a security guarantee. . . .

Partition Does Not Resolve Ethnic Hatreds

It is not clear that it is in anyone's power to resolve ethnic hatreds once there has been large-scale violence, especially murders of civilians. In the long run, however, separation may help reduce inter-ethnic antagonism; once real security threats are reduced, the plausibility of hypernationalist appeals may eventually decline. Certainly ethnic hostility cannot be reduced without separation. As long as either side fears, even intermittently, that it will be attacked by the other, past atrocities and old hatreds can easily be aroused. If, however, it becomes and remains implausible that the other group could ever seriously endanger the nation, hypernationalist drum-beating may fall on deafer and deafer ears.

The only stronger measure would be to attempt a thorough re-engineering of the involved groups' political and social systems, comparable to the rehabilitation of Germany after World War II. The costs would be steep, since this would require conquering the country and occupying it for a long time, possibly for decades. The apparent benignification of Germany suggests that, if the international community is prepared to go this far, this approach could succeed.

CONCLUSION

Humanitarian intervention to establish lasting safety for peoples endangered by ethnic civil wars is feasible, but only if the international community is prepared to recognize that some shattered states cannot be restored, and that population transfers are sometimes necessary.

Some observers attack separation and partition as immoral, suggesting that partitioning states like Bosnia would ratify the arguments of bloody-minded extremists such as Milošević and Tudjman that ethnic cleansing is necessitated by intractable ancient hatreds, when in fact they themselves whipped up hypernationalist fears for their own political ends. This argument is mistaken. The construction of ethnic hostility might have been contained by intervention in Yugoslav political discourses in the 1980s. It is too late now, but what the international community can still do is to provide surviving Muslims with physical security and a defensible homeland. The claims of justice demand that we go further, to the capture and trial of the aggressors, but that is beyond the scope of this article, the focus of which is the minimum requirements for protection of peoples endangered by ethnic war.

Alternatively, one could argue that the Bosnia record demonstrates that the international community cannot muster the will even for much lesser enterprises, let alone the campaigns of conquest envisaged in this paper. Even if this is true, the analysis above has four values. First, it tells us what apparent cheap and easy solutions are *not* viable. Second, it identifies the types of solutions to aim at through lesser means—aid or sanctions—if those are the most that outsiders are willing to do. Third, even if we are not prepared to intervene in certain cases, it explains what we would like other, more interested, powers to do and not do. Fourth, if Western publics and elites understood that the costs of military intervention in ethnic wars are lower, the feasibility higher, and the alternatives fewer than they now believe, perhaps this option would become more politically viable.

Ultimately we have a responsibility to be honest with ourselves as well as with the victims of ethnic wars all over the world. The world's major powers must decide whether they will be willing to spend any of their own soldiers' lives to save strangers, or whether they will continue to offer false hopes to endangered peoples.

NOTES

1 Constructivist scholars of nationalism would not agree, as they argue that ethnic identities are flexible social constructions, which can be manipulated by political entrepreneurs and more or less freely adopted or ignored by individuals. Key works include Paul

R. Brass, *Language, Religion, and Politics in North India* (Cambridge, England: Cambridge University Press, 1974); Benedict Anderson, *Imagined Communities: Reflections on the Origins and Spread of Nationalism* (London: Verso, 1983). Primordialists, by contrast, see ethnic identities as fixed by linguistic, racial, or religious background. Edward Shils, "Primordial, Personal, and Sacred Ties," *British Journal of Sociology*, Vol. 8 (1957), pp. 130–145; Clifford Geertz, "The Integrative Revolution: Primordial Sentiments and Civil Politics in the New States," in Geertz, ed., *Old Societies and New States* (New York: Free Press, 1963). For a recent defense, see Alexander J. Motyl, "Inventing Invention: The Limits of National Identity Formation," in Michael Kennedy and Ronald Gregor Suny, eds., *Intellectuals and the Articulation of the Nation*, book manuscript. A middle position, "perennialist," accepts that identities are social constructs but argues that their deep cultural and psychological roots make them extremely persistent, especially in literate cultures. See Walker Connor, *Ethnonationalism: The Quest for Understanding* (Princeton, N.J.: Princeton University Press, 1994). In this paper I do not take a position on the initial sources of ethnic identities or on their malleability under conditions of low conflict, but argue that massive ethnic violence creates conditions which solidify both ethnic boundaries and inter-ethnic hostility.

2 Barry R. Posen, "The Security Dilemma and Ethnic Conflict," in Michael Brown, ed., *Ethnic Conflict and International Security* (Princeton, N.J.: Princeton University Press, 1993), pp. 103–124. Posen argues that nationalism and hypernationalism are driven primarily by the need to supply recruits for mass armies, and are thus likely to be more extreme in new states which lack the capacity to field more capital-intensive and less manpower-intensive forces (pp. 106–107). See also Posen, "Nationalism, the Mass Army, and Military Power," *International Security*, Vol. 18, No. 2 (Fall 1993), pp. 80–124.

3 Increased geographic intermixing of ethnic groups often intensifies conflict, particularly if the state is too weak or too biased to assure the security of all groups. Increasing numbers of Jewish settlers in the West Bank had this effect on Israeli-Palestinian relations. A major reason for the failure of the negotiations that preceded the Nigerian civil war was the inability of northern leaders to guarantee the safety of Ibo living in the northern region. Harold D. Nelson, ed., *Nigeria: A Country Study* (Washington, D.C.: U.S. GPO, 1982), p. 55.

4 Lijphart, "Consociational Democracy," *World Politics*, Vol. 21, No. 2 (January 1969). In fact, Lijphart argues that diffuse or fluid ethnic identities are undesirable, because design of a power-sharing agreement requires clear identification of the players. Lijphart, "Power Sharing Approach," pp. 499–500.

5 Lijphart cites Belgium as an archetypical example, as well as Malaysia, Canada, India, and Nigeria. "Power-Sharing Approach," pp. 492, 494–96.

6 Lijphart admits that power-sharing is more difficult under conditions of high conflict but prefers it anyway, arguing that pessimism in difficult cases would be self-fulfilling; power-sharing cannot work when it is not tried. Ibid., p. 497.

7 This is why the strongest advocates of intervention in Bosnia have emphasized Serb crimes, while those opposed to intervention insist on the moral equivalence of the two sides. Anthony Lewis, "Crimes of War," *New York Times*, April 25, 1994; Charles G. Boyd, "Making Peace with the Guilty," *Foreign Affairs*, Vol. 74, No. 5 (September/October 1995), pp. 22–38.

8 Further, attempts at even-handed intervention rarely achieve their goals, leading either to nearly complete passivity, as in the case of UNPROFOR in Bosnia, or eventually to open combat against one or all sides. At worst, peace-keeping efforts may actually prolong fighting. See Richard K. Betts, "The Delusion of Impartial Intervention," *Foreign Affairs*, Vol. 73, No. 6 (November/December 1994), pp. 20–33.

Reading 6.4

The Troubled History of Partition

RADHA KUMAR

BOSNIA GOES THE WAY OF CYPRUS

The September [1996] elections in Bosnia highlighted what was until then an implicit aspect of the current peace: it is more likely to move Bosnia toward the ethnic states for which the war was fought than to reestablish the multiethnic Bosnia that once was. Indeed, as the Dayton process unfolds, it becomes clearer that the peace agreement signed in November 1995 after three and a half years of war was something historically familiar: a so-called peace accord that is in reality a partition agreement with an exit clause for outside powers.

At the same time, while key aspects of the document, such as the creation of two "entities" with virtually separate legislatures, administrations, and armies, tend toward partition, the pact attempts to get around some of the more hostile legacies of partition through a common economic space and arms control, and it creates structures that could reverse the partition process by returning refugees and rebuilding civil society. So far, these structures have been dormant, and the holding of national elections in a still highly uncertain peace marks the tilt toward partition. As was widely predicted, the Bosnians gave their ethnic leaders new mandates, and Bosnia took another step toward partition. However, the postponement of the municipal elections due to irregularities in voter registration means the international community is not yet in a position to accept partition as the democratically expressed will of the people.

The Bosnian war and the Dayton peace agreement have reignited a debate on whether partition is an effective solution to ethnic conflict. Although Bosnia is the starting point, the arguments in this debate have broad resonance at a time in which the rapid spread of ethnic and communal wars east and south of Bosnia is of increasing concern to the international community. Defenders of partition make an argument that runs as follows. When an ethnic war is far advanced, partition is probably the most humane form of intervention because it attempts to achieve through negotiation what would otherwise be achieved through fighting; it circumvents the conflict and saves lives. It might even save a country from disappearing altogether because an impartial intervenor will attempt to secure the rights of each contending ethnic group, whereas in war the stronger groups might oust the weaker ones. In fact, its advocates say, the

Source: Radha Kumar, "The Troubled History of Partition." Reprinted by permission of Foreign Affairs, Vol. 76, No. 1 (January/February 1997). Copyright 1997 by the Council on Foreign Relations Inc.

ideal strategy for resolving an ethnic conflict is to intervene and take partition to its logical conclusion by dividing a country along its communal battle lines and helping make the resulting territories ethnically homogeneous through organized population transfers. This will ensure that partition is more than a temporary means of containing conflict. Less thorough partitions, however, can still be a lasting means of containment.[1]

Partition, however, has its own sordid history, not arising as a means of realizing national self-determination, but imposed as a way for outside powers to unshoulder colonies or divide up spheres of influence—a strategy of divide and quit. Although described as the lesser of two evils, the partitions in Cyprus, India, Palestine, and Ireland, rather than separating irreconcilable ethnic groups, fomented further violence and forced mass migration. Even where partition enabled outside powers to leave, as in India, it also led to a disastrous war. Often thought of as a provisional solution, it has been unable to contain the fragmentation it triggers among dispersed or overlapping ethnic groups that are not confined by neat geographic boundaries, and it gives birth to weak civil institutions demanding supervision. Similar conditions ensure that the partition of Bosnia, which from the start should have been reintegrated, will also amount only to a policy of divide and be forced to stay. The Dayton accords should not evoke memories of Munich, but rather of Cyprus.

THE ROAD TO QUITTING

The argument for ethnic partition is not new, but its terms changed considerably over this century before settling upon the current rationale of the lesser of two evils. Before World War I, most partitions were effected for the needs of empire, to strengthen rule or simplify administration. After 1918, however, colonial empires were increasingly challenged, and subsequent partitions took place as part of a devolution of authority or a Cold War policy of spheres of influence. There were two distinct rationales for the partitions resulting from the fall of colonial empires: Wilsonian national self-determination, applied to Poland and Romania, and the British colonial policy of identifying irreconcilable nationhoods, applied in Ireland, India, and, as a delayed response, Cyprus and Palestine. Though both rationales took ethnic identity as an important determinant of political rights, Wilsonian policy supported ethnic self-determination as freedom from colonial rule, while the British reluctantly espoused partition as a lesser evil than constant civil war.

After the last attempt to ratify a partition—Cyprus after the Turkish invasion in 1974—the notion that partition was an effective solution to ethnic conflict fell into disuse for a quarter-century. Paradoxically, its revival followed hard on the heels of German reunification and the potential integration of Europe that it heralded. In the first phase of the revival of partition theory, Wilsonian self-determination was invoked more often than the lesser-evil argument. Indeed, the prevailing feeling was that the end of the Cold War—and the relatively peaceful dissolution of the Soviet Union—meant that separations could be negotiated. In the early 1990s the most frequently cited example of a peaceful negotiated division was Czechoslovakia's "velvet divorce." When asked on *The News Hour with Jim Lehrer* in November 1995 whether the Dayton agreement was a partition, Assistant Secretary of State Richard C. Holbrooke said he preferred the example of Czechoslovakia's voluntary dissolution. But fewer people now refer to the Czech split. That the Czech Republic and Slovakia were relatively homogeneous and that dissolution of the federation did not require an alteration of internal borders or a substantial displacement of people make the comparison with Bosnia untenable. A comparison between Bosnia and the partitions of Ireland, India, and Cyprus, or the incomplete partition of Palestine, would be better, because each involved ethnically mixed and dispersed populations and each was held to be a pragmatic recognition of irreconcilable ethnic identities.

It is worth examining these partitions' relevance to Bosnia in more detail. All relied heavily on the lesser-evil argument, but in at least two of them the decision for partition was prompted not by a desire for peace and self-determination, but because the colonial power, Britain, wanted to withdraw. The recognition of irreconcilable nationhoods followed as a consequence—it would be easier to withdraw quickly if the aims of the ethnic leaders were fulfilled by territorial grants. Looking back on the 1947 partition of India in 1961, former civil servant Penderel Moon summed up as "divide and quit," in a book of the same name, the British policy of pushing partition through without establishing the boundaries of new states or planning for the wars that might ensue; it was the post–World War II imperative of quitting that drove the decision to divide, he said. It was arguably the post–World War I imperative of quitting the Irish conflict that led the British to espouse a partition of Ireland.

That both divisions were driven by considerations extraneous to the needs and desires of the people displaced does not necessarily mean that partition was not a solution to their conflicts. However, as in India and Ireland, partition has more often been a backdrop to war than its culmination in peace; although it may originate in a situation of conflict, its effect has been to stimulate further and even new conflict. Indeed, India's experience raises the question of whether a peaceful transition to partition is possible. India's political leadership agreed to partition the country before the spread of large-scale conflict; the 1947 partition agreement between the Indian National Congress and the Muslim League was intended partly to prevent the spread of communal riots from Bengal in eastern India to northwestern India, which was also to be divided. But the riots that followed in 1947–48 left more than a million people dead in six months and displaced upwards of 15 million.

Moreover, partition arises in high-level negotiations long before it becomes evident on the ground. The British partition of Ireland in 1921 was a late addition to negotiations for home rule during the 1919–21 Anglo-Irish war for independence, but partition had been on the drawing board since 1912, when it was suggested by a group of conservative and liberal members of parliament that Protestant-majority counties be excluded from the proposed Irish Home Rule Bill. Calls for partition were renewed in 1914, 1916, and 1919; the offer of a double partition of Ireland and Ulster based on religion led to the spread of conflict between English and Irish across the south, west, and north of Ireland, escalating to guerrilla warfare when Catholic rebels formed the Irish Republican Army in 1919. Nor did the war end in 1921 when Britain negotiated a treaty with Sinn Fein, the political arm of the ira, offering dominion status to southern Ireland in return for a separate Ulster under British administration. The decision to accept partition led to a split in Sinn Fein, and internecine conflict was added to communal conflict, ending two years later with the defeat of the faction led by Eamon De Valera. It took almost four years of war to achieve the partition of Ireland, and those four years were themselves a culminating phase in a movement toward partition that had begun ten years earlier.

Significantly, the British rejected the partition option in Palestine in the same years that they espoused it in India. The two reasons they gave were infeasibility and the risk of a military conflict that would involve an expanded British presence. Although partition had been proposed in 1937 by the Peel Commission, which concluded that cooperation between Jews and Arabs in a Palestinian state was impossible, and had been the subject of debate in Britain throughout the 1930s, in 1946 the British members of the Anglo-American Committee of Inquiry argued that because ethnic groups were so dispersed, partition would entail massive forced population transfers, and that the territories created—a tiny Arab state, a Jewish state in two parts, and three blocs under continuing British administration—would be infeasible. Moreover, they said, moves toward partition could cause a war. In 1947 the British referred the dispute to the United Nations. The Security Council opted for partition, with a special U.N. regime for Jerusalem and a continuing economic union for the whole of Palestine. The plan required Britain to undertake a substantial role in its implementation, but after the Ministry of Defence forecast that Britain's military presence would have to be reinforced in the wars that would follow, Britain announced that it would withdraw in May 1948. In April the Jewish Agency, which represented the Jewish community under the British mandate, announced that it would declare a Jewish state when the British withdrew. War broke out, resulting in a kind of skewed partition by which one new state was created but not the other. Subsequently there have been three Arab-Israeli wars, and the issue of territorial feasibility continues to dog the peace process.

In many ways Cyprus offers the most striking parallels to Bosnia, and its history again raises the question of whether a peaceful transition to partition is possible. Although the British proposed the partition of the island in a divide-and-rule move in 1956, they subsequently rejected the plan on the same grounds as in Palestine—infeasibility and the risk of conflict. The British-brokered constitution of 1960 that made Cyprus independent was an attempt to avert division of the island between ethnic Turks and ethnic Greeks, but the idea that ethnic politics could be contained by providing for ethnic representation at every level proved a failure. The constitutional creation of separate municipalities and a distribution between the two ethnic groups in the presidency, legislature, civil service, police, and army added communal (that is, interreligious) conflict to internecine conflict. In 1963 the "Green Line," the first partition boundary to be drawn, divided Greek and Turkish Cypriots in Nicosia, the capital. Ethnic conflict only intensified, and a Turkish Cypriot declaration of support for partition followed in 1964. Although U.N. troops arrived that year, tensions escalated, with a counter-declaration of unification by Greece and Cyprus in 1966, a military coup in Greece, renewed conflict in Cyprus, a Turkish Cypriot announcement in 1967 of a Provisional Administration, increasing Greek support for the radical Greek underground in Cyprus, and finally a Turkish invasion in 1974 that reinforced the *de facto* partition of the island. Thus it took 14 years to establish what continues to be a shaky partition of Cyprus.

FOMENTING CONFLICT

How successful have these partitions been at reducing conflict and permitting outside powers to end their involvement? It is not clear that the partitions of Ireland and Cyprus can be said to have worked, even in the lesser-evil sense. Although the former was a move to divide and quit—in which all sides accepted division as the price of self-determination—the British are embroiled in a military operation in Northern Ireland that continues 70 years later. The troop presence curtailed the toll that communal conflict might otherwise have taken; indeed, it could be argued that it contained the Irish conflict and kept deaths to a minimum. But it also brought the conflict to the heart of Britain as the ira mounted terrorist attacks in London to increase pressure for a British withdrawal, and it could just as well be argued that from the British point of view independence would have been a more effective way to contain the conflict because it would have thrown the onus of peace onto the Irish; moreover, it might have encouraged regional compromises rather than a prolonged stalemate.

The partition of Cyprus can only be described as a partition by default that the U.N. presence inadvertently aided. The conflict following independence in 1960 was compounded by the fact that Turkey, Greece, and Britain were appointed protecting powers by the constitution. The formal structure this gave to a wider engagement in the conflict drew both the Greek and Turkish armies in and permitted international acceptance of Turkey's invasion in 1974 and what was until then a de facto partition. While casualties have been restricted since then, the division of Cyprus is little more than a long standoff that remains volatile and continues to require the presence of U.N. troops. Nor can the conflict be confined to Cyprus. Over the 20 years since partition, its short fuse is evident. A violent demonstration by Cypriots in August 1996 resulted in Greece and Turkey threatening war. The costs of containment, therefore, include permanent vigilance on the part of NATO and the Atlantic allies.

In many ways, despite the violence and displacements it produced, India's was the most successful ethnic partition, both because it allowed the British to quit and because the conflicts that ensued were by and large contained. But this had less to do with the wisdom of ethnic separation than with other factors, among them the subcontinent's distance from Europe. Unlike Ireland, Cyprus, and Bosnia, the Indian subcontinent is so large that a dozen or more new states could have been created. The deployment of the ethnic two-nation theory, however, which holds that Hindus and Muslims could not live together, had a paradoxical effect—the new state created, Pakistan, was divided into two parts by roughly 2,000 miles of Indian territory. The subsequent separation of those parts points up the inadequacy of the principle of ethnic separation for effecting stable territories. In the late 1960s, resentment at West Pakistani political and economic dominance led to a regional Bengali movement for independence, a war between the two parts in which India intervened in support of the Bengalis, and the birth of Bangladesh in 1971.

In regions of multiple ethnicities—where, for example, the same individual might have loyalties to one community defined by its religion and another by its language—attempts to make one ethnic identity dominant can trigger further fragmentation and conflict. The temporary success of the Indian People's Party in whipping up Hindu nationalism during the destruction of the Babri mosque in Ayodhya and in the riots that followed in the winter of 1992–93 ultimately led to the party's isolation and failure to form a government after the 1996 elections. The case of Kashmir is more poignant. Since 1947, India and Pakistan have been embroiled in a conflict that has twice flared into war, over what has been described, in a phrase dear to politicians on both sides, as "the unfinished business of partition": Kashmir. On ethnic grounds it can be argued that the conflict has continued because India retained the Muslim-majority Kashmir Valley, which should have gone to Pakistan. But following ethnic dividing lines could well entail a further three-way partition of the state—the valley, Buddhist Ladakh, and multiethnic Jammu—which would not only set the stage for intensified conflict and ethnic cleansing, as much of Jammu lies between Pakistan and the valley, but would also dissolve Kashmir.

BALKAN BEDLAM

Bosnia-Herzegovina, like these other partitioned territories, has problems of dispersed populations and continuing fragmentation, which the Dayton agreement shows little promise of resolving. It is difficult to contain a conflict when partition is still in progress. Thus NATO and Implementation Force (IFOR) officials under its auspices increasingly worry that hasty implementation of civilian aspects of the agreement such as elections might renew the conflict; instead of reversing partition or facilitating its peaceful execution, the prelude to the elections brought renewed low-level conflict in August. To this extent the Bosnian elections are to the Dayton process what last year's Israeli elections were to the Palestinian peace process: they prove that partition is still incomplete on the ground. Nearly half the pre-1992 population of Bosnia is still living as refugees outside Bosnia. Ethnically homogeneous territories can be created only if the refugees are refused repatriation to the towns and villages from which they were driven, which puts pressure on their host countries not to enforce repatriation. The refugees have become a key constituency that is used both to further and to challenge the consolidation of such ethnic territories, as in the Serb efforts to force refugees to vote from towns other than their prewar residences, and the subsequent threat of Bosnian Muslims to boycott the elections.

Both IFOR and the risibly named Office of the High Representative, which oversees the civilian implementation of Dayton under former Swedish Prime Minister Carl Bildt, make no secret of a concern the elections highlighted: the third partition that always hovered in Dayton's wings, between the Herzegovinian Croats and Bosnian Muslims now living together in the Bosnian Federation. Since the 1994 agreement signed in Washington that established the federation—which was intended to limit Bosnia's partition but produced a constitution remarkably similar to the 1960 Cyprus constitution—Herzegovinian Croats have asked: If a two-way partition is acceptable, why not a three-way one? Unsurprisingly, the answer, that Croatia has already been offered a far more substantial quid pro quo than Serbia and that a tiny and probably landlocked Muslim Bosnia would perpetuate Muslims' resentment, does not satisfy Herzegovinians. But Muslim resentment should at least give partition revivalists pause. Indeed, their argument that the United States should jettison the federation in favor of a tripartite partition begs both the resentment issue and a related matter Bosnian nationalists have raised: that they be given Serbia's predominantly Muslim Sandjak province as territorial compensation. Moreover, their argument ignores the problematic relationship between Croatian and Herzegovinian Croats, whose distrust of each other rivals that between Croats and Muslims.

NATO and IFOR have also pointed out an even more crucial concern: a partition dependent on the awkward boundary line between the Bosnian Federation and Republika Srpska, the Bosnian Serb entity, can last only so long as a large international force is there to enforce it. It is not Mostar in the federation but Banja Luka in the Serb entity that may bring the simmering partition war to a head. One look at the map of the Republika Srpska shows why. Like Pakistan after the partition of India, the Serb entity is divided into two parts, connected only by the narrow Posavina corridor, in which the disputed town of Breko is key; Serb attempts to rig local elections there were a major factor in the postponement of municipal elections in Bosnia last year. Additionally, the two main parts of the Serb entity lean in opposite directions, Banja Luka toward Zagreb and the eastern strip toward Belgrade. Normalization would again pull Banja Luka toward Zagreb economically and diminish its links to the east. That might mean a further division of the Republika Srpska, rather like the division of Pakistan that created Bangladesh, in which the Serb republic would be reduced to a strip of eastern Bosnia. Banja Luka, therefore, must be forced to look eastward, and is—with tacit U.S. support, if Richard Holbrooke's recent suggestions that the Bosnian Serbs make Banja Luka their capital are anything to go by. But Banja Luka's isolation amid federation territory can be maintained only if Serb leaders keep the city in a state of anarchy and mafia rule, like Mostar. Banja Luka's location, however, makes this task much more difficult because Mostar, which remains integrated with Croatia despite being incorporated into the Bosnian Federation, is close to the

Croatian border. It is debatable whether anything short of a fortified wall will keep Banja Luka isolated.

Thus, while elections may well be a step toward ratifying partition politically, efforts to consolidate a partition will not only perpetuate conflict but will eventually show that Bosnia can be successfully divided into two only if the Republika Srpska is further partitioned, with the western part reintegrated into Bosnia and the eastern part joining Serbia. Paradoxically, this may be the only way of ensuring a stable partition under the Dayton agreement, as the reintegration of Banja Luka will help keep the Croats in the federation. But if a multiethnic Bosnia can be re-created in one part, then why not in the whole, especially since a further partition will renew conflict around Goražde in eastern Bosnia?

ALL THE KING'S HORSES ...

As pressure mounts to accept the September elections as a mandate for partition, more emphasis is being placed on the reintegration option of the Dayton agreement, which assumes that economic interests and the provisions for a common economic space will erode the partition lines by making them irrelevant. It is being argued that the partial partition the Dayton agreement partly accepts is only a means of buying time for Bosnia to undergo this process. Historically, however, the failure to inject substantial and timely aid has only hardened ethnic divisions.

Partition has rarely been seen as anything other than a temporary solution to a crisis, which can be reversed as the crisis recedes. However, ethnic partitions have never been reversed; their implementation has inexorably driven communities further apart. Sinn Fein's acquiescence to the partition of Ireland was on the condition that there be a referendum on unification; the referendum did not take place, and now that negotiations on the status of Northern Ireland have been revived, Sinn Fein faces the ironic possibility that Ireland may no longer want unification.

Ethnic partition can often hamper the development of postwar economies. Although economic cooperation could improve South Asia's economies enormously, the ongoing conflict between India and Pakistan over Kashmir has impeded attempts to build it. The Dayton agreement's hope that economic interests will militate against ethnic boundaries was also voiced in Ireland and Palestine. Irish nationalists and the U.N. mediators in Palestine both hoped that mutual dependence, geographic proximity, and the benefits of shared infrastructure would gradually dissipate the aftermath of ethnic partition. Indeed, the U.N. plan for the partition of Palestine was based explicitly on the premise that economic union would compensate for the difficulties of the proposed territories. Instead, partition's legacies thwarted economic union and kept both Ireland and what was left of Palestine in poverty.

If the lessons of these examples are noteworthy, it may be because Bosnia will constitute a turning point in partition theory. The fact that NATO is preparing for an extended presence indicates that the alliance recognizes the unlikely success of a divide and quit approach in this situation. Though divide and quit was a motive in Britain's support for partition in Ireland, Palestine, and India, it got Britain out quickly only in India, and that was because South Asia is distant from Britain. From the sequence of events in Bosnia, it is clear that European and American leaders, and the rest of the international community, were prepared to accept partition if it would curtail Western intervention in the conflict and limit Western involvement in the region. But as the partition process unfolds, it is being recognized that divide and quit might turn into divide and be forced to stay. Unlike Somalia or Rwanda, Bosnia is a high-profile intervention because the Balkans have played an important and generally unwelcome part in European security. So far, the West has not been able to walk away from this war, and each halfhearted intervention, however delusory, has led to more rather than less involvement. As the realization takes hold that a Bosnian partition may mean an indefinitely prolonged commitment to a chronically volatile region, investment in reintegration may be discovered to be an easier route to withdrawal.

NOTE

1 For examples of this view, see John J. Mearsheimer, "Shrink Bosnia to Save It," *The New York Times*, March 31, 1993, p. A23; Mearsheimer and Stephen Van Evera, "When Peace Means War," *The New Republic*, December 18, 1995, pp. 16–21; and Chaim Kaufmann, "Possible and Impossible Solutions to Ethnic Civil Wars," *International Security*, Spring 1996, pp. 136–75. Kaufmann goes so far as to suggest that after an international military takeover, international forces should intern "civilians of the enemy ethnic group" and "exchange" them once peace is established.

Military Technology, Strategy, and Stability

Technology has always been the watchword of modern military strategy, and revolutionary technological change can affect the odds of war or peace. Such change, however, never controls everything and sometimes can prove less important than other factors in determining whether or how military power shapes diplomatic and political developments. Whatever shapes strategy in peacetime, expectations about what would happen in the event of war can have a big impact on decisions to risk war or not.

Analysts of international relations are usually interested in the causes and consequences of wars, but much less in their conduct. How war is fought is seen by many as a technical subject, something that happens in between the political causes and effects. The main message of the most serious philosopher of war, however, is that war is an instrument of policy and a continuation of politics.[1] As such, how it unfolds—or would be expected to unfold—affects whether, when, and how governments or groups decide to resort to force or to end violent struggles.

Thus military capabilities—and political leaders' understanding or misunderstanding of them—can exert an independent influence on decisions for or against war. Depending on which side in a conflict has the edge, the military factors make it easier or harder for a government to risk resorting to force against the status quo. Military means can also become causes of conflict in their own right, by altering the balance of power and perceptions of threats, aggravating anxieties about vulnerability, and creating incentives for preventive or preemptive attack.

For all these reasons, nations engaged in political competition in peacetime also tend to compete in military preparations for the possibility of war. Arms races manifest nations' concerns for preventing their adversaries from enjoying a military advantage should war break out. There has been remarkably little theorizing about arms races. One of the few serious examples, by Samuel P.

Huntington, looks at historical cases in Europe and elsewhere and discusses the differing implications of quantitative and qualitative competitions and other factors that affect the course and consequences of arms competition.[2] If military capabilities are to be reliable for protecting the nation, yet not a catalyst for war in their own right, they must be distributed in some manner that is conducive to stability. What does this mean?

A state is not likely to start a war unless either of two conditions exists. One is if the government's leaders not only wish to overturn the status quo but believe that they can do so successfully by force. That means the capability to win a war if they start it, and at a cost more bearable than continuing to live with the existing situation. If they think that their would-be victim can defend its own territory successfully, or can retaliate and inflict damage on them that outweighs their gains if they attack, peace should remain preferable to war. The other condition is if leaders have defensive objectives but believe that if they do not strike first their enemy will do so, forcing war upon them on less favorable terms and increasing the chances of defeat. This condition encourages preventive or preemptive attack.[3] On the other hand, if they know the enemy would like to attack but believe that they can fight more effectively by waiting to parry the blow when it falls—that is, if they can rely militarily on purely defensive tactics—they will not have reason to initiate the war themselves. (Of course such rational calculation does not always dominate policymaking, which may sometimes be driven by emotional or other subjective concerns, such as those discussed in Part IV, this volume.)

These notions about rational strategy are the foundation of deterrence theory, which became so prominent in the Cold War. When the basic source and dimensions of international conflict are clear, as they were once the East–West confrontation became institutionalized in the decade after World War II, attention turns to the instrumental questions. At first, theorists wanted to design strategies that would put the revolutionary power of nuclear weapons to the purpose of deterring enemy attack. Then, when fear of relying too much on nuclear weapons came to the fore, strategists turned to applying the logic of deterrence to conventional military power. For some time after the Soviet collapse, deterrence seemed beside the point among the great powers. Political tensions have reemerged, however, in the second decade of the twenty-first century, so the potential effects of military strategy on political stability are again becoming salient. (When conflicts are between grossly unequal powers—such as the United States against Saddam Hussein's Iraq—deterrence is less feasible for the weaker side. This situation creates an incentive for the weaker to obtain an equalizer—nuclear or other weapons of mass destruction.)

How should conventional military power affect the odds of war or peace from now on? Some states will want to be able to use force actively to change situations of which they disapprove or find threatening (as the United States has often done since the Cold War). Strategists who have that option in mind will focus on maintaining superior military capabilities, and thus the capacity to defeat and dictate to opponents. For Americans, that has not been difficult when confronting conventional opponents since no other country after the

Cold War has the military capacity of the United States. The question is fast returning, however, as relations between the West and Russia and China have become more conflictual. (Unconventional enemies pose different and militarily more vexing challenges; these problems are addressed in Part VIII, this volume.) On the other hand, if the aim is to preserve peace for its own sake, rather than to use force to make the world into what the users of force think it should be, strategists will seek ways to reduce the utility of military instruments.

Arms control negotiations were much more prominent in the strategic relations of the Cold War, as the two superpowers made agreements on limiting nuclear weaponry and conventional forces in Europe matters of high politics. Arms control is less prominent now in international diplomacy, although still significant in attempts to prevent the spread of weapons of mass destruction, and some other areas that would have been considered minor in periods of great power conflict (for example, land mines). Formalized arms limitations are likely to become important in some of the smaller conflicts that typify the post–Cold War world, if those conflicts are to be ended by agreement rather than by conquest. If local political entities in the tangled conflicts of the Balkans, or Palestine, or Kashmir are to find a modus vivendi, and to accept it with confidence, the deals are likely to involve limitations of quantity, quality, and disposition of military capabilities.

There is one solution, in principle, for arms control that can unite both realists satisfied with the status quo and liberals who want to deny the legitimacy of force as a means of change: military power should be distributed, configured, and usable only in ways that maximize confidence for defenders and risks for attackers. Force structures, strategies, and arms control agreements should be crafted to minimize the role of technologies that facilitate offensive operations and boost those that aid defensive tactics. The strategic implications of such "defense dominance" should be publicized in order to make governments realize that they do not need to strike first in order to protect themselves, and cannot succeed if they strike first for aggressive reasons. In "Cooperation Under the Security Dilemma," Robert Jervis outlines the logic behind these notions.[4] Can such norms be institutionalized to keep peace in the future? Critics question how far the principle of defense dominance can be taken. Jack S. Levy raises questions about how clearly the concept of defense dominance can even be defined in principle or identified in practice.[5]

If arms control agreements are to promote stability, they must logically rest on distributions of capability that make it unappealing for leaders to decide to initiate exchanges between those capabilities in combat. To institutionalize such a distribution, strategists and diplomats must understand what weapons are most important to limit, and how changes in the numbers and types of particular weapons will affect an overall balance of military power.[6] Nuclear weapons remain a special problem. The fewer of them in the world the better, according to conventional wisdom. In Part I of this volume, on the other hand, John J. Mearsheimer claimed that "managed" nuclear proliferation could be the least dangerous way to save Europe from the instability that will otherwise follow the end of the Cold War. The reasoning behind this disturbing argument was first elaborated by Kenneth N. Waltz in the essay included in this section. Many skeptics will remain unconvinced—and they should see the rebuttals to Waltz by Scott Sagan,[7] but they should ask themselves whether it is consistent to reject the idea that nuclear deterrence may be stabilizing for Third World countries if they believe, as so many do, that mutual nuclear deterrence between the United States and Soviet Union during the Cold War was quite stable.

By the same token, we should ask how much of what we learned from the Cold War lore of deterrence is applicable to a very different set of conflicts and contenders in the twenty-first century.[8] This question becomes more pressing as revolutionary developments in military technology progress. In the Cold War this concern revolved primarily around nuclear weapons. Today radical changes in information technology and automation make the question critical all around.[9]

Even prosaic developments in technology can interact with political, psychological, and strategic questions in significant ways. The contrasting assessments at the end of this section by Daniel Byman and Audrey Kurth Cronin, on the effects on counterterrorism of unmanned aircraft—"drones," as they are known—demonstrate the difficulty of knowing whether or how certain weapons do more to suppress threats or to aggravate them.

—RKB

NOTES

1 Carl von Clausewitz, *On War*, Michael Howard and Peter Paret, eds. and trans. (Princeton, N.J.: Princeton University Press, 1976).
2 Samuel P. Huntington, "Arms Races: Prerequisites and Results," in Carl J. Friedrich and Seymour E. Harris, eds., *Public Policy: Yearbook of the Graduate School of Public Administration* (Cambridge, Mass.: Harvard University,1958).
3 The importance of the distinction between these two forms of striking first is explained in Richard K. Betts, *American Force: Dangers, Delusions, and Dilemmas in National Security* (New York: Columbia University Press, 2012), chapter 6.
4 Other examples of literature that find bases of stability in configurations that advantage the defense include George Quester, *Offense and Defense in the International System*, Second edition (New Brunswick, N.J.: Transaction Books, 1988); Stephen Van Evera, *Causes of War: Power and the Roots of Conflict* (Ithaca, N.Y.: Cornell University Press, 1999), chaps. 6–8; Jack L. Snyder, *The Ideology of the Offensive: Military Decision Making and the Disasters of 1914* (Ithaca, N.Y.: Cornell University Press, 1984); and Sean Lynn-Jones, "Offense-Defense Theory and Its Critics," *Security Studies* 4, no. 4 (Summer 1995). For a skeptical view see Richard K. Betts, "Must War Find a Way?" *International Security* 24, no. 2 (Fall 1999).
5 Scott Sagan points out several reasons that technological defense dominance did not solve all the strategic problems of states in 1914, especially the challenge of supporting exposed allies (this showed up starkly in 1939 when the French and British let defense dominate on the western front while the Germans gobbled Poland). Scott D. Sagan, "1914 Revisited: Allies, Offense, and Instability," *International Security* 11, no. 2 (Fall 1986).

6 A classic brief for how negotiated configuration of military capabilities can promote stability is Thomas C. Schelling and Morton H. Halperin, *Strategy and Arms Control* (New York: Twentieth Century Fund, 1961). For illustrations of how unanticipated effects of arms control can be destabilizing, on the other hand, see Charles H. Fairbanks, Jr. and Abram Shulsky, "From 'Arms Control' to Arms Reductions: The Historical Experience," *The Washington Quarterly* 10, no. 3 (Summer 1987).

7 Scott D. Sagan and Kenneth N. Waltz, *The Spread of Nuclear Weapons: A Debate Renewed* (New York: W. W. Norton, 2003).

8 See Richard K. Betts, "The New Threat of Mass Destruction," *Foreign Affairs* 77, no. 1 (January/February 1998).

9 For example, see P. W. Singer, *Wired for War: The Robotics Revolution and Conflict in the 21st Century* (New York: Penguin Press, 2009), and Martin C. Libicki's discussion of cyber conflict in Part X of this volume.

Cooperation Under the Security Dilemma
ROBERT JERVIS

. . . The security dilemma: many of the means by which a state tries to increase its security decrease the security of others. In domestic society, there are several ways to increase the safety of one's person and property without endangering others. One can move to a safer neighborhood, put bars on the windows, avoid dark streets, and keep a distance from suspicious-looking characters. Of course these measures are not convenient, cheap, or certain of success. But no one save criminals need be alarmed if a person takes them. In international politics, however, one state's gain in security often inadvertently threatens others. In explaining British policy on naval disarmament in the inter-war period to the Japanese, Ramsay MacDonald said that "Nobody wanted Japan to be insecure."[1] But the problem was not with British desires, but with the consequences of her policy. In earlier periods, too, Britain had needed a navy large enough to keep the shipping lanes open. But such a navy could not avoid being a menace to any other state with a coast that could be raided, trade that could be interdicted, or colonies that could be isolated. When Germany started building a powerful navy before World War I, Britain objected that it could only be an offensive weapon aimed at her. As Sir Edward Grey, the Foreign Secretary, put it to King Edward VII: "If the German Fleet ever becomes superior to ours, the German Army can conquer this country. There is no corresponding risk of this kind to Germany; for however superior our Fleet was, no naval victory could bring us any nearer to Berlin." The English position was half correct: Germany's navy was an anti-British instrument. But the British often overlooked what the Germans knew full well: "in every quarrel with England, German colonies and trade were . . . hostages for England to take." Thus, whether she intended it or not, the British Navy constituted an important instrument of coercion. . . .[2]

How a statesman interprets the other's past behavior and how he projects it into the future is influenced by his understanding of the security dilemma and his ability to place himself in the other's shoes. The dilemma will operate much more strongly if statesmen do not understand it, and do not see that their arms—sought only to secure the status quo—may alarm others and that others may arm, not because they are contemplating aggression, but because they fear attack from the first state. These two failures of empathy are linked. A state which thinks that the other knows that it wants only to preserve the status quo and that its arms are meant only for self-preservation will conclude

Source: "Cooperation Under the Security Dilemma," by Robert Jervis, from World Politics, *Vol. 30, No. 2 (January 1978), pp. 167–214. Copyright © 1978. Trustees of Princeton University. Reprinted with permission of Cambridge University Press.*

that the other side will react to its arms by increasing its own capability only if it is aggressive itself. Since the other side is not menaced, there is no legitimate reason for it to object to the first state's arms; therefore, objection proves that the other is aggressive. Thus, the following exchange between Senator Tom Connally and Secretary of State Acheson concerning the ratification of the NATO treaty:

Secretary Acheson: [The treaty] is aimed solely at armed aggression.

Senator Connally: In other words, unless a nation . . . contemplates, meditates, or makes plans looking toward aggression or armed attack on another nation, it has no cause to fear this treaty.

Secretary Acheson: That is correct, Senator Connally, and it seems to me that any nation which claims that this treaty is directed against it should be reminded of the Biblical admonition that 'The guilty flee when no man pursueth.'

Senator Connally: That is a very apt illustration. What I had in mind was, when a State or Nation passes a criminal act, for instance, against burglary, nobody but those who are burglars or getting ready to be burglars need have any fear of the Burglary Act. Is that not true?

Secretary Acheson: The only effect [the law] would have [on an innocent person] would be for his protection, perhaps, by deterring someone else. He wouldn't worry about the imposition of the penalties on himself.[3]

The other side of this coin is that part of the explanation for détente is that most American decision makers now realize that it is at least possible that Russia may fear American aggression; many think that this fear accounts for a range of Soviet actions previously seen as indicating Russian aggressiveness. Indeed, even 36 percent of military officers consider the Soviet Union's motivations to be primarily defensive. Less than twenty years earlier, officers had been divided over whether Russia sought world conquest or only expansion.[4]

Statesmen who do not understand the security dilemma will think that the money spent is the only cost of building up their arms. This belief removes one important restraint on arms spending. Furthermore, it is also likely to lead states to set their security requirements too high. Since they do not understand that trying to increase one's security can actually decrease it, they will overestimate the amount of security that is attainable; they will think that when in doubt they can "play it safe" by increasing their arms. Thus it is very likely that two states which support the status quo but do not understand the security dilemma will end up, if not in a war, then at least in a relationship of higher conflict than is required by the objective situation.

The belief that an increase in military strength always leads to an increase in security is often linked to the belief that the only route to security is through military strength. As a consequence, a whole range of meliorative policies will be downgraded. Decision makers who do not believe that adopting a more conciliatory posture, meeting the other's legitimate grievances, or developing mutual gains from cooperation can increase their state's security, will not devote much attention or effort to these possibilities.

On the other hand, a heightened sensitivity to the security dilemma makes it more likely that the state will treat an aggressor as though it were an insecure defender of the status quo. Partly because of their views about the causes of World War I, the British were predisposed to believe that Hitler sought only the rectification of legitimate and limited grievances and that security could best be gained by constructing an equitable international system. As a result they pursued a policy which, although well designed to avoid the danger of creating unnecessary conflict with a status-quo Germany, helped destroy Europe.

GEOGRAPHY, COMMITMENTS, BELIEFS, AND SECURITY THROUGH EXPANSION

. . . Situations vary in the ease or difficulty with which all states can simultaneously achieve a high degree of security. The influence of military technology on this variable is the subject of the next section. Here we want to treat the impact of beliefs, geography, and commitments (many of which can be considered to be modifications of geography, since they bind states to defend areas outside their homelands). In the crowded continent of Europe, security requirements were hard to mesh. Being surrounded by powerful states, Germany's problem—or the problem created by Germany—was always great and was even worse when her relations with both France and Russia were bad, such as before World War I. In that case, even a status-quo Germany, if she could not change the political situation, would almost have been forced to adopt something like the Schlieffen Plan. Because she could not hold off both of her enemies, she had to be prepared to defeat one quickly and then deal with the other in a more leisurely fashion. If France or Russia stayed out of a war between the other state and Germany, they would allow Germany to dominate the Continent (even if that was not Germany's aim). They therefore had to deny Germany this ability, thus making Germany less secure. Although Germany's arrogant and erratic behavior, coupled with the desire for an unreasonably high level of security (which amounted to the desire to escape from her geographic plight), compounded the problem, even wise German statesmen would have been hard put to gain a high degree of security without alarming their neighbors. . . .

OFFENSE, DEFENSE, AND THE SECURITY DILEMMA

Another approach starts with the central point of the security dilemma—that an increase in one state's security decreases the security of others—and examines the conditions under which this proposition holds. Two crucial variables are involved: whether defensive weapons and policies can be distinguished from offensive ones, and whether the defense or the offense has the advantage. The definitions are not always clear, and many cases are difficult to judge, but these two variables shed a great deal of light on the question of whether status-quo powers will adopt compatible security policies. All the variables discussed so far leave the heart of the problem untouched. But when defensive weapons differ from offensive ones, it is possible for a state to make itself more secure without making others less secure. And when the defense has the advantage over the offense, a large increase in one state's security only slightly decreases the security of the others, and status-quo powers can all enjoy a high level of security and largely escape from the state of nature.

Offense-Defense Balance

When we say that the offense has the advantage, we simply mean that it is easier to destroy the other's army and take its territory than it is to defend one's own. When the defense has the advantage, it is easier to protect and to hold than it is to move forward, destroy, and take. If effective defenses can be erected quickly, an attacker may be able to keep territory he has taken in an initial victory. Thus, the dominance of the defense made it very hard for Britain and France to push Germany out of France in World War I. But when superior defenses are difficult for an aggressor to improvise on the battlefield and must be constructed during peacetime, they provide no direct assistance to him.

The security dilemma is at its most vicious when commitments, strategy, or technology dictate that the only route to security lies through expansion. Status-quo powers must then act like aggressors; the fact that they would gladly agree to forego the opportunity for expansion in return for guarantees for their security has no implications for their behavior. Even if expansion is not sought as a goal in itself, there will be quick and drastic changes in the distribution of territory and influence. Conversely, when the defense has the advantage, status-quo states can make themselves more secure without gravely endangering others. Indeed, if the defense has enough of an advantage and if the states are of roughly equal size, not only will the security dilemma cease to inhibit status-quo states from cooperating, but aggression will be next to impossible, thus rendering international anarchy relatively unimportant. If states cannot conquer each other, then the lack of sovereignty, although it presents problems of collective goods in a number of areas, no longer forces states to devote their primary attention to self-preservation. Although, if force were not usable, there would be fewer restraints on the use of nonmilitary instruments, these are rarely powerful enough to threaten the vital interests of a major state.

Two questions of the offense-defense balance can be separated. First, does the state have to spend more or less than one dollar on defensive forces to offset each dollar spent by the other side on forces that could be used to attack? If the state has one dollar to spend on increasing its security, should it put it into offensive or defensive forces? Second, with a given inventory of forces, is it better to attack or to defend? Is there an incentive to strike first or to absorb the other's blow? These two aspects are often linked: if each dollar spent on offense can overcome each dollar spent on defense, and if both sides have the same defense budgets, then both are likely to build offensive forces and find it attractive to attack rather than to wait for the adversary to strike.

These aspects affect the security dilemma in different ways. The first has its greatest impact on arms races. If the defense has the advantage, and if the status-quo powers have reasonable subjective security requirements, they can probably avoid an arms race. Although an increase in one side's arms and security will still decrease the other's security, the former's increase will be larger than the latter's decrease. So if one side increases its arms, the other can bring its security back up to its previous level by adding a smaller amount to its forces. And if the first side reacts to this change, its increase will also be smaller than the stimulus that produced it. Thus a stable equilibrium will be reached. Shifting from dynamics to statics, each side can be quite secure with forces roughly equal to those of the other. Indeed, if the defense is much more potent than the offense, each side can be willing to have forces much smaller than the other's, and can be indifferent to a wide range of the other's defense policies.

The second aspect—whether it is better to attack or to defend—influences short-run stability. When the offense has the advantage, a state's reaction to international tension will increase the chances of war. The incentives for pre-emption and the "reciprocal fear of surprise attack" in this situation have been made clear by analyses of the dangers that exist when two countries have first-strike capabilities.[5] There is no way for the state to increase its security without menacing, or even attacking, the other. Even Bismarck, who once called preventive war "committing suicide from fear of death," said that "no government, if it regards war as inevitable even if it does not want it, would be so foolish as to leave to the enemy the choice of time and occasion and to wait for the moment which is most convenient for the enemy."[6] In another arena, the same dilemma applies to the policeman in a dark alley confronting a suspected criminal who appears to be holding a weapon. Though racism may indeed be present, the security dilemma can account for many of the tragic shootings of innocent people in the ghettos.

Beliefs about the course of a war in which the offense has the advantage further deepen the security dilemma. When there are incentives to strike first, a successful attack will usually so weaken the other side that victory will be relatively quick, bloodless, and decisive. It is in these periods when conquest is possible and attractive that states consolidate power internally—for instance, by destroying the feudal barons—and expand externally. There are several consequences that decrease the chance of cooperation among status-quo states. First, war will be profitable for the winner. The costs will be low and the benefits high. Of course, losers will suffer; the fear of losing could induce states to try to form stable cooperative arrangements, but the temptation of victory will make this particularly difficult. Second, because wars are expected to be both frequent and short, there will be incentives for high levels of arms, and quick and strong reaction to the other's increases in arms. The state cannot afford to wait until there is unambiguous evidence that the other is building new weapons. Even large states that have faith in their economic strength cannot wait, because the war will be over before their products can reach the army. Third, when wars are quick, states will have to recruit allies in advance.[7]

Without the opportunity for bargaining and re-alignments during the opening stages of hostilities, peacetime diplomacy loses a degree of the fluidity that facilitates balance-of-power policies. Because alliances must be secured during peacetime, the international system is more likely to become bipolar. It is hard to say whether war therefore becomes more or less likely, but this bipolarity increases tension between the two camps and makes it harder for status-quo states to gain the benefits of cooperation. Fourth, if wars are frequent, statesmen's perceptual thresholds will be adjusted accordingly and they will be quick to perceive ambiguous evidence as indicating that others are aggressive. Thus, there will be more cases of status-quo powers arming against each other in the incorrect belief that the other is hostile.

When the defense has the advantage, all the foregoing is reversed. The state that fears attack does not pre-empt—since that would be a wasteful use of its military resources—but rather prepares to receive an attack. Doing so does not decrease the security of others, and several states can do it simultaneously; the situation will therefore be stable, and status-quo powers will be able to cooperate. When Herman Kahn argues that ultimatums "are vastly too dangerous to give because . . . they are quite likely to touch off a preemptive strike,"[8] he incorrectly assumes that it is always advantageous to strike first.

More is involved than short-run dynamics. When the defense is dominant, wars are likely to become stalemates and can be won only at enormous cost. Relatively small and weak states can hold off larger and stronger ones, or can deter attack by raising the costs of conquest to an unacceptable level. States then approach equality in what they can do to each other. Like the .45-caliber pistol in the American West, fortifications were the "great equalizer" in some periods. Changes in the status quo are less frequent and cooperation is more common wherever the security dilemma is thereby reduced.

Many of these arguments can be illustrated by the major powers' policies in the periods preceding the two world wars. Bismarck's wars surprised statesmen by showing that the offense had the advantage, and by being quick, relatively cheap, and quite decisive. Falling into a common error, observers projected this pattern into the future.[9] The resulting expectations had several effects. First, states sought semi-permanent allies. In the early stages of the Franco-Prussian War, Napoleon III had thought that there would be plenty of time to recruit Austria to his side. Now, others were not going to repeat this mistake. Second, defense budgets were high and reacted quite sharply to increases on the other side. It is not surprising that Richardson's theory of arms races fits this period well. Third, most decision makers thought that the next European war would not cost much blood and treasure.[10] That is one reason why war was generally seen as inevitable and why mass opinion was so bellicose. Fourth, once war seemed likely, there were strong pressures to pre-empt. Both sides believed that whoever moved first could penetrate the other deep enough to disrupt mobilization and thus gain an insurmountable advantage. (There was no such belief about the use of naval forces. Although Churchill made an ill-advised speech saying that if German ships "do not come out and fight in time of war they will be dug out like rats in a hole,"[11] everyone knew that submarines, mines, and coastal fortifications made this impossible. So at the start of the war each navy prepared to defend itself rather than attack, and the short-run destabilizing forces that launched the armies toward each other did not operate.)[12] Furthermore, each side knew that the other saw the situation the same way, thus increasing the perceived danger that the other would attack, and giving each added reasons to precipitate a war if conditions seemed favorable. In the long and the short run, there were thus both offensive and defensive incentives to strike. This situation casts light on the common question about German motives in 1914: "Did Germany unleash the war deliberately to become a world power or did she support Austria merely to defend a weakening ally," thereby protecting her own position?[13] To some extent, this question is misleading. Because of the perceived advantage of the offense, war was seen as the best route both to gaining expansion and to avoiding drastic loss of influence. There seemed to be no way for Germany merely to retain and safeguard her existing position.

Of course the war showed these beliefs to have been wrong on all points. Trenches and machine guns gave the defense an overwhelming advantage. The fighting became deadlocked and produced horrendous casualties. It made no sense for the combatants to bleed themselves to death. If they had known the power of the defense beforehand, they would have rushed for their own trenches rather than for the enemy's territory. Each side could have done this without increasing the other's incentives to strike. . . .

Technology and Geography   Technology and geography are the two main factors that determine whether the offense or the defense has the advantage. As Brodie notes, "On the tactical level, as a rule, few physical factors favor the attacker but many favor the defender. The defender usually has the advantage of cover. He characteristically fires from behind some form of shelter while his opponent crosses open ground."[14] Anything that increases the amount of ground the attacker has to cross, or impedes his progress across it, or makes him more vulnerable while crossing, increases the advantage accruing to the defense. When states are separated by barriers that produce these effects, the security dilemma is eased, since both can have forces adequate for defense without being able to attack. Impenetrable barriers would actually prevent war; in reality, decision makers have to settle for a good deal less. Buffer zones slow the attacker's progress; they thereby give the defender time to prepare, increase problems of logistics, and reduce the number of soldiers available for the final assault. At the end of the 19th century, Arthur Balfour noted Afghanistan's "non-conducting" qualities. "So long as it possesses few roads, and no railroads, it will be impossible for Russia to make effective use of her great numerical superiority at any point immediately vital to the Empire." The Russians valued buffers for the same reasons; it is not surprising that when Persia was being divided into Russian and British spheres of influence some years later, the Russians sought assurances that the British would refrain from building potentially menacing railroads in their sphere. Indeed, since railroad construction radically altered the abilities of countries to defend themselves and to attack others, many diplomatic notes and much intelligence activity in the late 19th century centered on this subject.[15]

Oceans, large rivers, and mountain ranges serve the same function as buffer zones. Being hard to cross, they allow defense against superior numbers. The defender has merely to stay on his side of the barrier and so can utilize all the men he can bring up to it. The attacker's men, however, can cross only a few at a time, and they are very vulnerable when doing so. If all states were self-sufficient islands, anarchy would be much less of a problem. A small investment in short defenses and a small army would be sufficient to repel invasion. Only very weak states would be vulnerable, and only very large ones could menace others. As noted above, the United States, and to a lesser extent Great Britain, have partly been able to escape from the state of nature because their geographical positions approximated this ideal.

Although geography cannot be changed to conform to borders, borders can and do change to conform to geography. Borders across which an attack is easy tend to be unstable. States living within them are likely to expand or be absorbed. Frequent wars are almost inevitable since attacking will often seem the best way to protect what one has. This process will stop, or at least slow down, when the state's borders reach—by expansion or contraction—a line of natural obstacles. Security without attack will then be possible. Furthermore, these lines constitute salient solutions to bargaining problems and, to the extent that they are barriers to migration, are likely to divide ethnic groups, thereby raising the costs and lowering the incentives for conquest.

Attachment to one's state and its land reinforce one quasi-geographical aid to the defense. Conquest usually becomes more difficult the deeper the attacker pushes into the other's territory. Nationalism spurs the defenders to fight harder; advancing not only lengthens the attacker's supply lines, but takes him through unfamiliar and often devastated lands that require troops for garrison duty. These stabilizing dynamics will not operate, however, if the defender's war materiel is situated near its borders, or if the people do not care about their state, but only about being on the winning side. In such cases, positive feedback will be at work and initial defeats will be insurmountable.[16]

Imitating geography, men have tried to create barriers. Treaties may provide for demilitarized zones on both sides of the border, although such zones will rarely be deep enough to provide more than warning. Even this was not possible in Europe, but the Russians adopted a gauge for their railroads that was broader than that of the neighboring states, thereby complicating the logistics problems of any attacker—including Russia.

Perhaps the most ambitious and at least temporarily successful attempts to construct a system that would aid the defenses of both sides were the interwar naval treaties, as they affected Japanese-American relations. As mentioned earlier, the problem was that the United States could not defend the Philippines without denying Japan the ability to protect her home islands.[17] (In 1941 this dilemma became insoluble when Japan sought to extend her control to Malaya and the Dutch East Indies. If the Philippines had been invulnerable, they could have provided a secure base from which the U.S. could interdict

Japanese shipping between the homeland and the areas she was trying to conquer.) In the 1920's and early 1930's each side would have been willing to grant the other security for its possessions in return for a reciprocal grant, and the Washington Naval Conference agreements were designed to approach this goal. As a Japanese diplomat later put it, their country's "fundamental principle" was to have "a strength insufficient for attack and adequate for defense."[18] Thus, Japan agreed in 1922 to accept a navy only three-fifths as large as that of the United States, and the U.S. agreed not to fortify its Pacific islands.[19] (Japan had earlier been forced to agree not to fortify the islands she had taken from Germany in World War I.) Japan's navy would not be large enough to defeat America's anywhere other than close to the home islands. Although the Japanese could still take the Philippines, not only would they be unable to move farther, but they might be weakened enough by their efforts to be vulnerable to counterattack. Japan, however, gained security. An American attack was rendered more difficult because the American bases were unprotected and because, until 1930, Japan was allowed unlimited numbers of cruisers, destroyers, and submarines that could weaken the American fleet as it made its way across the ocean.[20]

The other major determinant of the offense-defense balance is technology. When weapons are highly vulnerable, they must be employed before they are attacked. Others can remain quite invulnerable in their bases. The former characteristics are embodied in unprotected missiles and many kinds of bombers. (It should be noted that it is not vulnerability *per se* that is crucial, but the location of the vulnerability. Bombers and missiles that are easy to destroy only after having been launched toward their targets do not create destabilizing dynamics.) Incentives to strike first are usually absent for naval forces that are threatened by a naval attack. Like missiles in hardened silos, they are usually well protected when in their bases. Both sides can then simultaneously be prepared to defend themselves successfully.

In ground warfare under some conditions, forts, trenches, and small groups of men in prepared positions can hold off large numbers of attackers. Less frequently, a few attackers can storm the defenses. By and large, it is a contest between fortifications and supporting light weapons on the one hand, and mobility and heavier weapons that clear the way for the attack on the other. As the erroneous views held before the two world wars show, there is no simple way to determine which is dominant. "[T]hese oscillations are not smooth and predictable like those of a swinging pendulum. They are uneven in both extent and time. Some occur in the course of a single battle or campaign, others in the course of a war, still others during a series of wars." Longer-term oscillations can also be detected:

> The early Gothic age, from the twelfth to the late thirteenth century, with its wonderful cathedrals and fortified places, was a period during which the attackers in Europe generally met serious and increasing difficulties, because the improvement in the strength of fortresses outran the advance in the power of destruction. Later, with the spread of firearms at the end of the

fifteenth century, old fortresses lost their power to resist. An age ensued during which the offense possessed, apart from short-term setbacks, new advantages. Then, during the seventeenth century, especially after about 1660, and until at least the outbreak of the War of the Austrian Succession in 1740, the defense regained much of the ground it had lost since the great medieval fortresses had proved unable to meet the bombardment of the new and more numerous artillery.[21]

Another scholar has continued the argument: "The offensive gained an advantage with new forms of heavy mobile artillery in the nineteenth century, but the stalemate of World War I created the impression that the defense again had an advantage; the German invasion in World War II, however, indicated the offensive superiority of highly mechanized armies in the field."[22]

The situation today with respect to conventional weapons is unclear. Until recently it was believed that tanks and tactical air power gave the attacker an advantage. The initial analyses of the 1973 Arab-Israeli war indicated that new anti-tank and anti-aircraft weapons have restored the primacy of the defense. These weapons are cheap, easy to use, and can destroy a high proportion of the attacking vehicles and planes that are sighted. It then would make sense for a status-quo power to buy lots of $20,000 missiles rather than buy a few half-million dollar tanks and multi-million dollar fighter-bombers. Defense would be possible even against a large and well-equipped force; states that care primarily about self-protection would not need to engage in arms races. But further examinations of the new technologies and the history of the October War cast doubt on these optimistic conclusions and leave us unable to render any firm judgment. . . .[23]

Offense-Defense Differentiation

The other major variable that affects how strongly the security dilemma operates is whether weapons and policies that protect the state also provide the capability for attack. If they do not, the basic postulate of the security dilemma no longer applies. A state can increase its own security without decreasing that of others. The advantage of the defense can only ameliorate the security dilemma. A differentiation between offensive and defensive stances comes close to abolishing it. Such differentiation does not mean, however, that all security problems will be abolished. If the offense has the advantage, conquest and aggression will still be possible. And if the offense's advantage is great enough, status-quo powers may find it too expensive to protect themselves by defensive forces and decide to procure offensive weapons even though this will menace others. Furthermore, states will still have to worry that even if the other's military posture shows that it is peaceful now, it may develop aggressive intentions in the future.

Assuming that the defense is at least as potent as the offense, the differentiation between them allows status-quo states to behave in ways that are clearly different from those of aggressors. Three beneficial consequences follow.

First, status-quo powers can identify each other, thus laying the foundations for cooperation. Conflicts growing out of the mistaken belief that the other side is expansionist will be less frequent. Second, status-quo states will obtain advance warning when others plan aggression. Before a state can attack, it has to develop and deploy offensive weapons. If procurement of these weapons cannot be disguised and takes a fair amount of time, as it almost always does, a status-quo state will have the time to take countermeasures. It need not maintain a high level of defensive arms as long as its potential adversaries are adopting a peaceful posture. . . .

The third beneficial consequence of a difference between offensive and defensive weapons is that if all states support the status quo, an obvious arms control agreement is a ban on weapons that are useful for attacking. As President Roosevelt put it in his message to the Geneva Disarmament Conference in 1933: "If all nations will agree wholly to eliminate from possession and use the weapons which make possible a successful attack, defenses automatically will become impregnable, and the frontiers and independence of every national will become secure."[24] The fact that such treaties have been rare—the Washington naval agreements discussed above and the anti-ABM treaty can be cited as examples—shows either that states are not always willing to guarantee the security of others, or that it is hard to distinguish offensive from defensive weapons.

Is such a distinction possible? Salvador de Madariaga, the Spanish statesman active in the disarmament negotiations of the interwar years, thought not: "A weapon is either offensive or defensive according to which end of it you are looking at." The French Foreign Minister agreed (although French policy did not always follow this view): "Every arm can be employed offensively or defensively in turn. . . . The only way to discover whether arms are intended for purely defensive purposes or are held in a spirit of aggression is in all cases to enquire into the intentions of the country concerned." Some evidence for the validity of this argument is provided by the fact that much time in these unsuccessful negotiations was devoted to separating offensive from defensive weapons. Indeed, no simple and unambiguous definition is possible and in many cases no judgment can be reached. Before the American entry into World War I, Woodrow Wilson wanted to arm merchantmen only with guns in the back of the ship so they could not initiate a fight, but this expedient cannot be applied to more common forms of armaments.[25]

There are several problems. Even when a differentiation is possible, a status-quo power will want offensive arms under any of three conditions. (1) If the offense has a great advantage over the defense, protection through defensive forces will be too expensive. (2) Status-quo states may need offensive weapons to regain territory lost in the opening stages of a war. It might be possible, however, for a state to wait to procure these weapons until war seems likely, and they might be needed only in relatively small numbers, unless the aggressor was able to construct strong defenses quickly in the occupied areas. (3) The state may feel that it must be prepared to take the offensive either because the other side will make peace only if it loses territory or because the state has commitments to attack if the other makes war on a third party. As noted above, status-quo states with extensive commitments are often forced to behave like aggressors. Even when they lack such commitments, status-quo states must worry about the possibility that if they are able to hold off an attack, they will still not be able to end the war unless they move into the other's territory to damage its military forces and inflict pain. Many American naval officers after the Civil War, for example, believed that "only by destroying the commerce of the opponent could the United States bring him to terms."[26]

A further complication is introduced by the fact that aggressors as well as status-quo powers require defensive forces as a prelude to acquiring offensive ones, to protect one frontier while attacking another, or for insurance in case the war goes badly. Criminals as well as policemen can use bulletproof vests. Hitler as well as Maginot built a line of forts. Indeed, Churchill reports that in 1936 the German Foreign Minister said: "As soon as our fortifications are constructed [on our western borders] and the countries in Central Europe realize that France cannot enter German territory, all these countries will begin to feel very differently about their foreign policies, and a new constellation will develop."[27] So a state may not necessarily be reassured if its neighbor constructs strong defenses.

More central difficulties are created by the fact that whether a weapon is offensive or defensive often depends on the particular situation—for instance, the geographical setting and the way in which the weapon is used. "Tanks . . . spearheaded the fateful German thrust through the Ardennes in 1940, but if the French had disposed of a properly concentrated armored reserve, it would have provided the best means for their cutting off the penetration and turning into a disaster for the Germans what became instead an overwhelming victory."[28] Anti-aircraft weapons seem obviously defensive—to be used, they must wait for the other side to come to them. But the Egyptian attack on Israel in 1973 would have been impossible without effective air defenses that covered the battlefield. Nevertheless, some distinctions are possible. Sir John Simon, then the British Foreign Secretary, in response to the views cited earlier, stated that just because a fine line could not be drawn, "that was no reason for saying that there were not stretches of territory on either side which all practical men and women knew to be well on this or that side of the line." Although there are almost no weapons and strategies that are useful only for attacking, there are some that are almost exclusively defensive. Aggressors could want them for protection, but a state that relied mostly on them could not menace others. More frequently, we cannot "determine the absolute character of a weapon, but [we can] make a comparison . . . [and] discover whether or not the offensive potentialities predominate, whether a weapon is more useful in attack or in defense."[29]

The essence of defense is keeping the other side out of your territory. A purely defensive weapon is one that can do this without being able to penetrate the enemy's land. Thus a committee of military experts in an interwar disarmament conference declared that armaments "incapable of mobility by means of self-contained power," or movable only after long delay, were "only capable of being used for the defense of a State's territory."[30] The most obvious examples are fortifications. They can shelter attacking forces, especially when they are built right along the frontier,[31] but they cannot occupy enemy territory. A state with only a strong line of forts, fixed guns, and a small army to man them would not be much of a menace. Anything else that can serve only as a barrier against attacking troops is similarly defensive. In this category are systems that provide warning of an attack, the Russian's adoption of a different railroad gauge, and nuclear land mines that can seal off invasion routes.

If total immobility clearly defines a system that is defensive only, limited mobility is unfortunately ambiguous. As noted above, short-range fighter aircraft and anti-aircraft missiles can be used to cover an attack. And, unlike forts, they can advance with the troops. Still, their inability to reach deep into enemy territory does make them more useful for the defense than for the offense. Thus, the United States and Israel would have been more alarmed in the early 1970's had the Russians provided the Egyptians with long-range instead of short-range aircraft. Naval forces are particularly difficult to classify in these terms, but those that are very short-legged can be used only for coastal defense. . . .

FOUR WORLDS

The two variables we have been discussing—whether the offense or the defense has the advantage, and whether offensive postures can be distinguished from defensive ones—can be combined to yield four possible worlds.

The first world is the worst for status-quo states. There is no way to get security without menacing others, and security through defense is terribly difficult to obtain. Because offensive and defensive postures are the same, status-quo states acquire the same kind of arms that are sought by aggressors. And because the offense has the advantage over the defense, attacking is the best route to protecting what you have; status-quo states will therefore behave like aggressors. The situation will be unstable. Arms races are likely. Incentives to strike first will turn crises into wars. Decisive victories and conquests will be common. States will grow and shrink rapidly, and it will be hard for any state to maintain its size and influence without trying to increase them. Cooperation among status-quo powers will be extremely hard to achieve.

There are no cases that totally fit this picture, but it bears more than a passing resemblance to Europe before World War I. Britain and Germany, although in many respects natural allies, ended up as enemies. Of course much of the explanation lies in Germany's ill-chosen policy. And from the perspective of our theory, the powers' ability to avoid war in a series of earlier crises cannot be easily explained. Nevertheless, much of the behavior in this period was the product of technology and beliefs that magnified the security dilemma. Decision makers thought that the offense had a big advantage and saw little difference between offensive and defensive military postures. The era was characterized by arms races. And once war seemed likely, mobilization races created powerful incentives to strike first. . . .

	OFFENSE HAS THE ADVANTAGE	*DEFENSE HAS THE ADVANTAGE*
	1	2
OFFENSIVE POSTURE NOT DISTINGUISHABLE FROM DEFENSIVE ONE	Doubly dangerous	Security dilemma, but security requirements may be compatible.
	3	4
OFFENSIVE POSTURE DISTINGUISHABLE FROM DEFENSIVE ONE	No security dilemma, but aggression possible. Status-quo states can follow different policy than aggressors. Warning given.	Doubly stable

In the second world, the security dilemma operates because offensive and defensive postures cannot be distinguished; but it does not operate as strongly as in the first world because the defense has the advantage, and so an increment in one side's strength increases its security more than it decreases the other's. So, if both sides have reasonable subjective security requirements, are of roughly equal power, and the variables discussed earlier are favorable, it is quite likely that status-quo states can adopt compatible security policies. Although a state will not be able to judge the other's intentions from the kinds of weapons it procures, the level of arms spending will give important evidence. Of course a state that seeks a high level of arms might be not an aggressor but merely an insecure state, which if conciliated will reduce its arms, and if confronted will reply in kind. To assume that the apparently excessive level of arms indicates aggressiveness could therefore lead to a response that would deepen the dilemma and create needless conflict. But empathy and skillful statesmanship can reduce this danger. Furthermore, the advantageous position of the defense means that a status-quo state can often maintain a high degree of security with a level of arms lower than that of its expected adversary. Such a state demonstrates that it lacks the ability or desire to alter the status quo, at least at the present time. The strength of the defense also allows states to react slowly and with restraint when they fear that others are menacing them. So, although status-quo powers will to some extent be threatening to others, that extent will be limited.

This world is the one that comes closest to matching most periods in history. Attacking is usually harder than defending because of the strength of fortifications and obstacles. But purely defensive postures are rarely possible because fortifications are usually supplemented by armies and mobile guns which can support an attack.

. . . In the third world there may be no security dilemma, but there are security problems. Because states can procure defensive systems that do not threaten others, the dilemma need not operate. But because the offense has the advantage, aggression is possible, and perhaps easy. If the offense has enough of an advantage, even a status-quo state may take the initiative rather than risk being attacked and defeated. If the offense has less of an advantage, stability and cooperation are likely because the status-quo states will procure defensive forces. They need not react to others who are similarly armed, but can wait for the warning they would receive if others started to deploy offensive weapons. But each state will have to watch the others carefully, and there is room for false suspicions. The costliness of the defense and the allure of the offense can lead to unnecessary mistrust, hostility, and war, unless some of the variables discussed earlier are operating to restrain defection. . . .

The fourth world is doubly safe. The differentiation between offensive and defensive systems permits a way out of the security dilemma; the advantage of the defense disposes of the problems discussed in the previous paragraphs. There is no reason for a status-quo power to be tempted to procure offensive forces, and aggressors give notice of their intention by the posture they adopt. Indeed, if the advantage of the defense is great enough, there are no security problems. The loss of the ultimate form of the power to alter the status quo would allow greater scope for the exercise of nonmilitary means and probably would tend to freeze the distribution of values.

This world would have existed in the first decade of the 20th century if the decision makers had understood the available technology. In that case, the European powers would have followed different policies both in the long run and in the summer of 1914. Even Germany, facing powerful enemies on both sides, could have made herself secure by developing strong defenses. France could also have made her frontier almost impregnable. Furthermore, when crises arose, no one would have had incentives to strike first. There would have been no competitive mobilization races reducing the time available for negotiations.

NOTES

1 Quoted in Gerald E. Wheeler, *Prelude to Pearl Harbor* (Columbia, MO: University of Missouri Press, 1963).

2 Quoted in Leonard Wainstein, "The Dreadnought Gap," in Robert Art and Kenneth N. Waltz, eds., *The Use of Force* (Boston: Little, Brown 1971), 155; Raymond Sontag, *European Diplomatic History, 1871–1932* (New York: Appleton-Century-Crofts 1933), 147. The French had made a similar argument 50 years earlier; see James Phinney Baxter III, *The Introduction of the Ironclad Warship* (Cambridge: Harvard University Press 1933), 149. For a more detailed discussion of the security dilemma, see Jervis, *Perception and Misperception in International Politics* (Princeton: Princeton University Press 1976), 62–76.

3 U.S. Congress, Senate, Committee on Foreign Relations, *Hearings, North Atlantic Treaty*, 81st Cong., 1st sess. (1949), 17.

4 Bruce Russett and Elizabeth Hanson, *Interest and Ideology* (San Francisco: Freeman 1975), 260; Morris Janowitz, *The Professional Soldier* (New York: Free Press 1960), chap. 13.

5 Thomas Schelling, *The Strategy of Conflict* (New York: Oxford University Press 1963), chap. 9.

6 Quoted in Fritz Fischer, *War of Illusions* (New York: Norton 1975), 377, 461.

7 George Quester, *Offense and Defense in the International System* (New York: John Wiley 1977), 105–06; Sontag (fn. 5), 4–5.

8 Herman Kahn, *On Thermonuclear War* (Princeton: Princeton University Press 1960), 211.

9 For a general discussion of such mistaken learning from the past, see Jervis (fn. 5), chap. 6. The important and still not completely understood question of why this belief formed and was maintained throughout the war is examined in Bernard Brodie, *War and Politics* (New York: Macmillan 1973), 262–70; Brodie, "Technological Change, Strategic Doctrine, and Political Outcomes," in Klaus Knorr, ed., *Historical Dimensions of National Security Problems* (Lawrence: University Press of Kansas 1976), 290–92; and Douglas Porch, "The French Army and the Spirit of the Offensive, 1900–14," in Brian Bond and Ian Roy, eds., *War and Society* (New York: Holmes & Meier 1975), 117–43.

10 Some were not so optimistic. Gray's remark is well-known: "The lamps are going out all over Europe; we shall not see them lit again in our life-time." The German Prime Minister, Bethmann Hollweg, also feared the consequences of the war. But the controlling view was that it would certainly pay for the winner.

11 Quoted in Martin Gilbert, *Winston S. Churchill, III, The Challenge of War, 1914–1916* (Boston: Houghton Mifflin 1971), 84.

12 Quester (fn. 7), 98–99. Robert Art, *The Influence of Foreign Policy on Seapower*, II (Beverly Hills: Sage Professional Papers in International Studies Series, 1973), 14–18, 26–28.

13 Konrad Jarausch, "The Illusion of Limited War: Chancellor Bethmann Hollweg's Calculated Risk, July 1914," *Central European History*, II (March 1969), 50.

14 Bernard Brodie, *Strategy in the Missile Age* (Princeton: Princeton University Press 1959), 179.

15 Arthur Balfour, "Memorandum," Committee on Imperial Defence, April 30, 1903, pp. 2–3; see the telegrams by Sir Arthur Nicolson, in G. P. Gooch and Harold Temperley, eds., *British Documents on the Origins of the War*, Vol. 4 (London: H.M.S.O. 1929), 429, 524. These barriers do not prevent the passage of long-range aircraft; but even in the air, distance usually aids the defender.

16 See, for example, the discussion of warfare among Chinese warlords in Hsi-Sheng Chi, "The Chinese Warlord System as an International System," in Morton Kaplan, ed., *New Approaches to International Relations* (New York: St. Martin's 1968), 405–25.

17 Some American decision makers, including military officers, thought that the best way out of the dilemma was to abandon the Philippines.

18 Quoted in Elting Morrison, *Turmoil and Tradition: A Study of the Life and Times of Henry L. Stimson* (Boston: Houghton Mifflin 1960), 326.

19 The U.S. "refused to consider limitations on Hawaiian defenses, since these works posed no threat to Japan." William Braisted, *The United States Navy in the Pacific, 1909–1922* (Austin: University of Texas Press 1971), 612.

20 That is part of the reason why the Japanese admirals strongly objected when the civilian leaders decided to accept a seven-to-ten ratio in lighter craft in 1930. Stephen Pelz, *Race to Pearl Harbor* (Cambridge: Harvard University Press 1974), 3.

21 John Nef, *War and Human Progress* (New York: Norton 1963), 185. Also see *ibid.*, 237, 242–43, and 323; C.W. Oman, *The Art of War in the Middle Ages* (Ithaca, N.Y.: Cornell University Press 1953), 70–72; John Beeler, *Warfare in Feudal Europe, 730–1200* (Ithaca, N.Y.: Cornell University Press 1971), 212–14; Michael Howard, *War in European History* (London: Oxford University Press 1976), 33–37.

22 Quincy Wright, *A Study of War* (abridged ed.; Chicago: University of Chicago Press 1964), 142. Also see 63–70, 74–75. There are important exceptions to these generalizations—the American Civil War, for instance, falls in the middle of the period Wright says is dominated by the offense.

23 Geoffrey Kemp, Robert Pfaltzgraff, and Uri Ra'anan, eds., *The Other Arms Race* (Lexington, Mass.: D.C. Heath 1975); James Foster, "The Future of Conventional Arms Control," *Policy Sciences*, No. 8 (Spring 1977), 1–19.

24 Quoted in Merze Tate, *The United States and Armaments* (Cambridge: Harvard University Press 1948), 108.

25 Marion Boggs, *Attempts to Define and Limit "Aggressive" Armament in Diplomacy and Strategy* (Columbia: University of Missouri Studies, XVI, No. 1, 1941), 15, 40.

26 Kenneth Hagan, *American Gunboat Diplomacy and the Old Navy, 1877–1889* (Westport, Conn.: Greenwood Press 1973), 20.

27 Winston Churchill, *The Gathering Storm* (Boston: Houghton 1948), 206.

28 Bernard Brodie, *War and Politics* (New York: Macmillan 1973), 325.

29 Boggs (fn. 25), 42, 83. For a good argument about the possible differentiation between offensive and defensive weapons in the 1930's, see Basil Liddell Hart, "Aggression and the Problem of Weapons," *English Review*, Vol. 55 (July 1932), 71–78.

30 Quoted in Boggs (fn. 25), 39.

31 On these grounds, the Germans claimed in 1932 that the French forts were offensive (*ibid.*, 49). Similarly, fortified forward naval bases can be necessary for launching an attack; see Braisted (fn. 19), 643.

Reading 7.2

The Offensive/Defensive Balance of Military Technology
JACK S. LEVY

. . . While many of the hypotheses regarding the consequences of the offensive/defensive balance are inherently plausible, there are critical analytical problems which must be resolved before they can be accepted as meaningful or

---

Source: "The Offensive/Defensive Balance of Military Technology: A Theoretical and Historical Analysis," by Jack S. Levy, from International Studies Quarterly *Vol. 28, No. 2 (June 1984). Copyright © 1984 by International Studies Association. Reprinted by permission of Blackwell Publishers Ltd.*

valid. These problems have to do with the theoretical logic of the hypotheses, the definition of the offensive/defensive balance, and the empirical validity of the hypotheses.

The hypothesis that the likelihood of war is increased when the military technology favors the offense is theoretically plausible only on the basis of the rather strong assumption that decision makers correctly perceive the offensive/defensive balance. However, it is perceptions of one's psychological environment that determine decisions, not the 'objective' operational environment (Sprout and Sprout, 1965). The assumption of accurate perceptions is therefore open to question. The inherent difficulty of determining the offensive/defensive balance and the alleged tendency of the military to prepare for the last war rather than the next one may result in some profound misperceptions. It is widely agreed, for example, that in 1914 military technology favored the defense (Hart, 1932:75; Fuller, 1961: ch. 8–9; Montgomery, 1983:472) but that most decision makers perceived that it favored the offense. It was not the offensive/defensive balance that intensified worst-case analysis and increased the incentives for preemption, but decision makers' perceptions of that balance. If the offensive/defensive balance is not defined in terms of the perceptions of decision makers (and in most conceptualizations it is not so defined), then the hypothesis is technically misspecified. Hypotheses regarding the consequences of war, on the other hand, are properly defined in terms of the 'objective' balance.

The second problem relates to the definition of the offensive/defensive balance. What does it mean to say that the offense is superior to the defense, or *vice versa?* This will be treated at length in the following section, but one point should be made here. An hypothesis regarding the offensive/defensive balance has no explanatory power unless that concept can be nominally and operationally defined independently of its hypothesized effects. For example, Wright (1965:796–97) states that

> ... it is difficult to judge the relative power of the offensive and defensive except by a historical audit to determine whether on the whole, in a given state of military technology, military violence had or had not proved a useful instrument of political change. ... During periods when dissatisfied powers have, on the whole, gained their aims by a resort to arms, it may be assumed, on the level of grand strategy, that the power of the offensive has been greater. During the periods when they have not been able to do so, it may be assumed that the power of the grand strategic defensive has been greater.

It would be tautological to use this conception of the offensive/defensive balance to predict to the military success of the aggressor, though it would be legitimate to predict to the frequency of war. Similarly, it is meaningless to hypothesize that offensive superiority increases the incentive to strike first if the offensive/defensive balance is defined by the incentive to strike first. The separation of hypothesis construction from concept definition and the absence of rigorous definition has increased the dangers of tautological propositions.

The failure to subject these hypotheses to systematic empirical testing is another major problem. Most attempts to identify the offensive/defensive advantage in various historical eras are not guided by an explicit definition of the concept, and rarely is there a demonstration that a given balance had an effect on the frequency of wars occurring or on the decisions for a particular war. The apparent *a priori* plausibility of a particular hypothesis may derive more from its tautological construction than from its correspondence with reality. In the absence of a more thorough analytic treatment and a more systematic empirical analysis the validity of any of these hypotheses cannot be accepted.

DEFINITIONS OF THE OFFENSIVE/DEFENSIVE BALANCE

Use of the concept of offensive/defensive balance to refer to a variety of different things has led to a great deal of confusion. Theoretical propositions which are meaningful or interesting for one use of the term may not be very meaningful for another, and for this reason the various usages of the concept must be identified and examined.

Concern here is with the offensive/defensive distinction with respect to military technology and perhaps tactics but not with respect to policy. The question of whether national policy is offensive (aggressive) or defensive is not unimportant, but is analytically distinct and not directly relevant to the hypotheses surveyed earlier. These propositions all suggest that there is something about military technology itself that affects the likelihood or nature of war, and that what is important is whether technology gives an advantage to the offense or defense. This relative advantage may be one of several variables affecting the likelihood of war by affecting policy, but itself is analytically distinct from policy.

The offensive/defensive balance of military technology has been defined primarily in terms of the ease of territorial conquest, the characteristics of armaments, the resources needed by the offense in order to overcome the defense, and the incentive to strike first.

Territorial Conquest

The most common use of the concept of the offensive/defensive balance is based on territorial conquest and the defeat of enemy forces. Quester (1977:15) states that "the territorial fixation then logically establishes our distinction between offense and defense." Jervis (1978:187) argues that an offensive advantage means that "it is easier to destroy the other's army and take its territory than it is to defend one's own." "The essence of defense," on the other hand, "is keeping the other side out of your territory. A purely defensive weapon is one that can do this without being able to penetrate the enemy's land" (1978:203). A defensive advantage means that "it is easier to protect and hold than it is to move forward, destroy, and take" (Jervis, 1978:187). Wright (1965:793) includes these notions of defeat of enemy forces and territorial seizure in his rather complex definition:

> On a tactical level the offensive or defensive quality of a unit may be esti-mated by considering its utility in an attack upon an enemy unit like itself or in an attack upon some other concrete enemy objective, such as territory, commerce, or morale.

A primary purpose of protecting territory, of course, is the protection of people and property. What is perhaps implicit in the above definitions is made explicit by Tarr (1984): "Defense refers to techniques and action, both active and pas-sive, to repel attack, to protect people and property, to hold territory, and to minimize damage by the attacker." This linkage of territorial conquest to popu-lation defense creates a problem, however. While territorial defense was suffi-cient for the protection of people and property in the pre-nuclear era (or at least in the era before strategic bombardment), that is no longer true. As Schelling (1966:ch. 1) and others have noted, the uniqueness of the nuclear age lies in the fact that the defeat of the adversary's military forces and territorial penetra-tion are no longer necessary for the destruction of his population centers. The destruction of population and the coercive power that it makes possible are no longer contingent upon military victory. For this reason the protection of terri-tory (from invasion) is analytically distinct from the protection of population. The inclusion of both in a definition of the offensive/defensive distinction only creates confusion (unless the use of that concept is explicitly restricted to the pre-nuclear era), for the hypothesized effects of an "offensive" advantage are precisely the opposite for the two concepts. The likelihood of war presumably increases as territorial conquest becomes easier, because the probability of vic-tory increases while its expected costs decrease. But the ability to destroy enemy population and industrial centers contributes to deterrence in the nuclear age, and therefore it decreases the likelihood of war (or at least nuclear war).

It is because of the distinction between deterrence and defense (Snyder, 1961:14–16) that the meaning of the offensive/defensive balance may differ in the nuclear and pre-nuclear eras. Whereas in the pre-nuclear era both deter-rence and defense were based on the capacity to defeat the armed forces of the enemy, that is only true for defense in the nuclear age, for deterrence is ultimately based on countervalue punishment. The use of military force for the purpose of defeating enemy armed forces is analytically distinct from the use of force for coercion (Schelling, 1966:ch. 2). Consequently, traditional hypoth-eses (Wright and others) regarding the effects of the offensive/defensive balance of military technology are not necessarily applicable for nuclear powers at the strategic level. Neither the concepts nor the hypotheses are interchangeable.

Now let us return to the territorial conception of the offensive/defen-sive balance. Our earlier discussion leads to the question of what, besides the numbers of troops or weapons, contributes to the defeat of enemy forces and conquest of territory. One answer is provided at the tactical level, based on movement towards the armed forces, possessions, or territory of the enemy. A condition of relative passivity and immobility in waiting for the enemy to attack defines the strategic and tactical defensive (Wright, 1965:807). Clausewitz (as quoted in Boggs, 1941:68) states:

> What is defense in conception? The warding off a blow. What is then its characteristic sign? The state of expectancy (or of waiting for this blow) . . . by this sign alone can the defensive be distinguished from the offensive in war. . . .

Clausewitz also writes: "In tactics every combat, great or small, is defensive if we leave the initiative to the enemy, and wait for his appearance on our front" (as quoted in Boggs, 1941:68).

Both offensive and defensive modes of war on the tactical level are necessary, of course, for the achievement of either offensive or defensive objectives. The pursuit of any offensive goal requires a supporting defense, and the defense alone can never bring victory but only stalemate. Mahan refers to "the fundamental principle of naval war, that defense is insured only by offence" (Boggs, 1941:70). Clausewitz writes that an absolute defense is an "absurdity" which "completely contradicts the idea of war" (Boggs, 1941:71). At some point it is necessary to seize the tactical offensive in order to avoid defeat. Thus the familiar maxim: the best defense is a good offense. It is necessary, however, to distinguish between the strategic and tactical levels. A general fighting offensively in strategic terms needs only to invade and then hold territory to enable him to adopt the tactical defensive (Strachan, 1983). It may be strategically advantageous to maneuver the enemy into a position in which he is forced to take the tactical offensive under unfavorable conditions. As the elder Moltke stated in 1865, "our strategy must be offensive, our tactics defensive" (Dupuy, 1980:200). In addition, military tactics may be offensive in one theater and defensive in another. The Schlieffen Plan, for example, required a holding action against Russia in the east in order to move against France in the west. Nevertheless, with certain types of weapons systems more movement and tactical mobility is possible than with others. It is difficult to measure movement historically while controlling for non-technological factors, however. This leads us to the question of whether the offensive/defensive balance can be defined by the characteristics of weapons systems themselves.

The Characteristics of Armaments

While nearly all weapons can be used for either the strategic or tactical offensive or the strategic or tactical defensive, the question is whether there are some weapons systems which contribute disproportionately more to one than to the other. As stated by the Naval Commission of the League of Nations Conference for the Reduction and Limitation of Armaments (1932–1936) (Boggs, 1941:82):

> Supposing one state either a) adopts a policy of armed aggression or
> b) undertakes offensive operations against another state, what are the
> weapons which, by reason of their specific character, and without prejudice

to their defensive purposes, are most likely to enable that policy or those operations to be brought rapidly to a successful conclusion?

Hart (1932:73) argues that certain weapons "alone make it possible under modern conditions to make a decisive offensive against a neighboring country." What are the characteristics of such weapons?

Both Fuller and Hart identify mobility, striking power, and protection as the essential characteristics of an offensive weapon (Wright, 1965:808). Striking power (the impact of the blow) is not alone sufficient. A mobile gun contributes more to the tactical offensive than an immobile one, and its penetrating power is further enhanced if it is protected. But protection is even more important for the defense. Mobility and protection are inversely related, for it is easier to protect immobile weapons and wait passively for the enemy to attack. The offensive value of the medieval knight ultimately was negated by the heavy armor which protected him but restricted his mobility. Thus Dupuy and Eliot (1937:103) give particular emphasis to the offensive advantages of mobility and striking power, noting that they too may be in conflict. Boggs (1941:84–85) argues that "the defense disposes especially of striking power and protection, to a lesser degree of mobility, while the offense possesses mobility and striking power, and protection to a lesser degree." He concludes that mobility is the central characteristic of an offensive weapon and argues that "armament which greatly facilitates the forward movement of the attacker might be said tentatively to possess relatively greater offensive power than weapons which contribute primarily to the stability of the defender" (Boggs, 1941:85). Our later survey of attempts by military historians to identify the offensive/defensive balance in various historical eras will show that tactical mobility is the primary criterion used to identify an advantage to the offense.

In terms of the characteristics of armaments, then, tactical mobility and movement toward enemy forces and territory are the primary determinants of the offense, at least in land warfare; protection and holding power contribute more to the defense. Other weapon characteristics such as striking power, rapidity of fire, and the range of a weapons system do not contribute disproportionately to either the offense or the defense. Much more work needs to be done here, however, because of the lack of precision of some of these concepts.

The classification of weapons systems by their contribution to mobility and tactical movement toward enemy forces and territory is much less useful for naval warfare. This was evident from the proceedings of the League of Nations Conference for the Reduction and Limitation of Armaments, where the problems and disagreements confronting the Naval Commission were even more serious than those confronting the Land Commission and where technical arguments were even more likely to follow the flag (Boggs, 1941:50–60). The United States, among others, declared that the qualitative distinction could not be applied to navies. Hart, a proponent of the qualitative principle in general, restricted it to the materials of land warfare (Boggs, 1941:50, 81). The main problem with attempts to apply these principles of mobility and tactical movement to naval warfare is the absence of anything comparable to the territorial standard occurring in land warfare. The command of the seas, the ultimate objective of naval warfare (Mahan, 1957), can be served by passive as well as aggressive action, for the neutralization of the enemy fleet by a blockade may serve the same function as its defeat. Moreover, aggressive action toward the enemy fleet does not always result in battle, for an inferior navy can often avoid battle without sacrificing major territorial objectives, unlike land warfare.

Application of the territorially-based criterion of tactical mobility to aerial weapons systems raises the question of whether the offensive or defensive character of these weapons is determined independently of land warfare or by their contribution to the defeat of enemy ground forces and territorial conquest. Many aerial weapons systems do contribute to the tactical offensive on the ground because of their striking power, mobility, and surprise (for example, in the Nazi *blitzkrieg*). Yet air power also has an independent capability to destroy the enemy's war making industrial capabilities, and hence contributes to deterrence in the nuclear age. This deterrent effect of air power takes place independently of its effect on the tactical offensive on the ground but cannot easily be incorporated into a conception of the offensive/defensive balance based on tactical mobility.

Some armaments that traditionally have been considered as defensive and therefore assumed to be "stabilizing" (in the sense that they discourage aggression and reduce the likelihood of war) are often considered to be destabilizing in the nuclear age. Air defenses, anti-ballistic missile defenses, and even civil defenses are considered under the prevailing strategic doctrine to be destabilizing because by protecting populations they threaten to undermine deterrence. This reinforces our earlier point that the hypothesized consequences of a military technology favoring the offense (or the defense) may not be interchangeable between the nuclear and pre-nuclear eras.

The definition of the offensive/defensive balance, in terms of the characteristics of armaments, raises other questions as well. One is whether it is possible to define the offensive/defensive character of a weapon by its intrinsic performance characteristics alone, apart from the prevailing doctrine that determines it use. For example, essentially the same tank that was used in much of World War I as protected fire support was used in World War II as the organizing element of mobile offensive warfare (Fuller, 1945:ch. VI). The offensive character of Napoleonic warfare was due far more to the innovative tactics of Napoleon than to weapons systems themselves (Howard, 1976:75–76; Preston and Wise, 1979:189–191). It must be concluded that the offensive or defensive character of a weapons system must be defined by both its intrinsic characteristics and the tactical doctrine which determines its use.

What is important, of course, is not the characteristics of an individual weapon, but rather the aggregate impact of all weapons systems in a given arsenal. How is a given mixture of armaments, designed for different purposes and deployed for use in different theaters on land, sea, and air, to be aggregated so that their net effect on the offense and defense can be classified? This overall impact cannot be determined apart from the composition of an enemy's weapons systems and the terrain where the combat takes place. The offensive value of the tank, for example, was reduced by the development of new antitank technologies in the early 1970s. To complicate matters further, most hypotheses relating to the offensive/defensive balance treat that concept as a systemic-level attribute (the hypotheses that offensive superiority contributes to an increased frequency of war and to empire-building, for example). They suggest that at a given time the offensive/defensive balance can be characterized by a single value throughout the system. The balance must be aggregated not only over all weapons, functional roles, and theaters for a given state, but also over all states in the system. This is difficult given differential levels of industrialization and military power, uneven rates of technological diffusion, and doctrinal differences among various states in the system. Some of these problems are minimized, however, if the focus is restricted to the leading powers in the system, because they are often comparable in terms of power and technology.

Relative Resources Expended

Gilpin distinguishes between the offense and the defense in terms of an economic cost-benefit framework. "To speak of a shift in favor of the offense means that fewer resources than before must be expended on the offense in order to overcome the defense" (Gilpin, 1981:62–63). Gilpin goes on to say that "the defense is said to be superior if the resources required to capture territory are greater than the value of the territory itself; the offense is superior if the cost of conquest is less than the value of the territory" (p. 63).

Clearly the second definition does not follow from the first. Whereas the first uses the relative costs of overcoming the defense at two different times and independently of the resulting benefits, the second definition introduces an entirely new concept—the actual value of the territorial conquest itself. The value of territorial conquest is undoubtedly an important variable leading to war but it is analytically distinct from military technology and ought to be treated separately. Under Gilpin's second definition the hypothesis becomes equivalent to the statement that a positive (expected) utility of territorial conquest increases the likelihood of war. This may be true (Bueno de Mesquita, 1981), but it is not the hypothesis under consideration here. Moreover, the definition of the offensive/defensive balance by the utility of territorial conquest reduces to a tautology the hypothesis that offensive superiority increases the utility of territorial conquest.

One of the two conceptualizations of the offensive/defensive balance suggested by Jervis is more consistent with Gilpin's first formulation. Jervis (1978:188) poses the question as follows: "Does the state have to spend more or less than one dollar on defensive forces to offset each dollar spent by the other side on forces that could be used to attack?" That is, what is the relative marginal utility of devoting military spending to the offense rather than to the defense? This approach is potentially valuable, but it is incomplete. It defines what it means to say that the offense (or the defense) has an advantage, but fails to provide any criteria for specifying what constitutes the offense or the defense in the first place. The marginal utilities cannot be compared until the offense and defense are first defined, and until this is done the concept is not particularly useful.

The definition of the offensive/defensive balance by the relative resources that must be expended on the offense in order to overcome the defense can be conceptualized in another way and related to the conception based on territorial conquest. This refers to attack/defense ratios rather than military spending. What ratio of troops does an attacker need in order to overcome an enemy defending fixed positions? This notion is mentioned but not developed by Quester (1977:212): "The significant impact of defensive or offensive technology shows up in the minimum ratios of numerical superiority required for such an offensive." It follows the same logic as Foch's comment regarding the power of the offensive prior to World War I: "Formerly many guns were necessary to produce an effect. Today a few suffice" (Montross, 1960:686). The conventional wisdom is that the offense needs at least a three-to-one advantage, but the point here is that this ratio varies as a function of existing military technology and the tactical doctrine guiding its use. The offensive/defensive balance is then defined as being inversely proportional to the minimum ratio of forces needed by the attacker in order to overcome an adversary defending fixed positions. The greater the minimum ratio, the greater the advantage of the defense.

It is important to note here that the minimum *ratio* of forces needed by the attacker in a particular era is analytically distinct from the relative *numbers* of forces actually possessed by two adversaries in a particular situation. The probability of victory is a function of both. To say that the balance of military technology (as a function of attack/defense ratios) favors the offense does *not* mean the attacker is likely to win. That would be true only if the attacker actually possessed the requisite number of troops in a particular situation.

The problem arises as to what ratio should be used as a baseline, the zero-point indicating the transition from a defensive advantage to an offensive advantage. The most obvious ratio is one to one, but that is widely regarded as favoring the defense. While it would not be technically incorrect to say that the balance always favors the defense because the attacker always requires numerical superiority, this is neither interesting nor useful. If the offensive/defensive balance is defined as attack/defense ratios, it is preferable to conceive of this in relative rather than absolute terms. It is useful to speak of shifts in the balance and to compare the balance at different times, but not to speak about the absolute state of the balance. Thus the hypothesis should technically state that "the higher the minimum ratio of forces needed by the attacker in order to overcome an adversary defending fixed positions, the lower the likelihood of war."

This conception of the offensive/defensive balance is more useful than the others surveyed above, at least for land warfare. The attack/defense ratio could be measured in one of two ways. It could be determined empirically from an analysis of a variety of battles in a given era, with the force ratios and results determined for each and some kind of average computed. The problem, of course, would be the need to control for asymmetries in geography, troop quality, and doctrine. Alternatively, the ratio could be conceived in perceptual terms and measured by the perceptions of military and political elites of what ratio of forces is necessary for either attack or defense. While this information is not readily available it might be inferred from an examination of the war plans of the leading states. The methodological problems involved in either of these approaches are quite serious, however.

The Incentive to Strike First

One of the questions asked by Jervis (1978:188) of the offensive/defensive balance is the following: "With a given inventory of forces, is it better to attack or to defend? Is there an incentive to strike first or to absorb the other's blow?' This conceptualization is more flexible than earlier criteria based on tactical mobility and characteristics of armaments because it can incorporate considerations of deterrence and be applied to the nuclear age. It creates some problems, however, which Jervis may recognize but does not fully develop. For one thing, the hypothesis that a military technology favoring the offense increases the incentive to strike first is reduced to a tautology and hence carries no explanatory power. In focusing attention on the linkage between the incentive to strike first and war, it ignores the more basic question of what conditions create an incentive to strike first. These antecedent conditions possess the greatest explanatory power and operate through the intervening variable of the incentive to strike first. This leads to a related problem: there are numerous factors besides technology and doctrine affecting the incentive to strike first, including geographic constraints and diplomatic and domestic political considerations, factors which also have an independent effect on war. If the offensive/defensive balance is *defined* as the incentive to strike first, then it becomes confounded with these other variables and it becomes impossible to distinguish their independent effects. The incentive to strike first is best conceptualized as an intervening variable leading to war and as the product of several distinct variables, one of which is military technology and doctrine. One key issue is to elaborate the aspects of military technology or doctrine which affect the incentives to strike first, but this cannot be fully analyzed here.

It is important to distinguish the incentive to strike first from other concepts that have also been used to define the offensive/defensive balance. The incentive to strike first should not be confused with aggressive policy, which is influenced by a wide range of variables. A state may have revisionist ambitions but be constrained by a military technology favoring the tactical defense, as well as by other variables. Or, a state with purely defensive ambitions may rationally initiate war if it perceives that through a preemptive strike it can minimize its losses against an assumed aggressor. The distinction between the incentive to strike first and seizing territory is particularly likely to be confused. These are clearly distinct for naval and air warfare (particularly in the nuclear age) but the difference is more profound. One may simultaneously have a policy of not striking first *and* a strategy of active defense and territorial penetration in the event that war does break out. This was Bismarck's policy in the 1870s and

1880s (Langer, 1964) and perhaps Israel's in 1973. Germany's Schlieffen Plan called for passive defense (holding ground) in the East and rapid territorial penetration in northern France regardless of who initiated the war.

The failure to recognize these distinctions only creates confusion and may result in the incorrect use of hypotheses designed for other purposes. Hypotheses appropriate for a territorially-based definition of the offensive/defensive balance of military technology may not be valid for a definition based on the incentive to strike first. While the ease of territorial seizure may shorten wars and lower their costs (Wright, 1965:673), this may not necessarily be true for the incentive to strike first. Nor is an incentive to strike first in the nuclear age likely to have the same consequences as an attack/defense ratio which favors the offense. Further, it is not clear that the incentive to strike first itself has the same causes or consequences in the pre-nuclear period as it does in the nuclear age, though this might be an interesting area for future research.

The same types of problems arise with respect to the various other conceptualizations of the offensive/defensive balance examined above. The concept has been defined in terms of the defeat of enemy armed forces, territorial conquest, protection of population, tactical mobility, the characteristics of armaments, attack/defense ratios, the relative resources expended on the offense and the defense, and the incentive to strike first. These separate definitions are often not interchangeable, and hypotheses based on one definition are often either implausible or tautological for another definition. This is particularly true for applications of the offensive/defensive balance to the nuclear age. Because the most advanced weapons of this era are used primarily for coercive purposes and the weapons of earlier eras were used primarily to engage enemy armed forces, the concept of the offensive/defensive balance of military technology may mean entirely different things in the two different situations. Certainly one reason for the confusion and ambiguity among these hypotheses is the fact that they are based on common concepts such as "offense", "aggressor", and "initiator" which have ordinary language meanings apart from more precise technical meanings. This is all the more reason why any attempt to use such a concept must first define it explicitly and be very clear regarding precisely which hypotheses are relevant.

CLASSIFICATION OF THE OFFENSIVE/ DEFENSIVE BALANCE IN HISTORY

The third section of this article surveys a variety of efforts to classify the offensive/defensive balance of military technology in the Western international system over the last eight centuries. This survey will be useful because of the absence of any previous review of this body of literature and because of the general failure of earlier studies to acknowledge or build upon each other. More importantly, it may reveal whether or not the concept has acquired an informal definition in its empirical application, in spite of the conceptual ambiguity demonstrated above. While the concept of the offensive/defensive balance of military technology has taken on a variety of meanings, the question arises as to how the concept has been used in attempts to classify the offensive/defensive balance in past historical eras. If different authorities have generally used the offensive/defensive balance to mean the same thing (even in the absence of any formal nominal or operational definition), and if they have generally agreed on the state of the balance in various historical eras, then it can be concluded that the ambiguity of the concept has not precluded its effective use in empirical analysis. Consistent usage and agreement by various authorities on the state of the balance in different historical eras would permit "inter-coder agreement" to be used as the basis for accurate historical measurement (provided these measurements are independent). Lack of agreement on classification, however, would suggest that the collective judgment of authorities cannot be used as the basis for measurement. It would also support the earlier conclusion that the offensive/defensive concept needs to be defined much more explicitly and rigorously before it can be used in historical analysis. . . .

[*At this point in the original article Levy includes a survey of several pages on varying interpretations of the offense/defense balance in several historical epochs. (Ed.)*]

There is unanimous agreement among the references cited that the period from 1200 to 1450 was characterized by defensive superiority and that the period from 1450 to 1525 was characterized by offensive superiority. The authorities are split on the 1525 to 1650 period. There is complete agreement that the defense was superior from 1650 to 1740. Some argue that this defensive superiority continues until 1789, though Frederick's emphasis on the tactical offensive leads some to assert the opposite and others to make no specific evaluation. The 1789 to 1815 period is generally regarded to favor the offense but because of innovations in tactics rather than armaments. Little attention is given to the 1815–1850 period. The next hundred years pose a problem because of the gap between the objective and perceived balance and the uncertain conceptual status of the latter. These authorities generally agree that from 1850 to 1925 or so the balance favored the defense but that nearly all statesmen perceived that it favored the offense from 1870 to 1914. Similarly, from 1930 to 1945 the balance favored the offense but that the actors themselves perceived that it favored the defense.

A rough calculation shows the following degree of consensus among our authorities. Of the 450 years from 1495–1945, only two periods totaling 55 years claim a definite consensus of offensive superiority. Two periods totaling at most 130 years claim a consensus of defensive superiority. Four periods constituting a minimum of 265 years are uncertain, either because of diverging views, or because of the diametric opposition of the evaluations of actors and analysts and the ambiguous conceptual status of perceptions in definitions of the balance. The inescapable conclusion is that there exists considerable divergence of opinion among leading authorities regarding the offensive/defensive balance during the last five centuries of the modern era, and that a method of "intercoder agreement" cannot be used to provide a basis for classification during this period. . . .

To conclude, the concept of the offensive/defensive balance is too vague and encompassing to be useful in theoretical analysis. Many of the individual variables that have been incorporated into the more general idea may themselves be useful, however. Few would doubt the utility for deterrence theory of the concept of the incentive to strike first, for example, and the concept of attack/defense ratios suggested here deserves further exploration. Much more conceptualization is necessary before these individual variables can be effectively used in empirical analysis, however. There is already a body of theory regarding the consequences of an incentive to strike first. What is needed are comparable theories regarding the consequences of military technologies which contribute to tactical mobility or to the ease of territorial conquest, or which reduce the ratio of forces needed by the attacker to overcome an adversary defending fixed positions. Interaction effects between these separate variables also need to be explored. Further theoretical development of this kind is necessary, because in its absence there is little reason to believe that these individual concepts have an important impact on war, and therefore little reason to use these concepts in empirical analysis.

REFERENCES

Boggs, M. W. (1941) "Attempts to Define and Limit 'Aggressive' Armament in Diplomacy and Strategy." *University of Missouri Studies*, XVI, No. 1. Columbia, Missouri.

Bueno de Mesquita, B. (1981) *The War Trap*. New Haven: Yale University Press.

Dupuy, R. E. and G. F. Eliot (1937) *If War Comes*. New York: Macmillan.

Dupuy, T. N. (1980) *The Evolution of Weapons and Warfare*. Bloomington: Indiana University Press.

Fuller, J. F. C. (1945) *Armament and History*. New York: Charles Scribner's Sons.

———. (1961) *The Conduct of War, 1789–1961*. New Brunswick: Rutgers University Press.

Gilpin, R. (1981) *War and Change in World Politics*. Cambridge: Cambridge University Press.

Hart, B. H. L. (1932) "Aggression and the Problem of Weapons." *English Review* 55: 71–78.

Hart, B. H. L. (1964) *Strategy*. New York: Praeger.

Howard, M. (1976) *War in European History*. New York: Oxford University Press.

———. (1983) *Clausewitz*. Oxford: Oxford University Press.

Jervis, R. (1978) "Cooperation Under the Security Dilemma." *World Politics* 30: 167–214.

Langer, W. L. (1964) *European Alliances and Alignments, 1871–1890*, 2nd ed. New York: Vintage Books.

Mahan, A. T. (1957) *The Influences of Sea Power Upon History, 1660–1783*. New York: Hill and Wang.

Montgomery of Alamein, V. (1983) *A History of Warfare*. New York: William Morrow.

Montross, L. (1960) *War Through the Ages*, 3rd ed., rev. New York: Harper & Row.

Preston, R. A. and S. F. Wise (1979) *Men in Arms*. New York: Holt, Rinehart and Winston.

Quester, G. H. (1977) *Offense and Defense in the International System*. New York: Wiley.

Schelling, T. C. (1966) *Arms and Influence*. New Haven: Yale University Press.

Snyder, G. H. (1961) *Deterrence and Defense*. Princeton: Princeton University Press.

Sprout, H. and M. Sprout (1965) *The Ecological Perspective on Human Affairs*. Princeton: Princeton University Press.

Strachan, H. (1983) *European Armies and the Conduct of War*. London: George Allen & Unwin.

Tarr, D. (1984) 'Defense as Strategy: A Conceptual Analysis,' in S. J. Cimbala (ed.) *National Security Strategy*. New York: Praeger.

Wright, Q. (1949) 'Modern Technology and the World Order,' in W. F. Ogburn (ed.) *Technology and International Relations*. Chicago: University of Chicago Press.

———. (1965) *A Study of War*, rev. ed. Chicago: Chicago University Press.

Reading 7.3

Why Nuclear Proliferation May Be Good
KENNETH N. WALTZ

PREDICTING FROM STRUCTURE: HOW BIPOLARITY HAS CHANGED THE RELATIONS OF NATIONS

The world has enjoyed more years of peace since 1945 than had been known in this century—if peace is defined as the absence of general war among the major states of the world. The Second World War followed the first one within 21 years. As of 1978, 33 years had elapsed since the Allies' victory over the Axis powers. Conflict marks all human affairs. In the past third of a century, conflict has generated hostility among states and at times has resulted in violence among the weaker and smaller ones. Even though the more powerful states of the world have occasionally been direct participants (most noticeably the United States and China), war has been confined geographically and limited in the number of states engaged in the fighting. Remarkably, general war has been avoided in a period of rapid and far-reaching changes—decolonization; the rapid economic growth of some states; the formation, tightening, and eventual loosening of blocs; the development of new technologies; and the emergence of new strategies for fighting guerrilla wars and deterring nuclear ones. The prevalence of peace, together with the fighting of circumscribed wars, indicates a high ability of the postwar international system to absorb changes and to contain conflicts and hostility.

Presumably features found in the postwar system that were not present earlier account for the world's recent good fortune. The biggest changes from the pre- to the postwar world are the shift from multi- to bipolarity and the introduction of nuclear weapons.

Bipolarity has two outstandingly good effects, which can be seen by contrasting multipolar and bipolar worlds. First, in a multipolar world there are

---

Source: From an essay for a conference sponsored by the U.S. Central Intelligence Agency and Department of Defense: Kenneth N. Waltz, "What Will the Spread of Nuclear Weapons Do to the World?" in John Kerry King, ed., International Political Effects of the Spread of Nuclear Weapons *(Washington, D.C.: Government Printing Office, April 1979).*

too many powers to permit any of them to draw clear and fixed lines between allies and adversaries and too few to keep the effects of defection low. With three or more powers, flexibility of alliances keeps relations of friendship and enmity fluid and makes everyone's estimate of the present and future relation of forces uncertain. So long as the system is one of fairly small numbers, the actions of any of them may threaten the security of others. There are too many to enable anyone to see for sure what is happening, and too few to make what is happening a matter of indifference. In a bipolar world, the two great powers depend militarily mainly on themselves. This is entirely true at the strategic nuclear level and largely true at the tactical nuclear and conventional levels. . . .

PREDICTING THE FUTURE FROM THE PAST

The second force for good in the world since the war has been nuclear weapons. They make the cost of war seem frighteningly high and thus discourage states from starting any wars that might lead to the use of such weapons. Nuclear weapons have been good for the great powers and have not been bad for the few additional states that possess them (cf. Weltman 1978, pp. 5–7). Their further spread, however, causes widespread fear. This calls to mind statements often uttered in one breath earlier in the nuclear age: "Nuclear weapons make war impossible. We must abolish nuclear weapons." Much of the writing about the spread of nuclear weapons has this unusual trait: It tells us that what did not happen in the nuclear past is likely to happen in the nuclear future, that tomorrow's nuclear states are likely to do to one another what today's nuclear states have not done. A happy nuclear past leads many to expect an unhappy nuclear future. This is odd, and the oddity leads me to believe that we need to reconsider how weapons affect the situation of their possessors. . . .

Force may be used for offense, for defense, for deterrence, and for coercion. Consider offense first. Germany and France before World War I provide a classic case of two adversaries each neglecting its defense and both planning to launch major attacks at the outset of war. France favored offense over defense, because only by fighting an offensive war could Alsace-Lorraine be reclaimed. This illustrates one purpose of an offense: namely, conquest. Germany favored offense over defense, believing offense to be the best defense, or even the only defense possible. Hemmed in by two adversaries, it could avoid fighting a two-front war only by concentrating its forces in the West and defeating France before Russia could mobilize and move effectively into battle. This is what the Schlieffen Plan called for. The Plan illustrates another purpose of the offense: namely, security. Even if security were Germany's only goal, an offensive strategy seemed to be the way to obtain it (cf. Art and Waltz 1971, pp. 6–11).

The offense may have either or both of two aims: conquest and security. An offense may be conducted in either, or in some combination of two ways: preventively or preemptively. If two countries are unequal in strength and the weaker is gaining, the stronger may be tempted to strike before its advantage is lost. Following this logic, a country with nuclear weapons may be tempted to destroy the nascent force of a hostile country. This would be preventive war, a war launched against a weak country before it can become disturbingly strong. The logic of preemption is different. Two countries may be equally prepared, but their forces may be vulnerable. Mutual vulnerability of forces leads to mutual fear of surprise attack by giving each nuclear power a strong incentive to strike first. If either country can eliminate the other's bombers and missiles in one surprise blow, then both of them are encouraged to mount sudden attacks if only for fear that if one does not the other one will.

French and German plans for war against each other emphasized prevention over preemption—to strike before enemies can become fully ready to fight, but not to strike at their forces in order to destroy them before they can be used to strike back. Whether preemptive or preventive, an offensive first strike is a hard one, as logic suggests and history confirms. Whoever strikes first does so to gain a decisive advantage. A preemptive strike is designed to eliminate or decisively reduce the opponent's ability to retaliate. A preventive strike is designed to defeat an adversary before he can develop and deploy his full potential might.

How can one state dissuade another state from attacking? It can do so in either or in some combination of two ways. One way to counter an intended offense is to build fortifications and to muster forces that look forbiddingly strong. To build defenses so patently strong that no one would try to destroy or overcome them would make international life perfectly tranquil. I call this the defensive ideal. The other way to inhibit a country's intended aggressive moves is to scare that country out of making them by threatening to visit unacceptable punishment upon it. "To deter" literally means to stop someone from doing something by frightening him. In contrast to dissuasion by defense, dissuasion by deterrence operates by frightening a state out of attacking, not because of the difficulty of launching the attack and carrying it home, but because the expected reaction of the opponent will result in one's own severe punishment. Defense and deterrence are often confused. One frequently hears statements like this: A strong defense in Europe will deter a Russian attack. What is meant is that a strong defense will dissuade Russia from attacking. Deterrence is achieved not through the ability to defend but through the ability to punish. Purely deterrent forces provide no defense. The message of the strategy is this: Although we are defenseless, if you attack we will punish you to an extent that more than cancels your gains. Second-strike nuclear forces serve that kind of strategy. Purely defensive forces provide no deterrence. They offer no means of punishment. The message of the strategy is this: Although we cannot strike back at you, you will find our defenses so difficult to overcome that you will dash yourself to pieces against them. The Maginot Line was to serve that kind of strategy.

States may also use force for coercion. One state may threaten to harm another state not to deter it from taking a certain action but to compel one. Napoleon III threatened to bombard Tripoli if the Turks did not comply with his demands for Roman Catholic control of the Palestinian Holy Places. This is blackmail, which can now be backed by conventional or nuclear threats.

Are nuclear weapons good or bad for the world? The answer depends on whether nuclear weapons permit and encourage states to deploy forces in ways that make the active use of force more or less likely and in ways that promise to be more or less destructive. If the offense becomes more effective and if the blackmailer's threat becomes more compelling, nuclear weapons are bad for the world—the more so the more widely diffused nuclear weapons become. If defense and deterrence are made easier and more reliable by the spread of nuclear weapons, we may expect the opposite results. . . .

John Herz coined the term "security dilemma" to describe the condition in which states, unsure of one anothers' intentions, arm for the sake of security and in doing so set a vicious circle in motion. Having armed for the sake of security, states feel less secure and buy more arms because the means to anyone's security is a threat to someone else who in turn responds by arming (1950, p. 157). A dilemma cannot be solved; it can more or less readily be dealt with. The security dilemma is produced by the situation of states. Weapons and strategies change the situation of states in ways that make their security dilemma more or less intense, as Robert Jervis has brilliantly shown (1978).

If weapons are not well suited for conquest, neighbors have more peace of mind (cf. Hoag 1961). According to the defensive-deterrent ideal, we should expect war to become less likely when weaponry is such as to make conquest more difficult, to discourage preemptive and preventive war, and to make coercive threats less credible. Nuclear weapons have those effects.

A few points elaborating on this statement make its importance clear. 1) Wars can be fought in the face of deterrent threats, but the higher the stakes and the closer a country moves toward winning them, the more surely that country invites retaliation and risks its own destruction. States are not likely to run major risks for minor gains. Wars between nuclear states may escalate as the loser uses larger and larger warheads. Fearing that, states will want to draw back. Not escalation but de-escalation becomes likely. War remains possible, but victory in war is too dangerous to fight for. If states can only score small gains, because large ones risk retaliation, they have little incentive to fight. Why fight if you can't win much? 2) The question demands a negative answer all the more insistently when the deterrent deployment of nuclear weapons contributes more to a country's security than does conquest of territory. A country with a deterrent strategy does not need the extent of territory required by a country relying on a conventional defense in depth. A deterrent strategy makes it unnecessary for a country to fight for the sake of increasing its security, and this removes a major cause of war. 3) Deterrent effect depends both on one's capabilities and on the will one has to use them (cf. Brodie 1966, pp. 74, 78; Snyder 1961, p. 10; Schelling 1966, pp. 37, 78). The will of the attacked, striving to preserve its own territory, can be presumed stronger than the will of the attacker striving to annex someone's else's territory. Knowing this, the would-be attacker is further inhibited. 4) States act with less care if the expected costs of war are low and with more care if they are high. In 1853 and 1854 Britain and France thought that if war with Russia came, victory would be easy. Prestige abroad and political popularity at home would be gained, if not much else. The vagueness of their expectations was matched by the carelessness of their actions. In blundering into the Crimean War they acted hastily on scant information, pandered to their people's frenzy for war, showed more concern for an ally's whim than for the adversary's situation, failed to specify the changes in behavior that threats were supposed to bring, and inclined toward testing strength first and bargaining second (see Smoke 1977, pp. 175–88). In sharp contrast, the presence of nuclear weapons makes states exceedingly cautious. Think of Kennedy and Khrushchev in the Cuban missile crisis.

Certainty about the relative strength of adversaries also makes war less likely. From the late nineteenth century onward the speed of technological innovation increased the difficulty of estimating relative strengths and predicting the course of campaigns. Since World War II technology has advanced even faster, but short of an ABM breakthrough, this does not matter very much. It does not disturb the American-Russian military equilibrium because one side's missiles are not made obsolete by improvements in the other side's missiles. In 1906 the British Dreadnought, with the greater range and fire power of its guns, made older battleships obsolete. This does not happen to missiles aimed at cities. As Bernard Brodie has put it: "Weapons that do not have to fight their like do not become useless because of the advent of newer and superior types" (1973, p. 321).

Many wars might have been avoided had their outcomes been foreseen. "To be sure," Georg Simmel once said, "the most effective presupposition for preventing struggle, the exact knowledge of the comparative strength of the two parties, is very often only to be obtained by the actual fighting out of the conflict" (1904, p. 501). Miscalculation causes wars. One side expects victory at an affordable price, while the other side hopes to avoid defeat. Predicting the result of conventional wars has proved difficult. The outcome of battles and the course of campaigns are hard to foresee because so many things affect them. In a nuclear world prediction is easy. One reason it is easy is that it does not have to be very precise to be politically decisive. The number of one's cities that can be severely damaged is equal to the number of strategic warheads an adversary can deliver. Variations of number mean little within wide ranges. The expected effect of the deterrent achieves an easy clarity because wide margins of error in estimates of the damage one may suffer do not matter. Do we expect to lose one city or two, two cities or ten? When these are the pertinent questions, we stop thinking about running risks and worry about how to avoid them. Nuclear weapons make miscalculation difficult and politically pertinent prediction easy. The effects of nuclear weapons and of bipolarity reinforce each other. . . .

The likelihood of war decreases as deterrent and defensive capabilities increase. Whatever the number of nuclear states, a nuclear world is tolerable if those states are able to send convincing deterrent messages: It is useless to attempt to conquer because you will be severely punished. A nuclear world becomes even more tolerable if states are able to send convincing defensive messages: It is useless to attempt to conquer because you cannot. Dissuading an enemy from attack by throwing up a good-looking defense may be as effective as dissuading him through deterrence; it may be more effective. A contemplated defensive deployment of nuclear weapons, if it should fail to dissuade, would bring small nuclear weapons into use before the physical, political, and psychological environment had deteriorated. The chances of de-escalation are high if the use of nuclear weapons is carefully planned and is limited to the battlefield. Nuclear weapons and an appropriate doctrine for their use make it possible to approach the defensive-deterrent ideal, a condition that causes the chances of war to dwindle. . . .

PREDICTING THE FUTURE FROM THE FUTURE

Contemplating the nuclear past gives ground for hoping that the world will survive if further nuclear powers join today's six or seven. This tentative conclusion is called into question by the widespread belief that the infirmities of some new nuclear states and the delicacy of their nuclear forces will work against the preservation of peace and for the fighting of nuclear wars. The likelihood of avoiding destruction as more states become members of the nuclear club is often coupled with question of who those states will be. What are the likely differences in situation and behavior of new as compared to old nuclear powers?

The Effects of Nuclear Weapons on Their Owners

What are the principal worries? First, because of the importance of controlling nuclear weapons—of keeping them firmly in the hands of reliable officials—rulers of nuclear states may become more authoritarian and ever more given to secrecy. Second, some potential nuclear states are not politically strong and stable enough to ensure control of the weapons and control of the decision to use them. If neighboring, hostile, unstable states are armed with nuclear weapons, each fears attack by the other. Frightful feelings of insecurity may lead to intense arms races, which subordinate civil needs to military necessities. Fears are compounded by the danger of internal coups in which the control of nuclear weapons may be the main object of struggle and the key to gaining control of the government. Under these fearful circumstances, to maintain governmental authority and civil order may be impossible. The legitimacy of the state and the loyalty of its citizenry may dissolve because the state is no longer thought to be capable of maintaining external security and internal order. The first fear is that states become tyrannical; the second, that they lose control. Both fears may be realized either in different states or in the same state at different times (cf. Dunn 1977, pp. 102–107).

What can one say? Four things primarily may be specified. 1) Possession of nuclear weapons may slow arms races down, rather than speeding them up. . . . 2) For less developed countries to build nuclear arsenals requires a long lead time. The more unstable a government is the shorter the attention span of its leaders become. They have to deal with today's problems and hope for the best tomorrow (Van Evera 1976). 3) In countries where political control is difficult to maintain, governments are unlikely to initiate nuclear-weapons programs. In such states, soldiers help to maintain leaders in power or try to overthrow them. For those purposes nuclear weapons are not useful. Soldiers who have political clout or want it are not interested in nuclear weapons. They are not scientists and technicians. They like to command troops and squadrons. Their vested interests are in the military's traditional trappings. 4) If a coup does occur in a nuclear state, control of the armed forces, including their nuclear weapons, will bring victory. But what is impossible to comprehend is why any of the contenders should start using nuclear weapons. Who would they aim at? How would they use them as instruments for maintaining or gaining control? I see little more reason to fear that one faction or another in some less developed country will fire atomic weapons in a struggle for political control than they will be used in a crisis of succession in the Soviet Union or China. One or another nuclear state will experience uncertainty of succession, fierce struggles for power, and instability of regime. Those who fear the worst have not shown with any plausibility how those expected events lead to the use of nuclear weapons. Only a madman would seek political power by shooting nuclear weapons at targets in the country he was seeking to rule.

What Changes When More States Get Nuclear Weapons?

Nuclear weapons are not likely to be used at home. Are they likely to be used abroad? As nuclear weapons spread, what new causes may bring effects different from and worse than those known earlier in the nuclear age? Considering four ways in which the new world is expected to differ from the old reduces the expectation of perverse novelty.

First, new nuclear states may come in hostile pairs and share a common border. The United States and the Soviet Union, however, and the Soviet Union and China, are hostile enough; and the latter pair share a long border. China's nuclear weapons have made both sides more cautious and the tensions between them less likely to lead to anything more than a skirmish, even though they have shown little reluctance to threaten force elsewhere and to use it occasionally.

Second, the uneven development of the forces of new nuclear states may create the temptation to preempt. Yet the forces of all the present nuclear countries necessarily have developed unevenly in relation to each other. Nobody has preempted yet, for reasons I shall discuss in a moment.

Third, new nuclear states may have trouble controlling their forces if they are crudely designed and if civil control of the military is shaky. Yet everyone so far has been able to control forces at various levels of sophistication. Moreover, I can see no reason to think that civil control of the military is secure in the Soviet Union given the occasional presence of serving officers in the Politburo and some known and some surmised instances of military intervention in civil affairs at critical times. And in the People's Republic of China military and civil branches of government are not separated but fused. Although I like civil control, preventing a highly destructive war does not require it. What is required is that decisions be made that keep destruction within bounds, whether decisions are made by civilians or soldiers. Soldiers may be more cautious than civilians. Generals and admirals do not like uncertainty, and they do not lack patriotism. They do not like to fight conventional wars under unfamiliar conditions. The use of nuclear weapons, whether for offense, deterrence, or defense, multiplies uncertainties. Nobody knows what a nuclear battlefield would look like, and nobody knows what happens after the first city is hit. Uncertainty about the course that a nuclear war might follow, along with certainty that destruction may be immense, strongly inhibits the first use of nuclear weapons.

Fourth, new nuclear states may be politically radical and militarily reckless. States that are radical at home, however, may not be radical abroad. Few states have been radical in the conduct of their foreign policy, and fewer have remained so for long. Think of the Soviet Union and the People's Republic of China. States coexist in a competitive arena. The pressures of competition cause them to behave in ways that make the threats they face manageable, in ways that enable them to get along. States can remain radical in foreign policy only if they are outside of the international mainstream and of little interest to others because of their unimportance. States that acquire nuclear weapons will not be regarded with indifference. States that want to be freewheelers will have to stay out of the nuclear business. A nuclear Libya, for example, would have to show caution, even in rhetoric, lest it suffer retaliation in response to someone else's anonymous attack on a third state. That state, ignorant of who attacked, could easily claim that its intelligence identified Libya as the culprit and take the opportunity of silencing it by making a modest conventional attack. Nuclear weapons induce caution, especially in weak states.

Examining the supposedly unfortunate characteristics of new nuclear states removes some of one's worries. One wonders why their civil and military leaders should be less interested in avoiding self-destruction than leaders of other states have been (cf. Weltman 1978, pp. 30–31). Nuclear weapons have never been used in a world in which two or more states possessed them. Still, one's feeling that something new and awful will emerge as new nuclear powers are added to the present group is not easily quieted. The fear remains that one or another of the new nuclear states will fire them in a cooly calculated pre-emptive strike, or use them to end a long and bitter rivalry, or launch them in the despair of defeat. The next section considers some of the possibilities.

The Active Use of Nuclear Weapons

Many believe that temptations to launch preventive or preemptive wars, along with the possibility of accidental firings, pose the greatest dangers that nuclear weapons will be used. Again, people worry about future events that the past does not disclose.

Because of America's nuclear arsenal, the Soviet Union could hardly have destroyed the budding forces of Britain and France; but the United States could have struck the Soviet Union's early nuclear installations, and the United States and the Soviet Union could have struck China's. Preventive nuclear war has been treated as more than an abstract possibility. When Francis P. Matthews was President Truman's Secretary of the Navy, he made a speech that seemed to favor our waging preventive war. The United States, he argued, should be willing to pay "even the price of instituting a war to compel cooperation for peace (*New York Times*, August 26, 1950, p. 1). Moreover, press reports have revealed that the United States and the Soviet Union considered a preventive strike against China early in its nuclear career, with the one country wanting to make sure that the other would not think that an attack was the beginning of World War III.

No one has launched a preventive strike at anyone's embryonic nuclear forces.[1] If new opportunities for preemption appear, will they prove to be less easily resisted? The United States even today worries about the vulnerability of its vast and varied arsenal. Will not new nuclear states, slightly and crudely armed, be all the more worried about their "delicate balances of terror," with each of them tempted to strike before being struck?

For several reasons we need worry little about the crudity and imbalance of such forces. Small nuclear countries are not thinking about arsenals comparable to those that the United States and the Soviet Union believe they must have to maintain second-strike forces against each other. The main worry in a world with more nuclear states is that states of limited and roughly similar capabilities will use them against each other. But they do not want to risk nuclear devastation any more than we do. Preemptive strikes nevertheless seem likely because we assume that their forces will be "delicate." This is an assumption about the future that is thrown into doubt by experience. For minimum standards of safety a country's nuclear force must meet three requirements. First, a part of the force must be able to survive an attack and launch one of its own. Second, survival of the force must not require early firing in response to what may be false alarms. Third, weapons must not be susceptible to accidental or unauthorized use. Nobody wants vulnerable, hair-trigger, accident-prone forces. Will new nuclear states find ways to hide their weapons, to deliver them, and to control them?

How hard is it to do that? Not very. Atomic weapons are fairly small and light. They are easy to hide. Early in the nuclear age, people worried about atomic bombs concealed in packing boxes and in the holds of ships to be exploded when the signal was given. When Winston Churchill was asked in the House of Commons whether any instrument was available for the sure detection of hidden bombs, he said, as I recall: Yes, there is, and it's called a screwdriver. By prying the lids off all of the boxes you find out what is in them. If the survival of nuclear weapons requires their dispersal and concealment, however, do not problems of command and control become harder to solve? We think so because we think in large numbers. Small nuclear powers will neither have nor need them. They might deploy, say, ten real weapons and ten dummies, while permitting other countries to infer that the numbers are larger. The adversary need only believe that some warheads may survive his attack and be visited on him. That belief should not be hard to create without making command and control unreliable. Foreigners think in terms of worst cases, as we do. How can one be sure of destroying unknown numbers of warheads at unknown locations? This question cannot be comfortably answered even if the country in question is merely suspected of having an embryonic nuclear force. Egypt, for example, does not know whether Israel has zero, ten, or twenty warheads. And if the number is zero and Egypt could be sure of that, she would still not know how many days or hours are required for assembling components that may be on hand. Nor are delivery systems difficult to devise or procure. Bombs can be driven in by truck from neighboring countries. Ports can be torpedoed by small boats lying offshore. Moreover, a thriving arms trade in ever more sophisticated military equipment provides ready access to what may be wanted, including planes and missiles suited to the delivery of atomic warheads.

Hiding nuclear weapons, delivering them, and keeping them under control are tasks for which the ingenuity of other states is adequate. Lesser nuclear states can pursue deterrent strategies effectively. To deter, they need not appear to be capable of destroying two-thirds of another country, although in some cases that may be easily done. Would a nuclear Egypt strike Israeli forces at the risk of two bombs surviving to fall on the Aswan Dam and on Cairo? And what would be left of Israel if Tel Aviv and Haifa were destroyed?

The ease of achieving deterrence, whether or not forces are balanced, reduces incentives for arms racing. Fears of arms racing rest on the assumption that new nuclear states subscribe to the myths we live by. Deterrence requires the ability to inflict unacceptable damage on the country that strikes first. Unacceptable damage to the Soviet Union was variously defined by Robert McNamara as requiring the ability to destroy one-fifth to one-fourth of its population and one-half to two-thirds of its industrial capacity. Our estimates of what is required for deterrence have been absurdly high. Worse still, even our grossly inflated "unacceptable damage" calculations do not place effective limits on the size of our forces. We slip from asking what is enough to deter into comparing our force levels with the Soviet Union's. Since a disarming, first-strike attack is not possible, force comparisons are irrelevant; and strategic arms races become pointless. Lesser nuclear states are likelier to realize this than we are. Because they are economically hard pressed, they are not likely to want to have more than enough.

Some people believe that if India had "small-yield plutonium weapons," it "would be unlikely to present a credible deterrent" against China's "megaton-range thermonuclear weapons." Imbalance in explosive power plus the difficulty of developing modern methods of delivering warheads may make an Indian nuclear deterrent "obsolete at commission" (Bray and Moodie 1977, p. 115). That is the way we think, but not the way they think. Why compare weapons with weapons when they are to be used not against each other but against cities that cannot counter them? China may need quite a bit to deter Russia, but India needs little to deter China. What issue between the latter could justify Chinese leadership in risking a city or two? To do so would be the surest way for a government to discredit itself. We know from experience, or rather the Japanese do, how devastating "small-yield plutonium weapons" of 14 and 20 kilotons may be. Those who foresee intense arms racing among new nuclear states fail to make the distinction between war-fighting and war-deterring capabilities. Forces designed for war-fighting have to be compared with each other. Forces designed for war-deterring need not be compared. The question is not whether one country has less than another but whether it can do "unacceptable damage" to another, with unacceptable damage sensibly defined. More is not better if less is enough.

The logic of deterrence, which the United States has developed but not followed, eliminates incentives for arms racing. The lesser nuclear states have aimed for a modest sufficiency. This may be so of China and is obviously so of all of the others. New nuclear powers are more likely to follow policies of "git and sit" than to vie with each other for a meaningless superiority. Because nuclear arms races among lesser powers are so unlikely, the interesting question is not whether such races will be run but whether the possession of nuclear weapons for deterrent and defensive uses will dampen the conventional arms races that now flourish.

Prevention and preemption are difficult games because the costs are so high if the games are not perfectly played. Inhibitions against using nuclear force for such attacks are strong, although one cannot say they are absolute. Some of the inhibitions lie in the impossibility of knowing for sure that a disarming strike will totally destroy an opposing force. Some of the inhibitions are simply human. Can country A find self-justification for a preventive or preemptive nuclear strike against B when B in acquiring nuclear weapons is imitating A? The leader of the country that strikes first courts condemnation by his own people, by the world's people, and by history. Awesome acts are hard to perform. Some of the inhibitions are political. As Bernard Brodie has tirelessly and wisely said, war has to find a political objective that appears commensurate with its cost. Clausewitz's central tenet remains valid in the nuclear age (e.g., Brodie 1978, p. 12).

Can offensive uses of nuclear weapons, whether for attack or for blackmail, find political objectives commensurate with the costs of achieving them? In 1953, Eisenhower and Dulles may have convinced Russia and China that they would widen the Korean War and intensify it by using nuclear weapons if a settlement were not reached. Dulles' speech of January 12, 1954 seemed to threaten massive retaliation in response to mildly bothersome actions by others. The successful siege of Dien Bien Phu in the spring of that year showed the limitations of such threats. Capabilities foster policies that employ them. But monstrous capabilities then foster monstrous policies, which when contemplated are seen to be too horrible to carry through. In Korea we had gone so far that the threat to go further seemed plausible. The blackmailer's nuclear threat is not a cheap way of working one's will. The threat is simply incredible unless a considerable investment has already been made. Imagine an Arab state threatening to strike Tel Aviv if the West Bank is not evacuated by the Israelis. No state can make the threat with credibility because no state can expect to execute the threat with impunity. Some have feared that nuclear weapons may be fired anonymously—by radical Arab states, for example, to attack an Israeli city in order to block a peace settlement (cf. Dunn 1977, p. 101). But the state exploding the warhead could not be certain of remaining unidentified. Even if a country's leaders persuade themselves that chances of retaliation are low, who would run the risk?

Although nuclear weapons are poor instruments for blackmail, might they not provide a cheap and decisive offensive force when used against a conventionally armed enemy? Some people think that South Korea and Iran want nuclear weapons for offensive use. Yet one cannot say why South Korea would use nuclear weapons against fellow Koreans while trying to reunite them nor how it could use nuclear weapons against the North, knowing that China and Russia might retaliate. And what goals would a conventionally strong Iran entertain that would tempt her to risk using nuclear weapons? Far from lowering the expected cost of aggression, a nuclear offense against a non-nuclear state raises the possible costs of aggression to uncalculable heights because the aggressor cannot be sure of the reaction of other nuclear powers.

Nuclear weapons do not make nuclear war a likely prospect, as history has so far shown. One can imagine new nuclear states using their weapons for defense—Taiwan against China, for example—and for deterrence, as ever, but hardly for political blackmail or military offense. . . .

CONCLUSION

What will the spread of nuclear weapons do to the world? To see the question in proper perspective requires emphasizing the stability of the strategic balance as it has developed between the United States and the Soviet Union. Stability at the strategic level means that the United States and the Soviet Union need not alter or enlarge their forces in ways that stimulate an arms race between them in response to the arsenals of new nuclear states. Stability at the top reduces the worry that nuclear wars between lesser states will spiral out of control and draw one or both of the great powers in. The distance in power between the United States and the Soviet Union, on the one hand, and lesser nuclear states, on the other hand, means that the former will retain the ability to shield some states and to moderate the behavior of others. Indeed, other states cannot contemplate using nuclear weapons without first considering the likely reactions of the United States and the Soviet Union.

I have found many reasons for believing that with more nuclear states the world's future can be rosy. I reach this somewhat unusual conclusion for five main reasons.

First, international politics is a self-help system, and in such systems the principal parties do most to determine their own fate, the fate of other parties, and the fate of the system. This will continue to be so, with the United States and the Soviet Union filling their customary roles. For the United States and the Soviet Union to achieve nuclear maturity and to show this by behaving sensibly is more important than preventing the spread of nuclear weapons.

Second, given the massive numbers of American and Russian warheads, and given the impossibility of one side destroying militarily significant numbers of the other side's missiles, the balance of terror is indestructible. What can lesser states do to disrupt the nuclear equilibrium if even the mighty efforts of the United States and the Soviet Union cannot shake it? The international equilibrium will endure.

Third, at the strategic level each of the great powers has to gauge the strength only of itself in relation to the other. They do not have to make guesses about the strengths of opposing coalitions, guesses that involve such imponderables as the coherence of diverse parties and their ability to concert their efforts. The two great powers obsessively focus their attention on each other because each is the only party that can do the other grievous harm. Estimating effective forces is thus made easier. Wars come most often by miscalculation, and miscalculation will not come from carelessness and inattention in a bipolar world as it may in a multipolar one.

Fourth, nuclear weaponry makes miscalculation difficult because it is hard not to be aware of how much damage a small number of warheads can do. When the active use of force threatens to bring great losses, wars become less likely. This proposition is widely accepted, but insufficiently emphasized. Nuclear weapons have reduced the chances of war between the United States and the Soviet Union and between the Soviet Union and China. One may expect them to have similar effects elsewhere. Where nuclear weapons threaten to make the cost of wars immense, who will dare to start them? Nuclear weapons make it possible to approach the deterrent ideal, or perhaps the defensive-deterrent ideal, which would be better still.

Fifth, new nuclear states will confront the possibilities and feel the constraints that present nuclear states have experienced. New nuclear states will be more mindful of dangers and more concerned for their safety than some of the old ones have been. We worry about a conventional war between minor nuclear states becoming a nuclear war as one side loses, but we plan to use nuclear weapons in Europe if that happens to us. The Soviet Union's military leaders openly plan to use nuclear weapons to win wars. Looking at the situation of weaker nuclear states and at the statements and plans of stronger nuclear states, one suspects that weak countries are less likely to use nuclear weapons first than are strong ones. I expect weak states to be more cautious than strong ones. As ever, the biggest international dangers come from the strongest states.

While nuclear weapons have spread, conventional weapons have proliferated. Conventional wars fought by countries that do not have nuclear weapons are likelier than conventional or nuclear wars fought by states that have nuclear weapons.

NOTE

1 *Editor's Note: In 1981, after this was written, Israel destroyed Iraq's Osirak nuclear reactor, and in 2003 the United States invaded Iraq to eliminate its presumed chemical and biological weapons and to prevent it from developing nuclear weapons.*

REFERENCES

Art, Robert J., and Kenneth N. Waltz (1971). "Technology, Strategy, and the Uses of Force." In Art and Waltz, eds., *The Use of Force*. Boston: Little, Brown.

Bray, Frank T.J., and Michael L. Moodie (May/June 1977). "Nuclear Politics in India." *Survival*. London: Institute of International Studies.

Brodie, Bernard (1966). *Escalation and the Nuclear Option*. Princeton: Princeton University Press.

——— (1973). *War and Politics*. New York: Macmillan.

———— (February 1978). "The Development of Nuclear Strategy." ACIS Working Paper No. 11. Los Angeles: Center for Arms Control and International Security, University of California.

Dunn, Lewis A. (March 1977). "Nuclear Proliferation and World Politics." In Joseph I. Coffey, ed., *Nuclear Proliferation: Prospects, Problems, and Proposals*. Philadelphia: The Annals of the American Academy of Political Science.

Herz, John H. (January 1950). "Idealist Internationalism and the Security Dilemma." *World Politics*, vol. 2.

Hoag, Malcolm W. (July 1961). "On Stability in Deterrent Races." *World Politics*, vol. 13.

Jervis, Robert (January 1978). "Cooperation under the Security Dilemma." *World Politics*, vol. 30.

Schelling, Thomas (1966). *Arms and Influence*. New Haven: Yale University Press.

Simmel, Georg (January 1974 [1904]). "The Sociology of Conflict, I." *American Journal of Sociology*, vol. 9.

Smoke, Richard (1977). *War: Controlling Escalation*. Cambridge: Harvard University Press.

Snyder, Glenn H. (1961). *Deterrence and Defense*. Princeton, Princeton University Press.

Van Evera, Stephen (1976). "The Effects of Nuclear Proliferation." Unpublished paper.

Weltman, John J. (May 4, 1978). "Nuclear Devolution and World Order." Unpublished paper.

Reading 7.4

Drones: Technology Serves Strategy

DANIEL BYMAN

Critics . . . claim that drones kill thousands of innocent civilians, alienate allied governments, anger foreign publics, illegally target Americans, and set a dangerous precedent that irresponsible governments will abuse. Some of these criticisms are valid; others, less so. In the end, drone strikes remain a necessary instrument of counterterrorism. The United States simply cannot tolerate terrorist safe havens in remote parts of Pakistan and elsewhere, and drones offer a comparatively low-risk way of targeting these areas while minimizing collateral damage.

NOBODY DOES IT BETTER

The Obama administration relies on drones for one simple reason: they work. According to data compiled by the New America Foundation, since Obama has been in the White House, U.S. drones have killed an estimated 3,300 al Qaeda, Taliban, and other jihadist operatives in Pakistan and Yemen. That

Source: Daniel Byman, "Why Drones Work," Foreign Affairs 92, no. 4 (July/August 2013).

number includes over 50 senior leaders of al Qaeda and the Taliban—top figures who are not easily replaced. In 2010, Osama bin Laden warned his chief aide, Atiyah Abd al-Rahman, who was later killed by a drone strike in the Waziristan region of Pakistan in 2011, that when experienced leaders are eliminated, the result is "the rise of lower leaders who are not as experienced as the former leaders" and who are prone to errors and miscalculations. And drones also hurt terrorist organizations when they eliminate operatives who are lower down on the food chain but who boast special skills: passport forgers, bomb makers, recruiters, and fundraisers.

Drones have also undercut terrorists' ability to communicate and to train new recruits. In order to avoid attracting drones, al Qaeda and Taliban operatives try to avoid using electronic devices or gathering in large numbers. A tip sheet found among jihadists in Mali advised militants to "maintain complete silence of all wireless contacts" and "avoid gathering in open areas." Leaders, however, cannot give orders when they are incommunicado, and training on a large scale is nearly impossible when a drone strike could wipe out an entire group of new recruits. Drones have turned al Qaeda's command and training structures into a liability, forcing the group to choose between having no leaders and risking dead leaders.

Critics of drone strikes often fail to take into account the fact that the alternatives are either too risky or unrealistic. To be sure, in an ideal world, militants would be captured alive, allowing authorities to question them and search their compounds for useful information. Raids, arrests, and interrogations can produce vital intelligence and can be less controversial than lethal operations. That is why they should be, and indeed already are, used in stable countries where the United States enjoys the support of the host government. But in war zones or unstable countries, such as Pakistan, Yemen, and Somalia, arresting militants is highly dangerous and, even if successful, often inefficient. In those three countries, the government exerts little or no control over remote areas, which means that it is highly dangerous to go after militants hiding out there. Worse yet, in Pakistan and Yemen, the governments have at times cooperated with militants. If the United States regularly sent in special operations forces to hunt down terrorists there, sympathetic officials could easily tip off the jihadists, likely leading to firefights, U.S. casualties, and possibly the deaths of the suspects and innocent civilians.

Of course, it was a Navy SEAL team and not a drone strike that finally got bin Laden, but in many cases in which the United States needs to capture or eliminate an enemy, raids are too risky and costly. And even if a raid results in a successful capture, it begets another problem: what to do with the detainee. Prosecuting detainees in a federal or military court is difficult because often the intelligence against terrorists is inadmissible or using it risks jeopardizing sources and methods. And given the fact that the United States is trying to close, rather than expand, the detention facility at Guantánamo Bay, Cuba, it has become much harder to justify holding suspects indefinitely. It has become more politically palatable for the United States to kill rather than detain suspected terrorists.

Furthermore, although a drone strike may violate the local state's sovereignty, it does so to a lesser degree than would putting U.S. boots on the ground or conducting a large-scale air campaign. And compared with a 500-pound bomb dropped from an F-16, the grenadelike warheads carried by most drones create smaller, more precise blast zones that decrease the risk of unexpected structural damage and casualties. Even more important, drones, unlike traditional airplanes, can loiter above a target for hours, waiting for the ideal moment to strike and thus reducing the odds that civilians will be caught in the kill zone.

Finally, using drones is also far less bloody than asking allies to hunt down terrorists on the United States' behalf. The Pakistani and Yemeni militaries, for example, are known to regularly torture and execute detainees, and they often indiscriminately bomb civilian areas or use scorched-earth tactics against militant groups.

Some critics of the drone program, such as Ben Emmerson, the UN's special rapporteur on the promotion and protection of human rights and fundamental freedoms while countering terrorism, have questioned the lethal approach, arguing for more focus on the factors that might contribute to extremism and terrorism, such as poverty, unemployment, and authoritarianism. Such a strategy is appealing in principle, but it is far from clear how Washington could execute it. Individuals join anti-American terrorist groups for many reasons, ranging from outrage over U.S. support for Israel to anger at their own government's cooperation with the United States. Some people simply join up because their neighbors are doing so. Slashing unemployment in Yemen, bringing democracy to Saudi Arabia, and building a functioning government in Somalia are laudable goals, but they are not politically or financially possible for the United States, and even if achieved, they still might not reduce the allure of jihad. . . .

THE NUMBERS GAME

Despite the obvious benefits of using drones and the problems associated with the alternatives, numerous critics argue that drones still have too many disadvantages. First among them is an unacceptably high level of civilian casualties. Admittedly, drones have killed innocents. But the real debate is over how many and whether alternative approaches are any better. The Bureau of Investigative Journalism reports that in 2011, U.S. drone strikes killed as many as 146 noncombatants, including as many as 9 children. Columbia Law School's Human Rights Clinic also cites high numbers of civilian deaths, as does the Pakistani organization Pakistan Body Count. Peter Bergen of the New America Foundation oversees a database of drone casualties culled from U.S. sources and international media reports. He estimates that between 150 and 500 civilians have been killed by drones during Obama's administration. U.S. officials, meanwhile, maintain that drone strikes have killed almost no civilians. In June 2011, John Brennan, then Obama's top counterterrorism adviser, even contended that U.S. drone strikes had killed no civilians in the previous year. But these claims are based on the fact that the U.S. government assumes that all military-age males in the blast area of a drone strike are combatants—unless it can determine after the fact that they were innocent (and such intelligence gathering is not a priority).

The United States has recently taken to launching "signature strikes," which target not specific individuals but instead groups engaged in suspicious activities. This approach makes it even more difficult to distinguish between combatants and civilians and verify body counts of each. Still, as one U.S. official told *The New York Times* last year, "Al Qaeda is an insular, paranoid organization—innocent neighbors don't hitchhike rides in the back of trucks headed for the border with guns and bombs." Of course, not everyone accepts this reasoning. Zeeshan-ul-hassan Usmani, who runs Pakistan Body Count, says that "neither [the United States] nor Pakistan releases any detailed information about the victims . . . so [although the United States] likes to call everybody Taliban, I call everybody civilians."

The truth is that all the public numbers are unreliable. Who constitutes a civilian is often unclear; when trying to kill the Pakistani Taliban leader Baitullah Mehsud, for example, the United States also killed his doctor. The doctor was not targeting U.S. or allied forces, but he was aiding a known terrorist leader. In addition, most strikes are carried out in such remote locations that it is nearly impossible for independent sources to verify who was killed. In Pakistan, for example, the overwhelming majority of drone killings occur in tribal areas that lie outside the government's control and are prohibitively dangerous for Westerners and independent local journalists to enter.

The Pakistani government and militant groups frequently doctor casualty numbers, often making reports from local Pakistani organizations, and the Western organizations that rely on them, unreliable. After a strike in Pakistan, militants often cordon off the area, remove their dead, and admit only local reporters sympathetic to their cause or decide on a body count themselves. The U.S. media often then draw on such faulty reporting to give the illusion of having used multiple sources. As a result, statistics on civilians killed by drones are often inflated. One of the few truly independent on-the-ground reporting efforts, conducted by the Associated Press last year, concluded that the strikes "are killing far fewer civilians than many in [Pakistan] are led to believe."

But even the most unfavorable estimates of drone casualties reveal that the ratio of civilian to militant deaths—about one to three, according to the Bureau of Investigative Journalism—is lower than it would be for other forms of strikes. Bombings by F-16s or Tomahawk cruise missile salvos, for example, pack a much more deadly payload. In December 2009, the United States fired Tomahawks at a suspected terrorist training camp in Yemen, and over 30 people were killed in the blast, most of them women and children. At the time, the Yemeni regime refused to allow the use of drones, but had this not been the case, a drone's real-time surveillance would probably have spotted the large number of women and children, and the attack would have been aborted. Even if the strike had gone forward for some reason, the drone's far smaller warhead would have killed fewer innocents. Civilian deaths are tragic and pose political problems. But the data show that drones are more discriminate than other types of force.

FOREIGN FRIENDS

It is also telling that drones have earned the backing, albeit secret, of foreign governments. In order to maintain popular support, politicians in Pakistan and Yemen routinely rail against the U.S. drone campaign. In reality, however, the governments of both countries have supported it. During the Bush and Obama administrations, Pakistan has even periodically hosted U.S. drone facilities and has been told about strikes in advance. Pervez Musharraf, president of Pakistan until 2008, was not worried about the drone program's negative publicity: "In Pakistan, things fall out of the sky all the time," he reportedly remarked. Yemen's former president, Ali Abdullah Saleh, also at times allowed drone strikes in his country and even covered for them by telling the public that they were conducted by the Yemeni air force. When the United States' involvement was leaked in 2002, however, relations between the two countries soured. Still, Saleh later let the drone program resume in Yemen, and his replacement, Abdu Rabbu Mansour Hadi, has publicly praised drones, saying that "they pinpoint the target and have zero margin of error, if you know what target you're aiming at."

As officials in both Pakistan and Yemen realize, U.S. drone strikes help their governments by targeting common enemies. A memo released by the antisecrecy website WikiLeaks revealed that Pakistan's army chief, Ashfaq Parvez Kayani, privately asked U.S. military leaders in 2008 for "continuous Predator coverage" over antigovernment militants, and the journalist Mark Mazzetti has reported that the United States has conducted "goodwill kills" against Pakistani militants who threatened Pakistan far more than the United States. Thus, in private, Pakistan supports the drone program. As then Prime Minister Yousaf Raza Gilani told Anne Patterson, then the U.S. ambassador to Pakistan, in 2008, "We'll protest [against the drone program] in the National Assembly and then ignore it."

Still, Pakistan is reluctant to make its approval public. First of all, the country's inability to fight terrorists on its own soil is a humiliation for Pakistan's politically powerful armed forces and intelligence service. In addition, although drones kill some of the government's enemies, they have also targeted pro-government groups that are hostile to the United States, such as the Haqqani network and the Taliban, which Pakistan has supported since its birth in the early 1990s. Even more important, the Pakistani public is vehemently opposed to U.S. drone strikes.

A 2012 poll found that 74 percent of Pakistanis viewed the United States as their enemy, likely in part because of the ongoing drone campaign. Similarly, in Yemen, as the scholar Gregory Johnsen has pointed out, drone strikes can win the enmity of entire tribes. This has led critics to argue that the drone program is shortsighted: that it kills today's enemies but creates tomorrow's in the process. . . .

FOLLOW THE LEADER

The fact remains that by using drones so much, Washington risks setting a troublesome precedent with regard to extrajudicial and extraterritorial killings. Zeke Johnson of Amnesty International contends that "when the U.S.

government violates international law, that sets a precedent and provides an excuse for the rest of the world to do the same." And it is alarming to think what leaders such as Syrian President Bashar al-Assad, who has used deadly force against peaceful pro-democracy demonstrators he has deemed terrorists, would do with drones of their own. Similarly, Iran could mockingly cite the U.S. precedent to justify sending drones after rebels in Syria. Even Brennan has conceded that the administration is "establishing precedents that other nations may follow."

Controlling the spread of drone technology will prove impossible; that horse left the barn years ago. Drones are highly capable weapons that are easy to produce, and so there is no chance that Washington can stop other militaries from acquiring and using them. Nearly 90 other countries already have surveillance drones in their arsenals, and China is producing several inexpensive models for export. Armed drones are more difficult to produce and deploy, but they, too, will likely spread rapidly. . . .

The U.S. government also needs to guard against another kind of danger: that the relative ease of using drones will make U.S. intervention abroad too common. The scholars Daniel Brunstetter and Megan Braun have argued that drones provide "a way to avoid deploying troops or conducting an intensive bombing campaign" and that this "may encourage countries to act on just cause with an ease that is potentially worrisome.". . . .

In places where terrorists are actively plotting against the United States, however, drones give Washington the ability to limit its military commitments abroad while keeping Americans safe. Afghanistan, for example, could again become a Taliban-run haven for terrorists after U.S. forces depart next year. Drones can greatly reduce the risk of this happening. Hovering in the skies above, they can keep Taliban leaders on the run and hinder al Qaeda's ability to plot another 9/11.

Reading 7.5

Drones: Tactics Undermine Strategy

AUDREY KURTH CRONIN

Although terrorism is a tactic, it can succeed only on the strategic level, by leveraging a shocking event for political gain. To be effective, counterterrorism must itself respond with a coherent strategy. The problem for Washington today is that its drone program has taken on a life of its own, to the point where tactics are driving strategy rather than the other way around.

Source: Audrey Kurth Cronin, "Why Drones Fail," Foreign Affairs 92, no. 4 (July/August 2013).

The main goals of U.S. counterterrorism are threefold: the strategic defeat of al Qaeda and groups affiliated with it, the containment of local conflicts so that they do not breed new enemies, and the preservation of the security of the American people. Drones do not serve all these goals. Although they can protect the American people from attacks in the short term, they are not helping to defeat al Qaeda, and they may be creating sworn enemies out of a sea of local insurgents. It would be a mistake to embrace killer drones as the centerpiece of U.S. counterterrorism.

AL QAEDA'S RESILIENCE

At least since 9/11, the United States has sought the end of al Qaeda—not just to set it back tactically, as drones have surely done, but also to defeat the group completely. Terrorist organizations can meet their demise in a variety of ways, and the killing of their leaders is certainly one of them. Abu Sayyaf, an Islamist separatist group in the Philippines, lost its political focus, split into factions, and became a petty criminal organization after the army killed its leaders in 2006 and 2007. In other cases, however, including those of the Shining Path in Peru and Action Directe in France, the humiliating arrest of a leader has been more effective. By capturing a terrorist leader, countries can avoid creating a martyr, win access to a storehouse of intelligence, and discredit a popular cause.

Despite the Obama administration's recent calls for limits on drone strikes, Washington is still using them to try to defeat al Qaeda by killing off its leadership. But the terrorist groups that have been destroyed through decapitation looked nothing like al Qaeda: they were hierarchically structured, characterized by a cult of personality, and less than ten years old, and they lacked a clear succession plan. Al Qaeda, by contrast, is a resilient, 25-year-old organization with a broad network of outposts. The group was never singularly dependent on Osama bin Laden's leadership, and it has proved adept at replacing dead operatives. . . .

Not only has al Qaeda's propaganda continued uninterrupted by the drone strikes; it has been significantly enhanced by them. As Sahab (The Clouds), the propaganda branch of al Qaeda, has been able to attract recruits and resources by broadcasting footage of drone strikes, portraying them as indiscriminate violence against Muslims. Al Qaeda uses the strikes that result in civilian deaths, and even those that don't, to frame Americans as immoral bullies who care less about ordinary people than al Qaeda does. And As Sahab regularly casts the leaders who are killed by drones as martyrs. It is easy enough to kill an individual terrorist with a drone strike, but the organization's Internet presence lives on.

A more effective way of defeating al Qaeda would be to publicly discredit it with a political strategy aimed at dividing its followers. Al Qaeda and its various affiliates do not together make up a strong, unified organization. Different factions within the movement disagree about both long-term objectives and short-term tactics, including whether it is acceptable to carry out suicide attacks or kill other Muslims. And it is in Muslim-majority countries where jihadist violence has taken its worst toll. Around 85 percent of those killed by al Qaeda's attacks have been Muslims, a fact that breeds revulsion among its potential followers. The United States should be capitalizing on this backlash. In reality, there is no equivalence between al Qaeda's violence and U.S. drone strikes—under the Obama administration, drones have avoided civilians about 86 percent of the time, whereas al Qaeda purposefully targets them. But the foolish secrecy of Washington's drone program lets critics allege that the strikes are deadlier and less discriminating than they really are. Whatever the truth is, the United States is losing the war of perceptions, a key part of any counterterrorism campaign. Since 2010, moreover, U.S. drone strikes have progressed well beyond decapitation, now targeting al Qaeda leaders and followers alike, as well as a range of Taliban members and Yemeni insurgents. With its so-called signature strikes, Washington often goes after people whose identity it does not know but who appear to be behaving like militants in insurgent-controlled areas. The strikes end up killing enemies of the Pakistani, Somali, and Yemeni militaries who may not threaten the United States at all. Worse, because the targets of such strikes are so loosely defined, it seems inevitable that they will kill some civilians. The June 2011 claim by John Brennan, President Barack Obama's top counterterrorism adviser at the time, that there had not been a single collateral death from drone attacks in the previous year strained credulity—and badly undermined U.S. credibility. The drone campaign has morphed, in effect, into remote-control repression: the direct application of brute force by a state, rather than an attempt to deal a pivotal blow to a movement. Repression wiped out terrorist groups in Argentina, Brazil, Peru, and tsarist Russia, but in each case, it sharply eroded the government's legitimacy. Repression is costly, not just to the victims, and difficult for democracies to sustain over time. It works best in places where group members can be easily separated from the general population, which is not the case for most targets of U.S. drone strikes. Military repression also often results in violence spreading to neighboring countries or regions, which partially explains the expanding al Qaeda footprint in the Middle East and North Africa, not to mention the Caucasus.

KEEPING LOCAL CONFLICTS LOCAL

Short of defeating al Qaeda altogether, a top strategic objective of U.S. counterterrorism should be to prevent fighters in local conflicts abroad from aligning with the movement and targeting the United States and its allies. Military strategists refer to this goal as "the conservation of enemies," the attempt to keep the number of adversaries to a minimum. Violent jihadism existed long before 9/11 and will endure long after the U.S. war on terrorism finally ends. The best way for the United States to prevent future acts of international terrorism on its soil is to make sure that local insurgencies remain local, to shore up its allies' capacities, and to use short-term interventions such as drones rarely, selectively, transparently, and only against those who can realistically target the United States. The problem is that the United States can conceivably justify an attack on any individual or group with some plausible link to al Qaeda. Washington would like to disrupt any potentially powerful militant network, but it risks turning relatively harmless local jihadist groups into stronger organizations with eager new recruits. If al Qaeda is indeed becoming a vast collective of local and regional insurgents, the United States should let those directly involved in the conflicts determine the outcome, keep itself out, provide resources only to offset funds provided to radical factions, and concentrate on protecting the homeland. Following 9/11, the U.S. war on terrorism was framed in the congressional authorization to use force as a response to "those nations, organizations, or persons" responsible for the attacks. The name "al Qaeda," which does not appear in the authorization, has since become an ill-defined shorthand, loosely employed by terrorist leaders, counterterrorism officials, and Western pundits alike to describe a shifting movement. The vagueness of the U.S. terminology at the time was partly deliberate: the authorization was worded to sidestep the long-standing problem of terrorist groups' changing their names to evade U.S. sanctions. But Washington now finds itself in a permanent battle with an amorphous and geographically dispersed foe, one with an increasingly marginal connection to the original 9/11 plotters. In this endless contest, the United States risks multiplying its enemies and heightening their incentives to attack the country. . . .

Other threats to the U.S. homeland have actually been sparked by outrage over the drone campaign. Faisal Shahzad, a naturalized U.S. citizen, tried to bomb Times Square in May 2010 by loading a car with explosives. A married financial analyst, Shahzad was an unlikely terrorist. When he pleaded guilty, however, he cited his anger about U.S. policies toward Muslim countries, especially drone strikes in his native Pakistan.

Indeed, the situation in Pakistan demonstrates that drone attacks exact a clear price in growing animus toward the United States. According to the Pew Global Attitudes Project, only 17 percent of Pakistani respondents to a 2012 poll approved of American drone strikes against the leaders of extremist groups, even if they were jointly conducted with the government of Pakistan. Pakistanis aren't the only disapproving ones: the vast majority of people polled internationally in 2012 indicated strong opposition to the U.S. drone campaign. The opposition was strongest in Muslim-majority countries, including traditional U.S. allies, such as Turkey (81 percent against), Jordan (85 percent against), and Egypt (89 percent against).

Europeans are almost as unhappy: of those polled in a 2012 Pew survey, 51 percent of Poles, 59 percent of Germans, 63 percent of French, 76 percent of Spanish, and a full 90 percent of Greeks noted their disapproval of U.S. drone strikes. The only publics that even approach the positive attitudes of the United States—where 70 percent of respondents to a recent New York Times poll approved of drones and 20 percent disapproved—are in India and the United Kingdom, where public opinion is more or less evenly divided. Washington insiders commonly contend that these popular attitudes don't matter, since government officials in all these countries privately envy American capabilities. But no counterterrorism strategy can succeed over time without public support.

That is because a crucial element in the success of U.S. counterterrorism has been close collaboration with allies on issues of terrorist financing, the extradition of terrorist suspects, and, most important, the sharing of vital intelligence. Obama ran for office in 2008 on the promise that he would restore the United States' reputation abroad. But his administration's unilateralism and lack of transparency on targeted killings are undermining the connections that were painstakingly built over the past decade, particularly with Pakistan and Yemen. This decreases the likelihood that allies will cooperate with Washington and increases the chances of terrorist attacks against Americans.

Of course, if drones actually stop another major attack along the lines of 9/11, they might be worth all the international opprobrium. But for the moment, the only sure thing Washington is doing is driving down international support for the United States and alienating local populations. All this in pursuit of preventing what is almost impossible to stop: a small cell of determined jihadists trying to carry out a minor attack on U.S. soil. That much was made clear by the tragic Boston Marathon bombings in April.

The long-term effect of drone strikes may be that the al Qaeda threat continues to metastasize. An alphabet soup of groups with long-standing local grievances now claim some connection to al Qaeda, including al Qaeda in the Arabian Peninsula, al Qaeda in the Islamic Maghreb, al Qaeda in Iraq, al Shabab (in Somalia), and Boko Haram (in Nigeria). This diversification should come as no surprise. The spread of terrorist groups has historically resulted from campaigns of decapitation and repression. Russia's assassinations of Chechen leaders between 2002 and 2006, for example, changed the conflict in Chechnya from a separatist insurgency to a broader radical movement in the Caucasus. The Russians killed virtually every major Chechen leader, pummeled Grozny to rubble, and brought Chechnya firmly under Russian control. In that sense, the campaign worked. But violence spread to the nearby regions of Dagestan, Ingushetia, and North Ossetia. Those who argue that the United States should stay the course with drones tend to be the same people who warn that the al Qaeda threat is spreading throughout the Middle East and North Africa. They need to consider whether drone strikes are contributing to this dynamic.

For the moment, there is no conclusive evidence that can prove whether drone strikes create more enemies than they kill. Some academics, including the Pakistan scholar C. Christine Fair and Christopher Swift, who has studied Yemen, argue that no widespread blowback against the United States can yet be detected. They argue that many locals grudgingly support drones and recognize their utility in beating back al Qaeda. Others, however, including the Yemen scholar Gregory Johnsen, warn of a simmering resentment that is driving recruits to al Qaeda. Much of the evidence is highly contested, and the sample sizes used tend to be small and biased toward local officials and educated professionals, who are the easiest to interview but the least likely to become terrorists. In short, the picture is mixed: drones are killing operatives who aspire to attack the United States today or tomorrow. But they are also increasing the likelihood of attacks over the long term, by embittering locals and cultivating a desire for vengeance. . . .

Drones are undermining U.S. strategic goals as much as they are advancing them. For starters, devoting a large percentage of U.S. military and intelligence resources to the drone campaign carries an opportunity cost. The U.S. Air Force trained 350 drone pilots in 2011, compared with only 250 conventional fighter and bomber pilots trained that year. There are 16 drone operating and training sites across the United States, and a 17th is being planned. There are also 12 U.S. drone bases stationed abroad, often in politically sensitive areas. In an era of austerity, spending more time and money on drones means spending less on other capabilities—and drones are not well suited for certain emerging threats.

Very easy to shoot down, drones require clear airspace in which to operate and would be nearly useless against enemies such as Iran or North Korea. They also rely on cyber-connections that are increasingly vulnerable. Take into account their high crash rates and extensive maintenance requirements, and drones start to look not much more cost effective than conventional aircraft.

Another main problem with Washington's overreliance on drones is that it destroys valuable evidence that could make U.S. counterterrorism smarter and more effective. Whenever the United States kills a suspected terrorist, it loses the chance to find out what he was planning, how, and with whom—or whether he was even a terrorist to begin with. Drone attacks eliminate the possibility of arresting and interrogating those whom they target, precluding one of the most effective means of undermining a terrorist group.

It is worth noting that the most dramatic recent decapitation of a terrorist organization—the killing of bin Laden—was performed by humans, not drones. As a result, the most important outcome of the operation was not the death of bin Laden himself but the treasure trove of intelligence it yielded. Drones do not capture hard drives, organizational charts, strategic plans, or secret correspondence, and their tactical effectiveness is entirely dependent on the caliber of human intelligence on the ground. And if the unpopularity of drones makes it harder to persuade locals to work with U.S. intelligence services, then Washington will have less access to the kind of intelligence it needs for effective targeting. Yes, killing would-be terrorists saves American lives. But so does interrogating them, and drone strikes make that impossible.

Finally, the drone campaign presents a fundamental challenge to U.S. national security law, as evidenced by the controversial killing of four American citizens in attacks in Yemen and Pakistan. The president's authority to protect the United States does not supersede an individual's constitutional protections. All American citizens have a right to due process, and it is particularly worrisome that a secret review of evidence by the U.S. Department of Justice has been deemed adequate to the purpose. The president has gotten personally involved in putting together kill lists that can include Americans—a situation that is not only legally dubious but also strategically unwise.

PASS THE REMOTE

The sometimes contradictory demands of the American people—perfect security at home without burdensome military engagements abroad—have fueled the technology-driven, tactical approach of drone warfare. But it is never wise to let either gadgets or fear determine strategy.

There is nothing inherently wrong with replacing human pilots with remote-control operators or substituting highly selective aircraft for stand-off missiles (which are launched from a great distance) and unguided bombs. Fewer innocent civilians may be killed as a result. The problem is that the guidelines for how Washington uses drones have fallen well behind the ease with which the United States relies on them, allowing short-term advantages to overshadow long-term risks.

Drone strikes must be legally justified, transparent, and rare. Washington needs to better establish and follow a publicly explained legal and moral framework for the use of drones, making sure that they are part of a long-term political strategy that undermines the enemies of the United States. With the boundaries for drone strikes in Pakistan, Somalia, and Yemen still unclear, the United States risks encouraging competitors such as China, Iran, and Russia to label their own enemies as terrorists and go after them across borders. If that happens—if counterterrorism by drone strikes ends up leading to globally destabilizing interstate wars—then al Qaeda will be the least of the United States' worries.

Terrorism, Revolution, and Unconventional Warfare

Since the Cold War there has been plenty of political violence in the world, but most of it has been irregular revolutionary activity rather than conventional warfare. Terrorism is particularly prominent since it has occurred in most regions of the globe, and especially because it has a powerful psychological impact beyond its material effects.[1] Most dramatic in that sense was the emergence of Islamic State, which is most significant in the way it escalated from hit-and-run terrorism to enduring control of territory. A step up in military action from simple terrorism is guerrilla warfare and its opposite, counterinsurgency, which have been equally prevalent, from Iraq and Afghanistan, to Chechnya, Congo, Colombia, and elsewhere. The potential for regular conventional warfare or use of weapons of mass destruction always remains the most dangerous threats to peace, but in recent times unconventional warfare has been the most common.

When Al Qaeda hijackers flew airliners into the World Trade Center and Pentagon on September 11, 2001, people were stunned by an action that seemed entirely unprecedented. Many believed that everything in the realm of security policy had changed and that we had entered a new era for which the conflicts of history offered few lessons. For the most part, this common perception was untrue.

The specific tactic that the perpetrators of September 11th chose—using hijacked aircraft as bombers on a kamikaze mission—was indeed novel and unexpected. The rest of what happened on that day, however, was more or less anticipated by professional observers of terrorism. For several years experts had warned of the danger of catastrophic attack (although they tended to focus on the threat of terrorist use of biological or chemical weapons); such warnings simply did not register forcefully on normal people when they heard them.

Nor were the motives and logic of the Al Qaeda attackers as unusual or irrational as many assumed.[2] In many respects they reflected the strategic outlook of terrorists at other times and places in history, which in turn overlap the logic of unconventional or "asymmetric" warfare in general. Although some terrorists are clearly more fanatical than most political movements and make demands that seem impossible to their targets, few aim at mass murder for its own sake. (Islamic State may be one of those few.) Data on the social origins and motivations of jihadist terrorists also dispels myths that they are mentally ill, driven by the desperation of poverty, or otherwise socially or psychologically bizarre. The choice to use terror can be strategically quite rational.[3] As Martha Crenshaw argues in the essay that follows, terrorists use the tactics they do for instrumental reasons. They see terror as a means to an end—the achievement of a better political and social order on earth.[4] Osama bin Ladin's own words in this section show this clearly in a manner that surprises those who assumed his motives to be nihilistic. None of this, however, detracts from the salience of religious motives that animate so much of contemporary terrorism by radical Islamist groups, as they have often in history for deviant sects in many different religions.[5]

Guerrilla warfare is a form of unconventional war that has seemed, to many in the West, more sensible and legitimate than terrorism. This was not true until the mid-twentieth century, however, when anti-fascist resistance movements in occupied Europe and Asia cast a more positive light on the practice of irregular combat in the eyes of sympathetic Western liberals. For much of history, however, guerrilla warfare was lumped with terrorism as an illegal and unacceptable means of waging war.[6] Terrorist tactics, such as assassination, coercive threats against civilians, and combat out of uniform, have often merged into guerrilla war. Counterinsurgency forces in many different cases refer to insurgents as terrorists.

In fact, in terms of a neutral analysis of tactics, shorn of moral context, unconventional warfare forms a rough continuum from terrorism at the low end, when antigovernment forces (or those resisting a victorious foreign invader) lack any military capability, through small-scale episodic ambushes and other quasi-conventional forms of partisan warfare in the middle range, to increasingly large-scale conventional attacks at the high end, as the anti-regime movement gathers steam and becomes an effective challenger. Mao Tse-tung (Mao Ze-dong) emphasizes this transitional nature of guerrilla war, and the interdependence of political and military success in moving from one stage to another, in the selections from his work included here.[7]

The hallmark of both terrorism and guerrilla warfare is the effective wielding of force by a weak contender against an opponent that is far superior in conventional military power. In the essay that follows, T. E. Lawrence ("Lawrence of Arabia") explores the ways in which guerrilla forces differ in character and operation from regular military forces, and how they can exploit geography and demography to hamstring an occupying power. Although their political purposes may differ profoundly, the strategic incentive to find ways to use force despite relative weakness is the same for revolutionary or resistance movements within a given state or for transnational or subnational terrorist groups. Neither sort of group can compete with the resources of a government within a state, or of a more powerful invader who has defeated the home government, until the accelerating success of initial attacks mobilizes enough support to reach a higher level of power.

Lawrence and Mao's insights came from their experience in promoting irregular resistance to invaders—Turks and Japanese. In the second half of the twentieth century, however, guerrilla warfare was most often undertaken by ideological movements aiming to overthrow homegrown governments. This is the context that highlights the relevance of Huntington's discussion of the differences between dualistic intergovernmental war and tripartite antigovernmental war. His emphasis on the importance of the "target group" in unconventional warfare—the uncommitted segment of the population whose loyalty will tilt the balance in the political contest—carries over to today's global war on terror. If the Muslim world becomes yet more polarized, forcing choices between extremists such as Al Qaeda or Islamic State and those groups' conservative Islamic and liberal Western opponents, which way will Muslims in the middle tilt?

International peacekeeping operations that burgeoned in the 1990s embroiled many members of the United Nations in internal, unconventional wars. After September 11th, the United States in particular became entangled in prolonged irregular conflicts in Iraq and Afghanistan. These challenges led to an earnest revival of ideas about strategy for counterinsurgency. Three items in this section outline prominent theories of counterinsurgency, as well as criticism of the feasibility or strategic priority of the mission. The excerpt from David Galula's classic work, originally published in 1964, reflects the Cold War preoccupation with Communist insurgencies, but his logic still applies in many respects to contemporary rebellions.[8] The piece by Eliot Cohen et al. is a distillation of some of the main points in the U.S. military's official revision of doctrine on the subject, which became prominent in U.S. strategy after several years of shocks and stumbling in Iraq and Afghanistan.[9]

The rediscovery and refinement of counterinsurgency theory dominated official American thinking after 2004, but not all strategists considered the theory wise, practical, or deserving of the priority it got under the pressure of events. Colonel Gian P. Gentile's essay attacks the new American emphasis on counterinsurgency. Dismal results of counterinsurgency efforts in Iraq and Afghanistan prompted other analytical counterattacks on the idea.[10]

As the rest of this volume indicates, the vast bulk of thinking on war and peace has been about force and its alternatives in relations among states, and whether norms and institutions or specific distributions of power may hold impulses to war in check. Realists focus on material power, liberals on the moral power of particular ideological values, and culturalists or constructivists on the role of identity. All of these factors interact in the contests within states, or between Western societies and transnational opponents of globalization, that today fuel terrorism and irregular warfare. If any phenomenon reflects the inadequacy of any monocausal explanation of conflict, it is unconventional warfare in the forms discussed in this section.

—RKB

NOTES

1 In his book *Overblown: How Politicians and the Terrorism Industry Inflate National Security Threats, and Why We Believe Them* (New York: Free Press, 2006), John Mueller makes a strong argument that risks from terrorism are statistically tiny compared to other dangers, that public preoccupation with terrorism is irrational, and that government has grossly overreacted to the threat. He does not take sufficient account, however, of the link between the extent of counterterrorism efforts and the low incidence of successful terror attacks. See Richard K. Betts, "Maybe I'll Stop Driving," *Terrorism and Political Violence* 17, no. 4 (2005).

2 Trends in terrorism did change somewhat after the Cold War, as groups with leftist ideological agendas faded and those with religious, millenarian, or diffuse anti-Western motives grew in prominence. By some accountings the number of terrorist incidents declined while their average lethality increased. See Audrey Kurth Cronin, "Behind the Curve: Globalization and International Terrorism," *International Security* 27, no. 3 (Winter 2002/03); Steven Simon and Daniel Benjamin, *The Age of Sacred Terror: Radical Islam's War Against America* (New York: Random House, 2003); Michael Mousseau, "Market Civilization and Its Clash With Terror," *International Security* 27, no. 3 (Winter 2002/03); Martha Crenshaw, ed., *Terrorism in Context* (University Park: Pennsylvania State University Press, 1995); Rohan Gunaratna, *Inside Al Qaeda: Global Network of Terror* (New York: Columbia University Press, 2002); James F. Hoge, Jr. and Gideon Rose, eds., *How Did This Happen: Terrorism and the New War* (New York: Public Affairs, 2001). In general, see Bruce Hoffman, *Inside Terrorism*, Revised edition (New York: Columbia University Press, 2006).

3 For example, Mark Sageman, *Leaderless Jihad: Terror Networks in the Twenty-First Century* (Philadelphia: University of Pennsylvania Press, 2008) and Alan B. Krueger, *What Makes a Terrorist: Economics and the Roots of Terrorism* (Princeton, N.J.: Princeton University Press, 2007).

4 There is a widely shared alternative view, however, that emphasizes the unconscious psychic imperatives driving terrorists. See Jerrold M. Post, "Terrorist Psycho-Logic: Terrorist Behavior as a Product of Psychological Forces," in Walter Reich, ed., *Origins of Terrorism: Psychologies, Ideologies, Theologies, States of Mind* (Washington, D.C.: Woodrow Wilson Center Press, 1998). Evidence for this view of terrorists as psychologically disturbed comes more from examination of leftist terror groups in the Cold War than from the radical Islamist groups most prominent in recent times. See also the discussion of "solipsistic" terrorism in Ian S. Lustick, "Terrorism in the Arab-Israeli Conflict," in Crenshaw, ed., *Terrorism in Context*.

5 Mark Juergensmeyer, *Terror in the Mind of God: The Global Rise of Religious Violence* (Berkeley: University of California Press, 2000); David C. Rapoport, "Fear and Trembling: Terrorism in Three Religious Traditions," *American Political Science Review* 78, no. 3 (September 1984).

6 J. B. Firth, "The Guerrilla in History," *Fortnightly Review* (W. L. Courtney, ed.) 70, New Series (July–December 1901).

7 See the more detailed argument in Mao Tse-tung, *On the Protracted War* (Peking: Foreign Languages Press, 1954).

8 Examples of other old diagnoses and prescriptions that reflect some timeless problems and insights include Colonel C. E. Callwell, *Small Wars: Their Principles and Practice*, Third edition (London: HMSO, 1906); *Small Wars Manual, United States Marine Corps, 1940* (Manhattan, Kans.: Sunflower University Press, n.d.); and Sir Robert Thompson, *Defeating Communist Insurgency* (New York: Praeger, 1966). A more recent examination of British and American approaches is John A. Nagl, *Learning to Eat Soup With a Knife: Counterinsurgency Lessons From Malaya and Vietnam* (Chicago: University of Chicago Press, 2005).

9 Reprinted as *The U.S Army/Marine Corps Counterinsurgency Field Manual* (Chicago: University of Chicago Press, 2007).

10 See the book-length version of Gentile's critique: *Wrong Turn: America's Deadly Embrace of CounterInsurgency* (New York: New Press, 2013) and especially Douglas Porch, *Counterinsurgency: Exposing the Myths of the New Way of War* (New York: Cambridge University Press, 2013).

Reading 8.1

The Strategic Logic of Terrorism

MARTHA CRENSHAW

This chapter examines the ways in which terrorism can be understood as an expression of political strategy. It attempts to show that terrorism may follow logical processes that can be discovered and explained. For the purpose of presenting this source of terrorist behavior, rather than the psychological one, it interprets the resort to violence as a willful choice made by an organization for political and strategic reasons, rather than as the unintended outcome of psychological or social factors.[1]

In the terms of this analytical approach, terrorism is assumed to display a collective rationality. A radical political organization is seen as the central actor in the terrorist drama. The group possesses collective preferences or values and selects terrorism as a course of action from a range of perceived alternatives. Efficacy is the primary standard by which terrorism is compared with other methods of achieving political goals. Reasonably regularized decision-making procedures are employed to make an intentional choice, in conscious anticipation of the consequences of various courses of action or inaction. Organizations arrive at collective judgments about the relative effectiveness of different strategies of opposition on the basis of observation and experience, as much as on the basis of abstract strategic conceptions derived from ideological assumptions. This approach thus allows for the incorporation of theories of social learning.

Conventional rational-choice theories of individual participation in rebellion, extended to include terrorist activities, have usually been considered inappropriate because of the "free rider" problem. That is, the benefits of a successful terrorist campaign would presumably be shared by all individual supporters of the group's goals, regardless of the extent of their active participation. In this case, why should a rational person become a terrorist, given the high costs associated with violent resistance and the expectation that everyone who supports the cause will benefit, whether he or she participates or not? One answer is that the benefits of participation are psychological.

A different answer, however, supports a strategic analysis. On the basis of surveys conducted in New York and West Germany, political scientists suggest that individuals can be *collectively* rational.[2] People realize that their participation is important because group size and cohesion matter. They are sensitive

Source: Reich, Walter, ed. new foreword by Walter Laqueur. Origins of Terrorism: Psychologies, Ideologies, Theologies, States of Mind. *pp. 7–24.* © *1998 Woodrow Wilson Center Press. Reprinted with permission of Johns Hopkins University Press.*

to the implications of free-riding and perceive their personal influence on the provision of public goods to be high. The authors argue that "average citizens may adopt a collectivist conception of rationality because they recognize that what is individually rational is collectively irrational."[3] Selective incentives are deemed largely irrelevant.

One of the advantages of approaching terrorism as a collectively rational strategic choice is that it permits the construction of a standard from which deviations can be measured. For example, the central question about the rationality of some terrorist organizations, such as the West German groups of the 1970s or the Weather Underground in the United States, is whether or not they had a sufficient grasp of reality—some approximation, to whatever degree imperfect—to calculate the likely consequences of the courses of action they chose. Perfect knowledge of available alternatives and the consequences of each is not possible, and miscalculations are inevitable. The Popular Front for the Liberation of Palestine (PFLP), for example, planned the hijacking of a TWA flight from Rome in August 1969 to coincide with a scheduled address by President Nixon to a meeting of the Zionist Organization of America, but he sent a letter instead.[4]

Yet not all errors of decision are miscalculations. There are varied degrees of limited rationality. Are some organizations so low on the scale of rationality as to be in a different category from more strategically minded groups? To what degree is strategic reasoning modified by psychological and other constraints? The strategic choice framework provides criteria on which to base these distinctions. It also leads one to ask what conditions promote or discourage rationality in violent underground organizations.

The use of this theoretical approach is also advantageous in that it suggests important questions about the preferences or goals of terrorist organizations. For example, is the decision to seize hostages in order to bargain with governments dictated by strategic considerations or by other, less instrumental motives?

The strategic choice approach is also a useful interpretation of reality. Since the French Revolution, a strategy of terrorism has gradually evolved as a means of bringing about political change opposed by established governments. Analysis of the historical development of terrorism reveals similarities in calculation of ends and means. The strategy has changed over time to adapt to new circumstances that offer different possibilities for dissident action—for example, hostage taking. Yet terrorist activity considered in its entirety shows a fundamental unity of purpose and conception. Although this analysis remains largely on an abstract level, the historical evolution of the strategy of terrorism can be sketched in its terms.[5]

A last argument in support of this approach takes the form of a warning. The wide range of terrorist activity cannot be dismissed as "irrational" and thus pathological, unreasonable, or inexplicable. The resort to terrorism need not be an aberration. It may be a reasonable and calculated response to circumstances. To say that the reasoning that leads to the choice of terrorism may be logical is not an argument about moral justifiability. It does suggest, however, that the belief that terrorism is expedient is one means by which moral inhibitions are overcome. . . .

THE CONDITIONS FOR TERRORISM

The central problem is to determine when extremist organizations find terrorism useful. Extremists seek either a radical change in the status quo, which would confer a new advantage, or the defense of privileges they perceive to be threatened. Their dissatisfaction with the policies of the government is extreme, and their demands usually involve the displacement of existing political elites.[6] Terrorism is not the only method of working toward radical goals, and thus it must be compared to the alternative strategies available to dissidents. Why is terrorism attractive to some opponents of the state, but unattractive to others?

The practitioners of terrorism often claim that they had no choice but terrorism, and it is indeed true that terrorism often follows the failure of other methods. In nineteenth-century Russia, for example, the failure of nonviolent movements contributed to the rise of terrorism. In Ireland, terrorism followed the failure of Parnell's constitutionalism. In the Palestinian-Israeli struggle, terrorism followed the failure of Arab efforts at conventional warfare against Israel. In general, the "nonstate" or "substate" users of terrorism—that is, groups in opposition to the government, as opposed to government itself—are constrained in their options by the lack of active mass support and by the superior power arrayed against them (an imbalance that has grown with the development of the modern centralized and bureaucratic nation-state). But these constraints have not prevented oppositions from considering and rejecting methods other than terrorism. Perhaps because groups are slow to recognize the extent of the limits to action, terrorism is often the last in a sequence of choices. It represents the outcome of a learning process. Experience in opposition provides radicals with information about the potential consequences of their choices. Terrorism is likely to be a reasonably informed choice among available alternatives, some tried unsuccessfully. Terrorists also learn from the experiences of others, usually communicated to them via the news media. Hence the existence of patterns of contagion in terrorist incidents.[7]

Thus the existence of extremism or rebellious potential is necessary to the resort to terrorism but does not in itself explain it, because many revolutionary and nationalist organizations have explicitly disavowed terrorism. The Russian Marxists argued for years against the use of terrorism.[8] Generally, small organizations resort to violence to compensate for what they lack in numbers.[9] The imbalance between the resources terrorists are able to mobilize and the power of the incumbent regime is a decisive consideration in their decision making.

More important than the observation that terrorism is the weapon of the weak, who lack numbers or conventional military power, is the explanation for weakness. Particularly, why does an organization lack the potential to attract enough followers to change government policy or overthrow it?

One possibility is that the majority of the population does not share the ideological views of the resisters, who occupy a political position so extreme that their appeal is inherently limited. This incompatibility of preferences may be purely political, concerning, for example, whether or not one prefers socialism to capitalism. The majority of West Germans found the Red Army Faction's promises for the future not only excessively vague but distasteful. Nor did most Italians support aims of the neofascist groups that initiated the "strategy of tension" in 1969. Other extremist groups, such as the *Euzkadi ta Akatasuna* (ETA) in Spain or the Provisional Irish Republican Army (PIRA) in Northern Ireland, may appeal exclusively to ethnic, religious, or other minorities. In such cases, a potential constituency of like-minded and dedicated individuals exists, but its boundaries are fixed and limited. Despite the intensity of the preferences of a minority, its numbers will never be sufficient for success.

A second explanation for the weakness of the type of organization likely to turn to terrorism lies in a failure to mobilize support. Its members may be unwilling or unable to expend the time and effort required for mass organizational work. Activists may not possess the requisite skills or patience, or may not expect returns commensurate with their endeavors. No matter how acute or widespread popular dissatisfaction may be, the masses do not rise spontaneously; mobilization is required.[10] The organization's leaders, recognizing the advantages of numbers, may combine mass organization with conspiratorial activities. But resources are limited and organizational work is difficult and slow even under favorable circumstances. Moreover, rewards are not immediate. These difficulties are compounded in an authoritarian state, where the organization of independent opposition is sure to incur high costs. Combining violent provocation with nonviolent organizing efforts may only work to the detriment of the latter.

For example, the debate over whether to use an exclusively violent underground strategy that is isolated from the masses (as terrorism inevitably is) or to work with the people in propaganda and organizational efforts divided the Italian left-wing groups, with the Red Brigades choosing the clandestine path and Prima Linea preferring to maintain contact with the wider protest movement. In prerevolutionary Russia the Socialist-Revolutionary party combined the activities of a legal political party with the terrorist campaign of the secret Combat Organization. The ira has a legal counterpart in Sinn Fein.

A third reason for the weakness of dissident organizations is specific to repressive states. It is important to remember that terrorism is by no means restricted to liberal democracies, although some authors refuse to define resistance to authoritarianism as terrorism.[11] People may not support a resistance organization because they are afraid of negative sanctions from the regime or because censorship of the press prevents them from learning of the possibility of rebellion. In this situation a radical organization may believe that supporters exist but cannot reveal themselves. The depth of this latent support cannot be measured or activists mobilized until the state is overthrown.

Such conditions are frustrating, because the likelihood of popular dissatisfaction grows as the likelihood of its active expression is diminished.

Frustration may also encourage unrealistic expectations among the regime's challengers, who are not able to test their popularity. Rational expectations may be undermined by fantastic assumptions about the role of the masses. Yet such fantasies can also prevail among radical undergrounds in Western democracies. The misperception of conditions can lead to unrealistic expectations.

In addition to small numbers, time constraints contribute to the decision to use terrorism. Terrorists are impatient for action. This impatience may, of course, be due to external factors, such as psychological or organizational pressures. The personalities of leaders, demands from followers, or competition from rivals often constitute impediments to strategic thinking. But it is not necessary to explain the felt urgency of some radical organizations by citing reasons external to an instrumental framework. Impatience and eagerness for action can be rooted in calculations of ends and means. For example, the organization may perceive an immediate opportunity to compensate for its inferiority vis-à-vis the government. A change in the structure of the situation may temporarily alter the balance of resources available to the two sides, thus changing the ratio of strength between government and challenger.

Such a change in the radical organization's outlook—the combination of optimism and urgency—may occur when the regime suddenly appears vulnerable to challenge. This vulnerability may be of two sorts. First, the regime's ability to respond effectively, its capacity for efficient repression of dissent, or its ability to protect its citizens and property may weaken. Its armed forces may be committed elsewhere, for example, as British forces were during World War I when the ira first rose to challenge British rule, or its coercive resources may be otherwise overextended. Inadequate security at embassies, airports, or military installations may become obvious. The poorly protected U.S. Marine barracks in Beirut were, for example, a tempting target. Government strategy may be ill-adapted to responding to terrorism.

Second, the regime may make itself morally or politically vulnerable by increasing the likelihood that the terrorists will attract popular support. Government repressiveness is thought to have contradictory effects: it both deters dissent and provokes a moral backlash.[12] Perceptions of the regime as unjust motivate opposition. If government actions make average citizens willing to suffer punishment for supporting antigovernment causes, or lend credence to the claims of radical opponents, the extremist organization may be tempted to exploit this temporary upsurge of popular indignation. A groundswell of popular disapproval may make liberal governments less willing (as opposed to less able) to use coercion against violent dissent.

Political discomfort may also be internationally generated. If the climate of international opinion changes so as to reduce the legitimacy of a targeted regime, rebels may feel encouraged to risk a repression that they hope will be limited by outside disapproval. In such circumstances the regime's brutality may be expected to win supporters to the cause of its challengers. The current situation in South Africa furnishes an example. Thus a heightened sensitivity to injustice may be produced either by government actions or by changing public attitudes.

The other fundamental way in which the situation changes to the advantage of challengers is through acquiring new resources. New means of financial support are an obvious asset, which may accrue through a foreign alliance with a sympathetic government or another, richer revolutionary group, or through criminal means such as bank robberies or kidnapping for ransom. Although terrorism is an extremely economical method of violence, funds are essential for the support of full-time activists, weapons purchases, transportation, and logistics.

Technological advances in weapons, explosives, transportation, and communications also may enhance the disruptive potential of terrorism. The invention of dynamite was thought by nineteenth-century revolutionaries and anarchists to equalize the relationship between government and challenger, for example. In 1885, Johann Most published a pamphlet titled *Revolutionary War Science*, which explicitly advocated terrorism. According to Paul Avrich, the anarchists saw dynamite "as a great equalizing force, enabling ordinary workmen to stand up against armies, militias, and police, to say nothing of the hired gunmen of the employers."[13] In providing such a powerful but easily concealed weapon, science was thought to have given a decisive advantage to revolutionary forces.

Strategic innovation is another important way in which a challenging organization acquires new resources. The organization may borrow or adapt a technique in order to exploit a vulnerability ignored by the government. In August 1972, for example, the Provisional ira introduced the effective tactic of the one-shot sniper. ira Chief of Staff Sean MacStiofain claims to have originated the idea: "It seemed to me that prolonged sniping from a static position had no more in common with guerrilla theory than mass confrontations."[14] The best marksmen were trained to fire a single shot and escape before their position could be located. The creation of surprise is naturally one of the key advantages of an offensive strategy. So, too, is the willingness to violate social norms pertaining to restraints on violence. The history of terrorism reveals a series of innovations, as terrorists deliberately selected targets considered taboo and locales where violence was unexpected. These innovations were then rapidly diffused, especially in the modern era of instantaneous and global communications.

It is especially interesting that, in 1968, two of the most important terrorist tactics of the modern era appeared—diplomatic kidnappings in Latin America and hijackings in the Middle East. Both were significant innovations because they involved the use of extortion or blackmail. Although the nineteenth-century Fenians had talked about kidnapping the prince of Wales, the People's Will (Narodnaya Volya) in nineteenth-century Russia had offered to halt its terrorist campaign if a constitution were granted, and American marines were kidnapped by Castro forces in 1959, hostage taking as a systematic and lethal form of coercive bargaining was essentially new. This chapter later takes up the issue in more detail as an illustration of strategic analysis.

Terrorism has so far been presented as the response by an opposition movement to an opportunity. This approach is compatible with the findings of Harvey Waterman, who sees collective political action as determined by the calculations of resources and opportunities.[15] Yet other theorists—James Q. Wilson, for example—argue that political organizations originate in response to a threat to a group's values.[16] Terrorism can certainly be defensive as well as opportunistic. It may be a response to a sudden downturn in a dissident organization's fortunes. The fear of appearing weak may provoke an underground organization into acting in order to show its strength. The PIRA used terrorism to offset an impression of weakness, even at the cost of alienating public opinion: in the 1970s periods of negotiations with the British were punctuated by outbursts of terrorism because the PIRA did want people to think that they were negotiating from strength.[17] Right-wing organizations frequently resort to violence in response to what they see as a threat to the status quo from the left. Beginning in 1969, for example, the right in Italy promoted a "strategy of tension," which involved urban bombings with high numbers of civilian casualties, in order to keep the Italian government and electorate from moving to the left.

CALCULATION OF COST AND BENEFIT

An organization or a faction of an organization may choose terrorism because other methods are not expected to work or are considered too time-consuming, given the urgency of the situation and the government's superior resources. Why would an extremist organization expect that terrorism will be effective? What are the costs and benefits of such a choice, compared with other alternatives? What is the nature of the debate over terrorism? Whether or not to use terrorism is one of the most divisive issues resistance groups confront, and numerous revolutionary movements have split on the question of means even after agreeing on common political ends.[18]

The Costs of Terrorism   The costs of terrorism are high. As a domestic strategy, it invariably invites a punitive government reaction, although the organization may believe that the government reaction will not be efficient enough to pose a serious threat. This cost can be offset by the advance preparation of building a secure underground. *Sendero Luminoso* (Shining Path) in Peru, for example, spent ten years creating a clandestine organizational structure before launching a campaign of violence in 1980. Furthermore, radicals may look to the future and calculate that present sacrifice will not be in vain if it inspires future resistance. Conceptions of interest are thus long term.

Another potential cost of terrorism is loss of popular support. Unless terrorism is carefully controlled and discriminate, it claims innocent victims. In a liberal state, indiscriminate violence may appear excessive and unjustified and alienate a citizenry predisposed to loyalty to the government. If it provokes generalized government repression, fear may diminish enthusiasm for resistance. This potential cost of popular alienation is probably least in ethnically divided societies, where victims can be clearly identified as the enemy and where the government of the majority appears illegal to the minority. Terrorists try to compensate by justifying their actions as the result of the absence of choice or the need to respond to government violence. In addition, they may make their strategy highly discriminate, attacking only unpopular targets.

Terrorism may be unattractive because it is elitist. Although relying only on terrorism may spare the general population from costly involvement in the struggle for freedom, such isolation may violate the ideological beliefs of revolutionaries who insist that the people must participate in their liberation. The few who choose terrorism are willing to forgo or postpone the participation of the many, but revolutionaries who oppose terrorism insist that it prevents the people from taking responsibility for their own destiny. The possibility of vicarious popular identification with symbolic acts of terrorism may satisfy some revolutionaries, but others will find terrorism a harmful substitute for mass participation.

The Advantages of Terrorism   Terrorism has an extremely useful agenda-setting function. If the reasons behind violence are skillfully articulated, terrorism can put the issue of political change on the public agenda. By attracting attention it makes the claims of the resistance a salient issue in the public mind. The government can reject but not ignore an opposition's demands. In 1974 the Palestinian Black September organization, for example, was willing to sacrifice a base in Khartoum, alienate the Sudanese government, and create ambivalence in the Arab world by seizing the Saudi Arabian embassy and killing American and Belgian diplomats. These costs were apparently weighed against the message to the world "to take us seriously." Mainstream Fatah leader Salah Khalef (Abu Iyad) explained: "We are planting the seed. Others will harvest it. . . . It is enough for us now to learn, for example, in reading the Jerusalem Post, that Mrs. Meir had to make her will before visiting Paris, or that Mr. Abba Eban had to travel with a false passport."[19] George Habash of the PFLP noted in 1970 that "we force people to ask what is going on."[20] In these statements, contemporary extremists echo the nineteenth-century anarchists, who coined the idea of propaganda of the deed, a term used as early as 1877 to refer to an act of insurrection as "a powerful means of arousing popular conscience" and the materialization of an idea through actions.[21]

Terrorism may be intended to create revolutionary conditions. It can prepare the ground for active mass revolt by undermining the government's authority and demoralizing its administrative cadres—its courts, police, and military. By spreading insecurity—at the extreme, making the country ungovernable—the organization hopes to pressure the regime into concessions or relaxation of coercive controls. With the rule of law disrupted, the people will be free to join the opposition. Spectacular humiliation of the government demonstrates strength and will and maintains the morale and enthusiasm of adherents and sympathizers. The first wave of Russian revolutionaries claimed that the aims of terrorism were to exhaust the enemy, render the government's position untenable, and wound the government's prestige by delivering a moral, not a physical, blow. Terrorists hoped to paralyze the government by their presence merely by showing signs of life from time to time. The hesitation, irresolution, and tension they would produce would undermine the processes of government and make the Czar a prisoner in his own palace.[22] As Brazilian revolutionary Carlos Marighela explained: "Revolutionary terrorism's great weapon is initiative, which guarantees its survival and continued activity. The more committed terrorists and revolutionaries devoted to anti-dictatorship terrorism and sabotage there are, the more military power will be worn down, the more time it will lose following false trails, and the more fear and tension it will suffer through not knowing where the next attack will be launched and what the next target will be."[23]

These statements illustrate a corollary advantage to terrorism in what might be called its excitational function: it inspires resistance by example. As propaganda of the deed, terrorism demonstrates that the regime can be challenged and that illegal opposition is possible. It acts as a catalyst, not a substitute, for mass revolt. All the tedious and time-consuming organizational work of mobilizing the people can be avoided. Terrorism is a shortcut to revolution. As the Russian revolutionary Vera Figner described its purpose, terrorism was "a means of agitation to draw people from their torpor," not a sign of loss of belief in the people.[24]

A more problematic benefit lies in provoking government repression. Terrorists often think that by provoking indiscriminate repression against the population, terrorism will heighten popular disaffection, demonstrate the justice of terrorist claims, and enhance the attractiveness of the political alternative the terrorists represent. Thus, the West German Red Army Faction sought (in vain) to make fascism "visible" in West Germany.[25] In Brazil, Marighela unsuccessfully aimed to "transform the country's political situation into a military one. Then discontent will spread to all social groups and the military will be held exclusively responsible for failures."[26]

But profiting from government repression depends on the lengths to which the government is willing to go in order to contain disorder, and on the population's tolerance for both insecurity and repression. A liberal state may be limited in its capacity for quelling violence, but at the same time it may be difficult to provoke to excess. However, the government's reaction to terrorism may reinforce the symbolic value of violence even if it avoids repression. Extensive security precautions, for example, may only make the terrorists appear powerful.

Summary To summarize, the choice of terrorism involves considerations of timing and of the popular contribution to revolt, as well as of the relationship between government and opponents. Radicals choose terrorism when they want immediate action, think that only violence can build organizations and mobilize supporters, and accept the risks of challenging the government in a particularly provocative way. Challengers who think that organizational infrastructure must precede action, that rebellion without the masses is misguided, and that premature conflict with the regime can only lead to disaster favor gradualist strategies. They prefer methods such as rural guerrilla warfare, because terrorism can jeopardize painfully achieved gains or preclude eventual compromise with the government.

The resistance organization has before it a set of alternatives defined by the situation and by the objectives and resources of the group. The reasoning behind terrorism takes into account the balance of power between challengers and authorities, a balance that depends on the amount of popular support the resistance can mobilize. The proponents of terrorism understand this constraint and possess reasonable expectations about the likely results of action or inaction. They may be wrong about the alternatives that are open to them, or miscalculate the consequences of their actions, but their decisions are based on logical processes. Furthermore, organizations learn from their mistakes and from those of others, resulting in strategic continuity and progress toward the development of more efficient and sophisticated tactics. Future choices are modified by the consequences of present actions.

HOSTAGE TAKING AS BARGAINING

Hostage taking can be analyzed as a form of coercive bargaining. More than twenty years ago, Thomas Schelling wrote that "hostages represent the power to hurt in its purest form."[27] From this perspective, terrorists choose to take hostages because in bargaining situations the government's greater strength and resources are not an advantage. The extensive resort to this form of terrorism after 1968, a year that marks the major advent of diplomatic kidnappings and airline hijackings, was a predictable response to the growth of state power. Kidnappings, hijackings, and barricade-type seizures of embassies or public buildings are attempts to manipulate a government's political decisions.

Strategic analysis of bargaining terrorism is based on the assumption that hostage takers genuinely seek the concessions they demand. It assumes that they prefer government compliance to resistance. This analysis does not allow for deception or for the possibility that seizing hostages may be an end in itself because it yields the benefit of publicity. Because these limiting assumptions may reduce the utility of the theory, it is important to recognize them.

Terrorist bargaining is essentially a form of blackmail or extortion.[28] Terrorists seize hostages in order to affect a government's choices, which are controlled both by expectations of outcome (what the terrorists are likely to do, given the government reaction) and preferences (such as humanitarian values). The outcome threatened by the terrorist—the death of the hostages—must be worse for the government than compliance with terrorist demands. The terrorist has two options, neither of which necessarily excludes the other: to make the threat both more horrible and more credible or to reward compliance, a factor that strategic theorists often ignore.[29] That is, the cost to the government of complying with the terrorists' demands may be lowered or the cost of resisting raised.

The threat to kill the hostages must be believable and painful to the government. Here hostage takers are faced with a paradox. How can the credibility of this threat be assured when hostage takers recognize that governments know that the terrorists' control over the situation depends on live hostages? One way of establishing credibility is to divide the threat, making it sequential by killing one hostage at a time. Such tactics also aid terrorists in the process of incurring and demonstrating a commitment to carrying out their threat. Once the terrorists have murdered, though, their incentive to surrender voluntarily is substantially reduced. The terrorists have increased their own costs of yielding in order to persuade the government that their intention to kill all the hostages is real.

Another important way of binding oneself in a terrorist strategy is to undertake a barricade rather than a kidnapping operation. Terrorists who are trapped with the hostages find it more difficult to back down (because the government controls the escape routes) and, by virtue of this commitment, influence the government's choices. When terrorists join the hostages in a barricade situation, they create the visible and irrevocable commitment that Schelling sees as a necessary bond in bargaining. The government must expect desperate behavior, because the terrorists have increased their potential loss in order to demonstrate the firmness of their intentions. Furthermore, barricades are technically easier than kidnappings.

The terrorists also attempt to force the "last clear chance" of avoiding disaster onto the government, which must accept the responsibility for noncompliance that leads to the deaths of hostages. The seizure of hostages is the first move in the game, leaving the next move—which determines the fate of the hostages—completely up to the government. Uncertain communications may facilitate this strategy.[30] The terrorists can pretend not to receive government messages that might affect their demonstrated commitment. Hostage takers can also bind themselves by insisting that they are merely agents, empowered to ask only for the most extreme demands. Terrorists may deliberately appear irrational, either through inconsistent and erratic behavior or unrealistic expectations and preferences, in order to convince the government that they will carry out a threat that entails self-destruction.

Hostage seizures are a type of iterated game, which explains some aspects of terrorist behavior that otherwise seem to violate strategic principles. In terms of a single episode, terrorists can be expected to find killing hostages painful, because they will not achieve their demands and the government's desire to punish will be intensified. However, from a long-range perspective, killing hostages reinforces the credibility of the threat in the next terrorist incident, even if the killers then cannot escape. Each terrorist episode is actually a round in a series of games between government and terrorists.

Hostage takers may influence the government's decision by promising rewards for compliance. Recalling that terrorism represents an iterative game, the release of hostages unharmed when ransom is paid underwrites a promise in the future. Sequential release of selected hostages makes promises credible. Maintaining secrecy about a government's concessions is an additional reward for compliance. France, for example, can if necessary deny making concessions to Lebanese kidnappers because the details of arrangements have not been publicized.

Terrorists may try to make their demands appear legitimate so that governments may seem to satisfy popular grievances rather than the whims of terrorists. Thus, terrorists may ask that food be distributed to the poor. Such demands were a favored tactic of the *Ejercito Revolucionario del Pueblo* (ERP) in Argentina in the 1970s.

A problem for hostage takers is that rewarding compliance is not easy to reconcile with making threats credible. For example, if terrorists use publicity to emphasize their threat to kill hostages (which they frequently do), they may also increase the costs of compliance for the government because of the attention drawn to the incident.

In any calculation of the payoffs for each side, the costs associated with the bargaining process must be taken into account.[31] Prolonging the hostage crisis increases the costs to both sides. The question is who loses most and thus is more likely to concede. Each party presumably wishes to make the delay more costly to the other. Seizing multiple hostages appears to be advantageous to terrorists, who are thus in a position to make threats credible by killing hostages individually. Conversely, the greater the number of hostages, the greater the cost of holding them. In hijacking or barricade situations, stress and fatigue for the captors increase waiting costs for them as well. Kidnapping poses fewer such costs. Yet the terrorists can reasonably expect that the costs to governments in terms of public or international pressures may be higher when developments are visible. Furthermore, kidnappers can maintain suspense and interest by publishing communications from their victims.

Identifying the obstacles to effective bargaining in hostage seizures is critical. Most important, bargaining depends on the existence of a common interest between two parties. It is unclear whether the lives of hostages are a sufficient common interest to ensure a compromise outcome that is preferable to no agreement for both sides. Furthermore, most theories of bargaining assume that the preferences of each side remain stable during negotiations. In reality, the nature and intensity of preferences may change during a hostage-taking episode. For example, embarrassment over the Iran-*contra* scandal may have reduced the American interest in securing the release of hostages in Lebanon.

Bargaining theory is also predicated on the assumption that the game is two-party. When terrorists seize the nationals of one government in order to influence the choices of a third, the situation is seriously complicated. The hostages themselves may sometimes become intermediaries and participants. In Lebanon, Terry Waite, formerly an intermediary and negotiator, became a hostage. Such developments are not anticipated by bargaining theories based on normal political relationships. Furthermore, bargaining is not possible if a government is willing to accept the maximum cost the terrorists can bring to bear rather than concede. And the government's options are not restricted to resistance or compliance; armed rescue attempts represent an attempt to break the bargaining stalemate. In attempting to make their threats credible—for example, by sequential killing of hostages—terrorists may provoke military intervention. There may be limits, then, to the pain terrorists can inflict and still remain in the game.

CONCLUSIONS

This essay has attempted to demonstrate that even the most extreme and unusual forms of political behavior can follow an internal, strategic logic. If there are consistent patterns in terrorist behavior, rather than random idiosyncrasies, a strategic analysis may reveal them. Prediction of future terrorism can only be based on theories that explain past patterns.

Terrorism can be considered a reasonable way of pursuing extreme interests in the political arena. It is one among the many alternatives that radical organizations can choose. Strategic conceptions, based on ideas of how best to take advantage of the possibilities of a given situation, are an important determinant of oppositional terrorism, as they are of the government response. However, no single explanation for terrorist behavior is satisfactory. Strategic calculation is only one factor in the decision-making process leading to terrorism. But it is critical to include strategic reasoning as a possible motivation, at a minimum as an antidote to stereotypes of " terrorists" as irrational fanatics. Such stereotypes are a dangerous underestimation of the capabilities of extremist groups. Nor does stereotyping serve to educate the public—or, indeed, specialists—about the complexities of terrorist motivations and behaviors.

NOTES

1 For a similar perspective (based on a different methodology), see James DeNardo, *Power in Numbers: The Political Strategy of Protest and Rebellion* (Princeton, N.J.: Princeton University Press, 1985). See also Harvey Waterman, "Insecure 'Ins' and Opportune 'Outs': Sources of Collective Political Activity," *Journal of Political and Military Sociology* Vol. 8 (1980): 107–12, and "Reasons and Reason: Collective Political Activity in Comparative and Historical Perspective," *World Politics* Vol. 33 (1981): 554–89. A useful review of rational choice theories is found in James G. March, "Theories of Choice and Making Decisions," *Society* Vol. 20 (1982): 29–39.

2 Edward N. Muller and Karl-Dieter Opp, "Rational Choice and Rebellious Collective Action," *American Political Science Review* 80 (1986): 471–87.

3 Ibid., 484. The authors also present another puzzling question that may be answered in terms of either psychology or collective rationality. People who expected their rebellious behavior to be punished were more likely to be potential rebels. This propensity could be explained either by a martyr syndrome (or an expectation of hostility from authority figures) or intensity of preference—the calculation that the regime was highly repressive and thus deserved all the more to be destroyed. See pp. 482 and 485.

4 Leila Khaled, *My People Shall Live: The Autobiography of a Revolutionary* (London: Hodder and Stoughton, 1973), 128–31.

5 See Martha Crenshaw, "The Strategic Development of Terrorism," paper presented to the 1985 Annual Meeting of the American Political Science Association, New Orleans.

6 William A. Gamson, *The Strategy of Social Protest* (Homewood, Illinois: Dorsey Press, 1975).

7 Manus I. Midlarsky, Martha Crenshaw, and Fumihiko Yoshida, "Why Violence Spreads: The Contagion of International Terrorism," *International Studies Quarterly* 24 (1980): 262–98.

8 See the study by David A. Newell, *The Russian Marxist Response to Terrorism: 1878–1917* (Ph.D. dissertation, Stanford University, University Microfilms, 1981).

9 The tension between violence and numbers is a fundamental proposition in DeNardo's analysis; see *Power in Numbers*, chapters 9–11.

10 The work of Charles Tilly emphasizes the political basis of collective violence. See Charles Tilly, Louise Tilly, and Richard Tilly, *The Rebellious Century 1830–1930* (Cambridge: Harvard University Press, 1975), and Charles Tilly, *From Mobilization to Revolution* (Reading, Mass.: Addison-Wesley, 1978).

11 See Conor Cruise O'Brien, "Terrorism under Democratic Conditions: The Case of the IRA," in *Terrorism, Legitimacy, and Power: The Consequences of Political Violence*, edited by Martha Crenshaw (Middletown, Conn.: Wesleyan University Press, 1983).

12 For example, DeNardo, in *Power in Numbers*, argues that "the movement derives moral sympathy from the government's excesses" (p. 207).

13 Paul Avrich, *The Haymarket Tragedy* (Princeton: Princeton University Press, 1984), 166.

14 Sean MacStiofain, *Memoirs of a Revolutionary* (N.p.: Gordon Cremonisi, 1975), 301.

15 Waterman, "Insecure 'Ins' and Opportune 'Outs'" and "Reasons and Reason."

16 *Political Organizations* (New York: Basic Books, 1973).

17 Maria McGuire, *To Take Arms: My Year with the IRA Provisionals* (New York: Viking, 1973), 110–11, 118, 129–31, 115, and 161–62.

18 DeNardo concurs; see *Power in Numbers*, chapter 11.

19 See Jim Hoagland, "A Community of Terror," *Washington Post*, 15 March 1973, pp. 1 and 13; also *New York Times*, 4 March 1973, p. 28. Black September is widely regarded as a subsidiary of Fatah, the major Palestinian organization headed by Yasir Arafat.

20 John Amos, *Palestinian Resistance: Organization of a Nationalist Movement* (New York: Pergamon, 1980), 193; quoting George Habash, interviewed in *Life* Magazine, 12 June 1970, 33.

21 Jean Maitron, *Histoire du mouvement anarchiste en France (1880–1914)*, 2d ed. (Paris: Société universitaire d'éditions et de librairie, 1955), 74–5.

22 "Stepniak" (pseud. for Sergei Kravshinsky), *Underground Russia: Revolutionary Profiles and Sketches from Life* (London: Smith, Elder, 1883), 278–80.

23 Carlos Marighela, *For the Liberation of Brazil* (Harmondsworth: Penguin, 1971), 113.

24 Vera Figner, *Mémoires d'une révolutionnaire* (Paris: Gallimard, 1930), 206.

25 *Textes des prisonniers de la "fraction armée rouge" et dernières lettres d'Ulrike Meinhof* (Paris: Maspéro, 1977), 64.

26 Marighela, For the Liberation of Brazil, 46.

27 Schelling, *Arms and Influence* (New Haven, Conn.: Yale University Press, 1966), 6.

28 Daniel Ellsberg, *The Theory and Practice of Blackmail* (Santa Monica: Rand Corporation, 1968).

29 David A. Baldwin, "Bargaining with Airline Hijackers," in *The 50% Solution*, edited by William I. Zartman, 404–29 (Garden City, N.Y.: Doubleday, 1976), argues that promises have not been sufficiently stressed. Analysts tend to emphasize threats instead, surely because of the latent violence implicit in hostage taking regardless of outcome.

30 See Roberta Wohlstetter's case study of Castro's seizure of American marines in Cuba: " Kidnapping to Win Friends and Influence People," *Survey* 20 (1974): 1–40.

31 Scott E. Atkinson, Todd Sandler, and John Tschirhart, "Terrorism in a Bargaining Framework," *Journal of Law and Economics* 30 (1987): 1–21.

Reading 8.2

Speech to the American People

OSAMA BIN LADIN

Praise be to Allah who created the creation for his worship and commanded them to be just and permitted the wronged one to retaliate against the oppressor in kind. To proceed: Peace be upon he who follows the guidance: People of America this talk of mine is for you and concerns the ideal way to prevent another Manhattan, and deals with the war and its causes and results.

Before I begin, I say to you that security is an indispensable pillar of human life and that free men do not forfeit their security, contrary to Bush's claim that we hate freedom.

If so, then let him explain to us why we don't strike for example—Sweden? And we know that freedom-haters don't possess defiant spirits like those of the 19—may Allah have mercy on them.

No, we fight because we are free men who don't sleep under oppression. We want to restore freedom to our nation, just as you lay waste to our nation. So shall we lay waste to yours.

No one except a dumb thief plays with the security of others and then makes himself believe he will be secure. Whereas thinking people, when disaster strikes, make it their priority to look for its causes, in order to prevent it happening again.

But I am amazed at you. Even though we are in the fourth year after the events of September 11th, Bush is still engaged in distortion, deception and hiding from you the real causes. And thus, the reasons are still there for a repeat of what occurred.

So I shall talk to you about the story behind those events and shall tell you truthfully about the moments in which the decision was taken, for you to consider.

I say to you, Allah knows that it had never occurred to us to strike the towers. But after it became unbearable and we witnessed the oppression and tyranny of the American/Israeli coalition against our people in Palestine and Lebanon, it came to my mind.

The events that affected my soul in a direct way started in 1982 when America permitted the Israelis to invade Lebanon and the American Sixth Fleet helped them in that. This bombardment began and many were killed and injured and others were terrorized and displaced.

Source: English translation of speech delivered by videotape on Al Jazeera Television, October 30, 2004, http://english.aljazeera.net. Reprinted by permission of Al Jazeera.

I couldn't forget those moving scenes, blood and severed limbs, women and children sprawled everywhere. Houses destroyed along with their occupants and high rises demolished over their residents, rockets raining down on our home without mercy.

The situation was like a crocodile meeting a helpless child, powerless except for his screams. Does the crocodile understand a conversation that doesn't include a weapon? And the whole world saw and heard but it didn't respond.

In those difficult moments many hard-to-describe ideas bubbled in my soul, but in the end they produced an intense feeling of rejection of tyranny, and gave birth to a strong resolve to punish the oppressors.

And as I looked at those demolished towers in Lebanon, it entered my mind that we should punish the oppressor in kind and that we should destroy towers in America in order that they taste some of what we tasted and so that they be deterred from killing our women and children.

And that day, it was confirmed to me that oppression and the intentional killing of innocent women and children is a deliberate American policy. Destruction is freedom and democracy, while resistance is terrorism and intolerance.

This means the oppressing and embargoing to death of millions as Bush Sr did in Iraq in the greatest mass slaughter of children mankind has ever known, and it means the throwing of millions of pounds of bombs and explosives at millions of children—also in Iraq—as Bush Jr did, in order to remove an old agent and replace him with a new puppet to assist in the pilfering of Iraq's oil and other outrages.

So with these images and their like as their background, the events of September 11th came as a reply to those great wrongs, should a man be blamed for defending his sanctuary?

Is defending oneself and punishing the aggressor in kind, objectionable terrorism? If it is such, then it is unavoidable for us.

This is the message which I sought to communicate to you in word and deed, repeatedly, for years before September 11th.

And you can read this, if you wish, in my interview with Scott in *Time* Magazine in 1996, or with Peter Arnett on CNN in 1997, or my meeting with John Weiner in 1998.

You can observe it practically, if you wish, in Kenya and Tanzania and in Aden. And you can read it in my interview with Abdul Bari Atwan, as well as my interviews with Robert Fisk.

The latter is one of your compatriots and co-religionists and I consider him to be neutral. So are the pretenders of freedom at the White House and the channels controlled by them able to run an interview with him? So that he may relay to the American people what he has understood from us to be the reasons for our fight against you?

If you were to avoid these reasons, you will have taken the correct path that will lead America to the security that it was in before September 11th. This concerned the causes of the war.

As for its results, they have been, by the grace of Allah, positive and enormous, and have, by all standards, exceeded all expectations. This is due to many factors, chief among them, that we have found it difficult to deal with the Bush administration in light of the resemblance it bears to the regimes in our countries, half of which are ruled by the military and the other half which are ruled by the sons of kings and presidents.

Our experience with them is lengthy, and both types are replete with those who are characterised by pride, arrogance, greed and misappropriation of wealth. This resemblance began after the visits of Bush Sr to the region.

At a time when some of our compatriots were dazzled by America and hoping that these visits would have an effect on our countries, all of a sudden he was affected by those monarchies and military regimes, and became envious of their remaining decades in their positions, to embezzle the public wealth of the nation without supervision or accounting.

So he took dictatorship and suppression of freedoms to his son and they named it the Patriot Act, under the pretence of fighting terrorism. In addition, Bush sanctioned the installing of sons as state governors, and didn't forget to import expertise in election fraud from the region's presidents to Florida to be made use of in moments of difficulty.

All that we have mentioned has made it easy for us to provoke and bait this administration. All that we have to do is to send two mujahidin to the furthest point east to raise a piece of cloth on which is written al-Qaida, in order to make the generals race there to cause America to suffer human, economic, and political losses without their achieving for it anything of note other than some benefits for their private companies.

This is in addition to our having experience in using guerrilla warfare and the war of attrition to fight tyrannical superpowers, as we, alongside the mujahidin, bled Russia for 10 years, until it went bankrupt and was forced to withdraw in defeat.

All Praise is due to Allah.

So we are continuing this policy in bleeding America to the point of bankruptcy. Allah willing, and nothing is too great for Allah.

That being said, those who say that al-Qaida has won against the administration in the White House or that the administration has lost in this war have not been precise, because when one scrutinizes the results, one cannot say that al-Qaida is the sole factor in achieving those spectacular gains.

Rather, the policy of the White House that demands the opening of war fronts to keep busy their various corporations—whether they be working in the field of arms or oil or reconstruction—has helped al-Qaida to achieve these enormous results.

And so it has appeared to some analysts and diplomats that the White House and us are playing as one team towards the economic goals of the United States, even if the intentions differ.

And it was to these sorts of notions and their like that the British diplomat and others were referring in their lectures at the Royal Institute of International Affairs. [When they pointed out that] for example, al-Qaida spent $500,000 on the event, while America, in the incident and its aftermath, lost—according to the lowest estimate—more than $500 billion.

Meaning that every dollar of al-Qaida defeated a million dollars by the permission of Allah, besides the loss of a huge number of jobs.

As for the size of the economic deficit, it has reached record astronomical numbers estimated to total more than a trillion dollars.

And even more dangerous and bitter for America is that the mujahidin recently forced Bush to resort to emergency funds to continue the fight in Afghanistan and Iraq, which is evidence of the success of the bleed-until-bankruptcy plan—with Allah's permission.

It is true that this shows that al-Qaida has gained, but on the other hand, it shows that the Bush administration has also gained, something of which anyone who looks at the size of the contracts acquired by the shady Bush administration-linked mega-corporations, like Halliburton and its kind, will be convinced. And it all shows that the real loser is . . . you.

It is the American people and their economy. And for the record, we had agreed with the Commander-General Muhammad Ataa, Allah have mercy on him, that all the operations should be carried out within 20 minutes, before Bush and his administration notice.

It never occurred to us that the commander-in-chief of the American armed forces would abandon 50,000 of his citizens in the twin towers to face those great horrors alone, the time when they most needed him.

But because it seemed to him that occupying himself by talking to the little girl about the goat and its butting was more important than occupying himself with the planes and their butting of the skyscrapers, we were given three times the period required to execute the operations—all praise is due to Allah.

And it's no secret to you that the thinkers and perceptive ones from among the Americans warned Bush before the war and told him: "All that you want for securing America and removing the weapons of mass destruction—assuming they exist—is available to you, and the nations of the world are with you in the inspections, and it is in the interest of America that it not be thrust into an unjustified war with an unknown outcome."

But the darkness of the black gold blurred his vision and insight, and he gave priority to private interests over the public interests of America.

So the war went ahead, the death toll rose, the American economy bled, and Bush became embroiled in the swamps of Iraq that threaten his future. He fits the saying "like the naughty she-goat who used her hoof to dig up a knife from under the earth."

So I say to you, over 15,000 of our people have been killed and tens of thousands injured, while more than a thousand of you have been killed and more than 10,000 injured. And Bush's hands are stained with the blood of all those killed from both sides, all for the sake of oil and keeping their private companies in business.

Be aware that it is the nation who punishes the weak man when he cause the killing of one of its citizens for money, while letting the powerful one get off, when he causes the killing of more than 1000 of its sons, also for money.

And the same goes for your allies in Palestine. They terrorise the women and children, and kill and capture the men as they lie sleeping with their families on the mattresses, that you may recall that for every action, there is a reaction.

Finally, it behoves you to reflect on the last wills and testaments of the thousands who left you on the 11th as they gestured in despair. They are important testaments, which should be studied and researched.

Among the most important of what I read in them was some prose in their gestures before the collapse, where they say: "How mistaken we were to have allowed the White House to implement its aggressive foreign policies against the weak without supervision."

It is as if they were telling you, the people of America: "Hold to account those who have caused us to be killed, and happy is he who learns from others' mistakes."

And among that which I read in their gestures is a verse of poetry. "Injustice chases its people, and how unhealthy the bed of tyranny."

As has been said: "An ounce of prevention is better than a pound of cure."

And know that: "It is better to return to the truth than persist in error." And that the wise man doesn't squander his security, wealth and children for the sake of the liar in the White House.

In conclusion, I tell you in truth, that your security is not in the hands of Kerry, nor Bush, nor al-Qaida. No.

Your security is in your own hands. And every state that doesn't play with our security has automatically guaranteed its own security.

And Allah is our Guardian and Helper, while you have no Guardian or Helper. All peace be upon he who follows the Guidance.

Reading 8.3

Science of Guerrilla Warfare   *T. E. LAWRENCE*

This study of the science of guerrilla, or irregular, warfare is based on the concrete experience of the Arab Revolt against the Turks, 1916–1918. But the historical example in turn gains value from the fact that its course was guided by the practical application of the theories here set forth.

The Arab Revolt began in June, 1916, with an attack by the half-armed and inexperienced tribesmen upon the Turkish garrisons in Medina and about Mecca. They met with no success, and after a few days' effort withdrew out of range and began a blockade. This method forced the early surrender of Mecca, the more remote of the two centres. Medina, however, was linked by railway to the Turkish main army in Syria, and the Turks were able to reinforce the

Source: T. E. Lawrence, "Science of Guerrilla Warfare." Reprinted with permission from Encyclopaedia Britannica, 14th edition, Vol. 10. © 1929 by Encyclopaedia Britannica, Inc.

garrison there. The Arab forces which had attacked it then fell back gradually and took up a position across the main road to Mecca.

At this point the campaign stood still for many weeks. The Turks prepared to send an expeditionary force to Mecca, to crush the revolt at its source, and accordingly moved an army corps to Medina by rail. Thence they began to advance down the main western road from Medina to Mecca, a distance of about 250 miles. The first 50 miles were easy, then came a belt of hills 20 miles wide, in which were Feisal's Arab tribesmen standing on the defensive: next a level stretch, for 70 miles along the coastal plain to Rabegh, rather more than halfway. Rabegh is a little port on the Red Sea, with good anchorage for ships, and because of its situation was regarded as the key to Mecca. Here lay Sherif Ali, Feisal's eldest brother, with more tribal forces, and the beginning of an Arab regular army, formed from officers and men of Arab blood who had served in the Turkish Army. As was almost inevitable in view of the general course of military thinking since Napoleon, the soldiers of all countries looked only to the regulars to win the war. Military opinion was obsessed by the dictum of Foch that the ethic of modern war is to seek for the enemy's army, his centre of power, and destroy it in battle. Irregulars would not attack positions and so they were regarded as incapable of forcing a decision.

While these Arab regulars were still being trained, the Turks suddenly began their advance on Mecca. They broke through the hills in 24 hours, and so proved the second theorem of irregular war—namely, that irregular troops are as unable to defend a point or line as they are to attack it. This lesson was received without gratitude, for the Turkish success put the Rabegh force in a critical position, and it was not capable of repelling the attack of a single battalion, much less of a corps.

In the emergency it occurred to the author that perhaps the virtue of irregulars lay in depth, not in face, and that it had been the threat of attack by them upon the Turkish northern flank which had made the enemy hesitate for so long. The actual Turkish flank ran from their front line to Medina, a distance of some 50 miles: but, if the Arab force moved towards the Hejaz railway behind Medina, it might stretch its threat (and, accordingly, the enemy's flank) as far, potentially, as Damascus, 800 miles away to the north. Such a move would force the Turks to the defensive, and the Arab force might regain the initiative. Anyhow, it seemed the only chance, and so, in Jan. 1917, Feisal's tribesmen turned their backs on Mecca, Rabegh and the Turks, and marched away north 200 miles to Wejh.

This eccentric movement acted like a charm. The Arabs did nothing concrete, but their march recalled the Turks (who were almost into Rabegh) all the way back to Medina. There, one half of the Turkish force took up the entrenched position about the city, which it held until after the Armistice. The other half was distributed along the railway to defend it against the Arab threat. For the rest of the war the Turks stood on the defensive and the Arab tribesmen won advantage over advantage till, when peace came, they had taken 35,000 prisoners, killed and wounded and worn out about as many, and occupied 100,000 square miles of the enemy's territory, at little loss to themselves.

However, although Wejh was the turning point its significance was not yet realized. For the moment the move thither was regarded merely as a preliminary to cutting the railway in order to take Medina, the Turkish headquarters and main garrison.

Strategy and Tactics   However, the author was unfortunately as much in charge of the campaign as he pleased, and lacking a training in command sought to find an immediate equation between past study of military theory and the present movements—as a guide to, and an intellectual basis for, future action. The text books gave the aim in war as "the destruction of the organized forces of the enemy" by "the one process battle." Victory could only be purchased by blood. This was a hard saying, as the Arabs had no organized forces, and so a Turkish Foch would have no aim: and the Arabs would not endure casualties, so that an Arab Clausewitz could not buy his victory. These wise men must be talking metaphors, for the Arabs were indubitably winning their war . . . and further reflection pointed to the deduction that they had actually won it. They were in occupation of 99% of the Hejaz. The Turks were welcome to the other fraction till peace or doomsday showed them the futility of clinging to the window pane. This part of the war was over, so why bother about Medina? The Turks sat in it on the defensive, immobile, eating for food the transport animals which were to have moved them to Mecca, but for which there was no pasture in their now restricted lines. They were harmless sitting there; if taken prisoner, they would entail the cost of food and guards in Egypt: if driven out northward into Syria, they would join the main army blocking the British in Sinai. On all counts they were best where they were, and they valued Medina and wanted to keep it. Let them!

This seemed unlike the ritual of war of which Foch had been priest, and so it seemed that there was a difference of kind. Foch called his modern war "absolute." In it two nations professing incompatible philosophies set out to try them in the light of force. A struggle of two immaterial principles could only end when the supporters of one had no more means of resistance. An opinion can be argued with: a conviction is best shot. The logical end of a war of creeds is the final destruction of one, and Salammbo the classical textbook-instance. These were the lines of the struggle between France and Germany, but not, perhaps, between Germany and England, for all efforts to make the British soldier hate the enemy simply made him hate war. Thus the "absolute war" seemed only a variety of war; and beside it other sorts could be discerned, as Clausewitz had numbered them, personal wars for dynastic reasons, expulsive wars for party reasons, commercial wars for trading reasons.

Now the Arab aim was unmistakably geographical, to occupy all Arabic-speaking lands in Asia. In the doing of it Turks might be killed, yet "killing Turks" would never be an excuse or aim. If they would go quietly, the war would end. If not, they must be driven out: but at the cheapest possible price, since the Arabs were fighting for freedom, a pleasure only to be tasted by a man alive. The next task was to analyse the process, both from the point of view of strategy, the aim in war, the synoptic regard which sees everything by the standard of the whole, and from the point of view called tactics, the means towards the strategic end, the steps of its staircase. In each were found the same elements, one algebraical, one biological, a third psychological. The first seemed a pure science, subject to the laws of mathematics, without humanity. It dealt with known invariables, fixed conditions, space and time, inorganic things like hills and climates and railways, with mankind in type-masses too great for individual variety, with all artificial aids, and the extensions given our faculties by mechanical invention. It was essentially formulable.

In the Arab case the algebraic factor would take first account of the area to be conquered. A casual calculation indicated perhaps 140,000 square miles. How would the Turks defend all that—no doubt by a trench line across the bottom, if the Arabs were an army attacking with banners displayed . . . but suppose they were an influence, a thing invulnerable, intangible, without front or back, drifting about like a gas? Armies were like plants, immobile as a whole, firm-rooted, nourished through long stems to the head. The Arabs might be a vapour, blowing where they listed. It seemed that a regular soldier might be helpless without a target. He would own the ground he sat on, and what he could poke his rifle at. The next step was to estimate how many posts they would need to contain this attack in depth, sedition putting up her head in every unoccupied one of these 100,000 square miles. They would have need of a fortified post every four square miles, and a post could not be less than 20 men. The Turks would need 600,000 men to meet the combined ill wills of all the local Arab people. They had 100,000 men available. It seemed that the assets in this sphere were with the Arabs, and climate, railways, deserts, technical weapons could also be attached to their interests. The Turk was stupid and would believe that rebellion was absolute, like war, and deal with it on the analogy of absolute warfare.

Humanity in Battle   So much for the mathematical element; the second factor was biological, the breaking-point, life and death, or better, wear and tear. Bionomics seemed a good name for it. The war-philosophers had properly made it an art, and had elevated one item in it, "effusion of blood," to the height of a principle. It became humanity in battle, an art touching every side of our corporal being. There was a line of variability (man) running through all its estimates. Its components were sensitive and illogical, and generals guarded themselves by the device of a reserve, the significant medium of their art. Goltz had said that when you know the enemy's strength, and he is fully deployed, then you know enough to dispense with a reserve. But this is never. There is always the possibility of accident, of some flaw in materials, present in the general's mind: and the reserve is unconsciously held to meet it. There is a "felt" element in troops, not expressible in figures, and the greatest commander is he whose intuitions most nearly happen. Nine-tenths of tactics are certain, and taught in books: but the irrational tenth is like the kingfisher flashing across the pool and that is the test of generals. It can only be ensued by instinct, sharpened by thought practising the stroke so often that at the crisis it is as natural as a reflex.

Yet to limit the art to humanity seemed an undue narrowing down. It must apply to materials as much as to organisms: In the Turkish Army materials were scarce and precious, men more plentiful than equipment. Consequently the cue should be to destroy not the army but the materials. The death of a Turkish bridge or rail, machine or gun, or high explosive was more profitable than the death of a Turk. The Arab army just then was equally chary of men and materials: of men because they being irregulars were not units, but individuals, and an individual casualty is like a pebble dropped in water: each may make only a brief hole, but rings of sorrow widen out from them. The Arab army could not afford casualties. Materials were easier to deal with. Hence its obvious duty to make itself superior in some one branch, guncotton or machine guns, or whatever could be most decisive. Foch had laid down the maxim, applying it to men, of being superior at the critical point and moment of attack. The Arab army might apply it to materials, and be superior in equipment in one dominant moment or respect.

For both men and things it might try to give Foch's doctrine a negative twisted side, for cheapness' sake, and be weaker than the enemy everywhere except in one point or matter. Most wars are wars of contact, both forces striving to keep in touch to avoid tactical surprise. The Arab war should be a war of detachment: to contain the enemy by the silent threat of a vast unknown desert, not disclosing themselves till the moment of attack. This attack need be only nominal, directed not against his men, but against his materials: so it should not seek for his main strength or his weaknesses, but for his most accessible material. In railway cutting this would be usually an empty stretch of rail. This was a tactical success. From this theory came to be developed ultimately an unconscious habit of never engaging the enemy at all. This chimed with the numerical plea of never giving the enemy's soldier a target. Many Turks on the Arab front had no chance all the war to fire a shot, and correspondingly the Arabs were never on the defensive, except by rare accident. The corollary of such a rule was perfect "intelligence," so that plans could be made in complete certainty. The chief agent had to be the general's head (de Feuquière said this first), and his knowledge had to be faultless, leaving no room for chance. The headquarters of the Arab army probably took more pains in this service than any other staff.

The Crowd in Action   The third factor in command seemed to be the psychological, that science (Xenophon called it diathetic) of which our propaganda is a stained and ignoble part. It concerns the crowd, the adjustment of spirit to the point where it becomes fit to exploit in action. It considers the capacity for mood of the men, their complexities and mutability, and the cultivation of what in them profits the intention. The command of the Arab army had to arrange their men's minds in order of battle, just as carefully and as formally as other officers arranged their bodies: and not only their own men's minds, though them first: the minds of the enemy, so far as it could reach them: and thirdly, the mind of the nation supporting it behind the firing-line, and the mind of the hostile nation waiting the verdict, and the neutrals looking on.

It was the ethical in war, and the process on which the command mainly depended for victory on the Arab front. The printing press is the greatest weapon in the armoury of the modern commander, and the commanders of the Arab army being amateurs in the art, began their war in the atmosphere of the 20th century, and thought of their weapons without prejudice, not distinguishing one from another socially. The regular officer has the tradition of 40 generations of serving soldiers behind him, and to him the old weapons are the most honoured. The Arab command had seldom to concern itself with what its men did, but much with what they thought, and to it the diathetic was more than half command. In Europe it was set a little aside and entrusted to men outside the General Staff. But the Arab army was so weak physically that it could not let the metaphysical weapon rust unused. It had won a province when the civilians in it had been taught to die for the ideal of freedom: the presence or absence of the enemy was a secondary matter.

These reasonings showed that the idea of assaulting Medina, or even of starving it quickly into surrender, was not in accord with the best strategy. Rather, let the enemy stay in Medina, and in every other harmless place, in the largest numbers. If he showed a disposition to evacuate too soon, as a step to concentrating in the small area which his numbers could dominate effectively, then the Arab army would have to try and restore his confidence, not harshly, but by reducing its enterprises against him. The ideal was to keep his railway just working, but only just, with the maximum of loss and discomfort to him.

The Turkish army was an accident, not a target. Our true strategic aim was to seek its weakest link, and bear only on that till time made the mass of it fall. The Arab army must impose the longest possible passive defence on the Turks (this being the most materially expensive form of war) by extending its own front to the maximum. Tactically it must develop a highly mobile, highly equipped type of force, of the smallest size, and use it successively at distributed points of the Turkish line, to make the Turks reinforce their occupying posts beyond the economic minimum of 20 men. The power of this striking force would not be reckoned merely by its strength. The ratio between number and area determined the character of the war, and by having five times the mobility of the Turks the Arabs could be on terms with them with one-fifth their number.

Range Over Force   Success was certain, to be proved by paper and pencil as soon as the proportion of space and number had been learned. The contest was not physical, but moral, and so battles were a mistake. All that could be won in a battle was the ammunition the enemy fired off. Napoleon had said it was rare to find generals willing to fight battles. The curse of this war was that so few could do anything else. Napoleon had spoken in angry reaction against the excessive finesse of the 18th century, when men almost forgot that war gave licence to murder. Military thought had been swinging out on his dictum for 100 years, and it was time to go back a bit again. Battles are impositions on the side which believes itself weaker, made unavoidable either by lack of land-room, or by the need to defend a material property dearer than the lives of soldiers. The Arabs had nothing material to lose, so they were to defend nothing and to shoot nothing. Their cards were speed and time, not hitting power, and these gave them strategical rather than tactical strength. Range is more to strategy than force. The invention of bully-beef had modified land-war more profoundly than the invention of gunpowder.

The British military authorities did not follow all these arguments, but gave leave for their practical application to be tried. Accordingly the Arab forces went off first to Akaba and took it easily. Then they took Tafileh and the Dead Sea; then Azrak and Deraa, and finally Damascus, all in successive stages worked out consciously on these theories. The process was to set up ladders of tribes, which should provide a safe and comfortable route from the sea-bases (Yenbo, Wejh or Akaba) to the advanced bases of operation. These were sometimes 300 miles away, a long distance in lands without railways or roads, but made short for the Arab Army by an assiduous cultivation of desert-power, control by camel parties of the desolate and unmapped wilderness which fills up all the centre of Arabia, from Mecca to Aleppo and Baghdad.

The Desert and the Sea In character these operations were like naval warfare, in their mobility, their ubiquity, their independence of bases and communications, in their ignoring of ground features, of strategic areas, of fixed directions, of fixed points. "He who commands the sea is at great liberty, and may take as much or as little of the war as he will": he who commands the desert is equally fortunate. Camel raiding-parties, self-contained like ships, could cruise securely along the enemy's land-frontier, just out of sight of his posts along the edge of cultivation, and tap or raid into his lines where it seemed fittest or easiest or most profitable, with a sure retreat always behind them into an element which the Turks could not enter.

Discrimination of what point of the enemy organism to arrange came with practice. The tactics were always tip and run; not pushes, but strokes. The Arab army never tried to maintain or improve an advantage, but to move off and strike again somewhere else. It used the smallest force in the quickest time at the farthest place. To continue the action till the enemy had changed his dispositions to resist it would have been to break the spirit of the fundamental rule of denying him targets.

The necessary speed and range were attained by the frugality of the desert men, and their efficiency on camels. In the heat of summer Arabian camels will do about 250 miles comfortably between drinks: and this represented three days' vigorous marching. This radius was always more than was needed, for wells are seldom more than 100 miles apart. The equipment of the raiding parties aimed at simplicity, with nevertheless a technical superiority over the Turks in the critical department. Quantities of light machine guns were obtained from Egypt for use not as machine guns, but as automatic rifles, snipers' tools, by men kept deliberately in ignorance of their mechanism, so that the speed of action would not be hampered by attempts at repair. Another special feature was high explosives, and nearly every one in the revolt was qualified by rule of thumb experience in demolition work.

Armoured Cars On some occasions tribal raids were strengthened by armoured cars, manned by Englishmen. Armoured cars, once they have found a possible track, can keep up with a camel party. On the march to Damascus, when nearly 400 miles off their base, they were first maintained by a baggage train of petrol-laden camels, and afterwards from the air. Cars are magnificent fighting machines, and decisive whenever they can come into action on their own conditions. But though each has for [a] main principle that of "fire in movement," yet the tactical employments of cars and camel-corps are so different that their use in joint operations is difficult. It was found demoralizing both to use armoured and unarmoured cavalry together.

The distribution of the raiding parties was unorthodox. It was impossible to mix or combine tribes, since they disliked or distrusted one another. Likewise the men of one tribe could not be used in the territory of another. In consequence, another canon of orthodox strategy was broken by following the principle of the widest distribution of force, in order to have the greatest number of raids on hand at once, and fluidity was added to speed by using one district on Monday, another on Tuesday, a third on Wednesday. This much reinforced the natural mobility of the Arab army, giving it priceless advantages in pursuit, for the force renewed itself with fresh men in every new tribal area, and so maintained its pristine energy. Maximum disorder was, in a real sense its equilibrium.

An Undisciplined Army The internal economy of the raiding parties was equally curious. Maximum irregularity and articulation were the aims. Diversity threw the enemy intelligence off the track. By the regular organization in identical battalions and divisions information builds itself up, until the presence of a corps can be inferred on corpses from three companies. The Arabs, again, were serving a common ideal, without tribal emulation, and so could not hope for any *esprit de corps*. Soldiers are made a caste either by being given great pay and rewards in money, uniform or political privileges; or, as in England, by being made outcasts, cut off from the mass of their fellow-citizens. There have been many armies enlisted voluntarily: there have been few armies serving voluntarily under such trying conditions, for so long a war as the Arab revolt. Any of the Arabs could go home whenever the conviction failed him. Their only contract was honour.

Consequently the Arab army had no discipline, in the sense in which it is restrictive, submergent of individuality, the Lowest Common Denominator of men. In regular armies in peace it means the limit of energy attainable by everybody present: it is the hunt not of an average, but of an absolute, a 100-per-cent standard, in which the 99 stronger men are played down to the level of the worst. The aim is to render the unit a unit, and the man a type, in order that their effort shall be calculable, their collective output even in grain and in bulk. The deeper the discipline, the lower the individual efficiency, and the more sure the performance. It is a deliberate sacrifice of capacity in order to reduce the uncertain element, the bionomic factor, in enlisted humanity, and its accompaniment is *compound* or social war, that form in which the fighting man has to be the product of the multiplied exertions of long hierarchy, from workshop to supply unit, which maintains him in the field.

The Arab war, reacting against this, was *simple* and individual. Every enrolled man served in the line of battle, and was self-contained. There were no lines of communication or labour troops. It seemed that in this articulated warfare, the sum yielded by single men would be at least equal to the product of a compound system of the same strength, and it was certainly easier to adjust to tribal life and manners, given elasticity and understanding on the part of the commanding officers. Fortunately for its chances nearly every young Englishman has the roots of eccentricity in him. Only a sprinkling were employed, not more than one per 1,000 of the Arab troops. A larger proportion would have created friction, just because they were foreign bodies (pearls if you please) in the oyster: and those who were present controlled by influence and advice, by their superior knowledge, not by an extraneous authority.

The practice was, however, not to employ in the firing line the greater numbers which the adoption of a "simple" system made available theoretically. Instead, they were used in relay: otherwise the attack would have become too extended. Guerrillas must be allowed liberal work-room. In irregular war if two men are together one is being wasted. The moral strain of isolated action makes this simple form of war very hard on the individual soldier, and exacts from him special initiative, endurance and enthusiasm. Here the ideal was to make action a series of single combats to make the ranks a happy alliance of commanders-in-chief. The value of the Arab army depended entirely on quality, not on quantity. The members had to keep always cool, for the excitement of a blood-lust would impair their science, and their victory depended on a just use of speed, concealment, accuracy of fire. Guerrilla war is far more intellectual than a bayonet charge.

The Exact Science of Guerrilla Warfare By careful persistence, kept strictly within its strength and following the spirit of these theories, the Arab army was able eventually to reduce the Turks to helplessness, and complete victory seemed to be almost within sight when General Allenby by his immense stroke in Palestine threw the enemy's main forces into hopeless confusion and put an immediate end to the Turkish war. His too-greatness deprived the Arab revolt of the opportunity of following to the end the dictum of Saxe that a war might be won without fighting battles. But it can at least be said that its leaders worked by his light for two years, and the work stood. This is a pragmatic argument that cannot be wholly derided. The experiment, although not complete, strengthened the belief that irregular war or rebellion could be proved to be an exact science, and an inevitable success, granted certain factors and if pursued along certain lines.

Here is the thesis: Rebellion must have an unassailable base, something guarded not merely from attack, but from the fear of it: such a base as the Arab revolt had in the Red Sea ports, the desert, or in the minds of men converted to its creed. It must have a sophisticated alien enemy, in the form of a disciplined army of occupation too small to fulfill the doctrine of acreage: too few to adjust number to space, in order to dominate the whole area effectively from fortified posts. It must have a friendly population, not actively friendly, but sympathetic to the point of not betraying rebel movements to the enemy. Rebellions can be made by 2% active in a striking force, and 98% passively sympathetic. The few active rebels must have the qualities of speed and endurance, ubiquity and independence of arteries of supply. They must have the technical equipment to destroy or paralyze the enemy's organized communications, for irregular war is fairly Willisen's definition of strategy, "the study of communication," in its extreme degree, of attack where the enemy is not. In 50 words: Granted mobility, security (in the form of denying targets to the enemy), time, and doctrine (the idea to convert every subject to friendliness), victory will rest with the insurgents, for the algebraical factors are in the end decisive, and against them perfections of means and spirit struggle quite in vain.

Reading 8.4

On Guerrilla Warfare   MAO TSE-TUNG

WHAT IS GUERRILLA WARFARE?

In a war of revolutionary character, guerrilla operations are a necessary part. This is particularly true in a war waged for the emancipation of a people who inhabit a vast nation. China is such a nation, a nation whose techniques are undeveloped and whose communications are poor. She finds herself confronted with a strong and victorious Japanese imperialism. Under these circumstances, the development of the type of guerrilla warfare characterized by the quality of mass is both necessary and natural. This warfare must be developed to an unprecedented degree and it must coordinate with the operations of our regular armies. If we fail to do this, we will find it difficult to defeat the enemy.

These guerrilla operations must not be considered as an independent form of warfare. They are but one step in the total war, one aspect of the revolutionary struggle. They are the inevitable result of the clash between oppressor and oppressed when the latter reach the limits of their endurance. In our case, these hostilities began at a time when the people were unable to endure any more from the Japanese imperialists. Lenin, in *People and Revolution*, said: "A people's insurrection and a people's revolution are not only natural but inevitable." We consider guerrilla operations as but one aspect of our total or mass war because they, lacking the quality of independence, are of themselves incapable of providing a solution to the struggle.

Guerrilla warfare has qualities and objectives peculiar to itself. It is a weapon that a nation inferior in arms and military equipment may employ against a more powerful aggressor nation. When the invader pierces deep into the heart of the weaker country and occupies her territory in a cruel and oppressive manner, there is no doubt that conditions of terrain, climate, and society in general offer obstacles to his progress and may be used to advantage

Source: From On Guerrilla Warfare. *Copyright 1961 by Samuel B. Griffith (New York: Praeger, 1961), Chapters 1, 2, and 6. Reprinted by arrangement with Jane Griffith and Belle Gordon Griffith Heneberger. Used with permission of the University of Illinois Press.*

by those who oppose him. In guerrilla warfare, we turn these advantages to the purpose of resisting and defeating the enemy.

During the progress of hostilities, guerrillas gradually develop into orthodox forces that operate in conjunction with other units of the regular army. Thus the regularly organized troops, those guerrillas who have attained that status, and those who have not reached that level of development combine to form the military power of a national revolutionary war. There can be no doubt that the ultimate result of this will be victory.

Both in its development and in its method of application, guerrilla warfare has certain distinctive characteristics. We first discuss the relationship of guerrilla warfare to national policy. Because ours is the resistance of a semicolonial country against an imperialism, our hostilities must have a clearly defined political goal and firmly established political responsibilities. Our basic policy is the creation of a national united anti-Japanese front. This policy we pursue in order to gain our political goal, which is the complete emancipation of the Chinese people. There are certain fundamental steps necessary in the realization of this policy, to wit:

1. Arousing and organizing the people.
2. Achieving internal unification politically.
3. Establishing bases.
4. Equipping forces.
5. Recovering national strength.
6. Destroying enemy's national strength.
7. Regaining lost territories.

There is no reason to consider guerrilla warfare separately from national policy. On the contrary, it must be organized and conducted in complete accord with national anti-Japanese policy. It is only those who misinterpret guerrilla action who say, as does Jen Ch'i Shan, "The question of guerrilla hostilities is purely a military matter and not a political one." Those who maintain this simple point of view have lost sight of the political goal and the political effects of guerrilla action. Such a simple point of view will cause the people to lose confidence and will result in our defeat.

What is the relationship of guerrilla warfare to the people? Without a political goal, guerrilla warfare must fail, as it must if its political objectives do not coincide with the aspirations of the people and their sympathy, cooperation, and assistance cannot be gained. The essence of guerrilla warfare is thus revolutionary in character. On the other hand, in a war of counterrevolutionary nature, there is no place for guerrilla hostilities. Because guerrilla warfare basically derives from the masses and is supported by them, it can neither exist nor flourish if it separates itself from their sympathies and cooperation. There are those who do not comprehend guerrilla action, and who therefore do not understand the distinguishing qualities of a people's guerrilla war, who say: "Only regular troops can carry on guerrilla operations." There are others who, because they do not believe in the ultimate success of guerrilla action, mistakenly say: "Guerrilla warfare is an insignificant and highly specialized type of operation in which there is no place for the masses of the people" (Jen Ch'i Shan). Then there are those who ridicule the masses and undermine resistance by wildly asserting that the people have no understanding of the war of resistance (Yeh Ch, for one). The moment that this war of resistance dissociates itself from the masses of the people is the precise moment that it dissociates itself from hope of ultimate victory over the Japanese.

What is the organization for guerrilla warfare? Though all guerrilla bands that spring from the masses of the people suffer from lack of organization at the time of their formation, they all have in common a basic quality that makes organization possible. All guerrilla units must have political and military leadership. This is true regardless of the source or size of such units. Such units may originate locally, in the masses of the people; they may be formed from an admixture of regular troops with groups of the people, or they may consist of regular army units intact. And mere quantity does not affect this matter. Such units may consist of a squad of a few men, a battalion of several hundred men, or a regiment of several thousand men.

All these must have leaders who are unyielding in their policies—resolute, loyal, sincere, and robust. These men must be well educated in revolutionary technique, self-confident, able to establish severe discipline, and able to cope with counterpropaganda. In short, these leaders must be models for the people. As the war progresses, such leaders will gradually overcome the lack of discipline, which at first prevails; they will establish discipline in their forces, strengthening them and increasing their combat efficiency. Thus eventual victory will be attained.

Unorganized guerrilla warfare cannot contribute to victory and those who attack the movement as a combination of banditry and anarchism do not understand the nature of guerrilla action. They say: "This movement is a haven for disappointed militarists, vagabonds and bandits" (Jen Ch'i Shan), hoping thus to bring the movement into disrepute. We do not deny that there are corrupt guerrillas, nor that there are people who under the guise of guerrillas indulge in unlawful activities. Neither do we deny that the movement has at the present time symptoms of a lack of organization, symptoms that might indeed be serious were we to judge guerrilla warfare solely by the corrupt and temporary phenomena we have mentioned. We should study the corrupt phenomena and attempt to eradicate them in order to encourage guerrilla warfare, and to increase its military efficiency. "This is hard work, there is no help for it, and the problem cannot be solved immediately. The whole people must try to reform themselves during the course of the war. We must educate them and reform them in the light of past experience. Evil does not exist in guerrilla warfare but only in the unorganized and undisciplined activities that are anarchism," said Lenin, in *On Guerrilla Warfare.*

What is basic guerrilla strategy? Guerrilla strategy must be based primarily on alertness, mobility, and attack. It must be adjusted to the enemy situation, the terrain, the existing lines of communication, the relative strengths, the weather, and the situation of the people.

In guerrilla warfare, select the tactic of seeming to come from the east and attacking from the west; avoid the solid, attack the hollow; attack; withdraw; deliver a lightning blow, seek a lightning decision. When guerrillas engage a stronger enemy, they withdraw when he advances; harass him when he stops; strike him when he is weary; pursue him when he withdraws. In guerrilla strategy, the enemy's rear, flanks, and other vulnerable spots are his vital points, and there he must be harassed, attacked, dispersed, exhausted and annihilated. Only in this way can guerrillas carry out their mission of independent guerrilla action and coordination with the effort of the regular armies. But, in spite of the most complete preparation, there can be no victory if mistakes are made in the matter of command. Guerrilla warfare based on the principles we have mentioned and carried on over a vast extent of territory in which communications are inconvenient will contribute tremendously towards ultimate defeat of the Japanese and consequent emancipation of the Chinese people.

A careful distinction must be made between two types of guerrilla warfare. The fact that revolutionary guerrilla warfare is based on the masses of the people does not in itself mean that the organization of guerrilla units is impossible in a war of counterrevolutionary character. As examples of the former type we may cite Red guerrilla hostilities during the Russian Revolution; those of the Reds in China; of the Abyssinians against the Italians for the past three years; those of the last seven years in Manchuria, and the vast anti-Japanese guerrilla war that is carried on in China today. All these struggles have been carried on in the interests of the whole people or the greater part of them; all had a broad basis in the national manpower, and all have been in accord with the laws of historical development. They have existed and will continue to exist, flourish, and develop as long as they are not contrary to national policy.

The second type of guerrilla warfare directly contradicts the law of historical development. Of this type, we may cite the examples furnished by the White Russian guerrilla units organized by Denikin and Kolchak; those organized by the Japanese; those organized by the Italians in Abyssinia; those supported by the puppet governments in Manchuria and Mongolia, and those that will be organized here by Chinese traitors. All such have oppressed the masses and have been contrary to the true interests of the people. They must be firmly opposed. They are easy to destroy because they lack a broad foundation in the people.

If we fail to differentiate between the two types of guerrilla hostilities mentioned, it is likely that we will exaggerate their effect when applied by an invader. We might arrive at the conclusion that "the invader can organize guerrilla units from among the people." Such a conclusion might well diminish our confidence in guerrilla warfare. As far as this matter is concerned, we have but to remember the historical experience of revolutionary struggles.

Further, we must distinguish general revolutionary wars from those of a purely "class" type. In the former case, the whole people of a nation, without regard to class or party, carry on a guerrilla struggle that is an instrument of the national policy. Its basis is, therefore, much broader than is the basis of a struggle of class type. Of a general guerrilla war, it has been said: "When a nation is invaded, the people become sympathetic to one another and all aid in organizing guerrilla units. In civil war, no matter to what extent guerrillas are developed, they do not produce the same results as when they are formed to resist an invasion by foreigners" (*Civil War in Russia*). The one strong feature of guerrilla warfare in a civil struggle is its quality of internal purity. One class may be easily united and perhaps fight with great effect, whereas in a national revolutionary war, guerrilla units are faced with the problem of internal unification of different class groups. This necessitates the use of propaganda. Both types of guerrilla war are, however, similar in that they both employ the same military methods.

National guerrilla warfare, though historically of the same consistency, has employed varying implements as times, peoples, and conditions differ. The guerrilla aspects of the Opium War, those of the fighting in Manchuria since the Mukden incident, and those employed in China today are all slightly different. The guerrilla warfare conducted by the Moroccans against the French and the Spanish was not exactly similar to that which we conduct today in China. These differences express the characteristics of different peoples in different periods. Although there is a general similarity in the quality of all these struggles, there are dissimilarities in form. This fact we must recognize. Clausewitz wrote, in *On War*: "Wars in every period have independent forms and independent conditions, and, therefore, every period must have its independent theory of war." Lenin, in *On Guerrilla Warfare*, said: "As regards the form of fighting, it is unconditionally requisite that history be investigated in order to discover the conditions of environment, the state of economic progress, and the political ideas that obtained, the national characteristics, customs, and degree of civilization." Again: "It is necessary to be completely unsympathetic to abstract formulas and rules and to study with sympathy the conditions of the actual fighting, for these will change in accordance with the political and economic situations and the realization of the people's aspirations. These progressive changes in conditions create new methods."

If, in today's struggle, we fail to apply the historical truths of revolutionary guerrilla war, we will fall into the error of believing with T'ou Hsi Sheng that under the impact of Japan's mechanized army, "the guerrilla unit has lost its historical function." Jen Ch'i Shan writes: "In olden days, guerrilla warfare was part of regular strategy but there is almost no chance that it can be applied today." These opinions are harmful. If we do not make an estimate of the characteristics peculiar to our anti-Japanese guerrilla war, but insist on applying to it mechanical formulas derived from past history, we are making the mistake of placing our hostilities in the same category as all other national guerrilla struggles. If we hold this view, we will simply be beating our heads against a stone wall and we will be unable to profit from guerrilla hostilities.

To summarize: What is the guerrilla war of resistance against Japan? It is one aspect of the entire war, which, although alone incapable of producing the decision, attacks the enemy in every quarter, diminishes the extent of area under his control, increases our national strength, and assists our regular armies. It is one of the strategic instruments used to inflict defeat on our enemy. It is the one pure expression of anti-Japanese policy, that is to say, it is military strength organized by the active people and inseparable from them. It is a powerful special weapon with which we resist the Japanese and without which we cannot defeat them. . . .

THE RELATION OF GUERRILLA HOSTILITIES TO REGULAR OPERATIONS

The general features of orthodox hostilities, that is, the war of position and the war of movement, differ fundamentally from guerrilla warfare. There are other readily apparent differences such as those in organization, armament, equipment, supply, tactics, command; in conception of the terms "front" and "rear"; in the matter of military responsibilities.

When considered from the point of view of total numbers, guerrilla units are many; as individual combat units, they may vary in size from the smallest, of several score or several hundred men, to the battalion or the regiment, of several thousand. This is not the case in regularly organized units. A primary feature of guerrilla operations is their dependence upon the people themselves to organize battalions and other units. As a result of this, organization depends largely upon local circumstances. In the case of guerrilla groups, the standard of equipment is of a low order, and they must depend for their sustenance primarily upon what the locality affords.

The strategy of guerrilla warfare is manifestly unlike that employed in orthodox operations, as the basic tactic of the former is constant activity and movement. There is in guerrilla warfare no such thing as a decisive battle; there is nothing comparable to the fixed, passive defense that characterizes orthodox war. In guerrilla warfare, the transformation of a moving situation into a positional defensive situation never arises. The general features of reconnaissance, partial deployment, general deployment, and development of the attack that are usual in mobile warfare are not common in guerrilla war.

There are differences also in the matter of leadership and command. In guerrilla warfare, small units acting independently play the principal role, and there must be no excessive interference with their activities. In orthodox warfare, particularly in a moving situation, a certain degree of initiative is accorded subordinates, but in principle, command is centralized. This is done because all units and all supporting arms in all districts must coordinate to the highest degree. In the case of guerrilla warfare, this is not only undesirable but impossible. Only adjacent guerrilla units can coordinate their activities to any degree. Strategically, their activities can be roughly correlated with those of the regular forces, and tactically, they must cooperate with adjacent units of the regular army. But there are no strictures on the extent of guerrilla activity nor is it primarily characterized by the quality of cooperation of many units.

When we discuss the terms "front" and "rear," it must be remembered, that while guerrillas do have bases, their primary field of activity is in the enemy's rear areas. They themselves have no rear. Because an orthodox army has rear installations (except in some special cases as during the 10,000-mile march of the Red Army or as in the case of certain units operating in Shansi Province), it cannot operate as guerrillas can.

As to the matter of military responsibilities, those of the guerrillas are to exterminate small forces of the enemy; to harass and weaken large forces; to attack enemy lines of communication; to establish bases capable of supporting independent operations in the enemy's rear; to force the enemy to disperse his strength; and to coordinate all these activities with those of the regular armies on distant battle fronts.

From the foregoing summary of differences that exist between guerrilla warfare and orthodox warfare, it can be seen that it is improper to compare the two. Further distinction must be made in order to clarify this matter. While the Eighth Route Army is a regular army, its North China campaign is essentially guerrilla in nature, for it operates in the enemy's rear. On occasion, however, Eighth Route Army commanders have concentrated powerful forces to strike an enemy in motion, and the characteristics of orthodox mobile warfare were evident in the battle at P'ing Hsing Kuan and in other engagements.

On the other hand, after the fall of Feng Ling Tu, the operations of Central Shansi, and Suiyuan, troops were more guerrilla than orthodox in nature. In this connection, the precise character of Generalissimo Chiang's instructions to the effect that independent brigades would carry out guerrilla operations should be recalled. In spite of such temporary activities, these orthodox units retained their identity and after the fall of Feng Ling Tu, they not only were able to fight along orthodox lines but often found it necessary to do so. This is an example of the fact that orthodox armies may, due to changes in the situation, temporarily function as guerrillas.

Likewise, guerrilla units formed from the people may gradually develop into regular units and, when operating as such, employ the tactics of orthodox mobile war. While these units function as guerrillas, they may be compared to innumerable gnats, which, by biting a giant both in front and in rear, ultimately exhaust him. They make themselves as unendurable as a group of cruel and hateful devils, and as they grow and attain gigantic proportions, they will find that their victim is not only exhausted but practically perishing. It is for this very reason that our guerrilla activities are a source of constant mental worry to Imperial Japan.

While it is improper to confuse orthodox with guerrilla operations, it is equally improper to consider that there is a chasm between the two. While differences do exist, similarities appear under certain conditions, and this fact must be appreciated if we wish to establish clearly the relationship between the two. If we consider both types of warfare as a single subject, or if we confuse guerrilla warfare with the mobile operations of orthodox war, we fall into this error: We exaggerate the function of guerrillas and minimize that of the regular armies. If we agree with Chang Tso Hua, who says, "Guerrilla warfare is the primary war strategy of a people seeking to emancipate itself," or with Kao Kang, who believes that "Guerrilla strategy is the only strategy possible for an oppressed people," we are exaggerating the importance of guerrilla hostilities. What these zealous friends I have just quoted do not realize is this: If we do not fit guerrilla operations into their proper niche, we cannot promote them realistically. Then, not only would those who oppose us take advantage of our varying opinions to turn them to their own uses to undermine us, but guerrillas would be led to assume responsibilities they could not successfully discharge and that should properly be carried out by orthodox forces. In the meantime, the important guerrilla function of coordinating activities with the regular forces would be neglected.

Furthermore, if the theory that guerrilla warfare is our only strategy were actually applied, the regular forces would be weakened, we would be divided in purpose, and guerrilla hostilities would decline. If we say, "Let us transform the regular forces into guerrillas," and do not place our first reliance on a victory to be gained by the regular armies over the enemy, we may certainly expect to see as a result the failure of the anti-Japanese war of resistance. The concept that guerrilla warfare is an end in itself and that guerrilla activities can be divorced from those of the regular forces is incorrect. If we assume that guerrilla warfare does not progress from beginning to end beyond its elementary forms, we have failed to recognize the fact that guerrilla hostilities can, under specific conditions, develop and assume orthodox characteristics. An opinion that admits the existence of guerrilla war, but isolates it, is one that does not properly estimate the potentialities of such war.

Equally dangerous is the concept that condemns guerrilla war on the ground that war has no other aspects than the purely orthodox. This opinion is often expressed by those who have seen the corrupt phenomena of some guerrilla regimes, observed their lack of discipline, and have seen them used as a screen behind which certain persons have indulged in bribery and other corrupt practices. These people will not admit the fundamental necessity for guerrilla bands that spring from the armed people. They say, "Only the regular forces are capable of conducting guerrilla operations." This theory is a mistaken one and would lead to the abolition of the people's guerrilla war.

A proper conception of the relationship that exists between guerrilla effort and that of the regular forces is essential. We believe it can be stated this way: "Guerrilla operations during the anti-Japanese war may for a certain time and temporarily become its paramount feature, particularly insofar as the enemy's rear is concerned. However, if we view the war as a whole, there can be no doubt that our regular forces are of primary importance, because it is they who are alone capable of producing the decision. Guerrilla warfare assists them in producing this favorable decision. Orthodox forces may under certain conditions operate as guerrillas, and the latter may, under certain conditions, develop to the status of the former. However, both guerrilla forces and regular forces have their own respective development and their proper combinations."

To clarify the relationship between the mobile aspect of orthodox war and guerrilla war, we may say that general agreement exists that the principal element of our strategy must be mobility. With the war of movement, we may at times combine the war of position. Both of these are assisted by general guerrilla hostilities. It is true that on the battlefield mobile war often becomes positional; it is true that this situation may be reversed; it is equally true that each form may combine with the other. The possibility of such combination will become more evident after the prevailing standards of equipment have been raised. For example, in a general strategical counterattack to recapture key cities and lines of communication, it would be normal to use both mobile and positional methods. However, the point must again be made that our fundamental strategical form must be the war of movement. If we deny this, we cannot arrive at the victorious solution of the war. In sum, while we must promote guerrilla warfare as a necessary strategical auxiliary to orthodox operations, we must neither assign it the primary position in our war strategy nor substitute it for mobile and positional warfare as conducted by orthodox forces. . . .

THE POLITICAL PROBLEMS OF GUERRILLA WARFARE

. . . I mentioned the fact that guerrilla troops should have a precise conception of the political goal of the struggle and the political organization to be used in attaining that goal. This means that both organization and discipline of guerrilla troops must be at a high level so that they can carry out the political activities that are the life of both the guerrilla armies and of revolutionary warfare.

First of all, political activities depend upon the indoctrination of both military and political leaders with the idea of anti-Japanism. Through them, the idea is transmitted to the troops. One must not feel that he is anti-Japanese merely because he is a member of a guerrilla unit. The anti-Japanese idea must be an ever-present conviction, and if it is forgotten, we may succumb to the temptations of the enemy or be overcome with discouragements. In a war of long duration, those whose conviction that the people must be emancipated is not deep rooted are likely to become shaken in their faith or actually revolt. Without the general education that enables everyone to understand our goal of driving out Japanese imperialism and establishing a free and happy China, the soldiers fight without conviction and lose their determination.

The political goal must be clearly and precisely indicated to inhabitants of guerrilla zones and their national consciousness awakened. Hence, a concrete explanation of the political systems used is important not only to guerrilla troops but to all those who are concerned with the realization of our political goal. The Kuomintang has issued a pamphlet entitled *System of National Organization for War*, which should be widely distributed throughout guerrilla zones. If we lack national organization, we will lack the essential unity that should exist between the soldiers and the people.

A study and comprehension of the political objectives of this war and of the anti-Japanese front is particularly important for officers of guerrilla troops. There are some militarists who say: "We are not interested in politics but only in the profession of arms." It is vital that these simple-minded militarists be made to realize the relationship that exists between politics and military affairs. Military action is a method used to attain a political goal. While military affairs and political affairs are not identical, it is impossible to isolate one from the other.

It is to be hoped that the world is in the last era of strife. The vast majority of human beings have already prepared or are preparing to fight a war that will bring justice to the oppressed peoples of the world. No matter how long this war may last, there is no doubt that it will be followed by an unprecedented epoch of peace. The war that we are fighting today for the emancipation of the Chinese is a part of the war for the freedom of all human beings, and the independent, happy, and liberal China that we are fighting to establish will be a part of that new world order. A conception like this is difficult for the simple-minded militarist to grasp and it must therefore be carefully explained to him.

There are three additional matters that must be considered under the broad question of political activities. These are political activities, first, as applied to the troops; second, as applied to the people; and, third, as applied to the enemy. The fundamental problems are: first, spiritual unification of officers and men within the army; second, spiritual unification of the army and the people; and, last, destruction of the unity of the enemy. The concrete methods for achieving these unities are discussed in detail in pamphlet Number 4 of this series, entitled *Political Activities in Anti-Japanese Guerrilla Warfare*.

A revolutionary army must have discipline that is established on a limited democratic basis. In all armies, obedience of the subordinates to their superiors must be exacted. This is true in the case of guerrilla discipline, but the basis for guerrilla discipline must be the individual conscience. With guerrillas, a discipline of compulsion is ineffective. In any revolutionary army, there is unity of purpose as far as both officers and men are concerned, and, therefore, within such an army, discipline is self-imposed. Although discipline in guerrilla ranks is not as severe as in the ranks of orthodox forces, the necessity for discipline exists. This must be self-imposed, because only when it is, is the soldier able to understand completely why he fights and why he must obey. This type of discipline becomes a tower of strength within the army, and it is the only type that can truly harmonize the relationship that exists between officers and soldiers.

In any system where discipline is externally imposed, the relationship that exists between officer and man is characterized by indifference of the one to the other. The idea that officers can physically beat or severely tongue-lash their men is a feudal one and is not in accord with the conception of a self-imposed discipline. Discipline of the feudal type will destroy internal unity and fighting strength. A discipline self-imposed is the primary characteristic of a democratic system in the army.

A secondary characteristic is found in the degree of liberties accorded officers and soldiers. In a revolutionary army, all individuals enjoy political liberty and the question, for example, of the emancipation of the people must not only be tolerated but discussed, and propaganda must be encouraged. Further, in such an army, the mode of living of the officers and the soldiers must not differ too much, and this is particularly true in the case of guerrilla troops. Officers should live under the same conditions as their men, for that is the only way in which they can gain from their men the admiration and confidence so vital in war. It is incorrect to hold to a theory of equality in all things, but there must be equality of existence in accepting the hardships and dangers of war. Thus we may attain to the unification of the officer and soldier groups, a unity both horizontal within the group itself, and vertical, that is, from lower to higher echelons. It is only when such unity is present that units can be said to be powerful combat factors.

There is also a unity of spirit that should exist between troops and local inhabitants. The Eighth Route Army put into practice a code known as "The Three Rules and the Eight Remarks," which we list here:

Rules

1. All actions are subject to command.
2. Do not steal from the people.
3. Be neither selfish nor unjust.

Remarks

1. Replace the door when you leave the house.
2. Roll up the bedding on which you have slept.
3. Be courteous.
4. Be honest in your transactions.
5. Return what you borrow.
6. Replace what you break.
7. Do not bathe in the presence of women.
8. Do not without authority search the pocketbooks of those you arrest.

The Red Army adhered to this code for ten years and the Eighth Route Army and other units have since adopted it.

Many people think it impossible for guerrillas to exist for long in the enemy's rear. Such a belief reveals lack of comprehension of the relationship that should exist between the people and the troops. The former may be likened to water and the latter to the fish who inhabit it. How may it be said that these two cannot exist together? It is only undisciplined troops who make the people their enemies and who, like the fish out of its native element, cannot live.

We further our mission of destroying the enemy by propagandizing his troops, by treating his captured soldiers with consideration, and by caring for those of his wounded who fall into our hands. If we fail in these respects, we strengthen the solidarity of our enemy.

Reading 8.5

Patterns of Violence in World Politics
SAMUEL P. HUNTINGTON

THE CHANGING LOCUS OF VIOLENCE

"An arena is *military*," say Lasswell and Kaplan, "when the expectation of violence is high; *civic*, when the expectation of violence is low."[1] For three centuries in the West international politics has been viewed as a military arena, and the domestic politics of nation-states have been thought to be civic arenas. Continuing this pattern, after World War II the expectations and apprehensions of international war, particularly war between Communist and Western states, were high. In practice, however, international violence was relatively infrequent.

Source: Reprinted and edited with the permission of The Free Press, a Division of Simon & Schuster, Inc., from Changing Patterns of Military Politics *by Samuel P. Huntington. Copyright © 1962 by The Free Press. Copyright renewed © 1990 by Samuel P. Huntington. All rights reserved.*

The Korean War was the only major prolonged interstate war between 1945 and 1960. Previously, of course, much longer periods of time had passed with even fewer interstate wars. These, however, were also periods of relative harmony with few significant clashes of interest between states. The fifteen years after World War II were marked by intense international conflicts, not only between the Soviet bloc and the West, but also between many other states over local issues. Nonetheless, with a few exceptions, governments did not resort to war. Never before in human history, one might say, were such high expectations of interstate violence accompanied by so little interstate violence in actuality.

The willingness of governments to resort to interstate violence presumably is affected by considerations of domestic politics and calculations of international gains. The decision to go to war or to take action that seriously risks war is seldom made casually.[2] In the past, when governments "blundered" into wars they did not want or could not win, the result was usually caused not by a refusal to act in a rational manner but by deficiencies in knowledge concerning the intentions and capabilities of other states. As long as governments choose war or peace in terms of their own interests and sometimes miscalculate those interests, interstate war is never impossible.

After 1945, however, the evolution of international politics produced new inhibitions reinforcing the reluctance of governments to resort to violence. In the past interstate wars were almost always associated with changes in control or influence over territory. They were the natural concomitant of the "territoriality" of the nation-state.[3] In the mid-twentieth century, however, prospective gains in territorial control began to decrease in value compared to the risks and the costs involved in procuring them. Governments became more willing to live with disputed boundaries, unsettled claims, and irredentist hopes. In part this was due to the existence of nuclear weapons, and in part also it was the result of improvements in international communication and organization, which made more visible any resort to violence and provided mechanisms for avoiding violence or bringing it quickly to an end. Increasingly, in effect, the territorial status quo became stabilized and even sanctified beyond the ability of any one state, however powerful, unilaterally to change it. The destruction of Hiroshima and the humiliation of Suez were strong deterrents to the resort to force.

The decline in the likelihood of intergovernmental violence was marked by a change in the nature of the Cold War. In the early years of the struggle between the Soviet Union and the United States bipolarity prevailed, and the conflict between the two powers and their allies was largely over territory. A gain in territory (e.g., China) for one side was a direct loss for the other. In the mid-1950's, however, bipolarity began to decline, and the struggle between the two great powers shifted from territory to the "peaceful competition" of economic development, military build-ups, scientific achievements, and diplomatic successes. The relevant model for world politics was less a two-person zero-sum game than a multiperson nonzero-sum game. A gain for one country did not necessarily mean an equivalent loss for another. A finite limit existed on territory, but there were no limits on the goals which a government might set for itself in expanding its production, developing its military strength, and exploring outer space. All these activities served as substitutes for the actual recourse to violence.[4] In the international competition for prestige resort to violence was often a sign of weakness or failure.

As a result, the conflict between the major powers tended to become regularized or stabilized. The periodic threats made by one government or the other to destroy this stability were in themselves an index of its pervasiveness and value. The relative military power of the major states still remained decisively important. It was important, however, more for its contribution to Cold War diplomacy than for its potential contribution to hot war victory. In the early years of the Cold War statesmen on both sides seemed primarily concerned with ending the international deadlock. Increasingly, in the 1950's, they seemed more concerned with preserving it lest a worse fate befall them.

The inhibition of direct intergovernmental violence contrasted with the frequency and variety of violence in the domestic politics of the colonial territories and independent states of Latin America, Africa, the Middle East, and southern Asia. These were the principal military arenas in world politics. The Korean War was rivaled in either duration or intensity by the Chinese civil war, the Indonesian war for independence, the struggle between the French and the Viet Minh in Indochina. Insurrection, terrorism, or civil war occurred in Greece, Malaya, the Philippines, Kenya, Cyprus, Algeria, Cuba, the Congo, and Laos. In the Republic of Colombia 100,000 persons were killed in civil strife between 1948 and 1953.[5] In other Latin American countries, and in many Middle Eastern ones, coups d'état were a recurring phenomenon. The year 1960 could well be labeled the "year of revolt":[6] Korea, Turkey, the Congo, Cuba, the Dominican Republic, Ethiopia, Vietnam, Laos all shared in the pattern in one way or another. In Moscow and Washington strategists plotted and replotted the probable course of hypothetical wars between the Soviet Union and the United States. In the underdeveloped areas of the world, however, violence was an immediate actuality. The dominant pattern was not interstate war in the sense of sustained violence between the forces of two or more governments roughly comparable in structure and function, if not in power. Instead, it was insurrectionary violence, in which a nongovernmental body—a clique, a party, a movement—attempted to overthrow and to supersede the existing government. Territorial boundaries served not as the focus of conflict but as its parameters.

The frequency of violence in the domestic politics of the underdeveloped areas reflected the prevalence of rapid social and political change. "Social revolution," to quote Lasswell and Kaplan again, "occurs within a short time span only by the exercise of violence."[7] In the late 1950's the international situation was commonly described by such words as "stalemate," "deadlock," "equilibrium," and "balance." Within the principal countries of the West and even within the Soviet Union domestic politics was often spoken of in terms of "the absence of issues," "the end of ideology," "the apathy of the masses," "the prevalence of pragmatism," "other-directedness," and "organization men." In the underdeveloped areas, however, the key words were "development," "growth," "modernization," "westernization," "transition," and "independence." Here were the principal causes of insurrectionary violence.

DIFFERENCES BETWEEN INTERGOVERNMENTAL AND ANTIGOVERNMENTAL VIOLENCE

The classic theory of intergovernmental war was formulated by Clausewitz. When he said that war was a continuation of policy by other means, he meant that it was a continuation of foreign policy. He was concerned with the "war of a community—of whole nations and particularly of civilized nations. . . ."[8] For Clausewitz war was an instrument of governments and an interaction between governments. "War," he said, "is thus an act of force to compel our adversary to do our will. . . . Each of the adversaries forces the hand of the other, and a reciprocal action results which in theory can have no limit." Clausewitz's theory of war was dualistic, concerned solely with the interaction of two contestants. His analysis of the relation of military force to politics postulated a system of objective civilian control. His was the military theory of the nation-state, reflecting eighteenth-century practice and anticipating nineteenth-century developments. It is only partially relevant to intrastate war. Intrastate war is also the continuation of policy by other means, but it is the continuation of the policies of antigovernment and government within a common territory and society, each endeavoring to win support from at least some of the same groups. The patterns of intergovernmental war reflect the processes and structure of international politics; those of antigovernmental war reflect the processes and structure of domestic politics.

Intergovernmental war is initially symmetrical. The war begins between two independent governments, and it ends when one government succeeds in imposing its will on the other or when both governments conclude that their interests will no longer be served by continuing the struggle. The abstract pattern of insurrectionary war, on the other hand, is asymmetrical. It begins with a government confronting a nongovernment (institution, clique, movement, or party), and it ends with a similar relationship, although perhaps with the positions of the participants reversed. In the interval a symmetrical phase may occur, but prolonged symmetry means civil war in which two governments contend for authority within a single state. This closely resembles intergovernmental war. The American Civil War, for example, was a struggle between two governments each exercising effective authority over well-defined populations and territories. It differed little from the normal international war. A successful coup d'état, on the other hand, moves directly from one asymmetrical phase to another. The frequency of antigovernmental violence reflects the extent to which antigovernments monopolize the initiative in resorting to violence. They exist in greater numbers and variety than governments; possessing fewer responsibilities, they are restrained by fewer inhibitions. The distinctive characteristics of antigovernmental war stem from the fact that it is waged between qualitatively different types of organizations, each of which has its own liabilities and advantages.

In intergovernmental war the initiative is normally presumed to rest with the stronger of the two contestants: a three-to-one superiority, according to the traditional military maxim, was necessary to pass from the defensive to the offensive. In this sense, as Clausewitz maintained, defense was the stronger form of warfare because it could be sustained with weaker forces. In intrastate war, however, this relationship is reversed. As in nonviolent domestic politics, the offensive is the strategy of the weaker and the defensive that of the stronger. The strategic initiative always rests with the antigovernment, and larger forces are required by the defensive government than by the offensive clique or party. The offensive is the stronger form of warfare. In international warfare the offensive is the result of material superiority, while in domestic warfare the offensive is a means to material superiority. Inferiority can be converted to superiority, however, only because of the fundamentally tripartite nature of antigovernmental war as contrasted with the duality of intergovernmental war.

Abstractly, two general types of competitive situations can be distinguished: those in which the two parties interact directly and attempt to secure their aims by strengthening themselves and reducing the strength of their opponents and those in which the two contestants compete indirectly by attempting to win for themselves the support of third parties. The former situation, to adapt Spykman's terminology, involves "direct action," the latter "political action."[9] In actuality, of course, any competitive situation contains elements of both. To the extent, however, that only two parties exist, politics becomes impossible. Two men on a desert island can bargain or fight, but they cannot politick; when the waves wash up a third, however, politics begins. In competition between any two of the three, inherent differences in strength and cunning will still be important, but the extent to which one or the other can secure the support of the third will also be important. The classic recurring situations of politics always involve this tripartite relationship: two parties appealing for the vote of an electorate, two lobbyists attempting to influence legislators, two lawyers contesting before a judge, two states attempting to make an ally out of a neutral. In most interstate wars each participant has an interest in encouraging neutrality or belligerence in other powers. If, however, the support of a third party is essential to the victory of either of two participants in an interstate controversy, neither side is likely to risk war until it is assured of that support. In domestic violence, on the other hand, the essence of the conflict is the appeal to third parties. The direct action of the opponents upon each other, particularly in coups d'état, remains important, but the decisive characteristic of the struggle is the effort to gain the support of those who initially are neither friend nor foe. Apart from a prolonged intergovernmental civil war, the dichotomization of population and social institutions is seldom complete. All the distinctive methods of revolutionary war are devoted to the appeal for third-party support, and even in a coup d'état the great advantage of the quick seizure of the government is the opportunity it gives the insurrectionists to appeal to the uncommitted: the first act of the leaders of any successful coup invariably is the issuance of a manifesto demanding the support of the populace for "their" new government against the sinister forces of the counterrevolution.

The contestants in interstate wars are governments, and their goals may be limited to the acquisition of a particular piece of territory or some other specific value, or they may be total, requiring the elimination or complete subordination, of the opposing government. Insurrectionary war, on the other hand, is almost always total. The government aims at the elimination of the challenge to its authority; the insurrectionists aim at the capture or destruction of the government. Thus, the political character of domestic war, in the competing appeals of the contestants to third parties, tends to be stronger than that of interstate war. On the other hand, negotiation and compromise between the contestants, which often characterize intergovernmental war, are normally lacking in domestic wars. Neither side wants to recognize the legitimacy of the other, and negotiations, much less agreements, imply such recognition. Armistices and peace treaties are possible between governments, but rarely between governments and antigovernments. When they do exist, they are generally recognized as temporary in nature, similar to the "political truces" which in national emergencies momentarily suspend partisan competition in constitutional democracies. When discussion does take place between domestic contestants, it usually results in the surrender of one or the other.

Antigovernmental war encourages civil-military relations different from those stimulated by interstate conflict. Other things being equal, the more a state achieves a system of objective civilian control the more effective it is in providing for its external security and in conducting foreign wars. Domestic war, on the other hand, demands subjective civilian control. In particular, in the post–World War II period the strategies of deterrence and of limited war not only required types of military forces that were of little use in internal wars, but they also tended to demand a relationship between military institutions and the government opposite to that required by internal war. In terms of type of military force, deterrence and limited war demanded reasonably small, ready, professional "constabulary forces," in Morris Janowitz's happy phrase.[10] In terms of military relations to the government, both the deterrent force and the limited war force had clearly defined missions and had to be highly responsive to the political leaders of the government in the performance of these missions. In domestic war, on the other hand, the political and military roles of the principal actors are merged on both sides, and political and military means become indistinguishable. In a coup d'état generals play political roles and governmental leaders, if they are able, exercise military command. In domestic war, moreover, the targets of both contestants are political institutions, social groups, and the general population. Both insurrectionaries and the government attempt to arouse these groups on their behalf. The employment of arms, like the exercise of the franchise, becomes a concomitant of citizenship. Thus the military forces which are employed and the nature of their leadership, on both sides, tend to be directly opposed to that required for interstate wars. Traditionally, the European powers made a relatively sharp distinction between the colonial army and the metropolitan army.[11] Certainly, it is an open question whether a government can maintain simultaneously within the same territory the systems required for both international war and domestic war. As Raoul Girardet has demonstrated, the change in function from interstate to domestic conflict may have drastic effect upon the attitudes of military officers toward their government and upon their amenability to the traditional forms of objective civilian control.[12]

VARIETIES OF DOMESTIC VIOLENCE

Different forms of government are associated with different forms of war. The decline of limited war and the rise of total war normally ha[ve] been linked, for example, with the shift from absolute monarchy to democracy. Even monarchies, democracies, and totalitarian dictatorships, however, share much in common as governments, and the variations in the forms of war that they wage are neither numerous nor extensive. Insurrections, on the other hand, may be launched by the most varied groups, from a small junta of top military officers to a fanatic revolutionary party. Insurrectionary wars, consequently, seem to exist in an almost endless variety of forms. Perhaps for this reason the temptation to catalog them is virtually irresistible. Lasswell and Kaplan speak of palace revolutions, political revolutions, and social revolutions.[13] Bonnet distinguishes among *guerres civiles*, *guerres de libération*, and *guerres révolutionnaires*. *Guerres civiles* are subdivided into riots, insurrections, pronunciamentos, and revolutions. *La guerre révolutionnaire*, in turn, is a compound of *la guerre de partisans* plus *la guerre psychologique*.[14] Stokes, in his analysis of violence in Latin America, identifies *machetismo*, *cuartelazo*, *golpe de estado*, and *revolución* as means of direct action, and *imposición*, *candidato único*, *continuismo*, and election as outwardly peaceful means of obtaining power which "rest upon a foundation of force."[15] In his volume on Latin American violence Lieuwen discusses *caudillismo*, "predatory militarism," coups d'état, and social revolutions.[16] Other writers speak of subversion, *émeutes*, general strikes, and assassination, and almost everyone attempts to draw a line between national revolutions and social revolutions. The variety of forms reflects differences in the nature of the participants, their relations with each other, and the political culture of the society in which they exist.

Historically the classic form of domestic violence in Europe was the urban revolt or revolution in which the principal focus was the seizure or attempted seizure of power by one class or social group through violence directed primarily against the established government in the capital city. For this Gallic tradition, epitomized by Halévy's "Insurgent," 1789 was the model.

> There were [in the words of D. W. Brogan] the June Days of 1848; the resistance to the Coup d'Etat of 1851; the Commune of 1871. There were the less dramatic or less dramatized days of 1848 in Berlin and Vienna; there were riots and risings in the Romagna, in Valencia; there were the great strikes—and their bloody consequences, Fetherstonhaugh and the battle between the steel workers and the Pinkerton gunmen hired by Carnegie and Frick. There were Moscow and Petersburg in 1905; Paterson and Lowell; the 'Wobblies' and the mutineers of the 17th Infantry at Montpellier; all the tradition of insurrection and defiance that runs continuously from the first Fourteenth of July. . . .[17]

At the end of the line, there is Petersburg again in 1917. This type of insurrection reflected the politics of bourgeoisie, proletariat, and industrialism. A distinctive mark of the nineteenth century, it is out of date in the middle of the twentieth century.

After World War II politics in the underdeveloped areas centered about the struggle for independence and the processes of modernization and development. These were the principal causes of the two dominant forms of insurrectionary violence in these areas: revolutionary war and the reform coup d'état. The struggle for independence often took the form of revolutionary war. The processes of modernization and westernization often required either revolutionary war or a succession of coups d'état.

REVOLUTIONARY WAR AND GROUP ALIENATION

Revolutionary wars of the post–World War II period included the later phases of the Chinese civil war, the struggle between the Viet Minh and the French in Indochina, the guerrilla war of the Communist rebels in Greece, the Hukbalahap rebellion in the Philippines, the jungle fighting in Malaya, the Algerian insurrection, and the Castro revolt against Batista.[18] Revolutionary war is linked with the end of colonialism, agrarian movements, and the process of community definition and state creation. The difference between it and the old European urban revolution is the difference between the Chinese revolution and the Russian revolution.

Revolutionary wars occur when the government is distant—politically, socially, and even geographically—from a significant counterelite. Recourse to revolutionary war is a sign that the counterelite has failed to penetrate the existing political structure. Colonial revolts, consequently, often take the form of revolutionary wars. The base of the colonial government in its home territory is out of reach of the nationalist counter-elite, and this distance is normally reinforced by ethnic differences between the colonial rulers and the native population. Where revolutionary wars occur in noncolonial areas, similar obstacles usually prevent the permeation of the government by the counterelite. In the Philippines, for instance, the Hukbalahaps first attempted to achieve their goals through peaceful means, electing seven members of the Philippine legislature. When the legislature refused to seat them, the Huk leaders returned to the countryside to precipitate revolt.

Divorced from the existing political system, the counterelite attempts to develop a parallel structure independent of the government. Its goal is usually the overthrow of the entire existing political and social system. A long, arduous route to power, revolutionary war can only be pursued by dedicated parties or movements sustained by a coherent ideology or sense of mission. The war usually begins in an area distant from the capital and the main centers of governmental power. If successful, the instigating group gradually expands the locus of its authority, acquires more and more of the attributes of a government, and eventually exhausts and overwhelms the previously existing government. Lenin, it is reported, once said that "no revolution of the masses can triumph without the help of a portion of the armed forces that sustained the old regime."[19] The successful revolutionary wars in Asia and Africa and the Castro revolution in Cuba are exceptions to this rule. Revolutionary war proceeds on the premise that the government controls the armed forces of the state and that it is necessary to develop distinct revolutionary armed forces to employ against the state. In a successful revolutionary war a party creates an army, which, in turn, brings into existence a government.

The decisive aspect of the revolutionary war is the contest between the counterelite and the government for the support of a communal or socioeconomic group that is imperfectly integrated into the existing political system. The causes of the alienation of the group may stem either from the refusal of the government to recognize its distinctive characteristics and problems or the relegation of the group to a secondary position in society. As Lucien Pye has suggested, alienation often has its roots in the rationalism of modern government.[20] The doctrines of equality and individualism undermine the ties of the community to the government. The abolition of the Arab bureaus in Algeria was justified on the grounds that no distinction should be drawn between Frenchmen of different faiths. The Chinese secretariat in Malaya was emasculated because here "were no separate corps of officials to deal with Malay or Indian problems, and it bordered on the invidious to treat the Chinese as a special case."[21] In each case these actions symbolized an apparent indifference by the governing authorities to communal differences and hence encouraged feelings of alienation in the affected groups at the same time that they reduced the ability of the government to counteract them. Just as the educated Chinese in Malaya resented their "restricted citizenship," the Indochinese resented their "second class citizenship." Similarly, in the Philippines, "For too many years the government had been set apart from the common people in the farm lands of Central Luzon. . . . At the end of the war the peasants felt no obligation to support the government nor to be loyal to it in the struggle with the Huks."[22] The decline in identification and communication between communal group and the governmental authorities opens the group as a target for the counterelite.

The counterelite attempts to win the target group through terrorism and persuasion. In the "normal" intergovernmental war violence is directed primarily against the enemy; it is a means of reducing his numbers and of undermining his will to resist. In the initial phases of a revolutionary war, however, the counterelite directs its terrorism and violence primarily against the members of the target group. The aim of the violence is not to eliminate the forces of the government but to win the members of the target group. In Algeria between November, 1954, and April, 1957, the rebels killed 891 European civilians and 3,438 members of the French security forces but 5,576 Moslem civilians. In Malaya through June, 1957, the insurrectionists killed 106 Europeans, 226 Indians, 318 Malayans, and 1,700 Chinese civilians. In the first year of the Kenya emergency the Mau Mau killed eleven Asians, twenty-one Europeans, and at least 704 Africans. In Cyprus the EOKA killed three Greeks for every two non-Greeks.[23] In the Philippines the Huks killed farmers, burned homes, and raided villages in efforts to build up their support among the peasants. Similarly, the Viet Minh penetrated the Tonkin delta and established a codominion with the French, the one ruling by day and the other by night, through "its two most useful weapons, nationalism and terror."[24] Since the terrorism of the counterelite is useful only in the effects it has *pour encourager les autres*, it frequently includes blatant brutalities and atrocities. The elimination of prominent members of the target group who refuse to cooperate with the rebels convinces other members of the group that the only prudent course is to buy safety by contributing money to the rebels, furnishing them with information, or cooperating with them in other ways.

Simultaneously with their use of terror the counterelite and its military forces also employ persuasion. Propaganda and psychological war are the partners of terrorism. In Malaya, for example, Lucien Pye found that virtually all the surrendered Communist prisoners interviewed emphasized the importance of propaganda, identifying it with politics.[25] While the motivations of the counterelite may be ideological in character, the appeal to the target group is normally couched in the nationalistic or economic terms which are most meaningful to the target group. The revolutionaries particularly attempt to create and to maintain in the target group a sense of the ineptitude and weakness of the established government and a belief in the ultimate victory of the revolutionary group. The appearance of strength must be cultivated at the sacrifice of all else; a "bandwagon" psychology is essential in winning the target group.[26] In reply, the government attempts to convince the target group that it has the will and the strength to stamp out the insurrection. To win supporters in the target group, the government must guarantee not to abandon them at a later date. If it once breaks its word, it creates a doubt which will haunt it continuously. In a dualistic intergovernmental war the sense of inferiority, of fighting against great odds, may inspire great effort. In a tripartite revolutionary war, however, the decisive factor is the support of the target group. The members of the target group, in turn, want to be on the winning side. Whichever side can convince the target group that it is winning is in fact winning.

Terrorism, Brian Crozier argues, is the weapon of the weak.[27] It is a weapon, however, which is effective not against the strong but against the vulnerable. Though sporadic murders and bombings would never suffice to destroy the forces of the government, they may suffice to win the active or passive support of the target group. The protection of the target group against the terrorism may well strain the government's resources or impose upon it a burden that it does not wish to bear. The peculiar strength of the counterelite derives precisely from the fact that it is *not* a government and that it *is* pursuing an offensive strategy. Dramatic differences in strength usually exist between the antigovernmental and governmental forces. In Malaya, at their top strength, the Communists had 5,500 fighters in the jungle, while the British mobilized against them over 40,000 regular troops plus 100,000 men in auxiliary and constabulary forces. In Indochina the Viet Minh came out of World War II with slightly over 10,000 men. By the last year of the war their forces numbered 300,000 to 400,000 troops, including local militia, but the French Union forces were still more numerous. In March, 1956, FLN military strength in Algeria totalled 29,050 men, more than ever before, while French forces included about 200,000 men at that time and more than twice that number five months later.[28]

To carry out its efforts to conquer the target group, the counterelite and its military forces require a reasonably secure base of operations. One great weakness of the Hukbalahap movement was the inadequacy of the relatively restricted and heavily populated farm areas of central Luzon as a base for revolutionary operations. In Malaya the jungle furnished a base for the Communist guerrillas so long as they could procure food and supplies from villages and other settled areas. In Cuba the rugged terrain of the Sierra Maestrae furnished Castro with a base for operations against the peasants. In all three of these cases the rebel bases were within the territory of the government the rebels were attempting to overthrow. If a base can be established upon external territory, secure from governmental attack, the revolutionary movement has a much greater chance of success. Furnishing such a base for supplies and training purposes is the greatest assistance a foreign government can give a revolutionary movement. If the territory of the foreign government is contiguous with that of the target government, this assistance may be of decisive importance in the outcome of the revolutionary war. The withdrawal of Tito from the Comintern helped end the Greek war at the same time that the Communist victory in China insured the continuation of the Indochinese war. The Algerian Nationalists originally received extensive assistance from Egypt and then, after its independence, from Tunisia. Since a revolutionary war is a war of attrition, a relatively secure base is essential for its successful prosecution. A colonial power has an inherent advantage in fighting against a revolutionary movement that lacks a contiguous external base. On the other hand, a revolutionary movement with such a base has an inherent advantage in fighting an independent government without a home territory to draw upon. In the latter case, substantial support from allies, as in Greece, may be essential for the government to maintain itself. If the colonial government is secure in its home base and the revolutionary forces also possess a secure contiguous external base, it is possible that the war may, as in Indochina, drag on indefinitely with neither side able to force a decision.

Eventually, of course, if it is to achieve its ultimate goal, the revolutionary counterelite has to establish "liberated" base areas within the contested territory. As it gradually expands its locus of control, the revolutionary movement takes on more and more of the functions and characteristics of a government. Along with the collection of taxes and supplies from a liberated area, it also organizes the population into local militia units. The establishment of such units for the revolutionary forces, as for their opponents, is essential to free the mobile, "regular" forces for offensive operations in other areas. Terrorism gives way to guerrilla war and then to full-scale war.[29]

The reaction of the government in a revolutionary war normally goes through two phases. At first the government tends to treat the insurrection as a traditional problem for the police and the military. It minimizes the threat of the revolutionary forces and confidently proclaims that the "brigands" will be quickly eliminated and order restored. In 1946 the Philippine government declared that it would exterminate the Huks within sixty days. General Boucher confidently announced in the summer of 1948 that he would quickly clean up the Malayan guerrillas.[30] The government retains confidence in its superior conventional military forces, and it attempts to use those forces in the conventional fashion. The continued success of the revolutionary forces, however, precipitates a crisis within the government. It now recognizes that the revolution requires not only a much larger and different military effort to suppress it but also an integrated political-economic effort to counter the appeals of the revolutionaries to the target group. It also recognizes the need to overhaul its organizational structure dealing with the rebellion and to merge political and military responsibilities in a single individual. In November, 1952, for example, Oliver Lyttleton emphasized that the three great needs in Malaya were to unify civil-military authority, to secure Chinese cooperation in the antiguerrilla campaigns, and to organize Chinese militia units for the self-protection of the loyal Chinese population. Similarly, in the fall of 1950, the French were forced to the realization that "an effective end must be put to the antipathy between French civil and military authorities" in Indochina and that new efforts must be made to win the support of the Vietnamese in the struggle against the Viet Minh.[31]

As the government's response moves into its second phase, the new supreme political-military director of the effort plays a critical role. He not only concentrates in himself the direction of the war on all fronts, but he also dramatizes the determination and ability of the government to carry through the struggle and to maintain the safety of its supporters. In varying degrees this critically important role was played by Magsaysay in the Philippines, Templer in Malaya, Papagos in Greece, and de Lattre de Tassigny in Indochina. Above all, the leader plays the role of the politician in campaigning for the support and the confidence of the target group. Templer and Magsaysay devoted large portions of their time to touring the disturbed areas, restoring direct communications with the target group, and demonstrating personally the interests of the government in the well-being and safety of the target-group members.

The director of the counterrevolutionary effort may be a civilian cabinet officer (Magsaysay), a military theater commander (de Lattre), or military commander and civilian governor (Templer). Irrespective of his formal position, however, to be successful he must effectively exercise complete control of the counterrevolutionary effort. Magsaysay, for instance, insisted upon the unification of the Philippine Constabulary and the military forces, previously in separate departments, under a single chief of staff. Like Hoche in the pacification of the Vendée, he must be a "skilled politician as well as soldier." Magsaysay, for instance, although a civilian, personally commanded units in the field. The essential element is the vigor, determination, and ability of the individual, not his previous background or experience. Like the great colonial soldiers Bugeaud, Galliéni, and Lyautey, he must play both political and military roles; and, as Lyautey said, it is not the label but the man that matters, "the right man in the right place."[32]

The crucial step in the change in the approach of the government toward the revolutionary war is the recognition that the decisive aspect of the struggle is not the defeat of the enemy forces but the reconquest of the confidence of the contested population. To win the population, it is necessary to know the population, to win an audience with it, to detach it from the revolutionary forces, and eventually to control it.[33] The first necessity is for the government to convince the target group that it can provide for its security. This is the military job. Then, however, it must reintegrate the target group into the existing community. New organizational units devoted to this end provide help. In Algeria in 1955, for example, the government established the Special Administrative Sections to work with the Algerian Moslems and to carry on the activities which before 1945 had been performed by the Arab Bureaus. A nongovernmental group, the Malayan Chinese Association, founded in February, 1949, played an important role in combatting the appeal of the Communists to the Malayan Chinese and in bringing about their reintegration into the Malayan community. In the Philippines civil-affairs officers were appointed to undertake the "important tasks of interpreting the army to the people and of winning civilian support for the army activities against the Huks." The basic goal is to stimulate favorable attitudes toward the government on the part of the target group. In Malaya Templer taught the police that "in the long run their most important task was not to catch the terrorists but to persuade the public to look upon them as friends." In the Philippines Magsaysay ruthlessly suppressed police terrorism against the peasants and instituted a campaign of "attraction and fellowship."[34]

The reintegration of portions of the target group into the community may require extensive physical movement and resettlement. In Malaya, for instance, thousands of "squatters" making a meager living on government land close to the jungle became a major source of support and supplies for the guerrillas. One decisive action of the government in its struggles against the guerrillas was the movement and resettlement of these "squatters" in new villages, where they were provided with adequate work, land, and protection. According to one French officer the three most effective methods of pacification were the "tache d'huile" of Lyautey, the establishment of forbidden zones in which all nongovernment personnel were presumed to be enemies, and the regrouping of the population. In Cambodia, in 1952–1953, thousands of peasants were regrouped to provide for their own security and welfare.[35] In the Philippines Magsaysay created the EDCOR farms in Mindanao for the resettlement and rehabilitation of the Hukbalahaps. Significantly, one of the principal attractions of EDCOR to the rebels was the promise of peace and security which they offered.

The conduct of an effective counterrevolutionary action by a government thus requires a major change in the leadership, attitude, and functions of the military forces. The armed forces of the state become an instrument of persuasion as well as an instrument of coercion. The military become the chain which binds a potentially disaffected social group to the broader community. As one student of the Philippine anti-Huk campaign observed:

> The EDCOR farms created a radically new role for the army. No longer were the armed forces limited to defending the nation and destroying the enemy.

The army was to serve the people in a new way—constructively and creatively. It would rehabilitate the Huks and restore them to the nation as loyal productive citizens.

A foreign news correspondent [observing the EDCOR villages] . . . said, "I have seen many armies, but this one beats them all. This is an army with a social conscience."[36]

As Girardet makes clear in his essay in this volume, the French Army in Algeria not only developed nonmilitary functions and organizations but also a political program based on the continuing French presence in Algeria and social, economic, and political equality for the Moslem population. This "social conscience" of the French Army contrasted with the indecisiveness of the French government and the self-interested devotion to the status quo of the French colonies.

As a result of the weakness of the defense in revolutionary war, the security of the target group can be protected only by the mobilization of the group itself. Militarily speaking, the formation of local militia units for this purpose is absolutely essential, as the regular military forces of the government would never suffice to guarantee security. One French officer has estimated that at least a ten-to-one superiority is necessary for effective internal defense, and in some areas of Malaya it was necessary to have a ratio of sixty-five armed men to every known terrorist.[37] Local militia units not only serve to re-establish confidence and security within the target group but also tend to cement its commitment to the side of the government. By 1952 the British in Malaya had organized over 244,000 home guards for the protection of the villages. In the Philippines and Indochina similar units were found to be indispensable.[38]

The goals of the conflicting parties and the importance of maintaining confidence in victory generally render nugatory any efforts to arrive at truces or agreements between the government and antigovernment forces. Between 1946 and 1948 the Roxas and Quirino Administrations in the Philippines attempted to reach a peaceful settlement with the Huks. One three-month truce ended "in bitter fighting," and a subsequent suspension of hostilities came to naught when the Huks refused to surrender their arms. Efforts to work out a basis for cooperation between the Communists and the Nationalists in China inevitably failed. Repeated negotiations between the French and the Viet Minh in Indochina did not produce any basis for agreement. In 1955 efforts to arrange a peaceful settlement in Malaya also broke down. In most of these instances the government was willing to offer a general amnesty to rebels who would surrender their arms, abandon their revolutionary activities, and resume normal peacetime employment. The rebels, on the other hand, normally were willing to abandon temporarily the military struggle, but not to surrender their arms or to give up their organization and its revolutionary aims. For them the truce or armistice was a shift in tactics but not in goal. On the other hand, any compromise by the government or agreement with the revolutionaries inevitably would raise questions in the minds of members of the target group about the determination of the government to maintain itself and to maintain order. As Jacques Soustelle remarked about Algeria:

> If the conviction that France will remain in Algeria is not inculcated in everyone, no Moslem, no matter how closely he may be bound to us by heart or by interest, will remain at our side. . . . Any political movement, any statement, any article in the press giving the impression that we will come to terms with terrorism—in other words, that the terrorists will some day be in a position to settle outstanding scores—drives the Algerian Moslems further from us.[39]

The decisive aspect of revolutionary war thus is the struggle for the loyalty of the vulnerable sector. In a sense, the war is conducted like an agonizing and bloody electoral campaign. If the counterelite can establish and maintain itself as the leader of the alienated sector, it has won its battle. If that sector is insufficient to maintain a state, continued strife is inevitable. If a territorially defined and viable state is feasible, succession from the old political community is the only solution. Victory for the government, in turn, can only be achieved by the reintegration of the alienated group into the over-all community and its participation in the political system.

The ability of a government to react successfully to a revolutionary war depends upon the perception and political strength of its leaders. The operations required in the second phase of the war often run counter to traditional ideas and established interests. The more detached a government is from the society disrupted by revolutionary war, the more able it will be to surmount these obstacles. An imperial government, for instance, may develop a broad view of the relations among the various groups in the colonial society and possess the ability to impose upon that society the social, economic, and political reforms necessary to reintegrate the target group into the community. A non-imperial government faced with revolutionary war may be unable to deal effectively with the war because it depends upon the very groups which the counterelite is challenging. In such circumstances the guidance and discipline of an allied government may be necessary to institute the measures required to win the revolutionary war. The British government was able to handle the Chinese insurrection in Malaya much easier than a Malayan government could have. On the other hand, divisions of opinion in the home country of the imperial government may hamper the ability of that government to fight the war. If these divisions make the government unable to devise at the political level a strategy for the conduct of the war, subordinate groups, such as the French Army in Algeria, may well attempt to assume that responsibility.

Many French writers have called revolutionary war the most probable form of future conflict. It is, however, the product of peculiar conditions. The decline of colonialism removes its best breeding ground. The revolutionary wars of the late 1940's, moreover, were in many respects an outgrowth of World War II: the insurrectionary counterelites usually began as anti-Axis guerrillas and accumulated weapons and experience which they used in the postwar period.[40] In southeast Asia the tactics of the Communist parties were shaped by the Chinese Communist victory; the revolutionary wars in the Philippines, Malaya, Indochina, and the attempted insurrections in Indonesia, Burma, and India, all reflected the Communist line of the moment. That line may again, of course, endorse these tactics. In the independent states of Asia and Africa, however, this hardly seems necessary. Their governments are often too weak to require it, and easier routes to power exist through propaganda, infiltration, and coup d'état. The Cold War competition of the major powers, however, could lead them to intervene to strengthen incipient revolutionary movements or tottering counter-revolutionary governments. Such interventions would then increase the ability of both sides to wage a prolonged revolutionary war.

Revolutionary war is most likely in a society occupying an extensive territory and divided between different communities and races in which one group predominates in the government. Potentialities for revolutionary war exist in many Latin American countries: the "Prestes column" of the 1920's in Brazil could well be the embryonic prototype of more elaborate movements to come. Conceivably the struggles between settler governments and African natives could also take this form. In South Africa, and possibly elsewhere, however, the lines may become so tightly drawn that the violence will take the form of direct intercommunal warfare rather than political competition between government and counterelite for support from the same group. . . .

INTERNATIONAL TENSION AND DOMESTIC VIOLENCE—THE DOCTRINES OF LA GUERRE REVOLUTIONNAIRE AND INDIRECT AGGRESSION

Various attempts have been made in the West to interpret and explain the violence in the politics of the underdeveloped areas. One common interpretation sees the rise of the new forms of domestic violence as directly related to the decline of the old forms of intergovernmental violence. In its most general form, the argument that a decrease in the frequency of intergovernmental conflict is likely to increase the frequency of domestic violence usually assumes that mankind's propensity to fight remains roughly constant. War is inevitable, and if it becomes unprofitable in one locale, it reappears in another. As a general truth, however, this proposition is not valid. To be sure, some relationship exists between the internal and external conflicts of a state, and external conflict does tend to increase internal unity and cohesion.[41] It does not, however, follow that external peace stimulates internal conflict, and the students of conflict have produced no significant evidence to show that such a relationship exists. Sweden and Switzerland have enjoyed both internal and external peace for decades. Governments, on the other hand, may attempt to stave off internal war with a nongovernment at home by instigating external war with a foreign government abroad. To the extent that the new inhibitory factors on interstate wars tend to close off this course of action, they also tend to make it more difficult to avoid domestic violence. Governments, however, are fairly ingenious. As alternatives to foreign wars as unifiers, they may resort to more intensive domestic action to suppress the embryonic conflict, in which case "police state" measures are the result of the absence rather than the presence of external conflict. In addition, governments may engage in nonviolent, peaceful adventurism, in which an external enemy is identified and castigated and serves as a target for group hostility, although the government carefully refrains from resorting to violence. The government may instead go to some lengths to provoke the opposing government to use violence first. Also, the reduction in interstate wars moderates one of the causes of domestic strife. "Civil war," as Sir George Clark observed of the seventeenth century, "was often a sequel to external victory . . . [and] a consequence of external defeat."[42]

While there may be no necessary general relationship between the inhibition of interstate violence and the prevalence of intrastate violence, this does not exclude the possibility of a relationship existing between the two in the special circumstances of the mid-twentieth century. That such a relationship does exist is a key assumption of the French doctrine of *la guerre révolutionnaire* and the American concept of indirect aggression. For both theories the new forms of domestic violence are primarily methods of intergovernmental conflict.

The French doctrine of *la guerre révolutionnaire* was in many respects the counterpart to the American doctrine of limited war.[43] The American doctrine was a reaction to a traumatic military experience in Korea, the French doctrine to similar experiences in Indochina and Algeria. To American thinkers the logical result of the balance of terror was limited war; to French military men it was insurrectionary war. While American theory distinguished between general war involving thermonuclear weapons, on the one hand, and limited war with conventional or tactical nuclear weapons, on the other, French theory drew a threefold distinction. "La guerre classique," the traditional form of general war, was now highly improbable. The two relevant types of military action were "la guerre nucléaire" and "la guerre révolutionnaire."[44] The former, the French emphasized, was likely to include all forms of interstate war; it was expensive, destructive, and relatively unlikely. While American theorists saw limited war as the most probable form of future Soviet military action, French writers assigned a similar role to *la guerre révolutionnaire*. In both countries it was argued that this new phenomenon required a major reorientation of military thought and new military doctrines. Yet, while the novel features of the new form of warfare were emphasized, in both countries extensive efforts were also made to develop its historical precedents. In both countries also it was emphasized that the new form of warfare was peculiarly suited to Marxist-Leninist theory and practice.

The parallels in the development of the doctrines of limited war and *la guerre révolutionnaire* should not obscure significant differences in the substances of these doctrines. The doctrine of limited war was a pure theory of intergovernmental war. The model for it was derived from the eighteenth-century world of territorial nation-states in which absolute governments exercised strict control over their military forces and used them as instruments in their diplomacy, and in which the struggles among the states were normally over specific pieces of territory and did not involve either the existence of the state or the overthrow of its political and social system. The basic model for the French doctrine, on the other hand, was not eighteenth-century Europe but twentieth-century China. While the limited-war theorists harked back to Clausewitz, those of *la guerre révolutionnaire* invoked Mao Tse-tung. *La guerre révolutionnaire*, they emphasized, was total war within a society. In it, to be sure, war was the instrument of politics, but its distinguishing characteristic was the intermingling of economic, political, and military means. The theory of limited war, in many respects so classically military, was in large part articulated in the United States by civilian social scientists. The theory of *la guerre révolutionnaire*, on the other hand, involving the intimate mixture of political and military roles, techniques, and forces, was to a much larger extent the product of professional military officers.

The theorists of *la guerre révolutionnaire* recognized that it was a form of domestic war. It was, however, they insisted, a product of interstate conflict. They argued that it was primarily an instrument of one government, the Soviet Union, against another government, France, waged through satellites and political instruments. "The Algerian rebellion," one official French document stated, "is incontestably a movement inspired and actively supported by foreign countries which interfere impudently in the internal affairs of France."[45] *La guerre révolutionnaire*, Claude Delmas said, is the means whereby one state can make war against another without provoking general conflict and without even appearing to be resorting to war. The peculiar nature of *la guerre révolutionnaire* (guerrilla warfare plus psychological warfare) bore the imprint of the doctrine and tactics of international Communism. As Delmas declared, "la guerre révolutionnaire n'existerait pas (ou en resterait au stade de la guerilla) si les parties communistes n'etaient pas des instruments de la politique soviétique."[46] In some cases the French thinkers suggested that *la guerre révolutionnaire* was always the instrument of Communists; in others they argued that even where it was not the product of Communism the Communists always benefitted from its use; always, however, they maintained that the methods of *la guerre révolutionnaire* were inspired by Communist theory and practice, and that the Communists were the instruments of the Soviet Union.[47] Having linked the origins of *la guerre révolutionnaire* with the deterrence of intergovernmental wars and the nature of it with Communist theory and practice, the French thinkers inevitably were drawn to argue that every manifestation of *la guerre révolutionnaire* was the product of Communist action on behalf of the Soviet Union. The French military thus arrived at the conclusion shared by many civilian leaders of the government that in Algeria as in Indochina the real enemy was international Communism.[48]

Like the doctrine of *la guerre révolutionnaire*, the concept of indirect aggression was stimulated initially by the struggle with the Communist movements of southeast Asia. The Manila pact of September, 1954, provided that the parties would cooperate not only "to resist armed aggression" but also "to prevent and counter subversive activities directed from without against their territorial integrity and political stability." Although the operative terms of the pact in Article II were directed primarily at what Professor W. Macmahon Ball has called "subversion from without," the actual antisubversive activities jointly undertaken by members of the pact have been largely directed at "subversion from within." Committees and a staff established under the pact help to coordinate the antisubversive efforts of the members and to provide for the exchange of information.[49] The invocation of indirect aggression as a justification for direct American counteraction did not come until the 1958 coup d'état in Baghdad and the American intervention in Lebanon. Here the evidence of subversion from without was much more definite. American action was justified, the President argued, because the "Cairo, Damascus and Soviet radios" had encouraged an insurrection against the established government of Lebanon and the insurrectionists were being supplied with "sizeable amounts of arms, ammunition, and money and by personnel infiltrated from Syria to fight against the lawful authorities." The aim of these actions was to "overthrow the legally constituted Government of Lebanon and to install by violence a government which would subordinate the independence of Lebanon to the policies of the United Arab Republic."[50]

The doctrine of *la guerre révolutionnaire* began with the result—the struggles in Indochina, Algeria, and elsewhere—and argued that the Soviet Union and its subservient international Communist movement were in large part causes of this result. The doctrine of indirect aggression, on the other hand, began with the causes—the means by which one government can encourage violence against another government—and then argued that these causes could produce calamitous results. "Through use of inflammatory radio broadcasts; through infiltration of weapons, agents, and of bribe money," Mr. Dulles said, "through incitement to murder and assassination; and through threats of personal violence it becomes possible for one nation to destroy the genuine independence of another." Toleration of indirect aggression, he warned, would lead to a third world war.[51] Thus, while the doctrine of *la guerre révolutionnaire* stressed the extent to which Communist influence was responsible for actual revolutionary wars, the doctrine of indirect aggression stressed the extent to which one government, without resort to force, can produce revolution in another. The existence of an external base of support beyond the territory of the target government is, of course, a major aid to revolutionary forces. The basis for the revolution, however, must exist within the society in which it takes place. The techniques mentioned by President Eisenhower and Mr. Dulles can only serve to encourage and to support already existing antigovernmental forces in the target country.

The doctrine of indirect aggression tends to underestimate its pervasiveness and to overestimate its effectiveness. If "indirect aggression were to be admitted as a legitimate means of promoting international policy," Mr. Dulles declared, "small nations would be doomed and the world would become one of constant chaos, if not of war." Any change of government in any country, however, whether by violence or otherwise, presumably affects the interests of the major world powers. Governments attempt to encourage favorable changes in foreign governments and to prevent unfavorable ones. The pervasiveness of indirect aggression in this broad sense is, however, no testimony to its effectiveness. Because all domestic violence has implications for interstate conflict, it cannot be concluded that all domestic violence is caused by interstate conflict.

The tendency to overestimate the ease with which the Soviet Union can subvert or overthrow foreign governments leads to the conclusion that the United States can also profitably employ such tactics. "In the perfection of the instrument of subversion," one writer has said, for example, "the Soviets may have fashioned a form of unconventional military action capable of achieving victories as great as any expected from the more conventional forms of war." From this he concluded that "Subversion is not a form of action reserved for use by the Soviets alone; it can be fully as powerful if turned against them."[52] The Administration which Mr. Dulles served, however, came into power committed to a program of indirect aggression—liberation and political warfare—against the Soviet satellites. Its protestations were sufficient to make the Soviet Union until 1957 a leading advocate of un condemnation of indirect aggression.[53] Its accomplishments, however, are a significant index of the effectiveness of the tactic.

Insurrection and subversion are primarily the weapons of indigenous antigovernments. Foreign governments, of course, may encourage antigovernments. Intervention by one government against another, however, has the potentialities and the limitations of intervention by outside personnel and money in a local election campaign. Though it can influence the result, it cannot create support where the basis for that support does not already exist, and it cannot reverse a drastically unfavorable balance of forces within the contested area. Intervention on behalf of an established government, moreover, is usually easier than intervention against it. Traditional liberal thinking has often been criticized for analyzing war and international relations in terms of the ideas and categories of domestic politics. The doctrines of *la guerre révolutionnaire* and indirect aggression, on the other hand, tend to apply to domestic political struggles the assumptions and concepts of international politics. Domestic violence, obviously, is influenced by the intensity and nature of international conflict, but it cannot be explained *simply* as the result of that conflict.

Foreign governmental intervention more often is the result of domestic violence than is domestic violence the product of foreign intervention. The longer the domestic violence continues, moreover, the more likely are foreign governments to become involved on one side or another. The Soviet Union initiated neither the Indochinese and Algerian insurrections nor the Castro revolution, but once these became established facts of political life, it could hardly be expected not to capitalize upon them. Thus, a quick coup d'état is more likely to minimize the involvement of external powers and maximize international stability than a prolonged revolutionary war. From the Western viewpoint, even a coup that topples a friendly government, such as the Kassim coup of 1958, but that installs a government with whom one can negotiate, might be preferable to an unsuccessful coup degenerating into extensive civil strife, which inevitably would involve the Soviet Union and the Western powers.

VIOLENCE AND TRANSNATIONAL COMMUNITY

While the principal manifestations of domestic violence cannot be explained only by reference to *international* politics, neither can they be explained on an individual basis without reference to the general patterns of *world* politics. Outbreaks of domestic violence tend to occur in waves. In his study of Latin American politics Lieuwen identifies one wave of radical reform coups beginning with Peron's conquest of power in Argentina in 1943 and including coups or revolts in Bolivia in 1943, Ecuador and Guatemala in 1944, Brazil in 1945, El Salvador and Costa Rica in 1948, Panama and Bolivia in 1952, and Colombia in 1953. In addition, reformers came to power peacefully in Venezuela and Peru in 1945. Overlapping the reform wave was a progression of conservative coups: Venezuela and Peru in 1948, Haiti in 1950, Cuba in 1952, Guatemala and Brazil in 1954, Panama and Argentina in 1955, and Colombia in 1957.[54] In other waves of domestic violence the individual manifestations were much more closely grouped in time. In 1948, as the Communist line in Asia shifted, revolutionary wars or insurrections began in the Philippines, Burma, Indonesia, India, and Malaya. In 1956 anti-Soviet disorders shook the eastern European satellites, particularly Hungary and Poland. In 1958 military coups d'état took place in Iraq, the Sudan, Thailand, Burma, and Pakistan. In 1960 student demonstrations and riots helped to overturn the existing regimes in South Korea and Turkey, to cancel President Eisenhower's visit to Japan, and to stimulate the abortive insurrection of the Algerian colons.[55]

The reasons for these waves of violence undoubtedly vary. All of them, however, reflect the shrinking of world politics, the similarity of political conditions and forces in different countries, and the extent to which events in one country may affect those in another. At least three possible explanations exist for the waves of violence. First, they may be the result of common direction. This was certainly the case with the Communist-inspired revolutionary wars and insurrections of 1948 and 1949. Presumably it could be the case again if the Kremlin should decide that insurrection on a broad scale was a desirable way of achieving its objectives in the underdeveloped areas. Common direction, however, will not explain most of the waves of violence in domestic politics. Nor will the alternative extreme explanation of isolated parallelism, that is, the emergence in different countries of similar but unrelated situations that lead to similar and almost simultaneous coups or domestic wars. Undoubtedly, the processes of evolution in newly independent countries do follow certain broad common channels. But even if the paths of development were much more closely parallel than they are, this would still not completely explain the waves of violence. Parallelism does not necessarily imply simultaneity.

In addition to similarity of political condition, emulation is also necessary to create a wave. The power of example, the influence exercised by the "pacesetter," is a critically important result of the improvement in worldwide communications. A successful coup or insurrection by one party or group in one country inspires similar parties or groups in other countries to similar action. The conditions breeding insurrection or coup d'état must be present in these other countries, while the action of the "pacesetting" country indicates that the time may well be ripe. The success of Peron in Argentina stimulated radical military reformers in other Latin American states. The revolt in Bolivia a few months later was "obviously an echo of the events in Buenos Aires."[56] Similarly, the fall of Peron in 1955 stimulated the efforts to remove Rojas Pinilla in Colombia. The defeat of the French in one revolutionary war in Indochina directly encouraged the launching of another in Algeria. The successful toppling of Syngmann Rhee's government by student, civilian, and military action in 1960 demonstrated that the United States would not intervene to uphold an unpopular ally against a popular uprising and directly encouraged students, liberals, and soldiers to undertake similar successful action in Turkey.

A wave of violence presupposes a degree of transnational political community, involving some similarity of political conditions in the different countries and some influence by the political events in one country on the political events of another. A successful coup by conservative groups in Venezuela may stimulate action by conservative groups in Peru, but it is not likely to produce any comparable response in the United States, France, or Pakistan. In this sense, Peru and Venezuela are part of a political community from which the other three countries are excluded. On the other hand, a swing to the right in the United States may be the product of conditions that also produce a shift to the right in Canada, and the change in the United States may hasten the change in Canada. Or a military coup in Pakistan may serve as a model for comparable coups in other southern Asian states, but it is not likely to be relevant to political developments in Italy, Japan, or the Congo. Revolutions (and other forms of domestic violence reflecting changing political tides) are seldom exported, but they are often imitated. They can only be imitated, however, in countries where the necessary raw materials already exist.

The dominant forms of violence of each age reflect the politics of the age. The violence of the seventeenth century reflected the decline of the Hapsburg Empire and the conflicts over religion. The limited wars and colonial wars of the eighteenth century were the natural products of the national monarchies of the old regime. The nineteenth century encompassed insurrections devoted to liberalism, democracy, and social change, on the one hand, and renewed colonial wars on the other. The first half of the twentieth century saw nationalistic rivalries and expansion produce two world wars. The rapid political and economic change in Latin America, Africa, and southern Asia has produced and will continue to produce its own distinctive patterns of violence. This violence may take the form of revolutionary wars or reform coups, and it may assume still different forms. In the new states traditionalist elements are likely to reassert themselves and to challenge the nationalist leaders who led the fight against the colonial power. Wars of secession and integration are likely between the regions of artificially defined "nationstates." In Africa intertribal wars are still possible, and intercommunal wars between white settlers and natives seem unavoidable. Governments which have achieved their independence through revolutionary war or other forms of violence have their own distinctive problems in breaking the patterns of violence established in the pre-independence era.[57] All of these forms of violence are likely to involve military forces and civil-military relations very different from those usually associated with interstate wars along European lines. Most violence will be civil violence in that it occurs within the accepted boundaries of particular political units. All violence will be civil violence in that it occurs within the great society of world politics in which almost all nations and governments recognize a common interest in minimizing intergovernmental war and in which domestic violence in one country resembles and is influenced by the patterns of violence in other countries belonging to the same transnational political community.

For the future, the "general mêlée" of the seventeenth century may be a more applicable model than the calculated wars of the eighteenth. The distinction between intergovernmental and domestic wars may fade, with violence becoming more pervasive, more dispersed, and less within the control of governments. In a sense, vast areas of the world may evolve in the direction of Europe at the beginning of the seventeenth century when

> wars were not continuations of religious or dynastic or any other policy by the use of organized force, but collisions of communities. Some of these communities were the imperfect and improvised assemblages of civil war, others were the comparatively complete societies called monarchies or republics. They sometimes blundered into their struggles and sometimes went into them methodically, with their eyes open, through the regular procedure of negotiation, ultimatum, and declaration of war; sometimes they managed hostilities equally methodically, but sometimes their forces, even if they did not become mutinous or barbarous, were not servants at all but were moved by a will of their own. Peace sometimes came by rational stages, but sometimes by exhaustion and anarchy. Any component part of society might break loose and smash or obstruct any other in its movements.[58]

As in the seventeenth century, however, the proliferation of new forms of violence may herald the emergence of new and more stable political institutions.

NOTES

1 Harold D. Lasswell and Abraham Kaplan, *Power and Society* (New Haven, 1950), p. 252.

2 See, e.g., T. Abel, "The Element of Decision in the Pattern of War," *American Sociological Review*, Vol. 6 (December, 1941), 853–859. The assumption that decisions to risk or to provoke war are carefully calculated was, of course, basic to the entire strategy of deterrence pursued by the United States after World War II.

3 See John H. Herz, *International Politics in the Atomic Age* (New York, 1959), Part One.

4 On the conditions under which arms races may substitute for war, see my "Arms Races: Prerequisites and Results," *Public Policy* (Yearbook of the Graduate School of Public Administration, Harvard University), 8 (1958), 41–86.

5 See Vernon Lee Fluharty, Dance of the Millions: Military Rule and the Social Revolution in Colombia, 1930–1956 (Pittsburgh, 1957), pp. 2, 234, 250.

6   New York Herald Tribune, Dec. 6, 1960, p. 24.

7   Lasswell and Kaplan, *op. cit.*, p. 274. See also Quincy Wright, *A Study of War* (Chicago, 1942), I, 256–257.

8   Karl von Clausewitz, *On War*, trans. O. J. Matthijs Jolles (Washington, 1950), pp. 15–16. Cf. Herz, *op. cit.*, p. 60.

9   Nicholas Spykman, *America's Strategy in World Politics* (New York, 1942), p. 13. See also Simmel's comments on the dyad and the triad, *The Sociology of Georg Simmel* trans. and ed. Kurt H. Wolff (Glencoe, Ill., 1950), pp. 135–169.

10   Morris Janowitz, The Professional Soldier: A Social and Political Portrait (Glencoe, Ill., 1960), ch. 20.

11   See Maury Feld, "A Typology of Military Organization," *Public Policy*, 8 (1958), 3–40.

12   See his essay, *infra*, pp. 123–129.

13   Lasswell and Kaplan, *op. cit.*, pp. 274–275.

14   Gabriel Bonnet, Les Guerres insurrectionelles et révolutionnaires (Paris, 1958), pp. 34ff.

15   W. S. Stokes, "Violence as a Power Factor in Latin American Politics," *Western Political Quarterly*, 5 (Summer, 1952), 445–468.

16   Edwin Lieuwen, Arms and Politics in Latin America (New York, 1960), passim.

17   D. W. Brogan, *The Price of Revolution* (New York, 1951), pp. 19–20.

18   This discussion deals with the *phenomenon* of revolutionary war. For analysis of the French *doctrine* of *la guerre révolutionnaire*, see *infra*, pp. 40–44, and the two excellent discussions of Raoul Girardet, *infra*, pp. 127–134, and Peter Paret, "The French Army and La Guerre Révolutionnaire," *Journal of the Royal United Service Institution*, 104 (February, 1959), 59–69.

19   Quoted in Lieuwen, *op. cit.*, p. 134. See also Katherine Chorley, *Armies and the Art of Revolution* (London, 1943), p. 23.

20   Lucien Pye, *Guerrilla Communism in Malaya* (Princeton, 1956), ch. 15.

21   Lennox A. Mills, *Malaya: A Political and Economic Appraisal* (Minneapolis, 1958), pp. 48–49; Michael K. Clark, *Algeria in Turmoil* (New York, 1959), pp. 8, 131.

22   lvin H. Scaff, *The Philippine Answer to Communism* (Stanford, 1955), p. 135; Mills, *op. cit.*, pp. 54–55; Ellen J. Hammer, *The Struggle for Indochina* (Stanford, 1954), pp. 71–75.

23   Clark, *op. cit.*, p. 453; Mills, *op. cit.*, p. 51; D. H. Rawcliffe, *The Struggle for Kenya* (London, 1954), p. 93; Brian Crozier, *The Rebels: A Study of Post-War Insurrections* (Boston, 1960), p. 53.

24   Hammer, *op. cit.*, p. 292.

25   Pye, *op. cit.*, pp. 182ff.

26   *Ibid.*, pp. 8, 67–69; Clark, *op. cit.*, pp. 6, 133; Robert A. Smith, *Philippine Freedom 1946–1958* (New York, 1958), p. 142.

27   See Crozier, *op. cit.*, pp. 159–191, for an enlightening analysis of the successes and limitations of terrorism as a weapon.

28   Pye, *op. cit.*, pp. 91, 96n.; Mills, *op. cit.*, p. 53; Hammer, *op. cit.*, p. 287; E. L. Katzenbach, Jr., "Indo-China: A Military-Political Appreciation," *World Politics*, 4 (January, 1952), 205–206; Clark, *op. cit.*, pp. 299, 307.

29   See Girardet, *infra*, pp. 130–137; Crozier, *op. cit.*, pp. 127ff.

30   Scaff, *op. cit.*, p. 28; Harry Miller, *The Communist Menace in Malaya* (New York, 1954), pp. 92–93.

31   Katzenbach, *loc. cit.*, 192–193; Mills, *op. cit.*, p. 61.

32   Jean Gottmann, "Bugeaud, Galliéni, Lyautey: The Development of French Colonial Warfare," in Edward Mead Earle (ed.), *Makers of Modern Strategy* (Princeton,

1943), pp. 240–241; G. J. Younghusband, *Indian Frontier Warfare* (London, 1898), pp. 54–55; Scaff, *op. cit.*, p. 36; Smith, *op. cit.*, pp. 154–157.

33 Ximenes, "La guerre révolutionnaire et ses données fondamentales," *Revue militaire d'information* (February–March, 1957), 19–20.

34 Girardet, *infra*, pp. 135–137; Clark, *op. cit.*, pp. 8–9; Mills, *op. cit.*, pp. 63–72ff.; Scaff, *op. cit.*, p. 36; Lt. Col. T. C. Tirona, "The Philippine Anti-Communist Campaign," *Air University Quarterly Review*, 7 (Summer, 1954), 50.

35 J. Hogard, "Guerre révolutionnaire et pacification," *Revue militaire d'information* (January, 1957), 19.

36 Scaff, *op. cit.*, p. 38.

37 Col. Nemo, "Suggestions pour l'établissement d'une doctrine," *Revue militaire générale* (April, 1958), 490; Mills, *op. cit.*, p. 54.

38 Mills, *op. cit.*, p. 54; Tirona, *loc. cit.*, 54.

39 Quoted in Clark, *op. cit.*, p. 6; Scaff, *op. cit.*, pp. 28–30; Crozier, *op. cit.*, p. 16.

40 See Crozier, *op. cit.*, pp. 106–107.

41 See Georg Simmel, *Conflict*, trans. Kurt H. Wolff (Glencoe, Ill., 1955), pp. 87ff.; Lewis A. Coser, *The Functions of Social Conflict* (Glencoe, Ill., 1956), pp. 87ff.; Wright, *op. cit.*, I, 253ff.; R. F. Murphy, "Intergroup Hostility and Social Cohesion," *American Anthropologist*, 59 (December, 1957), 1018ff. Cf. David Rapoport, "Praetorianism" (Ph.D. Thesis, Univ. of California at Berkeley, 1960), pp. 85–86, 155ff., 230.

42 Sir George Clark, *War and Society in the Seventeenth Century* (Cambridge, 1958), p. 20.

43 For analyses of the French doctrine, see Girardet, *infra*, and Paret, *loc. cit.* The literature on *la guerre révolutionnaire* is immense. Between 1956 and 1960, almost every issue of the *Revue de défense nationale*, the *Revue militaire d'information* and the *Revue militaire générale* contained something on the subject. Among leading expositions are: Claude Delmas, *La guerre révolutionnaire* (Paris, 1959); Gabriel Bonnet, *op. cit.*; *Revue militaire d'information* (February–March, 1957); *Contre Révolution: stratégie et tactique* (Paris, 1958); J. Hogard, "Guerre révolutionnaire et pacification," *Revue militaire d'information* (January, 1957), 7–24. The first three items include helpful bibliographies.

44 See, e.g., Général d'Armée Jean Valluy, "Le corps des officiers devant la Nation," *Revue militaire générale* (December, 1958), 591–611; Delmas, *op. cit.*, pp. 9, 17; Gen. Paul Gerardot, "La renaissance militaire et le problème militaire français," *Revue militaire générale* (February, 1958), 173–195.

45 1956 Supplement to dossier on Algeria prepared for French un delegation, quoted in Crozier, *op. cit.*, pp. 130–31.

46 Delmas, *op. cit.*, p. 44.

47 See e.g., Gen. Coche, "Armée et guerre subversive," *Revue militaire générale* (March, 1959), 367–399; Contre-Amiral Peltier, "La pensée militaire soviétique," *Revue militaire générale* (December, 1957), 649–679; Chef d'escadrons Louis Pichon, "Caractères généraux de la guerre insurrectionnelle," *Revue militaire générale* (July, 1957), 158–186; *Revue militaire d'information* (February–March, 1957), 25; Delmas, *op. cit.*, p. 50.

48 Paret, *loc. cit.*, 67.

49 M. Margaret Ball, "Seato and Subversion," *Political Science*, 11 (March, 1959), 25ff.; W. Macmahon Ball, "Political Re-examination of SEATO," *International Organization*, 12 (Winter, 1958), 21–23.

50 Dwight D. Eisenhower, Message to Congress, July 15, 1958, *Department of State Bulletin*, 39 (August 4, 1958), 182.

51 John Foster Dulles, "Foundations of Peace," Address, Veterans of Foreign Wars, New York, N.Y., *Department of State Bulletin*, 39 (September 8, 1958), 375f.

52 Theodore Wyckoff, "War by Subversion," *South Atlantic Quarterly*, 59 (Winter, 1960), 35, 45.

53 See Geoffrey Barraclough, "What Is Indirect Aggression?" *The Listener*, 60 (September 18, 1958), 403–405. For a stimulating analysis of the relations between internal and external conflict, see George Modelski, *The International Relations of Internal War* (Princeton University, Center of International Studies, Research Monograph No. 11, May 24, 1961).

54 Lieuwen, *op. cit.*, pp. 63–65.

55 See the fears expressed in London of the tendency toward "government by students," *New York Times*, June 17, 1960, p. 11.

56 Lieuwen, *op. cit.*, p. 65.

57 D.E. Ashford, "Politics and Violence in Morocco," *Middle East Journal*, 13 (Winter, 1959), 11–25. See also R.A. LeVine, "Anti-European Violence in Africa: A Comparative Analysis," *Conflict Resolution*, 3 (December, 1959), 420–429.

58 Sir George Clark, *op. cit.*, pp. 73–74

Reading 8.6

Insurgency and Counterinsurgency

DAVID GALULA

The importance of a cause, an absolute essential at the outset of an insurgency, decreases progressively as the insurgent acquires strength. The war itself becomes the principal issue, forcing the population to take sides, preferably the winning one. . . .

WEAKNESS OF THE COUNTERINSURGENT

Let us assume now that our minute group of insurgent leaders in Country X has found several good causes, some acute, some latent, some even artificial, on which to base their insurgency. They all have agreed on a potent platform. Can they start operating? Not unless another preliminary condition has been met. The insurgent, starting from almost zero while his enemy still has every means at his disposal, is as vulnerable as a new-born baby. He cannot live and grow without some sort of protection, and who but the counterinsurgent himself can protect him? Therefore, we must analyze what makes a body politic resistant to infection.

Strengths and Weaknesses of the Political Regime

1. *Absence of problems.* A country fortunate enough to know no problem is obviously immune from insurgency. But since we have assumed that our potential insurgent leaders have found a cause, let us eliminate these countries—if there are any—from our consideration.

2. *National consensus.* The solidity of a regime is primarily based upon this factor. Thailand may live under a dictatorship or a democratic system, but her national consensus—which is not apathy, for the Thais would react vigorously to any attempt against their King and their way of life—has so far always strengthened the regime in power. On the other hand, no national consensus backs up East Germany's government.

3. *Resoluteness of the counterinsurgent leadership.* Resoluteness is a major factor in any sort of conflict, but particularly so in a revolutionary war for the reasons that (a) the insurgent has the initial benefit of a dynamic cause; (b) an insurgency does not grow suddenly into a national danger and the people's reaction against it is slow. Consequently, the role of the counterinsurgent leaders is paramount.

4. *Counterinsurgent leaders' knowledge of counterinsurgency warfare.* It is not enough for the counterinsurgent leaders to be resolute; they must also be aware of the strategy and tactics required in fighting an insurgency. Generalissimo Chiang Kai-shek's determination cannot be questioned; he proved it against Japan and still shows it in Taiwan. But did he know how to cope with the Communists' methods?

5. *The machine for the control of the population.* Four instruments of control count in a revolutionary war situation: the political structure, the administrative bureaucracy, the police, the armed forces.

   a. *The political structure.* If Country X is located behind the Iron Curtain, where political opposition is not tolerated and where the population is kept under a system of terror and mutual suspicion, the initial group of insurgents has no chance to develop; at best, the group will be able to survive in total secrecy—and hence be completely inactive—while waiting for better times.

Since there are people who dream of unleashing insurgencies in certain Communist countries—"Don't the people hate the regime there?"—it may be useful to give an idea of the extent of population control achieved by the Communist techniques of terror and mutual suspicion, of which the Red Chinese are past masters.

In Canton, in 1954, a neighbor saw an old Chinese lady giving some rice to her cat.

"I am sorry, but I will be obliged to report you at the next street meeting," said the neighbor to the owner of the cat.

"Why?" asked the old lady.

"Because rice is rationed and you have been wasting it on your cat."

"If you report me, they will cut off my rice ration. Why don't you just keep silent?"

"Suppose someone else saw you and reports you. What will happen to me, your neighbor, if I have not reported you first? I am your friend. If they suppress your ration I will give you half of mine."

This is exactly what happened, in a city where, according to some Western visitors, Chinese Communist control was less efficient than elsewhere in China.

At the end of 1952, a European was expelled from Hainan Island, where he had lived for many years. On reaching Hong Kong, he reported that the peasants "hated" the regime, and he gave much convincing evidence of it. He mentioned later that the Nationalists had twice attempted to drop agents in his area from Taiwan. In each case, the militia on duty at night heard the planes, saw the parachutes coming down, gave the alert, and the Nationalist agents were cornered and captured by several hundred armed villagers.

The European was challenged on this: "Isn't there a contradiction between your statement concerning the feelings of the peasants toward the regime and the attitude of the militiamen, who, after all, are peasants too? Why didn't they keep silent?"

"Put yourself in the place of one of these militiamen," he explained. "How does he know whether the other members of the militia won't give the alert? If they do and he hasn't, he will be in great trouble when the Communist cadres make their usual post-mortem investigations."

In July, 1953, during the Korean War, the Nationalists decided to make a raid on the mainland of China. They selected as their objective the small peninsula of Tungshan, jutting out of the Fukien coast, which is transformed into an island at high tide. The Communist garrison was made up of a regular battalion plus a thousand-man militia. The latter, the Nationalists thought, would put up no real fight. Indeed, every piece of available intelligence indicated that the population was thoroughly fed up with the Communists. The plan was to drop a regiment of paratroopers to neutralize the Communist battalion and to control the isthmus in order to prevent reinforcement from the mainland; an amphibious landing would follow to wipe out the opposition.

Because of a miscalculation in computing the local tide, the amphibious landing was delayed, and the Nationalist paratroopers bore the brunt of the opposition alone. They were virtually annihilated. The militia fought like devils. How could they act otherwise when they knew that the Nationalist action was just a raid?

A control of this order rules out the possibility of launching an insurgency. As long as there is no privacy, as long as every unusual move or event is reported and checked, as long as parents are afraid to talk in front of their children, how can contacts be made, ideas spread, recruiting accomplished?

What is possible is terrorism in a limited way, because a single man, even though completely isolated, can conduct a terrorist campaign; witness the case of the "mad bomber" in New York. But terrorism itself has far less value than the publicity that it is expected to produce, and it is rather doubtful that Communist authorities would complacently furnish publicity.

Another tactic that continues to be possible was one used in Greece by the Communists—unsustained command-type operations where terrain conditions are favorable.

At the other extreme, if anarchy prevails in Country X, the insurgent will find all the facilities he needs in order to meet, to travel, to contact people, to make known his program, to find and organize the early supporters, to receive and to distribute funds, to agitate and to subvert, or to launch a widespread campaign of terrorism.

In between these extremes lies a wide range of political structures that in varying degrees facilitate or hinder the task of the insurgent: dictatorship with a one-party system, dictatorship with no link to the grass roots, vigilant democracy, indolent democracy, etc.

b. *The administrative bureaucracy.* A country is run in its day-to-day life by its bureaucracy, which has a force of its own that has sometimes no relation to the strength or weakness of the top political leadership. France under the Third and Fourth Republics had a weak leadership but a strong administrative apparatus; the opposite appears to be the case in South Vietnam today. Since an insurgency is a bottom-to-top movement, an administrative vacuum at the bottom, an incompetent bureaucracy, plays into the hands of the insurgent.

The case of Algeria may be taken as an example. The territory was notoriously underadministered on the eve of the insurgency, not because the civil servants were incompetent but rather because the bureaucratic establishment had no relation to the size of the country and its population. Algeria (not counting the Sahara) extends more than 650 miles along the Mediterranean Sea and 350 miles inland, with an area of 115,000 square miles and a population of 10,500,000, of whom 1,200,000 are of European stock.

Under a governor general in Algiers, the territory was divided into three *départements* with seats in Oran, Algiers, and Constantine, each under a *préfet* assisted by a large staff. A *département* was in turn divided into *sous-préfectures*; for instance, in the *département* of Algiers, there was the *sous-préfecture* of Kabylia, with its seal in Tizi-Ouzou. Kabylia consisted of 5,000 square miles of rugged mountain terrain, with 1,200,000 inhabitants, of whom 90 per cent were Moslems.

The lower echelon in predominantly Moslem areas was the *commune-mixte* under a French administrator with 1 or 2 assistants and 5 gendarmes; the *commune-mixte* of Tigzirt, in Kabylia, measured 30 miles by 20 miles, with some 80,000 inhabitants.

At the lowest level was the *douar*, where the power of the state was embodied in a *garde-champêtre*, a native rural policeman armed with an old pistol in a holster on which shone a brass sign engraved with the awe-inspiring words: *"La Loi."* One such *douar* covered an area of 10 miles by 6 miles, with a population of 15,000 Kabylias.

With this setup, the insurgents had a field day.

c. *The police.* The eye and the arm of the government in all matters pertaining to internal order, the police are obviously a key factor in the early stages of an insurgency; they are the first counterinsurgent organization that has to be infiltrated and neutralized.

Their efficiency depends on their numerical strength, the competency of their members, their loyalty toward the government, and, last but not least, on the backing they get from the other branches of the government—particularly the judicial system. If insurgents, though identified and arrested by the police, take advantage of the many normal safeguards built into the judicial system and are released, the police can do little. Prompt adaptation of the judicial system to the extraordinary conditions of an insurgency, an agonizing problem at best, is a necessity. Algeria may again serve as an example. The total police force in 1954 was less than 50,000, barely larger than the police force for the city of Paris. When the insurgency was brewing, the Algerian police gave timely warnings, which were not heeded. A year after the insurgency broke out, the French National Assembly finally granted the government the "special powers" required to deal with the situation. By that time, the police—particularly its Moslem members—had been engulfed in the chaos.

d. *The armed forces.* Leaving aside the factors of strength applicable to the armed forces in all wars, those that are relevant in a revolutionary war are:

i. The numerical strength of the armed forces in relation to the size and the population of the country. An insurgency is a two-dimensional war fought for the control of the population. There is no front, no safe rear. No area, no significant segment of the population can be abandoned for long—unless the population can be trusted to defend itself. This is why a ratio of force of ten or twenty to one between the counterinsurgent and the insurgent is not uncommon when the insurgency develops into guerrilla warfare. The French forces in Indochina never approached this ratio, a fact that, more than any other, explains why the French could not have won there even if they had been led by Napoleon, regardless of the power of the nationalist cause initially.

ii. The composition of the armed forces. A conventional war today requires a modern, well-balanced force, with its air, sea, and ground components. But a revolutionary war is primarily a war of infantry. Paradoxically, the less sophisticated the counterinsurgent forces, the better they are. France's NATO divisions were useless in Algeria; their modern equipment had to be left behind, and highly specialized engineer or signal units had to be hurriedly converted into ordinary infantry. Naval operations by the insurgent being unlikely, all a navy needs is a sufficient force to blockade the coast line effectively. As for an air force, whose supremacy the insurgent cannot challenge, what it needs are slow assault fighters, short take-off transport planes, and helicopters.

iii. The feeling of the individual soldier toward the insurgent's cause and toward the counterinsurgent regime. Whereas the insurgent initially can use only a few combatants and can therefore select volunteers, the counterinsurgent's manpower demands are so high that he is condemned to draft soldiers, and he may well be plagued by the problem of loyalty. A few cases of collective desertions may cast so much suspicion on counterinsurgent units that their value may evaporate altogether. This happened with Algerian Rifle units in the early stage of the war in Algeria; although basically sound and trustworthy, these units had to be retired from direct contact with the population and used in a purely military capacity.

iv. The time lapse before intervention. Because of the gradual transition from peace to war in a revolutionary war, the armed forces are not ordered into action as fast as they would be in a conventional war. This delay is another characteristic of revolutionary wars. To reduce it is a political responsibility of the country's leaders.

6. *Geographic conditions.* Geography can weaken the strongest political regime or strengthen the weakest one. This question will subsequently be examined in more detail.

It is the combination of all these factors that determines whether an insurgency is possible or not once the potential insurgent has a cause.

Crisis and Insurgency

The insurgent cannot, of course, choose his opponent; he must accept him as he is. If he is confronted by a powerful counterinsurgent, he has no recourse but to wait until his opponent is weakened by some internal or external crisis.

The recent series of colonial insurgencies is, no doubt, a consequence of World War II, which constituted a formidable crisis for the colonial powers. The record shows that no insurgency or revolt succeeded in colonial territories before 1938, although the situation then was no less revolutionary than after the war. Few were even attempted—a revolt in the Dutch East Indies in 1926–27 and the extraordinary passive-resistance movement headed by Gandhi in India virtually exhaust the list.

The history of the Chinese Communist insurgency offers another example of the exploitation of a crisis. After a slow climb from 50 members in 1921 to 1,000 in 1925, the Chinese Communist Party associated itself with the Kuomintang, and its membership rose suddenly to 59,000 in 1926. The expansion was facilitated by the state of anarchy prevailing in China and by the popularity of the struggle led by the Kuomintang against the warlords and the imperialists. The two parties split in 1927, and the CCP went into open rebellion. Immediately, the membership fell to 10,000. A Communist group with Mao Tse-tung took refuge in the Kiangsi-Hunan area, while other groups scattered in various places. They slowly initiated guerrilla warfare, and, although at first they committed the mistake of attacking well-defended towns, they managed to develop their military strength. Membership rose to 300,000 in 1934. The Kuomintang had succeeded by that time in establishing itself as central government of China, and the Communists alone presented a challenge to its authority. The Kuomintang, by now a strong power, was energetically trying to stamp out the rebellion. After several unsuccessful offensives against the Communists, the Nationalist forces pressed them so hard that the CCP was really fighting for its survival. In order to escape annihilation, the Communists set off on their Long March, from Kiangsi to a remote area in the north of Shensi. In 1937, after the Long March, membership had fallen again to 40,000. Chiang Kai-shek was preparing another powerful offensive to finish off the Reds when they were saved by a crisis, the Japanese aggression against China. By V-J day, the Party had grown to 1,200,000, controlled an area of 350,000 square miles with a population of 95 million, and had a regular army of 900,000 men and a militia force of 2,400,000. It was no longer vulnerable. . . .

LAWS AND PRINCIPLES OF COUNTERINSURGENCY WARFARE

Limits of Conventional Warfare

Let us assume that the political and economic difficulties have been magically solved or have proved manageable, and that only one problem remains, the military one—how to suppress the insurgent forces. It is not a problem of means since the counterinsurgent forces are still largely superior to the insurgent's, even though they may be dispersed. It is primarily a problem of strategy and tactics, of methods and organization.

The strategy of conventional warfare prescribes the conquest of the enemy's territory, the destruction of his forces. The trouble here is that the enemy holds no territory and refuses to fight for it. He is everywhere and nowhere. By concentrating sufficient forces, the counterinsurgent can at any time penetrate and garrison a red area. Such an operation, if well sustained, may reduce guerrilla activity, but if the situation becomes untenable for the guerrillas, they will transfer their activity to another area and the problem remains unsolved. It may even be aggravated if the counter-insurgent's concentration was made at too great risk for the other areas.

The destruction of the insurgent forces requires that they be localized and immediately encircled. But they are too small to be spotted easily by the counterinsurgent's direct means of observation. Intelligence is the principal source of information on guerrillas, and intelligence has to come from the population, but the population will not talk unless it feels safe, and it does not feel safe until the insurgent's power has been broken.

The insurgent forces are also too mobile to be encircled and annihilated easily. If the counterinsurgent, on receiving news that guerrillas have been spotted, uses his ready forces immediately, chances are they will be too small for the task. If he gathers larger forces, he will have lost time and probably the benefit of surprise.

True, modern means of transportation—particularly helicopters, when available—allow the counterinsurgent to combine strength with swiftness. True, systematic large-scale operations, because of their very size, alleviate somewhat the intelligence and mobility deficiency of the counterinsurgent. Nevertheless, conventional operations by themselves have at best no more effect than a fly swatter. Some guerrillas are bound to be caught, but new recruits will replace them as fast as they are lost. If the counterinsurgent operations are sustained over a period of months, the guerrilla losses may not be so easily replaced. The question is, can the counterinsurgent operations be so sustained?

If the counterinsurgent is so strong as to be able to saturate the entire country with garrisons, military operations along conventional lines will, of course, work. The insurgent, unable to grow beyond a certain level, will slowly wither away. But saturation can seldom be afforded.

Why Insurgency Warfare Does Not Work
for the Counterinsurgent

Insurgency warfare is specifically designed to allow the camp afflicted with congenital weakness to acquire strength progressively while fighting. The counterinsurgent is endowed with congenital strength; for him to adopt the insurgent's warfare would be the same as for a giant to try to fit into a dwarf's clothing. How, against whom, for instance, could he use his enemy's tactics? He alone offers targets for guerrilla operations. Were he to operate as a guerrilla, he would have to have the effective support of the population guaranteed by his own political organization among the masses; if so, then the insurgent would not have it and consequently could not exist; there would be no need for the counterinsurgent's guerrilla operations. This is not to say that there is no place in counterinsurgency warfare for small commando-type operations. They cannot, however, represent the main form of the counterinsurgent's warfare.

Is it possible for the counterinsurgent to organize a clandestine force able to defeat the insurgent on his own terms? Clandestinity seems to be another of those obligations-turned-into-assets of the insurgent. How could the counterinsurgent, whose strength derives precisely from his open physical assets, build up a clandestine force except as a minor and secondary adjunct? Furthermore, room for clandestine organizations is very limited in revolutionary war. Experience shows that no rival—not to speak of hostile—clandestine movements can coexist for long; one is always absorbed by the other. The Chinese Communist maquis succeeded in suppressing almost entirely their Nationalist counterparts in the Japanese-occupied areas of north and central China. Later on, during the final round of the revolutionary war in China, ordinary bandits (almost a regular and codified profession in some parts of China) disappeared as soon as Communist guerrillas came. Tito eliminated Mikhailovitch. If the Greek Communist ELAS did not eliminate the Nationalist resistance groups, it was due to the restraint they had to show since they were entirely dependent on the Western Allies' support. More recently, the FLN in Algeria eliminated, for all practical purposes, the rival and older MNA group. Because the insurgent has first occupied the available room, attempts to introduce another clandestine movement have little chance to succeed.

Can the counterinsurgent use terrorism too? It would be self-defeating since terrorism is a source of disorder, which is precisely what the counterinsurgent aims to stop.

If conventional warfare does not work, if insurgency warfare cannot work, the inescapable conclusion is that the counterinsurgent must apply a warfare of his own that takes into account not only the nature and characteristics of the revolutionary war, but also the laws that are peculiar to counterinsurgency and the principles deriving from them.

The First Law: The Support of the Population Is as Necessary for the Counterinsurgent as for the Insurgent

What is the crux of the problem for the counterinsurgent? It is not how to clean an area. We have seen that he can always concentrate enough forces to do it, even if he has to take some risk in order to achieve the necessary concentration. The problem is, how to keep an area clean so that the counterinsurgent forces will be free to operate elsewhere.

This can be achieved only with the support of the population. If it is relatively easy to disperse and to expel the insurgent forces from a given area by purely military action, if it is possible to destroy the insurgent political organizations by intensive police action, it is impossible to prevent the return of the guerrilla units and the rebuilding of the political cells unless the population cooperates.

The population, therefore, becomes the objective for the counterinsurgent as it was for his enemy. Its tacit support, its submission to law and order, its consensus—taken for granted in normal times—have been undermined by the insurgent's activity. And the truth is that the insurgent, with his organization at the grass roots, is tactically the strongest of opponents where it counts, at the population level.

This is where the fight has to be conducted, in spite of the counterinsurgent's ideological handicap and in spite of the head start gained by the insurgent in organizing the population.

The Second Law: Support Is Gained Through an Active Minority

The original problem becomes now: how to obtain the support of the population—support not only in the form of sympathy and approval but also in active participation in the fight against the insurgent.

The answer lies in the following proposition, which simply expresses the basic tenet of the exercise of political power:

In any situation, whatever the cause, there will be an active minority for the cause, a neutral majority, and an active minority against the cause.

The technique of power consists in relying on the favorable minority in order to rally the neutral majority and to neutralize or eliminate the hostile minority.

In extreme cases, when the cause and the circumstances are extraordinarily good or bad, one of the minorities disappears or becomes negligible, and there may even be a solid unanimity for or against among the population. But such cases are obviously rare.

This holds true for every political regime, from the harshest dictatorship to the mildest democracy. What varies is the degree and the purpose to which it is applied. Mores and the constitution may impose limitations, the purpose may be good or bad, but the law remains essentially valid whatever the variations, and they can indeed be great, for the law is applied unconsciously in most countries.

It can no longer be ignored or applied unconsciously in a country beset by a revolutionary war, when what is at stake is precisely the counterinsurgent's power directly challenged by an active minority through the use of subversion and force. The counterinsurgent who refuses to use this law for his own purposes, who is bound by its peacetime limitations, tends to drag the war out without getting closer to victory.

How far to extend the limitations is a matter of ethics, and a very serious one, but no more so than bombing the civilian population in a conventional war. All wars are cruel, the revolutionary war perhaps most of all because every citizen, whatever his wish, is or will be directly and actively involved in it by the insurgent who needs him and cannot afford to let him remain neutral. The cruelty of the revolutionary war is not a mass, anonymous cruelty but a highly personalized, individual one. No greater crime can be committed by the counterinsurgent than accepting, or resigning himself to, the protraction of the war. He would do as well to give up early.

The strategic problem of the counterinsurgent may be defined now as follows: "To find the favorable minority, to organize it in order to mobilize the population against the insurgent minority." Every operation, whether in the military field or in the political, social, economic, and psychological fields, must be geared to that end.

To be sure, the better the cause and the situation, the larger will be the active minority favorable to the counterinsurgent and the easier its task. This truism dictates the main goal of the propaganda—to show that the cause and the situation of the counterinsurgent are better than the insurgent's. More important, it underlines the necessity for the counterinsurgent to come out with an acceptable countercause.

Victory in Counterinsurgency Warfare

We can now define negatively and positively what is a victory for the counterinsurgent.

A victory is not the destruction in a given area of the insurgent's forces and his political organization. If one is destroyed, it will be locally re-created by the other; if both are destroyed, they will both be re-created by a new fusion of insurgents from the outside. A negative example: the numerous mopping-up operations by the French in the Plain of Reeds in Cochinchina all through the Indochina War.

A victory is that plus the permanent isolation of the insurgent from the population, isolation not enforced upon the population but maintained by and with the population. A positive example: the defeat of the FLN in the Oran region in Algeria in 1959–60. In this region, which covers at least a third of the Algerian territory, FLN actions—counting everything from a grenade thrown in a café to cutting a telephone pole—had dwindled to an average of two a day.

Such a victory may be indirect; it is nonetheless decisive (unless of course, as in Algeria, the political goal of the counterinsurgent government changes).

The Third Law: Support From the Population is Conditional

Once the insurgent has established his hold over the population, the minority that was hostile to him becomes invisible. Some of its members have been eliminated physically, thereby providing an example to the others; others have escaped abroad; most have been cowed into hiding their true feelings and have thus melted within the majority of the population; a few are even making a show of their support for the insurgency. The population, watched by the active supporters of the insurgency, lives under the threat of denunciation to the political cells and prompt punishment by the guerrilla units.

The minority hostile to the insurgent will not and cannot emerge as long as the threat has not been lifted to a reasonable extent. Furthermore, even after the threat has been lifted, the emerging counterinsurgent supporters will not be able to rally the bulk of the population so long as the population is not convinced that the counterinsurgent has the will, the means, and the ability to win. When a man's life is at stake, it takes more than propaganda to budge him.

Four deductions can be made from this law. Effective political action on the population must be preceded by military and police operations against the guerrilla units and the insurgent political organizations.

Political, social, economic, and other reforms, however much they ought to be wanted and popular, are inoperative when offered while the insurgent still controls the population. An attempt at land reform in Algeria in 1957 fell flat when the FLN assassinated some Moslem peasants who had received land.

The counterinsurgent needs a convincing success as early as possible in order to demonstrate that he has the will, the means, and the ability to win.

The counterinsurgent cannot safely enter into negotiations except from a position of strength, or his potential supporters will flock to the insurgent side.

In conventional warfare, strength is assessed according to military or other tangible criteria, such as the number of divisions, the position they hold, the industrial resources, etc. In revolutionary warfare, strength must be assessed by the extent of support from the population as measured in terms of political organization at the grass roots. The counterinsurgent reaches a position of strength when his power is embodied in a political organization issuing from, and firmly supported by, the population.

The Fourth Law: Intensity of Efforts and Vastness of Means Are Essential

The operations needed to relieve the population from the insurgent's threat and to convince it that the counterinsurgent will ultimately win are necessarily of an intensive nature and of long duration. They require a large concentration of efforts, resources, and personnel.

This means that the efforts cannot be diluted all over the country but must be applied successively area by area.

STRATEGY OF THE COUNTERINSURGENCY

Translated into a general strategy, the principles derived from these few laws suggest the following step-by-step procedure:

In a Selected Area

1. Concentrate enough armed forces to destroy or to expel the main body of armed insurgents.
2. Detach for the area sufficient troops to oppose an insurgent's comeback in strength, install these troops in the hamlets, villages, and towns where the population lives.
3. Establish contact with the population, control its movements in order to cut off its links with the guerrillas.
4. Destroy the local insurgent political organizations.
5. Set up, by means of elections, new provisional local authorities.

6. Test these authorities by assigning them various concrete tasks. Replace the softs and the incompetents, give full support to the active leaders. Organize self-defense units.
7. Group and educate the leaders in a national political movement.
8. Win over or suppress the last insurgent remnants.

Order having been re-established in the area, the process may be repeated elsewhere. It is not necessary, for that matter, to wait until the last point has been completed.

The operations outlined above will be studied in more detail, but let us first discuss this strategy. Like every similar concept, this one may be sound in theory but dangerous when applied rigidly to a specific case. It is difficult, however, to deny its logic because the laws—or shall we say the facts—on which it is based can be easily recognized in everyday political life and in every recent revolutionary war.

This strategy is also designed to cope with the worst case that can confront a counterinsurgent, i.e., suppressing an insurgency in what was called a "red" area, where the insurgent is already in full control of the population. Some of the operations suggested can obviously be skipped in the "pink" areas, most can be skipped in the "white" ones. However, the general order in which they must be conducted cannot be tampered with under normal conditions without violating the principles of counterinsurgency warfare and of plain common sense. For instance, small detachments of troops cannot be installed in villages so long as the insurgent is able to gather a superior force and to overpower a detachment in a surprise attack; Step 2 obviously has to come after Step 1. Nor can elections be staged when the insurgent cells still exist, for the elections would most likely bring forth the insurgent's stooges. . . .

COMMAND PROBLEMS

Single Direction

Destroying or expelling from an area the main body of the guerrilla forces, preventing their return, installing garrisons to protect the population, tracking the guerrilla remnants—these are predominantly military operations.

Identifying, arresting, interrogating the insurgent political agents, judging them, rehabilitating those who can be won over—these are police and judicial tasks.

Establishing contact with the population, imposing and enforcing control measures, organizing local elections, testing the new leaders, organizing them into a party, doing all the constructive work needed to win the wholehearted support of the population—these are primarily political operations.

The expected result—final defeat of the insurgents—is not an addition but a multiplication of these various operations; they all are essential and if one is nil, the product will be zero. Clearly, more than any other kind of warfare, counterinsurgency must respect the principle of a single direction. A single boss must direct the operations from beginning until the end.

The problem, unfortunately, is not simple. Tasks and responsibilities cannot be neatly divided between the civilian and the soldier, for their operations overlap too much with each other. The soldier does not stay in his garrison with nothing to do, once the early large-scale operations have been concluded; he constantly patrols, ambushes, combs out; at some time in the process, he will have to organize, equip, train, and lead self-defense units. The policeman starts gathering intelligence right from the beginning; his role does not end when the political cells have been destroyed, because the insurgent will keep trying to build new ones. The civil servant does not wait to start his work until the army has cleared away the guerrillas.

Furthermore, no operation can be strictly military or political, if only because they each have psychological effects that alter the over-all situation for better or for worse. For instance, if the judge prematurely releases unrepentant insurgents, the effects will soon be felt by the policeman, the civil servant, and the soldier.

Another fact complicates the situation. However developed the civil administration may be in peacetime, it is never up to the personnel requirements of a counterinsurgency. When the broad objective of winning the support of the population is translated into concrete field tasks, each multiplied by the given number of villages, towns, and districts, the number of reliable personnel needed is staggering. Usually, the armed forces alone can supply them promptly. As a result, the counterinsurgent government is exposed to a dual temptation: to assign political, police, and other tasks to the armed forces; to let the military direct the entire process—if not in the whole country, at least in some areas.

The first one cannot be avoided. To confine soldiers to purely military functions while urgent and vital tasks have to be done, and nobody else is available to undertake them, would be senseless. The soldier must then be prepared to become a propagandist, a social worker, a civil engineer, a schoolteacher, a nurse, a boy scout. But only for as long as he cannot be replaced, for it is better to entrust civilian tasks to civilians. This, incidentally, is what the Chinese Communists have always tended to do. During the spring and summer of 1949, on the eve of their drive into south China, they recruited and trained in special schools more than 50,000 students whose mission was to follow the army and assist it by taking over "army servicing, publicity work, education and mobilization of the masses." To imitate this example is not easy for the counterinsurgent. Where does one find such a large group of reliable civilians when the loyalty of almost everyone is open to question? But it will have to be done eventually. The second temptation—to let the military direct the entire process—on the other hand, is so dangerous that it must be resisted at all costs.

Primacy of the Political Over the Military Power

That the political power is the undisputed boss is a matter of both principle and practicality. What is at stake is the country's political regime, and to defend it is a political affair. Even if this requires military action, the action is constantly directed toward a political goal. Essential though it is, the military action is secondary to the political one, its primary purpose being to afford the political power enough freedom to work safely with the population.

The armed forces are but one of the many instruments of the counter insurgent, and what is better than the political power to harness the non-military instruments, to see that appropriations come at the right time to consolidate the military work, that political and social reforms follow through?

"A revolutionary war is 20 per cent military action and 80 per cent political" is a formula that reflects the truth. Giving the soldier authority over the civilian would thus contradict one of the major characteristics of this type of war. In practice, it would inevitably tend to reverse the relative importance of military versus political action and move the counterinsurgent's warfare closer to a conventional one. Were the armed forces the instrument of a party and their leaders high-ranking members of the party, controlled and assisted by political commissars having their own direct channel to the party's central direction, then giving complete authority to the military might work; however, this describes the general situation of the insurgent, not of his opponent.

It would also be self-defeating, for it would mean that the counterinsurgent government had acknowledged a signal defeat: Unable to cope with the insurgency through normal government structures, it would have abdicated in favor of the military who, at once, become the prime and easy target of the insurgent propaganda. It would be a miracle if, under these circumstances, the insurgent did not succeed in divorcing the soldier from the nation.

The inescapable conclusion is that the over-all responsibility should stay with the civilian power at every possible level. If there is a shortage of trusted officials, nothing prevents filling the gap with military personnel serving in a civilian capacity. If the worst comes to the worst, the fiction, at least, should be preserved.

Coordination of Efforts

The counterinsurgent leader, whom we now assume to be a civilian, has to take into account the problems of the various civilian and military components of his forces before reaching a decision, especially when their actions interrelate intricately and when their demands often conflict with each other. He has also to coordinate and to channel their efforts in a single direction. How can he do it? Among the theoretical solutions in terms of organization, two are obvious: (1) the committee, as in Malaya, for example, where control of an area at district level was invested in a committee under the chairmanship of the district officer, with the members drawn from the police, local civilians (European planters and representative Chinese and Malayans), and the soldiers; (2) or the integrated civilian-military staff, where the soldier is directly subordinated to the local civil authority (the author knows of no example of this setup, but the opposite case—with the civil authority directly subordinated to the local military one—is easy to find, as in the Philippines, where army officers took the place of a nonexistent civil administration, or in Algeria, where all powers were invested in the military for a brief period in 1958–59).

Each formula has its merits and its defects. A committee is flexible, affords more freedom to its members, and can be kept small, but it is slow. An integrated staff allows a more direct line of command and is speedier, but it is more rigid and prone to bureaucratism. There seems to be room for both in counterinsurgency warfare. The committee is better for the higher echelons concerned with long- and medium-range affairs, the integrated staff for the lower echelons, where speed is essential. For counterinsurgency, at the bottom levels, is a very small-scale war, with small-scale and fugitive opportunities that must be seized upon instantly.

At the higher echelons, where the committee system prevails and where the civilian and military components retain their separate structures, they should each be organized in such a way as to promote their cooperation still more. In conventional warfare, the staff of a large military unit is composed roughly of two main branches—"intelligence/operations" and "logistics." In counterinsurgency warfare, there is a desperate need for a third branch—the "political" one—which would have the same weight as the others. The officer in charge of it would follow the developments in all matters pertaining to political and civic action, advise his chief, make his voice heard when operations are in the planning stage and not have to wait until they are too advanced to be altered. Similarly, the civilian staff, which in conventional warfare usually has little to do with military affairs, should have its military branch, with a corresponding role toward the civilian chief. With these two organic branches working closely together, the danger of divergent efforts by the civilian and the military might be reduced.

Whatever system is chosen, however, the best organization is only as good as its members. Even with the best conceivable organization, personality conflicts are more than likely to be the order of the day. Although the wrong member can sometimes be fired and replaced, this will not solve the problem for all committees or integrated staff.

The question, then, is how to make these mixed organizations work at their maximum effectiveness in a counterinsurgency, regardless of the personality factors. Assuming that each of these organizations works more or less with its own over-all personality, how is the disjointed, mosaic effect of their operations to be avoided? If the individual members of the organizations were of the same mind, if every organization worked according to a standard pattern, the problem would be solved. Is this not precisely what a coherent, well-understood, and accepted doctrine would tend to achieve? More than anything else, a doctrine appears to be the practical answer to the problem of how to channel efforts in a single direction.

Primacy of the Territorial Command

The counterinsurgent's armed forces have to fulfill two different missions: to break the military power of the insurgent and to ensure the safety of the territory in each area. It seems natural that the counterinsurgent's forces should be organized into two types of units, the mobile ones fighting in a rather conventional fashion, and the static ones staying with the population in order to protect it and to supplement the political efforts.

The static units are obviously those that know best the local situation, the population, the local problems; if a mistake is made, they are the ones who will bear the consequences. It follows that when a mobile unit is sent to operate temporarily in an area, it must come under the territorial command, even if the military commander of the area is the junior officer. In the same way as the U.S. ambassador is the boss of every U.S. organization operating in the country to which he is accredited, the territorial military commander must be the boss of all military forces operating in his area. . . .

Reading 8.7

Principles, Imperatives, and Paradoxes of Counterinsurgency

ELIOT COHEN; LIEUTENANT COLONEL CONRAD CRANE, U.S. ARMY, RETIRED; LIEUTENANT COLONEL JAN HORVATH, U.S. ARMY; AND LIEUTENANT COLONEL JOHN NAGL, U.S. ARMY

America began the 20th century with military forces engaged in counterinsurgency (COIN) operations in the Philippines. Today, it is conducting similar operations in Afghanistan, Iraq, and a number of other countries around the globe. During the past century, Soldiers and Marines gained considerable experience fighting insurgents in Southeast Asia, Latin America, Africa, and now in Southwest Asia and the Middle East.

Conducting a successful counterinsurgency requires an adaptive force led by agile leaders. While every insurgency is different because of distinct environments, root causes, and cultures, all successful COIN campaigns are based on common principles. All insurgencies use variations of standard frameworks and doctrine and generally adhere to elements of a definable revolutionary campaign plan. In the Information Age, insurgencies have become especially dynamic. Their leaders study and learn, exchange information, employ seemingly leaderless networks, and establish relationships of convenience with

Source: Eliot Cohen, Conrad Crane, Jan Horvath, and John Nagl, "Principles, Imperatives, and Paradoxes of Counterinsurgency," Reprinted with the permission of Military Review, the Professional Journal of the U.S. Army, Combined Arms Center, Fort Leavenworth, Kansas. Originally published in the March–April 2006 issue of Military Review.

criminal gangs. Insurgencies present a more complex problem than conventional operations, and the new variants have a velocity that previous historical insurgencies never possessed.

PRINCIPLES OF COUNTERINSURGENCY

The principles and imperatives of modern counterinsurgency provide guideposts for forces engaged in COIN campaigns. However, counterinsurgency is a strange and complicated beast. Following the principles and imperatives does not guarantee success, which is just one of the several paradoxes of counterinsurgency. Understanding such paradoxes helps illuminate the extraordinary challenges inherent in defeating an insurgency.

Legitimacy as the Main Objective A legitimate government derives its just powers from the governed and competently manages collective security and political, economic, and social development. Legitimate governments are inherently stable. They engender the popular support required to manage internal problems, change, and conflict. Illegitimate governments are inherently unstable. Misguided, corrupt, and incompetent governance inevitably fosters instability. Thus, illegitimate governance is the root cause of and the central strategic problem in today's unstable global-security environment.

Five actions that are indicators of legitimacy and that any political actor facing threats to stability should implement are—

- Free, fair, and frequent selection of leaders.
- A high level of popular participation in and support for the political process.
- A low level of corruption.
- A culturally acceptable level or rate of political, economic, and social development.
- A high level of regime support from major social institutions.

Governments that attain these goals usually garner the support of enough of the population to create stability. The primary objective of any counterinsurgent is to establish such a government. While military action can deal with the symptoms of loss of legitimacy, restoring it can only be accomplished using all elements of national power. Unless the government achieves legitimacy, counterinsurgency efforts cannot succeed.

Unity of Effort Ideally, a counterinsurgent would have unity of command over all elements of national power involved in COIN operations. However, the best that military commanders can generally hope for is unity of effort through communication and liaison with those responsible for the nonmilitary elements of power. The ambassador and country team must be key players in higher level planning, while similar connections are achieved down the chain of command. Even nongovernmental organizations (NGOs) can play important roles in improving lives. Many such players will resist being overtly involved with military units, but they must make an effort to establish some kind of liaison.

Connecting with joint, interagency, coalition, and indigenous organizations is important to ensuring that objectives are shared and that actions and messages are synchronized. The resulting synergy is essential for effective counterinsurgency. Unity of effort must pervade every level of activity, from national to neighborhood. Otherwise, well-intentioned but uncoordinated actions can cancel each other out or provide a competent insurgent with many vulnerabilities to exploit.

Political Primacy   While all the elements of national power have a role in successful counter-insurgency, political objectives must retain primacy. All actions, kinetic or nonkinetic, must be planned and executed with consideration of their contribution toward strengthening the host government's legitimacy and achieving the U.S. Government's political goals. The political and military aspects of an insurgency are usually so bound together as to be inseparable, and most insurgents recognize this fact. In counterinsurgencies, military actions conducted without proper analysis of their political effects will at best be ineffective and at worst aid the enemy.

Understanding the Environment   A key aspect in an insurgency is the population. Analyzing the effect of any operation is impossible without understanding the society and culture within which the COIN operation occurs. Soldiers and Marines must understand demographics, history, and the causes, ideologies, aims, organizations, capabilities, approaches, and supporting entities for every player in the conflict. The interconnected politico-military nature of insurgency requires the counterinsurgent to immerse himself in the lives of the people in order to achieve victory. Successful U.S. COIN operations require Soldiers and Marines to possess a clear, nuanced, empathetic appreciation of the essential nature of the conflict, particularly the motivation, strengths, and weaknesses of insurgents and indigenous actors.

Intelligence as the Driver for Operations   Without understanding the environment, one cannot understand and properly apply intelligence. Without good intelligence, a counterinsurgent is like a blind boxer wasting energy flailing at an unseen opponent. With good intelligence, a counterinsurgent is like a surgeon cutting out the cancers while keeping the vital organs intact. All operations must be shaped by carefully considered actionable intelligence gathered and analyzed at the lowest possible levels and disseminated and distributed throughout the force.

Isolating Insurgents From Their Cause and Support   Cutting an insurgency off to die on the vine is easier than it is to kill every insurgent. Dynamic insurgencies regenerate quickly, so a skillful counterinsurgent must cut off the sources of that recuperative power. Ideological support can be sundered by redressing the grievances that fuel the insurgency. Physical support can be cut off by population control or border security. In the 20th century, population control often meant resettling people; in the 21st century, biometric identification cards will accomplish the same objectives with much less disruption to people's lives. International or local legal action might be required to limit foreign financial support to insurgents.

As the host government increases its own legitimacy, the people will more actively help achieve this principle. Victory will be gained when this isolation is permanently maintained by the people's active support.

Security Under the Rule of Law   The cornerstone of any COIN effort is security for the populace. Without security, no permanent reforms can be implemented, and disorder will spread. To establish legitimacy, security activities must move from the realm of major combat operations into the realm of law enforcement. Insurgents seen as criminals will lose public support. If they are dealt with by an established legal system in line with local culture and practices, the legitimacy of the host government will be enhanced. This process will take time, but Soldiers must be aware of the legal procedures applicable to their conduct and support them. They must also help establish indigenous institutions (police forces, court systems, and penal facilities) that will sustain that legal regime.

Long-term Commitment   Insurgencies tend to be protracted conflicts. Counterinsurgency always demands considerable expenditures of time and resources. The insurgent wins if he does not lose. The counterinsurgent loses if he does not win. Insurgents are strengthened by the belief that a few casualties or a few years will cause adversaries to abandon the conflict. Only constant reaffirmations of commitment backed by deeds will bolster public faith in government survivability. People will not support a government until they are convinced the counterinsurgent has the means, ability, stamina, and will to win.

CONTEMPORARY IMPERATIVES
OF COUNTERINSURGENCY

Recent experiences with Counterinsurgency highlight the following additional imperatives that we must keep in mind for success.

Manage Information and Expectations   Information and expectations are related, and a skillful counterinsurgent must carefully manage both. To limit discontent and build support, a counterinsurgent and host government must create and maintain realistic expectations among the populace, friendly military forces, and even the international community. Information operations will be a key tool to accomplish this.

Americans have a disadvantage because of our reputation for accomplishment, resulting in what has been termed the Man on the Moon syndrome. To people in Afghanistan and Iraq, it seems unbelievable that a nation that can put a man on the moon cannot restore electricity. American agencies trying to fan enthusiasm for their efforts must avoid making exorbitant promises. In some cultures, failing to deliver promised results is interpreted as deliberate deception, not simply good intentions gone awry.

Managing expectations also involves showing economic and political progress as part of the campaign to show the populace how life is improving. In the end, the people must be convinced that their lives will be better with the counterinsurgent in control rather than with the insurgent in control. Both the counterinsurgent and the host nation must ensure that their deeds match their words. Any action has an information reaction, so they must carefully consider its effect on the many audiences involved and work to shape responses that further desired ends.

Use Measured Force Any use of force generates a series of reactions, so it is best to use the minimum possible force in resolving any situation. At times, an overwhelming effort is necessary to intimidate an opponent or reassure the populace, but the amount of force and who wields it should be carefully calculated. Mounting an operation that kills 5 insurgents is futile if collateral damage leads to the recruitment of 50 more. Often it is better that police handle urban raids, even if they are not as well-armed or as capable as military units, because the populace is likely to view that application of force as more legitimate. Also, a local police force reinforces the rule of law.

Learn and Adapt A COIN force must be a learning organization. Insurgents shift between military and political phases and approaches. In addition, networked insurgents constantly exchange information about enemy vulnerabilities. A skillful counterinsurgent must be able to adapt at least as fast as the opponent. Every unit must be able to make observations, draw lessons, apply them, and assess results. Higher headquarters must develop an effective system to circulate lessons learned throughout the organization. Insurgents shift their areas of operations looking for weak links, so widespread competence is required throughout the counterinsurgent force.

Empower the Lowest Levels The learning process must go on at every level of the COIN effort. The mosaic nature of an insurgency means that local commanders have the best grasp of their own situations. They must have the assets to produce actionable intelligence and manage information operations. Also, COIN operations must be decentralized, and higher commanders owe it to their subordinates to push as many capabilities as possible down to lower levels. Lower level initiative has to be supported and encouraged in order to create a COIN force that can adapt as quickly as insurgents.

Support the Host Nation American forces must remember that they are conducting COIN operations to help a host government. The long-term goal is for that government to stand on its own. In the end, the host nation must win its own war. While U.S. forces and agencies can provide invaluable assistance, they must be able to hand off responsibilities to indigenous elements. And, while it might be easier for U.S. military units to conduct operations them-selves, it is far better for them to help strengthen local forces. In successful COIN operations, host governments have the final responsibility to solve their own problems.

PARADOXES OF COUNTERINSURGENCY

COIN operations present complex, often unfamiliar missions and consider-ations. In many ways, conducting COIN operations is counterintuitive to the traditional American approach to war and combat operations. Some represen-tative paradoxes follow:

The More You Protect Your Force, the Less Secure You Are   The counterinsur-gent gains ultimate success by protecting the populace, not himself. If military forces stay locked up in compounds, they lose touch with the people who are the ultimate arbiters of victory and who could concede the streets and fields to the insurgent. Forces must conduct patrols, share risk, and maintain contact to obtain the intelligence to drive operations and to reinforce the connections with the people who establish legitimacy.

The More Force You Use, the Less Effective You Are   Any use of force produces many effects, not all of which can be foreseen. The more force applied, the greater the chance of collateral damage and mistakes. Enemy propaganda will portray kinetic military activities as brutal. Restrained force also strengthens the rule of law the counterinsurgent is trying to establish.

Sometimes Doing Nothing is the Best Reaction   Often an insurgent will carry out a terrorist act or guerrilla raid to entice the counterinsurgent to overreact or, at least, react in a way that the insurgent can exploit. If a careful analysis of the effects of a response reveals that more negatives than positives might result, Soldiers should consider an alternative.

The Best Weapons for Counterinsurgency Do Not Fire Bullets   Counterinsur-gents achieve the most meaningful success by gaining popular support and legitimacy for the host government, not by killing insurgents. Security is important in setting the stage for other kinds of progress, but lasting vic-tory will come from a vibrant economy, political participation, and restored hope. Dollars and ballots will have a more important effect than bombs and bullets; information is even more powerful when correctly wielded. T. E. Lawrence once observed that "[t]he printing press is the greatest weapon in the armoury of the modern commander. . . ."[1] This is even truer today than it was when Lawrence wrote it nearly a century ago—except that the truly effective counterinsurgent requires not just a printing press, but radio and television programs and an Internet presence. Soldiers and Marines must be prepared to engage in a host of traditional nonmilitary missions to support COIN operations.

Them Doing Something Poorly is Sometimes Better than us Doing it Well Who performs an operation is just as important as how well it is done. The United States is and will be supporting host nations in a counterinsurgency, and long-term success requires establishing viable institutions that can continue without significant U.S. support. The longer that process takes, the more popular support in the United States will wane and the more the local populace will question the legitimacy of their own forces. Lawrence said of his experience leading the Arab Revolt against the Ottoman Turkish Empire: "Do not try and do too much with your own hands. Better the Arabs do it tolerably than you do it perfectly. It is their war, and you are to help them, not win it for them."[2]

If a Tactic Works This Week, it Will Not Work Next Week; if it Works in This Province, it Will Not Work in the Next Today's competent insurgents are adaptive and are often part of a widespread network that constantly and instantly communicates. Successful COIN practices and appropriate countermeasures pass rapidly throughout the insurgency, and insurgents can implement changes quickly. COIN leaders must avoid complacency and be at least as adaptive as the adversary.

Tactical Success Guarantees Nothing When Colonel Harry Summers told a North Vietnamese counterpart in 1975 that "[y]ou know you never defeated us on the battlefield." the reply was: "That may be so, but it is also irrelevant."[3] Military actions alone cannot achieve success. Tactical actions must be linked to operational and strategic military objectives and essential political goals. Without those connections, we might waste lives and resources for no real gain.

THE FUTURE OF WARFARE

America's extraordinary conventional military power makes it likely that many of our future opponents will choose irregular means, including terrorism and insurgency, to achieve their political objectives and prevent us from achieving ours. The U.S. Army prides itself on its system of lessons learned. We must understand that others study us no less carefully than we study them. We reflect on tactics, techniques, and procedures; our enemies consider those as well, but they also pay attention to the operational and strategic levels of irregular warfare.

To the extent that our reaction to new manifestations of old forms of war consists chiefly of improved ways to protect vehicles against improvised explosive devices, or refined sniper tactics, or more adroit cordon and search techniques, we expose vulnerabilities that others will exploit. As painful as it might be to admit, future opponents have already drawn comfort from our missteps in Afghanistan and Iraq and, before that, in Somalia, Haiti, and elsewhere. They respect our immense firepower and logistical capabilities; they do not have equal regard for our strategic acumen or operational skill in fighting such wars.

After Vietnam, the U.S. Army reacted to the threat of irregular warfare chiefly by saying "never again." The study of counterguerrilla and COIN operations was leached from the various military college curricula, and the hard-won experience of a generation of officers was deliberately ignored. The Army told itself that the failure in Vietnam was the fault of an overweening civilian leadership, a timorous high command, a feeble domestic base of support, a hostile press, and the sheer impossibility of the task. These judgments were grounded in reality, but the Army's institutional failures deserved no less attention. Instead, although Army officers developed skills and achieved successes in irregular warfare in places like El Salvador and the former Yugoslavia, the institution continued to treat irregular warfare as an exception, an additional duty, or simply as a mistake. The result was an Army that was not as well-prepared to battle sophisticated insurgent enemies in Iraq and Afghanistan as it could have been.

We are at a turning point in the Army's institutional history. By considering the principles, imperatives, and paradoxes of counterinsurgency presented here, we can learn the lessons from Iraq and Afghanistan needed to prepare for the insurgencies and small wars we will have to fight in the future. Our enemies are fighting us as insurgents because they think insurgency is their best chance for victory. We must prove them wrong.

NOTES

1 T. E. Lawrence. "The Evolution of a Revolt." *Army Quarterly and Defense Journal* (October 1920). Reprinted by the Combat Studies Institute, US. Army Command and General Staff College, Fort Leavenworth, Kansas, with permission On-line at <www.cgsc.army.mil/carl/resources/csi/Lawrence/Lawrence.asp>, accessed 2 March 2006.

2 Lawrence, "The 27 Articles of T.E. Lawrence." *The Arab Bulletin* (20 August 1917). on-line at <www.d-n-i.net/fcs/lawrence_27_articles.htm>, accessed 1 March 2006.

3 COL Harry Summers, quoted in COL Robert Killebrew, "Winning Wars," Professional Writing Collection, *Army Magazine* (April 2005): on-line at www.army.mil/professional writing/volumes/volume3/may_2005/5_05_2_pf.html, accessed 1 March 2006.

Reading 8.8

A Strategy of Tactics: The Folly of Counterinsurgency
COLONEL GIAN P. GENTILE, U.S. ARMY

Population-centric counterinsurgency (COIN) has become the American Army's new way of war. The principles and ideas that emerged out of the Army's counterinsurgency field manual (FM), FM 3–24, published in late

---

Source: Gian P. Gentile, "A Strategy of Tactics: Population-centric COIN and the Army," Parameters: The Journal of the Army War College *(Autumn 2009).* © 2009 Gian P. Gentile. Reprinted by permission of the author.

2006, have become transcendent. The field manual has moved beyond simple Army doctrine for countering insurgencies to become the defining characteristic of the Army's new way of war. In the American Army today, everyone is a counterinsurgent. It is easy to find examples of FM 3–24's permeating effect in other Army doctrinal manuals such as FM 3–0, *Operations*, and FM 3–07, *Stability Operations*, Lieutenant General William B. Caldwell, IV, the American Army general charged with writing the Army's doctrine, recently stated:

> The future is not one of major battles and engagements fought by armies on battlefields devoid of population; instead, the course of conflict will be decided by forces operating among the people of the world. Here, the margin of victory will be measured in far different terms than the wars of our past. The allegiance, trust, and confidence of populations will be the final arbiters of success.[1]

The idea of populations as the prize in war, that they are the focus, is drawn directly from the pages of FM 3–24.[2]

In a sense, population-centric counterinsurgency has perverted a better way of American war which has primarily been one of improvisation and practicality. Over the course of American history there have been strategic shifts in terms of the threats and enemies that the United States had faced. With each of these shifts came a different approach, or way, to fighting wars or preparing for them in peacetime. For example, in the American Civil War, General Ulysses S. Grant carried out a strategy of exhausting the southern armies through large-scale combat. A quarter of a century later in the Philippines, the American Army improvised and adapted to fight and ultimately defeat an insurgency against the US colonial government. As historian Brian Linn has shown in criticism of Russell Weigley's classic *The American Way of War*, the US military's approach has not been an ideological one of only wanting to fight wars consisting of big battles. A close reading of Linn's work shows that the true American way of war has been one of adaptation and flexibility, and not a rigid ideological attachment to seeking out the next Napoleonic battle of Austerlitz.[3]

Regrettably, the American Army's new way of war, otherwise called population-centric counterinsurgency, has become the only operational tool in the Army's repertoire to deal with problems of insurgency and instability throughout the world. Population-centric COIN may be a reasonable operational method to use in certain circumstances, but it is not a strategy. There are flaws and limitations that need to be exposed and considered.

A MILITARY METHODOLOGY

Population-centric counterinsurgency is a military operation, a method, nothing more and nothing less. Its ideas and rules of tactics and operations should be familiar to anyone who has studied or thought about various approaches to COIN. They are:

- Populations are always the focus, the center of gravity, and they have to be protected.

- The enemy insurgent as a rule cannot be as important or given the same level of emphasis as the population.
- Population-centric COIN requires patience on the part of the American people.
- It demands a certain tactical approach of dispersion into small outposts to live amongst the people to win their hearts and minds; this has become the concept of clear, hold, and build.
- Population-centric counterinsurgency equals nation-building, and it requires a major investment in time to be successful.
- Its historical model of success is the British in Malaya.
- Its supreme historical failure is the United States' involvement in Vietnam.
- Its current narrative is that the techniques of population-centric counterinsurgency practiced by several additional combat brigades as part of the Surge of forces in Iraq produced success after February 2007.
- Its historical "how-to" text is *Counterinsurgency Warfare* by a French Army officer who fought in Algeria, David Galula.
- Its current set of rules are prescribed in FM 3–24. As the rules dictate, an Army unit must learn and adapt to improved population-centric tactics and operations; the unit cannot learn and adapt other methods in place of population-centric counterinsurgency.

Good strategy, however, demands the consideration of alternatives, yet the American Army's fixation on population-centric COIN precludes choice. We may have become adept at appearing to apply Galula's principles in Iraq and Afghanistan, but we are not good strategists. Strategy is about choice, options, and the wisest use of resources in war to achieve policy objectives. Yet in the American Army's new way of war, tactics—that is, the carrying out of the "way"—have utterly eclipsed strategy.

Nation-building using population-centric COIN as its centerpiece should be viewed as an operation. It should not be viewed as strategy, or even policy for that matter. But what is occurring now in Afghanistan, for example, at least for the American Army, is a "strategy of tactics." If strategy calls for nation-building as an operational method to achieve policy objectives, and it is resourced correctly, then the population-centric approach might make sense. But because the United States has "principilized" population-centric COIN into the only way of doing any kind of counterinsurgency, it dictates strategy.

TACTICAL ORIENTATION

Ironically, the new approach has inverted political scientist Andrew Krepinevich's damning criticism of the American Army in his hugely influential but deeply flawed 1986 book, *The Army in Vietnam*. Krepinevich's strategy of tactics argument for Vietnam was that the American Army was so conventionally minded and hidebound that it was unable to see a better way of population-centric COIN.[4] Now the American Army has done the inverse. The Army is so tactically oriented toward population-centric counterinsurgency that it cannot think of doing anything else. General Stanley McChrystal's recently released command guidance to forces in Afghanistan employs all of the dictums of population-centric counterinsurgency and confirms this strategy of tactics. His statement that success in Afghanistan will not be determined by the number of enemy killed but by the "shielding" of the civilian population could have easily come out of the pages of FM 3–24, or commander's talking points during the Iraq Surge.[5]

These population-centric COIN principles have been turned into immutable rules that are dictating strategy in Afghanistan and having a powerful shaping effect on reorganizing the American Army. A few months ago, when asked about the way ahead for the American military in Afghanistan and how Iraq was comparable to Afghanistan, General David Petraeus acknowledged that the two were very different. But the thing to remember, according to General Petraeus, was that the principles of COIN that the Army has learned in Iraq over the past couple of years are applicable to Afghanistan.[6]

Those principles belong to the population-centric COIN methodology. If we accept that the principles are applicable, then we have already chosen the way ahead in Afghanistan, which is population-centric nation-building requiring large numbers of American ground combat forces, dispersed into the local population in an effort to win their hearts and minds away from the insurgent enemy, and to eventually build a nation.

It is a recipe for a long-term American combat presence in the world's troubled spots. At present in the American Army there does not seem to be any alternatives. The inability to realistically consider alternatives reveals that the Army has become dogmatic, bound like a Gordian knot to the methods of population-centric counterinsurgency as the sole solution in Afghanistan and, potentially, in any other part of the world where instability and insurgencies are brewing.[7]

How did this happen? How did we get to a point where the American Army has developed a mentality, a worldview, a zeitgeist, of population-centric counterinsurgency, reflecting the American Army's new way of war? The genesis for all of this was the US Army's experience in Vietnam. The American Army lost that war, as Krepinevich argued, because under General William Westmoreland it tried to fight World War II all over again, a conventional war. The American Army did not understand population-centric COIN, could only think in terms of conventional warfare, and therefore lost, according to Krepinevich and others. Derivatives of this argument by author Lewis Sorley in his book *A Better War* say there was a radical change between General Westmoreland and his successor, General Creighton Abrams, and that Abrams redirected the American Army's strategy and could have won if the American people and their policymakers had not lost their will.[8]

The British counterinsurgency campaign in Malaya is viewed in a similar way. As the standard understanding goes, just as with the radical change between Westmoreland and Abrams, so too in Malaya there was a substantial shift in strategy between Generals Harold Briggs and Gerald Templer with their respective search-and-destroy and hearts-and-minds campaigns. Briggs, according to the stock explanations, focused too much on large-unit, conventional operations using search-and-destroy techniques trying to kill enemy insurgents, or what later commentators referred to as the enemy-centric approach. But it was Briggs's replacement, Sir Gerald Templer, who understood the importance of winning the hearts and minds of the population and shifted strategy to the classic population-centric counterinsurgency approach utilizing techniques designed to persuade the population to support the government and reject the insurgents.[9]

These historical interpretations have been seriously challenged and in a number of instances overturned by current historical scholarship. Regarding Vietnam, American scholars such as Andrew Birtle and Dale Andrade have shown that there was not a radical change between Westmoreland and Abrams, and that Westmoreland's strategy, at least in 1965 when faced with a conventional Communist threat inside South Vietnam, made sense. With regard to the British in Malaya, new scholarship by British historian Karl Hack strongly suggests that there was more continuity than discontinuity between Briggs and Templer and that the insurgency was actually broken during the Briggs years, not under Templer. Briggs, as this revisionist interpretation argues, based on newly released primary sources, broke the back of the insurgency through the use of military force directed against the insurgents, combined with an effective population resettlement program that took away the insurgents' base of support.[10]

COIN IN IRAQ

From the history of the Vietnam War, fast forward to the Iraq War and the beginning of the Surge of forces in February 2007. At that time and even in the year before, one began to hear arguments that the reason things were going so badly in Iraq was because the American Army up to the point when the Surge was initiated did not fully understand how to execute COIN, and in the early years of the conflict was making the same mistakes it did in Vietnam and that the British initially made in Malaya. The primary mistake, as this standard explanation goes, was that the American Army was trying to fight a war of big battles in the Sunni triangle instead of using the proper approach—to apply Galula and win hearts and minds.[11]

In short, the conventionally minded American Army did not prepare for COIN before the war, did not understand how to execute it once the war started (except for a few exceptional units such as the 101st Airborne Division in Mosul, 3d Armored Cavalry Regiment in Talafar, or 1st Brigade of the 1st Armored Division in Ramadi), and this lack of knowledge, experience, and training caused things to turn out so badly. But then things quickly turned around in February 2007 with the Surge of forces armed with a new counterinsurgency manual called FM 3–24. Under inspired new leadership the American Army started doing counterinsurgency correctly.[12] Best-known of the books that have espoused this narrative are Thomas Ricks's *Fiasco* and *The Gamble*, Linda Robinson's *Tell Me How This Ends*, and Kimberly Kagan's *The Surge: A Military History*.[13]

The triumph narrative associated with the Surge can best be summarized as follows. Prior to the Surge, the conventionally minded Army under General George Casey, when he was commander of Multi-National Force-Iraq, had allowed the insurgency to grow and by the end of 2006 had withdrawn from the rural regions and hunkered down on Forward Operating Bases while the Iraq civil war raged. But with the Surge, the new commander, General David Petraeus, armed his army with the new COIN doctrine in the form of FM 3–24 and deployed American combat forces into major population areas. Once in these locations, the US Army in Iraq began executing population-centric COIN correctly; they were able to secure the population, win the hearts and minds, and from this new position of power the deals cut with the Sons of Iraq, Moqtada al Sadr's retreat, and all the other successes flowed from the population-centric actions of the American Army.[14]

Consider these historical analogies that appear to perfectly support such a narrative. In Malaya, the failing Briggs to the successful Templer; in Vietnam, the anachronistic, conventionally minded Westmoreland to the enlightened, counterinsurgency-minded Abrams; and in Iraq, the Fulda Gap, big-battle strategy of Casey to the new way of population-centric counterinsurgency of Petraeus. More recently in Afghanistan, the change between General David McKiernan and General Stanley McChrystal, with the former being cast as the general who did not necessarily comprehend America's new way of war and was viewed as being a member of the "old school" Army.[15]

Quite possibly, the will of the Sunni insurgency broke long before the Surge went into full effect in the summer of 2007. A combination of brutal attacks by Shia militia in conjunction with the actions of the Iraqi Shia government and the continuing persecution by al Qaeda against the Sunni community convinced the insurgents that they could no longer counter all these forces and it was to their advantage to cut a deal with the Americans. To be sure, the reduction in violence that began in the summer of 2007 in Iraq had multiple causes, and the Surge did contribute. But to think that the reduction of violence was primarily the result of American military action is hubris run amuck.[16]

POINTS OF CRITICISM

This combined Malaya, Vietnam, Iraq, and Afghanistan War narrative has turned the American Army's new counterinsurgency doctrine outlined in FM 3–24 into an oracle, a cipher that unlocks the keys to success in any counterinsurgency as long as its precepts, principles, and rules are adhered to. But there are points of criticism to the new doctrine that need to be seriously considered. First, it provides for only one way to counter insurgencies and deal with the world's instabilities, and that way is population-centric counterinsurgency. The manual offers no other alternatives, no other strategies or methodologies. There is a short five-line paragraph in Chapter 5 that considers more limited options. That short paragraph should have been turned into half of the manual.

Second, history has shown that insurgencies can be defeated by means other than the population-centric approach. Consider the recent defeat of the Tamil Tigers by the Sri Lankan military. Or consider what actually broke the back of the Malayan insurgency in the early 1950s, which was not so much the hearts-and-minds persuasion of Templer but the hard-handed use of military force against civilians, combined with a major resettlement program. FM 3–24 actually serves as a restatement of the counter-Maoist approach to insurgencies that military officers such as Galula and Sir Robert Thompson developed in the 1950s and 1960s.[17] The end result is a counterinsurgency doctrine that has become a guiding set of operational principles for today's American Army and greater defense establishment. A doctrine based on lessons learned while combating the FLN insurgents in Algeria, Malaya Communist insurgents, and other Communist-inspired insurgencies some 50 years ago.

The American Army has become ahistorical in the manner in which it thinks about counterinsurgency, meaning it has difficulty thinking in a historical context. In a sense, it is as if the world of counterinsurgency warfare began suddenly around 1945 with the end of World War II and the rise of the Cold War, along with the numerous people's wars inspired by nationalism and communism. The term itself "counterinsurgency" is so heavily loaded with historical context, assumptions, myths, and absurdities that it has become almost meaningless. A set of case studies of counterinsurgency operations has been extracted from their historical context and turned into a large historical trope used to define and judge any small war, imperial war, or insurgency.[18]

What is needed to correct this fallacy is for this ahistorical view of counterinsurgency warfare to be integrated back to its historical context and combined with a much longer view of small-war history dating to the early 1800s.[19] Most worrisome for those concerned with the future of the American Army is that there has not been a wide-ranging debate over the efficacy and utility of this new way of war. Between 1976 and 1982, more than 110 published articles appeared in the professional journal, *Military Review*, fundamentally challenging the Army's doctrine at the time, the Active Defense. There has been no similar debate following the publication of FM 3–24 almost three years ago. What has appeared is a series of articles touting the triumph of the Surge, a narrative that has steamrolled the American Army into accepting this new way of war.

Some strategists say that if the United States is going to conduct nation-building, then the population-centric approach is the best. That may be true, but this article's thesis is that because this new way of war has become so dominant, it precludes America's Army from thinking in other more limited ways for dealing with instability and insurgencies.

This intellectual straightjacket of population-centric counterinsurgency has had other deleterious effects on the Army. It has pushed America's Army and other parts of the American defense establishment into fanciful thinking. The authors of FM 3–24 declare that counterinsurgency is the graduate level of warfare. Implicit in this statement is that conventional war is the undergraduate level. A respected counterinsurgency professional in the US Army, Colonel

Robert Cassidy, said in a widely cited 2004 essay that conducting counterinsurgency warfare was "more difficult" than conventional war. Another counterinsurgency expert, David Ucko, in a recent book on what he calls the "new counterinsurgency era," argues that COIN with all of its associated political and economic tasks is "far more demanding" than the relatively simple process of "locating and striking targets."[20]

In fact, COIN is arguably less complex precisely because it is less "kinetic." There is very little room for commander or soldier error in high-intensity combat. People are killed immediately, and sometimes many of them. COIN is executed at a slower pace and, thus, can be more forgiving. People get killed, yes, but far fewer than in fighting at the higher end of the conflict spectrum; and more importantly in COIN there is a great deal more time to assess, judge, and decide.

SOMETHING REVOLUTIONARY?

Counterinsurgency experts in the American defense establishment have gone to great lengths to turn their new way of war into something revolutionary, something radically different from the past, something more complex and qualitatively more difficult than what came before.[21] The Prussian theorist of war, Carl von Clausewitz, said that "everything in war is very simple . . . but the simplest thing is difficult." To be fair, it is not that COIN or conventional warfare is the harder or easier. All warfare is demanding and difficult, that is why it is called war. In the 1920s, the German Army, as it thought its way through the lessons of the First World War, understood this point. Under the leadership of the brilliant German General Hans von Seeckt, they believed that the nature of war was essentially unchanging even if the means, machines, and milieu of it do change. Von Seeckt and his officers rejected what they referred to as any "schema" for war that tried to reduce its nature to a list of principles and rules.[22]

The COIN experts seem to believe that they are "young Turks" who have figured out the true political nature of war compared to the old, conventionally minded American military leaders who did not care about such things and only wanted to focus on tactics. Since population-centric COIN involves political activities at low levels such as platoons, companies, and battalions (for example, establishing village governing councils, etc.), its proponents then assume that the tactical activities that involve politics in the execution of COIN mean that those executing this doctrine understand the political nature of war writ large.[23] But in theory, there is nothing more political in a platoon leader in the Korengal Valley talking to a sheik about local governance then there was of a rifle platoon leader storming the beach at Normandy. Again, to cite the old Prussian, "War in all of its action and forms is fundamentally a political act."

With the new American way of war as population-centric counterinsurgency, the Army has lost track of what has happened to its conventional warfighting skills. In 2008, three US Army colonels, all former combat brigade commanders in Iraq, told Army Chief of Staff General George Casey that after seven years of conducting almost nothing but population-centric counterinsurgency operations in Iraq and Afghanistan, the Army's field artillery branch had lost its ability to fight and had become a "dead branch walking." Others have also expressed concern over the atrophying of core fighting competencies. Commenting on the widely read *Small Wars Journal* blog, Major Ike Sallee, an infantry officer with two combat tours in Iraq, stated:

> The Army, if we want to remain a profession, is best served in adhering to core values, principles, and capabilities. If the core is strong . . . then we are able to transfer capability to other methods. But if we focus on methods (area-specific tactics, techniques, and procedures) at the expense of core capabilities (offensive, defensive, protection, battle drills, marksmanship, physical fitness) we will be chasing our tails and may find ourselves lacking identity and relevance. . . . If forced to prioritize (inevitable for the foreseeable future)—focus on core capabilities . . . what our Army can do exclusively for our Nation. If we are thrown into a condition requiring counterinsurgency tactics, we will be able to adapt because of our well-trained competencies.

The essential point and concern expressed by Major Sallee is that an army's core capability is to fight at every level of command. If it can do that, it can do almost anything.[24] This is not an argument to stop the focus on COIN operations, since they are the missions the Army has been assigned by the nation's political leaders. The critique of population-centric COIN is a call for the American Army to honestly look at itself and the risks that it is taking.

There are indeed risks. History and more recent events show what happens when armies trained and organized for counterinsurgencies and small wars have to rapidly adapt to missions at the higher end of the conflict spectrum. The French Army's failure in the Franco-Prussian War of 1871 was partly due to the influence from colonial warfare, as was the British Army's experience in the early months of the Second Boer War.

The Israeli Defense Forces' recent experience in Lebanon is another good example. There were many reasons for its failure, but one of them, as validated by scholars and analysts, is that its army had done almost nothing but COIN in the Palestinian territories, and its ability to fight against a strident enemy had atrophied. During the past few months a number of studies have been published on Israel's 2008 operations in Gaza. What these reports show is that the Israeli military, especially its army, realized what had happened to them in Lebanon and took the intervening two years to get back to the basics of war fighting; critical competencies such as synchronizing fire, maneuver, and intelligence at all levels of command against a hostile force.[25] The American Army would do well to pay attention to what the Israeli army has undergone in the past two years.

The COIN zeitgeist has convinced many observers that conventionally trained and minded armies cannot do counterinsurgency warfare. This belief is not supported by history. Examples of success are the American Army in the Philippines, the British Army in Malaya, and the US Army in Vietnam and moreover in Iraq starting in 2003, not 2007.[26] It is dangerous, however, to think that this principle can operate in reverse, as the example of the Israelis in Lebanon demonstrates. Imagine how well the drive on Baghdad would have gone in 2003 if the American Army had spent the majority of its training time in the years prior learning to talk to sheiks, rebuild schools, or conduct negotiations.

But the most damaging consequence to the American Army from the new zeitgeist of COIN is that it has taken the Army's focus off of strategy. Currently, US military strategy is really nothing more than a bunch of COIN principles, massaged into catchy commander's talking points for the media, emphasizing winning the hearts and minds and shielding civilians. The result is a strategy of tactics and principles.

CONCLUSION

Instead of American Army officers reading the so-called COIN classic texts of Galula, Thompson, Kitson, and Nagl, they should be reading the history of the British Empire in the latter half of the nineteenth century. It is in this period that if they did nothing else right the British Army and government did understand the value of strategy. They understood the essence of linking means to ends. In other words, they did not see military operations as ends in themselves but instead as a means to achieve policy objectives. And they realized that there were costs that had to be paid.[27]

The new American way of war has eclipsed the execution of sound strategy, producing never-ending campaigns of nation-building and attempts to change entire societies in places like Afghanistan. One can only guess at the next spot on the globe for this kind of crusade.[28] Former Army officer and writer Craig Mullaney, who recently penned a book-portrait of himself and what he learned in combat, said that the "Achilles' heel for Americans is our lack of patience." But perhaps not; perhaps America's lack of patience in wars like Iraq and Afghanistan should be seen as a virtue in that it could act as a mechanism to force the US military to execute strategy in a more efficient and successful manner. Doing strategy better would leverage the American Army out of its self-inflicted box of counterinsurgency tactics and methodologies into a more open assessment of alternatives to current military actions in Afghanistan.

The new American way of war commits the US military to campaigns of counterinsurgency and nation-building in the world's troubled spots. In essence it is total war—how else can one understand it any differently when COIN experts talk about American power "changing entire societies"—but it is a total war without the commensurate total support of will and resources from the American people. This strategic mismatch might prove catastrophic in the years ahead if the United States cannot figure out how to align means with ends in a successful strategy. The new American way of war perverts and thus prevents us from doing so.

The ancient Chinese philosopher of war Sun Tzu had this to say about the conduct of war and implicitly about its nature:

> Strategy without tactics is the slowest route to victory. . . . Tactics without strategy is the noise before defeat. . . . There is no instance of a nation benefitting from prolonged warfare. . . . Speed is the essence of war.[29]

The new American way of war—wars amongst the people—has turned Sun Tzu's maxim on its head. These days it is customary to think of war and conflict as prolonged affairs that afflict the farthest-flung precincts of US influence, thereby demanding a long-term American military presence on the ground. We are told by the experts that this new way of war requires time, patience, modest amounts of blood, and vast amounts of treasure. Sun Tzu was highlighting strategy, and strategy is about choice, options, and the wisest use of resources in war to achieve political objectives. Yet in the new way of American war, tactics have buried strategy, and it precludes any options other than an endless and likely futile struggle to achieve the loyalty of populations that, in the end, may be peripheral to American interests.

NOTES

1 William B. Caldwell, IV, and Steven M. Leonard, "Field Manual 3–07, Stability Operations: Upshifting the Engine of Change," *Military Review*, 88 (July/August 2008), 6.

2 Department of the Army, Field Manual 3–24, *Counterinsurgency* (Washington: Headquarters Department of the Army, 2006), 1–1, 1–28, 5–18.

3 Brian M. Linn, *"The American Way of War* Revisited," *Journal of Military History*, 66 (April 2002), 505. Also see Linn's superb intellectual history of the US Army, *The Echo of Battle: The Army's Way of War* (Cambridge, Mass.: Harvard Univ. Press, 2007).

4 Andrew F. Krepinevich, Jr., *The Army and Vietnam* (Baltimore, Md.: Johns Hopkins Univ. Press, 1986), 164–68.

5 See Stanley A. McChrystal, "Initial Commander's Guidance as of: 13 June 09," Headquarters International Security Assistance Force, 13 June 2009; and Jason Straziuso, "New US Battle Rule: No Fighting Near Afghan Homes," *Associated Press*, 22 June 2009.

6 Fred W. Baker, III, "Petraeus Parallels Iraq, Afghanistan Strategies," *American Forces Press Service*, 28 April 2009.

7 On COIN and dogmatism in the American Army, see Gian P. Gentile, "The Dogmas of War," *Armed Forces Journal* (November 2007).

8 Lewis Sorley, *A Better War: The Unexamined Victories and Final Tragedy of America's Last Years in Vietnam* (New York: Harcourt Brace, 1999), 17–18, 383–86; for a better interpretation of America's last years in Vietnam, see James H. Willbanks, *Abandoning Vietnam: How America Left and South Vietnam Lost Its War* (Lawrence: Univ. Press of Kansas, 2004).

9 For the stock explanations on Malaya, see John A. Nagl, *Learning to Eat Soup with a Knife: Counterinsurgency Lessons from Malaya and Vietnam* (Chicago, Ill.: Univ. of Chicago Press, 2005); Thomas R. Mockaitis, *British Counterinsurgency, 1919–1960* (New York: St. Martin's Press, 1990); and Richard Stubbs, *Hearts and Minds in Guerrilla Warfare: The Malayan Emergency, 1948–1960* (New York: Oxford Univ. Press, 1989).

10 On revising the stock explanations of Vietnam, see Andrew J. Birtle, "PROVN, Westmoreland, and the Historians: A Reappraisal," *Journal of Military History*, 72 (October 2008), 1213–47; and Dale Andrade, "Westmoreland Was Right: Learning the Wrong Lessons from the Vietnam War," *Small Wars and Insurgencies*,

19 (June 2008), 145–81. On revising the Malaya counterinsurgency paradigm, see Paul Dixon, "'Hearts and Minds'? British Counter-Insurgency from Malaya to Iraq," *Journal of Strategic Studies*, 32 (June 2009), 353–81; and Karl Hack, "The Malayan Emergency as Counter-Insurgency Paradigm," *Journal of Strategic Studies*, 32 (June 2009), 383–414.

11 See "Making a Fiasco," interview with Tom Ricks. Amazon.com, http://www.amazon.com/Fiasco-Amertcan-Military-Adventure-Iraq/dp/l 59420103X.

12 For a hagiographic view of these players, see Tom Ricks, *The Gamble: General David Petraeus and the American Military Adventure in Iraq, 2006–2008* (New York: Penguin Books, 2009).

13 For excellent criticism and analysis on how narratives are constructed in war, see Jill Lepore, *The Name of War: King Phillip's War and the Origins of American Identify* (New York: Alfred A. Knopf, 1998); and Douglas Porch, *The Conquest of Morocco* (New York: Farrar, Straus, and Giroux, 2005).

14 The most strident book in promoting American military agency as the primary causative factor for the lowering of violence is Kimberly Kagan's *The Surge: A Military History* (New York: Encounter Books. 2009); in this line also see Michael Yon, *The Moment of Truth in Iraq: How a New "Greatest Generation" of American Soldiers is Turning Defeat and Disaster into Victory and Hope* (Minneapolis, Minn.: Richard Vigilante Books, 2008). For a critique of the Surge narrative, see Gian P. Gentile, "A (Slightly) Better War: A Narrative and Its Defects," *World Affairs*, 171 (Summer 2008), 57–64.

15 Rajiv Chandrasekaran, "Pentagon Worries Led to Command Change," *The Washington Post*, 17 August 2009, Al.

16 For a critical view of the Surge, see Steven Simon, "The Price of the Surge: How U.S. Strategy Is Hastening Iraq's Demise," *Foreign Affairs*, 87 (May/June 2008), 57–76.

17 For two scholarly reviews of FM 3–24 that support the author's criticism of it being simply a rehash of counter-Maoist doctrine, see reviews by Stathis N. Kalyvas and Wendy Brown in "The New U.S. Army/Marine Corps Counterinsurgency Field Manual as Political Science and Political Praxis," *Perspectives on Politics*, 6 (June 2008), 351–57.

18 Gian P. Gentile, "The Selective Use of History in the Development of American Counterinsurgency Doctrine," *Army History* (Summer 2009), 21–35.

19 An excellent general history of western empires, in which counterinsurgency should be seen as historically embedded, is Douglas Porch, *Wars of Empire* (London: Cassell, 2000).

20 Robert M Cassidy, "Winning the War of the Flea: Lessons from Guerrilla Warfare," *Military Review*, 84 (September/October 2004), 41; and David H. Ucko, *The New Counterinsurgency Era: Transforming the U.S. Military for Modern Wars* (Washington: Georgetown Univ. Press, 2009), 2.

21 See John Nagl, "Foreword," in Michael I. Burgoyne and Albert J. Marckwardt, *The Defense of Jisr Al-Doreaa* (Chicago, Ill.: Univ. of Chicago Press, 2009); also see John Nagl, review of *The Echo of Battle: The Army's Way of War*, by Brian M. Linn, *RUSI Journal*, 153 (April 2008), 82–84.

22 See Robert M. Citino, *The German Way of War: From the Thirty Years' War to the Third Reich* (Lawrence: Univ. Press of Kansas, 2005), xiii.

23 See Peter R. Mansoor, review of *The Centurions*, by Jean Larteguy, *Military Review*, 86 (November/December 2006), 102–03.

24 Ike Sallee, comment on "One Army or Two?" *Small Wars Journal* blog, 19 July 2009, http://smallwarsjournal.com/blog/2Q09/06/one-army-or-two/#c003418; and

Sean MacFarland, Michael Shields, and Jeffrey Snow, "The King and I: The Impending Crisis in Field Artillery's Ability to Provide Fire Support to Maneuver Commanders," available on the National Public Radio Web site, http://www.npr.org/documents/2008/may/artil-lerywhilepaper.pdf. For an argument on the need for a fighting general-purpose Army, see Gian P. Gentile, "The Imperative for an American General Purpose Army that Can Fight," *Obis*, 53 (Summer 2009), 457–70.

25 For the latest analysis on the Israeli Defense Forces in Lebanon and Gaza, see Matt M. Matthews, "The Israeli Defense Forces Response to the 2006 War with Hezbollah," *Military Review*, 89 (July/August 2009), 41–51.

26 On the American Army in Iraq and how it learned and adapted from 2003 to 2005, see Donald P. Wright and Timothy R. Reese, *On Point II: Transition to the New Campaign; The United Stales Army in Operation Iraqi Freedom, May 2003–January 2005* (Fort Leavenworth, Kans.: Combat Studies Institute Press, 2008).

27 See Thomas Pakenham, The Scramble for Africa: White Man's Conquest of the Dark Continent from 1876 to 1912 (New York: HarperCollins, 1992).

28 See, for example, Michael O'Hanlon's call for a new type of American Army unit called a "Peace Operations Division" that could intervene in the Congo, "U.S. Boots on Congo Ground: A New Kind of Force Could Provide Security," *The Washington Post*, 14 August 2009, A17.

29 Sun Tzu, *The Art of War*, Samuel B. Griffith, trans. (London: Oxford Univ. Press, 1963).

Threat Assessment and Misjudgment: Recurrent Dilemmas

Too often bitter hindsight makes wars seem to have been unnecessary, terrible mistakes that wiser decision-makers could have avoided had they better understood the threats they faced—that is, if they had neither underestimated nor overestimated those threats. Some wars could have been averted if the victim had exerted more effective deterrence in peacetime, denying the aggressor an opening to use force. Some wars arise out of unintended escalation in crises where neither side started out wanting war. Some wars turn out to be unwinnable at a cost commensurate with the stakes at issue. How should statesmen use such lessons from hindsight—some of which contradict each other—to find the right strategy in peacetime and to preserve peace while avoiding losses?

The dominant thinking for great powers' strategists has been "*Si vis pacem para bellum*"—the hoary Latin adage meaning "If you want peace, prepare for war." Peaceful governments hope that having potent military capabilities for defense—by developing their own forces and enlisting foreign allies—will convince predatory enemies not to attack them. If the enemy is indeed aggressive, hoping for an opportunity to pounce, then the stronger the defensive preparations, the better. If the enemy happens to be equally fearful rather than predatory, however, maximizing military capability in that way may provoke rather than deter.

A situation where both adversaries prefer peace to war, yet mistrust each other and feel the need to prepare for the worst, is fraught with uncertainty. Both can misread each other's defensive preparations as aggressive, and as evidence of the need to ratchet up their own capabilities further—which in turn may be seen by the other as confirming their suspicions of the adversary's

546

malign intent. This "security dilemma," the concept developed by John Herz and elaborated by Robert Jervis in Part VII of this volume, risks producing a tragic spiral of action and reaction. At their worst, miscalculations risk unintended or inadvertent war. Against a ruthless aggressor, maximum military power and deterrence make sense; in a security dilemma, restraint and reassurance of the adversary make sense. How do powers satisfied with the status quo know whether they face a predatory aggressor or a security dilemma? This is the main task of threat assessment.

In this section of the volume, historic and current cases of competing threat assessments illustrate the problem starkly. World Wars I and II were the greatest military catastrophes in history. Why did policymakers fail to adapt appropriately in peacetime to prevent them? After World War I, many believed that decision-makers had stumbled into it because they assumed the worst about their enemies, allowed the 1914 crisis to get out of control, and lurched into combat precipitously. In this view they had been too bound by the logic of the famous Crowe Memorandum. Following the carnage of that war, the Sanderson critique of Crowe, which had made the case for empathizing with Germany, seemed wiser to many. Consequently, the communications from Ambassador Neville Henderson at the time of the Munich crisis in 1938 reflected the logic of empathy with German interests and the incentive for the British to choose reassurance rather than resistance. Of course, this turned out to be a mistake—quite the opposite of the spiraling escalation of 1914—enabling German aggression rather than blocking it. Together these cases illustrate the difficulty of choosing between opposite risks.

The two subsequent items concerning Russian intervention in Ukraine present a contemporary case that poses such issues of judgment. President Vladimir Putin's address asserts a host of defensive justifications for annexation of Crimea and support of separatists in Eastern Ukraine, while Eliot A. Cohen sees Russia's action as just as outrageous as Germany's at Munich and after. Should policymakers today worry more about repeating the mistake of 1914 or the mistake of 1938? The Betts and Christensen essay in turn applies the questions to the rise of China, an issue of threat assessment that has been more and more prominent as China grows toward superpower status. Will this development produce a war of hegemonic transition as Gilpin presented the historic phenomenon? An unintended but tragic security dilemma of the sort described by Jervis? A new order of cooperative interdependence a la Angell, Schumpeter, Rosecrance, or Ikenberry? A clash of civilizations that escalates to war as Huntington fears?

Determining whether the main threat a country faces is aggression or the security dilemma is primarily a question of discerning the adversary's intentions. Sometimes, on the other hand, crucial misjudgments flow from faulty assessment of one's own interest, the adversary's capabilities, and the balance of costs and benefits in pursuing military conflict. The Vietnam War was such a case for the United States. James C. Thomson, Jr.'s essay is a classic examination of the dynamics in the policymaking process that allowed exaggeration of the value of the stakes in Washington, and underestimation of the difficulty of overcoming Communist capabilities.[1] Stephen Biddle presents an analysis that raises similar questions about the more recent American involvement in Afghanistan.

The main point of these various illustrations is that confidence in understanding of an adversary's intentions and capabilities is always greater after war starts, when failure to avoid it testifies to mistaken judgment, than before it. Yet it is in peacetime that the task of threat assessment matters most, if unnecessary wars are to be avoided. Often this task is performed adequately, policy adapts appropriately, and peace is preserved. This happened, more or less, in the long Cold War. In that case, the avoidance of World War III—which could have annihilated modern civilization as we know it—may rank as the greatest human achievement of the twentieth century. The risk that intelligent decision-makers can often fail to link correct judgments and adaptive responses effectively, however, should not be underestimated, and that risk remains extraordinary even after the Cold War, as rivalries revive and weapons of mass destruction persist.

—RKB

NOTE

1 For a thorough examination of this process, see Leslie H. Gelb with Richard K. Betts, *The Irony of Vietnam* (Washington, D.C.: Brookings Institution, 1979).

Reading 9.1

The German Threat? 1907

EYRE CROWE AND THOMAS SANDERSON

The general character of England's foreign policy is determined by the immutable conditions of her geographical situation on the ocean flank of Europe as an island State with vast oversea colonies and dependencies, whose existence and survival as an independent community are inseparably bound up with the possession of preponderant sea power. The tremendous influence of such preponderance has been described in the classical pages of Captain Mahan. No one now disputes it. Sea power is more potent than land power, because it is as pervading as the element in which it moves and has its being. Its formidable character makes itself felt the more directly that a maritime State is, in the literal sense of the word, the neighbour of every country accessible by sea. It would, therefore, be but natural that the power of a State supreme at sea should inspire universal jealousy and fear, and be ever exposed to the danger of being overthrown by a general combination of the world. Against such a combination no single nation could in the long run stand, least of all a small island kingdom, not possessed of the military strength of a people trained to arms, and dependent for its food supply on oversea commerce. The danger can in practice only be averted—and history shows that it has been so averted—on condition that the national policy of the insular and naval State is so directed as to harmonize with the general desires and ideals common to all mankind, and more particularly that it is closely identified with the primary and vital interests of a majority, or as many as possible, of the other nations. Now, the first interest of all countries is the preservation of national independence. It follows that England, more than any other non-insular Power, has a direct and positive interest in the maintenance of the independence of nations, and therefore must be the natural enemy of any country threatening the independence of others, and the natural protector of the weaker communities.

Second only to the ideal of independence, nations have always cherished the right of free intercourse and trade, in the world's markets, and in proportion as England champions the principle of the largest measure of general freedom of commerce, she undoubtedly strengthens her hold on the interested friendship of other nations, at least to the extent of making them feel less apprehensive of naval supremacy in the hands of a free trade England than they would in the face of a predominant protectionist Power. This is an aspect of the free trade question which is apt to be overlooked. It has been well said

Source: "Memorandum on the Present State of British Relations with France and Germany," *January 1, 1907, in G. P. Gooch and Harold Temperley, eds.,* Documents on the Origins of the War, 1898–1914, vol. III: The Testing of the Entente, 1904–6 *(London: His Majesty's Stationery Office, 1928).*

that every country, if it had the option, would, of course, prefer itself to hold the power of supremacy at sea, but that, this choice being excluded, it would rather see England hold that power than any other State.

History shows that the danger threatening the independence of this or that nation has generally arisen, at least in part, out of the momentary predominance of a neighbouring State at once militarily powerful, economically efficient, and ambitious to extend its frontiers or spread its influence, the danger being directly proportionate to the degree of its power and efficiency, and to the spontaneity or "inevitableness" of its ambitions. The only check on the abuse of political predominance derived from such a position has always consisted in the opposition of an equally formidable rival, or of a combination of several countries forming leagues of defence. The equilibrium established by such a grouping of forces is technically known as the balance of power, and it has become almost an historical truism to identify England's secular policy with the maintenance of this balance by throwing her weight now in this scale and now in that, but ever on the side, opposed to the political dictatorship of the strongest single, State or group at a given time.

If this view of British policy is correct, the opposition into which England must inevitably be driven to any country aspiring to such a dictatorship assumes almost the form of a law of nature, as has indeed been theoretically demonstrated, and illustrated historically, by an eminent writer on English national policy.

By applying this general law to a particular case, the attempt might be made to ascertain whether, at a given time, some powerful and ambitious State is or is not in a position of natural and necessary enmity towards England; and the present position of Germany might, perhaps, be so tested. Any such investigation must take the shape of an inquiry as to whether Germany is, in fact, aiming at a political hegemony with the object of promoting purely German schemes of expansion, and establishing a German primacy in the world of international politics at the cost and to the detriment of other nations . . .

With the events of 1871 the spirit of Prussia passed into the new Germany. In no other country is there a conviction so deeply rooted in the very body and soul of all classes of the population that the preservation of national rights and the realization of national ideals rest absolutely on the readiness of every citizen in the last resort to stake himself and his State on their assertion and vindication. With "blood and iron" Prussia had forged her position in the councils of the Great Powers of Europe. In due course it came to pass that, with the impetus given to every branch of national activity by the newly-won unity, and more especially by the growing development of oversea trade flowing in ever-increasing volume through the now Imperial ports of the formerly "independent" but politically insignificant Hanse Towns, the young empire found opened to its energy a whole world outside Europe, of which it had previously hardly had the opportunity to become more than dimly conscious. Sailing across the ocean in German ships, German merchants began for the first time to divine the true position of countries such as England, the United States, France, and even the Netherlands, whose political influence extends to distant seas and continents. The colonies and foreign possessions of England more especially were seen to give to that country a recognized and enviable status in a world where the name of Germany, if mentioned at all, excited no particular interest. The effect of this discovery upon the German mind was curious and instructive. Here was a vast province of human activity to which the mere title, and rank of a European Great Power were not in themselves a sufficient passport. Here in a field of portentous magnitude, dwarfing altogether the proportions of European countries, others, who had been perhaps rather looked down upon as comparatively smaller folk, were at home and commanded, whilst Germany was at best received but as an honoured guest. Here was distinct inequality, with a heavy bias in favour of the maritime and colonizing Powers.

Such a state of things was not welcome to German patriotic pride. Germany had won her place as one of the leading, if not, in fact, the foremost Power on the European continent. But over and beyond the European Great Powers there seemed to stand the "World Powers." It was at once clear that Germany must become a "World Power." The evolution of this idea and its translation into practical politics followed with singular consistency the line of thought that had inspired the Prussian Kings in their efforts to make Prussia great. "If Prussia," said Frederick the Great, "is to count for something in the councils of Europe, she must be made a Great Power." And the echo: "If Germany wants to have a voice in the affairs of the larger oceanic world she must be made a 'World Power.'" "I want more territory," said Prussia. "Germany must have Colonies," says the new world-policy. And Colonies were accordingly established, in such spots as were found to be still an appropriated, or out of which others could be pushed by the vigorous assertion of a German demand for "a place in the sun": Damaraland, Cameroons, Togoland, German East Africa, New Guinea, and groups of other islands in the Pacific. The German example, as was only natural, found ready followers, and the map of unclaimed territories was filled up with surprising rapidity. When the final reckoning was made up the actual German gain seemed, even in German eyes, somewhat meagre. A few fresh possessions were added by purchase or by international agreement—the Carolines, Samoa, Heligoland. A transaction in the old Prussian style secured Kiao-chau. On the whole, however, the "Colonies" have proved assets of somewhat doubtful value.

Meanwhile the dream of a Colonial Empire had taken deep hold on the German imagination. Emperor, statesmen, journalists, geographers, economists, commercial and shipping houses, and the whole mass of educated and uneducated public opinion continue with one voice to declare: We must have real Colonies, where German emigrants can settle and spread the national ideals of the Fatherland, and we must have a fleet and coaling stations to keep together the Colonies which we are bound to acquire. To the question, "Why must?" the ready answer is: "A healthy and powerful State like Germany, with its 60,000,000 inhabitants, must expand, it cannot stand still, it must have territories to which its overflowing population can emigrate without giving up its nationality." When it is objected that the world is now actually parcelled out among independent States, and that territory for colonization cannot be had except by taking it from the rightful possessor, the reply again is: "We cannot enter into such considerations. Necessity has no law. The world belongs to the strong. A vigorous nation cannot allow its growth to be hampered by blind adherence to the *status quo*. We have no designs on other people's possessions, but where States are too feeble to put their territory to the best possible use, it is the manifest destiny of those who can and will do so to take their places" . . .

So long, then, as Germany competes for an intellectual and moral leadership of the world in reliance on her own national advantages and energies England can but admire, applaud, and join in the race. If, on the other hand, Germany believes that greater relative preponderance of material power, wider extent of territory, inviolable frontiers, and supremacy at sea are the necessary and preliminary possessions without which any aspirations to such leadership must end in failure, then England must expect that Germany will surely seek to diminish the power of any rivals, to enhance her own by extending her dominion, to hinder the co-operation of other States, and ultimately to break up and supplant the British Empire.

Now, it is quite possible that Germany does not, nor ever will, consciously cherish any schemes of so subversive a nature. Her statesmen have openly repudiated them with indignation. Their denial may be perfectly honest, and their indignation justified. If so they will be most unlikely to come into any kind of armed conflict with England, because, as she knows of no causes of present dispute between the two countries, so she would have difficulty in imagining where, on the hypothesis stated, any such should arise in the future. England seeks no quarrels, and will never give Germany cause for legitimate offence.

But this is not a matter in which England can safely run any risks. The assurances of German statesmen may after all be no more genuine than they were found to be on the subject of the Anglo-French *entente* and German interests in Morocco, or they may be honestly given but incapable of fulfilment. It would not be unjust to say that ambitious designs against one's neighbours are not as a rule openly proclaimed, and that therefore the absence of such proclamation, and even the profession of unlimited and universal political, benevolence are not in themselves conclusive evidence for or against the existence of unpublished intentions. The aspect of German policy in the past, to which attention has already been called, would warrant a belief that a further development on the same general lines would not constitute a break with former traditions, and must be considered as at least possible. In the presence of such a possibility it may well be asked whether it would be right, or even prudent, for England to incur any sacrifices or see other, friendly, nations sacrificed merely in order to assist Germany in building up step by step the fabric of a universal preponderance, in the blind confidence that in the exercise of such preponderance Germany will confer unmixed benefits on the world at large, and promote the welfare and happiness of all other peoples without doing injury to any one. There are, as a matter of fact, weighty reasons which make it particularly difficult for England to entertain that confidence. These will have to be set out in their place.

Meanwhile it is important to make it quite clear that a recognition of the dangers of the situation need not and does not imply any hostility to Germany. England herself would be the last to expect any other nation to associate itself with her in the active support of purely British interests, except in cases where it was found practicable as a matter of business to give service for counter-service. Nevertheless, no Englishman would be so foolish as to regard such want of foreign co-operation for the realization of British aims as a symptom of an anti-British animus. All that England on her part asks—and that is more than she has been in the habit of getting—is that, in the pursuit of political schemes which in no way affect injuriously the interests of third parties, such, for instance, as the introduction of reforms in Egypt for the sole benefit of the native population, England shall not be wantonly hampered by factious opposition. The same measure, and even a fuller measure, England will always be ready to mete out to other countries, including Germany. Of such readiness in the past instances are, as numerous as they are instructive; and this is perhaps the place where to say a few words respecting the peculiar complexion of the series of transactions which have been characteristic of Anglo-German relations in recent years.

It has been so often declared, as to have become almost a diplomatic platitude, that between England and Germany, as there has never been any real clashing of material interests, so there are no unsettled controversies over outstanding questions. Yet for the last twenty years, as the archives of our Foreign Office show, German Governments have never ceased reproaching British Cabinets with want of friendliness and with persistent opposition to German political plans. A review of British relations during the same period with France, with Russia, and with the United States reveals ancient and real sources of conflict, springing from imperfectly patched-up differences of past centuries, the inelastic stipulations of antiquated treaties, or the troubles incidental to unsettled colonial frontiers. Although with these countries England has fortunately managed to continue to live in peace, there always remained sufficient elements of divergence to make the preservation of good, not to say cordial, relations an anxious problem requiring constant alertness, care, moderation, good temper, and conciliatory disposition. When particular causes of friction became too acute, special arrangements entered into succeeded as a rule in avoiding an open rupture without, however, solving the difficulties, but rather leaving the seed of further irritation behind. This was eminently the ease with France until and right up to the conclusion of the Agreement of the 8th April, 1904.

A very different picture is presented by the succession of incidents which punctuate the record of contemporary Anglo-German relations, 1884 onward, when Bismarck first launched his country into colonial and maritime enterprise, numerous quarrels arose between the two countries. They all have in common this feature—that they were opened by acts of direct and unmistakable hostility to England on the part of the German Government, and that this hostility was displayed with a disregard of the elementary rules of straightforward and honourable dealing which was deeply resented by successive British Secretaries of State for Foreign Affairs. But perhaps even more remarkable is this other feature, also common to all these quarrels, that the British Ministers, in spite of the genuine indignation felt at the treatment to which they were subjected, in each case readily agreed to make concessions or accept compromises which not only appeared to satisfy all German demands, but were by the avowal of both parties calculated and designed to re-establish, if possible, on a firmer basis the fabric of Anglo-German friendship. To all outward appearance absolute harmony was restored on each occasion after these separate settlements, and in the intervals of fresh outbreaks it seemed true, and was persistently reiterated, that there could be no further occasion for disagreement.

[*A long listing and discussion of controversies and incidents of British-German conflict over imperial interests in Africa, the Pacific, and China, and alleged German aggressiveness and duplicity, followed in the original.*—Ed.]

. . . There is no pretence to completeness in the foregoing survey of Anglo-German relations, which, in fact, gives no more than a brief reference to certain salient and typical incidents that have characterized those relations during the last twenty years. The more difficult task remains of drawing the logical conclusions. The immediate object of the present inquiry was to ascertain whether there is any real and natural ground for opposition between England and Germany. It has been shown that such opposition has, in fact, existed in an ample measure for a long period, but that it has been caused by an entirely one-sided aggressiveness, and that on the part of England the most conciliatory disposition has been coupled with never-failing readiness to purchase the resumption of friendly relations by concession after concession.

It might be deduced that the antagonism is too deeply rooted in the relative position of the two countries to allow of its being bridged over by the kind of temporary expedients to which England has so long and so patiently resorted. On this view of the case it would have to be assumed that Germany is deliberately following a policy which is essentially opposed to vital British interests, and that an armed conflict cannot in the long run be averted, except by England either sacrificing those interests, with the result that she would lose her position as an independent Great Power, or making herself too strong to give Germany the chance of succeeding in a war. This is the opinion of those who see in the whole trend of Germany's policy conclusive evidence that she is consciously aiming at the establishment of a German hegemony, at first in Europe, and eventually in the world.

After all that has been said in the preceding paragraphs, it would be idle to deny that this may be the correct interpretation of the facts. There is this further seemingly corroborative evidence that such a conception of world-policy offers perhaps the only quite consistent explanation of the tenacity with which Germany pursues the construction of a powerful navy with the avowed object of creating slowly, but surely, a weapon fit to overawe any possible enemy, however formidable at sea.

There is, however, one obvious flaw in the argument. If the German design were so far-reaching and deeply thought out as this view implies, then it ought to be clear to the meanest German understanding that its success must depend very materially on England's remaining blind to it, and being kept in good humour until the moment arrived for striking the blow fatal to her power. It would be not merely worth Germany's while, it would be her imperative duty, pending the development of her forces, to win and retain England's friendship by every means in her power. No candid critic could say that this elementary strategical rule had been even remotely followed hitherto by the German government.

It is not unprofitable in this connection to refer to a remarkable article in one of the recent numbers of the "Preussische Jahrbücher," written by Dr. Hans Delbrück, the distinguished editor of that ably conducted and influential magazine. This article discusses very candidly and dispassionately the question whether Germany could, even if she would, carry out successfully an ambitious policy of expansion which would make her follow in the footsteps of Louis XIV and of Napoleon I. The conclusion arrived at is that, unless Germany wishes to expose herself to the same overwhelming combinations which ruined the French dreams of a universal ascendency, she must make up her mind definitely and openly to renounce all thoughts of further extending her frontiers, and substitute for the plan of territorial annexations the nobler ambition of spreading German culture by propagating German ideals in the many quarters of the globe where the German language is spoken, or at least taught and understood.

It would not do to attribute too much importance to the appearance of such an article in a country where the influence of public opinion on the conduct of the affairs of State is notoriously feeble. But this much may probably be rightly gathered from it, that the design attributed by other nations to Germany has been, and perhaps is still being, cherished in some indeterminate way by influential classes, including; perhaps, the Government itself, but that responsible statesmen must be well aware of the practical impossibility of carrying it out.

There is then, perhaps, another way of looking at the problem: It might be suggested that the great German design is in reality no more than the expression of a vague, confused, and unpractical statesmanship, not fully realizing its own drift. A charitable critic might add, by way of explanation, that the well-known qualities of mind and temperament distinguishing for good or for evil the present Ruler of Germany may not improbably be largely responsible for the erratic, domineering, and often frankly aggressive spirit which is recognizable at present in every branch of German public life, not merely in the region of foreign policy; and that this spirit has called forth those manifestations of discontent and alarm both at home and abroad with which the world is becoming familiar; that, in fact, Germany does not really know what she is driving at, and that all her excursions and alarums, all her underhand intrigues do not contribute to the steady working out of a well-conceived and relentlessly followed system of policy, because, they do not really form part of any such system. This is an hypothesis not flattering to the German Government, and it must be admitted that much might be urged against its validity. But it remains true that on this hypothesis also most of the facts of the present situation could be explained.

It is, of course, necessary to except the period of Bismarck's Chancellorship. To assume that so great a statesman was not quite clear as to the objects of his policy would be the *reductio ad absurdum* of any hypothesis. If, then, the hypothesis is to be held sound, there must be forthcoming a reasonable explanation for Bismarck's conduct towards England after 1884, and a different explanation for the continuance of German hostility after his fall in 1890. This view can be shown to be less absurd than it may at first sight appear.

Bismarck suffered from what Count Schuvaloff called *le cauchemar des coalitions*. It is beyond doubt that he particularly dreaded the hostile combination against his country of France and Russia, and that, as one certain means of counteracting that danger, he desired to bring England into the Triple Alliance, or at least to force her into independent collision with France and Russia, which would inevitably have placed her by Germany's side. He knew England's aversion to the entanglement of alliances, and to any policy of determined assertion of national rights, such as would have made her a Power to be seriously reckoned with by France and Russia. But Bismarck had also a poor opinion of the power of English Ministers to resist determined pressure. He apparently believed he could compel them to choose between Germany and a universal opposition to England. When the colonial agitation in Germany gave him an opening, he most probably determined to bring it home to England that meekness and want of determination in foreign affairs do not constitute a policy; that it was wisest, and certainly least disagreeable, for her to shape a decided course in a direction which would secure her Germany's friendship; and that in co-operation with Germany lay freedom from international troubles as well as safety, whilst a refusal to, co-operate brought inglorious conflicts, and the prospect of finding Germany ranged with France and Russia for the specific purpose of damaging British interests.

Such an explanation gains plausibility from the fact that, according to Bismarck's own confession, a strictly analogous policy was followed by him before 1866 in his dealings with the minor German States. Prussia deliberately bullied and made herself disagreeable to them all, in the firm expectation that, for the sake of peace and quiet, they would follow Prussia's lead rather than Austria's. When the war of 1866 broke out Bismarck had to realize that, with the exception of a few small principalities which were practically enclaves in the Kingdom of Prussia, the whole of the minor German States sided with Austria. Similarly he must have begun to see towards the end of his career that his policy of browbeating England into friendship had failed, in spite of some fugitive appearance of success. But by that time the habit of bullying and offending England had almost become a tradition in the Berlin Foreign Office, and Bismarck's successors, who, there is other evidence to show, inherited very little of his political capacity and singleness of purpose, seem to have regarded the habit as a policy in itself, instead of as a method of diplomacy calculated to gain an ulterior end. Whilst the great Chancellor made England concede demands objectionable more in the manner of presentation than in themselves, treating her somewhat in the style of Richard III wooing the Lady Ann, Bismarck's successors have apparently come to regard it as their ultimate and self-contained purpose to extract valuable Concessions from England by offensive bluster and persistent nagging, Bismarck's experience having shown her to be amenable to this form of persuasion without any risk of her lasting animosity being excited.

If, merely by way of analogy and illustration, a comparison not intended to be either literally exact or disrespectful be permitted, the action of Germany towards this country since 1890 might be likened not inappropriately to that of a professional blackmailer, whose extortions are wrung from his victims by the threat of some vague and dreadful consequences in case of a refusal. To give way to the blackmailer's menaces enriches him, but it has long been proved by uniform experience that, although this may secure for the victim temporary peace, it is certain to lead to renewed molestation and higher demands after ever-shortening periods of amicable forbearance. The blackmailer's trade is generally ruined by the first resolute stand made against his exactions and the determination rather to face all risks of a possibly disagreeable situation than to continue in the path of endless concessions. But, failing such determination, it is more than probable that the relations between the two parties will grow steadily worse.

If it be possible, in this perhaps not very flattering way, to account for the German Government's persistently aggressive demeanour towards England, and the resulting state of almost perpetual friction, notwithstanding the pretence of friendship, the generally restless, explosive, and disconcerting activity of Germany in relation to other States would find its explanation partly in the same attitude towards them and partly in the suggested want of definite political aims and purposes. A wise German statesman would recognise the limits within which any world-policy that is not to provoke a hostile combination of all the nations in arms must confine itself. He would realize that the edifice of Pan-Germanism, with its outlying bastions in the Netherlands, in the Scandinavian countries, in Switzerland, in the German provinces of Austria, and on the Adriatic, could never be built up on any other foundation than the wreckage of the liberties of Europe. A German maritime supremacy must be acknowledged to be incompatible with the existence of the British Empire, and even if that Empire disappeared, the union of the greatest military with the greatest naval Power in one State would compel the world to combine for the riddance of such an incubus. The acquisition of colonies fit for German settlement in South America cannot be reconciled with the Monroe doctrine, which is a fundamental principle of the political faith of the United States. The creation of a German India in Asia Minor must in the end stand or fall with either a German command of the sea or a German conquest of Constantinople and the countries intervening between Germany's present south-eastern frontiers and the Bosphorus. Whilst each of these grandiose schemes seems incapable of fulfilment under anything like the present conditions of the world, it looks as if Germany were playing with them all together simultaneously, and thereby wilfully concentrating in her own path all the obstacles and oppositions of a world set at defiance. That she should do this helps to prove how little of logical and consistent design and of unrelenting purpose lies behind the impetuous mobility, the bewildering surprises, and the heedless disregard of the susceptibilities of other people that have been so characteristic of recent manifestations of German policy.

If it be considered necessary to formulate and accept a theory that will fit all the ascertained facts of German foreign policy, the choice must lie between the two hypotheses here presented :

Either Germany is definitely aiming at a general political hegemony and maritime ascendency, threatening the independence of her neighbours and ultimately the existence of England;

Or Germany, free from any such clear-cut ambition, and thinking for the present merely of using her legitimate position and influence as one of the leading Powers in the council of nations, is seeking to promote her foreign commerce, spread the benefits of German culture, extend the scope of her national energies, and create fresh German interests all over the world wherever and whenever a peaceful opportunity offers, leaving it to an uncertain future to decide whether the occurrence of great changes in the world may not some day assign to Germany a larger share of direct political action over regions not now a part of her dominions, without that violation of the established rights of other countries which would be involved in any such action under existing political conditions. In either case Germany would clearly be wise to build as powerful a navy as she can afford.

The above alternatives seem to exhaust the possibilities of explaining the given facts. The choice offered is a narrow one, nor easy to make with any close approach to certainty. It will, however, be seen, on reflection, that there is no actual necessity for a British Government to determine definitely which of the two theories of German policy it will accept. For it is clear that the second scheme (of semi-independent evolution, not entirely unaided by statecraft) may at any stage merge into the first, or conscious, design scheme. Moreover, if ever the evolution scheme should come to be realized, the position thereby accruing to Germany would obviously constitute as formidable a menace to the rest of the world as would be presented by any deliberate conquest of a similar position by "malice aforethought."

It appears, then, that the element of danger present as a visible factor in one case, also enters, though under some disguise, into the second; and against such danger, whether actual or contingent, the same general line of conduct seems prescribed. It should not be difficult briefly to indicate that line in such a way as to command the assent of all persons competent to form a judgment in this matter.

So long as England remains faithful to the general principle of the preservation of the balance of power, her interests would not be served by Germany being reduced to the rank of a weak Power, as this might easily lead to a Franco-Russian predominance equally, if not more, formidable to the British Empire. There are no existing German rights, territorial or other, which this country could wish to see diminished. Therefore, so long as Germany's action does not overstep the line of legitimate protection of existing rights she can always count upon the sympathy and good-will and even the moral support, of England.

Further, it would be neither just nor politic to ignore the claims to a healthy expansion which a vigorous and growing country like Germany has a natural right to assert in the field of legitimate endeavour. The frank recognition of this right has never been grudged or refused by England to any foreign country. It may be recalled that the German Empire owes such expansion as has already taken place in no small measure to England's co-operation or spirit of accommodation, and to the British principle of equal opportunity and no favour. It cannot be good policy for England to thwart such a process of development where it does not directly conflict either with British interests or with those of other nations to which England is bound by solemn treaty obligations. If Germany, within the limits imposed by these two conditions, finds the means peacefully and honourably to increase her trade and shipping, to gain coaling stations or other harbours, to acquire landing rights for cables, or to secure concessions for the employment of German capital or industries, she should never find England in her way.

Nor is it for British Governments to oppose Germany's building as large a fleet as she may consider necessary or desirable for the defence of her national interests. It is the mark of an independent State that it decides such matters for itself, free from any outside interference, and it would ill become England with her large fleets to dictate to another State what is good for it in matters of supreme national concern. Apart from the question of right and wrong, it may also be urged that nothing would be more likely than any attempt at such dictation, to impel Germany to persevere with her shipbuilding programmes. And also, it may be said in parenthesis, nothing is more likely to produce in Germany the impression of the practical hopelessness of a never-ending succession of costly naval programmes than the conviction, based on ocular demonstration, that for every German ship England will inevitably lay down two, so maintaining the present, relative British preponderance.

It would be of real advantage if the determination not to bar Germany's legitimate and peaceful expansion, nor her schemes of naval development, were made as patent and pronounced as authoritative as possible, provided care were taken at the same time to make it quite clear that this benevolent attitude will give way to determined opposition at the first sign of British or allied interests being adversely affected. This alone would probably do more to bring about lastingly satisfactory relations with Germany than any other course.

It is not unlikely that Germany will before long again ask, as she has so often done hitherto, for a "close understanding" with England. To meet this contingency, the first thing to consider is what exactly is meant by the request. The Anglo-French *entente* had a very material basis and tangible object—namely, the adjustment of a number of actually-existing serious differences. The efforts now being made by England to arrive at an understanding with Russia are justified by a very similar situation. But for an Anglo-German understanding on the same lines there is no room, since none could be built up on the same foundation. It has been shown that there are no questions of any importance now at issue between the two countries. Any understanding must therefore be entirely different in object and scope. Germany's wish may be for an understanding to co-operate for specific purposes, whether offensive or defensive, or generally political or economical, circumscribed by certain geographical limits, or for an agreement of a self-denying order, binding the parties not to do, or not to interfere with, certain things or acts. Or the coveted arrangement might contain a mixture of any or all of these various ingredients. Into offensive or defensive alliances with Germany there is, under the prevailing political conditions, no occasion for England to enter, and it would hardly be honest at present to treat such a possibility as an open question. British assent to any other form of co-operation or system of non-interference must depend absolutely on circumstances, on the particular features, and on the merits of any proposals that may be made. All such proposals England will be as ready as she always has been to weigh and discuss from the point of view of how British interests will be affected. Germany must be content in this respect to receive exactly the same treatment as every other Power.

There is no suggestion more untrue or more unjust than that England has on any recent occasion shown, or is likely to show in future, a *parti pris* against Germany or German proposals as such, or displayed any unfairness in dealing strictly on their own merits with any question having a bearing on her relations with Germany. This accusation has been freely made. It is the stock-in-trade of all the inspired tirades against the British Government which emanate directly or indirectly from the Berlin Press Bureau. But no one has ever been able to bring forward a tittle of evidence in its support that will bear examination. The fact, of course, is that, as Mr. Balfour felt impelled to remark to the German Ambassador on a certain occasion, German communications to the British Government have not generally been of a very agreeable character, and, unless that character is a good deal modified, it is more than likely that such communications will in future receive unpalatable answers. For there is one road which, if past experience is any guide to the future, will most certainly not lead to any permanent improvement of relations with any Power, least of all Germany, and which must therefore be abandoned: that is the road paved with graceful British concessions—concessions made without any conviction either of their justice or of their being set off by equivalent counter-services. The vain hopes that in this manner Germany can be "conciliated" and made more friendly must be definitely given up. It may be that such hopes are still honestly cherished by irresponsible people, ignorant, perhaps necessarily ignorant, of the history of Anglo-German relations during the last twenty years, which cannot be better described than as the history of a systematic policy of gratuitous concessions, a policy which has led to the highly disappointing result disclosed by the almost perpetual state of tension existing between the two countries. Men in responsible positions, whose business it is to inform themselves and to see things as they really are, cannot conscientiously retain any illusions on this subject.

Here, again, however, it would be wrong to suppose that any discrimination is intended to Germany's disadvantage. On the contrary, the same rule will naturally impose itself in the case of all other Powers. It may, indeed, be useful to cast back a glance on British relations with France before and after 1898. A reference to the official records will show that ever since 1882 England had met a growing number of French demands and infringements of British rights in the same spirit of ready accommodation which inspired her dealings with Germany. The not unnatural result was that every successive French Government embarked on a policy of "squeezing" England, until the crisis came in the year of Fashoda, when the stake at issue was the maintenance of the British position on the Upper Nile. The French Minister for Foreign Affairs of that day argued, like his predecessors, that England's apparent opposition was only half-hearted, and would collapse before the persistent threat of French displeasure. Nothing would persuade him that England could in a question of this kind assume an attitude of unbending resistance. It was this erroneous impression, justified in the eyes of the French Cabinet by their deductions from British political practice, that brought the two countries to the verge of war. When the Fashoda chapter had ended with the just discomfiture of France, she remained for a time very sullen, and the enemies of England rejoiced, because they believed that an impassable gulf had now been fixed between the two nations. As a matter of fact, the events at Fashoda proved to be the opening of a new chapter of Anglo-French relations. These, after remaining for some years rather formal, have not since been disturbed by any disagreeable incidents. France behaved more correctly and seemed less suspicious and inconsiderate than had been her wont, and no fresh obstacle arose in the way which ultimately led to the Agreement of 1904.

Although Germany has not been exposed to such a rebuff as France encountered in 1898, the events connected with the Algeciras Conference appear to have had on the German Government the effect of an unexpected revelation, clearly showing indications of a new spirit in which England proposes to regulate her own conduct towards France on the one hand and to Germany on the other. That the result was a very serious disappointment to Germany has been made abundantly manifest by the turmoil which the signature of the Algeciras Act has created in the country, the official, semi-official, and unofficial classes vying with each other in giving expression to their astonished discontent. The time which has since elapsed has, no, doubt, been short. But during that time, it may be observed that our relations with Germany, if not exactly cordial, have at least been practically free from all symptoms of direct friction, and there is an impression that Germany will think twice before she now gives rise to any fresh disagreement. In this attitude she will be encouraged if she meets on England's part with unvarying courtesy and consideration in all matters of common concern, but also with a prompt and firm refusal to enter into any one-sided bargains or arrangements, and the most unbending determination to uphold British rights and interests in every part of the globe. There will be no surer or quicker way to win the respect of the German Government and of the German nation.

Observations on Printed Memorandum on Relations With France and Germany, January 1907[1]

THOMAS HENRY SANDERSON

FOREIGN OFFICE, FEBRUARY 21, 1907

. . . I have written these notes, partly because the circumstances themselves are of considerable interest, partly because they tend to show that the history of German policy towards this Country is not the unchequered record of black deeds which the memorandum seems to portray. There have been many occasions on which we have worked comfortably in accord with Germany, and not a few cases on which her support has been serviceable to us. There have been others in which she has been extremely aggravating, sometimes unconsciously so, sometimes with intention. The Germans are very tight bargainers, they have earned the nickname of "*les Juifs se la diplomatie.*" The German Foreign office hold to a traditional view of negotiation that one of the most effective methods of gaining your point is to show how intensely disagreeable you can make yourself if you do not. They are surprised that the recollection of these methods should rankle, and speaking generally the North Germans combine intense susceptibility as regards themselves with a singular inability to appreciate the susceptibilities of others.

(25.) On the other hand it is undeniable that we have at times been compelled to maintain an attitude in defence of British interests which has been very inconvenient to German ambitions. And of late years while the British Gov[ernmen]t has remained calm and conciliatory, the press and public opinion here have interfered seriously with our working so much together as would otherwise have been desirable. It is not at all unnatural that the German Ambassador, who has seen better days, should feel this rather keenly.

(26.) In considering the tendencies and methods of German policy, we have to remember that the Empire took its present place among the Great Powers of Europe only 35 years ago, after some 50 years of helpless loggings for united national existence. It was inevitable that a nation flushed with success which had been obtained at the cost of great sacrifices, should be somewhat arrogant and over-eager, impatient to realise various long-suppressed aspirations, and to claim full recognition of its new position. The Government was at the same time suffering from the constant feeling of insecurity caused by the presence on the East and West of two [powerful, jealous and discontented neighbours. It is not surprising that with the traditions of the Prussian monarchy behind it, it should have shown itself restless and scheming, and have had frequent recourse to tortuous methods, which have not proved wholly successful.

(27.) It is not, I think, to be expected that Germany will renounce her ambition for oversea possessions, which shall assist and support the development of her commerce, and afford openings for her surplus population. But, as time goes on, her manner of pursuing these objects will be less open to exception, and popular opinion, which in Germany is on the whole sound and prudent, will exercise an increasing wholesome restraint. If the mere acquisition of territory were in itself immoral, I conceive that the sins of Germany since 1871 are light in comparison to ours, and it must be remembered that, from and outside point of view, a Country which looks to each change as a possible chance of self-aggrandisement is not much more open to criticism than one which sees in every such change a menace to its own interests, existing or potential, and founds on this theory continued claims to interference or compensation. It has sometimes seemed to me that to a foreigner reading our press the British Empire must appear in the light of some huge giant sprawling over the globe, with gouty fingers and toes stretching in every direction, which cannot be approached without eliciting a scream. The sentiment was aptly expressed by a member of a Deputation form South Africa who concluded an address to the late Lord Salisbury with the remark "My Lord, we are told that the Germans are good neighbours, but we prefer to have no neighbours at all." That is an attitude which no Government can successfully maintain, and it appears to me that Mr. Rhodes was better advised when in order to draw off the attention of the German Government from South African affairs, he mentioned to the Emperor William "that blessed word Mesopotamia," and suggested opportunities for the development of German energy in a different quarter of the globe.

(28.) The moral which I should draw form the events of recent years is that Germany is a helpful, though somewhat exacting, friend, that she is a tight and tenacious bargainer, and a most disagreeable antagonist. She is oversensitive about being consulted on all questions on which she claim a voice, either as a Great Power or on account of special interests, and it is never prudent to neglect her on such occasions. Her diplomacy is, to put it mildly, always watchful, and any suspicion of being ignored rouses an amount of wrath disproportionate to the offence. However tiresome such discussions may be, it is, as a general rule, less inconvenient to take her at once into counsel, and to state frankly within what limits you can accept her views, than to have a claim for interference suddenly launched on you at some critical moment. It would of course be absurd to make her any concessions of importance except as a matter of bargain and in return for value received. Her motto has always been "Nothing for nothing in this world, and very little for sixpence." But I do not think it can be justly said that she is ungrateful for friendly support. It is at all events unwise to meet her with an attitude of pure obstruction, such as is advocated by part of our press. A great and rowing nation cannot be repressed. It is altogether contrary to reason that Germany should wish to be in a position to face a quarrel with more chances of success, than she can be said now to have. But it would be a misfortune that she should be led to believe that in whatever direction she seeks to expand she will find the British lion in her path, there must be places in which German enterprise can find a field without injury to any important British interests, and it would seem wise that in any policy of development which takes due account of these interests she would be allowed to expect our good will.

NOTE

1 In Gooch and Temperley, eds., *Documents on the Origins of the War.*

Reading 9.2

The German Threat? 1938 NEVILLE HENDERSON

Letter from Sir N. Henderson to Viscount Halifax (Received July 29)

BRITISH EMBASSY, BERLIN,
JULY 26, 1938

DEAR SECRETARY OF STATE,

Your talk with Wiedemann and the Prime Minister's with von Dirksen have eased my mind in the sense that both confirm my opinion that the Germans, apart from a section of extremists, are just as afraid of war as anybody else—or even more so. Yet nothing will convince the pessimists that Germany is not actually and definitely contemplating war. Personally I am certain to-day that she does not but, like the rest of us, she appreciates the fact that circumstances may be too strong for her, and consequently is prepared or preparing for all emergencies. All the war talk here has its origin in this fact.

Cui bono is not a bad basis for argument in policy as well as detective stories. War would doubtless serve the purposes of all the Jews, communists and doctrinaires in the world for whom Nazism is anathema, but it would be a terrible risk to-day for Germany herself and particularly for the new Nazi Germany which Hitler has built up in the past five years. The roots have not yet gone down far enough. That this is not apparent to Hitler I cannot believe. I hate the excessive nationalism of Nazism myself but the remedy of war would be worse than the disease.

On the other hand there is Hitler's prestige and German stupidity. I told Weizsäcker the other day that I should not be the least nervous, if it were not for German stupidity. If they could do a stupid thing at the wrong moment they always went off and did it. He was taken aback but he was unable to deny it. It is, unfortunately, a fact and when—quite apart from this caprice of dictators—one realises the strength of the forces in every country which are praying for war as the only remedy for anti-communism, anti-Judaism and against a strong Germany one must remain nervous. If it comes, it will not be Hitler or the mass of the Germans who have sought it, this year at any rate. They will be, of course, blamed for it. Unjustly, in my opinion: but by my contemporaries my opinion will be regarded as worthless.

I do not envy Lord Runciman the difficult and thankless job which he is undertaking. The Czechs are a pig-headed race and Benes not the least pig-headed among them. And with it all, a master of words and formulae, which

Source: E. L. Woodward and Rohan Butler, eds., assisted by Margaret Lambert, Documents on British Foreign Policy 1919–1939, Third Series, Vol II: 1938 *(London: His Majesty's Stationery Office, 1949). Reprinted by permission.*

sound magnificent but are really empty. Ask anyone who has worked with him at Geneva. I remember well the opinion King Alexander and his Yugoslavs had of him when I was at Belgrade. I perjure myself about him to the Germans but I have few illusions in my heart. And the Germans, from past experience, have less than none and I perjure myself, Heaven forgive me and alas, in vain.

There are two points which I think have to be borne in mind. The first is that so long as the Germans trust us and have confidence in the sincerity and impartiality of our effort, the battle is not lost. But this means that we shall have at long last to put our foot down very firmly and say to Benes 'You must'. He will yield to nothing less. The new Statute has got to be a genuine Nationalities Statute and not a camouflaged Minorities one. This means a fundamental change in the Czech proposals as at present contemplated.

The second point is that the Germans have adopted and will continue to adopt the line that they are not influencing the Sudeten and will not exercise any pressure on them. Merely to say that we don't believe them, while obvious and necessary, does not alter the situation in the least. It is a definite and set policy, with moreover certain useful aspects from our own and a peace point of view as well as from the German angle. It enables us, for instance, to send observers and Lord Runciman and to act at Prague generally as seems good to us without regard to German criticism. Had Weizsäcker raised objection to the Runciman mission, the retort was obvious.

At the same time it does not bind the German Government to this, that or the other specific solution. If the German Government had clamoured for pre-announced concessions and the Sudeten did not get them, German honour would be involved and it would probably prove impossible to find a compromise solution. To that extent therefore the German attitude is helpful rather than the reverse for the moment. The tug of war will come when the deadlock comes. It is then—but not till then—that we shall have to say to the Germans, 'If we are prepared to put the thumbscrews on Benes, you must help by putting pressure on Henlein to accept this or that, which may be short of his desiderata'.

It will not be easy, for Hitler has assumed the line (see my telegram No. 295[1] of July 4th) that he will put no pressure on the Sudeten and that a non-agreed solution is worthless, in as much as it only means prolonging the tension indefinitely. Unfortunately there is much force in this contention, but if the solution really is a just one we shall have to insist on it. Will it be just? That is the great question. My United States colleague (among others) who is a shrewd and objective observer, will not even admit my 5 to 10 per cent chance of keeping indefinitely the Sudeten in Czechoslovakia. Are we then merely ramming our heads against a brick wall? And would not the plebiscite to-day be the only practical answer?

I personally do not feel that. The compromise solution may and probably will be only temporary but we must try it out in the interests of world peace. Later it may not be the same danger to world peace and that consideration to me is everything. We may feel a certain inevitable compassion for the Czechs as a small and heroic race (even though their own acts during the last twenty years have not justified it) and superficial and sentimental public opinion in England will cry out, yet the whole is greater than the part and there is much in the present position which is morally untenable. If Germany was a weak country like Hungary and if it was not Nazi, public opinion in England would have adopted a very different outlook to this problem. Yet the basic moral position remains, however big and dangerous Germany may be.

YOURS EVER,
NEVILE HENDERSON

Letter from Sir N. Henderson to Mr. Strang (Received July 29)

BRITISH EMBASSY, BERLIN,
JULY 27, 1938

MY DEAR STRANG,

Your letter of July 21st[1] on the subject of Germany's military preparations.

I enclose (1) a detailed commentary drawn up by Colonel Mason-MacFarlane on the specific points you mention, and (2) his general remarks thereon.

As you are aware from my reports, the latter are in conformity with my views. In order to form one's opinion one must also try to understand the German point of view. If we were in Germany's place what would we, in the midst of all this war psychosis, be doing: exactly what I think the Germans are today doing, namely (1) omitting nothing, short of actual mobilisation, calculated to prepare the army for all emergencies and (ii) strengthening Germany's defensive fortifications in the west. If there is to be a show down with Czechoslovakia, Germany, for obvious reasons, wants a stalemate in the West as well as to impress upon France that, if she comes to Czechoslovakia's assistance—as she has announced so often and so solemnly that she intends to do, it will cost her dear. The Siegfried line is at any rate not aggressive, so far as France is concerned.

The reports which you receive and those which reach us in Berlin can in my opinion be attributed to a variety of causes:

(*a*) Logical and natural precautionary measures in view of the political situation and the war-talk in all countries.

(*b*) Fear of war, which is almost, if not quite, as general here as in England.

(*c*) Bluff or intimidation, i.e. to encourage His Majesty's Government to continue their pressure at Prague and to warn the Czechs what to expect if they are not reasonable (incidentally the press campaign has the same basis).

(*d*) Aggressiveness on the part of the war-party here.

For there is a war-party which would like to make the German Heaven at once without waiting. Moreover its motives are mixed and not solely confined to the bellicose young hotheads or extremists. There are even some Germans who would like a war as affording the only chance of upsetting both a *régime* which they hate and its present gang of leaders. Every Jew and communist in the world probably shares this theory. If I were a German desirous of peace I should be anxious myself. Hence their military precautions.

The only specific comment I would make as regards Colonel Mason-Mac-Farlane's general remarks is the following. He observes that 'under certain circumstances Hitler will almost certainly march against Czechoslovakia without warning'. I am not so certain that he will begin marching without warning. I think that it is equally possible that he will do nothing irrevocable without giving us a possibly 24 hour chance to prevent the irrevocable. If we want to stop bloodshed, it is then that we would have, without waiting, to say 'Plebiscite'.

YOURS EVER,
NEVILE HENDERSON

Sir N. Henderson (Berlin) to Viscount Halifax (Received August 19, 7.15 p.m.)

BERLIN,
AUGUST 19, 1938

Military Attaché saw General Tippelskirch, Chief of Intelligence at Ministry of War, this morning. Military Attaché opened conversation by pointing out that foreign press were in some cases attributing greater significance to German military manœuvres this autumn than would appear to be justified by information previously given him by Ministry of War. He asked if he could be given the same detailed information of locality, scope, and nature of these manœuvres as is normally procured by the press of other countries when dealing with such a subject. The General said he could not give exact information as regards military measures at present in progress. It was not worth his while making detailed enquiries on Military Attaché's behalf as he was quite certain that detailed information would not be given. He confirmed the fact that the scope of measures now in progress was as outlined to Military Attaché in his previous talks on the subject at Ministry of War. He said that care must be taken not to exaggerate the number of reservists being called up. Active formations require very few reservists to complete to war strength, and number of reserve formations being embodied was limited. He stressed the unsatisfactory state of affairs in Austria and doubted whether it would be possible to do much in the way of embodying reserve formations in that country. The large quantity of material of all kinds which had admittedly been streaming into Austria by road and rail was the least amount required to make Austrian army effective. Contrary to previous information on this point he said many of the reservists being called up were of 'E' type who have only done short time reserve training. The General was at great pains to explain how necessary from military point of view the measures now in progress are. He said the only reason that French did not take similar measures on a similar scale was fact that they unhappily for them suffered from democratic government. He refused to admit that German military programme this autumn could be regarded as a disturbing factor in the admittedly very tense European situation. Really serious factors were of a very different kind. It was quite false to assume that measures now being taken were preliminaries to military action against Czechoslovakia. On the other hand as a soldier the Military Attaché would understand that in view of present critical situation German army must clearly do all it can to be 100 per cent. ready for eventualities. Everything this year had come with a rush. The 'Anschluss' had come like a bolt from the blue owing to Dr. Schuschnigg's ill-advised action and German army naturally had at the moment to work at abnormal speed in order to cope with possibilities of a situation which had been created by 6½ millions of Germans in Austria now being Reich Germans, while their 3½ million fellow Germans of old Austrian Empire were still clamouring without very much hope for the same right. The General gave no indication that he knew of our recent communication to Herr Hitler and the Military Attaché naturally made no reference to it. Military Attaché made it clear that as a soldier he quite understood the force of the General's arguments and that his sole wish was to be able to give me the exactest possible information to enable me to appreciate the situation correctly in face of the many rumours which are now current. General Tippelskirch was most friendly throughout the interview and gave no indication of ill-feeling. He was, however, manifestly more than perturbed by present situation and said he found it very hard to see daylight.

Reading 9.3

The Threat to Ukraine From the West

VLADIMIR PUTIN

. . . A referendum was held in Crimea on March 16 in full compliance with democratic procedures and international norms. More than 82 percent of the electorate took part in the vote. Over 96 percent of them spoke out in favour of reuniting with Russia. These numbers speak for themselves.

To understand the reason behind such a choice it is enough to know the history of Crimea and what Russia and Crimea have always meant for each other . . .

Crimea is a unique blend of different peoples' cultures and traditions. This makes it similar to Russia as a whole, where not a single ethnic group has been lost over the centuries. Russians and Ukrainians, Crimean Tatars and people of other ethnic groups have lived side by side in Crimea, retaining their own identity, traditions, languages and faith.

Incidentally, the total population of the Crimean Peninsula today is 2.2 million people, of whom almost 1.5 million are Russians, 350,000 are

Source: Address by the President of the Russian Federation, 18 March 2014. http://en.kremlin.ru/events/president/news/20603.

Ukrainians who predominantly consider Russian their native language, and about 290,000–300,000 are Crimean Tatars, who, as the referendum has shown, also lean towards Russia . . .

In people's hearts and minds, Crimea has always been an inseparable part of Russia. This firm conviction is based on truth and justice and was passed from generation to generation, over time, under any circumstances, despite all the dramatic changes our country went through during the entire 20th century.

After the revolution, the Bolsheviks, for a number of reasons—may God judge them—added large sections of the historical South of Russia to the Republic of Ukraine. This was done with no consideration for the ethnic make-up of the population, and today these areas form the southeast of Ukraine. Then, in 1954, a decision was made to transfer Crimean Region to Ukraine, along with Sevastopol, despite the fact that it was a federal city. This was the personal initiative of the Communist Party head Nikita Khrushchev. What stood behind this decision of his—a desire to win the support of the Ukrainian political establishment or to atone for the mass repressions of the 1930's in Ukraine—is for historians to figure out.

What matters now is that this decision was made in clear violation of the constitutional norms that were in place even then. The decision was made behind the scenes. Naturally, in a totalitarian state nobody bothered to ask the citizens of Crimea and Sevastopol. They were faced with the fact. People, of course, wondered why all of a sudden Crimea became part of Ukraine. But on the whole—and we must state this clearly, we all know it—this decision was treated as a formality of sorts because the territory was transferred within the boundaries of a single state. Back then, it was impossible to imagine that Ukraine and Russia may split up and become two separate states. However, this has happened.

Unfortunately, what seemed impossible became a reality. The USSR fell apart. Things developed so swiftly that few people realised how truly dramatic those events and their consequences would be. Many people both in Russia and in Ukraine, as well as in other republics hoped that the Commonwealth of Independent States that was created at the time would become the new common form of statehood. They were told that there would be a single currency, a single economic space, joint armed forces; however, all this remained empty promises, while the big country was gone. It was only when Crimea ended up as part of a different country that Russia realised that it was not simply robbed, it was plundered.

At the same time, we have to admit that by launching the sovereignty parade Russia itself aided in the collapse of the Soviet Union. And as this collapse was legalised, everyone forgot about Crimea and Sevastopol—the main base of the Black Sea Fleet. Millions of people went to bed in one country and awoke in different ones, overnight becoming ethnic minorities in former Union republics, while the Russian nation became one of the biggest, if not the biggest ethnic group in the world to be divided by borders. . . .

We accommodated Ukraine not only regarding Crimea, but also on such a complicated matter as the maritime boundary in the Sea of Azov and the

Kerch Strait. What we proceeded from back then was that good relations with Ukraine matter most for us and they should not fall hostage to deadlock territorial disputes. However, we expected Ukraine to remain our good neighbour, we hoped that Russian citizens and Russian speakers in Ukraine, especially its southeast and Crimea, would live in a friendly, democratic and civilised state that would protect their rights in line with the norms of international law.

However, this is not how the situation developed. Time and time again attempts were made to deprive Russians of their historical memory, even of their language and to subject them to forced assimilation. Moreover, Russians, just as other citizens of Ukraine are suffering from the constant political and state crisis that has been rocking the country for over 20 years.

I understand why Ukrainian people wanted change. They have had enough of the authorities in power during the years of Ukraine's independence. Presidents, prime ministers and parliamentarians changed, but their attitude to the country and its people remained the same. They milked the country, fought among themselves for power, assets and cash flows and did not care much about the ordinary people. They did not wonder why it was that millions of Ukrainian citizens saw no prospects at home and went to other countries to work as day labourers. I would like to stress this: it was not some Silicon Valley they fled to, but to become day labourers. Last year alone almost 3 million people found such jobs in Russia. According to some sources, in 2013 their earnings in Russia totalled over $20 billion, which is about 12% of Ukraine's GDP.

I would like to reiterate that I understand those who came out on Maidan with peaceful slogans against corruption, inefficient state management and poverty. The right to peaceful protest, democratic procedures and elections exist for the sole purpose of replacing the authorities that do not satisfy the people. However, those who stood behind the latest events in Ukraine had a different agenda: they were preparing yet another government takeover; they wanted to seize power and would stop short of nothing. They resorted to terror, murder and riots. Nationalists, neo-Nazis, Russophobes and anti-Semites executed this coup. They continue to set the tone in Ukraine to this day.

The new so-called authorities began by introducing a draft law to revise the language policy, which was a direct infringement on the rights of ethnic minorities. However, they were immediately 'disciplined' by the foreign sponsors of these so-called politicians. One has to admit that the mentors of these current authorities are smart and know well what such attempts to build a purely Ukrainian state may lead to. The draft law was set aside, but clearly reserved for the future. Hardly any mention is made of this attempt now, probably on the presumption that people have a short memory. Nevertheless, we can all clearly see the intentions of these ideological heirs of Bandera, Hitler's accomplice during World War II.

It is also obvious that there is no legitimate executive authority in Ukraine now, nobody to talk to. Many government agencies have been taken over by the impostors, but they do not have any control in the country, while they themselves—and I would like to stress this—are often controlled by radicals. In some cases, you need a special permit from the militants on Maidan to meet with certain ministers of the current government. This is not a joke—this is reality.

Those who opposed the coup were immediately threatened with repression. Naturally, the first in line here was Crimea, the Russian-speaking Crimea. In view of this, the residents of Crimea and Sevastopol turned to Russia for help in defending their rights and lives, in preventing the events that were unfolding and are still underway in Kiev, Donetsk, Kharkov and other Ukrainian cities.

Naturally, we could not leave this plea unheeded; we could not abandon Crimea and its residents in distress. This would have been betrayal on our part.

First, we had to help create conditions so that the residents of Crimea for the first time in history were able to peacefully express their free will regarding their own future. However, what do we hear from our colleagues in Western Europe and North America? They say we are violating norms of international law. Firstly, it's a good thing that they at least remember that there exists such a thing as international law—better late than never.

Secondly, and most importantly—what exactly are we violating? True, the President of the Russian Federation received permission from the Upper House of Parliament to use the Armed Forces in Ukraine. However, strictly speaking, nobody has acted on this permission yet. Russia's Armed Forces never entered Crimea; they were there already in line with an international agreement. True, we did enhance our forces there; however—this is something I would like everyone to hear and know—we did not exceed the personnel limit of our Armed Forces in Crimea, which is set at 25,000, because there was no need to do so.

Next. As it declared independence and decided to hold a referendum, the Supreme Council of Crimea referred to the United Nations Charter, which speaks of the right of nations to self-determination. Incidentally, I would like to remind you that when Ukraine seceded from the USSR it did exactly the same thing, almost word for word. Ukraine used this right, yet the residents of Crimea are denied it. Why is that?

Moreover, the Crimean authorities referred to the well-known Kosovo precedent—a precedent our western colleagues created with their own hands in a very similar situation, when they agreed that the unilateral separation of Kosovo from Serbia, exactly what Crimea is doing now, was legitimate and did not require any permission from the country's central authorities. Pursuant to Article 2, Chapter 1 of the United Nations Charter, the UN International Court agreed with this approach and made the following comment in its ruling of July 22, 2010, and I quote: "No general prohibition may be inferred from the practice of the Security Council with regard to declarations of independence," and "General international law contains no prohibition on declarations of independence." Crystal clear, as they say.

I do not like to resort to quotes, but in this case, I cannot help it. Here is a quote from another official document: the Written Statement of the United States America of April 17, 2009, submitted to the same UN International Court in connection with the hearings on Kosovo. Again, I quote: "Declarations of independence may, and often do, violate domestic legislation. However, this does not make them violations of international law." End of quote. They wrote this, disseminated it all over the world, had everyone agree and now they are outraged. Over what? The actions of Crimean people completely fit in with these instructions, as it were. For some reason, things that Kosovo Albanians (and we have full respect for them) were permitted to do, Russians, Ukrainians and Crimean Tatars in Crimea are not allowed. Again, one wonders why.

We keep hearing from the United States and Western Europe that Kosovo is some special case. What makes it so special in the eyes of our colleagues? It turns out that it is the fact that the conflict in Kosovo resulted in so many human casualties. Is this a legal argument? The ruling of the International Court says nothing about this. This is not even double standards; this is amazing, primitive, blunt cynicism. One should not try so crudely to make everything suit their interests, calling the same thing white today and black tomorrow. According to this logic, we have to make sure every conflict leads to human losses.

I will state clearly—if the Crimean local self-defence units had not taken the situation under control, there could have been casualties as well. Fortunately this did not happen. There was not a single armed confrontation in Crimea and no casualties. Why do you think this was so? The answer is simple: because it is very difficult, practically impossible to fight against the will of the people. Here I would like to thank the Ukrainian military—and this is 22,000 fully armed servicemen. I would like to thank those Ukrainian service members who refrained from bloodshed and did not smear their uniforms in blood.

Other thoughts come to mind in this connection. They keep talking of some Russian intervention in Crimea, some sort of aggression. This is strange to hear. I cannot recall a single case in history of an intervention without a single shot being fired and with no human casualties. . . .

Like a mirror, the situation in Ukraine reflects what is going on and what has been happening in the world over the past several decades. After the dissolution of bipolarity on the planet, we no longer have stability. Key international institutions are not getting any stronger; on the contrary, in many cases, they are sadly degrading. Our western partners, led by the United States of America, prefer not to be guided by international law in their practical policies, but by the rule of the gun. They have come to believe in their exclusivity and exceptionalism, that they can decide the destinies of the world, that only they can ever be right. They act as they please: here and there, they use force against sovereign states, building coalitions based on the principle "If you are not with us, you are against us." To make this aggression look legitimate, they force the necessary resolutions from international organisations, and if for some reason this does not work, they simply ignore the UN Security Council and the UN overall.

This happened in Yugoslavia; we remember 1999 very well. It was hard to believe, even seeing it with my own eyes, that at the end of the 20th century, one of Europe's capitals, Belgrade, was under missile attack for several weeks, and then came the real intervention. Was there a UN Security Council resolution on this matter, allowing for these actions? Nothing of the sort. And then, they hit Afghanistan, Iraq, and frankly violated the UN Security Council resolution on Libya, when instead of imposing the so-called no-fly zone over it they started bombing it too.

There was a whole series of controlled "colour" revolutions. Clearly, the people in those nations, where these events took place, were sick of tyranny and poverty, of their lack of prospects; but these feelings were taken advantage of cynically. Standards were imposed on these nations that did not in any way correspond to their way of life, traditions, or these peoples' cultures. As a result, instead of democracy and freedom, there was chaos, outbreaks in violence and a series of upheavals. The Arab Spring turned into the Arab Winter.

A similar situation unfolded in Ukraine. In 2004, to push the necessary candidate through at the presidential elections, they thought up some sort of third round that was not stipulated by the law. It was absurd and a mockery of the constitution. And now, they have thrown in an organised and well-equipped army of militants.

We understand what is happening; we understand that these actions were aimed against Ukraine and Russia and against Eurasian integration. And all this while Russia strived to engage in dialogue with our colleagues in the West. We are constantly proposing cooperation on all key issues; we want to strengthen our level of trust and for our relations to be equal, open and fair. But we saw no reciprocal steps.

On the contrary, they have lied to us many times, made decisions behind our backs, placed us before an accomplished fact. This happened with NATO's expansion to the East, as well as the deployment of military infrastructure at our borders. They kept telling us the same thing: "Well, this does not concern you." That's easy to say.

It happened with the deployment of a missile defence system. In spite of all our apprehensions, the project is working and moving forward. It happened with the endless foot-dragging in the talks on visa issues, promises of fair competition and free access to global markets.

Today, we are being threatened with sanctions, but we already experience many limitations, ones that are quite significant for us, our economy and our nation. For example, still during the times of the Cold War, the US and subsequently other nations restricted a large list of technologies and equipment from being sold to the USSR, creating the Coordinating Committee for Multilateral Export Controls list. Today, they have formally been eliminated, but only formally; and in reality, many limitations are still in effect.

In short, we have every reason to assume that the infamous policy of containment, led in the 18th, 19th and 20th centuries, continues today. They are constantly trying to sweep us into a corner because we have an independent position, because we maintain it and because we call things like they are and do not engage in hypocrisy. But there is a limit to everything. And with Ukraine, our western partners have crossed the line, playing the bear and acting irresponsibly and unprofessionally.

After all, they were fully aware that there are millions of Russians living in Ukraine and in Crimea. They must have really lacked political instinct and common sense not to foresee all the consequences of their actions. Russia found itself in a position it could not retreat from. If you compress the spring all the way to its limit, it will snap back hard . . .

Let me note too that we have already heard declarations from Kiev about Ukraine soon joining NATO. What would this have meant for Crimea and Sevastopol in the future? It would have meant that NATO's navy would be right there in this city of Russia's military glory, and this would create not an illusory but a perfectly real threat to the whole of southern Russia. These are things that could have become reality were it not for the choice the Crimean people made, and I want to say thank you to them for this.

But let me say too that we are not opposed to cooperation with NATO, for this is certainly not the case. For all the internal processes within the organisation, NATO remains a military alliance, and we are against having a military alliance making itself at home right in our backyard or in our historic territory. I simply cannot imagine that we would travel to Sevastopol to visit NATO sailors. Of course, most of them are wonderful guys, but it would be better to have them come and visit us, be our guests, rather than the other way round. . . .

I understand the people of Crimea, who put the question in the clearest possible terms in the referendum: should Crimea be with Ukraine or with Russia? We can be sure in saying that the authorities in Crimea and Sevastopol, the legislative authorities, when they formulated the question, set aside group and political interests and made the people's fundamental interests alone the cornerstone of their work. The particular historic, population, political and economic circumstances of Crimea would have made any other proposed option—however tempting it could be at the first glance—only temporary and fragile and would have inevitably led to further worsening of the situation there, which would have had disastrous effects on people's lives. The people of Crimea thus decided to put the question in firm and uncompromising form, with no grey areas. The referendum was fair and transparent, and the people of Crimea clearly and convincingly expressed their will and stated that they want to be with Russia.

Russia will also have to make a difficult decision now, taking into account the various domestic and external considerations. What do people here in Russia think? Here, like in any democratic country, people have different points of view, but I want to make the point that the absolute majority of our people clearly do support what is happening.

The most recent public opinion surveys conducted here in Russia show that 95 percent of people think that Russia should protect the interests of Russians and members of other ethnic groups living in Crimea—95 percent of our citizens. More than 83 percent think that Russia should do this even if it will complicate our relations with some other countries. A total of 86 percent of our people see Crimea as still being Russian territory and part of our country's lands. And one particularly important figure, which corresponds exactly with the result in Crimea's referendum: almost 92 percent of our people support Crimea's reunification with Russia.

Thus we see that the overwhelming majority of people in Crimea and the absolute majority of the Russian Federation's people support the reunification of the Republic of Crimea and the city of Sevastopol with Russia. . . .

Reading 9.4

The Threat From Russia   *ELIOT A. COHEN*

Whether we fully realize it or not, the West in general and NATO in particular face a new crisis—by far the most serious and dangerous of the post–Cold War era. It is not a crisis about the intricacies of NATO reform, the mechanisms of European security, the finer points of cyber-warfare, or the coordination and financing of Transatlantic defense policy. It is rather about something far deeper and far more fundamental. The fact that many seem not to realize it is both part of the problem and starkly symptomatic of it.

The crisis has a name—Ukraine—but the crisis is about more than one country, and it is even about more than Ukraine's aggressor, Russia. It is, quite possibly, a foundational crisis in an early stage whose potential for menace is as great as the crises that enveloped our civilization in the century past: its two world wars and the Cold War, when the high civilization of the West trembled before the onslaught of totalitarian enemies. We have not yet reached a level of danger of the same magnitude as 1917 or 1941 or 1949, and strong, state-based totalitarian threats do not properly define the crisis. But we are in some ways beyond the level of danger of most of the Cold War crises of the past century—Berlin 1961 or the December 1979 Soviet invasion of Afghanistan, for example.

In the three great crises of the 20th century the United States ultimately stepped forward; as Churchill put it in a particularly dark moment, the New World came forth to rescue and liberate the Old. In part for that very reason, the United States is today as much the front line of crisis as Europe. Whether the United States will or indeed can do anything like that again remains to be seen. But we are getting ahead of ourselves. First we need to sort out how the new crisis resembles or echoes those of the past century, in what ways it is different, and how we should approach it going forward.

The crisis of the moment is, as noted above, "Ukraine." In and of itself the crisis consists of, some believe, an unfortunate set of not especially critical or dangerous events. This assessment is at best fractionally true; to explain why, we must again invoke the ghost of Winston Churchill.

Source: Eliot A. Cohen, "The 'Kind of Thing' Crisis," The American Interest, vol. 10, no. 3 (January/February 2015).

In September 1935, Vincent Sheean, an American journalist and novelist, was lodging in an elegant house in the south of France where Churchill, as was his wont, was visiting at the very end of summer. The talk of the day was the Ethiopian crisis. Here are Sheean's words:

He had a distinction which he tried to bring out in every talk about Ethiopia just then: it seemed to him very important. "It's not the thing we object to", he would say, "it's the kind of thing." I had not then succumbed as much to his genial charm as I did later, and I could not quite accept this. I mentioned the Red Sea, the route to India, the importance of Aden. Mr. Churchill brushed all that aside: "We don't need to worry about the Italians", he said. "It isn't that at all. It isn't the thing. It's the *kind* of thing. . . ."

Mr Churchill was pinned down firmly one day by an elegant lady, Mme Lepelletier, who said that an objection to the thing might be practical and necessary, but that England had no historical right to object to the kind of thing. England had too often profited by "the kind of thing."

"Ah, but you see, all that belongs to the unregenerate past, is locked away in the limbo of the old, the wicked days", Mr Churchill said, smiling benevolently upon her across the luncheon table. "The world progresses. We have endeavoured, by means of the League of Nations and the whole fabric of international law, to make it impossible for nations nowadays to infringe upon each other's rights. In trying to upset the empire of Ethiopia, Mussolini is making a most dangerous and foolhardy attack upon the whole established structure, and the results of such an attack are quite incalculable. Who is to say what will come of it in a year, or two, or three? With Germany arming at breakneck speed, England lost in a pacifist dream, France corrupt and torn by dissension, America remote and indifferent—Madame, my dear lady, do you not tremble for your children?"

That is just the point. It does not matter whether Khrushchev was wise in giving the Crimea to Ukraine in 1954, or how it came to be that eastern Ukraine is largely populated by native Russian speakers. Nor does it now matter what kind of policy it was prudent to pursue in the 1990s in terms of contemplating NATO entry for countries that had been part of the Soviet Union. Even the events that precipitated the crisis are not important. Such things perhaps used to matter, but we are beyond them now, not least because we cannot go back and mend our judgments even if we wished to do so.

It's *the kind of thing* we must understand. And the kind of thing is the dismemberment of a sovereign state, in this case one whose borders were guaranteed thusly under the first article of the Budapest Declaration of 1994:

The Russian Federation, the United Kingdom of Great Britain and Northern Ireland and the United States of America reaffirm their commitment to Ukraine, in accordance with the principles of the Final Act of the Conference on Security and Cooperation in Europe, to respect the independence and sovereignty and the existing borders of Ukraine. . . .

And it is dismemberment not only by economic pressure and subversion, but by violence and invasion, by fire and sword, by kidnapping and murder.

That is *the kind of thing*, and it has happened not in Africa or Asia or South America but in Europe, and it has happened not to a remote monarchy but to a reasonably free state whose sovereign rights are, to repeat, guaranteed in writing by the Great Powers.

And the reaction? Sanctions that mean little, and a nervous shuffling of feet and wringing of hands by the leaders of the so-called free world. The crisis consists just as much, if not more, in the implications of the Western reaction as it does to the aggression that stimulated the crisis in the first place. A case in point: Just a few months ago the new Secretary General of NATO, Jens Stoltenberg, began his tenure with this declaration: "My main message has been, today and for many years, that there is no contradiction between aspiring to a constructive relationship with Russia and at the same time being in favor of a strong NATO." In an even more invertebrate statement, the German Foreign Minister welcomed the new Secretary General by criticizing his predecessor: "I found some of the things that came in the last weeks from Brussels, from the NATO headquarters, not always helpful. I wasn't the only one in the German government who felt that way."

This is not prudence, or diplomacy, or finesse, or the fine-tuning of optics and options. It is cowardice. The Germans have coined the word *Russlandversteher*—people who *understand Russia*. It is not a derogatory term, even though the category includes a former Chancellor who has prostituted the dignity of that office by selling himself to Gazprom. It captures a kind of cravenness in the face of aggression that is not limited to a country many of whose leaders are paralyzed by guilt on the one hand and cupidity on the other.

Thus, in the early phases of this crisis British officials made clear that they could not abide sanctions that would make it impossible for the crooked Russian oligarchs who use London as their playground to bank, invest, live, educate their children, and go on debauches in discreet private clubs. It has been only with the deepest reluctance, too, that France has put on hold its transfer of advanced Mistral warships to Moscow—although, of course, the training of Russian crews continues.

The U.S. authorities have been a bit better, but not much. A few more training exercises in the East, yes. But stop shrinking the U.S. Army? Permanently station U.S. ground forces in Poland and the Baltic states? Supply Ukraine with weapons or training to defend itself? No, not yet; and from the looks of things, not at all. And the subsequent reaction to American reserve in Bratislava, Prague, and even Warsaw? To appease the Russians at the expense of NATO solidarity.

The Ukrainian crisis is therefore but a manifestation of something more deeply gone wrong in the West. This past September witnessed an astounding spectacle. Great Britain, formerly mistress of the greatest empire since Rome, the home of the mother of parliaments, and the source of notions of liberty and self-government that shaped this country and many others—was on the verge of dissolution. It was a would-be dissolution brought about by a feckless political class that allowed 16-year-olds, intoxicated by overheated commemorations of the 700th anniversary of a medieval battle, to vote to break up a Union older than the United States.

And when they suddenly realized that they could actually lose their country, what kind of arguments could British politicians come up with? There was precious little about shared values, an inspiring past, or a common destiny. It was all about whether Scottish banks would need very large sterling balances to maintain the pound, and co-payments for the National Health Service, and how North Sea oil would be divided. It is testimony to the good sense of the people of Scotland—or rather, to their innate caution—that they voted the independence resolution down. But Britain came close to voting itself out of existence in a moment of silliness and selfishness, even as clueless intellectuals and journalists chirped cheerfully about what a model of the democratic process this wanton recklessness was.

This combination of foolishness and fecklessness comes at a time, we all know, of economic lethargy in the West, of the increasingly severe crisis of the euro, whose success depended ultimately on a degree of political unification that the peoples of Europe would not accept, no matter what their betters believed. It comes at a time when for other reasons, too, the larger European project, shaped by elites whose attitude to their own populations was often contemptuous, has come up very short. Those elites are now being rewarded by the rise of parties well outside the social-democratic consensus, at times frighteningly so.

It also comes at a time when other threats hover on the horizon of the Transatlantic world, of which the most notable is the rise of armed radical Islamist movements. These are movements that delight in murder and destruction, and whose antipathy to the West is of the most profound type even if, for the time being, it is all they can do to battle their local antagonists as the para-states of the region dissolve into dust. The European response to all this, too, has been inadequate both materially and intellectually. European leaders are willing to see the United States kill a terrorist here and fire a missile from a drone there, but all the while they tut-tut about Guantánamo and Islamophobia and collateral damage and mutter, usually but not always below audible range, how anyway it's all the fault of the Israelis (read: Jews).

George Orwell captured the essence of our own situation in an essay published in April 1940:

> It is as though in the space of ten years we had slid back into the Stone Age. Human types supposedly extinct for centuries, the dancing dervish, the robber chieftain, the Grand Inquisitor, have suddenly reappeared, not as inmates of lunatic asylums, but as the masters of the world.

But by then we at least knew the kind of thing, and the kind of people, we were dealing with. We have yet to face those realities square on this time around.

The crisis of the West is both external and internal. It is molded partly by geopolitics—by the return of a Russia rich in resources and resentful at how the Cold War ended, and a Russia led by particular leaders whose skills we should respect and understand rather than dismiss as being "so 19th century", as one National Security Council staffer, callow even by the standards of this

Administration, put it. It has been facilitated, alas, by the tactical foolishness of U.S. leaders in several ways. But it is more profoundly a result of the hollowing out of certain Western ideas and values.

The ur-mistake of contemporary politics is its reduction of public life to a combination of manipulation in order to achieve office—tweeting, Facebooking, and generally acting like a teenager in order to curry favor with them; and mere administration when one gets there. In all Western countries the result is a political elite for which our publics—one used to say our citizenry, but that implies more engagement and above all responsibility than is typical these days—express a well-deserved contempt. In such a vacuum of purpose and leadership, other, darker forces can find purchase. Again, George Orwell, in his 1940 review of *Mein Kampf*, put his finger on the problem:

> Nearly all western thought since the last war, certainly all 'progressive' thought, has assumed tacitly that human beings desire nothing beyond ease, security and avoidance of pain. . . . Hitler, because in his own joyless mind he feels it with exceptional strength, knows that human beings don't only want comfort, safety, short working-hours, hygiene, birth-control and, in general, common sense; they also, at least intermittently, want struggle and self-sacrifice, not to mention drums, flags and loyalty parades. . . . Whereas Socialism, and even capitalism in a more grudging way, have said to people 'I offer you a good time', Hitler has said to them 'I offer you struggle, danger and death', and as a result a whole nation flings itself at his feet. Perhaps later on they will get sick of it and change their minds, as at the end of the last war. 'Greatest happiness of the greatest number' is a good slogan, but at this moment, 'Better an end with horror than a horror without end' is a winner. Now that we are fighting against the man who coined it, we ought not to underrate its emotional appeal.

We are not up against Hitler, to be sure, though we do face belief systems, at least in the Middle East, that are quite capable of dealing out death on the same scale if they ever get the weapons with which to do it. But we are up against the reality that a life of comfort and convenience, and a politics built exclusively around securing them, cannot withstand the forces from without that will prey on it, or the slow decay of values from within that depletes our will to resist. As others have pointed out, there seems to be something about liberalism that in time causes it to generate its own nemeses, or at least sap its own defenses against them.[1]

The new crisis of the West thus has many dimensions, including some—the steady aging of our populations, for example—about which little can be done. In the proximate case of Ukraine, for example, we could restore adequate levels of defense expenditure, commit forces to the frontline states of NATO, and aid the rump of Ukraine that might otherwise be abandoned to indirect if not direct Russian control. But behind any concrete policy actions there has to be something larger, something deeper, a kind of recovery of spirit. That will be hard, because no leaders seem to be available to offer the inspiration that a de Gaulle or a Churchill did in World War II, or that a Kennedy or a Thatcher did during the spikes of Cold War danger.

Nor am I speaking of political leaders only, or even chiefly. There is no Václav Havel to say "live in truth." There is no John Paul II to say over and over again, "Be not afraid." There are precious few intellectuals like Raymond Aron or Isaiah Berlin or Reinhold Neibuhr to explore what freedom means, and speak about how to use it wisely. There are few fierce and fearless journalists like Oriana Fallaci to scream uncomfortable truths at timid politicians.

But we can try, beginning perhaps with Havel's inspiration, by clinging to the truth. We can call things by their names—using words like *invasion* and *fanaticism*, for example, and not pretending that they are something tamer and less dangerous.

We can dismiss gestures like standing up yet another useless European rapid response unit or headquarters from the same pieces that are already on the military chessboard. We can recognize and name such pointless sops to our guilty consciences for what they are. We can admit openly, too, that the comfortable assumptions of several generations in the West, about the essential security of our states and institutions, may rest on as shaky premises as did those that were widely held in 1913.

We can also refrain from treating terms like "deterrence" or "Article 5 obligations" as a kind of strategic pixie dust to be sprinkled over problems in the hope of making them go away as if by magic. We can acknowledge that what deterrence and Article 5 are really about is a commitment to wage war under well understood circumstances. We can face the bracing fact that we need what John Paul II gave so many people: the courage to stand for freedom and principle in the face of danger and even death.

As a teenager, I had a summer job as a tour guide in the state house in Boston. It was then that I learned the meaning of the motto of my home state, the Commonwealth of Massachusetts: *Ense petit placidam, sub libertate quietem.* It means, "[This hand, hostile to tyrants] seeks with a sword a quiet peace, under liberty."

To the north of Massachusetts lies New Hampshire, whose motto is simpler: "Live free or die." The phrase, which may be found on license plates and makes many visitors and suburbanites fleeing high housing prices in Boston squirm, comes from a letter by a hero of New Hampshire, General John Stark. Stark fought in both the Seven Years' War and in the Revolution and, like Cincinnatus, returned to his farm when his duty was done. At age 81, too ill to travel to a reunion of his old comrades, he sent this greeting to them: "Live free or die: Death is not the worst of evils."

It's all very old-fashioned stuff. It is not at all sophisticated. And to most erudite people it is downright embarrassing to hear a professor cite it approvingly. But it is true, and free governments, and free peoples, had better believe these things. They have to believe that freedom is not about ample pensions and free college tuitions and a 35-hour work week, that it is about something vastly deeper and more important than that. One sometimes wonders if belief in big, deeper things itself has gone out of fashion in the postmodern West, as if the larger ideals of the past have somehow become an embarrassment. If so, we would probably ignore Churchill himself were he to return to us from beyond the grave and warn, as he warned his colleagues in the jubilant House of Commons following the Munich accords, that all would not be well; he quoted the Book of Daniel: "Thou art weighed in the balance and are found wanting."

What is happening now in Ukraine is not a new Munich. But thus far, we have indeed been weighed in the balance and found wanting. And what will get us out of the Ukraine crisis, with any luck at all, is the same thing Churchill invoked some seventy years ago: "Moral health and martial vigor", and a willingness to take a stand for "freedom, as in the olden time." Let us not merely hope so, but act now to make it happen.

NOTE

1 See Abram N. Shulsky, "Liberalism's Beleaguered Victory", *The American Interest* (September/October 2014).

Reading 9.5

How Could Vietnam Happen? An Autopsy
JAMES C. THOMSON, JR.

As a case study in the making of foreign policy, the Vietnam War will fascinate historians and social scientists for many decades to come. One question that will certainly be asked: How did men of superior ability, sound training, and high ideals—American policy-makers of the 1960s—create such costly and divisive policy?

As one who watched the decision-making process in Washington from 1961 to 1966 under Presidents Kennedy and Johnson, I can suggest a preliminary answer. I can do so by briefly listing some of the factors that seemed to me to shape our Vietnam policy during my years as an East Asia specialist at the State Department and the White House. I shall deal largely with Washington as I saw or sensed it, and not with Saigon, where I have spent but a scant three days, in the entourage of the Vice President, or with other decision centers, the capitals of interested parties. Nor will I deal with other important parts of the record: Vietnam's history prior to 1961, for instance, or the overall course of America's relations with Vietnam.

Yet a first and central ingredient in these years of Vietnam decisions does involve history. The ingredient was *the legacy of the 1950s*—by which I mean the so-called "loss of China," the Korean War, and the Far East policy of Secretary of State Dulles.

Source: James C. Thomson, Jr., "How Could Vietnam Happen? An Autopsy," Atlantic Monthly (April 1968).

This legacy had an institutional by-product for the Kennedy Administration: in 1961 the U.S. government's East Asian establishment was undoubtedly the most rigid and doctrinaire of Washington's regional divisions in foreign affairs. This was especially true at the Department of State, where the incoming Administration found the Bureau of Far Eastern Affairs the hardest nut to crack. It was a bureau that had been purged of its best China expertise, and of farsighted, dispassionate men, as a result of McCarthyism. Its members were generally committed to one policy line: the close containment and isolation of mainland China, the harassment of "neutralist" nations which sought to avoid alignment with either Washington or Peking, and the maintenance of a network of alliances with anti-Communist client states on China's periphery.

Another aspect of the legacy was the special vulnerability and sensitivity of the new Democratic Administration on Far East policy issues. The memory of the McCarthy era was still very sharp, and Kennedy's margin of victory was too thin. The 1960 Offshore Islands TV debate between Kennedy and Nixon had shown the President-elect the perils of "fresh thinking." The Administration was inherently leery of moving too fast on Asia. As a result, the Far East Bureau (now the Bureau of East Asian and Pacific Affairs) was the last one to be overhauled. Not until Averell Harriman was brought in as Assistant Secretary in December, 1961, were significant personnel changes attempted, and it took Harriman several months to make a deep imprint on the bureau because of his necessary preoccupation with the Laos settlement. Once he did so, there was virtually no effort to bring back the purged or exiled East Asia experts.

There were other important by-products of this "legacy of the fifties":

The new Administration inherited and somewhat shared *a general perception of China-on-the-march*—a sense of China's vastness, its numbers, its belligerence; a revived sense, perhaps, of the Golden Horde. This was a perception fed by Chinese intervention in the Korean War (an intervention actually based on appallingly bad communications and mutual miscalculation on the part of Washington and Peking; but the careful unraveling of that tragedy, which scholars have accomplished, had not yet become part of the conventional wisdom).

The new Administration inherited and briefly accepted *a monolithic conception of the Communist bloc*. Despite much earlier predictions and reports by outside analysts, policy-makers did not begin to accept the reality and possible finality of the Sino-Soviet split until the first weeks of 1962. The inevitably corrosive impact of competing nationalisms on Communism was largely ignored.

The new Administration inherited and to some extent shared *the "domino theory" about Asia*. This theory resulted from profound ignorance of Asian history and hence ignorance of the radical differences among Asian nations and societies. It resulted from a blindness to the power and resilience of Asian nationalisms. (It may also have resulted from a subconscious sense that, since "all Asians look alike," all Asian nations will act alike.) As a theory, the domino fallacy was not merely inaccurate but also insulting to Asian nations; yet it has continued to this day to beguile men who should know better.

Finally, the legacy of the fifties was apparently compounded by an uneasy sense of a worldwide Communist challenge to the new Administration after the Bay of Pigs fiasco. A first manifestation was the President's traumatic Vienna meeting with Khrushchev in June, 1961; then came the Berlin crisis of the summer. All this created an atmosphere in which President Kennedy undoubtedly felt under special pressure to show his nation's mettle in Vietnam—if the Vietnamese, unlike the people of Laos, were willing to fight.

In general, the legacy of the fifties shaped such early moves of the new Administration as the decisions to maintain a high-visibility SEATO (by sending the Secretary of State himself instead of some underling to its first meeting in 1961), to back away from diplomatic recognition of Mongolia in the summer of 1961, and most important, to expand U.S. military assistance to South Vietnam that winter on the basis of the much more tentative Eisenhower commitment. It should be added that the increased commitment to Vietnam was also fueled by a new breed of military strategists and academic social scientists (some of whom had entered the new Administration) who had developed theories of counter-guerrilla warfare and were eager to see them put to the test. To some, "counterinsurgency" seemed a new panacea for coping with the world's instability.

So much for the legacy and the history. Any new Administration inherits both complicated problems and simplistic views of the world. But surely among the policy-makers of the Kennedy and Johnson Administrations there were men who would warn of the dangers of an open-ended commitment to the Vietnam quagmire?

This raises a central question, at the heart of the policy process: Where were the experts, the doubters, and the dissenters? Were they there at all, and if so, what happened to them?

The answer is complex but instructive.

In the first place, the American government was sorely *lacking in real Vietnam or Indochina expertise.* Originally treated as an adjunct of Embassy Paris, our Saigon embassy and the Vietnam Desk at State were largely staffed from 1954 onward by French-speaking Foreign Service personnel of narrowly European experience. Such diplomats were even more closely restricted than the normal embassy officer—by cast of mind as well as language—to contacts with Vietnam's French-speaking urban elites. For instance, Foreign Service linguists in Portugal are able to speak with the peasantry if they get out of Lisbon and choose to do so; not so the French speakers of Embassy Saigon.

In addition, the *shadow of the "loss of China"* distorted Vietnam reporting. Career officers in the Department, and especially those in the field, had not forgotten the fate of their World War II colleagues who wrote in frankness from China and were later pilloried by Senate committees for critical comments on the Chinese Nationalists. Candid reporting on the strengths of the Viet Cong and the weaknesses of the Diem government was inhibited by the memory. It was also inhibited by some higher officials, notably Ambassador Nolting in Saigon, who refused to sign off on such cables.

In due course, to be sure, some Vietnam talent was discovered or developed. But a recurrent and increasingly important factor in the decisionmaking process was *the banishment of real expertise.* Here the underlying cause was the "closed politics" of policy-making as issues become hot: the more sensitive the issue, and the higher it rises in the bureaucracy, the more completely the experts are excluded while the harassed senior generalists take over (that is, the Secretaries, Undersecretaries, and Presidential Assistants). The frantic skimming of briefing papers in the back seats of limousines is no substitute for the presence of specialists; furthermore, in times of crisis such papers are deemed "too sensitive" even for review by the specialists. Another underlying cause of this banishment, as Vietnam became more critical, was the replacement of the experts, who were generally and increasingly pessimistic, by men described as "can-do guys," loyal and energetic fixers unsoured by expertise. In early 1965, when I confided my growing policy doubts to an older colleague on the NSC staff, he assured me that the smartest thing both of us could do was to "steer clear of the whole Vietnam mess"; the gentleman in question had the misfortune to be a "can-do guy," however, and is now highly placed in Vietnam, under orders to solve the mess.

Despite the banishment of the experts, internal doubters and dissenters did indeed appear and persist. Yet as I watched the process, such men were effectively neutralized by a subtle dynamic: *the domestication of dissenters.* Such "domestication" arose out of a twofold clubbish need: on the one hand, the dissenter's desire to stay aboard; and on the other hand, the nondissenter's conscience. Simply stated, dissent, when recognized, was made to feel at home. On the lowest possible scale of importance, I must confess my own considerable sense of dignity and acceptance (both vital) when my senior White House employer would refer to me as his "favorite dove." Far more significant was the case of the former Undersecretary of State, George Ball. Once Mr. Ball began to express doubts, he was warmly institutionalized: he was encouraged to become the inhouse devil's advocate on Vietnam. The upshot was inevitable: the process of escalation allowed for periodic requests to Mr. Ball to speak his piece; Ball felt good, I assume (he had fought for righteousness); the others felt good (they had given a full hearing to the dovish option); and there was minimal unpleasantness. The club remained intact; and it is of course possible that matters would have gotten worse faster if Mr. Ball had kept silent, or left before his final departure in the fall of 1966. There was also, of course, the case of the last institutionalized doubter, Bill Moyers. The President is said to have greeted his arrival at meetings with an affectionate, "Well, here comes Mr. Stop-the-Bombing. . . ." Here again the dynamics of domesticated dissent sustained the relationship for a while.

A related point—and crucial, I suppose, to government at all times—was *the "effectiveness" trap*, the trap that keeps men from speaking out, as clearly or often as they might, within the government. And it is the trap that keeps men from resigning in protest and airing their dissent outside the government. The most important asset that a man brings to bureaucratic life is his "effectiveness," a mysterious combination of training, style, and connections. The most ominous complaint that can be whispered of a bureaucrat is: "I'm afraid Charlie's beginning to lose his effectiveness." To preserve your effectiveness,

you must decide where and when to fight the mainstream of policy; the opportunities range from pillow talk with your wife, to private drinks with your
friends, to meetings with the Secretary of State or the President. The inclination to remain silent or to acquiesce in the presence of the great men—to live
to fight another day, to give on this issue so that you can be "effective" on later
issues—is overwhelming. Nor is it the tendency of youth alone; some of our
most senior officials, men of wealth and fame, whose place in history is secure,
have remained silent lest their connection with power be terminated. As for
the disinclination to resign in protest: while not necessarily a Washington or
even American specialty, it seems more true of a government in which ministers
have no parliamentary backbench to which to retreat. In the absence of such
a refuge, it is easy to rationalize the decision to stay aboard. By doing so, one
may be able to prevent a few bad things from happening and perhaps even
make a few good things happen. To exit is to lose even those marginal chances
for "effectiveness."

Another factor must be noted: as the Vietnam controversy escalated at
home, there developed *a preoccupation with Vietnam public relations as
opposed to Vietnam policy-making*. And here, ironically, internal doubters
and dissenters were heavily employed. For such men, by virtue of their own
doubts, were often deemed best able to "massage" the doubting intelligentsia.
My senior East Asia colleague at the White House, a brilliant and humane
doubter who had dealt with Indochina since 1954, spent three quarters of his
working days on Vietnam public relations: drafting presidential responses to
letters from important critics, writing conciliatory language for presidential
speeches, and meeting quite interminably with delegations of outraged Quakers, clergymen, academics, and housewives. His regular callers were the late
A. J. Muste and Norman Thomas; mine were members of the Women's Strike
for Peace. Our orders from above: keep them off the backs of busy policy-
makers (who usually happened to be nondoubters). Incidentally, my most discouraging assignment in the realm of public relations was the preparation of a
White House pamphlet entitled *Why Vietnam*, in September, 1965; in a gesture
toward my conscience, I fought—and lost—a battle to have the title followed
by a question mark.

Through a variety of procedures, both institutional and personal, doubt,
dissent, and expertise were effectively neutralized in the making of policy. But
what can be said of the men "in charge"? It is patently absurd to suggest
that they produced such tragedy by intention and calculation. But it is neither
absurd nor difficult to discern certain forces at work that caused decent and
honorable men to do great harm.

Here I would stress the paramount role of *executive fatigue*. No factor
seems to me more crucial and underrated in the making of foreign policy. The
physical and emotional toll of executive responsibility in State, the Pentagon,
the White House, and other executive agencies is enormous; that toll is of
course compounded by extended service. Many of today's Vietnam policy-
makers have been on the job for from four to seven years. Complaints may be
few, and physical health may remain unimpaired, though emotional health is

far harder to gauge. But what is most seriously eroded in the deadening process of fatigue is freshness of thought, imagination, a sense of possibility, a sense of priorities and perspective—those rare assets of a new Administration in its first year or two of office. The tired policy-maker becomes a prisoner of his own narrowed view of the world and his own clichéd rhetoric. He becomes irritable and defensive—short on sleep, short on family ties, short on patience. Such men make bad policy and then compound it. They have neither the time nor the temperament for new ideas or preventive diplomacy.

Below the level of the fatigued executives in the making of Vietnam policy was a widespread phenomenon: *the curator mentality* in the Department of State. By this I mean the collective inertia produced by the bureaucrat's view of his job. At State, the average "desk officer" inherits from his predecessor our policy toward Country X; he regards it as his function to keep that policy intact—under glass, untampered with, and dusted—so that he may pass it on in two to four years to his successor. And such curatorial service generally merits promotion within the system. (Maintain the status quo, and you will stay out of trouble.) In some circumstances, the inertia bred by such an outlook can act as a brake against rash innovation. But on many issues, this inertia sustains the momentum of bad policy and unwise commitments—momentum that might otherwise have been resisted within the ranks. Clearly, Vietnam is such an issue.

To fatigue and inertia must be added the factor of internal confusion. Even among the "architects" of our Vietnam commitment, there has been persistent *confusion as to what type of war we were fighting* and, as a direct consequence, *confusion as to how to end that war.* (The "credibility gap" is, in part, a reflection of such internal confusion.) Was it, for instance, a civil war, in which case counterinsurgency might suffice? Or was it a war of international aggression? (This might invoke SEATO or UN commitment.) Who was the aggressor—and the "real enemy"? The Viet Cong? Hanoi? Peking? Moscow? International Communism? Or maybe "Asian Communism"? Differing enemies dictated differing strategies and tactics. And confused throughout, in like fashion, was the question of American objectives; your objectives depended on whom you were fighting and why. I shall not forget my assignment from an Assistant Secretary of State in March, 1964: to draft a speech for Secretary McNamara which would, *inter alia*, once and for all dispose of the canard that the Vietnam conflict was a civil war. "But in some ways, of course," I mused, "it *is* a civil war." "Don't play word games with me!" snapped the Assistant Secretary.

Similar confusion beset the concept of "negotiations"—anathema to much of official Washington from 1961 to 1965. Not until April, 1965, did "unconditional discussions" become respectable, via a presidential speech; even then the Secretary of State stressed privately to newsmen that nothing had changed, since "discussions" were by no means the same as "negotiations." Months later that issue was resolved. But it took even longer to obtain a fragile internal agreement that negotiations might include the Viet Cong as something other than an appendage to Hanoi's delegation. Given such confusion as to the whos and whys of our Vietnam commitment, it is not surprising, as Theodore Draper has written, that policy-makers find it so difficult to agree on how to end the war.

Of course, one force—a constant in the vortex of commitment—was that of *wishful thinking*. I partook of it myself at many times. I did so especially during Washington's struggle with Diem in the autumn of 1963 when some of us at State believed that for once, in dealing with a difficult client state, the U.S. government could use the leverage of our economic and military assistance to make good things happen, instead of being led around by the nose by men like Chiang Kai-shek and Syngman Rhee (and, in that particular instance, by Diem). If we could prove that point, I thought, and move into a new day, with or without Diem, then Vietnam was well worth the effort. Later came the wishful thinking of the air- strike planners in the late autumn of 1964; there were those who actually thought that after six weeks of air strikes, the North Vietnamese would come crawling to us to ask for peace talks. And what, someone asked in one of the meetings of the time, if they don't? The answer was that we would bomb for another four weeks, and that would do the trick. And a few weeks later came one instance of wishful thinking that was symptomatic of good men misled: in January, 1965, I encountered one of the very highest figures in the Administration at a dinner, drew him aside, and told him of my worries about the air-strike option. He told me that I really shouldn't worry; it was his conviction that before any such plans could be put into effect, a neutralist government would come to power in Saigon that would politely invite us out. And finally, there was the recurrent wishful thinking that sustained many of us through the trying months of 1965–1966 after the air strikes had begun: that surely, somehow, one way or another, we would "be in a conference in six months," and the escalatory spiral would be suspended. The basis of our hope: "It simply can't go on."

As a further influence on policy-makers I would cite the factor of *bureaucratic detachment*. By this I mean what at best might be termed the professional callousness of the surgeon (and indeed, medical lingo—the "surgical strike" for instance—seemed to crop up in the euphemisms of the times). In Washington the semantics of the military muted the reality of war for the civilian policy-makers. In quiet, air-conditioned, thick-carpeted rooms, such terms as "systematic pressure," "armed reconnaissance," "targets of opportunity," and even "body count" seemed to breed a sort of games-theory detachment. Most memorable to me was a moment in the late 1964 target planning when the question under discussion was how heavy our bombing should be, and how extensive our strafing, at some midpoint in the projected pattern of systematic pressure. An Assistant Secretary of State resolved the point in the following words: "It seems to me that our orchestration should be mainly violins, but with periodic touches of brass." Perhaps the biggest shock of my return to Cambridge, Massachusetts, was the realization that the young men, the flesh and blood I taught and saw on these university streets, were potentially some of the numbers on the charts of those faraway planners. In a curious sense, Cambridge is closer to this war than Washington.

There is an unprovable factor that relates to bureaucratic detachment: the ingredient of *cryptoracism*. I do not mean I do not mean to imply any conscious contempt for Asian loss of life on the part of Washington officials. But I do mean to imply that bureaucratic detachment may well be compounded by a traditional Western sense that there are so many Asians, after all; that Asians have a fatalism about life and a disregard for its loss; that they are cruel and barbaric to their own people; and that they are very different from us (and all look alike?). And *I do* mean to imply that the upshot of such subliminal views is a subliminal question whether Asians, and particularly Asian peasants, and most particularly Asian Communists, are really people—like you and me. To put the matter another way: would we have pursued quite such policies—and quite such military tactics—if the Vietnamese were white?

It is impossible to write of Vietnam decision-making without writing about language. Throughout the conflict, words have been of paramount importance. I refer here to the impact of *rhetorical escalation* and to the *problem of oversell*. In an important sense, Vietnam has become of crucial significance to us *because we have said that it is of crucial significance*. (The issue obviously relates to the public relations preoccupation described earlier.)

The key here is domestic politics: the need to sell the American people, press, and Congress on support for an unpopular and costly war in which the objectives themselves have been in flux. To sell means to persuade, and to persuade means rhetoric. As the difficulties and costs have mounted, so has the definition of the stakes. This is not to say that rhetorical escalation is an orderly process; executive prose is the product of many writers, and some concepts—North Vietnamese infiltration, America's "national honor," Red China as the chief enemy—have entered the rhetoric only gradually and even sporadically. But there is an upward spiral nonetheless. And once you have *said* that the American Experiment itself stands or falls on the Vietnam outcome, you have thereby created a national stake far beyond any earlier stakes.

Crucial throughout the process of Vietnam decision-making was a conviction among many policy-makers: that Vietnam posed a *fundamental test of America's national will*. Time and again I was told by men reared in the tradition of Henry L. Stimson that all we needed was the will, and we would then prevail. Implicit in such a view, it seemed to me, was a curious assumption that Asians lacked will, or at least that in a contest between Asian and Anglo-Saxon wills, the non-Asians must prevail. A corollary to the persistent belief in will was a *fascination with power* and an awe in the face of the power America possessed as no nation or civilization ever before. Those who doubted our role in Vietnam were said to shrink from the burdens of power, the obligations of power, the uses of power, the responsibility of power. By implication, such men were soft-headed and effete.

Finally, no discussion of the factors and forces at work on Vietnam policy-makers can ignore the central fact of *human ego investment*. Men who have participated in a decision develop a stake in that decision. As they participate in further, related decisions, their stake increases. It might have been possible to dissuade a man of strong self-confidence at an early stage of the ladder of decision; but it is infinitely harder at later stages since a change of mind there usually involves implicit or explicit repudiation of a chain of previous decisions.

To put it bluntly: at the heart of the Vietnam calamity is a group of able, dedicated men who have been regularly and repeatedly wrong—and whose standing with their contemporaries, and more important, with history, depends, as they see it, on being proven right. These are not men who can be asked to extricate themselves from error.

The various ingredients I have cited in the making of Vietnam policy have created a variety of results, most of them fairly obvious. Here are some that seem to me most central:

Throughout the conflict, there has been *persistent and repeated miscalculation* by virtually all the actors, in high echelons and low, whether dove, hawk, or something else. To cite one simple example among many: in late 1964 and early 1965, some peace-seeking planners at State who strongly opposed the projected bombing of the North urged that, instead, American ground forces be sent to South Vietnam; this would, they said, increase our bargaining leverage against the North—our "chips"—and would give us something to negotiate about (the withdrawal of our forces) at an early peace conference. Simultaneously, the air-strike option was urged by many in the military who were dead set against American participation in "another land war in Asia"; they were joined by other civilian peace-seekers who wanted to bomb Hanoi into early negotiations. By late 1965, we had ended up with the worst of all worlds: ineffective and costly air strikes against the North, spiraling ground forces in the South, and no negotiations in sight. Throughout the conflict as well, there has been *a steady give-in to pressures for a military solution* and only minimal and sporadic efforts at a diplomatic and political solution. In part this resulted from the confusion (earlier cited) among the civilians—confusion regarding objectives and strategy. And in part this resulted from the self-enlarging nature of military investment. Once air strikes and particularly ground forces were introduced, our investment itself had transformed the original stakes. More air power was needed to protect the ground forces; and then more ground forces to protect the ground forces. And needless to say, the military mind develops its own momentum in the absence of clear guidelines from the civilians. Once asked to save South Vietnam, rather than to "advise" it, the American military could not but press for escalation. In addition, sad to report, assorted military constituencies, once involved in Vietnam, have had a series of cases to prove: for instance, the utility not only of air power (the Air Force) but of supercarrier-based air power (the Navy). Also, Vietnam policy has suffered from one ironic byproduct of Secretary McNamara's establishment of civilian control at the Pentagon: in the face of such control, interservice rivalry has given way to a united front among the military—reflected in the new but recurrent phenomenon of JCS unanimity. In conjunction with traditional congressional allies (mostly Southern senators and representatives) such a united front would pose a formidable problem for any President.

Throughout the conflict, there have been *missed opportunities, large and small, to disengage ourselves from Vietnam on increasingly unpleasant but still acceptable terms.* Of the many moments from 1961 onward, I shall cite only one, the last and most important opportunity that was lost: in the summer of

1964 the President instructed his chief advisers to prepare for him as wide a range of Vietnam options as possible for postelection consideration and decision. He explicitly asked that all options be laid out. What happened next was, in effect, Lyndon Johnson's slow-motion Bay of Pigs. For the advisers so effectively converged on one single option—juxtaposed against two other, phony options (in effect, blowing up the world, or scuttle-and-run)—that the President was confronted with unanimity for bombing the North from all his trusted counselors. Had he been more confident in foreign affairs, had he been deeply informed on Vietnam and Southeast Asia, and had he raised some hard questions that unanimity had submerged, this President could have used the largest electoral mandate in history to de-escalate in Vietnam, in the clear expectation that at the worst a neutralist government would come to power in Saigon and politely invite us out. Today, many lives and dollars later, such an alternative has become an elusive and infinitely more expensive possibility.

In the course of these years, another result of Vietnam decision-making has been *the abuse and distortion of history.* Vietnamese, Southeast Asian, and Far Eastern history has been rewritten by our policy-makers, and their spokesmen, to conform with the alleged necessity of our presence in Vietnam. Highly dubious analogies from our experience elsewhere—the "Munich" sell-out and "containment" from Europe, the Malayan insurgency and the Korean War from Asia—have been imported in order to justify our actions. And more recent events have been fitted to the Procrustean bed of Vietnam. Most notably, the change of power in Indonesia in 1965–1966 has been ascribed to our Vietnam presence; and virtually all progress in the Pacific region—the rise of regionalism, new forms of cooperation, and mounting growth rates—has been similarly explained. The Indonesian allegation is undoubtedly false (I tried to prove it, during six months of careful investigation at the White House, and had to confess failure); the regional allegation is patently unprovable in either direction (except, of course, for the clear fact that the economies of both Japan and Korea have profited enormously from our Vietnam-related procurement in these countries; but that is a costly and highly dubious form of foreign aid).

There is a final result of Vietnam policy I would cite that holds potential danger for the future of American foreign policy: *the rise of a new breed of American ideologues who see Vietnam as the ultimate test of their doctrine.* I have in mind those men in Washington who have given a new life to the missionary impulse in American foreign relations: who believe that this nation, in this era, has received a threefold endowment that can transform the world. As they see it, that endowment is composed of, first, our unsurpassed military might; second, our clear technological supremacy; and third, our allegedly invincible benevolence (our "altruism," our affluence, our lack of territorial aspirations). Together, it is argued, this threefold endowment provides us with the opportunity and the obligation to ease the nations of the earth toward modernization and stability: toward a fullfledged *Pax Americana Technocratica.* In reaching toward this goal, Vietnam is viewed as the last and crucial test. Once we have succeeded there, the road ahead is clear. In a sense, these men are our counterpart to the visionaries of Communism's radical left: they are technocracy's own Maoists. They do not govern Washington today. But their doctrine rides high.

Long before I went into government, I was told a story about Henry L. Stimson that seemed to me pertinent during the years that I watched the Vietnam tragedy unfold—and participated in that tragedy. It seems to me more pertinent than ever as we move toward the election of 1968.

In his waning years Stimson was asked by an anxious questioner, "Mr. Secretary, how on earth can we ever bring peace to the world?" Stimson is said to have answered: "You begin by bringing to Washington a small handful of able men who believe that the achievement of peace is possible.

"You work them to the bone until they no longer believe that it is possible.

"And then you throw them out—and bring in a new bunch who believe that it is possible."

Reading 9.6

Afghanistan's Legacy: Emerging Lessons
STEPHEN BIDDLE

The war in Afghanistan is not over. Nor is it ending any time soon. The U.S. role may end in 2016, in whole or in part, but the war will continue—and its ultimate outcome is very much in doubt. The conflict is now stalemated militarily, and will likely stay that way as long as outsiders pay the large bills needed to keep the Afghan National Security Forces (ANSF) in the field and fighting. The war will thus grind onward until this funding dries up or the two sides negotiate a compromise settlement, neither of which is imminent. Depending on how any talks unfold, historians in 2050 could thus look back on this war as a costly but tolerable outcome for the West, as a wasteful disaster, or as something in between; for now, all we know for sure is that it continues.

Yet, for many Americans the war is already receding in the rearview mirror. President Obama, for example, often suggests that by as early as 2014 "this long war will come to a responsible end."[1] It will not, in fact, but Americans could be excused for thinking otherwise, given such framing. Nor is the President alone in this thinking, though many of his compatriots are taking a notably less optimistic tone in their retrospectives.

Among the most important of these pre-postmortems is an emerging debate on the war's lessons. Perhaps the most common position is that

Source: Stephen Biddle, "Afghanistan's Legacy: Emerging Lessons," Washington Quarterly, vol. 37, no. 2 (Summer 1914). Copyright © The Elliott School of International Affairs, reprinted by Taylor and Francis Ltd on behalf of The Elliott School of International Affairs.

Afghanistan shows the futility of counterinsurgency (COIN). By contrast with the President's view, many now believe the war can already be deemed a failure in spite of massive investment. For critics such as Gian Gentile or Andrew Bacevich, this failure in Afghanistan shows how counterinsurgency's demands cannot be met, and how the United States should therefore avoid such wars at all costs in the future.[2] For many in this camp, Iraq, too, was a failure; others see Iraq as an eleventh-hour turnaround brought about by good luck in the idiosyncratic Sunni realignment of the Anbar Awakening.[3] Even the latter group, however, usually sees Afghanistan as evidence that COIN cannot succeed without the happy accident of the enemy changing sides. Within the military, debate on the future of COIN revolves as much around *how* the United States should wage counterinsurgency in the future as around *whether* it should. Formal studies of the lessons of the Afghan and Iraq wars are still very thin on the ground, perhaps unsurprisingly—with the Afghan war still ongoing, there is yet no equivalent to the post–World War II Strategic Bombing Survey or the post-1991 Gulf War Airpower Survey. But an emerging informal argument heard among many veterans of Afghanistan and Iraq holds that prevailing U.S. COIN doctrine now undervalues military security and combat relative to "softer" governance reform and economic development. Many view the doctrinal manual co-authored by then-Lieutenant Generals David Petraeus and James Amos in 2006 (FM 3–24, *Counterinsurgency*),[4] as advocating an approach centered on winning civilians' hearts and minds via superior public services. Yet, the actual conduct of both the Iraq and Afghanistan wars has proven far more violent than many readers of this manual have expected; even officers who see Iraq or Afghanistan as successes now often attribute this largely to the "kinetic" security campaign and the hard fighting it produced in both theaters. For them, the wars show that FM 3–24's "hearts and minds" provisions are overemphasized, and a central lesson is thus that future COIN doctrine should subordinate governance to security, and reemphasize the combat function.[5]

In an important sense, these debates are premature: because the Afghan war continues with results as yet unknown, there is no observable final outcome to explain, or from which to draw lessons. But the debates matter all the same. Wartime experience always shapes post-war policy, and the impressions formed first are often the most persistent and influential. For Afghanistan, ideas and interpretations are already taking shape and could easily become established well before the war is actually over. Hence, it makes sense to give them an early look, and to evaluate how well or badly they correspond with what can actually be observed in the war's conduct to date—premature as any such findings must necessarily be.

What we know so far suggests a more nuanced view than what one often finds in the emerging debate. There are important elements of truth in both of these early accounts (i.e. the "never again" school and the combat-emphasis camp within the military). But the first is overstated, and the second overlooks important flaws in the way governance reform has been undertaken in Afghanistan (and also Iraq, though my focus here is on the former).

COIN is obviously hard and slow. But the Afghan experience shows that current U.S. methods *can* return threatened districts to government control, when conducted with the necessary time and resources. This certainly does require combat and hard fighting. Counterinsurgency is not social work, and its purpose is not to make local civilians like Americans. But combat and security alone will have difficulty *sustaining* control if all they do is allow a predatory government to exploit the population for the benefit of unrepresentative elites. Yet, the governance reform approach in FM 3–24 misunderstands the issue and tends to make the problem worse rather than better, as I will explain later.

HARD? YES. IMPOSSIBLE? NO

For most of the post–Vietnam era, the conventional wisdom among Americans held that COIN was a hopeless project, especially for democracies like the United States. Defeat in Vietnam preconditioned many Americans to see insurgencies as intractable quagmires that would inevitably overwhelm any occupier's patience. Soviet defeat in Afghanistan just reinforced this view. Even the Bush administration shared it: its refusal to acknowledge a mounting insurgency in Iraq in 2003–04 and its reluctance to commit to a large-scale presence in Afghanistan in 2001 both stemmed in part from this widespread view that insurgencies could not be defeated, hence avoiding them was the only sensible approach.[6]

The Iraq surge led to a brief reversal of this orthodoxy. After reaching murderous heights in early 2007, violence in Iraq then plunged by a factor of about ten in a period of just a few months.[7] This nose-dive in violence followed the deployment of about 30,000 U.S. reinforcements and the appointment of FM 3–24's co-author, David Petraeus, to command in Baghdad. Many saw this reduction in violence as validation of the new COIN doctrine and a demonstration that one could tame insurgencies in brief campaigns with the right methods.

COIN critics see this reassessment as a wave of unwarranted enthusiasm which led the Obama administration down a primrose path to a misbegotten repeat in the Afghan surge of 2009. Speaking only for the analysts who wrote General Stanley McChrystal's assessment report in spring 2009 (I served as a member of the analysis team), I can say that none saw Afghanistan as a meaningful analog to Iraq, or thought COIN was a cheap and easy ticket to success in the war. I doubt anyone in the Obama administration thought so, either. But the Iraq surge did suggest that COIN was not impossible, and that if the United States was willing to invest the time and resources, then it could eventually defeat an insurgency.

The ensuing 2009–12 surge in Afghanistan certainly looked different than Iraq's in 2007. No Iraq-like sudden turnaround occurred. Five years after surge forces arrived in Afghanistan, the Taliban remain militarily viable and continue to control strategically important terrain, especially in the east but also in parts of the south and southwest. U.S. casualties were lower in 2013 than in 2009,[8] but by nothing like Iraq's 2007 factor-of-ten plummet, and many now expect at least a temporary increase in Taliban attacks as they test the ANSF to see whether it can function after Western combat forces withdraw. Anyone who thought the Iraq surge had created a new template for rapid success in COIN must surely be disabused of this notion by now.

But does this warrant a return to the general COIN pessimism of the Vietnam-to-2006 era? Does the Afghan surge show that COIN is as hopeless as many now believe? In fact, what the Afghan experience shows is that counterinsurgents can indeed re-establish government control of threatened areas, hold them against insurgent counterattacks, and hand that control off to indigenous security forces. What COIN cannot do, though, is to accomplish this quickly or cheaply.

Among the Afghan surge's earliest targets were the districts and subdistricts of Nawa, Marjah, Garmser, and Nad Ali in the central Helmand River Valley.[9] By mid-2009, these had become Taliban strongholds with little to no government presence, populations who complied with Taliban edicts, and dense networks of improvised explosive devices and ambush sites confronting any government effort to patrol or penetrate the area. By early 2010, the arrival of U.S. surge forces enabled systematic offensives to clear these districts of insurgents. Taliban defenders resisted, and the result was a spike in violence with heavy U.S. and insurgent casualties. Following FM 3–24-prescribed methods of dismounted patrolling, forward basing among the population, and intensive efforts to build intelligence networks for guiding operations, clearance forces that met or exceeded the doctrinal norm of 20 troops per thousand members of the population succeeded in driving the Taliban from their strongholds, defeating a series of counterattacks, and establishing government control with substantial freedom of movement.[10]

As a result, violence fell: by May 2011, Marines in Nawa had gone over a year without a serious firefight; in Nad Ali, reported violence fell by 85 percent by June 2010; in Garmser, attacks fell by 90 percent by March 2011; in Marjah, Taliban-initiated attacks fell from almost 1,600 in 2011 to 782 in 2012, and have continued to decline since.[11] By early 2012, shops had reopened, displaced populations were returning, and visiting American civilians were able to walk through marketplaces without body armor.[12] By late 2013, lead security responsibility was transferred to the Afghan Army, U.S. forces had largely withdrawn, violence was continuing to decrease, and all four areas remain in government control today despite repeated Taliban efforts to retake them following the U.S. handoff to the ANSF.[13] Similar experiences accompanied offensives in Arghendab, Zari, Panjway, and many other districts in which large U.S. or other Western forces were introduced into Taliban-held areas, displaced insurgents, held the results against counterattack, and eventually handed security over to Afghan forces.[14]

None of these offensives were cheap. Not only did they require large forces relative to the size of the population to be secured, but clearing the Taliban and establishing government control cost many lives: in Marjah alone, 28 U.S. Marines were killed in the first twelve months.[15] Nor were any of these operations quick. The Allied command initially hoped that it could mostly re-establish government control in such places within a single fighting season, after which the ANSF could take over; that rule of thumb then stretched into a year, then eighteen months.[16] The Taliban have proven themselves as tough opponents capable of sustained resistance against better-equipped, numerically superior forces.

The results have also fallen a good deal short of creating Eden in the Helmand River Valley. The Taliban there are not annihilated; counterattacks never disappeared altogether, and will probably increase now to test the ANSF. Many Afghans continue to see insecurity as a significant problem in their daily lives.

But the Taliban could not prevent properly trained forces from seizing and holding contested areas. Nor have Taliban counterattacks made much net headway to date against ANSF defenders in regaining districts the Taliban lost to the surge. Modern counterinsurgency methods have shown in Afghanistan that, when properly resourced, they can indeed drive insurgents out, and mostly keep them out, even after transition to indigenous control. And this means that U.S. forces can progressively expand the government's zone of control by using the pattern of clearing districts, holding them against counterattack, handing off to indigenous forces, then moving on to repeat the process elsewhere while indigenous forces hold the cleared areas left behind. This suggests that such "ink spot" processes can eventually clear enough of a country to compel insurgents to end the war on terms the government can accept.

Nor have the Taliban been able simply to move from cleared areas to others, increasing violence elsewhere in a balloon-squeezing phenomenon. After an initial spike, violence nationwide fell in Afghanistan during the surge. Moreover, in areas where violence increased after 2009 (especially the country's east), there were new U.S. clearance operations ongoing as forces swung from the initially reinforced south into regions that had not previously received surge forces.[17] Offensives for clearance always increase local violence before stabilizing an area under government control; this means that an ink-spot strategy will rarely show a large drop in nationwide violence until all the local offensives are complete everywhere (in the meantime, drops in violence in one locality where the process is complete will be counterbalanced by local increases in violence elsewhere where the process is only beginning). In fact, there is little evidence that the Taliban made compensating gains elsewhere to offset its losses in the surge.

The commonplace narrative that Afghanistan shows how COIN is impossible is thus overstated. What experience to date suggests is that it can work—but only where counterinsurgents invest the lives, forces, and time needed. Neither FM 3–24 nor any other contemporary COIN technique can produce quick or inexpensive results. Anyone who employs it expecting otherwise will be deeply disappointed—and would be better advised not to start the process at all.

HEARTS, MINDS, AND FIREPOWER

Many felt the early U.S. military response to Iraq's insurgency was heavy-handed and overly violent.[18] This built on a common impression of U.S. tactics in Vietnam, which have been criticized for applying conventional-style firepower to destroy an elusive enemy, rather than protecting and winning over the civilian population.[19] When FM 3–24 appeared in 2006, its emphasis on the latter was widely seen as a response to this criticism, and the manual itself goes to great lengths to contrast the less violent methods needed for COIN with the kind of firepower dominance emphasized in conventional warfare. In fairness, the manual does not present COIN as armed humanitarianism. The manual clearly intends a balance that includes a major combat function which will have to be violent, but the contrast with conventional doctrine is striking by design. And given this, it is perhaps predictable that many would feel the manual swung the pendulum too far.

When General McChrystal took command in Kabul in 2009, one of his first major initiatives was to reduce civilian casualties in consonance with the doctrine's emphasis on protecting the population. He never meant this to suggest that killing the enemy was unimportant, or that troops in contact could not use firepower to protect themselves. But communicating a nuanced message of balance and change-by-degree across a sprawling organization of more than 100,000 people, many nations, and multiple military services proved very difficult in practice. The result was an unhappy combination of persistent heavy-handedness in some places, and widespread resentment in many others among troops who felt hamstrung by the new restrictions.

This frustration interacted with widespread awareness among the troops that COIN was continuing to involve bitter combat with sometimes heavy U.S. firepower. Certainly the Iraq surge was anything but soft or non-violent: in a single day on January 10, 2008, for example, U.S. aircraft dropped 47,000 pounds of bombs in support of Operation Marne Thunderbolt, south of Baghdad.[20] And when General Petraeus replaced McChrystal in Kabul in 2010, he both re-emphasized the need to kill the enemy and de-emphasized governance reform, in an effort to prioritize near-term security progress of the kind he thought necessary to secure support for the war in Washington.

Taken together, these things have promoted a view among many within the military that recent experience shows how FM 3–24 swung the pendulum too far toward an almost humanitarian conception of victory through popularity and away from traditional military concerns with violent combat, combat that was continuing in any case. FM 3–24 is now under review for revision; one widespread and influential view of Afghanistan's lessons thus holds that this revision should swing the pendulum back toward combat and away from governance.

Yet, this view risks over-shooting the target in the opposite direction. Combat and violence are clearly essential for successful COIN. But the biggest problem with FM 3–24 is not an underemphasis on combat and an overemphasis on governance—it is the manual's prescription for the wrong *kind* of governance effort. Whereas FM 3–24 advocates apolitical capacity building, what Afghanistan actually shows is that governance problems are about political *interests* at least as much as administrative capacity. Merely improving the capacity of government actors who seek to prey on their population makes things worse, not better.

The underlying problem here is a tacit assumption throughout FM 3–24 that U.S. political interests align with the host's. The manual implicitly assumes that the host government wants to be an effective, disinterested, broadly representative defender of its people's well-being. The host thus theoretically shares with the United States a mutual ambition for what the manual refers to as legitimacy—the host just lacks the means to achieve it. Hence, the manual focuses on providing the means: equipping would-be Jeffersonian democrats in the host government with schools, clinics, judges and prosecutors, trained administrators and police, well-equipped soldiers. The doctrine also emphasizes connecting this more capable government to the people, so the public will see their stake in the government's success and sacrifice on its behalf.

In Afghanistan, this assumption has proven badly mistaken. Much of the Afghan government operates as a collection of patronage networks that systematically extract resources from the population for the benefit of those networks and the power brokers who run them. This is hardly a disinterested attempt to improve the lives of average Afghans. And it happens not because the government lacks an adequate supply of trained administrators or roads or schools—it happens because the elites who run the system profit from it and want it to function this way. Hence, this problem will not diminish merely by the West increasing Afghanistan's material capacity to govern. On the contrary, poorly monitored "capacity building" often makes the problem worse by supplying patronage networks with the money and resources needed to reward their allies, punish their rivals, and extract resources from the public more effectively. Worse still, U.S. attempts to connect the public to local government organs that the public sees as predatory implicate the United States in official predation and suggest to prospective victims that they have nowhere to turn for succor but the insurgency.

Nor is this problem limited to Afghanistan. In Iraq, the biggest challenge was sectarianism rather than profiteering (though plenty of the latter also existed), but in Iraq, too, U.S. interests and the host government's were badly misaligned.

In fact, U.S. interests will rarely align naturally with the host's in COIN. Local governments which actively promote a fair distribution of resources rarely face major insurgencies in the first place—hence, Americans are rarely asked to wage counterinsurgency at all in such places. It is no accident that the U.S. military does little COIN in Switzerland or Canada. If there is an insurgency to counter, then the odds are good that the local government is ruling in the interest of elites who do not want to redistribute power toward groups they distrust or exploit. The basic premise underlying governance reform doctrine in FM 3–24 is thus almost always false. Afghanistan shines a spotlight on the problem, but it is anything but unique to Kabul.

This does not make governance reform impossible for counterinsurgents. Among the reasons Iraq's violence fell in 2007 is that Petraeus and U.S. Ambassador Ryan Crocker forced Iraqi Prime Minister Nouri al-Maliki to replace known sectarians in the Iraqi security forces, and to moderate Iraqi government behavior toward Sunnis (for example, by tolerating the mostly-Sunni Sons of Iraq groups that actualized the Anbar Awakening). They did this by coercing Maliki via conditional provision of support: if Maliki refused to act, Petraeus and Crocker would deny essential U.S. logistical support to Iraqi army or police units, or they would withhold other U.S. support Maliki valued and needed.[21] Making COIN work here was not a process of benign, apolitical capacity building, a la FM 3–24. On the contrary, it was profoundly political and often highly coercive.

In Afghanistan, by contrast, the West has been systematically unwilling to use conditionality as leverage for reform. For some, especially in the military, the reason has been the absence of doctrinal guidance for this kind of coercive political bargaining. For others, the chief barrier has been fear that Afghans would call the bluff, assistance would have to be withheld, and this would delay the creation of a higher-capacity Afghan civil and military administration— which is usually seen as the key enabler for Western withdrawal. The net result is that the problem of government predation has grown worse, not better. Foreign presence has mostly served to aggravate the problem by fueling the corruption rather than solving it.

This in turn has contributed to the difficulty of truly eliminating the Taliban presence in Afghan population centers. Through combat, counterinsurgents can establish predominant control in which they regain freedom of movement and enable something like normal commerce. But even in major cities such as Kabul and Kandahar, resentment of government predation by some of its victims facilitates a shadow presence of Taliban fighters and sympathizers who can mount occasional attacks which keep the violence from truly disappearing. If government predation continues to worsen, the troop levels the ANSF will need to maintain control in such areas will leave them without the strength they need to expand the government's writ over time. This will consign the war to a future of grinding stalemate for as long as the ANSF's foreign funding holds up.

What Afghanistan suggests, then, is that if the U.S. military actually does wage counterinsurgency in the future, such apolitical "capacity building" is unlikely to work. Effective governance reform during insurgency is inherently political, typically coercive, and must proceed in a manner for which FM 3–24 offers little guidance. Yet, it cannot be ignored in favor of a unidimensional focus on security via combat. Without tolerable governance, the force levels and violence needed to sustain control of a threatened population will prove extreme even by doctrinal COIN standards, and residual instability is likely to remain unsatisfyingly high. It is not wooly-headed humanitarianism to suggest that voluntary public compliance with government edicts reduces security force requirements—or that public resentment increases them. Counterinsurgency is inherently slow, costly, and difficult; to conduct it amidst a population that views the government as a threat is to add substantially to an already substantial bill.

NEVER AGAIN?

Of course, it is too early to offer conclusive lessons from an ongoing war. But in the spirit of presenting hypotheses for definitive analysis later, and in the interest of spurring debate before conventional wisdom consolidates, two observations are worth considering now.

First, Afghanistan to date suggests that COIN can indeed restore government control of threatened areas, but not cheaply or quickly. Where counterinsurgent forces were committed in doctrinal numbers and stayed long enough, the Taliban have been driven out, and kept out—this is not mission impossible. But neither is it some kind of silver bullet that can win wars before democratic publics take notice.

Worse, it is not a method that adapts well to partial application. A year before the Obama administration's surge, there were already about 70,000 Western troops in Afghanistan; this did not yield half the stability for half the price of the 140,000-soldier peak Western presence.[22] On the contrary, it was the 70,000 soldiers' inability to prevent Taliban expansion that persuaded the administration to reinforce, lest the Taliban win the war outright. This makes it very hard to triangulate and serve limited interests with limited versions of COIN—the limited version attempted in Afghanistan before 2009 was well on its way to complete failure before the surge. Partial application is less likely to yield limited success than it is to produce a more expensive version of defeat.

This turns COIN into a thorny dilemma. In Afghanistan, the Obama administration has seen real but limited U.S. interests;[23] its instincts have been to seek some real but limited means to secure them at a cost that fits the stakes. There is no such means. COIN can secure the stakes, but at a cost which many find greater than the benefit. Withdrawal would be cheaper (certainly in the short run), but would sacrifice the U.S. security stakes in the conflict. If COIN were impossible, then sacrifice would be the only logical approach, and no dilemma would exist. If COIN were quick and cheap, it would be worth the stakes in Afghanistan, and again no dilemma would exist. Yet, COIN is neither.

This in turn makes answering the question of COIN's future more difficult than a simple verdict of "impossible, so never again." As Gentile and others rightly note, COIN is a means, not an end. To judge the means, one must therefore assess the ends, which are the U.S. interests at stake where the United States would wage counterinsurgency. This is challenging but tractable for specific wars and theaters. In Afghanistan, the Obama administration saw a close call, deciding in fall 2009 that the interests at stake there were worth the cost of counterinsurgency, if only barely so, then wrestled with buyer's remorse afterwards. For projections into uncertain futures in unknown theaters, the task of balancing interest and cost is harder still. The United States has interests of some kind in many places, the stakes vary in scale, and many conflicts affecting interests will probably not be anticipated before events bring them into focus.

Many COIN critics nevertheless think the stakes will never prove worth it; hence large, expensive, labor-intensive ground forces for COIN should shrink. This is not an unreasonable position. With dwindling budgets and pressing needs in the Pacific and elsewhere, the United States will surely have to reduce real capability of some kind; the least-damaging capability to divest might be that for large-scale COIN. But if so, this will not be a simple, cost-free call made easy by COIN's manifest impossibility as demonstrated in Afghanistan—the war offers no simple escape from the dilemmas posed by the need to accept expensive means if one wants to secure real but limited interests.

Nor does Afghanistan suggest that future counterinsurgencies can be waged more cheaply by dispensing with difficult governance programs and refocusing on security and combat. This brings in the second tentative observation of the war to date: the United States needs a different *approach* to governance in counterinsurgency. COIN can reinstate government control without meaningful reform, as the Helmand and Kandahar campaigns suggest. But to *sustain* control under predatory misgovernance adds great expense to an already expensive form of warfare. Afghanistan shows not that governance is unimportant, but that apolitical capacity building is the wrong approach.

Of course, COIN will remain expensive even with astute governance policies. Given this, Americans may choose to avoid it in the future. But this will probably not avoid the debates that hard decisions spur, and it is plausible that future U.S. administrations might resolve the dilemmas posed by real but limited interests via COIN as the Obama Administration did. So it is important to preserve, as much as possible, the skills and knowledge in COIN's conduct developed at such cost in Afghanistan and Iraq. This includes the knowledge of how to balance security with a more political understanding of governance reform. Overlooking this crucial balance under the influence of some popular early interpretations of the war's lessons would represent a great and unnecessary loss.

NOTES

1 See, e.g., "Obama: Afghan war to end in 2014," United Press International, January 11, 2013, http://www.upi.com/Top_News/US/2013/01/11/Obama-Afghan-war-to-end-in-2014/UPI-33701357891200/; Office of the Press Secretary, The White House, "Remarks by the President on the Way Forward in Afghanistan," June 22, 2011, http://www.whitehouse.gov/the-press-office/2011/06/22/remarks-president-way-forward-afghanistan.

2 For illustrative examples, see Gian P. Gentile, "A Requiem for American Counterinsurgency," *Orbis* 57, no. 4 (Autumn 2013), pp. 549–558; Andrew Bacevich, *Breach of Trust: How Americans Failed their Soldiers and their Country* (New York: Metropolitan Books, Henry Holt and Company, 2013), pp. 13, 109, 149; "The War in Afghanistan: Year Ten," *Salon*, October 7, 2010; also Karl Eikenberry, "The Limits of Counterinsurgency Doctrine in Afghanistan," *Foreign Affairs* (September/October 2013); Douglas Porch, *Counterinsurgency: Exposing the Myths of the New Way of War* (New York: Cambridge University Press, 2013).

3 On the Anbar Awakening, see, e.g., Austin Long, "The Anbar Awakening," *Survival* 50, no. 2 (April/May 2008), pp. 67–94; and Daniel R. Green, "The Fallujah Awakening: A Case Study in Counter-Insurgency," *Small Wars and Insurgencies* 21, no. 4 (December 2010), pp. 591–609, both of which attribute Iraq's 2007 violence reduction chiefly to the Awakening. For a counterargument, see Stephen Biddle, Jeffrey A. Friedman and Jacob N. Shapiro, "Testing the Surge: Why did Violence Decline in Iraq in 2007?" *International Security* 37, no. 1 (Summer 2012), pp. 7–40.

4 Headquarters, Department of the Army, *FM 3–24: Counterinsurgency* (Washington, DC: U.S. Government Printing Office, 2006), reprinted as United States Department of the Army, *The U.S. Army/Marine Corps Counterinsurgency Field Manual* (Chicago: University of Chicago Press, 2007).

5 Though this position is to date more widely held than published, for an illustrative articulation see Bing West, *The Wrong War: Grit, Strategy, and the Way Out of Afghanistan* (New York: Random House, 2011); also the views in U.S. Army Military History Institute, Iraq Surge Collection, esp. audio file 69.

6 See, e.g., Bob Woodward, *Bush at War* (New York: Simon and Schuster, 2002): pp. 220, 237, 241, 252–263, 310; Terry H. Anderson, *Bush's Wars* (NY: Oxford University Press, 2011): pp. 88, 159–67.

7 See "Operation Iraqi Freedom," iCasualties.org: Iraq Coalition Casualty Count, http://icasualties.org/Iraq/Index.aspx.

8 U.S. fatalities in Afghanistan totaled 317 in 2009 and 127 in 2013: "Operation Enduring Freedom," icasualties.org, http://icasualties.org/oef/.

9 For general accounts of the post-2009 fighting in Helmand, see, e.g., Jeffrey Dressler, *Counterinsurgency in Helmand* (Washington, DC: Institute for the Study of War, 2011); Rajiv Chandrasekaran, *Little America: The War within the War for Afghanistan* (New York: Knopf, 2012); Carter Malkasian, *War Comes to Garmser* (New York: Oxford University Press, 2013).

10 For the doctrinal troop density norm for COIN, see FM 3–24, para 1–67.

11 Rajiv Chandrasekaran, "Nawa turns into proving ground for U.S. strategy in Afghan War," *Washington Post*, December 12, 2010; Matt Millham, "Despite Lingering Reliance on US Aid, Afghanistan's Nawa District a Model of 'Transition,'" *Stars and Stripes*, May 28, 2011; Theo Farrell, *Operation Moshtarak: An Analysis of the Campaign in Nad-e-Ali District, Helmand*, Redacted version (British Army Land Warfare Centre, June 7, 2010), p. 16; Malkasian, *War Comes to Garmser*, figure 2, *Op. cit.*

12 See Tyrone C. Marshall Jr., "Carter's Walk Through Marjah Market Shows Progress," *American Forces Press Service*, February 24, 2012: http://www.defense.gov/news/newsarticle.aspx?id=67328.

13 UK House of Commons, Defense Committee, *Securing the Future of Afghanistan*, Vol. 1 (London: The Stationery Office Limited, 10 April 2013), p. EV-92.

14 See, e.g., Carl Forsberg, *Counterinsurgency in Kandahar* (Washington, DC: Institute for the Study of War, December 2010).

15 Nancy Montgomery, "One Year After Offensive: Signs of Progress in Marjah," *Stars and Stripes*, February 14, 2011, http://www.stripes.com/news/one-year-after-offensive-signs-of-progress-in-marjah-1.134822.

16 Author's observations, ISAF Headquarters, Kabul, June 2009, January 2010, June-July 2010, November 2010, March 2011, and November 2011.

17 For nationwide and provincial violence statistics, see the annual series *Report to the Congress on Progress Toward Security and Stability in Afghanistan* (Washington, DC: U.S. Department of Defense, various years).

18 See, e.g., Tom Ricks, *Fiasco: The American Military Adventure in Iraq, 2003 to 2005* (New York: Penguin, 2007); Michael Gordon and Bernard Trainor, *Endgame: The Inside Story of the Struggle for Iraq, from George W. Bush to Barack Obama* (New York: Pantheon, 2012).

19 See, e.g., Andrew Krepinevich, *The Army and Vietnam* (Baltimore: Johns Hopkins University Press, 1988); Jeffrey Record, *The Wrong War* (Annapolis: Naval Institute Press, 1998).

20 Dale Andrade, *Surging South of Baghdad: The Third Infantry Division and Task Force Marne in Iraq, 2007–2008* (Washington, DC: U.S. Army Center of Military History, 2010), p. 318.

21 See, e.g., Fred Kaplan, *The Insurgents: David Petraeus and the Plot to Change the American Way of War* (New York: Simon and Schuster, 2013), pp. 263–4, 341; Linda Robinson, *Tell Me How This Ends: General David Petraeus and the Search for a Way Out of Iraq* (New York: Public Affairs, 2008), pp. 81, 156, 261, 331.

22 For troop counts, see Ian S. Livingston and Michael O'Hanlon, *Afghanistan Index* (Washington, DC: Brookings, August 2013), figures 1.1 and 1.2; figures above are for March 2008.

23 Specifically, the administration has identified two chief U.S. interests in Afghanistan: that the country not again become a base for al-Qaeda to attack the West, and that it not become a base for militants to destabilize Afghanistan's neighbors. On the Administration's interest calculus in Afghanistan, see Stephen Biddle, "Is It Worth It? The Difficult Case for War in Afghanistan," *The American Interest* 4, no. 6 (July/August 2009), pp. 4–11.

Reading 9.7

China: Can the Next Superpower Rise Without War?

RICHARD K. BETTS AND THOMAS J. CHRISTENSEN

The challenge presented by a rising China is the principal issue facing American foreign policy. This is not always obvious to most Americans or even to many of our leaders. Since the end of the Cold War, defense policy has been absorbed in second-order problems of deterring or defeating mid-level powers such as Iraq, North Korea and Serbia, and in third-order problems of peacekeeping and humanitarian intervention. Over the long term, however, the first priority of a serious foreign policy is to handle challenges from discontented, nuclear-armed, major powers.

It is hardly inevitable that China will be a threat to American interests, but the United States is much more likely to go to war with China than it is with any other major power. Other current or emerging great powers either are aligned with the United States (NATO countries and Japan), are struggling against crippling decline (Russia), or, while having a tense diplomatic relationship with Washington, have no plausible occasion for war with America (India). China, by contrast, is a rising power with high expectations, unresolved grievances and an undemocratic government.

Source: Richard K. Betts and Thomas J. Christensen, "China: Getting the Question Right," The National Interest, No. 62 (Winter 2000/01), pp. 17–29. This article is reprinted with the permission of The National Interest. *All rights reserved.*

Debate about whether and how China might threaten U.S. security interests has often been simplistically polarized. Views range from alarmist to complacent: from those who see China emerging as a hefty and dangerous superpower, to those who believe the country's prospects are vastly overrated; and from those who see its economic growth as an engine for building threatening military capabilities, to those who see that growth as a welcome force for political liberalization and international cooperation.

Most strategic debate about China still focuses on a few simple questions. With respect to capabilities, these revolve mainly around whether the Chinese armed forces will develop to the point that they rival U.S. military power, and whether the economic surge—with its implications for military transformation—will continue indefinitely or stall. With regard to intentions, China watchers want to know how thoroughly and how soon the country will integrate into a global economy that allegedly constrains conflict; whether Beijing will adopt aggressive aims as its power grows; and whether political liberalization will occur as its wealth grows. Concern also zeroes in on whether the People's Republic of China (PRC) has the ability to take Taiwan by force.

These are relevant questions at the most basic level, but they are the wrong ones to generate progress in a mature debate. The most worrisome possibilities are those that lie beyond the answers to these questions, and between alarmist and complacent viewpoints. The truth is that China can pose a grave problem even if it does not become a military power on the American model, does not intend to commit aggression, integrates into a global economy, and liberalizes politically. Similarly, the United States could face a dangerous conflict over Taiwan even if it turns out that Beijing lacks the capacity to conquer the island.

WILL CHINA'S MILITARY POWER RIVAL AMERICA'S?

There is little disagreement that the People's Liberation Army (PLA), a generic designation for all the Chinese armed forces, remains a threadbare force, well below Western standards. Pockets of excellence notwithstanding, most personnel are poorly educated and trained. Weapons systems are old, and even those acquired most recently are inferior to those in Western arsenals. Many units spend a good deal of time in non-military activities; staffs do not practice complex, large-scale operations; exercises and training regimens are limited; and equipment is not well maintained. Even according to the highest estimates, defense spending per soldier is low by First World standards, indicating the dominance of quantity over quality in the Chinese forces.

The main disagreement among Western analysts of China's military is about whether the PLA is poised to move out of its unimpressive condition and into a new era of modernity, efficiency and competitiveness, as anticipated economic reform and growth translate into military improvement. Arguments to that effect are supported by a number of PLA writings about a prospective Chinese "revolution in military affairs" (RMA).[1] The current backwardness of the PLA reflects its low priority in the country's modernization efforts since the

1970s, and the diversion of the energy of the military into business activities (which are now supposed to be curtailed). In this view, the military potential of the PLA will be liberated when the political leadership decides to give it significantly more of the resources generated by economic development.

For China to develop a military on the model of the United States would be a tremendous stretch. The main issue is not whether Beijing will have high defense budgets or access to cutting-edge technology. A rich China might well be able to acquire most types of advanced weaponry. Deeply ingrained habits of threat assessment in the U.S. defense community encourage focusing on these factors. Unfortunately, however, basic "bean counts" of manpower and units and the quality of weapons platforms are poor measures of truly modern military capability. More fundamental to that assessment is whether the PLA establishment is capable of using whatever increase in resources it might receive to build the complex supporting infrastructure necessary to make Chinese forces competitive in combat. The PLA's current mediocrity—like that of many armed forces in the world—may be rooted in a history, ideology and culture that are incompatible with the patterns of organization and social interaction necessary to rival the best First World militaries. This does not mean that the PLA can never break out of this box. It does mean that it will not be easy to do, and will not occur quickly.

Modern military effectiveness has become more a matter of quality than of quantity, and less a matter of pure firepower than of the capacity to coordinate complex systems. The essence of the American RMA lies in the interweaving of capacities in organization, doctrine, training, maintenance, support systems, weaponry and the overall level of professionalism. These factors are harder to measure, but they are what make it feasible to assimilate and apply state-of-the-art weapons effectively. Those capacities require high levels of education throughout a military force, a culture of initiative and innovation, and an orientation toward operating through skill networks as much as through traditional command and obedience hierarchies. Few militaries have developed these capabilities. Indeed, experience in the Persian Gulf [in 1991] and Kosovo indicate that the United States is in a class by itself in these respects. If the PLA has the resources to integrate complexity and a willingness to delegate authority to overcome its mediocrity, it is a well-kept secret. As yet it is not obvious that PLA effectiveness is likely to be closer to that of the American military than to that of, say, Iraq.

If the PLA remains second-rate, should the world breathe a sigh of relief? Not entirely. First, American military power is not the only relevant standard of comparison. Other armed forces in Asia that the PLA could come up against are much closer to the Chinese standard than to the American. (This is true even of Taiwan's technologically sophisticated military, whose long isolation has eroded its quality.[2]) Second, the United States has global interests and often finds itself distracted or pinned down in other regions. Third, the Chinese do not need to match U.S. capabilities to cope with them. Rather than trying to match an American revolution in military affairs, they might do better to develop a *counter*-revolution by devising asymmetrical strategic options on various parts of the technological spectrum that can circumvent U.S. advantages.

One such example could be "cyberwar" attacks on the complex network of information systems that stitches American military superiority together. Another could be the use of new weapons like land attack cruise missiles or lower tech weapons such as naval mines to impede American access to the region. Still another could be the modification of China's no first-use policy on nuclear weapons, making an exception for repelling an invasion of Chinese territory. Although it is almost unimaginable that China would use nuclear weapons in an effort to gain political concessions from Taiwan, it might threaten their use to deter U.S. military action on behalf of the island. As Disarmament Ambassador Sha Zukang said in 1996, "As far as Taiwan is concerned it is a province of China. . . . So the policy of no-first-use does not apply."[3] Even though the Foreign Ministry subsequently repudiated the statement, nothing makes a future adaptation of doctrine in that direction unthinkable.

Pundits on defense policy commonly observe that China lacks power projection capabilities—the ability to send and sustain combat forces far from home. By U.S. standards this is true. Talk about obtaining aircraft carriers has produced nothing deployable, the navy and air forces lack the requisite assets for "lift" (transporting and supplying large units for operations abroad), and Chinese forces have negligible logistical capacity as we know it. For those worried about facing a Chinese force on the American model, these are all good grounds for optimism. Indeed, there is general agreement that Beijing lacks the capability at present to invade Taiwan and that it could take decades to overcome the obstacles. But China does not need to match American standards to reshape the Asian strategic environment. This becomes especially clear when one considers *where* power projection will be an issue.

Taiwan is both the most dangerous and most likely instance of Chinese power projection (more on which below), but it is not the only one. China has conceivable points of conflict in several places that would not require its forces to cross large bodies of water, and where it would not be facing opposition as potent as Taiwan's military. Although less likely than conflict over Taiwan, an imbroglio in Korea would be scarcely less dangerous if the Pyongyang regime were to collapse and South Korean or American forces were to move into the vacuum without Beijing's agreement. Far too little attention has been focused on the odds of miscalculation in a confused situation of this sort. The PLA does not have the American army's logistical capacity, but even a half century ago it managed to project a force of hundreds of thousands of men deep into Korea.

While the Chinese navy is weak, some of its neighbors' navies are weaker still. Two of these neighbors, Vietnam and the Philippines, have outstanding sovereignty disputes with China and have not fared well in naval skirmishes in the past three decades. We also cannot rule out the possibility of a land attack. The PLA did poorly in its invasion of Vietnam over twenty years ago, but the Vietnamese army is now less than half the size it was then, and the Vietnamese economic base is far more inferior to China's than it was in 1978. Logistical limitations would hamper, but not preclude, PRC action in Mongolia, or in the Russian Far East, if that region were to fall out of Moscow's effective control.

Granted, conflict over these places is improbable. The problem is that the same could have been said of most wars before they happened. . . .

WILL CHINA BE PACIFIED BY GLOBALIZATION?

To pessimists steeped in realpolitik, a rich China will necessarily be a threat, because economic power can be translated into military power and power generates ambition. To optimists impressed with the revolutionary implications of globalization, however, a more powerful China will not be a threat because it will have too much to lose from disrupting international trade and investment. The latter view is more common in the West than the former, which seems to many to reek of old thinking.

The notion that a web of commercial ties discourages war, however, is itself quite old, if not exactly venerable. It was popularized by Henry Thomas Buckle in the 1850s, by Norman Angell just a year before World War I erupted, and again in the 1970s, when interdependence was said to have reduced the utility of force. Most recently, at a White House rally for permanent normal trade relations, Al Gore quoted his father as saying, "When goods do not cross borders, armies will."

The argument this time around is that the proposition is finally true because the nature of interdependence has changed in a crucial way. A century ago it was characterized by vertical trade between imperial centers and colonies, trade in final products between wealthier nations, and portfolio investments. Today there is much more direct investment and transnational production of goods, which fosters "a growing interpenetration of economies, in the sense that one economy owns part of another."[4] With the PRC, Taiwan, Japan and the United States all owning pieces of each other, how can they fight without destroying their own property? As the Chinese elite make more and more money from bilateral investments with Taiwan, simple greed will prevent huffing and puffing from crossing the line to war. If development thoroughly enmeshes the PRC in the globalized economy, therefore, peace will follow.

There are at least two problems with this latest version of interdependence theory. One is that *both* sides in a political dispute have a stake in not overturning profitable economic integration. The PRC might not want to kill the golden goose, but neither would Taiwan or the United States. Why, then, should Beijing be any more anxious to back down in a crisis than Taipei or Washington? Mutual dependence makes a political conflict a game of chicken, in which each side expects the other to bow to the stakes, and in which collision may result rather than concession.

The second problem is that there is little reason to assume that sober economic interest will necessarily override national honor in a crisis. A tough stand by Beijing may be viewed from the inside as essential for regime survival, even if it is not seen by detached observers as being in China's "national interest." In an imbroglio over Taiwan, which capitals will feel the strongest emotional inhibitions against backing down? Beijing and Taipei both have a greater material, moral and historical stake in the outcome than does the United States.

The global economy does indeed change logical incentives to compromise in political conflict, but not to the degree that it makes Beijing likely to be more "reasonable" than anyone else. Economic globalization does not eliminate the high priority that nations place on their political identity and integrity. Drawing China into the web of global interdependence may do more to encourage peace than war, but it cannot guarantee that the pursuit of heartfelt political interests will be blocked by a fear of economic consequences.

WILL CHINA BECOME AGGRESSIVE?

Whether China has aggressive motives is what most policymakers want to know about Beijing's strategic intentions. Optimists say the answer is no, because the PRC is ideologically anti-imperialist and seeks only respect as a status quo great power. Pessimists say the answer is yes, because a seething set of Chinese grudges and territorial ambitions are on hold only for a lack of confidence in capability, or simply because all great powers tend to become aggressive when they get the chance.

But such focusing on the unlikely odds of deliberate aggression diverts attention from possibilities that are both much more likely and almost as dangerous. Most countries viewed as aggressors by their adversaries view their own behavior as defensive and legitimate. Whether Beijing is a tiger in waiting, about to set out deliberately on a predatory rampage, is not the most relevant question. No evidence suggests that Chinese leaders have an interest in naked conquest of the sort practiced by Genghis Khan, Napoleon Bonaparte or Adolf Hitler. The model more often invoked by pessimists is Kaiser Wilhelm's Germany. Like Germany a century ago, China is a late-blooming great power emerging into a world already ordered strategically by earlier arrivals; a continental power surrounded by other powers who are collectively stronger but individually weaker (with the exception of the United States and, perhaps, Japan); a bustling country with great expectations, dissatisfied with its place in the international pecking order, if only with regard to international prestige and respect. The quest for a rightful "place in the sun" will, it is argued, inevitably foster growing friction with Japan, Russia, India or the United States.

Optimists do not have a hard time brushing off this analogy to a state of a different culture on a different continent at a different time, a long-gone era when imperialism was the norm for civilized international behavior. Their benign view, that economic development and trade will inevitably make China fat and happy, uninterested in throwing its weight around, strikes them as common sense. It could turn out to be true. It is more an article of faith, however, than a prediction grounded in historical experience. The United States, for example, is quite interested in gaining the goodies from globalization, yet on the world stage it sometimes throws its weight around with righteous abandon.

Indeed, the most disturbing analogy for China's future behavior may not be Germany but the United States. If China acts with the same degree of caution and responsibility in its region in this century as the United States did in its neighborhood in the past century, Asia is in for big trouble. Washington intervened frequently in Mexico, Central America and the Caribbean for reasons most Americans consider legitimate, defensive, altruistic and humane. The United States and its allies in Asia, however, would see comparable Chinese regional policing as a mortal threat. Even if China does not throw its weight around, the fact that there are others who can respond to the growth of Chinese power sets up the possibility of a classic spiral of tense actions and reactions. China faces alliances involving the United States, Japan, Australia and South Korea, and potential alliances in Southeast Asia.

WOULD CHINESE LIBERALIZATION GUARANTEE PEACE?

Many assume that as long as democratization accompanies the growth of Chinese power, China will not necessarily pose a security challenge. This would hold true even if China proves able to maintain high levels of economic and technological growth, a healthy degree of government accumulation of the increasing national wealth, and, thereby, military modernization. This theory of the democratic peace—that developed democracies virtually never fight one another—is currently the most influential political science theory among American foreign policy elites.

Even if we accept the democratic peace theory at face value, there are several problems with applying it to China. First, as Fareed Zakaria has noted, the theory really applies only to liberal democracies on the Western model, ones with restraints on government action and guarantees of minority rights. Democratization in China could just as conceivably turn in an illiberal direction, on the model of post-Tito Yugoslavia, Iran or other unpleasant examples of violent activism.

Second, the democratic peace theory does not apply clearly to civil war. Democracies must recognize each other as democracies for the theory to apply.[5] They also have to view each other as legitimate, independent and sovereign states. No matter how many Americans and Taiwanese believe that Taiwan is or should be a sovereign state, this view is widely rejected on the mainland (and is not a premise of past or current U.S. policy).

Third, while liberal democracy is pacific, the process of becoming a democracy can be violent and destabilizing. This is particularly true of democratizing states that lack developed civil societies, independent news media, healthy outlets for popular grievances, and a marketplace for ideas where countervailing views can be debated. This gives elites incentives to manipulate populist or nationalist themes and to adopt tough international policies as an electoral strategy.[6]

The Chinese Communist Party has behaved like many authoritarian regimes, but with much more success. It has systematically prevented the rise of both an independent press and a civil society. Although the foreign press has penetrated China, domestic political publications are still strictly circumscribed by the state. As the recent crackdown on the Falun Gong demonstrates, the Party is afraid of any group that organizes for any purpose without state sanction, regardless of how apolitical it appears to be.

The Chinese government's concerns about its legitimacy are not mere expressions of paranoia. The intensity of criticism of the leadership that one hears privately in places ranging from taxi cabs to government offices is astonishing. Awareness of its unpopularity gives the government in Beijing incentives to use nationalism as a replacement for the now hollow shell of communist ideology. But the Party is also aware that nationalism is not an inert tool to be pulled out of a kit and manipulated at the whim of the government. It is double-edged. Volatile and potentially uncontrollable, especially on emotional issues such as relations with Japan and Taiwan, nationalism is powerful enough to prop up a communist party in a capitalist society, but it could also severely damage the party if it were turned against the state. Officials in Beijing are aware that nationalism was a major force in the Communist Party's overthrow of the Kuomintang, as it was in the 1911–12 revolution that overthrew the Qing dynasty. This is probably why, during the row with Japan over the Senkaku Islands in the summer of 1996, the Party actively prevented students and workers from marching in protest to the Japanese embassy.

According to one prominent Chinese foreign affairs expert, since the May 1999 NATO bombing of the embassy in Belgrade, the authorities in Beijing have been very concerned about an increasing trend in public opinion that views the leaders as soft in responding to international humiliations, and sees them even as "traitors" (*maiguo zei*) interested only in business prospects. He and others argue that the protests outside the American embassy in Beijing were not so much instigated by the Communist Party, as many in the West assumed, but rather were managed, controlled and ultimately suppressed by the Party. One retired Chinese military officer touched on a similar theme during the 1996 Senkaku crisis. He maintained that, if the Party allowed the people to protest unhindered, the first day they would be protesting against Japan, the next day against the lack of response by the government, and on the third day against the government itself.

In the early phases of democratization, China should be ripe for jingoism. Hypernationalism could be exploited to mobilize popular support and to deflect criticism of the state, especially given the existence of irredentist claims, and the danger of ethnic and regional "splittism" on the mainland and in Taiwan. If democratization were to occur in the current context of weak institutions, political leaders and opposition parties would have incentives to appeal to nationalism in ways that could destabilize the region. In fact, this is a favorite, though perhaps cynical, argument offered to foreigners by communist opponents of multiparty democracy.

There are, however, plausible scenarios in which Chinese democratization might reduce international conflict. Democratization could make the mainland more imaginative with regard to the frameworks for unification offered to Taiwan, thus making meaningful cross-strait political dialogue more likely. Political liberalization might also make the prospect of eventual accommodation with the mainland more palatable to Taiwan and discourage the island's diplomatic adventurism. But that possibility is not necessarily more likely than its opposite: a renewed belief by Taiwan that the island has its own national identity, that unification with the mainland under any circumstances is unacceptable, and that democratization on the mainland is a threat to Taiwanese goals. Taiwan may see a closing window of opportunity, with the hopes of gaining true independence reduced as the West's sympathy for Taiwan's opposition to unification hardens.

If Americans view mainland democratization as genuine, such fears on Taiwan are well placed. Would the United States risk war to prevent a democratic Taiwan from becoming part of a larger democratic China? The main reasons a president could currently use to mobilize Americans around action in defense of Taiwan's democracy would simply disappear. Many observers view democracy as Taiwan's biggest security asset, because it increases U.S. support. They are right. But it is not just democracy that provides Taiwan's security; it is the current contrast between Taiwan's democracy and the mainland's authoritarianism.

CAN THE MAINLAND CONQUER TAIWAN?

The possibility of war with China over Taiwan is arguably the most dangerous threat that U.S. security policy faces in the coming decade. No other flashpoint is more likely to bring the United States into combat with a major power, and no other contingency compels Washington to respond with such ambiguous commitment. U.S. policy regarding the defense of Taiwan is uncertain, and thus so is the understanding in Beijing and Taipei—and in Washington—over how strongly the United States might react in different circumstances. Because Taiwan is more independent than either Washington or Beijing might prefer, neither great power can fully control developments that might ignite a crisis. This is a classic recipe for surprise, miscalculation and uncontrolled escalation.

Traditional questions about Chinese intentions and capabilities miss the mark in analyzing the likelihood of war and the probable course war would take. A PRC attack on a Taiwan following the pursuit of formal independence from the Chinese nation would be viewed (quite sincerely) in Beijing as purely defensive, to preserve generally recognized territorial sovereignty. Many outside China would view the attack as a sign of belligerence. But military activity against an independence-minded Taiwan might have little relevance to Beijing's behavior on other issues, even for other sovereignty disputes such as those over the Senkaku or Spratly Islands.

The niceties of balance of power calculations could prove relatively unimportant in determining whether China would use force over Taiwan and whether it would do so effectively. U.S. efforts to create a stable balance across the Taiwan Strait might deter the use of force under certain circumstances, but certainly not all. Moreover, such efforts would miss the major point of cross-strait strategic interaction. China's military strategy in a conflict over Taiwan would likely be to punish and coerce rather than to control, tasks for which its military may be able to use force to great effect. The PLA's ability to mount a

Normandy-style assault on the island is not the toughest question. Geography (the water barrier), together with U.S. supplies, would provide powerful means to Taiwan for blocking such an invasion, even without direct U.S. combat involvement.

A greater challenge would be a blockade by the PRC, which has a large number of submarines and mines. Taiwan's proximity to the mainland and its dependence on international trade and investment enhance the potential effect of blockades—or coercive campaigns involving ballistic and cruise missiles— even if the military impact would be modest. The PRC might thus be able to damage severely the island's economy regardless of the number of F-16s, AWACS aircraft and theater missile defense batteries the island can bring to bear. Moreover, to break a blockade by sweeping the seas would likely require a direct attack on Chinese vessels. If Chinese forces had not already targeted U.S. ships by that point, it would be up to Washington to decide to fire the first shots against a nuclear-armed country that was attempting to regain limited control of what it believes is its own territory.

Some think that the United States should give Taiwan military assistance or defend it directly even in the extreme case that it openly declares legal independence. Many assume that the United States could deter an attack from the mainland and that, if worse came to worst, the United States would prevail in a war should deterrence fail. These assumptions, unfortunately, are suspect. Before being deterred, Beijing would have to weigh the costs of inaction against action. The perceived cost of inaction against Taiwanese independence is very high. No leader can count on survival if labeled the next Li Hongzhang, the diplomat who ceded Taiwan to Japan in the 1895 Treaty of Shimonoseki.

Many in Beijing believe that the United States lacks the national will to pursue a war against China to save Taiwan. If the prospect of casualties did not deter the United States from intervening, the reasoning goes, even low levels of casualties would frighten it into early withdrawal. Following this logic, China need not defeat the U.S. military in wartime or close the gap in military power in peacetime. Rather, the strategic requirement is much lower: to put a number of American soldiers, sailors and airmen at risk.

It is dangerous that so many Chinese seem to subscribe to this "Somalia analogy." Washington would probably not be deterred by fears of casualties if it decided that Taiwan was being bullied without serious provocation, any more than it was deterred from attacking Iraq in 1991 by high pre-war casualty estimates. Nor is it likely that, once the United States had made the momentous decision to gear up for combat against a power like China, it would quit easily after suffering a small number of casualties.

Thinking over the long term, however, it is hard to imagine how the United States could "win" a war to preserve Taiwan's independence against a resolute China. Too many analyses inside the Beltway stop at the operational level of analysis, assuming that tactical victories answer the strategic question. Sinking the Chinese navy and defeating an invasion attempt against the island would not be the end of the story. Unless the U.S. Air Force were to mount a massive and sustained assault against mainland targets, the PRC would maintain the capability to disrupt commerce, squeeze Taiwan, and keep U.S. personnel at risk. As one American naval officer put it, as a nation much larger than Iraq or Yugoslavia, "China is a cruise missile sponge." This will be doubly true once China builds more road-mobile, solid-fuel missiles and learns better ways to hide its military assets.

Moreover, strikes against the mainland would involve huge risks. Recall that for three years, while Chinese forces were killing U.S. soldiers in Korea, the Truman administration refrained from carrying combat to the mainland for fear of a wider war—and this at a time when China had no nuclear weapons and its Soviet allies had fewer than China now has. China maintains the capacity to strike the U.S. homeland with nuclear missiles, and to strike U.S. bases in the region with both conventional and nuclear missiles. China has or is feverishly obtaining increasingly sophisticated systems, including Russian SA-10 air defense batteries, stealth detection technologies, anti-ship missiles, land attack cruise missiles, accurate ballistic missiles, and new submarines. Any of these could give the United States and its regional allies pause before widening a campaign against the Chinese mainland.

And if the issue is a PRC blockade of Taiwan, who will bear the onus of starting a war between China and the United States? If a conventional engagement leaves U.S. naval forces in control of the Taiwan Strait, can anyone be confident that Beijing would not dream of using a nuclear weapon against the Seventh Fleet? And then what? Such a scenario of nuclear escalation seems fancifully alarmist to many in the post–Cold War era. But is it any more so than such concerns ever were when defense planning focused on crises with the Soviet Union? Is this an experiment a U.S. commander-in-chief should run?

Even if we dismiss entirely any nuclear danger, there are still considerable problems for the United States. If Chinese conventional capabilities do not deter American escalation, and if Chinese forces prove relatively ineffective against U.S. weaponry, a broader question remains: How long would the United States be willing to continue a war of attrition against a country of more than a billion people? How long would it be willing even to camp multiple aircraft carrier battle groups and minesweepers off the Chinese coast? What would American allies such as Japan—where crucial U.S. bases are located—do? Taiwan will always be just 100 miles from mainland China, and Chinese nationalism is extremely unlikely to wither under American bombardment. Indeed, it would probably harden. What, then, is the endgame? A negotiated deal that rejected Taiwanese independence but protected *de facto* autonomy would be tempting in this situation. In this limited but very real sense, the effort to defend an independent Taiwan would have failed and China would be victorious, since occupation and direct control of Taiwan is not Beijing's stated strategic goal.

The point here is not that a U.S. commitment to defend Taiwan is meaningless. It could be a major factor in deterring more activist impulses in Beijing among those who might want to do more than just prevent a declaration of independence, or those who view current trends in cross-strait relations with much more pessimism than their colleagues. But we should not overestimate the U.S. ability to deter and defeat China in all circumstances.

REASONS FOR PESSIMISM

Optimists on the China challenge are often guilty of contradictory arguments. On the one hand, they argue that China will only become a dangerous enemy if the United States treats it like one. At the same time, they attempt to demonstrate why China will not be able to develop the military capacity to pose any appreciable threat to us for a very long time. How can China be both hopelessly weak and potentially dangerous?

There are ways to square this circle by asking the right questions. China can pose security challenges to the United States even if it is unlikely to narrow the gap in military power. This is true because of geography; because of America's reliance on alliances to project power; and because of China's capacity to harm U.S. forces, U.S. regional allies, and the American homeland, even while losing a war in the technical, military sense.

Optimists are correct to focus on Chinese intentions and the potentially pacifying influences that the United States and other international actors can have on China. But they often assume too much about the positive effects of globalization, interdependence and political liberalization, because they underestimate the role of nationalist emotion and the possibility of misperceptions and inadvertence in war. They also forget that interdependence is a two-way street that restrains not only the Chinese, but China's potential adversaries as well.

In addressing the China challenge, the United States needs to think hard about three related questions: first, how to avoid crises and war through prudent, coercive diplomacy; second, how to manage crises and fight a war if the avoidance effort fails; third, how to end crises and terminate war at costs acceptable to the United States and its allies.

In terms of coercive diplomacy, the United States needs to balance deterrence and reassurance, recognizing that, on the one hand, deterrence is complicated by the increasing capabilities of the PLA, and that, on the other hand, if certain core interests of China are disregarded by the United States, even a relatively weak China might resort to force. The essence of deterrence and war planning lies in considering military responses—including crisis management and diplomacy—to a Chinese attack. It might be advantageous to have the capacity to sink a Chinese destroyer pre-emptively before it launched its missiles, but an American admiral might never receive authorization to do so in a real crisis. Similarly, it might be beneficial to have the capacity to strike theater missile sites pre-emptively, but such action might cause unwanted escalation and alienate needed allies. This is one reason that effective local missile defenses are a good idea, even though they may be much less effective and much more expensive than "shooting the archer."

The United States also needs to consider for how long and at what cost it is willing to fight for certain goals. For how long would the United States be willing to fight to keep Taipei from an agreement with Beijing in which Taipei maintains a very high degree of military and political autonomy, but is nonetheless, in terms of abstract sovereignty, part of China? (In answering this question, remember that the United States made similar concessions to

Belgrade regarding Kosovo after defeating Yugoslavia militarily.) It is better to ask such questions about the end of a war before the unpredictable forces of emotion regarding sunk costs and reputation take hold after a war breaks out.

China's growing power causes so many headaches largely because its strategic implications are not fully clear. But before one laments the rise of Chinese power, one should consider an even more uncertain alternative: Chinese weakness and collapse. Nothing ordains that China's march to great power status cannot be derailed. Severe economic dislocation and political fragmentation could throw the country into disorder, and the central government could prove too crippled to use external adventures to rally support and maintain unity. Hard-bitten realists should hesitate before hoping for such developments, however. The last time China was weak and disunified—in the era of warlordism and revolution in the first half of the twentieth century—it was a disaster, not only for China, but also for international peace and stability

NOTES

1 Michael Pillsbury, ed., *Chinese Views of Future Warfare* (Washington, DC: National Defense University Press, 1997), part 4.
2 See James Lilley and Carl Ford, "China's Military: A Second Opinion," *The National Interest* (Fall 1999).
3 Quoted in *China, Nuclear Weapons, and Arms Control* (New York: Council on Foreign Relations, 2000), p. 31n.
4 Richard Rosecrance, *The Rise of the Trading State* (New York: Basic Books, 1986), pp. 146–147.
5 John M. Owen IV, *Liberal Peace, Liberal War: American Politics and International Security* (Ithaca, NY: Cornell University Press, 1997).
6 Edward D. Mansfield and Jack L. Snyder, "Democratization and the Danger of War," *International Security* (Summer 1995).

New Threats and Strategies for Peace

What is to be done? The secular trend in international politics may be away from war, as Pinker and Goldstein argue, but exceptions to the trend can be quite costly, and in the modern era, potentially catastrophic. The preceding nine sections outlined a range of theories and issues that bear on the causes of war or peace and the ways in which balances of power, political and economic institutions, tactical and strategic choices for the conduct of war, understanding or misunderstanding of threats, and other factors affect those causes. This concluding section first notes two examples of huge new challenges to traditional concerns about national security, then presents two approaches to problems of conflict in the future. These approaches reflect some of the preoccupations of the broader schools of thought surveyed in Parts I–IV. None is unreservedly optimistic or pessimistic, but each lays out an argument for the criteria by which to judge the odds that peace may prevail.

At the end of the twentieth century analysts began to anticipate sources of conflict linking economy and ecology. These potential conflicts transcend borders and may not be caused or controlled by specific governments. Such problems were not well recognized during the Cold War era, or seemed less important then because the East–West struggle absorbed concern. With superpower threats like that of the Cold War no longer front and center, and consciousness growing about global warming, energy problems, food production, pandemic disease, and other threats to the underpinnings of social stability, such challenges to international order may become a higher priority. The extent to which they will be addressed in terms of national security, however, is an open question. It would be a traditionalist conceit to ignore the emergence of novel grounds of conflict, yet not all new international problems turn into security problems.

The idea that security should be redefined to cover nonmilitary dangers, a popular view at the end of the Cold War,[1] can be a cover. It diverts attention earmarked for security studies from military matters that the redefiners consider narrow and *passé* to problems they consider to be of real importance. Depletion of the ozone layer, coral reefs, arctic ice, or rain forests may indeed prove to be a greater threat to human survival than the Russians of yesteryear, the Islamic State of today, or the China of tomorrow. These dangers, apart from the use of force, should properly be considered matters of *human* security. If they are counted as matters of *national* security, however, that term becomes so inclusive as to be meaningless. If national security is synonymous with interests in general, or with human safety, we might as well include educational policy and medicine in security studies.

Some environmental disasters, nevertheless, may affect security in the sense in which the term is traditionally used. The point at which the line should be drawn is where issues not traditionally addressed in security studies may cause social conflict and *political violence*. If some country were to contemplate using force against another to prevent it from releasing ozone-destroying chemicals into the atmosphere, for example, the ozone issue would qualify as a matter of national security policy. Similarly, disputes over natural resources (especially water) or major population displacements might easily become a source of armed conflict between states.[2] Thomas F. Homer-Dixon's analysis here suggests how a wide range of developments that degrade the environment and thereby put pressure on economies and societies (especially in Third World countries that live closer to the margin of subsistence) could also lead to significant political violence.[3]

The emerging problem that is newest but potentially most dangerous in the immediate future is cybersecurity. In an amazingly short time the world has become thoroughly dependent, and unthinkingly so, on high-tech information systems and the Internet. Criminals and governments have been energetically developing ways to exploit vulnerabilities of computers and the Internet for theft, subversion, or other malign purposes. The possibility of catastrophic economic or military damage beyond anything yet seen cannot be dismissed. How should strategic options for countering cyber threats be conceived? How do they resemble or differ from preventive, deterrent, or defensive military options of the past? Martin Libicki's entry here explores the complexities of the challenge.

Threats to the economic and environmental viability of modern society may generate political violence, and cyber conflict spans the spectrum of national interests. These threats may prove to be added to traditional sources of conflict rather than replacing them. How do the various visions that underlie statesmen's approaches to the future imply diagnoses and solutions? The entry by G. John Ikenberry and Anne-Marie Slaughter in this section is the executive summary of the report of the Princeton Project on National Security, which surveyed a range of issues, objectives, and strategies for the United States in the twenty-first century. In a manner uncannily appropriate for a product of the graduate school named for Woodrow Wilson, this summary is a quintessential example of liberal institutionalist thinking. It identifies national security with international collective security and multilateral organizations, endorses "military predominance of liberal democracies" rather than balance of power as an underpinning of world order, deemphasizes the military dimension of national security compared to other threats to well-being, emphasizes the importance of international law, and asserts a "responsibility to protect" that would commit the "international community" to intervene against governments that murder their own citizens. This is a forthright brief against realist principles and an implicit endorsement of the progressive homogenizing tendencies of globalization rather than the tolerance and preservation of non-Western political cultures.[4]

In stark contrast is the final selection by Huntington, from the last chapter of his book, which greatly elaborated and refined his initial article on the clash of civilizations, which appears in Part I of this volume. When it first appeared, that article was misread by some as a hawkish attack on threats posed by non-Western cultures. Here Huntington shows clearly that he supports the integration of the West, but not its extension beyond the West, which requires imperialism. He opposes the assumption of liberals that Western culture is universal because "it is false; it is immoral; and it is dangerous." He sees commitment to nonintervention in other civilizations as the best way to prevent a clash of civilizations from becoming a war of civilizations.

There are many respects in which the various visions of the sources of war and peace surveyed in this volume overlap or can be kept compatible, and many limits to the predictive power of any of them. It is also rare for practical policymakers to recognize explicitly their allegiance to any of these theories. Real policymakers nevertheless make very few diagnoses, predictions, or recommendations that are not implicitly grounded in one or another of these sets of assumptions about how the world works in the realm of political and military conflict. Specific policy problems in the real world are always more complex and contingent than any theoretical model suggests, but which elements are essential and which secondary or minor in import depends a great deal on the relative validity of the model in the observer's mind. Strategies that are simple, bold, and consistent will be impressively successful *if* the simple vision on which they are based is *the* right one. Otherwise, successful strategies will have to be eclectic, and wisdom will consist in figuring out which elements of which theories do and do not apply to component parts of whatever specific challenge is at issue.

—RKB

NOTES

1 Richard Ullman, "Redefining Security," *International Security* 8, no. 1 (Summer 1983); Jessica Tuchman Mathews, "Redefining Security," *Foreign Affairs* 68, no. 2 (Spring 1989).
2 See John K. Cooley, "The War Over Water," *Foreign Policy* No. 54 (Spring 1984); Roy L. Thompson, "Water as a Source of Conflict," *Strategic Review* 6, no. 2 (Spring 1978); Myron Weiner, "Security, Stability, and International Migration," *International Security* 17, no. 3 (Winter 1992/93).

3 For the full version of the analysis, see Thomas Homer-Dixon, *Environment, Scarcity, and Violence* (Princeton, N.J.: Princeton University Press, 2001). The exact causes and effects of the interactions Homer-Dixon considers are disputed. See Indra de Soysa, "Ecoviolence: Shrinking Pie or Honey Pot?" *Global Environmental Politics* 2, no. 4 (November 2002). See also Norman Myers, "Environment and Security," *Foreign Policy* no. 74 (Spring 1989); and Robert L. Paarlberg, "Ecodiplomacy," in Kenneth Oye, Robert Lieber, and Donald Rothchild, eds., *Eagle in a New World* (New York: HarperCollins, 1992).

4 For a lengthy exposition of Ikenberry's ideas, see his *Liberal Leviathan: The Origins, Crisis, and Transformation of the American World Order* (Princeton, N.J.: Princeton University Press, 2011). For criticism see Richard K. Betts, "Institutional Imperialism," *The National Interest* no. 113 (May/June 2011).

Reading 10.1

Environmental Changes as Causes of Acute Conflict THOMAS F. HOMER-DIXON

How might environmental change lead to acute conflict? Some experts propose that environmental change may shift the balance of power between states either regionally or globally, producing instabilities that could lead to war.[1] Or, as global environmental damage increases the disparity between the North and South, poor nations may militarily confront the rich for a greater share of the world's wealth.[2] Warmer temperatures could lead to contention over new ice-free sea-lanes in the Arctic or more accessible resources in the Antarctic.[3] Bulging populations and land stress may produce waves of environmental refugees[4] that spill across borders with destabilizing effects on the recipient's domestic order and on international stability. Countries may fight over dwindling supplies of water and the effects of upstream pollution.[5] In developing countries, a sharp drop in food crop production could lead to internal strife across urban-rural and nomadic-sedentary cleavages.[6] If environmental degradation makes food supplies increasingly tight, exporters may be tempted to use food as a weapon.[7] Environmental change could ultimately cause the gradual impoverishment of societies in both the North and South, which could aggravate class and ethnic cleavages, undermine liberal regimes, and spawn insurgencies.[8] Finally, many scholars indicate that environmental degradation will "ratchet up" the level of stress within national and international society, thus increasing the likelihood of many different kinds of conflict and impeding the development of cooperative solutions. . . .[9]

Poor countries will in general be more vulnerable to environmental change than rich ones; therefore, environmentally induced conflicts are likely to arise first in the developing world. In these countries, a range of atmospheric, terrestrial, and aquatic environmental pressures will in time probably produce, either singly or in combination, four main, causally interrelated social effects: reduced agricultural production, economic decline, population displacement, and disruption of regular and legitimized social relations. These social effects, in turn, may cause several specific types of acute conflict, including scarcity disputes between countries, clashes between ethnic groups, and civil strife and insurgency, each with potentially serious repercussions for the security interests of the developed world. . . .

Source: Thomas F. Homer-Dixon, "On the Threshold: Environmental Changes as Causes of Acute Conflict," International Security, Vol. 16, No. 2 (Fall 1991), pp. 76–116. © 1991 by the President and Fellows of Harvard College and the Massachusetts Institute of Technology. Some portions of this article were published previously in Thomas F. Homer-Dixon, "Environmental Change and Human Security," Behind the Headlines, Vol. 48, No. 3 (Spring, 1991), by permission of the Canadian Institute of International Affairs.

THE SALIENCE OF ENVIRONMENTAL ISSUES

. . . The environmental system, in particular the earth's climate, used to be regarded as relatively resilient and stable in the face of human insults. But now it is widely believed to have multiple local equilibria that are not highly stable.[10] In 1987, for example, geochemist Wallace Broecker reflected on recent polar ice-core and ocean sediment data: "What these records indicate is that Earth's climate does not respond to forcing in a smooth and gradual way. Rather, it responds in sharp jumps which involve large-scale reorganization of Earth's system. . . . We must consider the possibility that the main responses of the system to our provocation of the atmosphere will come in jumps whose timing and magnitude are unpredictable."[11]

A paradigm-shattering example of such nonlinear or "threshold" effects in complex environmental systems was the discovery of the Antarctic ozone hole in the mid-1980s. The hole was startling evidence of the instability of the environmental system in response to human inputs, of the capacity of humankind to significantly affect the ecosystem on a global scale, and of our inability to predict exactly how the system will change.

This altered perception of the nature of the environmental system has percolated out of the scientific community into the policymaking community. It may also be influencing the broader public's view of environmental problems. Scientists, policymakers, and laypeople are beginning to interpret data about environmental change in a new light: progressive, incremental degradation of environmental systems is not as tolerable as it once was, because we now realize that we do not know where and when we might cross a threshold and move to a radically different and perhaps highly undesirable system. . . .

Angus MacKay examines the relationship between climate change and civil violence in the kingdom of Castile (much of modern-day Spain).[12] During the fifteenth century, there were numerous well-documented episodes of popular unrest in Castile, and some seem to have been produced directly by climate-induced food shortages. In March 1462, for instance, rioters rampaged through Seville after floods forced the price of bread beyond the means of the poor. Usually, however, the causal connections were more complex. An important intervening factor was the fabric of religious and social beliefs held by the people and promoted by preachers, especially those beliefs attributing weather fluctuations to the sin of someone in the community.[13] MacKay thus argues against a simplistic "stimulus-response" model of environment-conflict linkages and instead for one that allows for "culturally mediated" behavior.

Addressing a modern conflict, William Durham has analyzed the demographic and environmental pressures behind the 1969 "Soccer War" between El Salvador and Honduras.[14] Because of the prominence in this conflict of previous migration from El Salvador to Honduras, and because of the striking evidence of population growth and land stress in the two countries (most notably El Salvador), a number of analysts have asserted that the Soccer War is a first-class example of an ecologically driven conflict.[15] A simple Malthusian interpretation does not seem to have credibility when one looks at the aggregate data.[16] But Durham shows that changes in agricultural practice and land distribution—to the detriment of poor farmers—were more powerful inducements to migration than sheer population growth. Land scarcity developed not because there was too little to go around, but because of "a process of competitive exclusion by which the small farmers [were] increasingly squeezed off the land" by large land owners.[17] Durham thus contends that ecologists cannot directly apply to human societies the simple, density-dependent models of resource competition they commonly use to study asocial animals: a distributional component must be added, because human behavior is powerfully constrained by social structure and the resource access it entails.[18]

Others have analyzed environment-conflict linkages in the Philippines. Although the country has suffered from serious internal strife for many decades, its underlying causes may be changing: population displacement, deforestation, and land degradation appear to be increasingly powerful forces driving the current communist-led insurgency. Here, too, the linkages between environmental change and conflict are complex, involving numerous intervening variables, both physical and social. The Filipino population growth rate of 2.5 percent is among the highest in Southeast Asia. To help pay the massive foreign debt, the government has encouraged the expansion of large-scale lowland agriculture. Both factors have swelled the number of landless agricultural laborers. Many have migrated to the Philippines' steep and ecologically vulnerable uplands where they have cleared land or established plots on previously logged land. This has set in motion a cycle of erosion, falling food production, and further clearing of land. Even marginally fertile land is becoming hard to find in many places, and economic conditions are often dire for the peasants.[19] Civil dissent is rampant in these peripheral areas, which are largely beyond the effective control of the central government.

While these studies are commendable, a review of all of the recent work on environmental change and conflict reveals a number of difficulties, some methodological and some conceptual. First, researchers often emphasize human-induced climate change and ozone depletion to the neglect of severe terrestrial and aquatic environmental problems such as deforestation, soil degradation, and fisheries depletion. Second, much of the recent writing on the links between environmental change and conflict is anecdotal. These pieces do not clearly separate the "how" question (how will environmental change lead to conflict?) from the "where" question (where will such conflict occur?). . . .

Third, environmental-social systems are hard to analyze. They are characterized by multiple causes and effects and by a host of intervening variables, often linked by interactive, synergistic, and nonlinear causal relations. Empirical data about these variables and relations are rarely abundant. Although the underlying influence of environmental factors on conflict may be great, the complex and indirect causation in these systems means that the scanty evidence available is always open to many interpretations. Furthermore, understanding environmental-social systems involves specifying links across levels of analysis usually regarded as quite independent.

Fourth, the prevailing "naturalistic" epistemology and ontology of social science may hinder accurate understanding of the links between physical and social variables within environmental-social systems. In particular, it may be a mistake to conjoin, in causal generalizations, types of physical events with types of intentional social action. Fifth, researchers must acquire detailed knowledge of a daunting range of disciplines, from atmospheric science and agriculture hydrology to energy economics and international relations theory.

Sixth and finally, the modern realist perspective that is often used to understand security problems is largely inadequate for identifying and explaining the links between environmental change and conflict. Realism focuses on states as rational maximizers of power in an anarchic system; state behavior is mainly a function of the structure of power relations in the system. But this emphasis on states means that theorists tend to see the world as divided into territorially distinct, mutually exclusive countries, not broader environmental regions or systems. Realism thus encourages scholars to deemphasize transboundary environmental problems, because such problems often cannot be linked to a particular country, and do not have any easily conceptualized impact on the structure of economic and military power relations between states. Realism induces scholars to squeeze environmental issues into a structure of concepts including "state," "sovereignty," "territory," "national interest," and "balance of power." The fit is bad, which may lead theorists to ignore, distort, and misunderstand important aspects of global environmental problems.

MAPPING CAUSES AND EFFECTS

. . . The total effect of human activity on the environment in a particular ecological region is mainly a function of two variables: first, the product of total population in the region and physical activity per capita, and second, the vulnerability of the ecosystem in that region to those particular activities. Activity per capita, in turn, is a function of available physical resources (which include nonrenewable resources such as minerals, and renewable resources such as water, forests, and agricultural land) and ideational factors, including institutions, social relations, preferences, and beliefs. . . . Environmental effects may cause social effects that in turn could lead to conflict. For example, the degradation of agricultural land might produce large-scale migration, which could create ethnic conflicts as migratory groups clash with indigenous populations. There are important feedback loops from social effects and conflict to the ideational factors and thence back to activity per capita and population. Thus, ethnic clashes arising from migration could alter the operation of a society's markets and thereby its economic activity. . . .

The Range of Environmental Problems

Developing countries are likely to be affected sooner and more severely by environmental change than rich countries. By definition, they do not have the financial, material, or intellectual resources of the developed world; furthermore, their social and political institutions tend to be fragile and riven with discord. It is probable, therefore, that developing societies will be less able to apprehend or respond to environmental disruption.[20]

Seven major environmental problems might plausibly contribute to conflict within and among developing countries: greenhouse warming, stratospheric ozone depletion, acid deposition, deforestation, degradation of agricultural land, overuse and pollution of water supplies, and depletion of fish stocks. These problems can all be crudely characterized as large-scale human-induced problems, with long-term and often irreversible consequences, which is why they are often grouped together under the rubric "global change." However, they vary greatly in spatial scale: the first two involve genuinely global physical processes, while the last five involve regional physical processes, although they may appear in locales all over the planet. These seven problems also vary in time scale: for example, while a region can be deforested in only a few years, and severe ecological and social effects may be noticeable almost immediately, human-induced greenhouse warming will probably develop over many decades and may not have truly serious implications for humankind for a half century or more after the signal is first detected. In addition, some of these problems (for instance, deforestation and degradation of water supplies) are much more advanced than others (such as greenhouse warming and ozone depletion) and are already producing serious social disruption. This variance in tangible evidence for these problems contributes to great differences in our certainty about their ultimate severity. The uncertainties surrounding greenhouse warming, for example, are thus far greater than those concerning deforestation.

Many of these problems are causally interrelated. For instance, acid deposition damages agricultural land, fisheries, and forests. Greenhouse warming may contribute to deforestation by moving northward the optimal temperature and precipitation zones for many tree species, by increasing the severity of windstorms and wildfires, and by expanding the range of pests and diseases.[21] The release of carbon from these dying forests would reinforce the greenhouse effect. The increased incidence of ultraviolet radiation due to the depletion of the ozone layer will probably damage trees and crops, and it may also damage the phytoplankton at the bottom of the ocean food chain. . . .[22]

Four Principal Social Effects

Environmental degradation may cause countless often subtle changes in developing societies. These range from increased communal cooking as fuel-wood becomes scarce around African villages, to worsened poverty of Filipino coastal fishermen whose once-abundant grounds have been destroyed by trawlers and industrial pollution. Which of the many types of social effect might be crucial links between environmental change and acute conflict? This is the first part of the "how" question. To address it, we must use both the best knowledge about the social effects of environmental change and the best knowledge about the nature and causes of social conflict.

In thus working from both ends toward the middle of the causal chain, I hypothesize that four principal social effects may, either singly or in combination, substantially increase the probability of acute conflict in developing countries: decreased agricultural production, economic decline, population displacement, and disruption of legitimized and authoritative institutions and social relations. These effects will often be causally interlinked, sometimes with reinforcing relationships. For example, the population displacement resulting from a decrease in agricultural production may further disrupt agricultural production. Or economic decline may lead to the flight of people with wealth and education, which in turn could eviscerate universities, courts, and institutions of economic management, all of which are crucial to a healthy economy.

Agricultural Production . . . Decreased agricultural production is often mentioned as potentially the most worrisome consequence of environmental change. . . . The Philippines provides a good illustration of deforestation's impact. . . . Since the Second World War, logging and the encroachment of farms have reduced the virgin and second-growth forest from about sixteen million hectares to 6.8–7.6 million hectares. Across the archipelago, logging and land-clearing have accelerated erosion, changed regional hydrological cycles and precipitation patterns, and decreased the land's ability to retain water during rainy periods. The resulting flash floods have damaged irrigation works while plugging reservoirs and irrigation channels with silt. These factors may seriously affect crop production. For example, when the government of the Philippines and the European Economic Community commissioned an Integrated Environmental Plan for the still relatively unspoiled island of Palawan, the authors of the study found that only about half of the 36,000 hectares of irrigated farmland projected within the Plan for 2007 will actually be irrigable because of the hydrological effects of decreases in forest cover.[23]

. . . Degradation and decreasing availability of good agricultural land [are] problems that deserve much closer attention than they usually receive. Currently, total global cropland amounts to about 1.5 billion hectares. Optimistic estimates of total arable land on the planet, which includes both current and potential cropland, range from 3.2 to 3.4 billion hectares, but nearly all the best land has already been exploited. What is left is either less fertile, not sufficiently rainfed or easily irrigable, infested with pests, or harder to clear and work.

For developing countries during the 1980s, cropland grew at just 0.26 percent a year, less than half the rate of the 1970s. More importantly, in these countries arable land per capita dropped by 1.9 percent a year. In the absence of a major increase in arable land in developing countries, experts expect that the world average of 0.28 hectares of cropland per capita will decline to 0.27 hectares by the year 2025, given the current rate of world population growth. Large tracts are being lost each year to urban encroachment, erosion, nutrient depletion, salinization, waterlogging, acidification, and compacting. The geographer Vaclav Smil, who is generally very conservative in his assessments of environmental damage, estimates that two to three million hectares of cropland are lost annually to erosion; perhaps twice as much land goes to urbanization, and at least one million hectares are abandoned because of excessive salinity. In addition, about one-fifth of the world's cropland is suffering from some degree of desertification. Taken together, he concludes, the planet will lose about 100 million hectares of arable land between 1985 and 2000. . . .[24]

Economic Decline   . . . A great diversity of factors might affect wealth production. For example, increased ultraviolet radiation caused by ozone depletion is likely to raise the rate of disease in humans and livestock,[25] which could have serious economic results. Logging for export markets may produce short-term economic gain for the country's elite, but increased runoff can damage roads, bridges, and other valuable infrastructure, while the extra siltation reduces the transport and hydroelectric capacity of rivers. As forests are destroyed, wood becomes scarcer and more expensive, and it absorbs an increasing share of the household budget for the poor families that use it for fuel.

Agriculture is the source of much of the wealth generated in developing societies. Food production soared in many regions over the last decades because the green revolution more than compensated for inadequate or declining soil productivity; but some experts believe this economic relief will be short-lived. Jeffrey Leonard writes: "Millions of previously very poor families that have experienced less than one generation of increasing wealth due to rising agricultural productivity could see that trend reversed if environmental degradation is not checked."[26] Damage to the soil is already producing a harsh economic impact in some areas.

Gauging the actual economic cost of land degradation is not easy. Current national income accounts do not incorporate measures of resource depletion: "A nation could exhaust its mineral reserves, cut down its forests, erode its soils, pollute its aquifers, and hunt its wildlife to extinction—all without affecting measured income."[27] The inadequacy of measures of economic productivity reinforces the perception that there is a policy trade-off between economic growth and environmental protection; this perception, in turn, encourages societies to generate present income at the expense of their potential for future income.

Population Displacement   Some commentators have suggested that environmental degradation may produce vast numbers of "environmental refugees." Sea-level rise may drive people back from coastal and delta areas in Egypt; spreading desert may empty Sahelian countries as their populations move south; Filipino fishermen may leave their depleted fishing grounds for the cities. The term "environmental refugee" is somewhat misleading, however, because it implies that environmental disruption could be a clear, proximate cause of refugee flows. Usually, though, environmental disruption will be only one of many interacting physical and social variables, including agricultural and economic decline, that ultimately force people from their homelands. For example, over the last three decades, millions of people have migrated from Bangladesh to neighboring West Bengal and Assam in India. While detailed data are scarce (in part because the Bangladeshi government is reluctant to admit there is significant out-migration), many specialists believe this movement is a result, at least in part, of shortages of adequately fertile land due to a rapidly growing population. Flooding, caused by deforestation in watersheds upstream on the Ganges and Brahmaputra rivers, might also be driving people from the area. In the future, this migration could be aggravated by rising sea-levels coupled with extreme weather events (both perhaps resulting from climate change).

Disrupted Institutions and Social Relations   The fourth social effect especially relevant to the connection between environment change and acute conflict is the disruption of institutions and of legitimized, accepted, and authoritative social relations. In many developing societies, the three social effects described above are likely to tear this fabric of custom and habitual behavior. A drop in agricultural output may weaken rural communities by causing malnutrition and disease, and by encouraging people to leave; economic decline may corrode confidence in the national purpose, weaken the tax base, and undermine financial, legal, and political institutions; and mass migrations of people into a region may disrupt labor markets, shift class relations, and upset the traditional balance of economic and political authority between ethnic groups. . . .

Cornucopians and Neo-Malthusians

Experts in environmental studies now commonly use the labels "cornucopian" for optimists like Simon and "neo-Malthusian" for pessimists like Paul and Anne Ehrlich. Cornucopians do not worry much about protecting the stock of any single resource, because of their faith that market-driven human ingenuity can always be tapped to allow the substitution of more abundant resources to produce the same end-use service. Simon, for example, writes: "There is no physical or economic reason why human resourcefulness and enterprise cannot forever continue to respond to impending shortages and existing problems with new expedients that, after an adjustment period, leave us better off than before the problem arose."[28] Neo-Malthusians are much more cautious. For renewable resources, they often distinguish between resource "capital" and its "income": the capital is the resource stock that generates a flow (the income) that can be tapped for human consumption and well-being. A "sustainable" economy, using this terminology, is one that leaves the capital intact and undamaged so that future generations can enjoy an undiminished income stream.

Historically, cornucopians have been right to criticize the idea that resource scarcity places fixed limits on human activity. Time and time again, human beings have circumvented scarcities, and neo-Malthusians have often been justly accused of "crying wolf." But in assuming that this experience pertains to the future, cornucopians overlook seven factors.

First, whereas serious scarcities of critical resources in the past usually appeared singly, now we face multiple scarcities that exhibit powerful interactive, feedback, and threshold effects. An agricultural region may, for example, be simultaneously affected by degraded water and soil, greenhouse-induced precipitation changes, and increased ultraviolet radiation. This makes the future highly uncertain for policymakers and economic actors; tomorrow will be full of extreme events and surprises. Furthermore, as numerous resources become scarce simultaneously, it will be harder to identify substitution possibilities that produce the same end-use services at costs that prevailed when scarcity was less severe. Second, in the past the scarcity of a given resource usually increased slowly, allowing time for social, economic, and technological adjustment. But human populations are much larger and activities of individuals are, on a global average, much more resource-intensive than before. This means that debilitating scarcities often develop much more quickly: whole countries may be deforested in a few decades; most of a region's topsoil can disappear in a generation; and critical ozone depletion may occur in as little as twenty years. Third, today's consumption has far greater momentum than in the past, because of the size of the consuming population, the sheer quantity of material consumed by this population, and the density of its interwoven fabric of consumption activities. The countless individual and corporate economic actors making up human society are heavily committed to certain patterns of resource use; and the ability of our markets to adapt may be sharply constrained by these entrenched interests.

These first three factors may soon combine to produce a daunting syndrome of environmentally induced scarcity: humankind will face multiple resource shortages that are interacting and unpredictable, that grow to crisis proportions rapidly, and that will be hard to address because of powerful commitments to certain consumption patterns.

The fourth reason that cornucopian arguments may not apply in the future is that the free-market price mechanism is a bad gauge of scarcity, especially for resources held in common, such as a benign climate and productive seas. In the past, many such resources seemed endlessly abundant; now they are being degraded and depleted and we are learning that their increased scarcity often has tremendous bearing on a society's well-being. Yet this scarcity is at best reflected only indirectly in market prices. In addition, people often cannot participate in market transactions in which they have an interest, either because they lack the resources or because they are distant from the transaction process in time or space; in these cases the true scarcity of the resource is not reflected by its price.

The fifth reason is an extension of a point made earlier: market-driven adaptation to resource scarcity is most likely to succeed in wealthy societies, where abundant reserves of capital, knowledge, and talent help economic actors invent new technologies, identify conservation possibilities, and make the transition to new production and consumption patterns. Yet many of the societies facing the most serious environmental problems in the coming decades will be poor; even if they have efficient markets, lack of capital and know-how will hinder their response to these problems.

Sixth, cornucopians have an anachronistic faith in humankind's ability to unravel and manage the myriad processes of nature. There is no *a priori* reason to expect that human scientific and technical ingenuity can always surmount all types of scarcity. Human beings may not have the mental capacity to understand adequately the complexities of environmental-social systems. Or it may simply be impossible, given the physical, biological, and social laws governing these systems, to reduce all scarcity or repair all environmental damage. Moreover, the chaotic nature of these systems may keep us from fully anticipating the consequences of various adaptation and intervention strategies. Perhaps most important, scientific and technical knowledge must be built incrementally—layer upon layer—and its diffusion to the broader society often takes decades. Any technical solutions to environmental scarcity may arrive too late to prevent catastrophe.

Seventh and finally, future environmental problems, rather than inspiring the wave of ingenuity predicted by cornucopians, may instead reduce the supply of ingenuity available in a society. The success of market mechanisms depends on an intricate and stable system of institutions, social relations, and shared understandings. . . . Cornucopians often overlook the role of *social* ingenuity in producing the complex legal and economic climate in which *technical* ingenuity can flourish. Policymakers must be clever "social engineers" to design and implement effective market mechanisms. Unfortunately, however, the syndrome of multiple, interacting, unpredictable, and rapidly changing environmental problems will increase the complexity and pressure of the policymaking setting. It will also generate increased "social friction" as elites and interest groups struggle to protect their prerogatives. The ability of policymakers to be good social engineers is likely to go *down*, not up, as these stresses increase. . . .

TYPES OF CONFLICT

. . . I hypothesize that severe environmental degradation will produce three principal types of conflict. These should be considered ideal types: they will rarely, if ever, be found in pure form in the real world.

Simple Scarcity Conflicts [We would expect] simple scarcity conflicts . . . when state actors rationally calculate their interests in a zero-sum or negative-sum situation such as might arise from resource scarcity. We have seen such conflicts often in the past; they are easily understood within the realist paradigm of international relations theory, and they therefore are likely to receive undue attention from current security scholars. . . . I propose that simple scarcity conflicts may arise over three types of resources in particular: river water, fish, and agriculturally productive land. These renewable resources seem particularly likely to spark conflict because their scarcity is increasing rapidly in some regions, they are often essential for human survival, and they can be physically seized or controlled. There may be a positive feedback relationship between conflict and reduced agricultural production: for example, lower food supplies caused by environmental change may lead countries to fight over irrigable land, and this fighting could further reduce food supplies.

The current controversy over the Great Anatolia Project on the Euphrates River illustrates how simple scarcity conflicts can arise. By early in the next century, Turkey plans to build a huge complex of twenty dams and irrigation systems along the upper reaches of the Euphrates.[29] This $21 billion project, if fully funded and built, would reduce the average annual flow of the Euphrates within Syria from 32 billion cubic meters to 20 billion.[30] The water that passes through Turkey's irrigation system and on to Syria will be laden with fertilizers, pesticides, and salts. Syria is already desperately short of water, with an annual water availability of only about 600 cubic meters per capita. Much of the water for its towns, industries, and farms comes from the Euphrates, and the country has been chronically vulnerable to drought. Furthermore, Syria's population growth rate, at 3.7 percent per year, is one of the highest in the world, and this adds further to the country's demand for water.

Turkey and Syria have exchanged angry threats over this situation. Syria gives sanctuary to guerrillas of the Kurdish Workers Party (the PKK), which has long been waging an insurgency against the Turkish government in eastern Anatolia. Turkey suspects that Syria might be using these separatists to gain leverage in bargaining over Euphrates River water. Thus in October, 1989, then Prime Minister Turgut Ozal suggested that Turkey might impound the river's water if Syria did not restrain the PKK. Although he later retracted the threat, the tensions have not been resolved, and there are currently no high-level talks on water sharing.

Group-Identity Conflicts Group-identity conflicts are . . . likely to arise from the large-scale movements of populations brought about by environmental change. As different ethnic and cultural groups are propelled together under circumstances of deprivation and stress, we should expect intergroup hostility, in which a group would emphasize its own identity while denigrating, discriminating against, and attacking outsiders. The situation in the Bangladesh-Assam region may be a good example of this process; Assam's ethnic strife over the last decade has apparently been provoked by migration from Bangladesh.[31]

As population and environmental stresses grow in developing countries, migration to the developed world is likely to surge. "The image of islands of affluence amidst a sea of poverty is not inaccurate."[32] People will seek to move from Latin America to the United States and Canada, from North Africa and the Middle East to Europe, and from South and Southeast Asia to Australia. This migration has already shifted the ethnic balance in many cities and regions of developed countries, and governments are struggling to contain a xenophobic backlash. Such racial strife will undoubtedly become much worse.

Relative-Deprivation Conflicts Relative-deprivation [conflicts may arise] as developing societies produce less wealth because of environmental problems; their citizens will probably become increasingly discontented by the widening gap between their actual level of economic achievement and the level they feel they deserve. The rate of change is key: the faster the economic deterioration, it is hypothesized, the greater the discontent. Lower-status groups will be more frustrated than others because elites will use their power to maintain, as best they can, access to a constant standard of living despite a shrinking economic pie. At some point, the discontent and frustration of some groups may cross a critical threshold, and they will act violently against other groups perceived to be the agents of their economic misery or thought to be benefiting from a grossly unfair distribution of economic goods in the society. . . .

Conflict Objectives and Scope

Table 1 compares some attributes of the principal types of acute conflict that I hypothesize may result from environmental change. The table lists the objectives sought by actors involved in these conflicts (which are, once again, ideal types). There is strong normative content to the motives of challenger groups involved in relative-deprivation conflicts: these groups believe the distribution of rewards is unfair. But such an "ought" does not necessarily drive simple-scarcity conflicts: one state may decide that it needs something another state has, and then try to seize it, without being motivated by a strong sense of unfairness or injustice.

Comparison of Conflict Types		
Conflict Type	Objective Sought	Conflict Scope
Simple scarcity	Relief from scarcity	International
Group identity	Protection and reinforcement of group identity	International or domestic
Relative deprivation	Distributive justice	Domestic (with international repercussions)

The table also shows that the scope of conflict can be expected to differ. Although relative-deprivation conflicts will tend to be domestic, we should not underestimate their potentially severe international repercussions. The correlation between civil strife and external conflict behavior is a function of the nature of the regime and of the kind of internal conflict it faces. For example, highly centralized dictatorships threatened by revolutionary actions, purges, and strikes are especially prone to engage in external war and belligerence. In comparison, less centralized dictatorships are prone to such behavior when threatened by guerrilla action and assassinations.[33] External aggressions may also result after a new regime comes to power through civil strife: regimes born of revolution, for example, are particularly good at mobilizing their citizens and resources for military preparation and war.[34]

While environmental stresses and the conflicts they induce may encourage the rise of revolutionary regimes, other results are also plausible: these pressures might overwhelm the management capacity of institutions in developing countries, inducing praetorianism[35] or widespread social disintegration. They may also weaken the control of governments over their territories, especially over the hinterland (as in the Philippines). The regimes that do gain power in the face of such disruption are likely to be extremist, authoritarian, and abusive of human rights.[36] Moreover, the already short time horizons of policy makers in developing countries will be further shortened. These political factors could seriously undermine efforts to mitigate and adapt to environmental change. Soon to be the biggest contributors to global environmental problems, developing countries could become more belligerent, less willing to compromise with other states, and less capable of controlling their territories in order to implement measures to reduce environmental damage.

If many developing countries evolve in the direction of extremism, the interests of the North may be directly threatened. Of special concern here is the growing disparity between rich and poor nations that may be induced by environmental change. Robert Heilbroner notes that revolutionary regimes "are not likely to view the vast difference between first class and cattle class with the forgiving eyes of their predecessors." Furthermore, these nations may be heavily armed, as the proliferation of nuclear and chemical weapons and ballistic missiles continues. Such regimes, he asserts, could be tempted to use nuclear blackmail as a "means of inducing the developed world to transfer its wealth on an unprecedented scale to the underdeveloped world."[37] Richard Ullman, however, argues that this concern is overstated. Third world nations are unlikely to confront the North violently in the face of the "superior destructive capabilities of the rich."[38] In light of the discussion in this article, we might conclude that environmental stress and its attendant social disruption will so debilitate the economies of developing countries that they will be unable to amass sizeable armed forces, conventional or otherwise. But the North would surely be unwise to rely on impoverishment and disorder in the South for its security.

NOTES

1 For example, see David Wirth, "Climate Chaos," *Foreign Policy*, No. 74 (Spring 1989), p. 10.

2 Robert Heilbroner, An Inquiry into the Human Prospect (New York: Norton, 1980), pp. 39 and 95; William Ophuls, *Ecology and the Politics of Scarcity: A Prologue to a Political Theory of the Steady State* (San Francisco: Freeman, 1977), pp. 214–217.

3 Fen Hampson, "The Climate for War," *Peace and Security*, Vol. 3, No. 3 (Autumn 1988), p. 9.

4 Jodi Jacobson, *Environmental Refugees: A Yardstick of Habitability*, Worldwatch Paper No. 86 (Washington, D.C.: Worldwatch Institute, 1988).

5 Peter Gleick, "Climate Change," p. 336; Malin Falkenmark, "Fresh Waters as a Factor in Strategic Policy and Action," in Westing, *Global Resources*, pp. 85–113.

6 Peter Wallensteen, "Food Crops as a Factor in Strategic Policy and Action," Westing, *Global Resources*, pp. 151–155.

7 Ibid., pp. 146–151.

8 Ted Gurr, "On the Political Consequences of Scarcity and Economic Decline," *International Studies Quarterly*, Vol. 29, No. 1 (March 1985), pp. 51–75.

9 "The disappearance of ecological abundance seems bound to make international politics even more tension ridden and potentially violent than it already is. Indeed,

the pressures of ecological scarcity may embroil the world in hopeless strife, so that long before ecological collapse occurs by virtue of the physical limitations of the earth, the current world order will have been destroyed by turmoil and war." Ophuls, *Ecology*, p. 214.

10 The development of chaos theory has contributed to this understanding. A chaotic system has nonlinear and feedback relationships between its variables that amplify small perturbations, thereby rendering accurate prediction of the system's state increasingly difficult the further one tries to project into the future. In chaos (not to be confused with randomness), deterministic causal processes still operate at the micro-level and, although the system's state may not be precisely predictable for a given point in the future, the boundaries within which its variables must operate are often identifiable. See James Crutchfield, J. Doyne Farmer, and Norman Packard, "Chaos," *Scientific American*, Vol. 255, No. 6 (December 1986), pp. 46–57; James Gleick, *Chaos: Making of a New Science* (New York: Viking, 1987).

11 Wallace Broecker, "Unpleasant Surprises in the Greenhouse?" *Nature*, Vol. 328, No. 6126 (July 9, 1987), pp. 123–126.

12 Angus MacKay, "Climate and Popular Unrest in Late Medieval Castile," in T.M. Wigley, M.J. Ingram, and G. Farmer, *Climate and History: Studies in Past Climates and Their Impact on Man* (Cambridge: Cambridge University Press, 1981), pp. 356–376. For other historical case studies of climate–society interaction, see Hubert Lamb, *Weather, Climate and Human Affairs* (London: Routledge, 1988).

13 Anger over food scarcity was sometimes turned against Jews and *conversos* (Jews who had converted to Christianity after Iberian pogroms in the late fourteenth century), and sometimes against small shopkeepers who were accused of the "sins" of creating shortages and overpricing food.

14 William Durham, *Scarcity and Survival in Central America: The Ecological Origins of the Soccer War* (Stanford, Calif.: Stanford University Press, 1979).

15 For instance, see Paul Ehrlich, Anne Ehrlich, and John Holdren, *Ecoscience: Population, Resources, Environment* (San Francisco: Freeman, 1977), p. 908.

16 El Salvador was the most densely populated country in the Western Hemisphere (190 people per square kilometer in 1976; compare India at 186), with a population growth rate of 3.5 percent per year (representing a doubling time of about twenty years). Most of the country had lost its virgin forest, land erosion and nutrient depletion were severe, and total food production fell behind consumption in the mid-50s. Per capita farmland used for basic food crops fell from 0.15 hectares in 1953 to 0.11 hectares in 1971.

17 Durham, Scarcity and Survival, p. 54.

18 The importance of variables intervening between population density and conflict is emphasized in Nazli Choucri, ed., *Multidisciplinary Perspectives on Population and Conflict* (Syracuse, N.Y.: Syracuse University Press, 1984); see also Jack Goldstone, *Revolution and Rebellion in the Early Modern World* (Berkeley, Calif.: University of California Press, 1991).

19 Leonard notes that, around the planet, population growth, inequitable land distribution, and agricultural modernization have caused huge numbers of desperately poor people to move to "remote and ecologically fragile rural areas" or to already overcrowded cities. See Jeffrey Leonard, "Overview," *Environment and the Poor: Development Strategies for a Common Agenda* (New Brunswick, N.J.: Transaction, 1989), p. 5.

20 Gurr, "Political Consequences of Scarcity," pp. 70–71.

21 WRI, et al., *World Resources 1990–91*, p. 111.

22 Robert Worrest, Hermann Gucinski, and John Hardy, "Potential Impact of Stratospheric Ozone Depletion on Marine Ecosystems," in John Topping, Jr., ed., *Coping
with Climate Change: Proceedings of the Second North American Conference on
Preparing for Climate Change* (Washington, D.C.: The Climate Institute, 1989), pp.
256–262.

23 Christopher Finney and Stanley Western, "An Economic Analysis of Environmental
Protection and Management: An Example from the Philippines," *The Environmen-
talist*, Vol. 6, No. 1 (1986), p. 56.

24 Smil gives a startling account of the situation in China. From 1957 to 1977 the
country lost 33.33 million hectares of farmland (30 percent of its 1957 total), while
it added 21.2 million hectares of largely marginal land. He notes that "the net loss
of 12 million hectares during a single generation when the country's population
grew by about 300 million people means that per capita availability of arable land
dropped by 40 per cent and that China's farmland is now no more abundant than
Bangladesh's—a mere one-tenth of a hectare per capita!" See Vaclav Smil, *Energy,
Food, Environment* (Oxford, U.K.: Oxford University Press, 1987), pp. 223, 230.

25 Janice Longstreth, "Overview of the Potential Health Effects Associated with Ozone
Depletion," in Topping, *Coping with Climate Change*, pp. 163–167.

26 Leonard, Environment and the Poor, p. 27.

27 Robert Repetto, "Wasting Assets: The Need for National Resource Accounting,"
Technology Review, January 1990, p. 40.

28 Julian Simon, *The Ultimate Resource* (Princeton: Princeton University Press, 1981),
p. 345.

29 Alan Cowell, "Water Rights: Plenty of Mud to Sling," *New York Times*, February 7,
1990, p. A4; "Send for the Dowsers," *The Economist*, December 16, 1989, p. 42.

30 On January 13, 1990, Turkey began filling the giant reservoir behind the Ataturk
Dam, the first in this complex. For one month Turkey held back the main flow of the
Euphrates River, which cut the downstream flow in Syria to about a quarter of its
normal rate.

31 Myron Weiner, "The Political Demography of Assam's Anti-Immigrant Movement,"
Population and Development Review, Vol. 9, No. 2 (June 1983), pp. 279–292.

32 Richard Ullman, "Redefining Security," *International Security*, Vol. 8, No. 1 (Summer, 1983), p. 143.

33 Jonathan Wilkenfeld, "Domestic and Foreign Conflict Behavior of Nations," *Journal of Peace Research*, Vol. 5 (1968), pp. 56–69.

34 See Theda Skocpol, "Social Revolutions and Mass Military Mobilization," *World
Politics*, Vol. 40, No. 2 (January 1988), pp. 147–168.

35 "Praetorian" is a label used by Samuel P. Huntington for societies in which the level
of political participation exceeds the capacity of political institutions to channel,
moderate, and reconcile competing claims to economic and political resources. "In
a praetorian system, social forces confront each other nakedly; no political institutions, no corps of professional political leaders are recognized or accepted as the
legitimate intermediaries to moderate group conflict." Samuel P. Huntington, *Political Order in Changing Societies* (New Haven: Yale University Press, 1968), p. 196.

36 Ophuls notes that ecological scarcity "seems to engender overwhelming pressures
toward political systems that are frankly authoritarian by current standards." Ophuls, *Ecology*, p. 163.

37 Heilbroner, *Inquiry*, pp. 39 and 95. These North-South disputes would be the international analogues of domestic relative-deprivation conflicts.

38 llman, "Redefining Security," p. 143.

Reading 10.2

Why Cyberdeterrence Is Different

Martin C. Libicki

Cyberdeterrence seems like it would be a good idea. Game theory supports the belief that it might work. The nuclear standoff between the United States and the Soviet Union during the Cold War—which never went hot—provides the historical basis for believing cyberdeterrence should work.

It may well work. This chapter, however, lays out nine questions—three critical and six ancillary—that would differentiate cyberdeterrence from nuclear deterrence or general military deterrence. Such differences all work to the detriment of cyberdeterrence as a policy, and they illustrate why and how cyberdeterrence may be quite problematic. Expressed in terms of questions that are far less urgent when applied to, say, nuclear deterrence, the critical ones (*we* being the deterrer) are

- Do we know who did it?
- Can we hold their assets at risk?
- Can we do so repeatedly?

Six ancillary reasons are

- If retaliation does not deter, can it at least disarm?
- Will third parties join the fight?
- Does retaliation send the right message to our own side?
- Do we have a threshold for response?
- Can we avoid escalation?
- What if the attacker has little worth hitting?

This list, in toto, applies to the case of cyberretaliation following a cyberattack. Yet the relevance of individual elements is somewhat broader. Issues related to who did it, whether they can be disarmed, the right message, thresholds, and escalation apply to any retaliation following a cyberattack. Similarly, issues related to holding assets at risk, repeated retaliation, third parties, and escalation apply to cyberretaliation in response to other kinds of attacks. The little-worth-hitting argument applies primarily to cyberdeterrence in kind.

The contrast with Cold War—era nuclear deterrence is obvious, but here it is, anyway. In a nuclear war, who did it is usually clear, and targets can be held at risk. Attacks can be continued as long as weapons and delivery vehicles survive. Nuclear storage and delivery infrastructures can be disabled by nuclear

---

Source: Martin C. Libicki, Cyberdeterrence and Cyberwar *(Santa Monica, CA: RAND Corporation, 2009), chap. 3. Reprinted by permission.*

attacks—which is precisely the role of counterforce targeting. The involvement of a third-party nuclear-armed state, much less nonstate nuclear warriors during an exchange, is highly unlikely. Private fortifications are of limited use (no one ever pretended that fallout shelters could prevent all damage). The consensus is pretty strong that any nuclear use (with its telltale residues) would be clear and would cross a major threshold. Nuclear warfare trumps all other forms. All states had their survival at stake. Very similar statements can also be made about conventional deterrence, such as using the threat of strategic bombing to inhibit land-based aggression. . . .

DO WE KNOW WHO DID IT?

The notion that the one should know who attacked before retaliating seems clear enough. If deterrence is to work before the first retaliation takes place, others must have confidence that the deterring state will know who attacked it. Hitting the wrong person back not only weakens the logic of deterrence (if innocence does not matter, why be innocent?) but makes a new enemy. Instead of facing one potential cyber-war (against the original attacker), the defender may now face two (the second against the one incorrectly identified as the original attacker).

The value of attribution, and hence its difficulties, go deeper than that. The defender must not only convince itself but should also convince third parties that the attribution is correct (unless retaliation is kept quiet, and only the victim of retaliation can tell that is has taken place). Finally, and most importantly, the attacker has to be convinced that the attribution is correct. If the attacker believes the retaliator is just guessing or that the retaliator has ulterior motives for retaliating, it may conclude that carrying out further attacks will have no effect on whether or not it will face further punishment.

The need to convince third parties that an attribution is correct depends on the importance of third parties. In contrast to the bilateral nuclear standoff of the Cold War, third parties matter these days; over 100 countries are supposedly developing what are described as cyberattack capabilities (many may just be CNE [Computer Network Exploitation]). There is not even a *single* dominant threat; the most putatively capable threats (e.g., China) are not the most hostile to the United States. Unlike the attacker, which is likely to know that it attacked (but not necessarily whether it did so successfully), third parties may not even be convinced that the retaliator was really attacked or had struck back for unrelated reasons. If the purpose of an attack was to corrupt a target system, effects will be apparent only to the attacker and the target (if even then). Even if the effects are public, the cause of the malfunction may be apparent only to the target (if correct) and the attacker (who will likely correlate the failure of the target system with its having been attacked). If retaliation is to be public, deterrence must likewise be public. . . . much less the particulars, of the cited attack. Instead, it may reflect other events—a bureaucratic tussle within the retaliating state, a nasty trade dispute, an attempt to win a third state's favor. So thinking, the attacker may decide to halt attacks anyway and give the retaliator no further excuse. Or it may figure that further attacks are unlikely to raise the odds that it will be subject to retaliation, especially if the retaliator offers no evidence that implicated the attacker.

Attribution may be so uncertain that the odds that any one cyberattack could evoke a response would be fairly low. How low can the odds of attribution fall without destroying the empirical basis for deterrence? The raw calculus of deterrence is fairly straightforward: The lower the odds of getting caught, the higher the penalty required to convince potential attackers that what they might achieve is not worth the cost. Unfortunately, the higher the penalty for any one cyberattack, the greater the odds that the punishment will be viewed as disproportionate—at least by third parties (who will not know what the attacker did get away with) and perhaps even by the attacker. In other domains with low catch rates (e.g., traffic violations, marijuana possession), the accused at least know that they were caught because they were guilty.

What makes attribution so hard? In a medium where "nobody knows you're a dog," it is equally hard to know whether you are a hacker. Computers do not leave distinct physical evidence behind. The world contains billions of nearly identical machines capable of sending nearly identical packets. Attacks can come from anywhere. State-sponsored hackers could operate from a cybercafé, a public library with Wi-Fi access, or a cutout. Finding rogue packets that can be traced back to the network (IP) address of a government bureaucracy reveals a bureaucracy that is stupid, is arrogant, runs so many hackers that it cannot be anything less than obvious, or operates a network that has been hijacked by others. Packets can be bounced through multiple machines on their way to the target. They can be routed through a bot that only needs to erase the packet's originating address and substitute its own to mask the true origin. Attacks can be implanted beforehand in any machine that has been compromised.

The test that presumes that the beneficiary of action was its most likely instigator (*cui bono*) can be misleading. If the attack appears to have been made on behalf of a cause (e.g., Palestinian rights), one of several states—or none of them at all—may be behind it. A greater risk is the possibility of false-flag operations designed to get another state in trouble. Indeed, the more serious the threat of retaliation, the greater the incentive for false-flag operations on the part of the presumed attacker's enemies. A state's failure to cooperate with the investigation of a particular incident may be telling (and, as discussed later, can be made more telling) and may thus be construed as an indication of guilt—or nothing more than evidence that someone has some other state secrets to protect. Even friends whose cooperation may be needed to trace packets back to their source may hesitate if they think successful attribution will lead to a crisis. Furthermore, rejection may be entirely innocent; U.S. (or European) courts, for instance, could reject some investigative techniques other states employ because they violate privacy rights. . . .

When attribution can be localized to a country, or even to government networks, that fact does not in itself prove that the attack came from that state, that is, from someone operating under national command. It could be. But it could also be an element in the government, perhaps operating on behalf of what it perceives to be state interests but without specific or at least not clear authorization (it may have permission to spy but not to tamper). Or the attacker could believe its activities were winked at by a government that wanted to preserve deniability. Or the attacker could be a proactive bureaucratic faction that acted when it deemed command authority wimpy. Or an attacker could be an entrepreneurial group of hackers who were looking to steal information (if CNE) or to create effects that it was confident would be appreciated and perhaps even rewarded—in outright cash, by future contracts, or by having its other illicit activities overlooked. A large proportion of all those with DoD network addresses are actually support contractors, creating the (admittedly largely theoretical) possibility that these individuals are answering to their employers, not the government (if they are cutouts, the government is responsible). Hackers may be off the government payroll but linked to a particular political faction or to individual politicians (more likely in non-Western states). They may want to further state interests as their friends perceive them or may want to get the current regime in trouble—the better for their friends to assume (more) power. The hackers may be organized criminals (e.g., the Russian mafiya noted above) who have co-opted the state. The hackers could be "superpatriots" who have no connection to the government or ruling elites but are striking at adversaries in lieu of or in advance of where they are sure the government would go. . . .

Finally a third class of hackers, those organized and financed by criminal enterprises, are likely to have some attributes of both state and freelance hackers but can be differentiated according to their targets and aims. Nevertheless, distinctions between states and freelance hackers (and/or criminal hackers) are probabilistic and are not based on a great deal of revealed real-world experience.

None of this is to say that attribution is necessarily impossible. Attackers may be stupid (e.g., in operating from an address linked to the state). They may be arrogant and thus sloppy. They may be brazen and not care whether they drop hints, because hints are not proof, or because they simply do not care. Open chatter may prove a state's unmaking, especially if it uses hackers who are currently freelancing or have previously freelanced and then talked about what they did. Finally, states may be penetrated. . . .

As hard as attribution is today, when a state caught with its virtual hand in the virtual cookie jar faces few penalties, it would likely be much harder if attackers faced retribution if caught. Deterrence may inhibit states from attacking in the first place, but it is just as likely to persuade them to cover their tracks more carefully and continue attacking. After all, as already noted, they have many ways to do so, including working from overseas and avoiding tools, techniques, and hackers with which they have already been associated.

Incidentally, recovery may suffer if the threat of retaliation persuades attackers to hide better. Attribution permits diagnostic forensics (insofar as specific states have signature MOs [Mode of Operation]), which, in turn, helps reveal the source of the damage and thus may hint at how to reverse it. Anything that persuades the attacker to erase evidence that may lead to attribution also tends to reduce the amount of information that defenders can use in system repair. . . .

CAN WE HOLD THEIR ASSETS AT RISK?

Battle damage is a multifaceted issue. Before the attack (or retaliation) is launched, the attacker does not have a good idea what the sum of its effects will be—and the target does not know what the attacker is capable of damaging. Even afterward, neither the attacker nor even the target may know for sure what the damage was. It is one thing to assess an attack that blows up a refinery and thereby eliminates a source of gasoline; it is another to assess an attack that corrupts the refinery control system to introduce subtle but vehicle-damaging changes to the chemical mix in the gasoline.

Battle damage prediction is critical in establishing deterrence at all. All deterrence requires the ability to hold something at risk. Yet without knowing which targets are vulnerable to what degree—and, more unpredictably, how quickly they can be recovered—it is difficult to know, much less promise, what damage retaliation can wreak. From the retaliator's point of view, the worst outcome would be to huff and puff after the attack, announce that retaliation would follow, carry it out—*and no one notices*. Waiting too long and claiming success after the one act of retaliation that manages to succeed enough to catch the attacker's attention creates other ambiguities: Was the return strike a retaliatory blow, or will it be perceived as aggression and thus start a new cycle? Without a declaration, is it certain that the retaliator carried out a delayed strike, or did the retaliator claim success for an attack that some third party actually carried out for other reasons? After all, no single target in this world has just one potential attacker. This is why claiming to put any specific target at risk from a cyberattack is foolish: The more specific the asset put at risk (e.g., China's Three Gorges' Dam in exchange for messing with the Hoover Dam), the more likely that asset will receive additional protection (or merely be yanked offline) and therefore be placed out of risk.

Even if the effects of retaliation on any one target are unpredictable, might not multiple attacks produce some statistical level of certainty? They might, were not failures often correlated with one another (e.g., the target has unseen defenses against a particular class of attack). Beyond that, difficulties in predicting human performance (security sensitivity, damage mitigation, repair) bedevil even order-of-magnitude guesses. Also bear in mind that the point is not to create just *any* effect by retaliation but enough effects to catch enough of the attention of policymakers that they begin to calculate that the costs of carrying out further attacks would not exceed whatever benefits they might gain.

For this reason, it is unclear how policymakers can gauge the effectiveness of a contemplated retaliation, a prerequisite for a deterrence policy. They may remember that, from World War II to Vietnam and onward, strategic targeteers have overstated how long enemy infrastructures would be unavailable if destroyed—and cyberspace is a far more difficult environment to make such calculations for.

Potential retaliators also face the prospect that, without a true understanding of which downstream computer processes depend on the targeted system or software, a retaliatory attack will cripple or corrupt operations well beyond those intended. This may create problems for the retaliator. If the damage is disproportional, others may condemn it as such. The defender may conclude that it is escalatory and respond with counterescalation. The retaliator may also have lost the opportunity to declare certain classes of targets off limits in hopes that the attacker may observe similar thresholds.

For either attacker or retaliator, good battle damage assessment (BDA) requires answering many questions correctly: Was the target penetrated? Did the attack affect the functioning of the target (and is the damage real or feigned)? If the system supports human decisionmaking (or if its malfunctioning would be important to decisionmakers), were the effects noticed—and by the decisionmakers? If the intent was to coerce, how do we know it was persuasive? Negative answers here show that an attack can succeed in technical terms and fail to register in operational terms. Has collateral damage been minimized or at least accounted for? After all, the target of a cyberattack is a system that was not supposed to be easy for random hackers to get into (otherwise it would have been hit already). If the vector of the attack had any self-replicating code, access to the target system may be yanked (even literally, if a network wire is pulled) after the code was inserted but well before the full damage has taken place. Absent a monitor resident in the target system, the only way an attacker might know what happened is if the attack was designed to disrupt a service available to the public, e.g., the lights go out. But such targets are not necessarily the best ones in terms of the kind of damage they can cause.

This dilemma holds with even greater force for retaliation. Since its *primary* purpose is to communicate displeasure, it may be even more necessary to make only the attacks that produce obvious effects—even though they are not necessarily the most damaging attacks to the victim (the original attacker) and may be easier to reverse than the more-subtle attacks are. Otherwise, it may not be known whether the message has been received on the other end.

One might think that the target, at least, knows what the damage has been. This will be mostly true for disruption—but only if the target knows that the disruption was caused by an attack rather than some malfunction. This may not be always be true for corruption—the point, after all, is to ruin processes in ways that defy detection and correction but are not immediately recognized as such (ruining processes in ways that obviously require restoration can only be second best from the attacker's perspective). Ironically, the attacker may have a better fix on what happened because it knows which systems or processes were being targeted, while the target can only guess. But the attacker may have no good sense of which systems or processes relied on the corrupted systems or processes; only the target will know that. . . .

CAN WE DO SO REPEATEDLY?

Deterrence can be fragile if hitting back today prevents hitting back tomorrow and thereafter. For most forms of deterrence, this is not a problem. Some deterrents are so awful that no one tempts them. For others, one hit does not preclude another. In cyberspace, the problem is vexing. Serial reapplication of retaliation may be necessary, but each use tends to diminish the expected consequences of the next use.

As previously discussed, the ability to penetrate a system and make it do what it was not designed to do requires the target system to have a vulnerability. If the system is attacked and if the attack is recognized as such (rather than, say, dismissed as a normal glitch), sysadmins will understand they have a vulnerability of some sort. If the vulnerability is known but is not attended to, sysadmins will likely hasten to catch up on their repairs (e.g., installing the requisite patch, closing the offending port). If a fresh vulnerability is discovered, efforts will be made to repair the vulnerability directly or, if the software came from elsewhere, tell the software vendor and press for a solution. If the fact but not the nature of the vulnerability is known, sysadmins may route around the offending system or code (e.g., by disallowing functions or settings that activate the code). Granted, success is not assured. The attack may not be correctly identified. The discovered vulnerability may be a manifestation of a deeper problem that goes uncorrected. The fix may break something else or open up new vulnerabilities. But repetition is not assured, either.

If the attack works by looking for vulnerabilities in the periphery—e.g., user-managed systems—there is little guarantee that the same human weaknesses (e.g., clicking on a rogue Web site, yielding password information to tricksters) will not lead to subsequent problems ad infinitum. Whether or not peripheral vulnerabilities are consequential and, if so, how consequential, is another question. . . .

The difficulty of continuing attacks (whether original or retaliatory) complicates predicting what a follow-on retaliation might achieve. If the retaliator is to threaten a similar attack the next time, it may know what the first one achieved but can only guess how the victim fixed (or routed around) its hitherto-vulnerable systems in response to the first retaliation. In contrast to most forms of warfare, repeated use does not necessarily improve anyone's understanding of weapon effects.

This problem has direct ramifications for the attacker's behavior. Even if the initial retaliation was painful, the attacker may be convinced that its fix was enough to safeguard it sufficiently. So the attacker continues its mischief. Thus, a second retaliatory attack may be required. Even then, the attacker may be convinced that that the second fix worked. Proving to a stubborn attacker that diminishing returns are not setting in may require multiple attacks—if possible. Conversely, all this may be an academic quibble: Despite professional optimism that the original vulnerability has been laid to rest, the public may believe otherwise, and it is the public's reaction that may shape the attacking state's behavior.

All this depletion and fragility applies to the attacker as well. That is, the undeterred attacker will find it continually harder to hit similar targets because they harden as they recover from each new attack. It is possible to argue that, while the quality of retaliation is depleting, so too is the quality of the attack that retaliation was meant to deter. From another perspective, this means that the importance of deterrence vis-à-vis defense is likely to decline with repeated use. . . .

IF RETALIATION DOES NOT DETER, CAN IT AT LEAST DISARM?

Retaliation attacks are useful only for deterrence. Unlike conventional or nuclear retaliation attacks, they are generally incapable of disarming the attacker. If retaliation does not build deterrence, there is no second prize here. This is why.

The prerequisites for a cyberattack are few: talented hackers, intelligence on the target, exploits to match the vulnerabilities found through such intelligence, a personal computer or any comparable computing device, and any network connection. Powerful hardware may be needed for breaking codes or decompiling software, but it need not be online. If that hardware is not online, it is very difficult to break with a cyberattack. Botnet attacks are certainly useful, albeit less sophisticated, but botnets can be rented and cannot be destroyed through cyberattack, almost by definition. No botnets are easy to dent, much less destroy, through cyber counterattack. Indeed, since hackers need only an arbitrary computer and one network connection, it is not clear that even a physical attack could destroy a state's cyberattack capabilities (unless their hackers cluster in one physical location).

That being so, there are serious drawbacks to an active defense—defined as automatic targeting of the attacking computers. Perhaps it is satisfying to stop an attacking machine while an attack is in progress or to see if one can capture attack tools from such a machine. But an active defense may also automate retaliation decisions that could profit from more-careful consideration. An attacker who anticipates active defense can easily make the attack appear to come from somewhere else, ranging from the sensitive (e.g., an orphanage, mosque), to the ticklish (e.g., an opposition newspaper, a trusted ally), to a computer within the target system itself. The attacker could also establish a honey pot in front of the attacking computer to capture the return packets and thereby analyze the target's retaliatory capabilities. Some types of attacks, notably those involving bots, do not necessarily have a single point of origin. Finally, even if the attacker's computer were destroyed, the attacker would be out only a few hundred dollars.

Combining the last two tenets suggests that a state's cyberattack capability is more likely to lose its punch by being used than by being attacked.

The inability to disarm attackers has three silver linings. First, the inability to destroy a cyberattack capability means that preemption is not a rational motive for attacking others; hence, this is one less reason to start a fight. Second, the attacker can see retaliation for what it is more clearly, rather than as an opportunity to blunt the attacker's cyberweapons; this improves the fidelity of the signal. Third, and most important, if it is not possible to disarm the cyberattacker, there is little point to rushing into retaliation. More important than speed is the ability to convince the attacker not to try again. Ironically for a medium that supposedly conducts its business at warp speed, the urgency of retaliation is governed by the capacity of the human mind to be convinced, not the need to disable the attacking computer before it strikes again.

WILL THIRD PARTIES JOIN THE FIGHT?

To *deter* is to signal a potential attacker that certain acts will have undesirable consequences. As previously discussed, problems in attribution and BDA can interfere with the signal. There is another form of interference: Attacks and counterattacks may also come from third parties, thereby confusing everyone.

This problem emerges if attacks and counterattacks are visible to the hacker community. At a minimum, such an exchange would legitimize hacking to a community that is otherwise constantly lectured on how immoral and immature such activities are. After all, if states that adhere to "rule of law" do it, the only difference between legitimate and illegitimate hacking is official imprimatur. Hackers are not particularly impressed by imprimatur.

An exchange of cyberattacks between states may also excite the general interest of superpatriot hackers or those who like a dog pile—particularly if the victim of the attack or the victim of retaliation, or both, are unpopular in certain circles. The very nature of the attacks is likely to reveal the victim's general vulnerabilities (X is not impregnable) and perhaps even specific vulnerabilities (this is how to get into X). They put certain assets "in play" in the same sense that a takeover bid for a corporation makes it a feasible target for others. Both attacker and retaliator may have to face the possibility that third-party hackers may continue to plague the target even after the original attacker has pulled back.

Outside participation matters because hacking is one of the activities in which third parties can play in the same league as states. Software, after all, comes from the commercial world; it is broken by individual hackers and repaired by other individual hackers. It is not unknown for single individuals to break copyright locks that corporations put into the market. States may have a larger panoply of attack methods than individuals do, but that is of little help in determining whether a state or an individual carried out a single particular attack.

The emergence of third-party hackers could further complicate attribution and make it difficult to understand the relationships among attack, retaliation, and counterretaliation. The prospect that attacks may continue after the attacker and the target have found out how to live with one another will complicate efforts to restore status quo conditions or even promise as much as a condition to cease hostilities.

All this weakens an implied promise of deterrence: If you stop, we stop. With the existence of third-party hackers, the "we" loses its strength. What attackers want to hear—if you stop, it stops—may not be something the retaliator can promise. Fortunately, third-party attackers may strengthen an implied threat of deterrence: Do not even start because who knows where it will lead.

DOES RETALIATION SEND THE RIGHT MESSAGE TO OUR OWN SIDE?

Some potential cybertargets are government systems and some are private. The latter set includes almost all U.S. energy, communications, and financial infrastructures. Severe attacks on them are likely to get the public's attention. With a few exceptions . . . government systems are not so essential to day-to-day life.

The defense of private systems is largely in private hands. Although the government can play a key indirect role in protecting such systems (e.g., through the development of policies, standards, and law enforcement), it can do little directly. The government has no privileged insight into specific vulnerabilities of private systems, and there is little evidence that private system owners are interested in telling it.

Ironically, a government deterrence policy may weaken rather than strengthen the private sector's incentive to protect its own systems if that policy alters who is responsible for third-party damage. If the power industry, for instance, fails to protect its supervisory control and data acquisition system, and it then gets hacked into and shut down, the cost to its users (i.e., blackouts) far outweighs the lost revenue to the power company. The threat that angry customers could sue the company and recover damages (or that regulators will get angry) has to be uppermost in the minds of the power company's security managers. The same holds in general for public or at least publicly accessible infrastructures.

Any policy that stipulates or even hints that a cyberattack is an act of war (or even terrorism) tends to immunize infrastructure owners against such risk. A cyberattack would be considered on a par with other acts (e.g., abnormal weather) that are beyond the power of the infrastructure owner to abate. Infrastructure providers could, in effect, declare force majeure and thereby evade their obligation to provide continuous service. Similarly, persuading the public that such attacks are beyond what infrastructure owners can protect themselves against would reduce political pressure on them to keep their systems clean. Indemnification, in turn, reduces their incentives to protect their own systems.

A deterrence policy, as such, creates a moral hazard that could induce owners to postpone the vigorous search for vulnerabilities in their own systems.

DO WE HAVE A THRESHOLD FOR RESPONSE?

How bad must an attack be to justify retaliation? The defender (perhaps backed by a global consensus) can choose to retaliate against *any* intrusion into its systems that leaves systems less capable. Alternatively, it can define a threshold of damage beyond which a response would be called for.

Choosing a zero-tolerance policy is asking for trouble. If CNE is (unwisely) included, the potential for a *casus belli* will always exist, and the difference between retaliating and not retaliating will have much more to do with accidents of discovery than attack activity. If implants are (somewhat unwisely) included, the crossover point will likewise be breached continually. Even if every state is fastidious about not crossing the line, can a fastidious target state afford to investigate every bot it finds to determine whether those who planted it work for some potentially hostile state? Thus, at minimum, the class of events labeled as attacks should include only those known to involve disruption or corruption; even then, DDOS attacks may merit partial exception. To repeat an earlier point, if retaliation is more likely to follow the occasional discovery than the constant activity, the supposed attacker cannot help but ask, "Why me, why now?" and perhaps draw the wrong lessons from retaliation. The proportionality issue also weighs against a zero-tolerance policy. Minor attacks leave minor damage, generally too small to merit the attention of what would be a U.S. small claims court. Cranking up the machinery of retaliation for something so small, unless it is repeated in very large quantities, would exceed the actual damage by several orders of magnitude. Any retaliation large enough to be noticed on its own—unless announced as such—would have to be fairly large or very precisely targeted and would therefore be viewed as much more serious than the original infraction. If the target did not believe retaliation of such magnitude was deserved and therefore also responded disproportionately, escalation would loom. Strict adherence to a no-threshold policy of response also implies a no-threshold policy of investigation of cyberattacks, one that is untenable and, in any case, unaffordable.

True, a zero-threshold policy has one big advantage: A state could demonstrate its will to retaliate for large attacks (that have not happened yet) by retaliating, even if in lesser measure, for small attacks. But the smaller the attack, the smaller the signature. Although it is possible to argue that very large attacks can come only from states, no such relationship covers small attacks. It is unlikely that the attacker will confess to a small charge; no state has yet to own up to conducting CNE, much less a small cyberattack. Ditto for BDA; if retaliation for small attacks is correspondingly small but undertaken just to prove a point, the attacker (as the target of retaliation) may have a problem determining that it was, in fact, retaliated against. The smaller the disruption, the more likely it is to have looked like an accident. Even if the attacker received some specific indication that the attack was an act of retaliation, such signals may not necessarily reach the attacker's public (or the third parties the retaliator wishes to impress). Small attacks may, anyway, appear to lend themselves to prosecution rather than retaliation because they look like the acts of a single person or a small group. Thus *any* retaliation could seem provocative. Meanwhile, the attacker may have learned a cheap lesson from low-level retaliation—not about the foolishness of cyberattacks but about the importance of covering one's tracks. It may also gain insight about what kind of attacks are likely to be caught or, if it is lucky, something about the forensic methods the target uses. Still, in a zero-threshold posture, this may inhibit the aggressor's contemplation of a cat's-paw gambit: The target did not retaliate against *this*, so I will try *that* next. If adversary believes that it can carefully calibrate increasing levels of attack—extremely hard to do in practice—it may hope to replicate what happens to frogs put in slowly boiling water: No gradient of added pain is sharp enough to make them jump out.

Unfortunately, selecting and monitoring activity against any one threshold is no picnic either, even if the state allows itself and the suspected attacker wiggle room. Loss of life might be one threshold; in terms of clarity, death has the advantage of being unambiguous. The U.S. strike against Libya in 1986 was justified as retaliation against an allegedly Libyan-sponsored bombing in Berlin that killed two Americans. Few in the United States thought that this was an arbitrary flash point. Yet cyberattacks can kill people only as a secondary, rather than primary, consequence, and 20-plus years of cyber mischief have yet to claim their first clear casualty. Chances are that the first casualty from a cyberattack (unless it takes place in the context of war) is likely to come because some accident was made more likely or because some warning and control system was knocked offline. Given the indirect chain of events cited here, justifying retaliation based on such an event would hardly be simple.

Economic criteria—e.g., retaliation will follow if the attack cost more than $1 million—are tractable, and offer the promise of some reasonable proportionality, but are hard to define. How does one put a price on lost secrets, lost privacy, or lost trust (admittedly, these are consequences of CNE more than they are of cyberattack)? An attacker could easily cross the threshold by accident—although, in legal terms, this is not much of a mitigating circumstance (someone who takes a deliberate but random shot into a sparse crowd and, contrary to odds, kills someone can be indicted for murder). The potential retaliator would have a double burden: not only establishing causality between an attack and the subsequent damage but also, unless the threshold was low or the damage clearly high, making a convincing case that the damage exceeded the threshold. There would also have to be some consensus about how to measure the cost of monitoring the attacked system for nonobvious damage and putting in additional safeguards to prevent the next such attack. Such expenses are not inherent in the attack but are decided on afterward by the target.

The economic threshold problem can be mitigated by requiring, say, a ten-to-one ratio between measured damage and the threshold, leaving room for error. This only works if the number of attacks whose damage exceeds the nominal threshold (i.e., $1 million worth of damage from all related attacks) but not the actionable threshold ($10 million) is small, so that retaliation against the big attack does not seem arbitrary when other attacks that could have crossed the announced threshold are ignored.

The threshold question pertains even if states respond to cyberattacks with admonishment rather than punishment. A norms-based threshold would require defining, or helping the community of nations define, what bad behavior is (e.g., hacking is not simply "boys will be boys" or "spies will be spies"). But with cyberretaliation, the stakes in getting it right are higher, and the arguments about proportionality may surface only after it is too late to take things back.

CAN WE AVOID ESCALATION?

Nuclear deterrence strategists did not worry about escalation beyond the nuclear level. If the attacker had used nuclear weapons, it was hard to argue that retaliation would induce them to do something much worse than what they had already proved they were willing to do.

Cyberdeterrence strategists *do* have to worry about such issues. The attacker may respond to retaliation by escalating into the violent or even nuclear realm. Indeed, for a while, it was Russia's declared policy to react to a strategic cyberattack with the choice of any strategic weapon in its arsenal. Attackers are likely to escalate if they (1) do not believe cyberretaliation is merited, (2) face internal pressures to respond in an obviously painful way, or (3) believe they will lose in a cyber tit-for-tat but can counter in domains where they enjoy superiority.

Attackers are also likely to escalate if the retaliation crosses a threshold in their own perception—even if the retaliation is in kind and appears proportionate to the retaliator. Accidental and inadvertent escalation exists in the real world. In cyberspace, where the ultimate effects of the attack are so uncertain and the ground rules are practically nonexistent, the risks are even higher.

Attackers could threaten physical counterretaliation in hopes of reducing the credibility of the target to that of a bluff. Those who would forestall a cyberattack by threatening retaliation in kind may lose to an attacker who counterthreatens escalatory counterretaliation.

Incidentally, any state that carries out a seriously damaging cyberattack on a nuclear-armed state necessarily runs the risk—small, perhaps, but not zero—that nuclear war may result from its actions. If it decides to attack regardless, it may be because it believes that the benefits from attacking (or the costs from *not* attacking) are sufficiently large. If the attacker believes that the benefits merit running the risk of nuclear war, how much would it be daunted by the additional (albeit more plausible) risks of cyberretaliation?

WHAT IF THE ATTACKER HAS LITTLE WORTH HITTING?

Perfectly symmetric warfare does not exist, particularly when the United States is involved. Yet cyberwarfare may be more asymmetric than most. The U.S. economy and society are heavily networked; so is its military. The attacker, by contrast, may have no targets of consequence, either because it is not particularly digitized, because its digital assets are not networked to the outside world, or because such assets are not terribly important to its government. The DDOS attacks that knocked out servers in the well-wired nation of Estonia (or "E-stonia" as some of its countrymen like to boast) in May 2007 were greeted with shock. Those against Georgia (August 2008) were greeted with some dismay. Finally, the January 2009 attacks against Kyrgyzstan, in central Asia, were hardly noticed at all. Conversely, when unwired states do get digital equipment, they tend to buy it from others, which makes them potentially vulnerable to supply-chain attacks, a hit-or-miss proposition that may reverberate (by ruining the vendors thought responsible for the damage).

The prospect of retaliating after a cyberattack from a target with nothing important to lose is not pleasant. If nothing else, this makes a declaratory policy that contemplates staying in the cyberlanes look a little foolish. The results of going ahead with such a policy may be completely successful yet altogether trivial. If the United States escalates using kinetic means, it loses whatever advantage it may garner from keeping others in cyberlanes and must explain why it was the first to use violence (unless the opening cyberattack itself created casualties).

YET THE *WILL* TO RETALIATE IS MORE CREDIBLE FOR CYBERSPACE

A key paradox of nuclear deterrence arises from the question of whether someone who threatened retaliation would, in fact, carry it out when the time came. The very concept of deterrence presumed that would-be attackers were rational and that they, being rational, would conclude that whatever was to be gained by aggression would be more than overwhelmed by the nuclear retaliation that followed. The problem in such a formulation is the presumption that the victim of aggression had to be at least somewhat irrational, particularly if there was valid cause to believe the original aggression had limited scope. The gains from retaliation—such as having one's threats be taken seriously— paled before the destruction that might arise if both sides started emptying out their nuclear arsenals on one another. Yet if the aggressor believed that the victim would not act irrationally and retaliate, deterrence could fail. Several strategic scholars tried to deal with the problem in different ways. Thomas Schelling argued for a deterrence that "left something to chance." Herman Kahn argued that building enough bomb shelters could make a U.S. threat to fight a nuclear war more credible. Patrick Morgan argued that "rationality" may be the wrong standard and that thinking in terms of a "sensible," rather than a rational, deterrence policy might avoid some of the conundrum.[1] Nevertheless, the question of "will" was central to strategic thought, and there was also considerable debate on how a state would express its will to retaliate before actually having to do so.

The question of will is not absent in cyberspace, but it is much less of an issue, especially if the odds are sufficiently high that war in cyberspace can be decoupled from more-violent forms of war. The key difference between nuclear deterrence and cyberdeterrence is that a full-fledged cyberattack may be burdensome, expensive, and highly unpleasant but also survivable. When the registers clear, systems will be reestablished, and deterrence, if it makes sense at all, would have to be reestablished for the next time. Thus, it could very well be rational to retaliate because it would help later and would boost the credibility of other deterrents, as Appendix B suggests—especially if the retaliator had declared its intentions beforehand.

Conversely, rejecting retaliation, even after declaring the intention to use it, does not bespeak irrationality. For example, a specific instance of refusing to retaliate might be due to the realization that this particular attack succeeded because of some oversight on the part of the target's sysadmins, that they would correct the mistake, that no such attack would henceforth take place, and that therefore this one incident could be ignored. The alternative would be committing to a confrontation with the attacker that might lead to further damage all around—not just in cyberspace.

Thus, while attackers may doubt the target state's willingness to retaliate, such doubts and how to resolve them in the opponent's mind do not play the central role in cyberdeterrence that they do in nuclear deterrence. Of greater importance may be whether or not the target state has, in fact, retaliated against an attack. As Chapter Five describes in more detail, a failure to retaliate could be a failure of will, a failure to detect the attack (e.g., a corruption attack), a failure to attribute the attack, or a failure of the response to register.

A GOOD DEFENSE ADDS FURTHER CREDIBILITY

Although a successful cyberdeterrence posture can be justified by the money that one can save on defense, cyberdefense adds credibility to a cyberdeterrence posture.

The first effect is straightforward: The better one's defenses, the less likely it is that an attack will succeed and so the less often a cyberdeterrence policy will be tested. The longer such a policy goes untested, the more credibility it acquires, if only through precedent.

Second, a good defense adds credibility to the threat to retaliate, much in the way Herman Kahn argued that having bomb shelters made nuclear deterrence more credible. Likewise, demonstrating the ability to absorb counter-retaliation without flinching increases the likelihood in the attacker's mind of being retaliated against because the costs of sparking at full-fledged cyberwar would fall disproportionately on the other side. Unfortunately for the analogy, such credibility tends to be associated with what Kahn labeled Type III deterrence: the ability to get one's way on nonnuclear matters (e.g., a conventional attack in Europe) by threatening nuclear action. Finding an analogy in cyberspace requires identifying issues *below* the cyberwar level, where the threat of escalation to cyberwar could decide the issue in one's favor—a prospect that may be defeated by the many uncertainties and ambiguities of cyberwar.

Third, good defenses have a way of filtering out third-party attacks, *if* third parties are incapable of rising to the level of sophistication of state attackers. This means that one argument against retaliation—putting one's infrastructure at risk from emerging hackers—loses much of its force.

Fourth, to the extent that good defenses filter out third-party attacks, they facilitate attribution by elimination. This should not be overstated, since the differences between state and nonstate attackers may be subtle, and the problem of distinguishing between attacks from two or more cybercompetent states (e.g., was it Russia or China?) remains.

NOTE

1 See Patrick Morgan, *Deterrence, a Conceptual Analysis*, Beverly Hills, Calif.: Sage Library of Social Research 40, 1977, esp. pp. 103–126.

Reading 10.3

A World of Liberty Under Law

G. JOHN IKENBERRY AND ANNE-MARIE SLAUGHTER

In the first decade of the 21st century the United States must assess the world not through the eyes of World War II, or the Cold War, or even 9/11. Instead, Americans need to recognize that ours is a world lacking a single organizing principle for foreign policy like anti-fascism or anticommunism. We face many present dangers, several long-term challenges, and countless opportunities. This report outlines a new national security strategy tailored both to the world we inhabit and the world we want to create.

Objectives   The basic objective of U.S. strategy must be to protect the American people and the American way of life. This overarching goal should comprise three more specific aims: 1) *a secure homeland*, including protection against attacks on our people and infrastructure and against fatal epidemics; 2) *a healthy global economy*, which is essential for our own prosperity and security; and 3) *a benign international environment*, grounded in security cooperation among nations and the spread of liberal democracy.

Criteria   To achieve these goals in the 21st century, American strategy must meet six basic criteria. It needs to be: 1) *multidimensional*, operating like a Swiss army knife, able to deploy different tools for different situations on a moment's notice; 2) *integrated*, fusing hard power—the power to coerce—and soft power—the power to attract; 3) *interest-based rather than threat-based*, building frameworks of cooperation centered on common interests with other nations rather than insisting that they accept our prioritization of common threats; 4) *grounded in hope rather than fear*, offering a positive vision of the world and using our power to advance that vision in cooperation with other nations; 5) *pursued inside-out*, strengthening the domestic capacity, integrity, and accountability of other governments as a foundation of international order and capacity; and 6) *adapted to the information age*, enabling us to be fast and flexible in a world where information moves instantly, actors respond to it instantly, and specialized small units come together for only a limited time for a defined purpose—whether to make a deal, restructure a company, or plan and execute a terrorist attack.

Source: *Executive Summary of Forging A World of Liberty Under Law: U.S. National Security in the 21st Century, Final Report of the Princeton Project on National Security, Woodrow Wilson School of Public and International Affairs, Princeton University, September 2006. Reprinted courtesy of the Woodrow Wilson School of Public and International Affairs at Princeton University.*

FORGING A WORLD OF LIBERTY UNDER LAW

America must stand for, seek, and secure a world of liberty under law. Our founders knew that the success of the American experiment rested on the combined blessings of order and liberty, and by order they meant law. Internationally, Americans would be safer, richer, and healthier in a world of countries that have achieved this balance—mature liberal democracies. Getting there requires:

Bringing Governments up to PAR Democracy is the best instrument that humans have devised for ensuring individual liberty over the long term, but only when it exists within a framework of order established by law. We must develop a much more sophisticated strategy of creating the deeper preconditions for successful liberal democracy—preconditions that extend far beyond the simple holding of elections. The United States should assist and encourage Popular, Accountable, and Rights-regarding (PAR) governments worldwide.

To help bring governments up to PAR, we must connect them and their citizens in as many ways as possible to governments and societies that are already at PAR and provide them with incentives and support to follow suit. We should establish and institutionalize networks of national, regional, and local government officials and nongovernmental representatives to create numerous channels for PAR nations and others to work on common problems and to communicate and inculcate the values and practices that safeguard liberty under law.

Building a Liberal Order The system of international institutions that the United States and its allies built after World War II and steadily expanded over the course of the Cold War is broken. Every major institution—the United Nations (U.N.), the International Monetary Fund (IMF), the World Bank, the World Trade Organization (WTO), the North Atlantic Treaty Organization (NATO)—and countless smaller ones face calls for major reform. The United States has the largest stake of any nation in fixing this system, precisely because we are the most powerful nation in the world. Power cannot be wielded unilaterally, and in the pursuit of a narrowly drawn definition of the national interest, because such actions breed growing resentment, fear, and resistance. We need to reassure other nations about our global role and win their support to tackle common problems.

However, it is clear that America can no longer rely on the legacy institutions of the Cold War; radical surgery is required. The United Nations is simultaneously in crisis and in demand. Its structures are outdated and its performance is inadequate, yet it remains the world's principal forum for addressing the most difficult international security issues. America must make sweeping U.N. reform a political priority. Necessary reforms include: expanding the Security Council to include India, Japan, Brazil, Germany, and two African states as permanent members without a veto; ending the veto for all Security Council resolutions authorizing direct action in response to a crisis; and requiring all

U.N. members to accept "the responsibility to protect," which acknowledges that sovereign states have a responsibility to protect their own citizens from "avoidable catastrophe," but that when they are unwilling or unable to do so, that responsibility must be borne by the international community.

While pushing for reform of the United Nations and other major global institutions, the United States should work with its friends and allies to develop a global "Concert of Democracies"—a new institution designed to strengthen security cooperation among the world's liberal democracies. This Concert would institutionalize and ratify the "democratic peace." If the United Nations cannot be reformed, the Concert would provide an alternative forum for liberal democracies to authorize collective action, including the use of force, by a supermajority vote. Its membership would be selective, but self-selected. Members would have to pledge not to use or plan to use force against one another; commit to holding multiparty, free-and-fair elections at regular intervals; guarantee civil and political rights for their citizens enforceable by an independent judiciary; and accept the responsibility to protect.

The United States must also: revive the NATO alliance by updating its grand bargains and expanding its international partnerships; build a "networked order" of informal institutions, such as private networks and bilateral ties; and reduce the sharply escalating and politically destabilizing inequalities among and within states that result from the generally beneficial process of globalization.

Rethinking the Role of Force   At their core, both liberty and law must be backed up by force. Instead of insisting on a doctrine of primacy, the United States should aim to sustain the military predominance of liberal democracies and encourage the development of military capabilities by like-minded democracies in a way that is consistent with their security interests. The predominance of liberal democracies is necessary to prevent a return to destabilizing and dangerous great power security competition; it would also augment our capacity to meet the various threats and challenges that confront us.

America must dust off and update doctrines of deterrence. The United States should announce—preferably with our allies—that in the case of an act of nuclear terrorism, we will hold the source of the nuclear materials or weapon responsible. We must also ensure that our deterrent remains credible against countries with different strategic cultures and varied military national security doctrines. And we must find ways of deterring suppliers of nuclear weapons materials from transferring them—deliberately or inadvertently—to terrorists.

America should develop new guidelines on the preventive use of force against terrorists and extreme states. Preventive strikes represent a necessary tool in fighting terror networks, but they should be proportionate and based on intelligence that adheres to strict standards. The preventive use of force against states should be very rare, employed only as a last resort and authorized by a multilateral institution—preferably a reformed Security Council, but alternatively by the existing Security Council or another broadly representative multilateral body like NATO.

MAJOR THREATS AND CHALLENGES

The Middle East   Preventing the cradle of civilizations from becoming the cradle of global conflict must be a top priority. Any long-term solution in the Middle East must include a comprehensive two-state solution in Israel and Palestine; the United States should take the lead in doing everything possible to advance this goal or get caught trying. This push for peace should be accompanied by a steady process of institution building to establish a framework of liberty under law among Middle Eastern nations. In an effort to combat radicalization in Middle Eastern states, the United States should make every effort to work with Islamic governments and Islamic/Islamist movements, including fundamentalists, as long as they disavow terrorism and other forms of civic violence.

America must take considerable risks to ensure that Iran does not develop a nuclear weapons capacity. However, we must also be prepared to offer Iran assurances that assuage its legitimate fears, such as a negative security assurance, the reliable provision to it of peaceful fissile materials, and international influence commensurate with its position. On the other hand, the United States should make it clear that life as a nuclear weapons power, if it came to pass, would be a thoroughly miserable experience for Iran.

The United States should make it clear to Iraqis that we remain willing and ready to do everything we can to rebuild Iraq and to train and support a government that is up to PAR, but that this will not be sustainable in the context of a full-scale civil war. In cooperation with the Iraqi government, America should establish a series of benchmarks that would allow U.S. forces to redeploy inside Iraq—to places where they can be useful in building order and avoid becoming entangled in internecine civil conflict—and outside Iraq. The United States must also work with the European Union and Russia to prevent a spillover of the Iraqi conflict into the rest of the region; this effort should include the provision of incentives to regional powers to behave responsibly and the imposition of costs on those countries that exacerbate the crisis.

Global Terror Networks   Framing the struggle against terrorism as a war similar to World War II or the Cold War lends legitimacy and respect to an enemy that deserves neither; the result is to strengthen, not degrade, our adversary. Labeling terrorists as Islamic warriors has a similar effect. Terror networks represent a global insurgency with a criminal core; our response must take the form of a global counterinsurgency that utilizes a range of tools, particularly law enforcement, intelligence, and surgical military tools, such as special forces. Our priorities must be to prevent the formation of a nexus between terror networks and nuclear weapons, to destroy the hard core of terrorists, and to peel away terrorist supporters and sympathizers. The ability of terror networks to dictate the agenda of the world's leading powers is a crucial source of their strength; the United States must not dance to this tune. In the longer run, building a world of liberty under law will make it harder for specific grievances and fanatical ideologies to take root and grow into global violence.

The Proliferation and Transfer of Nuclear Weapons The world is on the cusp of a new era of nuclear danger. Life in a nuclear crowd promises to be unstable and fraught with peril, from the risk of the collapse of a nuclear state to the potential failure of deterrence in a sea of uncertainty. These problems are not separate but part of a general breakdown of the global non-proliferation regime. Thus, we must reform and revive the Nuclear Non-Proliferation Treaty (NPT) by revising Article IV to allow non-nuclear weapons states nuclear energy but not nuclear capacity and by taking concrete steps to live up to our commitment under Article VI to reduce our dependence on nuclear weapons. We should also use aggressive counter-proliferation measures, including locking down all insecure nuclear weapons and materials, building on the Proliferation Security Initiative (PSI) to interdict the trade in nuclear materials, and developing plans to intervene effectively if a nuclear-weapons state like Pakistan or North Korea collapses.

The Rise of China and Order in East Asia The rise of China is one of the seminal events of the early 21st century. America's goal should not be to block or contain China, but rather to help it achieve its legitimate ambitions within the current international order and to become a responsible stakeholder in Asian and international politics. In Asia more broadly, America should aim to build a trans-Pacific, rather than pan-Asian, regional order— that is, one in which the United States plays a full part. The U.S.-Japan alliance should remain the bedrock of American strategy in East Asia, but the United States should also seek the creation of an East Asian security institution that brings together the major powers—China, Japan, South Korea, Russia, and America—for ongoing discussions about regional issues. At the same time, we should continue to strengthen ties with Asia's other emerging power, India, and should formulate policies throughout the region based on the principle that sustained economic growth in Asian countries other than China is the key to managing China's rise.

A Global Pandemic Highly infectious diseases represent a national security threat of the first order—even though they are not guided by a human hand. Health experts currently warn of the apocalyptic danger of an avian influenza pandemic, which has the potential to kill hundreds of millions of people. Indeed, AIDS already poses a grave security threat. To combat the threat of another global pandemic, we must invest more in our public health system, provide adequate resources and training to our first responders, build the capacity of foreign governments that are least equipped to deal with disease outbreaks, and create an incentive structure in at-risk countries to ensure that they take necessary public health measures in a timely fashion.

Energy   Massive U.S. consumption of oil threatens American security by transferring an enormous amount of wealth from Americans to autocratic regimes and by contributing to climate change and degradation of the environment. The only solution to these problems is to decrease our dependence on oil and provide incentives for investments in energy alternatives. Toward this end the United States should adopt a national gasoline tax that would start at fifty cents per gallon and increase by twenty cents per year for each of the next ten years. This measure should be accompanied by stricter automobile fuel efficiency standards. The United States should also lead international efforts to deal with climate change, seeking a third way between the Kyoto Protocol's requirements for emission reductions and opposition to any binding constraints.

Building a Protective Infrastructure   The United States must build a stronger protective infrastructure—throughout our society, our government, and the wider world—that helps prevent threats and limits the damage once they materialize. In our society, we must strengthen our public health system, repair a broken communications system, and reform public education so that students attain the skill sets required to achieve our national security objectives. In our government, we need to create "joined-up government;" de-politicize threat assessment; integrate relevant but neglected portfolios, such as economics and health, into the national security policy-making process; and reach out to the private sector. In the wider world, we must work through networks of security officials to contain immediate threats before they reach our shores and should consider defining our border protections beyond our actual physical borders.

Reading 10.4

Peace Among Civilizations?

SAMUEL P. HUNTINGTON

THE RENEWAL OF THE WEST?

History ends at least once and occasionally more often in the history of every civilization. As the civilization's universal state emerges, its people become blinded by what Toynbee called "the mirage of immortality" and convinced

---

that theirs is the final form of human society. So it was with the Roman Empire, the 'Abbasid Caliphate, the Mughal Empire, and the Ottoman Empire. The citizens of such universal states "in defiance of apparently plain facts . . . are prone to regard it, not as a night's shelter in the wilderness, but as the Promised Land, the goal of human endeavors." The same was true at the peak of the Pax Britannica. For the English middle class in 1897, "as they saw it, history for them, was over. . . . And they had every reason to congratulate themselves on the permanent state of felicity which this ending of history had conferred on them."[1] Societies that assume that their history has ended, however, are usually societies whose history is about to decline.

Is the West an exception to this pattern? The two key questions were well formulated by Melko:

First, is Western civilization a new species, in a class by itself, incomparably different from all other civilizations that have ever existed?

Second, does its worldwide expansion threaten (or promise) to end the possibility of development of all other civilizations?[2]

The inclination of most Westerners is, quite naturally, to answer both questions in the affirmative. And perhaps they are right. In the past, however, the peoples of other civilizations thought similarly and thought wrong.

The West obviously differs from all other civilizations that have ever existed in that it has had an overwhelming impact on all other civilizations that have existed since 1500. It also inaugurated the processes of modernization and industrialization that have become worldwide, and as a result societies in all other civilizations have been attempting to catch up with the West in wealth and modernity. Do these characteristics of the West, however, mean that its evolution and dynamics as a civilization are fundamentally different from the patterns that have prevailed in all other civilizations? The evidence of history and the judgments of the scholars of the comparative history of civilizations suggest otherwise. The development of the West to date has not deviated significantly from the evolutionary patterns common to civilizations throughout history. The Islamic Resurgence and the economic dynamism of Asia demonstrate that other civilizations are alive and well and at least potentially threatening to the West. A major war involving the West and the core states of other civilizations is not inevitable, but it could happen. Alternatively the gradual and irregular decline of the West which started in the early twentieth century could continue for decades and perhaps centuries to come. Or the West could go through a period of revival, reverse its declining influence in world affairs, and reconfirm its position as the leader whom other civilizations follow and imitate.

In what is probably the most useful periodization of the evolution of historical civilizations, Carroll Quigley sees a common pattern of seven phases.[3] . . . In his argument, Western civilization gradually began to take shape between A.D. 370 and 750 through the mixing of elements of Classical, Semitic, Saracen, and barbarian cultures. Its period of gestation lasting from the middle of the eighth century to the end of the tenth century was followed by movement, unusual among civilizations, back and forth between phases of expansion and phases of conflict. In his terms, as well as those of other civilization scholars, the West now appears to be moving out of its phase of conflict. Western civilization has become a security zone; intra-West wars, apart from an occasional Cold War, are virtually unthinkable. The West is developing . . . its equivalent of a universal empire in the form of a complex system of confederations, federations, regimes, and other types of cooperative institutions that embody at the civilizational level its commitment to democratic and pluralistic politics. The West has, in short, become a mature society entering into what future generations, in the recurring pattern of civilizations, will look back to as a "golden age," a period of peace resulting, in Quigley's terms, from "the absence of any competing units within the area of the civilization itself, and from the remoteness or even absence of struggles with other societies outside." It is also a period of prosperity which arises from "the ending of internal belligerent destruction, the reduction of internal trade barriers, the establishment of a common system of weights, measures, and coinage, and from the extensive system of government spending associated with the establishment of a universal empire."

In previous civilizations this phase of blissful golden age with its visions of immortality has ended either dramatically and quickly with the victory of an external society or slowly and equally painfully by internal disintegration. What happens within a civilization is as crucial to its ability to resist destruction from external sources as it is to holding off decay from within. Civilizations grow, Quigley argued in 1961, because they have an "instrument of expansion," that is, a military, religious, political, or economic organization that accumulates surplus and invests it in productive innovations. Civilizations decline when they stop the "application of surplus to new ways of doing things. In modern terms we say that the rate of investment decreases." This happens because the social groups controlling the surplus have a vested interest in using it for "nonproductive but ego-satisfying purposes . . . which distribute the surpluses to consumption but do not provide more effective methods of production." People live off their capital and the civilization moves from the stage of the universal state to the stage of decay. This is a period of

> acute economic depression, declining standards of living, civil wars between the various vested interests, and growing illiteracy. The society grows weaker and weaker. Vain efforts are made to stop the wastage by legislation. But the decline continues. The religious, intellectual, social, and political levels of the society began to lose the allegiance of the masses of the people on a large scale. New religious movements begin to sweep over the society. There is a growing reluctance to fight for the society or even to support it by paying taxes.

Decay then leads to the stage of invasion "when the civilization, no longer *able* to defend itself because it is no longer *willing* to defend itself, lies wide open to 'barbarian invaders,' " who often come from "another, younger, more powerful civilization."[4] . . .

THE WEST IN THE WORLD

A world in which cultural identities—ethnic, national, religious, civilizational— are central, and cultural affinities and differences shape the alliances, antagonisms, and policies of states has three broad implications for the West generally and for the United States in particular.

First, statesmen can constructively alter reality only if they recognize and understand it. The emerging politics of culture, the rising power of non-Western civilizations, and the increasing cultural assertiveness of these societies have been widely recognized in the non-Western world. European leaders have pointed to the cultural forces drawing people together and driving them apart. American elites, in contrast, have been slow to accept and to come to grips with these emerging realities. The Bush and Clinton administrations supported the unity of the multicivilizational Soviet Union, Yugoslavia, Bosnia, and Russia, in vain efforts to halt the powerful ethnic and cultural forces pushing for disunion. They promoted multicivilizational economic integration plans which are either meaningless, as with APEC, or involve major unanticipated economic and political costs, as with NAFTA and Mexico. They attempted to develop close relationships with the core states of other civilizations in the form of a "global partnership" with Russia or "constructive engagement" with China, in the face of the natural conflicts of interest between the United States and those countries. At the same time, the Clinton administration failed to involve Russia wholeheartedly in the search for peace in Bosnia, despite Russia's major interest in that war as Orthodoxy's core state. Pursuing the chimera of a multicivilizational country, the Clinton administration denied self-determination to the Serbian and Croatian minorities and helped to bring into being a Balkan one-party Islamist partner of Iran. In similar fashion the U.S. government also supported the subjection of Muslims to Orthodox rule, maintaining that "Without question Chechnya is part of the Russian Federation."[5]

Although Europeans universally acknowledge the fundamental significance of the dividing line between Western Christendom, on the one hand, and Orthodoxy and Islam, on the other, the United States, its secretary of state said, would "not recognize any fundamental divide among the Catholic, Orthodox, and Islamic parts of Europe." Those who do not recognize fundamental divides, however, are doomed to be frustrated by them. The Clinton administration initially appeared oblivious to the shifting balance of power between the United States and East Asian societies and hence time and again proclaimed goals with respect to trade, human rights, nuclear proliferation, and other issues which it was incapable of realizing. Overall the U.S. government has had extraordinary difficulty adapting to an era in which global politics is shaped by cultural and civilizational tides.

Second, American foreign policy thinking also suffered from a reluctance to abandon, alter, or at times even reconsider policies adopted to meet Cold War needs. With some this took the form of still seeing a resurrected Soviet Union as a potential threat. More generally people tended to sanctify Cold War alliances and arms control agreements. NATO must be maintained as it was in the Cold War. The Japanese-American Security Treaty is central to East Asian security. The ABM treaty is inviolate. The CFE treaty must be observed. Obviously none of these or other Cold War legacies should be lightly cast aside. Neither, however, is it necessarily in the interests of the United States or the West for them to be continued in their Cold War form. The realities of a multicivilizational world suggest that NATO should be expanded to include other Western societies that wish to join and should recognize the essential meaninglessness of having as members two states each of which is the other's worst enemy and both of which lack cultural affinity with the other members. An ABM treaty designed to meet the Cold War need to insure the mutual vulnerability of Soviet and American societies and thus to deter Soviet-American nuclear war may well obstruct the ability of the United States and other societies to protect themselves against unpredictable nuclear threats or attacks by terrorist movements and irrational dictators. The U.S.-Japan security treaty helped deter Soviet aggression against Japan. What purpose is it meant to serve in the post–Cold War era? To contain and deter China? To slow Japanese accommodation with a rising China? To prevent further Japanese militarization? Increasingly doubts are being raised in Japan about the American military presence there and in the United States about the need for an unreciprocated commitment to defend Japan. The Conventional Forces in Europe agreement was designed to moderate the NATO-Warsaw Pact confrontation in Central Europe, which has disappeared. The principal impact of the agreement now is to create difficulties for Russia in dealing with what it perceives to be security threats from Muslim peoples to its south.

Third, cultural and civilizational diversity challenges the Western and particularly American belief in the universal relevance of Western culture. This belief is expressed both descriptively and normatively. Descriptively it holds that peoples in all societies want to adopt Western values, institutions, and practices. If they seem not to have that desire and to be committed to their own traditional cultures, they are victims of a "false consciousness" comparable to that which Marxists found among proletarians who supported capitalism. Normatively the Western universalist belief posits that people throughout the world should embrace Western values, institutions, and culture because they embody the highest, most enlightened, most liberal, most rational, most modern, and most civilized thinking of humankind.

In the emerging world of ethnic conflict and civilizational clash, Western belief in the universality of Western culture suffers three problems: it is false; it is immoral; and it is dangerous. That it is false has been the central thesis of this book, a thesis well summed up by Michael Howard: the "common Western assumption that cultural diversity is a historical curiosity being rapidly eroded by the growth of a common, western-oriented, Anglophone world-culture, shaping our basic values . . . is simply not true."[6] A reader not by now convinced of the wisdom of Sir Michael's remark exists in a world far removed from that described in this book.

The belief that non-Western peoples should adopt Western values, institutions, and culture is immoral because of what would be necessary to bring it about. The almost-universal reach of European power in the late nineteenth century and the global dominance of the United States in the late twentieth century spread much of Western civilization across the world. European globalism, however, is no more. American hegemony is receding if only because it is no longer needed to protect the United States against a Cold War—style Soviet military threat. Culture, as we have argued, follows power. If non-Western societies are once again to be shaped by Western culture, it will happen only as a result of the expansion, deployment, and impact of Western power. Imperialism is the necessary logical consequence of universalism. In addition, as a maturing civilization, the West no longer has the economic or demographic dynamism required to impose its will on other societies and any effort to do so is also contrary to the Western values of self-determination and democracy. As Asian and Muslim civilizations begin more and more to assert the universal relevance of their cultures, Westerners will come to appreciate more and more the connection between universalism and imperialism.

Western universalism is dangerous to the world because it could lead to a major intercivilizational war between core states and it is dangerous to the West because it could lead to defeat of the West. With the collapse of the Soviet Union, Westerners see their civilization in a position of unparalleled dominance, while at the same time weaker Asian, Muslim, and other societies are beginning to gain strength. Hence they could be led to apply the familiar and powerful logic of Brutus:

> Our legions are brim-full, our cause is ripe.
> The enemy increaseth every day;
> We at the height, are ready to decline.
> There is a tide in the affairs of men,
> Which taken at the flood, leads on to fortune;
> Omitted, all the voyage of their life
> Is bound in shallows and miseries.
> On such a full sea are we now afloat,
> And we must take the current when it serves,
> Or lose our ventures.

This logic, however, produced Brutus's defeat at Philippi, and the prudent course for the West is not to attempt to stop the shift in power but to learn to navigate the shallows, endure the miseries, moderate its ventures, and safeguard its culture.

All civilizations go though similar processes of emergence, rise, and decline. The West differs from other civilizations not in the way it has developed but in the distinctive character of its values and institutions. These include most notably its Christianity, pluralism, individualism, and rule of law, which made it possible for the West to invent modernity, expand throughout the world, and become the envy of other societies. In their ensemble these characteristics are peculiar to the West. Europe, as Arthur M. Schlesinger, Jr., has said, is "the source—the *unique* source" of the "ideas of individual liberty, political democracy, the rule of law, human rights, and cultural freedom. . . . These are

European ideas, not Asian, nor African, nor Middle Eastern ideas, except by adoption."[7] They make Western civilization unique, and Western civilization is valuable not because it is universal but because it *is* unique. The principal responsibility of Western leaders, consequently, is not to attempt to reshape other civilizations in the image of the West, which is beyond their declining power, but to preserve, protect, and renew the unique qualities of Western civilization. Because it is the most powerful Western country, that responsibility falls overwhelmingly on the United States of America.

To preserve Western civilization in the face of declining Western power, it is in the interest of the United States and European countries:

> to achieve greater political, economic, and military integration and to coordinate their policies so as to preclude states from other civilizations exploiting differences among them;
>
> to incorporate into the European Union and NATO the Western states of Central Europe that is, the Visegrad countries, the Baltic republics, Slovenia, and Croatia;
>
> to encourage the "Westernization" of Latin America and, as far as possible, the close alignment of Latin American countries with the West;
>
> to restrain the development of the conventional and unconventional military power of Islamic and Sinic countries;
>
> to slow the drift of Japan away from the West and toward accommodation with China;
>
> to accept Russia as the core state of Orthodoxy and a major regional power with legitimate interests in the security of its southern borders;
>
> to maintain Western technological and military superiority over other civilizations;
>
> and, most important, to recognize that Western intervention in the affairs of other civilizations is probably the single most dangerous source of instability and potential global conflict in a multicivilizational world.

In the aftermath of the Cold War the United States became consumed with massive debates over the proper course of American foreign policy. In this era, however, the United States can neither dominate nor escape the world. Neither internationalism nor isolationism, neither multilateralism nor unilateralism, will best serve its interests. Those will best be advanced by eschewing these opposing extremes and instead adopting an Atlanticist policy of close cooperation with its European partners to protect and advance the interests and values of the unique civilization they share.

CIVILIZATIONAL WAR AND ORDER

A global war involving the core states of the world's major civilizations is highly improbable but not impossible. Such a war, we have suggested, could come about from the escalation of a fault line war between groups from different civilizations, most likely involving Muslims on one side and non-Muslims on the other. Escalation is made more likely if aspiring Muslim core states compete to provide assistance to their embattled coreligionists. It is made less likely by the interests which secondary and tertiary kin countries may have in not becoming deeply involved in the war themselves. A more dangerous source of a global intercivilizational war is the shifting balance of power among civilizations and their core states. If it continues, the rise of China and the increasing assertiveness of this "biggest player in the history of man" will place tremendous stress on international stability in the early twenty-first century. The emergence of China as the dominant power in East and Southeast Asia would be contrary to American interests as they have been historically construed.[8] . . .

In the coming era, . . . the avoidance of major intercivilizational wars requires core states to refrain from intervening in conflicts in other civilizations. This is a truth which some states, particularly the United States, will undoubtedly find difficult to accept. This *abstention rule* that core states abstain from intervention in conflicts in other civilizations is the first requirement of peace in a multicivilizational, multipolar world. The second requirement is the *joint mediation rule* that core states negotiate with each other to contain or to halt fault line wars between states or groups from their civilizations.

Acceptance of these rules and of a world with greater equality among civilizations will not be easy for the West or for those civilizations which may aim to supplement or supplant the West in its dominant role. In such a world, for instance, core states may well view it as their prerogative to possess nuclear weapons and to deny such weapons to other members of their civilization. Looking back on his efforts to develop a "full nuclear capability" for Pakistan, Zulfikar Ali Bhutto justified those efforts: "We know that Israel and South Africa have full nuclear capability. The Christian, Jewish and Hindu civilizations have this capability. Only the Islamic civilization was without it, but that position was about to change."[9] The competition for leadership within civilizations lacking a single core state may also stimulate competition for nuclear weapons. Even though it has highly cooperative relations with Pakistan, Iran clearly feels that it needs nuclear weapons as much as Pakistan does. On the other hand, Brazil and Argentina gave up their programs aimed in this direction, and South Africa destroyed its nuclear weapons, although it might well wish to reacquire them if Nigeria began to develop such a capability. While nuclear proliferation obviously involves risks, as Scott Sagan and others have pointed out, a world in which one or two core states in each of the major civilizations had nuclear weapons and no other states did could be a reasonably stable world.

Most of the principal international institutions date from shortly after World War II and are shaped according to Western interests, values, and practices. As Western power declines relative to that of other civilizations, pressures will develop to reshape these institutions to accommodate the interests of those civilizations. The most obvious, most important, and probably most controversial issue concerns permanent membership in the U.N. Security Council. That membership has consisted of the victorious major powers of World War II and bears a decreasing relationship to the reality of power in the world. Over the longer haul either changes are made in its membership or other less formal procedures are likely to develop to deal with security issues, even as the G-7 meetings have dealt with global economic issues. In a multicivilizational world ideally each major civilization should have at least one permanent seat on the Security Council. At present only three do. The United States has endorsed Japanese and German membership but it is clear that they will become permanent members only if other countries do also. Brazil has suggested five new permanent members, albeit without veto power, Germany, Japan, India, Nigeria, and itself. That, however, would leave the world's 1 billion Muslims unrepresented, except in so far as Nigeria might undertake that responsibility. From a civilizational viewpoint, clearly Japan and India should be permanent members, and Africa, Latin America, and the Muslim world should have permanent seats, which could be occupied on a rotating basis by the leading states of those civilizations, selections being made by the Organization of the Islamic Conference, the Organization of African Unity, and the Organization of American States (the United States abstaining). It would also be appropriate to consolidate the British and French seats into a single European Union seat, the rotating occupant of which would be selected by the Union. Seven civilizations would thus each have one permanent seat and the West would have two, an allocation broadly representative of the distribution of people, wealth, and power in the world.

THE COMMONALITIES OF CIVILIZATION

Some Americans have promoted multiculturalism at home; some have promoted universalism abroad; and some have done both. Multiculturalism at home threatens the United States and the West; universalism abroad threatens the West and the world. Both deny the uniqueness of Western culture. The global monoculturalists want to make the world like America. The domestic multiculturalists want to make America like the world. A multicultural America is impossible because a non-Western America is not American. A multicultural world is unavoidable because global empire is impossible. The preservation of the United States and the West requires the renewal of Western identity. The security of the world requires acceptance of global multiculturality.

Does the vacuousness of Western universalism and the reality of global cultural diversity lead inevitably and irrevocably to moral and cultural relativism? If universalism legitimates imperialism, does relativism legitimate repression? Once again, the answer to these questions is yes and no. Cultures are relative; morality is absolute. Cultures, as Michael Walzer has argued, are "thick"; they prescribe institutions and behavior patterns to guide humans in the paths which are right in a particular society. Above, beyond, and growing out of this maximalist morality, however, is a "thin" minimalist morality that embodies "reiterated features of particular thick or maximal moralities." Minimal moral concepts of truth and justice are found in all thick moralities and cannot be divorced from them. There are also minimal moral "negative injunctions, most likely, rules against murder, deceit, torture, oppression, and tyranny." What people have in common is "more the sense of a common enemy [or evil] than the commitment to a common culture." Human society is "universal because it is human, particular because it is a society." At times we march with others; mostly we march alone.[10] Yet a "thin" minimal morality does derive from the common human condition, and "universal dispositions" are found in all cultures.[11] Instead of promoting the supposedly universal features of one civilization, the requisites for cultural coexistence demand a search for what is common to most civilizations. In a multicivilizational world, the constructive course is to renounce universalism, accept diversity, and seek commonalities.

A relevant effort to identify such commonalities in a very small place occurred in Singapore in the early 1990s. The people of Singapore are roughly 76 percent Chinese, 15 percent Malay and Muslim, and 6 percent Indian Hindu and Sikh. In the past the government has attempted to promote "Confucian values" among its people but it has also insisted on everyone being educated in and becoming fluent in English. In January 1989 President Wee Kim Wee in his address opening Parliament pointed to the extensive exposure of the 2.7 million Singaporeans to outside cultural influences from the West which had "put them in close touch with new ideas and technologies from abroad" but had "also exposed" them "to alien lifestyles and values." "Traditional Asian ideas of morality, duty and society which have sustained us in the past," he warned, "are giving way to a more Westernized, individualistic, and self-centered outlook on life." It is necessary, he argued, to identify the core values which Singapore's different ethnic and religious communities had in common and "which capture the essence of being a Singaporean."

President Wee suggested four such values: "placing society above self, upholding the family as the basic building block of society, resolving major issues through consensus instead of contention, and stressing racial and religious tolerance and harmony." His speech led to extensive discussion of Singaporean values and two years later a White Paper setting forth the government's position. The White Paper endorsed all four of the president's suggested values but added a fifth on support of the individual, largely because of the need to emphasize the priority of individual merit in Singaporean society as against Confucian values of hierarchy and family, which could lead to nepotism. The White Paper defined the "Shared Values" of Singaporeans as:

> Nation before [ethnic] community and society above self;
> Family as the basic unit of society;
> Regard and community support for the individual;
> Consensus instead of contention;
> Racial and religious harmony.

While citing Singapore's commitment to parliamentary democracy and excellence in government, the statement of *Shared Values* explicitly excluded political values from its purview. The government emphasized that Singapore was "in crucial respects an Asian society" and must remain one. "Singaporeans are not Americans or Anglo-Saxons, though we may speak English and wear Western dress. If over the longer term Singaporeans became indistinguishable from Americans, British or Australians, or worse became a poor imitation of them [i.e., a torn country], we will lose our edge over these Western societies which enables us to hold our own internationally."[12]

The Singapore project was an ambitious and enlightened effort to define a Singaporean cultural identity which was shared by its ethnic and religious communities and which distinguished it from the West. Certainly a statement of Western and particularly American values would give far more weight to the rights of the individual as against those of the community, to freedom of expression and truth emerging out of the contest of ideas, to political participation and competition, and to the rule of law as against the rule of expert, wise, and responsible governors. Yet even so, while they might supplement the Singaporean values and give some lower priority, few Westerners would reject those values as unworthy. At least at a basic "thin" morality level, some commonalities exist between Asia and the West. In addition, as many have pointed out, whatever the degree to which they divided humankind, the world's major religions—Western Christianity, Orthodoxy, Hinduism, Buddhism, Islam, Confucianism, Taoism, Judaism—also share key values in common. If humans are ever to develop a universal civilization, it will emerge gradually through the exploration and expansion of these commonalities. Thus, in addition to the abstention rule and the joint mediation rule, the third rule for peace in a multicivilizational world is the *commonalities rule*: peoples in all civilizations should search for and attempt to expand the values, institutions, and practices they have in common with peoples of other civilizations.

This effort would contribute not only to limiting the clash of civilizations but also to strengthening Civilization in the singular (hereafter capitalized for clarity). The singular Civilization presumably refers to a complex mix of higher levels of morality, religion, learning, art, philosophy, technology, material well-being, and probably other things. These obviously do not necessarily vary together. Yet scholars easily identify highpoints and lowpoints in the level of Civilization in the histories of civilizations. The question then is: How can one chart the ups and downs of humanity's development of Civilization? Is there a general, secular trend, transcending individual civilizations, toward higher levels of Civilization? If there is such a trend, is it a product of the processes of modernization that increase the control of humans over their environment and hence generate higher and higher levels of technological sophistication and material well-being? In the contemporary era, is a higher level of modernity thus a prerequisite to a higher level of Civilization? Or does the level of Civilization primarily vary within the history of individual civilizations?

This issue is another manifestation of the debate over the linear or cyclical nature of history. Conceivably modernization and human moral development produced by greater education, awareness, and understanding of human society and its natural environment produce sustained movement toward higher and higher levels of Civilization. Alternatively, levels of Civilization may simply reflect phases in the evolution of civilizations. When civilizations first emerge, their people are usually vigorous, dynamic, brutal, mobile, and expansionist. They are relatively unCivilized. As the civilization evolves it becomes more settled and develops the techniques and skills that make it more Civilized.

As the competition among its constituent elements tapers off and a universal state emerges, the civilization reaches its highest level of Civilization, its "golden age," with a flowering of morality, art, literature, philosophy, technology, and martial, economic, and political competence. As it goes into decay as a civilization, its level of Civilization also declines until it disappears under the onslaught of a different surging civilization with a lower level of Civilization.

Modernization has generally enhanced the material level of Civilization throughout the world. But has it also enhanced the moral and cultural dimensions of Civilization? In some respects this appears to be the case. Slavery, torture, vicious abuse of individuals, have become less and less acceptable in the contemporary world. Is this, however, simply the result of the impact of Western civilization on other cultures and hence will a moral reversion occur as Western power declines? Much evidence exists in the 1990s for the relevance of the "sheer chaos" paradigm of world affairs: a global breakdown of law and order, failed states and increasing anarchy in many parts of the world, a global crime wave, transnational mafias and drug cartels, increasing drug addiction in many societies, a general weakening of the family, a decline in trust and social solidarity in many countries, ethnic, religious, and civilizational violence and rule by the gun prevalent in much of the world. In city after city—Moscow, Rio de Janeiro, Bangkok, Shanghai, London, Rome, Warsaw, Tokyo, Johannesburg, Delhi, Karachi, Cairo, Bogota, Washington—crime seems to be soaring and basic elements of Civilization fading away. People speak of a global crisis in governance. The rise of transnational corporations producing economic goods is increasingly matched by the rise of transnational criminal mafias, drug cartels, and terrorist gangs violently assaulting Civilization. Law and order is the first prerequisite of Civilization and in much of the world—Africa, Latin America, the former Soviet Union, South Asia, the Middle East—it appears to be evaporating, while also under serious assault in China, Japan, and the West. On a worldwide basis Civilization seems in many respects to be yielding to barbarism, generating the image of an unprecedented phenomenon, a global Dark Ages, possibly descending on humanity.

In the 1950s Lester Pearson warned that humans were moving into "an age when different civilizations will have to learn to live side by side in peaceful interchange, learning from each other, studying each other's history and ideals and art and culture, mutually enriching each others' lives. The alternative, in this overcrowded little world, is misunderstanding, tension, clash, and catastrophe."[13] The futures of both peace and Civilization depend upon understanding and cooperation among the political, spiritual, and intellectual leaders of the world's major civilizations. In the clash of civilizations, Europe and America will hang together or hang separately. In the greater clash, the global "real clash," between Civilization and barbarism, the world's great civilizations, with their rich accomplishments in religion, art, literature, philosophy, science, technology, morality, and compassion, will also hang together or hang separately. In the emerging era, clashes of civilizations are the greatest threat to world peace, and an international order based on civilizations is the surest safeguard against world war.

NOTES

1 Arnold J. Toynbee, *A Study of History* (London: Oxford University Press, 12 vols., 1934–1961), VII, 7–17; *Civilization on Trial: Essays* (New York: Oxford University Press, 1948), 17–18; *Study of History*, IX, 421–422.
2 Matthew Melko, *The Nature of Civilizations* (Boston: Porter Sargent, 1969), p. 155.
3 Carroll Quigley, *The Evolution of Civilizations: An Introduction to Historical Analysis* (New York: Macmillan, 1961), pp. 146ff.
4 Ibid., pp. 138–139, 158–160.
5 Richard Holbrooke, "America: A European Power," *Foreign Affairs*, 74 (March/April 1995), 49.
6 Michael Howard, *America and the World* (St. Louis: Washington University, the Annual Lewin Lecture, 5 April 1984), p. 6.
7 Arthur M. Schlesinger, Jr., *The Disuniting of America: Reflections on a Multicultural Society* (New York: W. W. Norton, 1992), p. 127.
8 For a 1990s statement of this interest, see "Defense Planning Guidance for the Fiscal Years 1994–1999," draft, 18 February 1992, *New York Times*, 8 March 1992, p. 14.
9 Z. A. Bhutto, *If I Am Assassinated* (New Delhi: Vikas Publishing House, 1979), pp. 137–138, quoted in Louis Delvoie, "The Islamization of Pakistan's Foreign Policy," *International Journal*, 51 (Winter 1995–1996), 133.
10 Michael Walzer, *Thick and Thin: Moral Argument at Home and Abroad* (Notre Dame: University of Notre Dame Press, 1994), pp. 1–11.
11 James Q. Wilson, *The Moral Sense* (New York: Free Press, 1993), p. 225.
12 Government of Singapore, *Shared Values* (Singapore: Cmd. No. 1 of 1991, 2 January 1991), pp. 2–10.
13 Lester Pearson, *Democracy in World Politics* (Princeton: Princeton University Press, 1955), pp. 83–84.